Handbook of Canadian Foreign Policy

Handbook of Canadian Foreign Policy

Edited by
PATRICK JAMES, NELSON MICHAUD,
and
MARC J. O'REILLY

LEXINGTON BOOKS

A division of
ROWMAN & LITTLEFIELD PUBLISHERS, INC.
Lanham • Boulder • New York • Toronto • Oxford

LEXINGTON BOOKS

A division of Rowman & Littlefield Publishers, Inc.
A wholly owned subsidiary of The Rowman & Littlefield Publishing Group, Inc.
4501 Forbes Boulevard, Suite 200
Lanham, MD 20706

PO Box 317
Oxford
OX2 9RU, UK

Copyright © 2006 by Lexington Books

All rights reserved. No part of this publication may be reproduced, stored in a retrieval system, or transmitted in any form or by any means, electronic, mechanical, photocopying, recording, or otherwise, without the prior permission of the publisher.

British Library Cataloguing in Publication Information Available

Library of Congress Cataloging-in-Publication Data

Handbook of Canadian foreign policy / [edited by] Patrick James, Nelson Michaud, and Marc O'Reilly.
    p. cm.
    ISBN-13: 978-0-7391-0694-5 (cloth : alk. paper)
    ISBN-10: 0-7391-0694-5 (cloth : alk. paper)
    ISBN-13: 978-0-7391-1493-3 (pbk. : alk. paper)
    ISBN-10: 0-7391-1493-X (pbk. : alk. paper)
    1. Canada—Foreign relations. 2. Canada—Foreign relations—Handbooks, manuals, etc. I. James, Patrick, 1957– I. Michaud, Nelson, 1960– III. O'Reilly, Marc, 1969–
F1029.H27 2006
327.71—dc22   2005030657

Printed in the United States of America

∞ ™ The paper used in this publication meets the minimum requirements of American National Standard for Information Sciences—Permanence of Paper for Printed Library Materials, ANSI/NISO Z39.48–1992.

Contents

Acknowledgments ix

Abbreviations xi

1 Canadian Foreign Policy in a New Millennium: The Search for Understanding 1
 Patrick James, Nelson Michaud, and Marc J. O'Reilly

2 The Prime Minister, PMO, and PCO: Makers of Canadian Foreign Policy? 21
 Nelson Michaud

Part I: Refocused Efforts

3 Forty Years of Neglect, Indifference, and Apathy: The Relentless Decline of Canada's Armed Forces 51
 Andrew Richter

4 The Evolution of Liberalization in Canada's Trade Policy 83
 Michael Lusztig

5 Foreign Policy by Other Means: Paradiplomacy and the Canadian Provinces 105
 Richard Vengroff and Jason Rich

Part II: Multicultural Challenges

6 "There Are No Half-Countries": Canada, La Francophonie, and the Projection of Canadian Biculturalism, 1960–2002 133
 Greg Donaghy and Neal Carter

7	Lending Forces: Canada's Military Peacekeeping *Kimberly Marten*	165
8	International Conflict Prevention: An Assessment of Canadian Perceptions and Policies *Koren Marriott and David Carment*	189
9	Canadian Official Development Assistance Policy: Juggling the National Interest and Humanitarian Impulses *Jean-Sébastien Rioux*	209
10	Canadian Foreign Policy and International Human Rights *Bethany Barratt*	235
11	Canada and International Financial Policy: Non-Hegemonic Leadership and Systemic Stability *Duncan Wood*	265

Part III: Canada and World Regions

12	Canada as a Northern Nation: Finding a Role for the Arctic Council *Douglas C. Nord*	289
13	Canada in Latin America: A Foreign Policy of Ambivalence, Pragmatism, or Inconsistency? *Athanasios Hristoulas*	317
14	Canadian Foreign Policy in the Middle East: Reflexive Multilateralism in an Evolving World *Marc J. O'Reilly*	337
15	The Political Economy of Canada's Relations with the European Union *Axel Hülsemeyer*	365
16	Canada-U.S. Relations: Personality, Pattern, and Domestic Politics *Charles F. Doran*	389

Part IV: External Viewpoints into Canada

17 Canada's Military Capability and Sovereignty at the Dawn of the New Century — 411
Thomas G. Barnes

18 The Foundations of Canadian Foreign Policy: Federalism, Confederalism, International Law, and the Quebec Precedent — 431
James McHugh

Part V: Internal Perspectives

19 Civil-Military Relations and Canadian Foreign Policy: The Case of Gender Integration and the Canadian Navy — 457
Carolyn C. James

20 Civil Society Participation in Canadian Foreign Policy: Expanded Consultation in the Chrétien Years — 491
Jeffrey M. Ayres

21 Conclusion: Understanding Canada's Foreign Policy Challenges — 513
Patrick James, Nelson Michaud, and Marc J. O'Reilly

Bibliography — 527

Index — 577

About the Editors and Contributors — 601

Acknowledgments

This book is the result of a team effort. The contributors deserve our wholehearted thanks for sharing with us the fruit of their research and their analysis. Their patience during the process of bringing individual efforts into a common endeavor will be rewarded by what, we think, is a sum even better than its very impressive parts.

We would like to thank Lexington Books, especially Serena Krombach and Martin Hayward, for proposing that we edit a major book on Canadian foreign policy and remaining supportive throughout the process. We would also like to thank others at Lexington that ensured the successful completion of this lengthy project. Sheila Zwiebel did excellent work preparing the manuscript for publication, and Katie Funk and MacDuff Stewart provided timely assistance.

We would also like to thank Charis Egland, Bailey Trenchard, Greg Trumble, Sarah Lippitt, Jenny Coletta, Sean Bacon, Nicolas Moquin, and Balkan Devlen for their research and editorial assistance. Patrick James is grateful to the faculty, staff, and students of the Department of Political Science at the University of Missouri, Columbia, for providing an intellectually stimulating environment within which to carry out a project such as this volume. Nelson Michaud thanks the École nationale d'administration publique for its support and his assistant, Véronique Dumesnil, for her efficient assistance. Marc O'Reilly thanks Heidelberg College for its support of this endeavor.

Finally, we would like to thank readers, who, by acquiring this book, have accepted our invitation to explore the vast and complex realm of Canadian foreign policy.

Patrick James, Nelson Michaud, and Marc J. O'Reilly
January 2006

Abbreviations

ACCT	Agence de Coopération Culturelle et Technique
ALDE	Group of the Alliance of Liberals and Democrats for Europe
AMAP	Arctic Monitoring and Assessment Program
APEC	Asia-Pacific Economic Cooperation
ASW	Anti-Submarine Warfare
AU	African Union
BC	British Columbia
BCBS	Bank for International Settlements' Basel Committee on Banking Supervision
BCNI	Business Council on National Issues
BENELUX countries	Belgium, the Netherlands and Luxemburg
BNA Act	British North America Act
BPG	Binational Planning Group
CAFF	Conservation of Arctic Flora and Fauna
CAP	Common Agricultural Policy
CAR	Canadian Airborne Regiment
CAST	Canadian Air-Sea Transportable Brigade Group
CBCIIA	National Capital Branch of the Canadian Institute of International Affairs
CCCE	Canadian Council of Chief Executives
CCFDP	Canadian Centre for Foreign Policy Development
CCPC	Canadian Conflict Prevention Committee
CCPI	Canadian Conflict Prevention Initiative
CF	Canadian Forces
CFIB	Canadian Federation of Independent Business
CFSP	Common and Foreign Security Policy
CGR	Committee on Government Representatives for the Participation of Civil Society

CIBC	Canadian Imperial Bank of Commerce
CIDA	Canadian International Development Agency
CIMIC	Civil-Military Cooperation
CMA	Canadian Manufacturers Association
CME	Canadian Manufacturers and Exporters
CMS	Chief of Maritime Staff
CoR	uropean Union's Committee of the Regions
CREW	Combat-Related Employment of Women
CUSFTA	Canada-U.S. Free Trade Agreement
CUSO	Canadian University Service Overseas
DFAIT	Department of External Affairs and International Trade
DND	Department of National Defence
DOD	U.S. Department of Defense
DRS	Defence Structure Review
EC	European Community
ECB	European Union Central Bank
ECCP	European Centre for Conflict Prevention
ECJ	European Union Court of Justice
EFM	Emergency Financing Mechanism
EPPR	Emergency and Preparedness and Response
ERDF	European Regional Development Fund
ERT	European Roundtable of Industrialists
EU	European Union
EUFOR	European Union Force in Bosnia and Herzegovina
EUROPOL	European Law Enforcement Organization
FAC	Foreign Affairs of Canada
FSF	Financial Stability Forum
FTA	Free Trade Agreement
FTAA	Free Trade Area of the Americas
GATT	General Agreement on Tariffs and Trade
GUE/NGL	Confederal Group of the European United Left/ Nordic Green Left
HIPC	Highly Indebted Poorest Countries
HST	Hegemonic Stability Theory
IAIS	International Association of Insurance Supervisions
IBRD	International Bank for Reconstruction an Development
ICBL	International Campaign to Ban Landmines

ICC	International Criminal Court
IFIs	International Financial Institutions
IMF	International Monetary Fund
IND/DEM	Independence/Democracy Group
INF	Intermediate Range Nuclear Forces Treaty
IOSCO	International Organization of Securities Commissions
IRDC	International Development Research Center
ISAF	International Security Assistance Force
JHA	European Union's Justice and Home Affairs
LTCM	Long Term Capital Management
MAI	Multilateral Agreement Investment
MARCOM	Maritime Command
MFN	Most-Favored Nation
MGU	Mixed Gender Unit
NACU	North American Customs Union
NAFTA	North American Free Trade Agreement
NAMU	North American Monetary Union
NATO	North Atlantic Treaty Organization
NCGs	Non-Central Governments
NCM	Canadian Forces Non-Commissioned Members
NDP	New Democratic Party
NEP	National Energy Programme
NEPAD	New Economic Partnership for Africa's Development
NGOs	Non-Governmental Organizations
NORAD	North American Aerospace Defense Command
OAS	Organization of American States
OAU	Organization of African Unity
ODA	Official Development Assistance
OIRP	Office of International Relations and Protocol
PAME	Protection of Arctic Marine Environment
PC	Conservative Party of Canada
PCN	Pro-Canada Network
PCO	Private Council Office
PMO	Prime Minister's Office
PNWER	Pacific Northwest Economic Region
PQ	Parti Québécois
PSE	Socialist Group in the European Parliament

PTA	Preferential Trading Arrangements
QMV	Qualified Majority Voting
RAF	British Royal Air Force
RCMP	Royal Canadian Mounted Police
RCN	Royal Canadian Army
RDC	Democratic Republic of Congo
RMA	Revolution in Military Affairs
ROO	Rules of Origin
ROTC	Reserve Officer Training Corps
RTAA	Reciprocal Trade Agreements Act
SARS	Severe Acute Respiratory Syndrome epidemic
SEA	Single European Act
SCFAIT	Standing Committee on Foreign Affairs and International Trade
SFOR	Stabilization Force in Bosnia
SWINTER trials	Service Women in Non-Traditional Environments Role
TEU	Treaty of Maastricht on European Union
TIEA	Trade and Investment Enhancement Agreement
TNA	Trade Negotiations and Agreements
UEN	Union for Europe of the Nations Group
UK	United Kingdom
UN	United Nations
UNEF	United Nations Emergency Force
UNESCO	United Nations Economic, Social, and Cultural Organization
UNICEF	United Nations Children's Fund
UNSC	United Nations Security Council
USN	United Sates Navy
U.S.S.R.	Soviet Union
Verts/ALE	Group of Greens/European Free Alliance
WEU	West European Union
WMD	Weapons of Mass Destruction
Wren	Women's Royal Canadian Naval Service
WTO	World Trade Organization
YMP	Youth Millennium Project

1

Canadian Foreign Policy in a New Millennium: The Search for Understanding

PATRICK JAMES, NELSON MICHAUD, AND MARC J. O'REILLY

People from around the world perceive Canada in a variety of ways. From a North American perspective, it can be considered either a reliable U.S. ally in NORAD, for example, the Canadian-American organization responsible for North American defense, or an angry, intransigent neighbor intent on getting its way on softwood lumber, fisheries, and other issues deemed vital to Canadian economic interests, regardless of their impact on the country's standing in Washington or Mexico City. Canada's foreign policy may endear it to the United Nations and other multinational institutions, on which Canadians rely somewhat extensively, but recent restricted spending on defense and a refusal to endorse U.S. policy on Iraq have vexed the White House, which expects Canada to contribute its fair share to North American security, especially in a post-9/11 world. Most Canadians bristle at such chiding, however, eager to contrast Canada's identity—considered a mix of western European and North American values—with that of the United States.

Beyond North America, Canada's international reputation still earns it respect in various world fora, although the luster of Canadian foreign policy has faded in recent decades. Countries expect Ottawa, for instance, to temper U.S. policy excesses in the Americas and French high-handedness within La Francophonie, an organization whose members have in common the French language. As a result of Canada's efforts abroad, many foreigners perceive Canadians as staunch defenders of human rights, peacekeepers, and honest brokers—an assessment most Canadians not only believe true, but approve of wholeheartedly.

These ascribed qualities may stoke Canada's *amour-propre*, but increasingly they are based largely on past glories. One might even ask whether these traits should be considered more myth than fact. The country may not be a haven for international terrorists, despite Washington's complaints about Canada's lax pre-9/11 immigration policies and flimsy border security, but Canadian peacekeeping, once the nation's hallmark, should not be romanticized, as fewer Canadian soldiers serve in zones of conflict and Canada's contribution trails that of many countries. Such unnerving consequences of Ottawa's recent policies reflect the country's reorientation in the past dozen or so years. Following the end of the Cold War, a momentous event that resulted in a reevaluation of Canadian foreign policy, the governments of Brian Mulroney and Jean Chrétien tried to harmonize Canada's external relations with its domestic imperatives— e.g., reducing the sizeable federal budget deficit and reforming the ailing health care system. Unfortunately for Canada, these efforts lessened Ottawa's role abroad and underscored a post–World War II Canadian transition from a country that mattered internationally in the 1940s and 1950s to one often overlooked or even dismissed since the 1990s.

Canadian foreign policy in the wake of World War II took advantage of a very atypical international context. As "total war" devastated much of Europe and some of Asia, Canada achieved a level of power and influence it never could have envisaged at the onset of hostilities in 1939. Ottawa joined the war effort out of loyalty to the United Kingdom, which granted Canada its domestic independence in 1867 but dictated its foreign policy until 1931. As they did in World War I, Canadians fought bravely throughout the conflict, and their efforts on D-Day and in countless other battles helped secure victory for the Allies. As a result of this notable achievement, undoubtedly a contender for the country's finest moment, Canada emerged from World War II with assets previously unavailable to it—that is, a thriving economy, potent military force, and diplomatic clout—and its territory unscathed. While Great Britain and France, the two principal sources of Canada's European heritage, staggered into the postwar era, one soon to be characterized by the Cold War competition between the

United States and the Soviet Union and their respective allies, Canada strode into it confidently. In the heady years before and following V-J Day, Canadian diplomats helped establish the Bretton Woods economic system, the United Nations (UN), and the North Atlantic Treaty Organization (NATO), hallmarks of a new world order—unlike in recent centuries, one not dominated by European Great Powers.

Because the United States, and to a lesser extent the Soviet Union, United Kingdom, and France, overshadowed Canada, scholars of Canadian foreign policy referred to the country as a "principal power" or "middle power" (i.e., one that could make a variety of political, economic, and military contributions but lacked the capabilities and influence of the great powers and superpowers). Other analysts, however, mindful of Canada's economic and other ties to the United States, deemed the country no more than a "satellite power."

This book seeks not to revisit such debates, which persist and which Andrew Cooper and Kim Richard Nossal have effectively reviewed in their well-regarded books.[1] As Cooper, Nossal, and others clearly state, Canada differs markedly from countries such as the United States and Great Britain as well as from so-called developing countries, which make up the majority of the world's polities. By spotlighting Canadian idiosyncrasies within a global context defined by wrenching juxtapositions—e.g., opulence for the few, impoverishment for many; amazing scientific discoveries coupled with potentially catastrophic environmental degradation; optimism for some, despair for millions—this volume offers an updated examination of Canada's international role some fifteen years after the dismantling of the Berlin Wall ushered in a new era in world politics.

Given that many works offer fine treatments of various aspects (i.e., issue areas and the evolution) of Canadian foreign policy, this volume tackles recent developments, which authors in this collection seek to understand. The specialists who have contributed their expertise to this book provide sophisticated analysis—conceptual as well as historical—rather than simply impressionistic judgments about contemporary events. This volume, the first in a series that examines the foreign policies of a diversity of nations, does not examine every important issue in Canadian foreign policy; instead, it tries to highlight both well-known and understudied topics. This marriage of the familiar and the underappreciated enables readers to grasp much of the complexity of current Canadian foreign policy and appreciate the challenges policymakers must meet in the early twenty-first century.

With the book's *raison d'être* in mind, the next section of this introductory chapter examines in greater detail the volume's rationale.

CONTEMPORARY CANADIAN FOREIGN POLICY: AN OVERVIEW

In his recent bestseller, *While Canada Slept*, Andrew Cohen details the demise of Canada's post–World War II foreign policy.[2] In his book, Cohen explains that Canadians once possessed competent and influential diplomats, a well-equipped and well-trained military that performed capably, especially in its favored peacekeeping role, and a generous policy of foreign assistance. The so-called Golden Age ended in the 1960s, however, as the Canadian government reconsidered its priorities and world politics attenuated some of Canada's previous advantages—as a respected middle power, it had influenced both great and small powers.

Lacking the political will to rehabilitate its flagging international reputation, Ottawa spotlighted domestic matters, especially welfare and constitutional issues. With the francophone province of Québec threatening to secede from Canada, prime ministers from Pierre Trudeau to Jean Chrétien worked assiduously to ensure Canadian unity. Their efforts, while mostly successful, kept the country whole; yet, ironically, Canada mattered less and less internationally. Ottawa occasionally made a noteworthy contribution to world peace and betterment (e.g., it helped end apartheid in South Africa, successfully promoted the international community's right to intervene in a given country to preserve democracy and human rights, and sponsored the 1997 anti-personnel land mine treaty—known as the Ottawa treaty), but, as John Manley pointed out while foreign minister under Chrétien, its actions rarely matched its lofty "human-security" rhetoric. Regrettably, many Canadians remained oblivious to this fact—they still thought of their country as "Dudley Do-Right" rather than "Dudley Can't-Do" or "Dudley Won't-Do."

As Cohen and scholars such as Denis Stairs, Kim Richard Nossal, and Michael Ignatieff have noted, not even the seminal events of 9/11 and their aftermath awoke Ottawa from its torpor.[3] As the United States, Canada's leading trading partner and ultimate guarantor of its security, searched for the proverbial monsters to destroy—Osama bin Laden, al-Qaeda, the Taliban, and Saddam Hussein—Chrétien hesitated to support Washington wholeheartedly. Content to utter the pithy clichés of a reflexive multilateralism egregiously out of step with America's instinctive unilateralism and the seemingly boorish "you're with us or against us" attitude of the George W. Bush administration, the prime minister and his cabinet dithered and stumbled as they tried to assert their country's independence, work through the United Nations, and accommodate U.S. security needs.

While Chrétien often neglected foreign policy during his ten years in office (1993–2003)—thereby exasperating an already discouraged bureaucracy—academic writing on the subject continued, mostly in publications such as the *International Journal*[4] and *Canadian Foreign Policy*.[5] In 1997, Andrew Cooper published an excellent textbook, one that, like Kim Nossal's 1989 work, offered a useful analytical framework and relied on illuminating case studies.[6] The *Canada Among Nations* series, published annually, also provided, and continues to make available, informative articles on different facets of Canadian foreign policy. In recent years, the topic of Canadian decline has pervaded the annual volume with subtitles such as "Vanishing Borders" (2000), "Fading Power" (2002), and "Coping with the American Colossus" (2003).

The bleak assessment of Canadian foreign policy seemed unanimous. Yet, could Canada really have lost all clout and relevance in the world since the end of the Cold War? Canadians might have forfeited their conventional place in the world, but perhaps they had pursued different objectives and tackled different kinds of global problems in the past fifteen or so years. Hence, the rationale for this volume, which seeks to emulate the *Canada Among Nations* books but broaches the subject from a distinctly political science perspective, while also incorporating interdisciplinary concerns (e.g., political economy) and historical perspective. Political scientists rely on theories as well as on various qualitative and quantitative methodologies to explain international phenomena. That kind of social science expertise enables the scholars in this book to examine issues in Canadian foreign policy in a variety of insightful ways. Furthermore, while several contributors explore familiar topics such as Canada–U.S. relations and peacekeeping, others spotlight less familiar matters, such as Arctic policy, La Francophonie, and paradiplomacy.

Every chapter contributes something unique, but the visual representation of the volume—or "map" of Canadian foreign policy—found in the next section places each topic at a given location as a function of its range of inclusion in geographic and issue-based terms. The map summarizes what the book contributes collectively to an understanding of Canadian foreign policy. It also draws attention to components that lack coverage and might be given higher priorities for inclusion in a future study. The final section of this chapter contains individual chapter summaries. Each one provides a sense of what the chapter contributes both in a particular area and in a more general way to an understanding of Canadian foreign policy.

A MAP OF THE BOOK & OF CANADIAN FOREIGN POLICY

Figure 1.1 provides a sense of the contributions of this volume as conveyed by its respective chapters. The figure displays the contents along two dimensions: geographic and issue-based. Along the vertical axis is the range of issue coverage, from comprehensive, through partial, to single. A dividing line between security and political economy issues is adopted here. A given chapter will be seen to cover one or both types of issue; to be regarded as comprehensive, it must contain a wide selection from each.[7] Geographic coverage, which ranges from global, through regional, to intrastate or single state, appears as the horizontal axis. Substantive contributions made by respective chapters in this volume are mapped out within the figure. For example, chapter 16, by Charles F. Doran, appears at the upper-right corner and is designated by its substantive focus: the United States. This chapter examines contending explanations for U.S.-Canada relations. It focuses on a single country, the United States, in relation to Canada, and is comprehensive in terms of the issues addressed. All other chapters of the volume are assigned positions within this figure in the same manner.

While many other schemes of classification might be proposed, geographic range and the scope of issues included are fundamental to mapping out the analysis of public policy. *Where* events occur, and *what* is on the agenda, emerge as the most basic questions to answer in identifying the boundaries for a policy-oriented investigation. The most obvious additional dimension, perhaps, would be time frame, but this is regarded as less central than those considered here. A summary of the figure's contents will reveal (a) what is covered by the present study and (b) areas

Geographic Coverage

	global	regional	single state/intrastate
comprehensive	political economy and military effectiveness; trade; provincial diplomacy	Arctic	United States; Canadian prime ministers
partial	La Francophonie	Latin American Security; Middle Eastern Security; EU political economy	military capability; Quebec sovereignty
single	peacekeeping; conflict prevention; overseas development assistance; human rights; international financial architecture		gender integration in the navy; civil society participation

Issue Coverage

FIGURE 1.1
A Map of Canadian Foreign Policy

that, for constraints of space more than anything else, are not addressed. The discussion progresses from the most to the least aggregated sectors within the figure.

Comprehensive coverage of issues at the global level is threefold. The chapters here include both political economy and security issues. They also encompass institutions and political processes. Chapter 3, by Andrew Richter, focuses on both political economy and military effectiveness as related to the armed forces, while chapter 4, by Michael Lusztig, pertains to trade writ large. A third contribution within this sector, chapter 5 by Richard Vengroff and Jason Rich, pertains to the provincial role in foreign policy. Moreover, this treatment of subnational government involvement in policy beyond Canadian borders—one of several understudied topics in this volume—is a feature that helps to separate the present collection from others that might be consulted.

Next at the global level are chapters with an issue range that is partial in nature. La Francophonie, which extends to various locations around the world and includes very diverse French-speaking countries and sub-national entities (i.e., states or provinces), is included here. Chapter 6 by Greg Donaghy and Neal Carter examines the activities of the members of this linguistically based organization across several issues. Subject matter includes cultural issues, trade, human rights and governance, but not military security.

Several individual issues are assessed on a global basis. In chapter 7, Kimberly Marten addresses peacekeeping. This chapter is security-oriented and conveys the story of Canada's role as a middle power. Chapter 8, by Koren Marriott and David Carment, provides a sense of Canadian views on conflict prevention in the most relevant communities, including practitioners. In chapter 9, Jean-Sébastien Rioux discusses overseas development assistance, and in chapter 10, Bethany Barratt tackles human rights, especially its relevance to peacekeeping and foreign aid. In chapter 11, Duncan Wood analyzes Canada's financial "architecture," the final single issue. Wood spotlights the Canadian role in the evolution of various international financial institutions, an important subject in the study of political economy.

Some of the contributions to this volume are regional in focus and one is comprehensive in coverage—chapter 12 by Douglas C. Nord on the Arctic. While important to Canada in particular and the future viability of the world in general, this region is relatively neglected in foreign-policy studies. The chapter covers the region comprehensively, most notably in relation to development of the multifaceted Arctic Council.

Three regionally oriented chapters are partial in issue coverage. Chapter 13 by Athanasios Hristoulas on Latin America and chapter 14 by Marc J. O'Reilly on the Middle East focus on security issues; chapter 15 by Axel Hüelsemeyer on the European Union (EU) addresses political economy. Given the way events and issues have played out in each region, the time frames vary among these chapters. The chapter on Latin America spotlights the past decade—before that, Canada's involvement in the region's security was minimal. The chapter on the European Union also draws upon the previous ten or so years—not due to lack of history, but rather owing to the 1993 Maastricht treaty and its transformative effect on Canada–EU relations. Unlike chapters 13 and 15, the chapter on the Middle East draws upon two case studies separated by nearly fifty years to highlight the evolving Canadian role in conflict management.

One chapter in this volume is comprehensive in issue coverage and also pertains to a single state—chapter 16 by Charles F. Doran. Not surprisingly, given its central importance to Canada, this chapter focuses on the United States.

Two chapters are partial in issue coverage and pertain to the intrastate level. In chapter 17, Thomas G. Barnes examines Canada's lack of military capability. In chapter 18, James McHugh analyzes the issue of Québec sovereignty and its impact on Canadian foreign policy.

Finally, two chapters focus on the intrastate level and a single issue in each instance. In chapter 19, Carolyn C. James spotlights gender integration in the Canadian armed forces, specifically the navy, and relates that three-decades-old story to Ottawa's policy-making. In chapter 20, Jeffrey M. Ayres addresses the increasingly significant role of civil society participation in Canadian foreign policy.

Figure 1.1 allows for nine locations, which political scientists call ideal types. As evidenced by the preceding overview, only one location—a regional focus on a single issue—is without a chapter. Perhaps this absence stems from a methodological bias in the sub-discipline of area studies, which tends to look at a geographic region or sub-region more comprehensively or holistically—with at least a few issues studied in relation to each other. Despite not having a chapter in the ninth location, the map of Canadian foreign policy found in figure 1.1 features currently or increasingly significant topics such Canada–U.S. relations, national defense, La Francophonie, paradiplomacy, and the Arctic. Since it is worthwhile to address basic as well as underappreciated issues, the contents of figure 1.1 serve as a reasonable approximation to full coverage of Canadian foreign policy in terms of geographic scope and issues for a volume of this kind.

CONTRIBUTIONS TO THE VOLUME: A CLOSER LOOK
Although the matrix in figure 1.1 divides this book's nineteen substantive chapters into eight "easy-to-understand" categories, each contribution helps answer a fundamental question: Is Canada becoming less relevant internationally? While some authors in this volume underscore the country's inability or unwillingness to follow, if not shape, global trends, others spotlight its capacity and willingness to exercise influence in what, until recently, would have been considered unconventional ways. If, in fact, the world in the twenty-first century differs markedly from that of the twentieth, then maybe Canada is trying, albeit often tentatively and without much success, to forge a new role for itself. Canadians (and others) may barely recognize such a transition—and may continue to yearn for a mythical Golden Age policy wholly unsuited to Ottawa's current fiscal reality and international clout—but decades from now historians may point to these years as critical to the establishment of a Canadian foreign policy more in sync with the country's assets (political, economic, military, and sociocultural) and the hallmarks of global politics in the age of the Internet, al-Qaeda, and the American Colossus.

To assess whether Canada can reinvent itself internationally, a reader must first familiarize him/herself with the country's foreign policy-making institutions. In chapter 2, which, together with this chapter, serves as the introduction to this volume, Nelson Michaud explains who formulates and implements Canadian foreign policy. As in other parliamentary democracies such as the United Kingdom, the executive branch of government, led by a prime minister, who serves as Canada's head of government,[8] takes the policy lead. Unlike in the United States, the Canadian legislature—a bicameral institution made up of an elected House of Commons and an appointed Senate—provides minimal input into foreign-policy matters. A professional bureaucracy—known originally as the Department of External Affairs, renamed the Department of Foreign Affairs and International Trade in 1993, and dubbed Foreign Affairs Canada in early 2004—assists the prime minister, currently Stephen Harper, whose Conservative Party narrowly won the January 2006 federal election, and the minister of foreign affairs as they formulate and implement Canadian foreign policy. Other departments, especially those involving defense, development aid, and international trade, provide additional expertise, as do the Prime Minister's Office and the Privy Council Office, both of which cater exclusively to the prime minister's political and bureaucratic needs. This type of organizational structure resembles that found in the United States, France, and many other countries.

Although Canada's prime minister is not the head of state, a title which the U.S. president holds in addition to that of head of government, Paul Martin possesses more decision-making authority than his counterpart, George W. Bush—during the negotiations that would culminate in the 1988 Canada-U.S. Free Trade Agreement, President Ronald Reagan often reminded his friend Canadian Prime Minister Brian Mulroney of that fact. Due to the United States' diffused system of government, whereby the three branches of government—executive, legislative, and judicial—check each other, the president must often persuade others rather than dictate to them, whereas the prime minister can opt for the latter approach far more easily and at minimal political cost. With this basic information in mind, the following chapters in this book, which divide into five parts, examine a variety of important issues.

Part I

In chapter 3, the initial contribution to part I, which spotlights aggregated issue areas, Andrew Richter analyzes the most visible aspect of Canada's so-called recent decline: the demise of its military. Not only does Richter expertly chronicle decisions and developments since 1968; he also seeks to understand why Ottawa allowed Canadian Forces to wither, a condition that persists. Richter explains how governments since Pierre Trudeau deemed military matters of secondary importance. Not merely content to describe a policy debacle, Richter proposes how the country can rehabilitate its tattered military so that it can resume its historic role and/or fashion a new one.

In chapter 4, Michael Lusztig tackles trade and other economic matters often considered "low politics" and thus less important than military issues, which rank as "high politics." Although Canada relies on plentiful exports and imports to sustain its economic development, trade remains a "hidden component" of Canadian foreign policy, according to Lusztig. Examining twenty-five years of trade history, he detects a unique era when both the Liberals and the Progressive Conservatives (who recently merged with the Canadian Alliance to form the Conservative Party of Canada) evolved into free traders, thereby eschewing protectionism. To explain this transformation, he provides an insightful and well-documented historical overview, which spotlights the protectionists' loss of clout and the commensurate expansion of Canadian trade in the twenty-first century.

The final chapter of this first section probes an issue not often associated with foreign policy, namely, the role of subnational entities, in this case provinces—ten of them and three territories make up the Canadian federation. In an age of globalization, a phenomenon that often involves matters of provincial jurisdiction, Canada's provinces have sought to protect their economic and other interests while pursuing growth and other opportunities. Referring to this proclivity as "paradiplomacy," Richard Vengroff and Jason Rich point out in chapter 5 that Québec and other Canadian provinces possess a higher international profile than most U.S. states. In their chapter, Vengroff and Rich examine the origins of paradiplomacy while seeking to explain the proliferation of this type of foreign-policy activity, which could significantly alter Canada's foreign policy in the coming years.

Part II

Part II of this volume offers studies of more circumscribed issue areas. Though it is the lengthiest section of the book, it is by no means exhaustive. Thus, several important topics could not be included. With this caveat in mind, the chapters in part II offer a sample of some of the challenges—some well known, others less so—that confront Canada.

In chapter 6, Greg Donaghy and Neal Carter tackle one issue of paradiplomacy of particular importance to Québec, Canada's French-majority province, namely, La Francophonie. In their study, Donaghy and Carter describe effectively the evolution of this post-colonial institution (which includes countries such as Sénégal, Haïti, and France) while highlighting the shortcomings of this somewhat obscure organization: its size, identity problem, and the habits of some of its members—who regularly violate human rights. This chapter illustrates how Canada, a country committed to multilateralism, adjusted its foreign policy (not always willfully, mind you) to accommodate the heartfelt desire of one of its provinces to make its presence, views, and aspirations known internationally via a forum that celebrates French culture. Finally, like its predecessor, this chapter expands the scope of Canadian foreign policy.

In chapter 7, Kimberly Marten addresses an issue very familiar to most Canadians: peacekeeping. To end the 1956 Suez crisis, Foreign Minister Lester B. Pearson called for the establishment of the first ever UN peacekeeping force. For his diplomatic efforts, Pearson received the Nobel Peace Prize, the only Canadian to do so. Canadians so revere international peacekeeping, and their country's participation in dozens of missions, that a monument stands near Parliament honoring the "blue helmets" for their service and sacrifice. The reverse side of the ten-dollar bill also pays tribute to Canadian peacekeepers. To differentiate themselves from Americans, Canadians spotlight their government's commitment to peacekeeping, which contrasts with Washington's preference for non-UN military solutions.

Peacekeeping today, however, differs from that of Pearson's era. New political, economic, military, and sociocultural challenges have resulted in post–Cold War UN interventions in various civil wars, especially in Africa. As a result, "blue helmets" must engage in peacemaking and peacebuilding as well as traditional peacekeeping. Although the demand for well-trained peacekeepers exceeds the supply, the Canadian contribution to UN missions has declined as Ottawa's defense expenditures have shrunk in the past four decades. Despite its thriftiness, Canada continues to earmark its soldiers for both UN and NATO peacekeeping duty. Middle-power status and strategic culture imperatives usually explain Ottawa's commitment to collective and regional security, yet Marten emphasizes the "complex interactions of domestic party and bureaucratic politics" and underscores Canada's "unique location within NATO and in relation to the United States." Marten's contention may presage long-term Canadian policy, as the country adjusts to a post-9/11 world.

To avert another cataclysmic event (possibly involving weapons of mass destruction) and to prevent disputes which necessitate peacekeeping and other methods of conflict resolution, conflict prevention must occur. In chapter 8, Koren Marriott and David Carment study this issue, one in sync with Canadian values and consistent with the country's twenty-first century "human-security" foreign-policy agenda. Having carried out a survey on behalf of the Canadian Government, Marriott and Carment explain Canada's approach to conflict resolution and discuss policy implications.

While chapters 7 and 8 assess diplomatic and defense matters, chapters 9 and 10 tackle the third *d*—development—in what is now Canada's 3-D foreign policy. In chapter 9, Jean-Sébastien Rioux examines Ottawa's official development assistance (ODA) policy. In another example of reality belying rhetoric, Ottawa (echoing Canadians) says it values ODA, as it does peacekeeping, but does not fund it adequately. Not only is Canadian foreign aid well below the United Nations' target of 0.7% of Gross Domestic Product; analysts also characterize it as "a mile wide, but an inch thick" owing to Ottawa's habit of disbursing small sums to many countries. Rioux recounts the history of these shortcomings, explains who made the policy choices and why, and spotlights Prime Minister Chrétien's Kananaskis G-8 Summit commitment to assist impoverished African countries. But will the Canadian government honor Chrétien's pledge to help Africa, a decision that could reorient Canada's foreign policy and enable the country to carve out a new international role?

Even if the Canadian government pursues an African initiative, a Canadian policy reversal could still ensue should African autocrats continue to violate their citizens' human rights, yet another issue dear to Canadians. In chapter 10, Bethany Barratt discusses the foreign aid–human rights nexus and asserts that, given Canadians' mass/elite concern for human rights and historic support for international sanctions that targeted violators from South Africa to Haïti, "of Western donor countries, Canada could be expected a priori to be the most likely to link aid to human rights." By comparing human rights to other Canadian policy priorities in the context of foreign aid from 1980 to 1996, Barratt asks an important question: "Are human rights something for which states are willing to sacrifice gains in other arenas, or are they only pursued when it is not costly to do so?" Barratt's answer offers Canadians a way to intertwine their values and foreign policy.

The final chapter of part II highlights economic issues. In chapter 11, Duncan Wood analyzes Canada's international financial policy. To compensate for its eroding military relevance, Ottawa invested in economic fora such as the G-8 to maintain the country's global status. Addressing various theoretical issues, Wood details how Canada helped reform the international financial system's architecture. Interestingly, Wood underscores the Department of Finance's lead role (eclipsing that of the Department of Foreign Affairs and International Trade) and valuable contributions to this process. Wood spotlights Canada's emphasis on multilateralism in the G-8 and G-20, which enabled the country to secure an emerging structure consonant with its own economic preferences. Again, such a tack may portend Canada's policy in the coming years.

Part III

The study of these circumscribed issues would not be complete, however, without an examination of regions. While part III emphasizes areas of traditional importance to Canadians (the United States and Europe), it also highlights other types of regions: obscure (the Arctic), nascent (Latin America), and prominent (the Middle East). This juxtaposition of the familiar and unfamiliar makes a valuable contribution to the study of contemporary Canadian foreign policy, yet omits Asia, Oceania, and Africa, though Donaghy and Carter as well as Rioux discuss events within that continent that pertain to La Francophonie and foreign aid. Part III, then, offers a selective, rather than exhaustive, viewpoint.

In chapter 12, Douglas Nord assesses Canada's Arctic policy, one that has endowed Canadian foreign policy with a "distinctive northern dimension" since World War II. In examining this dimension, considered more relevant than ever these days, Nord underscores sovereignty, defense, security, and environmental issues as well as the Arctic Council, a recently created multilateral forum where Canada serves as a leader. Nord analyzes the creation of this organization, particularly the Canadian–U.S. negotiations. For Canadians, this institution accords with their values and affords opportunities for international cooperation in an increasingly critical region of the world. Nord concludes his chapter by probing the future, thereby highlighting Canada's "changing national foreign policy."

Such a transition applies to the southern section of the Americas as well. In Canada's early history, the then colony served as a hub in the French and British mercantile systems, which relied heavily on Caribbean sugar and other goods. Following its independence, however, Canada mostly ignored Latin America, even failing to join—other than as an observer—the oldest multilateral organization in the world, the Organization of American States, until 1990. In chapter 13, Athanasios Hristoulas examines Canadian-Mexican ties. His study illustrates how, if previously neglected, a relationship will not yield the benefits one might otherwise have expected under different circumstances. His insight reinforces one of the main conclusions of this book.

In chapter 14, Marc J. O'Reilly spotlights Canada's involvement in the Middle East, a volatile region beset with protracted conflict, insurgency, arms proliferation, authoritarianism, and economic stagnation. Unlike Washington, Ottawa has involved itself only intermittently in Middle Eastern affairs since World War II. Nevertheless, Canadians proudly recall their country's contribution to the denouement of the 1956 Suez crisis, which vaulted Canada into international prominence and won Lester Pearson the Nobel Peace Prize. In 2003, when another Middle East crisis divided NATO members, Ottawa sought to reprise its Suez role. On that occasion, however, Canada's UN diplomacy failed. In comparing both events, O'Reilly posits that "reflexive multilateralism succeeded only when the global context allowed Canadian diplomats to make significant contributions to conflict resolution."

Although Canadians remain mostly unfamiliar with the Middle East, they know Europe much better thanks to their heritage, involvement in both World Wars, and NATO membership. Canada's economic ties with the European Union (EU) are less well known, however. As Axel Hüelsemeyer points out in chapter 15, European integration required a different Canadian policy. Whereas previous to the 1993 Maastricht treaty Ottawa dealt separately with France, Germany, the United Kingdom, and the nine other members (three others joined in 1995, ten in 2004) on matters of political economy, since Maastricht Canada has addressed EU as well as national concerns. To engage the twenty-five countries that make up the new Europe in the most beneficial way possible, Canadians must understand the European Union's complex institutions, a task Hüelsemeyer greatly facilitates.

Canadians may not yet grasp the intricacies of the European Union, but they possess much knowledge of the United States, their mighty neighbor, number one trading partner, and most important ally. Though Washington and Ottawa regularly invoke the world's longest undefended border as evidence of an unshakeable U.S.–Canadian bond, discord often characterizes the relationship—to wit, the acrimony of both the Diefenbaker-Kennedy, Trudeau-Reagan, and Chrétien-Bush eras. In chapter 16, Charles F. Doran highlights such "disturbances" by examining personalities, cycles of accord and tension, and the use of foreign policy for domestic purposes. While these factors explain past and present Canadian-U.S. relations, they also presage their future.

Part IV

Part IV of the book adds exogenous (i.e., external) explanation to geographic analysis. Recognizing that sovereignty underpins the Westphalian system of nation-states, every country strives to assert its political and legal authority over the territory it calls its own. Given that Canada no longer attends to its own defense in a serious manner, how can it defend its borders and thus its sovereignty? In chapter 17, Thomas G. Barnes reviews U.S. foreign policy in the past century, especially since 9/11, in an effort to elucidate how Canada, a country driven by its multilateral instincts, should cope with its power politics–obsessed neighbor. His prescription calls into question the very axioms of Canadian foreign policy, and thus should shock many Canadians, yet his provocative analysis provides important insight into how Washington perceives Ottawa and how Canada's policy-makers must contend with U.S. national-security demands.

In chapter 18, James McHugh tackles Québec sovereignty, Canada's most divisive domestic issue. If that French-speaking province ever achieved independence, the Canadian nation-state might cease to exist. At the very least, its international influence would likely erode precipitously. In the wake of the Canadian Supreme Court's 1998 *Québec Reference Case*, however, whether or not Québec can legally separate from Canada remains in doubt. According to the Court, Québec cannot unilaterally withdraw from the Canadian federation. In McHugh's opinion, this decision therefore precludes Québec from pursuing its own foreign policy—a controversial assertion with potentially serious implications for Canadian foreign policy.

Part V

Although McHugh's chapter ends part IV, it could just as well be included in part V, which highlights endogenous (i.e., internal) explanations of Canadian foreign policy. In chapter 19, Carolyn C. James examines the role of women. Unlike most studies, which spotlight policy-making, James's work addresses policy implementation, specifically women in Canada's navy. Her chapter compares the U.S. and Canadian experiences, thereby underscoring similarities and differences between the two countries, especially as they pertain to civil rights and their impact on foreign policy.

In chapter 20, the final substantive chapter of the book, Jeffrey M. Ayres studies civil society and its ramifications for Canadian foreign policy. Though this topic remains somewhat obscure to most Canadians, civil society will no doubt exercise a profound impact upon Canadian policy-making in the coming decades. In his chapter, Ayres reviews the international and domestic contexts that have allowed staunch advocates of civil-society notions, such as democratization, to shape the Chrétien government's foreign-policy agenda and decision-making style.

The conclusion of this volume draws upon the previous nineteen chapters in an effort to identify, characterize, and understand Canadian foreign policy, as the country copes with the political, economic, military, and sociocultural trends of the new millennium. In a post-9/11 world, threats such as international terrorism and weapons of mass destruction ought to continue commanding Canada's full attention. Yet other threats, such as disease and environmental degradation, require immediate responses as well. This book shows that Canadians—whether elected officials, diplomats, bureaucrats, or ordinary citizens—remain attuned to the world's problems. They also seem aware of the possibilities before them: opportunities that should keep Ottawa awake and occupied.

NOTES

1. Andrew F. Cooper, *Canadian Foreign Policy: Old Habits and New Directions* (Scarborough, Ontario: Prentice Hall Allyn and Bacon Canada, 1997); Kim Richard Nossal, *The Politics of Canadian Foreign Policy*, 2nd Edition (Scarborough, ON: Prentice-Hall Canada, 1989).

2. Andrew Cohen, *While Canada Slept: How We Lost Our Place in the World* (Toronto: McClelland & Stewart, 2003).

3. Denis Stairs, "Trends in Canadian Foreign Policy: Past, Present, and Future," *Behind the Headlines* 59, no. 3 (Spring 2002): 1–7; Denis Stairs, "Myths, Morals, and Reality in Canadian Foreign Policy," *International Journal* 58, no. 2 (Spring 2003): 239–256; Kim Richard Nossal, "Canada: Fading Power or Future

Power?" *Behind the Headlines* 59, no. 3 (Spring 2002): 9–16; Michael Ignatieff, "Canada in the Age of Terror—Multilateralism Meets a Moment of Truth," *Policy Options* 24, no. 2 (February 2003): 14–18. See also Graham F. Walker, *Independence in an Age of Empire: Assessing Unilateralism and Multilateralism* (Halifax: Centre for Foreign Policy Studies, 2004).

4. See especially volume 58, no. 1 (Winter 2002–2003), which contains analyses of key issues of Canadian foreign policy, and volume 58, no. 4 (Autumn 2003), which offers advice to Paul Martin, the incoming prime minister of Canada.

5. See especially Louis Bélanger, Andrew Cooper, Heather Smith, Claire Turenne Sjolander, and Robert Wolfe, "Most Safely on the Fence? A Roundtable on the Possibility of a 'Canadian' Foreign Policy after 9/11," *Canadian Foreign Policy* 11, no. 1 (Spring 2004): 97–118.

6. Cooper, *Canadian Foreign Policy*; and Nossal, *The Politics of Canadian Foreign Policy*.

7. It is understood that security and political economy are not mutually exclusive categories. However, this dividing line is conventional and easily observed in practice, so it offers advantages to a survey of the kind conducted in this volume. Other, more arcane complications, such as what counts as an individual issue or where the boundaries of regions begin or end, are not considered here.

8. The British monarch, currently Queen Elizabeth II, remains Canada's head of state, a legacy of the country's long-time membership in the British Empire. The governor-general, currently Michaëlle Jean, represents the British sovereign in Canada.

2

The Prime Minister, PMO, and PCO: Makers of Canadian Foreign Policy?

NELSON MICHAUD

Before we study further the issue areas we have selected to obtain a better understanding of Canadian foreign policy and its future, it is important to become more familiar with some of the key actors involved in the Canadian foreign-policy-making process. In order to understand the differences between the Canadian and the U.S. systems, comparison can be useful. This chapter aims to anchor the similarities and outline distinctions.

From an American point of view, the role played by the Head of Government is of prime importance in the making of foreign policy. Of course, the State Department and Congress also play a role, but the President and the White House are obviously at the core of international conduct. Is something analogous also the case in Canada?

When one considers the formal organization of the Canadian government, it seems that, relative to the head of government's role, the department and the minister of External Affairs display, in relative terms, a more important involvement than does the American Secretary of State. After all, Lester B. Pearson under Louis St. Laurent, Joe Clark in the first years of the Mulroney government, or Lloyd Axworthy in the Chrétien cabinet seem to have been given ample room to maneuver in a quasi-autonomous fashion. This is both on paper and substantively in some issue areas. The

Canadian prime minister, however, plays a major role in Canadian foreign policy and even more so in the conduct of the Canadian–U.S. relationship.

This may vary from one individual to another, but largely, most Canadian prime ministers themselves have played a role of significance in how Canada conducted its foreign policy. In fact, the attention prime ministers have paid to international affairs—or lack thereof—has dictated in large part how Canada behaved on the international scene. And, as Doran clearly demonstrates in his chapter, with regard to the United States, the personal relationship entertained by the occupants of 1600 Pennsylvania Ave. and 24 Sussex Drive has considerable weight. It is a good indicator not only of the health of the Canadian–American bilateral relationship, but also of Canada's influence on the world stage. Finally, not only is the prime minister involved, but his or her involvement is supported by a host of bureaucratic and political personnel found in two central agencies with important powers and influence on the whole of the government. As we will see in this chapter, the Canadian organization of foreign policy management relies on institutions such as the Privy Council Office (PCO) and the prime minister's office (PMO).

Therefore, for any student of Canadian foreign policy, these particularities cannot be left unexplored. I suggest covering them in three steps. First, I look briefly at the principles inherent in the Canadian political system. This will tell us why and how the prime minister obtained this relatively important chunk of foreign policy decisional power. Second, to establish the nature of the institutions we are looking at, I sketch the institutional framing. This will be useful in helping to understand what role these institutions play. And thirdly, I review Canadian history to evaluate how different prime ministers exercised their influence over Canadian foreign policy-making, from the "pioneers' days," through the "Golden Age" and up to the "contemporary times." The chapter concludes with a look at what can be expected from Prime Minister Paul Martin Jr. in his conduct of foreign policy, his strengths, and the pitfalls he must watch out for.

THE BASIC PRINCIPLES

In order to fully understand and appreciate differences that exist between Canada and the United States and the impact of these differences on the conduct of foreign policy, it is first necessary to grasp key elements linked to political organization in both countries. We will see that, allowing for the fact that both are democracies, the Canadian system has not much in common with its U.S. counterpart.

While in the United States checks and balances between legislative, executive, and judicial branches of government are at the heart of the American democratic organization, in Canada the concept of "responsible government" plays the same role. By responsible government we do not merely mean "a government that takes responsibility." The concept instead refers to the fact that the executive is chosen among the legislators and is answerable to the elected House of Commons, the lower chamber of Canada's bicameral Parliament.[1] In other words, the Cabinet as a whole, as well as ministers individually, must have the support of a majority of the elected members of Parliament. If they fail to achieve that, they must resign, individually in the case of ministers, or as a government in the case of the Cabinet. This latter instance is of consequence because it almost invariably means that one of two important changes will occur. Either the opposition will be asked to form the government or, more usually, an election will be called so the people, and not only their elected representatives, will determine if the incumbent government deserves to be supported or replaced.

In a two-party system, which Canada experienced from 1867 to 1921, it was rather easy for the government in place to get support from a majority of members of the House, since the government members were chosen within this majority and party line and discipline historically were strongly enforced. However, when three or more parties are present in the House, this can mean that, although the government relies on the support of a plurality of elected members, the support of a majority is harder to get. This can be the case even with a single member simple plurality, or "first-past-the-post," electoral system, which is recognized to provide majority governments more easily than a proportional representation system. Indeed, since 1921, when more than two parties succeeded for the first time in having candidates elected, Canada experienced minority governments following federal elections in 1921, 1925, 1926, 1957, 1962, 1963, 1965, 1972, 1979, 2004, and 2006—or eleven out of twenty-five. This situation in itself explains in part why we see an actual shift of responsibility from ministers to the prime minister: leadership matters and prevails. Moreover, in many international fora, the prime minister interacts with other heads of government and heads of states and that favors a concentration of power in his or her hands.

Finally, one may look at historical precedents in order to find the third factor of importance that helps explain why prime ministers play a role that is not theirs either from a constitutional[2] or organizational point of view. From John A. Macdonald, at a time when Canada had no internationally recognized personality, to Stephen Harper, in an era of globalization, prime ministers have carried their weight in shaping Canada's world role. As we will see in the third section of this chapter, they have exercised a major influence in the crafting of Canadian foreign policy.

THE INSTITUTIONAL FRAMEWORK

A finer point is in order here. It is important to understand that, although most prime ministers have worked effectively to leave a personal imprint in the Canadian foreign policy landscape, they do not do that by themselves. They are supported by a host of analysts and advisors who are found in two central agencies, known as the political PMO and the bureaucratic PCO. In Canada, the public service is much less affected by the U.S. Jacksonian spoils system (i.e., government appointments go to supporters of the winning side after an election), so the distinction between the two is important. Together the PMO and PCO form what could be called the "Canadian White House."

The PMO is staffed with close personal political advisors to the prime minister. Their first and foremost role is to facilitate the prime minister's reelection. Their roles include handling correspondence, taking care of the prime minister's agenda, and managing press and media relations. Other officers take care of nominations, speech writing, or caucus liaison. And, since the prime minister is also a member of Parliament, his constituency personnel are also part of the PMO. Where does foreign policy find its place in this, at times, huge machinery? It all depends on the importance the prime minister devotes to such issues. As we will see, this can vary quite considerably.

For its part, PCO is the "department of the prime minister" and is staffed with nonpartisan civil servants. Originally, the PCO was an organization that dealt with occasional questions sent to the Privy Council—that is, the Cabinet and the governor-general—but its role has evolved to become a nexus of information from where policy advice to the prime minister emerges and interdepartmental coordination is orchestrated. This means that, for all intents and purposes, all departments must coordinate their actions through the PCO. Moreover, this mandatory coordination extends to the political level, since the Secretariat for the Cabinet, established in 1940, has always been housed within the PCO. This gives a good idea of its overreaching importance. Of course, exchanges between the PCO and PMO are quite frequent, for both agencies respond to the same master.

Regarding questions of foreign policy, the advisory role of PCO has varied as a function of the requests coming from the top of the hierarchy. However, when career foreign officers are handed senior responsibilities within PCO, as was the case with Norman Robertson, a former star of the Canadian foreign service who served as Clerk of the Privy Council and secretary to the Cabinet from 1949 to 1952, one can assume that foreign policy questions get an attentive ear.[3] Moreover, within PCO, foreign policy matters fall on the desk of a foreign policy advisor to the prime minister who also assumes the role of Assistant Secretary to the Cabinet (Foreign and Defence policy). Officially, the foreign policy advisor "supports the Prime Minister in dealings with other heads of government and heads of state (e.g., correspondence, visits to Canada, and foreign travel). In addition, he/she communicates directly, on behalf of the Prime Minister, with foreign government representatives in Canada and with senior officials of foreign leaders' offices."[4] As Assistant Secretary to the Cabinet, this person "provides advice to the Cabinet on major foreign policy and defence issues."[5]

These central agencies are no doubt very powerful because they have direct access to the apex of power that is, in a Westminster-style government, the prime minister. Scholars Colin Campbell and George Szablowski have nicknamed them "the super-bureaucrats."[6] What was descriptively accurate when they crafted this label is even more true today; as Donald Savoie has demonstrated,[7] the influence of the prime minister and his entourage in policy-making has increased significantly over recent decades.[8] As a result, the role of people working in PCO, by its own nature, brings them right on the thin line between bureaucrats and policy-makers. They will find their balance by setting foot on either side of the line, depending on the issue. However, even though these actors are no doubt influential in the crafting of policies, the prime minister has the final word.

As we will see in the following section, the way the prime minister perceives foreign affairs has an impact on Canada's place in the world.

HISTORICAL OVERVIEW

The principles that I referred to above, and which form the framework for the institutions I have just defined, were present from Canada's inception in 1867 as a Dominion. At the time of Confederation, however, Canada had full sovereignty over its domestic policies, but still had to defer to London in matters of foreign relations. Even Canada's foreign representation was ensured by British diplomats around the world. Canada had merely commercial agents in London and Paris. This explains why, in questions such as the Boer War, the Alaska border dispute, and World War I, Canada was not the locus of decision.

None of this means that Canadian prime ministers refrained from being involved in foreign policy-making. Early prime ministers had to open the way and settle the ground rules on which Canada would later intervene on the world scene. Canada established a foreign affairs department in 1909. These "pioneer days" lasted from the creation of Canada until 1946, when Louis St Laurent became Secretary of State for External Affairs.

After World War II, we can see flourishing what many Canadian foreign policy practitioners refer to, not without nostalgia, as the Golden Age of Canadian diplomacy. This period was symbolized by one man, Lester B. Pearson, who was, in turn, Canadian ambassador (most notably in Washington), deputy minister, minister, and prime minister. The Golden Age ends with his retirement from politics in 1968, when what might be referred to as "contemporary times" get under way.

It is always useful to "slice up" huge amounts of information. However, the divisions I suggest here are more than mere teaching artifacts that aim at rendering the information more digestible. They refer to important differences in how the Canadian government perceived its foreign policy. From each of the sections below, we will learn that these contextual dissimilarities need to be taken into consideration in order to fully understand the particulars of the foreign policy then conducted.

Pioneer Days

Canada was born as a dominion of the British Crown. This new strata in the family of nations was established to designate what was in fact a colony that acquired its independence for matters of domestic interest. Consequently, it is not surprising that the Canadian Constitution of 1867 (the *British North America Act*) was almost silent about who would take care of Canada's role in the world. Only one section (132) deals with matters of foreign interests. It states that "The Parliament and Government of Canada shall have all Powers necessary or proper for performing the Obligations of Canada or of any Province thereof, as Part of the British Empire, towards Foreign Countries, arising under Treaties between the Empire and such Foreign Countries." Chapters in this book dealing with the international role of provinces also refer to the same section, for it is the ground—or lack thereof—on which legitimacy for international action in the spheres of provincial jurisdiction is found. This absence of a legislative and constitutional frame of reference, however, did not prevent Canada from becoming involved in international affairs.

Of course, in the absence of guidelines, Canada's international initiatives were made in a haphazard fashion. Canada's first prime minister did not wait for long before seeking a role in foreign relations.[9] Not that John A. Macdonald was a strong autonomist—far from that. He was much more a proponent of Canada having an autonomous voice *within* the Empire. The need for such a link with the Empire was in part sentimental, but Macdonald also saw in it a much more pragmatic application: Canada with Great Britain was in a better position to resist any annexation attempt by the United States. This allowed Macdonald to conduct negotiations himself with the United States in view of settling any dispute that followed the American Civil War.

Macdonald's successor, Alexander Mackenzie (1873–1878), was the promoter of a better definition of Canada's interests within the Empire. Mackenzie was a little more audacious than Macdonald. As did his predecessor, but on a more constant basis, he dealt directly with Washington rather than via British diplomats. Moreover, he also conducted trade talks with France through consular channels. This opened the door to attempts for autonomous initiatives by different ministers in his cabinet. However, Mackenzie ensured that the prime minister would maintain control over these quasi-foreign policy operations. So, when John A. Macdonald was reelected as prime minister in 1878, the Canadian head of government's predominant role became well established and there to stay. Until his death in 1891, Macdonald built on those precedents in order to make progress toward acquiring autonomy for the conduct of Canada's foreign relations.

The period from 1891 to 1896 saw a succession of short-term governments, five prime ministers being sworn in during these few years. Of course, such political instability was reflected in the conduct of foreign relations and not much happened during this period. Stability returned with the election of Liberal Wilfrid Laurier (1896–1911).

One of Laurier's first important moves was to give the highest civil servant—his deputy minister, Sir Joseph Pope—responsibilities for foreign relations. In the following years, several international events put the new structure to use. The battle over the Alaska border saw London and Washington sign an agreement detrimental to Canadian interests. Also, in the realm of trade, the system of imperial preference went against the Liberal tradition. And when the Boer War erupted, Canada had to decide for itself which form of participation it would support. Looking for the middle ground, Laurier suggested a limited participation, which went against both Anglo-Canadian imperialists, who found such an answer weak, and the French-speaking Canadian nationalists, who followed Henri Bourassa in asking: "What do we owe to England?"[10] But what really inspired Laurier in terms of foreign relations was his participation in Queen Victoria's Jubilee in 1897, an occasion during which he was knighted. Mingling with heads of government and heads of state was an experience that most of his biographers consider a turning point in his vision of Canada and, I would add, Canada in the world.[11]

All of these factors converged with Governor-General Earl Grey's plans for a foreign affairs department and convinced Laurier that Canada needed a separate organization to manage its foreign policy. Thus, in 1909, Laurier introduced a bill to create the Secretariat of State for External Affairs. For all intents and purposes, the new entity would be under the prime minister's stewardship and, at first, it was conceived of in terms of the basic definition of a secretariat. Laurier aimed to ensure three things: first, departments would have to address more issues with a nondomestic component, so there was a danger that noncoordinated actions would result in a quagmire that the government might have difficulty to resolve; second, since all archives and papers related to Canada's exchanges in the world were consequently disseminated in all departments having to deal with issues abroad, there was an operational need to have them filed in one place so the government would more easily have access to complete and reliable information; and third, there was a need to develop Canada's expertise to provide advice to the government on questions with an external dimension. Nevertheless, even with the Secretariat, the country remained far from counting on a genuine foreign affairs department. The prime minister simply wanted to be able to rely on an appropriate tool to better manage Canada's foreign affairs.

The twentieth century, of course, brought its share of world crises from which Canada could not stay immune. As a consequence, when Laurier asked the governor-general to call an election in 1911, the two major issues discussed on the hustings were reciprocity with the United States and establishment of a Canadian navy. With regard to the latter, a look at the Liberal electoral program shows that the prime minister, once more mastering the art of the ambiguous compromise, championed a navy that would be "Canadian in times of peace, and British in times of war." As for reciprocity the imposition of the Dingly tariff following the defeat of President Grover Cleveland saw Laurier lobby Washington in vain in order to give Canada better trading conditions. As a result of pressures coming from prairie farmers, Laurier became an avid defender of free trade with the United States.

Both topics became hotly debated, but neither proposal met with the approval of the electorate.[12] Laurier was defeated, and Conservative Robert Laird Borden became Canada's prime minister. Once in power, Borden advocated an autonomous Canada.[13] Already a Canadian nationalist sentiment was emerging, stronger in Québec than elsewhere in the country. For Borden, dominions had to have a say in the formulation and the conduct of the British Empire's foreign policy. When World War I erupted, Canada entered in the conflict the same day the United Kingdom did. Canada then put forth a military effort of importance, accomplishing exploits as witnessed by the victory of Canadian troops at the battle of Vimy Ridge. This convinced Borden that Canada should not leave all war initiatives to London. Throughout the war, he attended meetings of the imperial war conference and, most importantly, of the imperial war cabinet. There, prime ministers met, allowing Canada—as well as the other dominions and India—to discuss the issue at the highest level and perhaps exert some influence on the Empire's decisions. From strategic issues to mundane matters, dominions were able to get involved in the policy-making process, although with limited impact. The Empire still saw foreign policy as the prerogative of the Crown, not of its dominions. However, all efforts were not in vain. Borden was able to convince London to consider the dominions when ordering war matériel, instead of systematically buying it from the United States.

Influence was not one-way, however. Returning from a war meeting in 1917, and profoundly impressed by what he had seen at the front, Borden was a laconic man when he disembarked the transatlantic liner that had brought him back to Québec City. As soon as he arrived in Ottawa, though, his government "tabled"—or introduced—a conscription bill, bringing Canada's contribution to the war effort to its utmost limits. In order to have the bill passed, he had to sacrifice party unity, lose a minister who resigned over the issue, and call an election that divided the country along the linguistic/cultural line of French- and English-speaking communities.[14] And even after the election gave Borden enough seats in his Union government to pass the bill, riots erupted in Québec City on Easter weekend 1918, resulting in casualties.[15]

The prime minister's leadership in foreign relations and the conduct of war almost broke the country in two. It also had two major consequences—one international and the other domestic. On the international stage, Canada was able to get a seat at the Versailles peace conference in 1919 and have Borden sign the treaty in the country's name. Following the conference, Canada also got a seat at the League of Nations, with Raoul Dandurand chairing the League at one point.[16] This was an important move toward Canada's full autonomy on the world stage. Domestically, Borden's action would alienate Québec from the Conservatives for more than sixty years, allowing for what some have labeled a Liberal hegemony over the Canadian government.[17] In the meantime, however, his government had passed a bill giving the prime minister full and exclusive authority over the foreign affairs portfolio, a major step in solidifying influence over these questions.

When the following election was called in 1921, Liberal Mackenzie King faced Conservative Arthur Meighen, the man who sponsored the conscription bill.[18] The results were easy to predict. Even though, for the first time in Canadian political history, a third party successfully ran candidates, it became obvious that King would win and have a major influence on the years to come. His mandates were interrupted twice: the first time for a few weeks during a constitutional crisis in 1925–1926[19]; and the second time, between 1930 and 1935, when Conservative leader Richard B. Bennett became prime minister. Bennett struggled to resolve domestic problems, so he did not leave a mark on Canadian foreign policy. He tried to cure the Great Depression by promoting Imperial trade, but this did not do much to alleviate Canada's economic problems. He got involved in the Washington discussions that aimed at a revitalization of world trade. He chaired the London World Conference on Wheat, but the meeting did not yield significant outcomes. The results would come once Bennett had left office. Overall, being prime minister during the Great Depression did not do much to secure your career as a politician. As a consequence, the man to look at during these years in order to understand the evolution of Canadian foreign policy is William Lyon Mackenzie King, the longest-serving Canadian prime minister.[20]

King was a career civil servant turned politician. He was not charismatic, and many analysts say that if he had to conduct his career in our time and age of communications and "packaged" messages, he would not last long. A bachelor, he literally turned to his crystal ball for advice from his mother, a habit that makes Nancy Reagan's practice of consulting her astrologer pale in comparison. Despite these eccentric aspects of his complex personality, it remains that King was an astute politician. While he was not the most sensitive prime minister when it came to foreign policy questions, he nevertheless can claim three major achievements: he laid the last "bricks" that finally led to Canada's full international autonomy, he developed a special relationship with Washington that allowed Canada to play a role of significance in the crafting of the post-war world order, and he favored the development of a highly competent foreign service and department. Let us look, in turn, at each of these three prime ministerial accomplishments that had a tremendous impact on Canadian foreign policy.

King's first success was to solidify Canada's autonomy on the world scene. Three events of minor magnitude on the world scale, but of major importance for the future of Canadian foreign policy, can be recalled here. The first one happened in 1921 at a conference on disarmament. Canada was able to convince Great Britain to end the Anglo-Japanese alliance. This stance favored the United States in the Pacific region. As a result, Canada first positioned itself as a valuable and credible negotiator between the United Kingdom and the United States. Canada then established a firm continental position, clearly distancing itself from its Imperial metropole.

The second event Canada used to its advantage was signing a treaty in 1923 that bore upon fisheries and more precisely the harvest of halibut near the Canada-U.S. Atlantic maritime border. In those days, Canada was not allowed to sign treaties by itself; the presence of a British representative was necessary. In this specific case, the Canadian negotiator, Minister of Fisheries Ernest Lapointe,[21] insisted that the British diplomat present at the signature ceremony keep his pen in his pocket. This precedent (the first such rebuff by a U.K. dominion) was a cornerstone in establishing Canada's autonomy from London in matters of international negotiations and signified the end of Great Britain's unified Imperial diplomacy.

Canada turned matters to its advantage a third time during the Chanak crisis, an incident involving "diplomatic poker." That incident finds its roots in World War I: Following the Versailles treaty, the Ottoman Empire was dislocated. France, Italy, and Great Britain shared among themselves part of the territory that now is Turkey, then led by the "Father of Modern Turkey," Mustafa Kemal, a nationalist who wanted to retrieve the territories taken by the western Europeans. A solution was arrived at with the Italian and French governments, but no agreement could be reached with the British Crown. The only solution seemed to be an armed conflict that most likely would happen in the strait of Chanak.

British Prime Minister James Ramsey Macdonald asked if the Dominion would be ready to shoulder British efforts. As newspapers hyped the story, King stated that Canada would not participate before the issue had been discussed in Parliament. Since all of this would happen over the summer, with Parliament in recess, King's stance amounted to a clever gamble. He knew that participation in an Imperial war effort would be divisive in Canada, so he wanted to "buy some time." The issue would never be discussed, for the crisis was resolved before Parliament reconvened.

Following his clever ploy, King articulated new rules for Canada's participation in Imperial war efforts. As a result, Canada would not automatically become a belligerent whenever Britain went to war. Ottawa would henceforth participate of its own will, as it would in World War II, after declaring war on Germany separately from the United Kingdom. Following these Canadian initiatives and a similar and growing need for autonomy in other dominions, the British Parliament voted the Statute of Westminster in 1931, thereby enacting the recommendation of the Balfour Report as agreed upon at the 1926 Imperial Conference. Britain thus gave its dominions full sovereignty, which included foreign policy. As Kim Nossal notes, "the Empire was negotiated out of existence."[22]

At the same time that he freed Canada from the remnants of colonialism, King showed awareness of the importance of developing Canada's continental personality, something he was not ready to consider a few years earlier. Thanks to the friendship King developed with U.S. President Franklin D. Roosevelt, he was able to lead Canada to decision-making tables of importance. During World War II the two men brought their countries closer together than ever. The cornerstone of this relationship was laid in the summer of 1940 when Roosevelt invited King to his Ogdensburg residence. The location in upstate New York was optimal, for it overlooked Prescott, Ontario, a town on the other side of the St. Lawrence River. King was almost at home and the leaders met midway—in fact, much closer to Ottawa than to Washington.

The direct result of this summit was the agreement on the Ogdensburg statement, in which the leaders established the Permanent Joint Board on Defence, the first continental security agreement, to be followed by many others. The following year, the two leaders met again, this time in Hyde Park in April. Their discussion of the economy—more precisely, the war economy—led to the issuing of a declaration on cooperation. This set the tone for Canada's involvement in future, more important meetings.

For instance, Canada hosted conferences in Québec City, where Roosevelt and Churchill planned the D-Day invasion of Normandy and the strategy to end the war. Canada was an even more active player in Bretton Woods, where economic institutions such as the World Bank, the International Monetary Fund (IMF), and later, the General Agreement on Tariffs and Trade (GATT) were established in view of rebuilding a devastated Europe. Canadian diplomats were able to bridge gaps between the U.S. and the British delegations. Both the United States and the United Kingdom agreed on the need for stable monetary relations, but not for the same reasons. For Canada, it was important to find a solution: if the interests of its two principal economic partners were well served, its own interests would be well served, too. Here, Canada established itself as a multilateralist country, a position still at the heart of Canadian foreign policy.

One may note that, since the Canadian delegation was composed of officials from the Department of Finance and of the Bank of Canada, King was not involved personally in Bretton Woods. However, the role Canada played would not have been possible if not for the good relationship King had previously established with Roosevelt.

This effort at institution-building would be followed by others, namely, in San Francisco in 1945, when the United Nations (UN) was founded, and in Washington in 1949, when the North Atlantic Treaty Organization (NATO) was chartered. The Prime Minister went twice to the San Francisco conference. Canada obtained two key elements to be included in the parameters from which the Security Council, the most influential body within the UN, would operate. First, countries affected by Security Council decisions would be involved in the decision-making process. Second, the first criterion of eligibility for nonpermanent seats around the council table would be a country's participation in achievement of peace-related goals, objectives, and actions. Canada was also influential in crafting the NATO Charter, succeeding in having Article 2 state that the military organization would pursue social and economic policies. The Prime Minister no doubt played some role in these foreign policy successes, but, more importantly, Canada counted on a team of high-level and highly dedicated diplomats, who comprised the third legacy King left to Canada's foreign relations.

The establishment of a high-quality foreign policy bureaucracy was important. It established Canada's foreign policy "tradition," which continues to this day. As King was sworn in as prime minister, the strong man in matters of Canada's international relations was no longer Sir Joseph Pope, but his successor, Loring Christie, who had been recruited by Borden. King was ill at ease with Christie's conservative acquaintances, to the extent that he kept most responsibilities far from his subordinate's desk. Attending a conference at Queen's University (in Kingston, Ontario), King was impressed by the presentation about "Canada and foreign policy" made by the Dean of the Faculty of Arts, Dr. O. D. Skelton. King invited Skelton to join the circle of his close advisors and appointed him member of the Canadian delegation at the League of Nations. In 1925, he made Skelton Under Secretary of State for External Affairs.

The ability to provide solid expertise to the prime minister was among Skelton's first needs to meet. To reach this goal, targeted recruitment started. The first wave of recruits, who joined the Department of External Affairs in the 1920s, brought in key individuals, such as Lester B. Pearson, who would shape Canadian foreign policy for decades. The next forty years would be deeply marked by Skelton's reforms and the diplomats he recruited. Despite the added personnel, King did not delegate much. The decision-making process rested in his hands, though he relied heavily on Skelton, who also kept for himself most of the department's workload.

Wartime diplomacy called for a major increase in resources, and the postwar context, which included the creation of multilateral organizations such as the UN, kept Canadian policy-makers busy. A fatigued King finally delegated responsibilities for the conduct of Canada's foreign policy when he appointed his right-hand man and Québec lieutenant, Louis St Laurent, as Secretary of State for External Affairs in September 1946.[23] With the exception of a few years in the Laurier and Borden governments, it was the first time in almost thirty years that it was not the Prime Minister who held the portfolio. With a competent foreign minister and Department of External Affairs, Canada was set to embark upon its "Golden Age."

The Golden Age

St. Laurent's arrival as head of the department coincided with that of a new deputy minister, Pearson, then Canadian ambassador to Washington. The two men had known each other during the negotiations that led to the creation of the UN. This type of collaboration between the two would last until 1948. Two years after St. Laurent had been sworn in as Secretary of State for External Affairs, King resigned, and St. Laurent was selected as his successor. Pearson took over St. Laurent's post as foreign minister. Together, they would steer Canada's foreign policy for nine more years. Both men were strongly convinced that Canada could not stay away from the great debates of the world and both strongly professed that internationalism was Canada's best approach to world questions.

From a foreign policy point of view, St. Laurent was an idealist, though he continued King's policy. St. Laurent's stance was grounded in five principles that he outlined in a lecture given at the University of Toronto in 1947 when he was Secretary of State for External Affairs.[24] What is now known as the "Gray Lecture" was, in fact, the first statement outlining the tenets of Canada's post-war foreign policy. The five principles outlined in the lecture were political freedom, application of the principle of the rule of law in international affairs, national unity, values of Christian civilization, and Canada's acceptance to play an international role.

This last item represented a major departure from previous Canadian foreign policy doctrine. It allowed Canada to get involved in key institutions, especially the UN and NATO. It was the basis on which Canada answered the UN call for participation in the 1950–1953 Korean War. It is also the principle underlying Pearson's initiative to solve the 1956 Suez crisis. St. Laurent and Pearson also reacted to the 1947 Truman Doctrine by establishing dialogue and a negotiation process that would lead to an agreement about North America's defense.[25] This was in tune with the Roosevelt–King talks of the 1940s and would result in the establishment of the North American Air Defense Command (NORAD) in 1958.

An important element to note is that, generally speaking, during the St. Laurent years, the prime minister, although still present and very much interested in matters of foreign policy, did not play a role as prominent as in the years before or the years to come. Due in large part to the close connection between St. Laurent and Pearson and the fact that Pearson was perceived by his department as "one of our own," the Canadian foreign affairs bureaucracy exercised a lot of influence on policy-making. It might very well be one of the reasons why the department's historians have labeled this period the "Golden Age." This does not mean that disagreements did not occur between the prime minister and his foreign minister. In such circumstances, St. Laurent's wishes prevailed. An example would be when St. Laurent and Pearson pondered what answer to offer the French government in 1952, as it tried to deliver arms to its beleaguered army in Indochina.

When St. Laurent lost power to the populist prairie lawyer John George Diefenbaker, a chapter in Canadian foreign policy closed.[26] In fact, for many people at External Affairs, the Golden Age ended on that day in 1957. For the purpose of this analysis, however, I will extend it for eleven more years—as did Hilliker and Barry in their history of the department—that is, until a definite change in how to perceive Canada's role in the world was brought forward. Moreover, the number of new countries emerging from colonialism at the end of the 1950s and during the first part of the 1960s allowed Canada to expand its diplomatic network and apply extensively its principles of internationalism.

Under Diefenbaker's stewardship, however, two major and closely linked changes happened. First, there was an abrupt rupture in the complicity that existed between bureaucrats and their political masters. Diefenbaker was distrustful of the "Pearsonalities" hanging around the department. As a consequence, he centralized and kept as his own most of the foreign policy decisions. This tendency to make the prime minister the locus of the foreign policy decision-making process was exacerbated by the fact that Diefenbaker was not able to find a "suitable" Secretary of State for External Affairs before 1959, when Howard Green got the job. In fact, the situation was so bad that the Clerk of the Privy Council convinced the Prime Minister to appoint a "liaison officer," Basil Robinson, to manage the relations, if not tensions, between the PMO and the department.[27]

Several examples illustrate Diefenbaker's inclination to centralize the decision-making process. For instance, when Canada agreed to form a continental defense alliance with the United States (i.e., NORAD), it was the Prime Minister's decision to sign the agreement, the Cabinet not even having the chance to review the documents. It is true that this project had been in the works for some time and that several people had an opportunity to look at different drafts, but it remains that the final agreement was worked out by one person, the Prime Minister himself. Indeed, it was an odd time for such a concentration of power in the hands of one man: the Cold War was raging and, if Diefenbaker had an excellent relationship with U.S. President Dwight Eisenhower, it was quite a different story with John F. Kennedy.[28] The relationship was bad enough that, during the 1962 Cuban Missile Crisis, Kennedy refused to get in touch with Diefenbaker; instead the White House contacted the associate minister of defense, Pierre Sévigny, asking him to relay the news about Soviet missiles in Cuba to his boss. In response, Diefenbaker publicly doubted the severity of the facts that were reported to him, delaying orders to put Canadian armed forces on full preparedness, thereby infuriating the White House.

Diefenbaker was sworn in as Prime Minister after the elections of 1957, 1958, and 1962, but only his second mandate was at the helm of a majority government. Although he stood on precarious ground, Diefenbaker continued to manage foreign policy questions in a centralized fashion. For instance, he opposed U.S. pressure to give Canadian armed forces nuclear capability. In the end, these questions cost him his prime ministership. Early in 1963, he lost three ministers, who resigned over the "vagueness" of Canadian defense policy: Douglas Harkness (Minister of National Defense), Georges Hees (Minister of Commerce) and Pierre Sévigny (Associate Minister of Defense). Instead of losing a vote of confidence in the House, Diefenbaker asked the Governor-General to call an election, which the Conservatives lost to the new Liberal leader, Lester Pearson.[29]

Pearson's return to the helm was warmly welcomed in Ottawa and abroad. In fact, warm is a mild word for, according to Peyton Lyon, "[t]he welcome accorded to Pearson by allied leaders and also by the Ottawa mandarins, bordered on impropriety."[30] Such reverence, however, could not compensate for successive minority governments (1963 and 1965). One might have expected this former diplomat to put an impressive stamp on Canadian foreign policy, especially given the uncertainties left by his predecessor. Who else could better lead the country on the international stage?

Instead of leading, though, Prime Minister Pearson relied on Foreign Minister Paul Martin Sr., knowing that the department he knew so well would continue to serve him well. Pearson got involved with issues only when Martin's other responsibilities (political or leadership hopes) kept him away from his portfolio. So, quite paradoxically, the Canadian Prime Minister who was best prepared to handle foreign policy questions left lots of room to maneuver to his ministers and his officials. In fact, his government's foreign policy was not that well received by the public, which, in the wave of opposition in the United States to the Vietnam War, was taking a larger interest in its formulation. To answer these criticisms, Pearson called for a review of Canadian foreign policy. But Pearson had already left office when the review was published in 1968.

Regarding Canada–U.S. relations, Pearson had established an excellent rapport with the Kennedy Administration and the President himself. The relationship began well with Lyndon B. Johnson—after all, in January 1965 both signed the Auto Pact, a major trade agreement between the two countries. However, the atmosphere became tense after Pearson delivered a speech at Temple University in Philadelphia in April that criticized American policy in Vietnam. For Pearson, a Nobel Peace Prize laureate, negotiation instead of bombing seemed the obvious way to go. The speech came as Johnson was committing more troops and, the following day, at a scheduled meeting at Camp David, Johnson angrily communicated his displeasure to the Canadian Prime Minister. The Canada–U.S. relationship would remain cool as Prime Minister Pierre Trudeau and President Richard Nixon did nothing to repair ties between Ottawa and Washington.

Contemporary Times

The Liberal Prime Minister and the Republican President were elected only a few months apart. As it would later be the case with Ronald Reagan, Trudeau did not find much in common with his counterpart in Washington. The relationship he established with Jimmy Carter was more cordial, but perhaps merely benign, as some analysts have portrayed it.

Pierre Trudeau entered in politics in 1965 mainly to achieve one very personal goal: turn Canada into a multilingual, multicultural federal state with its own constitution and a Charter of Rights and Freedoms.[31] In spite of extensive travel as a university student, Trudeau lacked a foreign policy philosophy, though he publicly opposed Pearson on nuclear issues (i.e., whether Canada should acquire warheads). Trudeau expressed a profound interest in foreign civilizations but did not consider international relations worth studying. As Prime Minister, his commitment to NATO was at first weak. He even toyed with the idea of having Canada withdraw from the organization. He was also open to developing relations with Cuba; he made Canada one of the first nations of the "second wave" to recognize Mao's China and did not believe that the Soviet Union posed a military threat to Canada. His first speech to the UN was delivered in 1978, ten years after he became Prime Minister. Trudeau's decisions and actions clearly indicated that the country had entered a new era in Canadian foreign policy, where values such as Pearsonian internationalism would be reconsidered and subordinated to domestic concerns and policies.

Due to his charisma, Trudeau was the center of attraction of his government and his will surpassed those of other ministers, including his various foreign affairs ministers. One of them, Mitchell Sharp, was instrumental, however, in articulating the Trudeau's government's "Third Option," its best-known foreign policy.

As mentioned previously, a foreign policy review was under way as Trudeau was sworn in as Prime Minister. His response to the review was to reorganize Canada's foreign policy priorities. For him, economic growth (a domestic concern) took precedence over peace, security, and sovereignty. This was his definition of the Canadian national interest. To fulfil Trudeau's wish, Sharp emphasized the need to diminish Canada's economic dependency on the United States. Instead of maintaining the status quo, which was not desirable, or integrating more closely Canada's economy with that of the U.S., which would have met strong opposition from Canadian nationalists, it was preferable to diversify Canada's partners and intensify Canada's economic ties elsewhere, notably with Europe. This was the Third Option. The results were minimal.

Trudeau's government also implemented domestic policies that had a significant impact on Canada's foreign relations. For instance, American investors saw the establishment of a Foreign Investment Review Agency as a series of unfriendly stumbling blocks thrown in their way to impair economic exchanges between the two countries. The National Energy Program also upset the United States, but in this case, it also angered the oil-producing province of Alberta, which saw most of its revenues capped by the policy.

In addition to those initiatives, Trudeau made his mark by spotlighting official development assistance and North-South issues. He became an advocate of summit meetings and, over the years, dwelled on the Soviet threat. In the last months of his last mandate, he embarked on a peace tour that did not produce much. His policy stances of the early years had "burnt too many bridges" that would then have been useful in order to promote his peace initiative. As a consequence, most analysts consider Trudeau's impact on international policy and Canadian foreign policy minimal. In fact, the first signs of Canada's decline in power occurred during his tenure as Prime Minister. Such a diagnosis was all Brian Mulroney, the Conservative leader chosen in 1983, needed to build his own foreign policy stance, which rested on a good dose of easy-to-grasp formulas and open criticisms of Trudeau's policies.

Though Mulroney inherited a weak foreign policy upon becoming Prime Minister in 1984, his nine years in power proved quite successful.[32] His government was one of Canada's most activist—and Mulroney himself one of the most involved prime ministers—in the area of foreign policy, taking the country in new and very different policy directions, breaking with a number of traditions in Canadian statecraft, and embracing policy positions that, from the perspective of September 1984, were radical departures.

By trade, Mulroney was a negotiator. He kept his skills honed during both of his terms at the head of the Canadian government and took full advantage of his personal relationships with world leaders. His successes included the 1988 Free Trade Agreement (FTA) with the United States and the 1994 North America Free Trade Agreement (which added Mexico to the FTA). During his tenure, Canada joined the Organization of American States and contributed to the establishment of La Francophonie—an issue Carter and Donaghy discuss (chapter 6 of this volume). Mulroney also clashed with British Prime Minister Margaret Thatcher over South African apartheid. As well, he mediated between African leaders so they could resolve a food shortage crisis in neighboring states. In all of these areas, he managed to leave his and Canada's imprint on the world scene.

Mulroney was also very much influential in having good governance and human rights at the center of foreign policy decisions. He ensured that there would be increased cooperation between government and nongovernmental organizations (NGOs) in the area of development assistance, a partnership he forged during the 1984 famine relief effort in Ethiopia—and which is now part of today's familiar development assistance landscape. Mulroney also increased significantly the involvement of Parliament in the policy-making process, a practice Jean Chrétien's Liberal government would largely abandon—it would seek to bypass members of Parliament in favor of more intense engagement with the NGO community.

In many cases—with the exception of Defence, where so many actors were influential that nobody really controlled the implementation of the government's policy[33]—Mulroney's personal involvement helped craft these major outcomes in Canadian foreign policy. None of them attracted more attention, however, than the close relationship he established with both the Reagan and Bush administrations. Mulroney had spent much of his professional life as a CEO for an American natural resources company and, from this experience, had developed respect for, but most importantly, knowledge of how to deal with Canada's southern neighbor. He took full advantage of these skills to iron out the creases left by the stormy Trudeau-Reagan era.

This "super-relationship," as Mulroney himself portrayed it, did not please everybody, however. His political foes—the Liberals—exploited what many Canadians perceived as a too cozy U.S.–Canadian relationship, one that could jeopardize Canadian sovereignty. In their electoral platforms of 1993, 1997, and 2000, the Liberals committed themselves to a foreign policy very different from the one implemented by their Progressive Conservative predecessors. For instance, in 1993, the new Liberal Prime Minister, Jean Chrétien, emphasized the need to base foreign policy on Canadian values, linking foreign and domestic policies. His government advocated a "voluntary, independent and internationalist" role for the government in world affairs and, like Trudeau, insisted on keeping its distance from the American administration. In 1997, the Liberals reprised Mitchell Sharp's Third Option when they talked of a strategic vision that looked beyond North America (i.e., the United States) and toward Europe. In 2000, the Liberals once more promoted Canadian values as the basis of Canada's international leadership.

What happened under Chrétien inspired many writings and analyses (referred to in chapter 1), which deplored Canada's declining influence and lack of clout on the world scene. Chrétien, like his political mentor Trudeau, was clearly more motivated by domestic policy than foreign policy. (His lack of concern for foreign policy matters clearly illustrates how important the Canadian prime minister is to the country's foreign policy process.) In another parallel to Trudeau-era foreign policy, the Chrétien government's White Paper on defense resembled the Macdonald paper of 1971. Thus, despite profound changes in world order following the end of the Cold War, Prime Minister Chrétien mostly refused to steer Canadian foreign policy in a new direction. The Prime Minister's attitude vis-à-vis foreign policy was well illustrated when he abolished the Cabinet Committee that dealt with foreign affairs. Chrétien's decision allowed Canada's foreign ministers to promote their own initiatives.

Most prominently, Lloyd Axworthy touted a human security agenda for Canada, which yielded the 1997 Ottawa protocol banning anti-personnel landmines. Axworthy also instructed the Department of Foreign Affairs and International Trade to work with a host of NGOs, including through the short-lived Centre for the Development of Foreign Policy. For Canadian foreign policy officers, this was an abrupt cultural change in how to deal with foreign policy questions. Grassroots activists, not the prime minister, provided directives. As well, when Canada tried to improve its relationship with the United States, it was not from Jean Chrétien's own desire; it was the priority of a newly sworn-in foreign minister,

John Manley, who wanted to differentiate himself from Axworthy, his predecessor.

The Prime Minister's lack of interest in foreign policy resulted in a series of diplomatic gaffes: misstatements in the Middle East by the Prime Minister himself, impolitic remarks about the American president by his staff, and sending his minister to a head of state's funeral. All of this eroded Canada's reputation abroad and diminished its middle power status. It is only slightly surprising, then, that, in the wake of the tragic events of September 11, 2001, President Bush forgot to thank Canada when he listed allies supporting the United States, even though Canadians had graciously hosted thousands of stranded U.S. airline passengers on 9/11 and in the days that followed. (Bush finally thanked Canada for its generosity when he visited in late 2004.)

Martin's mandate as Prime Minister was brief (January 2004–February 2006).[34] The early indications regarding his stance suggested better days for Canadian foreign policy. Martin, after all, grew up in a world where foreign policy was no doubt discussed, with his father (Paul Sr.) having served as Lester Pearson's Secretary of State for External Affairs. Moreover, Martin, as a long-time Minister of Finance in the Chrétien government, had the opportunity to build his own international network and was in a position to understand what it takes for Canada to play a prominent role in world affairs. Finally, his first acts as Prime Minister indicated a definite change of the guard: renewed dialogue with President Bush; the campaign to create a G20 at the level of the heads of state/heads of government, which will encourage a more open and more productive North-South dialogue; a commitment to come up with a redefined foreign policy; and a willingness to increase resources in foreign policy–related fields.

It is difficult to say how much of an imprint his short term in office has left on Canadian foreign policy. It is true that he was deeply involved in the reviewing of Canada's International Policy Statement and, after a *rapprochement* with the White House, the distance he took from President Bush—notably at the December 2005 Montreal conference on climate change—was in sharp contrast with previous indications he had given. Only time will tell what type of inheritance, if any, he has left as Prime Minister in terms of foreign policy.

With the past in mind, what does the future hold? Will Stephen Harper demonstrate a higher level of sensitivity and get involved more thoroughly in foreign policy–related matters? How will he handle the making and the implementation of Canadian foreign policy? Will he be able to warm up the relationship between Ottawa and Washington and, if so, at what price? It also remains to be seen if his government's minority status prevents him from being an activist foreign policy Prime Minister, a role most of his predecessors, from John A. MacDonald to Brian Mulroney, have carried out.

AN OVERALL EVALUATION

This chapter has focused on Canadian prime ministers and their vital role as managers of Canada's foreign policy. In order to grasp the importance of this role better, one has to first be familiar with the particulars of the Canadian parliamentary system. This system rests on the principle of responsible government, where ministers of the Crown are collectively and individually responsible before the elected House of Commons. In itself, this principle solidly anchors the leadership and the authority the prime minister exercises, especially in the realm of foreign relations. The fact that these relations are conducted with his/her counterparts around the world helps to explain why foreign affairs fall more easily under his or her purview. Moreover, this prominent role is reinforced by the support the prime minister receives from a bureaucratic and political framework. Together, the PMO and PCO provide advice and expertise, both from a political and policy point of view.

Over the years, the roles have varied. When one looks at the evolution of Canadian foreign policy, some characteristics can be outlined. First, from the three periods identified herein, it is possible to note that the initial efforts were to take Canada from a colonial status in terms of foreign policy and manage its integration into the concert of nations. This has been a constant effort to which almost all prime ministers of the period contributed significantly. Moreover, these efforts were characterized by a step-by-step process where personal relationships the prime minister entertained—be it Borden with other dominion leaders or King with Roosevelt—ensured the greatest progress. Then, during a period that some have portrayed as a "Golden Age," Canada quickly emerged as an actor that was known to "punch above its weight" as determined by its sole military or economic power. Those years established the values of Pearsonian internationalism, a set of principles and actions that are still very present in the minds of some Canadian foreign policy-makers.

Unfortunately, the contemporary period has seen a continuous decline in the role Canada plays in the world, due in large part to a sharp decline in resources allocated to foreign policy. During this period, two prime ministers—Trudeau and Chrétien—did not give the same importance to foreign policy questions as did their predecessors or, for that matter, their political opponent of the same period, Brian Mulroney, who nevertheless had to underfund the foreign policy apparatus due to harsher economic conditions and fiscal constraints. Moreover, in this latter case, a closer relationship with the United States (portrayed by the media and opponents as detrimental to Canada) and difficult domestic policy debates (such as the Meech Lake Accord, pensions, deficit fighting, and the implementation of the Goods and Services Tax) tarnished an image that was objectively much brighter—from a foreign policy standpoint—that many recall.

From these characteristics, two conclusions can be drawn. First, prime ministers have always played a key role in the conduct of Canadian policy—from the days when the country was not even recognized on the world stage as an autonomous actor up to today. Second, the importance of this role is borne out by the fact that the more prime ministers paid attention to and got involved in foreign policy making and implementation, the stronger Canada's position in the world became, and vice versa.

In sum, despite important differences between the Canadian and the American systems, the historical record shows that, in the Canadian context, probably even more than in the United States, the head of government exercises a very strong influence on the development and conduct of foreign policy. This is worth keeping in mind while reading the following chapters.

NOTES

1. In Canada, only the lower House (i.e., the House of Commons) is elected; senators are appointed, as they were in the United States until the early twentieth century (and are still today when there is a need to fill in-term vacancies). Canadian senators keep their seats until they reach the age of 75, resign, or die. There are also provisions for impeachment of senators, but this disciplinary measure is rarely used.

2. As a matter of fact, nowhere in the Canadian constitution is there any reference to the Prime Minister's roles.

3. Robertson is probably the most prominent example and his tenure at PCO coincided with Pearson's most influential period. Robertson headed External Affairs from 1941 to 1946, and again from 1958 to 1964. Two other high-ranking civil servants headed both External Affairs and PCO: Gordon Osbaldeston (External in 1982 and then PCO from 1982 to 1985) and Marcel Massé (PCO in 1979–1980 and External in 1982–1985). Massé also served as President of the Canadian International Development Agency.

4. "The Role and Structure of the Privy Council Office," Government of Canada Privy Council Office, http://www.pco.gc.ca/default.asp?page=publications&Language=E&doc=role/role_e.htm.

5. "The Role and Structure of the Privy Council Office," http://www.pco.gc.ca/default.asp?page=publications&Language=E&doc=role/role_e.htm.

6. Colin Campbell and George Szablowski, *The Super-Bureaucrats: Structures & Behaviour in Central Agencies* (Toronto: Macmillan, 1979).

7. Donald Savoie, *Governing from the Center: The Concentration of Power in Canadian Politics* (Toronto and Buffalo: University of Toronto Press, 1999).

8. The relationship between executive actors and central agencies presents several interesting particularities that cannot be covered here. For a good analysis of this phenomenon, see Colin Campbell, *Governments under Stress: Political Executives and Key Bureaucrats in Washington, London, and Ottawa* (Toronto and Buffalo: University of Toronto Press, 1983). Most of the conclusions reached in this study are still valid today.

9. Most studies on Canadian prime ministers are a bit dated, but still very accurate and useful. For instance, the most cited work on John A. Macdonald is Donald Creighton, *John A. Macdonald: The Old Chieftain* (Toronto: Macmillan, 1955).

10. This is the title of one of Bourassa's key published brochures. He resigned from his House of Commons Liberal seat in 1899 in protest of Canada's unpopular participation in the Boer War—although the government was required to answer the Empire's call to arms, Bourassa objected to the lack of public consultation prior to sending troops into battle. He founded, in 1910, *Le Devoir*, a "paper of opinion" still published today.

11. Réal Bélanger, *Wilfrid Laurier: Quand la politique devient passion* (Québec: Presses de l'Université Laval et Entreprises Radio-Canada, 1987); Laurier Lapierre, *Sir Wilfrid Laurier: Portrait intime* (Montréal: Éditions de l'Homme, 1996).

12. On this election, see Paul Stevens, *The 1911 General Election: A Study in Canadian Politics* (Toronto: Coop Clark, 1970).

13. On Borden, see Robert Craig Brown, *Robert Laird Borden, A Biography*, 2 volumes (Toronto: Macmillan, 1975); Robert Laird Borden, *His Memoirs* (Toronto: McClelland & Stewart, 1969).

14. See Nelson Michaud, *L'énigme du Sphinx* (Québec: Presses de l'Université Laval, 1998).

15. The Union Party that formed the government after the 1917 election was composed of conscriptionist Members of Parliament (almost all from English-speaking

Canada) formerly belonging to both the Liberal and the Conservative parties. They were opposed by Laurier and a group of non-conscriptionist Liberals (all of them being from French-speaking Canada).

16. On Dandurand, see his memoir, *Raoul Dandurand: Le Sénateur diplomate* (Québec: Presses de l'Université Laval and Institut québécois des hautes études internationales, 2000); *Études internationales* 31, no. 4, (December 2000), special issue titled "De la SDN à l'ONU: Raoul Dandurand et la vision idéaliste des relations internationales," ed. Charles-Philippe David.

17. Richard Jones, *Vers une hégémonie libérale* (Québec: Presses de la librairie des PUL, 1980).

18. Graham, Roger, *Arthur Meighen*, 3 volumes (Toronto: Clarke Irwin, 1960).

19. On this crisis, the most authoritative work is Eugene Forsey, *The Royal Power of Dissolution of Parliament in the British Commonwealth* (Toronto: Oxford University Press, 1968). For a shorter explanation, see Michaud, *L'énigme du Sphinx*, 169–172.

20. The key work on King is H. Blair Neatby, *William Lyon Mackenzie King*, 3 volumes (Toronto and Buffalo: University of Toronto Press, 1963).

21. On Lapointe and foreign policy, see John MacFarlane, *Ernest Lapointe and Québec's Influence on Canadian Foreign Policy* (Toronto and Buffalo: University of Toronto Press, 1999). Other works on his career cover foreign policy aspects. These include Paul Bernier, *Ernest Lapointe: Député de Kamouraska 1904–1919* (La Pocatière, Québec: Société historique de la Côte du Sud, 1979); Lita-Rose Betcherman, *Ernest Lapointe: Mackenzie King's Great Québec Lieutenant* (Toronto and Buffalo: University of Toronto Press, 2002).

22. Kim Richard Nossal, *The Politics of Canadian Foreign Policy*, 3rd ed. (Toronto: Prentice-Hall, 1997), 148.

23. On St. Laurent, see Dale C. Thompson, *Louis St-Laurent: Canadian* (Toronto: Macmillan, 1968); J. W. Pickersgill, *My Years with Louis St Laurent: A Political Memoir* (Toronto and Buffalo: University of Toronto Press, 1975).

24. In *Canadian Foreign Policy 1945–1954: Selected Speeches and Documents*, ed. R. A. Mackay (Toronto: McClelland & Stewart, 1970), 388–399.

25. John Hilliker and Donald Barry, *Le ministère des affaires extérieures du Canada, Volume II: L'essor (1946–1968)* (Québec: Presses de l'Université Laval et Institut d'administration publique du Canada, 1995), 32.

26. See John George Diefenbaker, *One Canada*, 3 volumes (Toronto: Macmillan, 1975); Peter Strusberg, *Diefenbaker: Leadership Gained: 1956–1962* (Toronto and Buffalo: University of Toronto Press, 1975); Peter Strusberg, *Diefenbaker: Leadership Lost: 1962–1967* (Toronto and Buffalo: University of Toronto Press, 1976); Denis Smith, *Rogue Tory: The Life and Legend of John G. Diefenbaker* (Toronto: Macfarlane, Walter & Ross, 1995).

27. From his unique standpoint, Robinson has provided an extensive reading of Diefenbaker's foreign policy management. See Basil Robinson, *Diefenbaker's World: A Populist in World Affairs* (Toronto and Buffalo: University of Toronto Press, 1989).

28. Nelson Michaud, *Genèse d'une politique syncopique : la défense du Canada et le*

livre blanc de 1987 (unpublished dissertation, Université Laval, 1998); Knowlton Nash, *Kennedy and Diefenbaker: Fear and Loathing across the Undefended Border* (Toronto: McClelland & Stewart, 1990).

29. Pearson's legacy is perceived by many as the core of Canadian foreign policy. See Lester B. Pearson, *Mike: The Memoirs of the Rt. Hon. Lester B. Pearson*, 3 volumes (Toronto and Buffalo: University of Toronto Press, 1975), as well as those of his Secretary of State for External Affairs, Paul Martin Sr. See Paul Martin, Sr., *A Very Public Life*, 2 volumes (Toronto: Deneau, 1985). For more on Pearson, see Peter Strusberg, *Lester Pearson and the Dream of Unity* (Toronto: Doubleday, 1978); Peter Strusberg, *Lester Pearson and the American Dilemma* (Toronto: Doubleday, 1980); John English, *The Life of Lester Pearson*, 2 volumes (Toronto: Vintage Books, 1993).

30. Peyton V. Lyon, "The Evolution of Canadian Diplomacy since 1945," in *From Mackenzie King to Pierre Trudeau: Forty Years of Canadian Diplomacy*, ed. Paul Painchaud (Québec: Les Presses de l'Université Laval, 1989), 24.

31. Trudeau has been a key figure in Canadian politics. An intellectual, he wrote several important works in which one can find most of his policy fundamentals. On his foreign policy, written with his close advisor, see Pierre Elliott Trudeau and Ivan Head, *The Canadian Way: Shaping Canada's Foreign Policy 1968–1984* (Toronto: McClelland & Stewart, 1995). Three of his foreign affairs ministers have written memoirs: Mitchell Sharp, *Which Reminds Me . . . A Memoir* (Toronto and Buffalo: University of Toronto Press, 1994); Don Jamieson, *The Political Memoirs of Don Jamieson*, ed. Carmelita McGrath (St. John's, Newfoundland: Breakwater, 1991); and a posthumous work by Mark MacGuigan, *An Inside Look at External Affairs During the Trudeau Years*, ed. P. Whitney Lackenbauer (Calgary: University of Calgary Press, 2002). For analyses of Trudeau foreign policy, see Bruce Thordarson, *Trudeau and Foreign Policy: A Study in Decision-Making* (Toronto: Oxford University Press, 1972); J. L. Granatstein and Robert Bothwell, *Pirouette: Trudeau and Canadian Foreign Policy* (Toronto and Buffalo: University of Toronto Press, 1990).

32. The Mulroney period, as well as subsequent periods, is well served with the analytical chronicle offered by the series *Canada Among Nations*, to which we have already referred in chapter 1. On the specifics of Mulroney's foreign policy, see *Diplomatic Departures: The Conservative Era in Canadian Foreign Policy 1984–1993*, ed. Nelson Michaud and Kim Richard Nossal (Vancouver: UBC Press, 2001). The book contains a bibliographical essay that provides an overview of the available works on the period. If some of Mulroney's trade and defense ministers have written their memoirs (for instance, Erik Nielsen, Kim Campbell, John Crosbie, and Pat Carney), it is interesting to note that none of the secretaries of state for external affairs during this period (Joe Clark, Barbara McDougall, and Perrin Beatty) has done so.

33. For an analysis of this struggle, see Nelson Michaud, "Bureaucratic Politics and the Shaping of Policies: Can We Measure Pulling and Hauling Games?" *Canadian Journal of Political Science* 35, no. 2 (June 2002): 269–300.

34. Martin succeeded in January 2004, won the election the following June, and was at the helm of a minority government until February 2006.

I

REFOCUSED EFFORTS

3

Forty Years of Neglect, Indifference, and Apathy: The Relentless Decline of Canada's Armed Forces

ANDREW RICHTER

According to a range of analysts, scholars, and observers, Canada's military is in decline.[1] Recent studies have concluded that Canada's Department of National Defence (DND) is underfunded and undermanned and will shortly face a "rust out" of both its equipment and war-fighting capabilities. However, largely unnoticed in such reports is how Canada got into this state of affairs in the first place. The reality is that the Canadian military's present condition is the result of decisions made over decades and represents a dramatic change from the pattern established in the early post–World War II period. In the 1950s and 1960s, Canada's military was large and well equipped. For the first two decades following the war, it accepted demanding responsibilities and tasks. Change occurred in the mid-1960s, however, when Canadian attitudes toward defense shifted and the lengthy process of military decay began. The purpose of this chapter, then, is to review the decisions and developments that have led to the current crisis of the Canadian Forces (C.F.) and to offer some suggestions that might see Canada reclaim its former military role.

This chapter will be divided into three parts. The first will establish the background for the contemporary defense and security debate. It will briefly review developments in the post-war period, and examine a few of the controversies that have had a long-lasting effect. The second will focus on successive Canadian governments over the period 1968 to the present, and how virtually each one of them considered military issues to be of secondary importance. Lastly, the third section will look at some of the chapter's findings and observations, as well as offer a few predictions on likely future developments.

PART ONE: CANADIAN DEFENSE
1945–1968: Paying the Price of Sovereignty

Following the conclusion of World War II (and the enormous contribution made by Canada), the Canadian military quickly demobilized, only to begin a period of rapid and sustained growth with the onset of the Korean War in 1950. Within a few years, the commitments undertaken during the war (and in particular the decision to station military personnel in Europe) essentially became permanent, and Canada irrevocably accepted the basic premise of liberal internationalism that was to guide this country's strategic policy for much of the next half-century. As such, the government was committed to developing and maintaining credible military forces. As Doug Bland has noted of this period, "it may seem unnatural that Canada would devise a strategy based, like those of the major powers, on force, but that was the reality."[2]

The decision to remain engaged in the international community represented a major change from Canada's traditional foreign policy orientation. From confederation until 1939 (with the brief exception of World War I), Canada was essentially isolationist, and had only limited international involvement. As Nelson Michaud points out in his chapter in this volume, the key declaration of this change came in a lecture given in 1947 by the newly named Secretary of State for External Affairs, Louis St. Laurent, who stated that from that time forward, Canada would assume greater global responsibilities, and its foreign policy would emphasize political liberty, democratic institutions, and humanitarian standards.[3] With the goal of internationalism established, Canada began playing a leadership role in several institutions, including the Commonwealth (where Canada immediately lobbied for Indian membership) and the formation of the North Atlantic Treaty Organization (1949).

A brief word might also be added about functionalism, which was introduced in Canada in 1942 by the diplomat Hume Wrong. While not a Canadian invention per se (rather, the concept can be traced to the work of David Mitrany in the 1930s[4]), in the late 1940 and early 1950s functionalism became the central tenant of Canadian foreign policy, and it helped elevate Canada's status within the international community. According to functionalist principles, in the post–World War II environment a new tier of states was to be created—middle powers.[5] Canada hoped to become one of the leading members of this emerging group of countries, but it realized that the maintenance and possession of military forces would play an important part of Canada's middle power role. As a result, the government began expanding defense capabilities, implicitly recognizing that if Canada wished to be taken seriously on the global stage, it would need to have the traditional elements of power to back up its verbal declarations.

That Canada maintained large military forces—and perhaps more importantly, accepted the *necessity* of such forces—is today often overlooked. It was, in fact, this country's military and the roles that it performed that sparked heated debate about Canada's role in the world.[6] Indeed, even peacekeeping, which would, with time, become the defense task most Canadians identified with and overwhelmingly supported, depended on the capabilities of the military.[7] While it would perhaps be an overstatement to say that Canada was a global military power in the 1950s, it is certainly accurate to note that Canada had serious military forces that were internationally respected.

As for what those forces did, the roles and tasks in the 1950s and 1960s were not very different from those of today. In the *1964 Defence White Paper*,[8] the objectives of Canadian defense policy were identified as: (1) to preserve the peace by supporting collective defense measures; (2) to support Canadian foreign policy, including our participation in international organizations; and (3) to provide for the protection and surveillance of Canadian territory. In many ways, this document was the first attempt to build a defense policy on a distinctly Canadian foundation, as earlier post-war defense statements had focused on Canada's alliance commitments and the tasks that resulted from them (a theme that Prime Minister Pierre Trudeau would pick up on a few years later).

In an attempt to implement these tasks, over time Canadian governments agreed to a number of commitments and obligations to the Western alliance, which, in turn, were translated into specific defense roles.[9]

Accordingly, during the Cold War, the primary defense missions of the C.F. were antisubmarine warfare (ASW) in the North Atlantic and contributing to the land and air defense of Western Europe. Canadian contributions were intended to promote international stability by providing the European allies with a degree of military and political confidence, thereby making the continent less vulnerable to Soviet aggression.[10] However, it should be noted that the Canadian defense contribution was part of the larger security strategy of the West, which was heavily dependent on American nuclear weapons to dissuade the Soviet Union from undertaking any foreign policy or security challenges.[11]

At the same time that Canada made defense commitments to NATO, it also solidified the security alliance it had with the United States (U.S.). That alliance, born during World War II, quickly strengthened in its aftermath, and especially once the Soviet Union (U.S.S.R.) developed nuclear weapons and long-range bombers in the late 1940s and early 1950s. As a result, in 1958, the two countries established the North American Air Defense Command (NORAD), which was responsible to both governments for the air defense of the continent.[12] Especially important to Canada was the command's division of responsibilities. As the larger and wealthier partner, the U.S. provided the bulk of NORAD's forces and financing, an arrangement that provided Canada with a measure of air sovereignty at a reduced financial cost. The agreement effectively freed Canadian defense resources for European commitments.[13] As Dan Middlemiss and Joel Sokolsky have noted, "the [NORAD] decision reflected Ottawa's assessment of the importance of Europe in maintaining overall allied security and of the need to maintain a visible Canadian presence in Europe for political purposes."[14]

The late 1950s and early 1960s was perhaps the most turbulent period in Canadian defense history. A series of controversies, including decisions regarding the Avro Arrow, the BOMARC surface-to-air missile, and whether or not to accept American nuclear weapons, all demanded responses.[15] The newly elected Conservative government of John Diefenbaker was ill-equipped to handle these issues, and during its six years in office (1957–1963) Canadian defense policy lurched from crisis to crisis. However, in spite of the controversies, Prime Minister Diefenbaker never questioned the basic requirement of military forces (or the need for Canada to maintain a credible defense establishment), and as a result funding for the military remained relatively stable through this difficult period. While this is not to suggest that this was in any way a positive time for the military (indeed, the debate over nuclear weapons ultimately tore the government apart in 1963[16]), in retrospect these years represent a dividing line between the "golden age" of the immediate post-war period and the under-funded, under-manned defense reality of the present.

The first indication of a general shift regarding the importance of the military came during the government of Lester Pearson (1963–1968). While Canada's Nobel Prize–winning Prime Minister was essentially supportive of the military—and certainly believed that states needed strong defenses to enforce global order—funding began to decline as demands for federal social programs grew rapidly (in particular Canada's health care and education programs). In real terms, then, the defense budget began to decline in the mid-1960s.[17] This was partially the result of the first-ever program of formula-funding, a decision that severely limited the spending options available to the government. The net effect was a military increasingly unable to replace dated equipment, and one that began to fall behind its allies in a variety of measures.

Defence Minister Paul Hellyer warned about the approaching challenge on several occasions in the mid-1960s. According to Hellyer, if Canada wished to contribute to and benefit from our participation in NATO and the United Nations, it had to have significant military forces to make a credible contribution.[18] This was becoming increasingly difficult, though, as defense systems were not only growing more costly to purchase and maintain, but their expected service lifespan was declining. By 1966, the choices facing the government were growing starker, and Hellyer warned that "either the defence budget had to be substantially increased or substantial cost reductions had to be made. Otherwise, funds would simply not be available for the capital expenditures that are essential to effective military forces." To buy Ottawa some time while it considered the need for increased defense spending, Hellyer proposed a sweeping reorganization that would have converted Canada's military into a mobile force that would be more deployable.[19] However, the Liberal government ignored both Hellyer's warning and plan, and consequently it fell to the next government, and to a new Prime Minister, to make the difficult decisions on the allocation of resources between economic, social, and military demands.

PART TWO: CANADIAN DEFENSE 1968–2004: ABDICATING CANADIAN DEFENSE RESPONSIBILITIES

The process of decline that began under Prime Minister Pearson greatly intensified under the leadership of Pierre Trudeau, who came into office in 1968 determined to reduce defense spending and make major changes to Canada's defense and foreign policy orientation. Indeed, one of the Prime Minister's first acts was to initiate major reviews of both Canadian foreign and defense policy. Even prior to assuming office, Trudeau believed that Canadian defense policy had determined this country's foreign policy for too long and a re-ordering of priorities was called for. In essence, Trudeau believed that Canadian defense policy needed to further national interests, and that Ottawa had options that had been overlooked in the post-war period.

In a general sense, Trudeau's fundamental foreign policy orientation was dramatically different from that of his predecessors. While not anti-American per se—at least not upon entering office—Trudeau had serious reservations regarding U.S. foreign policy, and had even been featured on an American blacklist of suspected pro-Communists (not surprising given his background and politics).[20] Trudeau did not accept American assertions about the aggressiveness of the U.S.S.R., and he was convinced that if detente between the two superpowers was to emerge, it was imperative for countries like Canada to achieve greater "balance" in their foreign policies. Thus, Trudeau wondered whether Canada's interests might be better served if this country were to become more accommodating to the Soviet Union.[21]

In April 1969, Trudeau issued a new set of Canadian defense priorities. These were: (1) the surveillance of Canadian territory and coastline; (2) the defense of North America in cooperation with the U.S.; (3) the fulfilment of such NATO commitments as may be agreed upon; and (4) the performance of international peacekeeping roles.[22] While the subsequent defense White Paper[23] did not assign priority to any of these roles and (somewhat ironically) stressed Canada's continued commitment to its alliances,[24] the emphasis was clearly on the first of these missions, i.e., sovereignty protection. As a result, the decision to reduce the Canadian Forces' presence in Europe by half (which had been announced in 1969) was rationalized by a discussion of the need for greater compatibility between European and Canadian-based forces.[25]

The move to reduce Canada's European presence generated significant negative allied reaction. In particular, the German government was incensed, as the decision had a direct impact on the Federal Republic, and yet Bonn had not been consulted prior to the announcement.[26] To the Germans, the reduction raised serious questions about Canada's reliability as an ally.[27] In addition, Britain feared that it would be called upon to compensate for the departing Canadian troops.[28] While the Canadian decision was not militarily significant, the unilateral nature of it demonstrated that NATO solidarity was not as strong as alliance supporters liked to assert. Further, at a time when U.S.–Soviet arms control negotiations were under way (and were nearing a long-awaited agreement), and coming shortly after the Soviet occupation of Czechoslovakia, Canada's decision was not particularly well timed.

Nonetheless, while sovereignty protection demanded an investment in new equipment and capabilities, none were immediately forthcoming for the C.F. The 1971 White Paper thus foreshadowed future uncertainty regarding defense spending as, rather than establish a funding program, it stated that spending would be determined "in relation to other government programs."[29] Continuing the pattern established under Pearson, the Trudeau government called for fiscal austerity in security matters, and within one year defense spending was effectively frozen (the result of which was that real spending declined by as much as 10 percent per year over the following few years). To cite but two examples of the consequences of limited spending, capital expenditures fell to a postwar low of 8 percent of the departmental budget, while personnel levels declined from 98,000 in 1968 to 81,000 in 1972.[30]

With defense spending stagnating (but effectively declining), the capabilities of the Canadian military diminished. By the mid-1970s, an emerging "commitment-capability" gap had become clear, as in spite of the low funding, Canada's total military commitments had remained steady (and, in point of fact, actually increased during the 1970s[31]). To address these (and other) concerns, in 1974 the government announced that a Defence Structure Review (DSR) would be undertaken, a three-phased process that involved examining the missions of the C.F. and the forces required to carry out those tasks.

Not surprisingly, the DSR concluded that the C.F. was in need of new equipment, and in 1975 the government committed itself to re-equipping both the ground and air forces in Europe. The result was a series of capital acquisitions for the C.F., including German battle tanks (the Leopard), American surveillance (Aurora) and fighter (F-18) aircraft, and an ambitious plan to design and build a new generation of patrol frigates in Canada (the Halifax class). In addition, the DSR established a new funding framework for Canada's military. While it did not set a specific spending goal, it indexed the defense budget to inflation, an important step at a time when price increases in many Western countries (including Canada) were at a post-war high. Further, capital expenditures were to be increased by 12 percent between 1977 and 1979.[32]

While certainly a step in the right direction, the DSR did not reverse the process of decline that was by this time well under way. In addition, spending increases did not match the goals that were established. For example, in 1978, the Trudeau government adopted the NATO target of 3 percent real growth in defense spending, but this goal was rarely attained. In addition, while the new weapons systems were certainly more capable than the ones they replaced, there were fewer of them. Thus, only 18 Auroras were bought to replace 33 Argus surveillance aircraft, and 128 Leopard tanks replaced 300 Centurions. Manpower levels also continued their steady decline, and the C.F. fell to a post-war low of 78,000 members in 1976.[33] The result was that by the time Trudeau left office in 1984, warnings were being raised about the decay of Canada's military, and the steps that were needed to reverse it.[34] As historians J. L. Granatstein and Robert Bothwell have summed up this period, the Trudeau years were a "long, dark night of the spirit" for the Canadian Forces.[35]

The landslide Conservative victory of Brian Mulroney seemed to signify better days for the Canadian military. During the 1984 election campaign, the Tory leader frequently spoke about the poor state of the C.F., and the need to overhaul and expand it. Further, Mulroney promised to preserve and strengthen Canada's alliances (particularly the country's relationship with the U.S.), restore tri-service traditions (independent defense services had been discontinued in 1964), and increase Canada's European force.[36] Indeed, shortly after taking office, the government reached an agreement with the United States to modernize the continent's northern radar installations, a development that suggested a level of concern with defense issues not seen in Ottawa in more than twenty years.[37]

But observers who had anticipated a quick departure and renewed emphasis on the military were to be disappointed. While the new Prime Minister certainly talked about the need for re-equipping the C.F., the government's actions did not match its rhetoric. In the financial statement presented in November 1984 by Minister Michael Wilson, the Tories actually *cut* $150 million CDN from the defense budget, and in their first two years in office defense spending under the Tories fell short of the increases that had been achieved in the last few years of the Liberal regime.[38] Further, while the government's foreign policy report, *Independence and Internationalism*,[39] was completed in 1985, it took two additional years before the updated defense White Paper, *Challenge and Commitment: A Defence Policy for Canada*, was completed.[40]

In many respects, the new White Paper was the most curious such document ever produced in Canada, and while it called for significant changes, it was soon overtaken by developments. Ignoring important, yet tenuous, political changes (i.e., *glasnost* and *perestroika*) in the Soviet Union, the 1987 White Paper presented the Soviet threat in stark, explicit Cold War terms and emphasized Soviet military developments.[41] As the report noted, "the realities of the present call for a more sober approach to international relations and the needs of security." As a result of the continued uncertainty in the global environment, the White Paper stressed the enduring importance of Canada's alliance commitments.

To combat the Soviet threat, the White Paper called for an extensive defense modernization program, highlighted by a proposal to purchase between ten and twelve nuclear-powered attack submarines (SSNs).[42] The submarines would contribute to the establishment of a "three ocean navy," one that would be able to provide surveillance and assert Canadian sovereignty in the far north. The sheer ambition of the plan was impressive, and for at least a brief time it appeared as if a new era in Canadian defense had arrived.

To pay for the procurement projects identified, the White Paper called for a funding framework of real spending increases of no less than 2 percent per year for fifteen years, a heady goal considering that military spending in Canada had either been declining or had barely kept up with inflation for the previous quarter century. In addition, the White Paper noted that major capital acquisition projects (like the SSNs) would require further funding in the years in which the procurements were made. Lastly, the cabinet would conduct an annual review of defense spending for the following five-year period.[43]

Without question, the proposal to buy nuclear-powered submarines was the most controversial component of the White Paper.[44] Critics contended that Ottawa was unwittingly—or perhaps intentionally—being drawn into Washington's controversial maritime strategy, which many argued was unnecessarily aggressive.[45] In response, DND maintained that Canada could not ignore recent maritime developments in the Arctic. In this regard, Defence Minister Perrin Beatty said that the Arctic was a region of growing strategic importance, and that "foreign submarines" were already operating there, which raised both security and sovereignty questions for Canada. The proposal also became entangled in the revival of the debate over the legal status of the Northwest Passage.[46]

In any event, the White Paper was quickly overtaken by political developments. Even prior to its release, at the 1986 Reykjavik summit between U.S. President Ronald Reagan and Soviet President Mikhail Gorbachev, the Soviet leader had called for improved bilateral relations, and had indicated that he was prepared to make significant cuts in Soviet defenses. The following year, in December 1987, the two countries signed the Intermediate-Range Nuclear Forces—or INF—Treaty, which eliminated medium-range ballistic missiles in Europe. Subsequently, the Soviet President announced plans to reorient Soviet armed forces in accordance with the new doctrines of "reasonable sufficiency" and "defensive defense."[47] And two years later, Soviet control over Eastern Europe effectively came to an end, as a string of countries announced their independence from Moscow. Suddenly, the U.S.S.R. no longer presented the stark threat that DND (not to mention virtually every other Western defense establishment) had anticipated just a few years earlier.

The changes in the strategic environment coincided with a deepening fiscal crisis in Canada, one that the Tory government appeared determined to tackle. In the 1989 fiscal year, the budget deficit reached almost $40 billion CDN, and the total federal debt soared to $380 billion CDN.[48] Given this fiscal reality, the Mulroney government concluded that its ambitious defense program no longer made financial (not to mention strategic) sense. In short order, the program envisioned in the White Paper was effectively canceled. In that year's federal budget, all of the big-ticket equipment items were discontinued, and the defense budget was reduced by $2.74 billion CDN to be spread over five years.[49]

Over the course of the following few years, defense cuts continued, as pressure grew to enjoy a "peace dividend" as a result of the end of the Cold War. While such a desire was understandable, it overlooked the fact that by 1990, defense spending in Canada as a percentage of Gross National Product (GNP) had been declining for almost thirty years, and that, in many ways, Canada had *already* enjoyed a peace dividend. Regardless, in 1991, further defense spending cuts were announced which threatened the viability of the continued Canadian commitments to NATO and European security.[50]

In September 1991, Defence Minister Marcel Masse announced that Canada would close its two military bases in Germany—Lahr and Baden-Soellingen—by 1995 and that it would withdraw its remaining 6,600 European soldiers. At the time, Masse promised that Canada would leave an emergency force of 1,100 troops and two squadrons of CF-18 fighter planes in Europe.[51] Prime Minister Mulroney subsequently reaffirmed the need to keep Canadian troops on the continent. But just five months later, in February 1992, the government announced that it would withdraw Canada's remaining European force by 1994. While the Defence Minister attempted to portray the decision as militarily and politically sensible,[52] allied reaction was swift and negative, reflective of the response a quarter century earlier when Canada had first reduced its continental presence.

To counter allied charges that Canada was effectively abandoning the continent, the government insisted that it was doing nothing of the sort. Rather, it stressed that Canada was still contributing a full battalion (complete with pre-positioned equipment) to serve with either the NATO Composite Force or the Allied Command European Land Force in Norway; that it would continue to join air and naval forces in operations in the Atlantic; that it would maintain a dedicated brigade and two squadrons of CF-18s in Canada which could be sent to Germany on short notice; and that it would provide about one hundred people to the NATO early warning system and two hundred more to staff headquarters in Brussels.[53] While these claims were all factually correct, they did little to alleviate alliance concern, much of which was linked to the unsettling possibility that if Canada could withdraw its European force, there was little to prevent the U.S. from doing the same. As Norman Ripsman has concluded of the Mulroney government, "not only did [the Tories] pare military spending to the bone, but they also cancelled the alliance commitment that had served as the pillar of Canadian defence and security policy for decades."[54]

By the end of his tenure in 1993, it was clear that Prime Minister Mulroney had backed off his commitment to expand and reequip the military. On the contrary, his government, which had come to power pledging a renewed emphasis on defense, left office leaving the C.F. in worse shape than it had originally found them. This decline was particularly notable in the size of the C.F., which shrank a further 10 percent (from 82,000 to 74,000) over the period 1984–1993. Perhaps appropriately, in the government's final budget in 1993, defense funding was slashed for repairs, spares, and overhaul activities, while the government placed "severe restraints" on training for operations.[55]

In many ways, the decline in the military that had been evident for thirty years by the time Jean Chrétien took office in 1993 served as a fitting backdrop for the even-greater cuts that were to come. The first security-related order of business for the new government was the cancellation of a major contract for EH-101 helicopters to replace the fleet of obsolete Sea Kings and Labradors (a contract which Prime Minister Mulroney had announced with great fanfare in 1992). While the decision entailed hundreds of millions of dollars in cancellation fees ($473 million CDN to be precise), Chrétien was effectively serving notice that the military would not be a priority for his government, and that whenever possible it would cancel modernization and reequipment projects.

Shortly after taking office, the government announced extensive (and public) reviews of foreign and defense policy, reviews that resulted in new policy White Papers in late 1994 and early 1995, respectively. With regards to the defense component of that task, the report was intended to replace the outdated—and by that time thoroughly discredited—1987 Cold War document. The White Paper was also expected to establish a strategic rationale for the Canadian Forces in the "new world order," a phrase coined by U.S. President George H. W. Bush in the aftermath of the 1991 Gulf War.[56] Further, the new paper was expected to examine the prospects for additional Canadian involvements in multilateral coalitions, a possibility that appeared more likely in the war's aftermath and Canada's participation in Operation Desert Storm.[57]

The result, the 1994 Defence White Paper,[58] was, in the words of defense analyst Dean Oliver, "a remarkably conservative document."[59] Rather than suggest sweeping changes—as many observers had predicted—the paper's primary recommendation was the need for Canada to retain robust defense capabilities across the range of military categories ("multi-purpose, combat capable forces"). The paper rejected the argument that Canada required a defense force focused around "constabulary tasks,"[60] and instead suggested that Canada "needs armed forces that are able to operate with the modern forces maintained by our allies and like-minded nations against a capable opponent—that is, able to fight alongside the best, against the best."[61] The White Paper thus left little doubt that Canada needed a modern defense establishment, one that could cooperate with a U.S. military that was the world leader in introducing and deploying sophisticated military technology.

With regard to equipment, the White Paper called for the Canadian Navy to eventually receive a replacement for the Sea Kings,[62] and more positively, to rejuvenate its submarine force, possibly by acquiring (slightly used) Upholder-class conventional vessels from the UK. In addition, the army would get new armored personnel carriers and replacements for its Cougar close fire–support vehicles. The service that came out the worst was the air force, which was to receive virtually nothing, and in fact would lose its entire C-5 fleet and a sizable number of CF-18s and face a 25 percent reduction in overall expenditures. And yet, despite the very modest equipment programs outlined, the White Paper was generally well received by both the academic and defense policy communities in Canada,[63] a reflection of the near-catastrophic predictions regarding the C.F. that had been made prior to its release.

As with prior defense White Papers, the devil was in the (funding) details, and it was here where the government's lack of concern with the military was most evident. With the total accumulated debt now at $750 billion CDN—and still growing at over $40 billion per year—the Chrétien government decided that defense would need to be slashed in the effort to bring financial sanity back to Canada. Thus, the White Paper warned that there "will be more reductions, cancellations, and delays." Although the paper recognized that DND had "already made a large contribution" in the effort to control the debt, it noted "additional cuts are both necessary and possible."[64] And it also cautioned that defense "must be mindful of other current issues," a reference that suggested that in a challenging fiscal environment, DND was just one of many government departments clamoring for more resources. Finally, recognizing that maintaining the existing C.F. on such an uncertain fiscal basis was essentially impossible, the White Paper called for an additional 15 percent reduction in the size of the military, so that by 1999 the Regular Force would consist of just 60,000 personnel.[65]

Within one year, the scale of the cuts became clear. In 1995, Finance Minister Paul Martin introduced a budget that called for massive spending reductions across the board. For DND, those cuts were to continue for three additional years, with the result that by 1998 the department budget had declined from $12 billion CDN to $9.4 billion, a staggering fall of almost 25 percent.[66] Measured differently, defense spending in Canada fell to just 1.1 percent of GNP, well below the NATO average of 2.2 percent, and the second lowest figure in the alliance (ahead of only Luxembourg).[67]

The accelerating decline of Canada's military was consistent with a dramatic change in Canada's foreign policy, one overseen by the Minister of Foreign Affairs in the mid-to-late 1990s, Lloyd Axworthy. Convinced that the end of the Cold War had transformed global politics, Axworthy believed that the traditional emphasis on state security—and the affiliated issues that were prioritized as a result—was no longer relevant in the new political environment. Rather, Axworthy argued that the principal threats to "human security" included economic privation, social inequality, and environmental catastrophe, and as a result there was an opportunity for Canada to play a leadership role in the alleviation of these issues.[68] The corollary was that traditional interstate conflict was on the decline, and there was thus little need to maintain costly armed forces which would be of little value in countering emerging threats. Lastly, Axworthy believed that "soft power"—that is, the attractiveness of a country's values, the appeal of its culture, and the strength of its institutions (among other attributes)—was far more important than traditional "hard power" resources, again reflecting a fundamental lack of concern with the military.

Canadians seemed to share Axworthy's views, as defense cuts from 1995 to 1997 generated little public reaction. Beginning in 1998, however, reports began to be released that warned that Canada's military was on the verge of collapse, the result of decades of spending cuts, reductions in capabilities, the cancellation of new equipment projects, and improper training.[69] Out of these reports came a gradual recognition that the military could not be starved indefinitely, and that if Canada wanted to play a role on the international stage then the defense status quo could not be continued for much longer.

A major development in this regard was the release of the 1998 Auditor General's report, part of which focused on DND and the difficulties it was having as a result of its declining budget. In blunt language, the Auditor General told Parliament that DND "cannot afford all the equipment forecast to fully modernize the forces."[70] In addition, the Auditor General warned that DND could be facing a $5 billion CDN capital budget shortfall unless defense spending was increased immediately. While the government had little to say in the military's defense, it was the first time since Prime Minister Mulroney's early years in office that anyone in Ottawa had spoken of the looming crisis in Canadian defense.[71]

In the spring of 1999, the Canadian military took part in its second campaign in less than a decade, the air war over Kosovo (designated Operation Allied Force). Canada, along with four other NATO members, participated in the bombing operation that was intended to diminish Serb president Slobodan Milosevic's capacity to wage war and to effectively force Serbia out of the disputed province.[72] While Canada played an important part in the air war,[73] a series of equipment shortcomings attracted attention[74] and focused concern on the increasingly dated CF-18s and the fact that the government had been unable to adequately modernize the fleet because of funding cuts.

Faced with the prospect that Canada's defense forces were becoming marginalized in coalition operations, in the war's aftermath both the government and DND began a concerted (albeit belated) effort to make sure that Canada's military remained at least *theoretically* capable of taking part in high-intensity combat operations. In 1999, the department released a major planning document intended to mold defense strategy for the first two decades of the new century. Titled *Shaping the Future of Canadian Defence: A Strategy for 2020*,[75] the document was focused on the rampaging Revolution in Military Affairs (RMA) that was by then well established in many countries (particularly the U.S.).[76] While the report was predictably cautious about what Canada might do about the RMA, it was apparent to many observers that unless the department's budget was dramatically increased, Canada would be largely incapable of transforming its military, and would thus be relegated to accepting missions at the lower end of the combat scale.

Over the following two years, there was a slight increase in defense spending, as the Chrétien government (somewhat grudgingly) attempted to restore the credibility of the Canadian Forces. However, the September 11, 2001, terrorist attacks on New York and Washington focused domestic attention on the limited capacity that Canada had to take part in the military campaign against global terrorism. While Canada ultimately did participate in the war against the Taliban and al-Qaeda in Afghanistan in the winter of 2002, that role was severely constrained by the C.F.'s diminished capabilities[77] and the fact that the U.S. had little need for allies that did not bring much to the military table.

In addition, the land forces contingent that Canada contributed (850 soldiers of the Princess Patricia's Canadian Light Infantry and an undisclosed number of special forces troops) had to deal with embarrassments of Ottawa's own making. As a result of budget cuts, no investment had been made in strategic airlift, and thus for three months the Canadian troops and their equipment waited on the ground in Canada, hoping to get a ride from the United States.[78] Once finally in Afghanistan, the Canadians sweltered in heavy green-black-and-brown uniforms better suited to the forests of the Canadian Shield, rather than the U.S.-style beige fatigues designed for the landscape of desert warfare. And while the Canadian troops performed their mission well,[79] in May 2002 the government announced that the force would be coming home at the end of their six-month tour in July. The explanation, as Andrew Cohen noted, "was that Canada couldn't stay any longer."[80]

It was around this time that more reports—many of which were penned by government officials and representatives—were released that outlined the extent of the crisis facing Canada's military.[81] Sadly, though, while there was no shortage of studies warning of the pending emergency, no statements from Ottawa were forthcoming that suggested major changes were planned.

First out of the blocks was a report by the Auditor General, Sheila Fraser, which served as a follow-up to the 1998 bombshell. In December 2001, Fraser reported that the armed forces lacked basic information about the condition of its equipment, suffered a shortage of personnel to fix it, and had trouble delivering spare parts for even urgent repairs.[82] And as for the government's declarations that the C.F. were in good shape, Ms. Fraser noted that "until steps are taken to manage equipment readiness more adequately, these claims should be taken with a grain of salt."[83] The report also listed a number of examples of declining readiness, including reduced maintenance of navy frigates and a shortage of operable army vehicles.

A few months later, the Standing Committee on National Defence and Veterans Affairs noted that the requirements of the *1994 Defence White Paper* could not be met and the government policies stated in the paper could no longer be maintained. Further, the Committee warned that there had been significant deterioration in the Forces' equipment, and thus an immediate infusion of $4 billion CDN was required (in addition to an increase in the department's annual budget of up to 50 percent).[84] As the Committee stated, "the status quo is not acceptable. . . . For too long, the CF have found it necessary to sacrifice one element in order to sustain another." Later in the report, the Committee recognized the enormous difficulties that the C.F. face and noted, "We are now in a situation where we will either have to increase funding or significantly restructure the CF."[85]

Adding its voice to the emerging consensus was the Council for Canadian Security in the 21st Century, which cautioned that "the Canadian Forces stands on a precipice between [being] a truly viable combat capable force and a constabulary force."[86] In July 2002, the Auditor General released an additional audit of DND that warned that the C.F. faced a serious shortage of skilled professionals.[87] And in perhaps the most troubling report of all, the Conference of Defence Associations warned that "unless the [Canadian Forces] are provided with more resources to execute the missions assigned to them . . . they will be forced to close-down entire operational capabilities. If that occurs, Canadian security and well-being, including national sovereignty, will be placed at significant risk."[88]

And yet, in spite of all the talk of imminent collapse, gross funding shortages, and equipment scandals, the government remained unmoved. In December 2001, the Prime Minister stated that the Canadian Forces were "well equipped" and suggested that the people calling for increases in defense spending—who, it should be reiterated, included not only Canada's Auditor General but several members of his own party—were essentially shills for Canada's (largely nonexistent) arms industry.[89] In effect, the Prime Minister signified that while the strategic environment may have changed (although it should be noted that it took the Canadian government several months post-9/11 to recognize this[90]), Canada's approach toward its military had not.

In that month's federal budget, $1.2 billion CDN was earmarked for the military (to be spread over five years), but of that total only $300 million was dedicated for capital spending. Adding insult to injury, approximately $100 million was taken out of DND's allocation and used to buy two new executive jets for the Prime Minister, a purchase that ignored all the established rules on the awarding of government contracts.[91] Subsequently, while the 2003 budget gave the military an additional $800 million (thereby raising DND's budget—at $12.7 billion—to just below what it had been in 1991), the Prime Minister again acknowledged that defense was not "the government's highest priority."[92] And in early 2004 came word that persistent funding shortages, and a $500 million budget shortfall, were likely to cause the closure of some of the country's biggest military bases.[93]

Prime Minister Chrétien departed Canadian politics in December 2003, leaving it to his successor, Paul Martin, to pick up the pieces of the country's once proud military. In a final assessment, then, Jean Chrétien oversaw the most dramatic reduction in Canadian defense capabilities in the forty-year period of near-uninterrupted military decline. It is hardly a proud legacy.

PART THREE: CONCLUSION

Canada's lax attitude toward defense and security has not gone unnoticed. In recent years, both NATO and the U.S. have called on Canada to increase its defense spending.[94] However, given that the needs of the military have long been ignored and/or disparaged, such calls have fallen largely on deaf ears.

And yet, this is not to suggest that Canada and the U.S. have ended their sixty-year history of close military cooperation. In the aftermath of September 11, the two governments managed to overcome a range of ideological and political differences and agreed to a number of measures to increase North American security.[95] In addition, in 2002, the two countries created the Binational Planning Group (BPG), whose mission is to improve bilateral arrangements to defend North America against maritime threats, and to respond to both land-based threats and natural disasters.[96]

That said, as American analyst Dwight Mason has recently noted, it is hard to overlook the fact that Canada's continuing military weakness is having a negative effect on the larger bilateral relationship.[97] Indeed, from a U.S. perspective, the Canadian government's neglect of its military threatens to diminish the relationship for several reasons. First, the smaller the C.F. becomes, the less likely that there can be meaningful (i.e., strategically significant) defense cooperation. Second, and perhaps more importantly, by continuously reducing its military, the Canadian government is sending a signal that it no longer much cares about the defense of North America, and that it is prepared to cede total control of the continent's defense to the U.S. While the U.S. is obviously willing (some critics might say eager) to assume complete control of North American defence, doing so would send a negative message internationally and potentially heighten tensions with other countries.

The decline of Canada's military has also had enormous repercussions on this country's ability to act as a sovereign state. By being dependent on the U.S. for its security, Canada runs the risk of looking foolish in the eyes of many countries. This tendency is exacerbated when Ottawa pursues foreign policies that are opposed to those of Washington (an example would be Canada's 2003 decision to oppose the Iraqi war). In such cases, it can appear as if Canada is intentionally tweaking the American nose, all the while enjoying the benefits of having the U.S. provide for Canadian security.

Furthermore, the refusal to pay the price of defense says something about Canada itself. As historian J. L. Granatstein has asked, "Does it matter if we are [defense] freeloaders? It does, to the military of course, but also to the nation and to the rest of the world. . . . Military strength has been and remains a key indicator of power because if a government leaves its military in decay . . . it is confessing an absence of will."[98] In the eyes of many, Canada's military weakness suggests a country that is not serious about countering threats, or of playing any significant role in the maintenance of international stability.

Canada's military weakness has had other consequences. As Marten has analyzed in her chapter in this volume, despite the public's (mis)perception,[99] Ottawa is no longer a leading contributor to international peacekeeping operations, a task that, in spite of recent scandals, remains very popular among Canadians. How far Canada has fallen is surprising to even veteran observers of the country's defense decline. At the end of 2002, Canada ranked 34th in terms of the total number of troops serving with UN-sponsored peacekeeping missions.[100] While, in fairness, the personnel that Canada contributes to the International Security Assistance Force (ISAF) in Afghanistan and the personnel serving in Bosnia in the Stabilization Force (SFOR) are not counted (as they are both NATO missions), even the inclusion of them would not vault Canada back onto the list of the world's leading peacekeeping/peace-supporting contributors.[101] To Canadian eyes, the fact that the U.S. contributes many-times more troops to global peacekeeping operations than Canada does is a particularly ruthless way of demonstrating just how much international politics has changed in the last few years.

In a nutshell, then, the issue is actually quite simple—in an increasingly dangerous world, does Canada believe that military forces are necessary? If one was to look at the record of the last forty years, the obvious answer would be "No." And yet, such a response contradicts more than one hundred years of Canadian statehood and the sacrifices that Canadians made in the battlefields of Europe and Asia in the century just ended. Thus, the question can and should be rephrased—is the current forty-year trend likely to continue, or will Canada reclaim the military role it once performed on the world stage so admirably?

As this chapter is written, there does not appear to be a clear answer, but there are some encouraging signs pointing to the latter possibility. First, the fact that so many Canadians—in both official and unofficial capacities—have begun to speak out about the weakness of the military is a positive development. Second, as noted, the government has taken some recent steps (albeit very tentative ones) to increase the funding available to DND.[102] Third, in April 2004, Canada's first-ever official statement on national security policy was released, one that identified basic principles intended to guide future defense decisions. The document, *Securing an Open Society: Canada's National Security Policy*,[103] while admittedly vague on several key issues, contained some important initiatives, including the creation of an Integrated Threat Assessment Centre, the development of a Critical Infrastructure Protection Strategy, and the convening of a Cyber-security Task Force. Fourth, in 2005, a new defense policy statement was released that called for "modern, combat-capable" military forces and emphasized the importance of the Canada–U.S. defense partnership.[104] And finally recent press reports suggest that the government had begun work on a plan to increase the size of the C.F. by 5,000 troops, the first such proposal in decades.[105] Add to this the fact that some of Ottawa's long-standing friends are beginning to voice their concerns about Canada's military weakness, and it is possible that the tide has turned.

If it has, it is not a moment too soon. In effect, successive Canadian governments have broken their agreement with both the public and the C.F. That agreement is based on the concept of the government providing the military with effective equipment, adequate funding, and tasks that do not involve unnecessary risk, and in return the military serves the state without regard for its institutional (or political) interest.[106] Perhaps even more worrisome, the endless cuts have resulted in a military that does not support the defense policies of the present—and previous—federal government(s). Officers widely believe that Canadian foreign policy (with its overwhelming emphasis on "soft power" and "human security") is flawed, and also believe that the C.F. have been asked to do too much, for too long, with too little.[107]

In sum, forty years of cuts have left the Canadian military in very poor shape. Should the situation continue much longer, there are good reasons to suspect that the military might effectively collapse under the combined weight of the lack of adequate finances, equipment, and effective leadership. And yet, the situation is far from hopeless. As Doug Bland has noted, "Canada today is an unmilitary nation by choice, not by character."[108] The century just ended demonstrated that Canada can play a military role far greater than its Middle Power status would suggest, provided that the political will exists. In an environment where spending money on defense is frequently characterized as wasteful and unnecessary, finding this will is not going to be easy. Ultimately, though, the decision will be made simpler by the realization that if Canada wishes to be considered a serious country on the international stage, it effectively has no choice.

NOTES

1. These reports have been produced by both government and interested observers. Among the former, see *Facing Our Responsibilities: The State of Readiness of the Canadian Forces* (Ottawa: Report of the Standing Committee on

National Defence and Veterans Affairs, 2002) and *For an Extra $130 Bucks: Update on Canada's Military Financial Crisis* (Ottawa: Report of the Standing Committee on National Security and Defence, 2002). For the latter, see *A Nation at Risk: The Decline of the Canadian Forces* (Ottawa: Conference of Defence Associations, 2002); *A Wake-Up Call for Canada: The Need for a New Military* (Toronto: Royal Canadian Military Institute, 2001); Joseph Jockel, *The Canadian Forces: Hard Choices, Soft Power* (Toronto: Canadian Institute of Strategic Studies, 1999); J. L. Granatstein, *Who Killed the Canadian Military?* (Toronto: Harper Collins, 2004). In addition, a recent report in *Jane's Defence Weekly* on Canada's military weakness attracted international attention. See "Readiness at a Price," *Jane's Defence Weekly*, September 17, 2003.

2. Douglas L. Bland, "A Sow's Ear from a Silk Purse," *International Journal* 54, no. 1 (Winter 1998–99): 149.

3. According to David Dewitt and John Kirton, the intent of St. Laurent's speech was to reinforce the belief that the pursuit of global economic and political stability and the avoidance of major international war required the establishment of a network of powerful states acknowledging the primacy of international law. See David Dewitt and John Kirton, *Canada as a Principal Power* (Toronto: John Wiley & Sons, 1983).

4. See David Mitrany, *The Progress of International Government* (London: George Allen & Unwin, 1933).

5. See Adam Chapnick, "The Canadian Middle Power Myth," *International Journal* 55, no. 2 (Spring 2000): 190. For works on the middle power paradigm, see Carsten Holbraad, *Middle Powers in International Politics* (London: Macmillan, 1984); *Canada's Role as a Middle Power*, ed. King Gordon (Toronto: Canadian Institute of International Affairs, 1966); John Holmes, "Most Safely in the Middle," *International Journal* 39, no. 2 (1984): 366–388.

6. Perhaps the best example of a book that generated significant public debate on the strategic and military choices facing Canada was written by a CBC reporter in 1960. See James Minifie, *Peacemaker or Powdermonkey? Canada's Role in a Revolutionary World* (Toronto: McClelland and Stewart, 1960).

7. Bland, 149. This argument can also be found in J. L. Granatstein, "Peacekeeping: Did Canada Make a Difference? And What Difference Did Peacekeeping Make to Canada?" in *Making a Difference: Canada's Foreign Policy in a Changing World Order*, ed. John English and Norman Hillmer (Toronto: Lester Publishing, 1993).

8. Department of National Defence, *White Paper on Defence* (Ottawa: Queen's Printer, 1964). Defence White Papers are completed every ten to twenty years, or when global conditions change in dramatic and unexpected ways. The intent is to

offer a general guideline of defense policy for the Canadian government, and a framework for strategy and major procurement programs. Douglas Bland has examined all five of the post-war White Papers in one volume. See *Canada's National Defence: Volume 1, Defence Policy*, ed. Douglas Bland (Kingston: Queen's University School of Policy Studies, 1997).

9. R. B. Byers, *Canadian Security and Defence: The Legacy and the Challenges*, Adelphi Paper no. 214 (London: International Institute for Strategic Studies, 1986), 6.

10. D. W. Middlemiss and J. J. Sokolsky, *Canadian Defence: Decisions and Determinants* (Toronto: Harcourt Brace, 1989), 20.

11. Among major works examining U.S. nuclear strategy of the period, see Colin Gray, *Strategic Studies and Public Policy: The American Experience* (Lexington: University of Kentucky Press, 1982); Lawrence Freedman, *The Evolution of Nuclear Strategy* (London: Macmillan, 1981); Saki Dockrill, *Eisenhower's New-Look National Security Policy, 1953–1961* (London: Macmillan, 1996).

12. On NORAD's formation, see Joseph Jockel, *No Boundaries Upstairs: Canada, the United States, and the Origins of North American Air Defence, 1945–1958* (Vancouver: UBC Press, 1987). For a recent look at contemporary issues facing the command, see D. F. Hollman, *NORAD in the New Millennium* (Toronto: Canadian Institute of International Affairs, 2000).

13. Middlemiss and Sokolsky, *Canadian Defence*, 22.

14. Middlemiss and Sokolsky, *Canadian Defence*, 22.

15. The best study of this period remains Jon B. McLin, *Canada's Changing Defense Policy, 1957–1963: The Problems of a Middle Power in Alliance* (Baltimore: Johns Hopkins University Press, 1967).

16. For more on the controversy, see J. L. Granatstein, *Canada 1957–1967: The Years of Uncertainty and Innovation* (Toronto: McClelland & Stewart, 1986).

17. Byers, 33. For a review of Pearson's defense program, see Marilyn Eustace, *Canada's Commitment to Europe: The European Force 1964–1971*, National Security Series no. 1 (Kingston, ON: Queen's University Centre for International Relations, 1979).

18. Bland, "A Sow's Ear from a Silk Purse," 150.

19. Bland, "A Sow's Ear from a Silk Purse," 151.

20. Robert Bothwell, *The Big Chill: Canada and the Cold War*, Contemporary Affairs no. 1 (Toronto: Canadian Institute of International Affairs, 1998), 88.

21. Bothwell, *The Big Chill*, 88.

22. As outlined in Desmond Morton, *A Military History of Canada: From Champlain to Kosovo* (Toronto: McClelland & Stewart, 1999), 255.

23. Department of National Defence, *Defence in the 1970s* (Ottawa: Queen's Printer, 1971).

24. The process by which this decision was made was unusual. During the 1968 election campaign, Trudeau had insisted that Canadian participation in its alliances would be reassessed once the government took office. Incoming Cabinet ministers Eric Kierans and Donald MacDonald argued publicly against continued Canadian membership in NATO, and there were numerous calls for Canada to declare itself a neutral country. Ultimately, Trudeau's advisor and close friend Ivan Head was recruited to draft a policy paper that accepted the continued need for Canadian participation in its alliances, but at the same time it called for Canada to work toward changing both NATO and NORAD from within. For Trudeau's and Head's recollection of these developments, see *The Canadian Way: Shaping Canada's Foreign Policy, 1968–1984* (Toronto: McClelland & Stewart, 1995). For a more objective account, see J. L. Granatstein and Robert Bothwell, *Pirouette: Pierre Trudeau and Canadian Foreign Policy* (Toronto: University of Toronto Press, 1990).

25. In September 1969, the Minister of National Defence, Leo Cadieux, announced that Canada's European defense force would be cut to a combat group of 2,800 troops and three squadrons of (increasingly obsolete) aircraft. As Robert Bothwell has noted of the decision, "in a half-hearted manner Canada was saying that . . . NATO, while not completely irrelevant. . . . was no longer as strategically important as it once had been." See *The Big Chill*, 89. At the same time, the government announced an end to the nuclear strike role that had been accepted by the Royal Canadian Air Force in 1959.

26. Bothwell, *The Big Chill*, 89.

27. Tom Keating and Larry Pratt, *Canada, NATO, and the Bomb: The Western Alliance in Crisis* (Edmonton: Hurtig Publishers, 1988), 34.

28. In addition, Denis Healey, the British Defence Minister, warned

> if the Canadians go through with their planned reductions, and, even more, if this leads to a chain reaction from the other countries, conventional strength would fall, the nuclear threshold would fall, and the point at which nuclear weapons would be used would arise much earlier.

As cited in Tom Keating, *Canada and World Order: The Multilateralist Tradition in Canadian Foreign Policy* (Don Mills, ON: Oxford University Press, 2002), 148.

29. As cited in Douglas Bland, "Controlling the Defence Policy Process in Canada: White Papers on Defense and Bureaucratic Politics in the Department of National Defense," in *Canada's Defence: Perspectives on Policy in the Twentieth Century*, ed. B. D. Hunt and R. G. Haycock (Toronto: Copp Clark Pitman, 1993), 217.

30. Middlemiss and Sokolsky, *Canadian Defence*, 35.

31. In 1968, the government decided to end the Canadian commitment to send

a reinforced brigade to Germany by sea in the event of war. In its place, the Canadian Air-Sea Transportable (CAST) Brigade Group would be available for deployment to either Norway or Denmark. As for the charge of a commitment-capability gap, it was not until the 1980s that this accusation became widespread. Besides the report by Byers (*Canadian Security and Defence: The Legacy and the Challenges*), additional studies making the allegation were issued by the Business Council of National Issues and a Senate Subcommittee. See, respectively, *Canada's Defence Policy: Capabilities Versus Commitments* (Ottawa: Business Council on National Issues, 1984) and *Canada's Maritime Forces* (Ottawa: Senate Subcommittee on National Defense and the Standing Committee on Foreign Affairs, 1983).

32. Byers, *Canadian Security and Defence: The Legacy and the Challenges*, 33.

33. Middlemiss and Sokolsky, *Canadian Defence*, 44.

34. See, in particular, Joseph Jockel and Joel Sokolsky, *Canada and Collective Security: Odd Man Out*, The Washington Papers, no. 121 (Washington, D.C.: Centre for Strategic and International Studies, 1986); R. B. Byers, "Canada's Defence Review: Strategic Doctrine and Military Commitments," *Canadian Defence Quarterly* 14, no. 4, (Spring 1985).

35. See Granatstein and Bothwell, *Pirouette*, 234. Even less charitable is Doug Bland's description of this period. Trudeau "simply and deliberately suffocated the armed forces and dismantled Canada's national military capabilities." See Bland, "A Sow's Ear from a Silk Purse," 152.

36. As the new prime minister stated in his first Throne Speech, "Canada will once again play its full part in the defense systems of NATO. Only in this way do we earn the right to full consultation and participation in the policies of that alliance." As cited in Keating, *Canada and World Order*, 157.

37. See Major T. J. Hochban, "North American Air Defense Modernization," *Canadian Defence Quarterly* 15, no. 3 (Winter 1985/86).

38. Joseph Jockel, "A Seat at the Table: Canada and Its Alliances," in Hunt and Haycock, *Canada's Defence*, 157.

39. Special Joint Committee of the Senate and House of Commons, *Independence and Internationalism: Report of the Special Joint Committee on Canada's International Relations* (Ottawa: Queen's Printer, 1985).

40. Department of National Defence, *Challenge and Commitment: A Defence Policy for Canada* (Ottawa: Supply and Services Canada, 1987). On the delays that slowed down the production of the White Paper, see Nelson Michaud, *Genèse d'une politique syncopique: La défense du Canada et le livre blanc de 1987* (unpublished dissertation thesis, Université Laval, 1998).

41. These terms reflected the enormous changes that were taking place in the U.S.S.R. in the late 1980s and early 1990s. Essentially, *perestroika* referred to eco-

nomic rejuvenation, specifically the need for major changes in the Soviet Union's industrial and business sectors. It also referred to changes to the organization of agricultural production and foreign trade practices. *Glasnost*, or political liberalization, consisted of measures to create electoral and legislative systems which would involve greater public participation. In addition, there would be changes to the role that the Communist Party played in daily life, a more candid and pluralistic media, and legal reforms to enhance the rights of citizens. For a discussion, see Leonard J. Cohen, "The Soviet Union and Eastern Europe in Transition: Trends and Implications for Canada," in *Canada Among Nations 1989: The Challenge of Change*, ed. Maureen Appel Molot and Fen Osler Hampson (Ottawa: Carleton University Press, 1990). Also see Richard Sakwa, *Gorbachev and His Reforms, 1985–1990* (London: Philip Allan, 1990).

42. Additional procurement programs identified in the White Paper included a second batch of six frigates, installation of an under-ice surveillance system in the Arctic, the development of a new sonar system for surface ships, the purchase of six additional maritime long-range patrol aircraft, and mine countermeasures vessels.

43. Middlemiss and Sokolsky, *Canadian Defence*, 53.

44. For an examination of the proposal, see S. Mathin Davis, "Nuclear Submarines for Canada: A Technical Critique," in *The U.S.–Canada Security Relationship: The Politics, Strategy, and Technology of Defense*, ed. David G. Haglund and Joel J. Sokolsky (Boulder, CO: Westview Press, 1989). Also see Sokolsky, "Parting of the Waves? The Strategy and Politics of the SSN Decision," in *The U.S.–Canada Security Relationship*.

45. See Joel J. Sokolsky, "The Bilateral Defense Relationship with the United States," in *Canada's International Security Policy*, ed. David B. Dewitt and David Leyton-Brown (Scarborough, ON: Prentice-Hall Canada, 1995). For more on the U.S. Maritime strategy of the period, see James D. Watkins, "The Maritime Strategy," *U.S. Naval Institute Proceedings* 4 (January 1986).

46. Sokolsky, "The Bilateral Defence Relationship with the United States," 180.

47. Dan W. Middlemiss, "Canadian Defence Policy: An Uncertain Transition," in *Canada Among Nations 1989*, 121.

48. See Norrin M. Ripsman, "Big Eyes and Empty Pockets: The Two Phases of Conservative Defense Policy," in *Diplomatic Departures: The Conservative Era in Canadian Foreign Policy, 1984–93*, ed. Nelson Michaud and Kim Richard Nossal (Vancouver: UBC Press, 2001), 107.

49. For a discussion of the 1989 budget and its consequences for DND, see Middlemiss, "Canadian Defence Policy," 123–129.

50. Ripsman, "Big Eyes and Empty Pockets," 108.

51. Andrew Cohen, "Security and NATO," in *Canada Among Nations 1993–94: Global Jeopardy*, ed. Christopher J. Maule and Fen Osler Hampson (Ottawa: Carleton University Press, 1993), 252.

52. As the minister noted, "it's not because we had 1,100 forces in Europe that we had a political voice. It is because we are a member of NATO and people know we are committed to Europe." See Cohen, "Security and NATO," 252.

53. Cohen, "Security and NATO," 254.

54. Ripsman, "Big Eyes and Empty Pockets," 108.

55. See Jockel, *The Canadian Forces*, 15.

56. For a discussion, see Manfred Bienefeld, "The New World Order: Echoes of a New Imperialism," *Third World Quarterly* 15 (March 1994): 31–48.

57. Ottawa's involvement in the Gulf represented the first time since Korea that Canada had gone to war. See Jean Morin and Richard H. Gimblett, *Operation Friction, 1990–1991: The Canadian Forces in the Persian Gulf* (Toronto: Dundurn Press, 1997); Martin Rudner, "Canada, the Gulf Crisis and Collective Security," in *Canada Among Nations 1990–91: After the Cold War*, eds. Fen Osler Hampson and Christopher J. Maule (Ottawa: Carleton University Press, 1991).

58. Department of National Defence, *1994 Defence White Paper* (Ottawa: Minister of Supply and Services, 1994).

59. Dean Oliver, "The Canadian Military After Somalia," in *Canada Among Nations 1998: Leadership and Dialogue*, ed. Fen Osler Hampson and Maureen Appel Molot (Don Mills, ON: Oxford University Press, 1998), 101.

60. This was the primary recommendation of a high-profile group of academics, former military officials, and policy advisors organized by the University of Toronto. See *Canada 21: Canada and Common Security in the Twenty-first Century* (Toronto: University of Toronto Centre for International Studies, 1994).

61. Department of National Defence, *1994 Defence White Paper*, 14.

62. It might be noted that in July 2004, a decade after the White Paper's release, a contract was finally signed for the Sea King's replacement, although the announcement did little to end the controversy over the helicopter saga. The government awarded the contract to U.S.-based Sikorsky, and their unproven H-92 design, over the competing bid from EH Industries and the updated version of the EH-101. Press reports suggested that political considerations played a critical role in the decision, and that the Liberal government simply could not purchase a variant of the helicopter that it had rejected ten years earlier. See "U.S. Firm Is Handed Ottawa's Helicopter Contract," *Globe and Mail*, 24 July 2004.

63. In a representative comment, John Marteinson, editor of *Canadian Defence Quarterly*, noted that "while we disagree with some aspects of the White Paper, all in all the new defence policy would appear to be well-conceived, farsighted and

sustainable." See John Marteinson, "Editorial," *Canadian Defence Quarterly* 24, no. 2 (December 1994).

64. Department of National Defence, *1994 Defence White Paper*, 9.

65. In addition to the decline in the Regular Force, the White Paper called for a significant reduction in the number of civilians working in DND, from 32,500 in 1994 to a goal of 20,000 in 1999. See *1994 Defence White Paper*, 46.

66. Jockel, *The Canadian Forces*, 13.

67. By way of comparison, figures for other allied countries are: the U.S. 3.2 percent, the U.K. 2.5 percent, Germany 1.5 percent, and France 2.6 percent. Figures from The International Institute for Strategic Studies, *The Military Balance 2002–2003* (London: Oxford University Press, 2002).

68. See Lloyd Axworthy, "Canada and Human Security: The Need for Leadership," *International Journal* 52, no. 2 (Spring 1997): 183–196. For a critical look at Axworthy's approach, see Fen Osler Hampson and Dean Oliver, "Pulpit Diplomacy: A Critical Assessment of the Axworthy Doctrine," *International Journal* 53, no. 3 (Summer 1998): 379–406.

69. An additional factor leading to the general sense of military decline was the Somalia inquiry, which was called to investigate the torture and murder of a Somali teenager by members of the Canadian Airborne Regiment in the spring of 1993. In 1997, the inquiry was unexpectedly cut short, just as it began uncovering developments that took place under the Chrétien government's tenure. See Commission of Inquiry into the Deployment of Canadian Forces to Somalia, *Dishonoured Legacy: The Lessons of the Somalia Affair* (Ottawa: Minister of Public Works and Government Services, 1997). Also see David Bercuson, *Significant Incident: Canada's Army, the Airborne, and the Murder in Somalia* (Toronto: McClelland & Stewart, 1996). In short order, a number of sensational stories appeared in the media detailing an array of physical and sexual abuses in the military, accounts that added to the sense of an institution in decline.

70. As cited in Jockel, *The Canadian Forces*, 118.

71. While not an official government report, Jockel's 1999 study *The Canadian Forces* also deserves noting. The author, a long-time observer of Canada's defense debate, warned that unless DND's budget was substantially increased, the department would shortly have to make difficult decisions regarding which combat capabilities to drop.

72. For a review of Canada's role in Kosovo, see David L. Bashow, Colonel Dwight Davies, and Colonel Andre Viens, "Mission Ready: Canada's Role in the Kosovo Air Campaign," *Canadian Military Journal* (Spring 2000): 55–62.

73. Canadian CF-18s flew a total of 678 combat sorties during the conflict. In addition, Canadian aircraft flew in nearly 10 percent of the battlefield air-interdiction missions, among the riskiest and most significant of the war.

74. For example, Canada did not have a strategic air-to-air refueling capability. In addition, Canada did not have any satellite-guided munitions, thus making it dependent on laser-guided missiles, of which the air force had only a small stockpile. Most importantly, Canada did not have a secure voice communication capability, a failing that forced the entire allied air effort to use single frequency (and thus jammable) equipment. For a discussion, see Bashow, Davies, and Viens, "Mission Ready."

75. Department of National Defence, *Shaping the Future of Canadian Defence: A Strategy for 2020* (Ottawa: Minister of Supply and Services, 1999).

76. Among general works on the RMA, see Admiral William Owens, *Lifting the Fog of War* (New York: Farrar, Straus & Giroux, 2000); and Michael O'Hanlon, *Technological Change and the Future of Warfare* (Washington, D.C.: Brookings Institution Press, 2000). Among studies that examine the Canadian approach to the RMA, see Andrew Richter, *The Revolution in Military Affairs and Its Impact on Canada: The Challenge and the Consequences*, Working Paper 28 (Vancouver: University of British Columbia Institute of International Relations, 1999); Elinor Sloan, "Canada and the Revolution in Military Affairs: Current Response and Future Opportunities," *Canadian Military Journal* (Autumn 2000).

77. While the military's official goal of 60,000 personnel—established in the *1994 Defence White Paper*—was still in effect, in reality the size of the C.F. in 2001 was closer to 52,000. Of that number, the army's official combat strength was 19,500, but the real figure was closer to 18,000. Once all of the various commitments were accounted for, it was undoubtedly a struggle to come up with any ground force for duty in Afghanistan. See Andrew Cohen, *While Canada Slept: How We Lost Our Place in the World* (Toronto: McClelland & Stewart, 2003), 58.

78. See "Our Bush League Armed Forces Hurry to Wait," *Globe and Mail*, 24 January 2002.

79. The Canadian troops provided airport security, performed land-mine removal, assisted in tracking and capturing remaining Taliban and al-Qaeda fighters, and helped protect aid operations. One indication of their value was the U.S. decision to recommend three Canadian soldiers for a Bronze Star.

80. Cohen, *While Canada Slept*, 58. As Defence Minister Art Eggleton noted, "the [U.S.] military indicated that they would like us to stay . . . [but] we were stretched [and] we needed time to rest and regroup our forces." See "Princess Pats to Return in Summer," *National Post* (Toronto), 22 May 2002.

81. Reports were prepared by, among other groups, the Senate Standing Committee on National Security and Defence, the House of Commons Standing Committee on National Defence and Veterans Affairs, the Centre for Military and Strategic Studies at the University of Calgary, the Council for Canadian Security in

the 21st Century, the Conference of Defence Associations, and the Center for Strategic and International Studies in Washington.

82. Cohen, *While Canada Slept*, 50.

83. Cohen, *While Canada Slept*, 50.

84. *Facing Our Responsibilities*, 2–3.

85. *Facing Our Responsibilities*, 1, 2, and 15.

86. Centre for Military and Strategic Studies, *To Secure a Nation: Canadian Defence and Security in the 21st Century* (Calgary: University of Calgary Press, 2002).

87. See "Military Faces Mass Exodus, Auditor Warns," *Kingston Whig-Standard*, 10 July 2002.

88. See *A Nation at Risk*, 1.

89. As the Prime Minister noted with his customary eloquence, "there is an industry that is very important that produces armaments for government . . . that [says] you should buy more of our stuff." See "Armed Forces 'Well Equipped,' Chrétien Fires Back," *National Post*, 21 December 2001.

90. For an unflattering look at the Chrétien government's response to 9/11, see Kim Richard Nossal, "Canadian Foreign Policy After 9/11: Realignment, Reorientation, or Reinforcement?" in *Foreign Policy Realignment in the Age of Terror*, ed. Leonard Cohen, Brian Job, and Alexander Moens (Toronto: The Canadian Institute of Strategic Studies, 2002).

91. See "Canadian DND Cash Used to Buy Jets for Prime Minister," *Jane's Defence Weekly*, April 17, 2002. In the Auditor General's February 2004 report, the purchase of the jets was harshly criticized. See "Ottawa Broke Rules for Jets It Didn't Need," *National Post*, 11 February 2004.

92. See "PM Vows to Raise Military Spending," *Ottawa Citizen*, 22 November 2002.

93. See "'Bankrupt' Forces May Shut 5 Bases," *National Post*, 24 February 2004.

94. While there was little foreign criticism of Canada's defense budget during the Cold War, that discretion has now disappeared. In 1999, NATO Secretary-General Lord Robertson referred to Canada's defense spending as "languishing" behind other alliance countries. A 1999 U.S. Department of Defense report similarly described Canada as one of the Western countries doing "substantially less than their fair share" of military spending. And in January 2004, the new NATO Secretary-General, Jaap de Hoop Scheffer, visited Ottawa and promptly told Canadian officials that he hoped "the financial means" will be provided to allow Canada to play a more active role in the alliance. See "We Stand on Guard, Barely," *Ottawa Citizen*, 22 December 2001; and "Canada's Defense Budget Targeted," *Halifax Herald*, 30 January 2004.

95. In December 2001, the Canadian and U.S. governments reached a general agreement on border issues, including surveillance, common enforcement measures, and increased cooperation on entry. The negotiation of the "Smart Border" has greatly speeded up the transshipment of goods, a critical consideration given that the two countries enjoy the world's largest bilateral trading relationship. The following summer, Canada and the United States announced the creation of five new integrated cross-border enforcement teams, including police, immigration, and customs officers. And while there has been no formal agreement on a North American defense perimeter, officials in both countries have repeatedly said that the level of bilateral cooperation is excellent. For a review of recent developments, see J. L. Granatstein, "A Friendly Agreement in Advance: Canada–U.S. Defense Relations Past, Present, and Future," *C. D. Howe Institute Commentary*, no. 166 (June 2002).

96. For more on the Bilateral Planning Group, see Dwight N. Mason, "The Canadian–American North American Defence Alliance in 2005," *International Journal* 55, no. 2 (Spring 2005). On the negative side, it might be noted that Ottawa decided in February 2005 to decline involvement in the U.S. missile defense program, a decision that suggested ongoing defense tensions.

97. Dwight N. Mason, "U.S.–Canada Defense Relations: A View from Washington," in *Canada Among Nations 2003: Coping with the American Colossus*, ed. David Carment, Fen Osler Hampson, and Norman Hillmer (Don Mills, ON: Oxford University Press, 2003), 151.

98. As cited by Granatstein, "A Friendly Agreement in Advance," 15–16.

99. A survey published in 1997 reported that 83 percent of Canadians believed that Canada played either a "substantial" or "very substantial" role in international peacekeeping. See Cohen, *While Canada Slept*, 61.

100. Granatstein, "A Friendly Agreement in Advance," 14.

101. A word on these two missions might be helpful. While the ISAF mission was originally established by the passage of a UN Security Council Resolution (1386) in December 2001, NATO formally took it over in August 2003. It might also be noted that Canada began scaling back its troop commitment in August 2004, reducing its presence by approximately 1,000 personnel (i.e., from 1,900 to about 900). Prior to the reduction, Canada had been the largest contributor to the 6,300-member force. However, the Canadian government has made a commitment to continue contributing to the force for several additional years. As for Canada's role in SFOR, the government has announced that it will end its participation in 2007. In the past year alone, the size of the Canadian commitment has been reduced by half. For a discussion of the ISAF mission, see Lewis Mackenzie, "Time to Go on the Offensive in Afghanistan," *National Post*, February 21, 2004.

See also "Canada to Reduce Overseas Military Operations," *CTV.ca*, June 25, 2004, http://www.ctv.ca/CTV News.

102. In the February 2005 budget, the Liberal government pledged an additional $13 billion to be spread over five years to DND. And in the 2006 election campaign, both the Liberals and the Conservatives emphasized the need for DND to receive more fiscal resources (even if Liberal funding promises were overshadowed by the controversy around an attack ad that suggested that a Conservative government would impose some form of martial law).

103. See *Securing an Open Society: Canada's National Security Policy*, released on April 27, 2004, http://www.pco-bcp.gc.ca.

104. See *Canada's International Policy Statement: A Role of Pride and Influence in the World* (Ottawa: Department of National Defence, 2005).

105. See "Planners Told to Prepare for Expanded Military," *Ottawa Citizen*, 17 August 2004.

106. Bland, "A Sow's Ear from a Silk Purse," 163–164.

107. Bland, "A Sow's Ear from a Silk Purse," 166.

108. Bland, "A Sow's Ear from a Silk Purse," 143. Bland has also written about the possible collapse of the Canadian military. See "A National Crisis for the Next Government," in *Canada Without Armed Forces?* ed. Bland (Montreal: McGill-Queen's University Press, 2004).

4

The Evolution of Liberalization in Canada's Trade Policy

MICHAEL LUSZTIG

For many Canadians, international trade is the hidden component of their country's foreign policy. This is not to suggest that Canadians find trade to be unimportant. Indeed, to note that foreign trade impacts upon the daily life of Canadians is trite; at some level the point informs the general consciousness of even those most casually acquainted with current events. At times trade is elevated to higher levels of consciousness, when flashpoints (typically involving the United States) capture headlines and lead off the evening news. On the whole, however, foreign trade does very little to stir the soul of the average Canadian.

At the same time, Canada's trade history has enough intrigue and political plot twists to make for a compelling tale. The past twenty-five years have witnessed fundamental policy shifts on the part of both the Conservative and Liberal parties on the issue of trade. For the first time since the early days of Confederation, both parties can be characterized as enthusiastic supporters of continental free trade. In addition, much of the business community has gone (if we are to take their public statements at face value) from needing high levels of import protection to permit their very survival to requiring increased liberalization of trade to permit their very survival. What changed and why? These questions serve as the mandate for this chapter.

WHAT CHANGED?

In terms of Canada's trade policy, the twenty-first century dawned far differently than did its predecessor. Today Canada is committed to liberalization of trade, both multilaterally through the World Trade Organization (WTO) and bilaterally under the auspices of trade deals signed with key trading partners in the Americas.[1] Moreover, Canada continues to play a leading role in the construction of the Free Trade Area of the Americas (FTAA)—a proposed hemispheric free trade zone that would include all non-communist states in the Americas. By contrast, the twentieth century began with the Canadian economy well insulated by high tariff walls, a product of the 1879 National Policy designed to promote the growth of industrial enterprises largely in Ontario and Quebec. So entrenched was the National Policy that Sir Wilfrid Laurier's political career was effectively wrecked when he tried to satisfy Western farmers by seeking to implement a continental free trade deal in 1911. Until Brian Mulroney came along, no Canadian Prime Minister would be so bold again.

Free trade has not been the watchword of Canada's economic history. From its earliest days, Canada's economy tended to keep market forces at bay. The trend started with the fur trade, which, in keeping with the prevailing economic philosophy in Europe, was mercantilist in orientation.[2] Both the French and British governments provided exclusive charters to companies as a means of exploiting the fur trade. Thus, the earliest disputes between English and French in what would become Canada began as a confrontation between two aspiring monopolies, the French Company of the West Indies and the British Hudson's Bay Company. Of course, these chartered companies were also the engines of settlement. They brought with them entire economic ecosystems, including banking structures, community infrastructure, and ultimately, through sponsor governments, community security. While certainly not the only source of disagreement between Britain and France during the late seventeenth century, competition over the fur trade ultimately led to armed conflict in North America. Within one hundred years, the French were defeated on the Plains of Abraham, and Britain controlled the Canadian colonies.[3]

British control hardly injected laissez-faire economics into its North American possessions. The British market was highly protected and would remain so until the repeal of the Corn Laws in 1846.[4] Under the terms of the Corn Laws, Canadian products—especially flour, wheat, and square timber—enjoyed privileged access to the lucrative British market. By contrast and for example, American wheat could gain like access to the Imperial market only if the wheat was ground in Canadian mills.[5]

As is often the case, when the government provides a free good, in this case import protection, a constituency develops for the retention of that good.[6] Such was the case in the Canadian colonies. Manufacturing and shipping interests in Montreal, Toronto, and Halifax became dependent on British protectionism for their livelihood. These interests lobbied the colonial and British governments not only for retention (and expansion) of Imperial privileges, but also for tariff protection against U.S. imports into the Canadian market. Until 1846, they were very successful.

The repeal of the Corn Laws was a trade policy revolution for the Canadian colonies. Long sheltered from the cruel winds of foreign competition, Canadian producers were now instantly exposed to global market forces. The results were felt quickly. Wheat and flour exports fell from 3.9 million bushels in 1847 to 2.2 million bushels in the subsequent year. Square timber exports from New Brunswick were almost halved during the same time frame.[7] The response to Corn Law repeal by the President of the Toronto Board of Trade is suggestive of the impact: "We are," he emoted, "in the same condition as a man suddenly precipitated from a lofty eminence. We are labouring under concussion of the brain."[8]

Truth be told, the response to repeal did have Canadian merchants acting a little strangely. So severe was the panic created by the loss of the protected British market that Canadian protectionists briefly flirted with radical reforms. In 1849, the most influential Montreal merchants issued the "Annexation Manifesto" which, if successful, would have seen the Province of Canada absorbed into the United States. Instead, in 1854, Canada entered into the Elgin-Marcy (Reciprocity) Treaty with the United States. The Reciprocity Treaty, however, was not to survive the cross-border tensions created by the U.S. Civil War, and in 1866 the United States abrogated the first continental free trade agreement.[9]

Meanwhile, Canada had come up with yet another plan for dealing with the loss of privileged access to the British market. Indeed, the economic imperative, combined with American jingoism in the West, which threatened the Pacific colony of British Columbia (B.C.), compelled the British North American colonies to enter into Confederation in 1867. Confederation, and particularly the terms of entry for B.C., conspired to doom the free trading sentiment that had arisen in the wake of Corn Law repeal. Part of the terms of entry for British Columbia was a promise to construct a continental railway. To make the railway cost effective, it was imperative to settle the West. In order to accomplish this, the Conservative government of Sir John A. Macdonald sought to emulate a similar development strategy—Henry Clay's American System[10]—utilized in the United States fifty years previously. Macdonald called his plan the National Policy.

The National Policy, enacted in 1879, became the cornerstone of Canadian protectionism for more than a century. It had three principal objectives: to finance completion of the railway; to populate the West; and to create a dynamic industrial base in Central Canada through the construction of a high tariff wall. These objectives were largely symbiotic. The tariff would generate revenues necessary to help fund the railway. It would also help foster an internal market for Canadian industrial products that, with the aid of an aggressive program of promoting immigration, would exist in Western Canada. Finally, the railway would transport Western agricultural goods and raw materials back to markets in Central Canada.[11]

While both political parties ultimately came to accept the continental protectionism embodied in the National Policy, there was some initial opposition.[12] The strongest challenge came from the Liberal Laurier government (1896–1911). By the early twentieth century, the international competitiveness of Western Canadian agricultural products created a constituency among farmers for liberalization of trade. As noted, the National Policy privileged industrialists with high tariffs. However, the result was that Canadian farmers had to pay higher prices for farm machinery and other durable goods that, but for the high tariffs, could have been had more cheaply south of the border. Moreover, reciprocal U.S. tariffs kept Canadian agricultural export levels to the United States modest. Instead of shipping their goods to lucrative and geographically proximate markets to the south, Western farmers were obliged to sell their wares in Central Canada, having to absorb high transport costs for their troubles. Acting as champion of the Western farmers, and seeking to expand his electoral coalition westward, Laurier hit upon the expedient of liberalizing agricultural trade with the United States. The result was a draft free trade deal, completed in January 1911 and subject to unofficial ratification in the general election later that year. The Laurier administration was careful to ensure that the free trade deal did not dismantle the industrial protectionism of the National Policy. The agreement seemed bound to satisfy farmers while not alienating industrialists.[13]

What seemed like a political tour de force, of course, ultimately proved disastrous. Later, social scientists would be able to explain that while voters tend to like the idea of free trade in theory, they typically respond negatively to specific agreements. If only Laurier had known! In reality, what he needed to know even more than the fickle nature of voters was the incentive structures of protectionists. Indeed, there exists an economic creature—known as the *rent-seeker*—that has wrecked the career of more than one politician.[14] Laurier was Canada's first victim.

Rent-seekers are protectionist producers, and they tend to get their way. One reason they get their way is that trade liberalization has a differential impact upon the people who produce goods than on the folk who consume them. Consumers benefit from free trade because competition among domestic and foreign producers typically generates cheaper goods that are of higher quality. The free market does a good job of regulating price and quality, a fact that explains why so few of us own durable goods produced in North Korea or Cuba. Producers who have enjoyed high levels of import protection (tariffs have traditionally been the most common form) lose from free trade for the same reason that consumers benefit: competition drives down prices and hence profits. Simply put, even though the aggregate benefit to consumers is larger than the total cost to producers, producers are far more intensely preferential on the issue. Most consumers will not man the metaphorical barricades in order to save $3 on a pair of pants, or to enjoy the comforts of pure duck cotton. Producers, however, who run the risk of losing their businesses, can be expected to react strongly if they feel their livelihood is threatened. Since governments are elected, they typically listen to whichever group—producers or consumers—demonstrates the strongest intensity of preference.[15]

A second reason why rent-seekers typically win is that it is far easier to sway public opinion in favor of protectionism than free trade. For example, there are obvious human-interest costs associated with free trade. Plants close, workers lose jobs, local economies are badly hurt. These sorts of stories are tailor-made for the evening news. Less gripping are stories about the economic advantages inherent in David Ricardo's theory of comparative advantage, prospects for larger economies of scale, and the altered incentive structures for direct and portfolio foreign investment. People can relate to others losing their jobs. Few have much knowledge or interest in theories that promise long-term aggregate economic gains.

Obviously there was no evening television news in Laurier's day. But rent-seekers were effective in exploiting other media. Hart[16] reprints an 1891 editorial cartoon entitled "A Mechanic's Home." In the top box, which bears the inscription "Under the National Policy," is a vigorous young man reading the newspaper in a comfortable chair in front of a warm fire. His family members busy themselves with homework, toys, and piano. The room is well lit and inviting. The lower box, by contrast, portrays life "Under a Free Trade or Revenue Tariff."[17] Here the young mechanic sits in Spartan surroundings. Gone are comfortable chairs, electric lighting, toys, and piano. Scattered bills demanding payment for coal, butcher, and rent have replaced his newspaper. His wife, head buried in despair, cannot muster the energy to comfort their wailing infant. Only the most heartless and callous reader, the cartoon implies, could wish to transform the life of this happy family and others like it by seeking to eliminate the National Policy tariffs.

We do not have the benefit of public opinion polls from 1911, so we cannot know for certain what motivated the Canadian electorate to turn the Laurier government out of office. For example, questions related to the Navy and Canadian autonomy within the British Empire received some attention. We can, however, make a pretty good guess about what mattered the most. We know that rent-seeking groups, led by the Canadian Manufacturers' Association (CMA), as well as financial, insurance, and transportation interests, sought to influence popular opinion through the Ontario manufacturing belt. We also know that free trade was the dominant issue in the election, in which the Conservatives secured a commanding victory. In Ontario, the Liberal Party seat total fell from 37 after the election of 1908, to 13; nationally, the Liberals went from 135 seats to 87, their lowest total in 24 years. The lesson that emerged appeared clear and lasting: free trade with the United States was a political nonstarter in Canada. It would remain that way until the mid-1980s.

Some movement on the continental free trading front did occur during the 1920s and 1930s. Prime Minister McKenzie King was a closet free trader. In the early 1920s, King advocated a "measure of reciprocity" between Canada and the United States, suggesting "it is well we should try again."[18] King's government ultimately did negotiate a free trade deal in secret with the United States immediately following World War II, but King decided not to publicize the accord, preferring to let it die rather than risk alienating the rent-seeking constituency that had doomed Laurier's political career.[19]

King did succeed in establishing more modest trade liberalization with the United States. Aided by the backdrop of the Great Depression and the imperative to undertake ameliorative economic reforms, the King government took modest steps toward greater continentalism. The administration of Franklin D. Roosevelt had established a new reciprocity regime under the auspices of the 1934 Reciprocal Trade Agreements Act (RTAA).[20] The most innovative part of the RTAA was that it extended the benefits of each bilateral reciprocal trade deal to each country that entered into a reciprocal trade deal with the United States. This system, whereby a concession to one was a concession to all, became the core operating principle of the GATT.[21] As a result, countries had a huge incentive to join the reciprocal trade plan. Canada's reciprocal trade deals (it entered into two) were fairly modest. They certainly did not constitute free trade in any meaningful sense, and tariffs against U.S. goods remained high by today's standards.[22]

While the reciprocity agreements with the United States might appear to be a reinvigoration of continentalism, the reality is that they set the stage for a new phase in Canada's foreign economic policy—multilateralism. Ironically, while facially dedicated to liberalizing trade, multilateralism actually served as a vehicle for continental protectionism after World War II. In those years, Canada sought to establish stronger trading relations with the rest of the world as a counterweight to its overwhelming and increasing reliance on the U.S. market. At the same time, logically enough, this policy mandated that Canada not engage in further continental trade liberalization, which would only serve to *reinforce* Canada's dependence on the United States.[23] Instead, Canada focused much of its post-war trade energy in the GATT.

Of course, it was not easy to resist the gravitational pull of the United States. By 1957, Prime Minister John Diefenbaker was so frustrated by Canada's reliance on the U.S. that he announced, absent any strategy toward achieving his objective, that Canada intended to divert 15 percent of its cross-border trade toward Great Britain.[24] The same basic objective, stated less baldly (albeit no more successfully), underscored the foreign policy of Prime Minister Pierre Trudeau. Articulated by Secretary of State for External Affairs Mitchell Sharp, and known as the Third Option, the Trudeau foreign policy explicitly rejected both the trade policy status quo and closer economic ties with the United States (the first two options) in favor of diversifying Canada's export markets and seeking to limit the effect of U.S. foreign investment in Canada.[25] It was an unqualified failure. In 1972, less than 70 percent of Canada's exports went to the United States. By the mid-1980s, at the end of the Third Option, the U.S. market absorbed 76.6 percent of Canada's exports.[26] At the same time, the Third Option managed to strain Canada–U.S. relations and alienate Western Canada.[27]

Although Canadian nationalists such as Diefenbaker, Lester Pearson, and Trudeau sought to use multilateralism as a counterweight to U.S. economic influence, I do not wish to leave the impression that Canadian governments of the 1960s and 1970s were rabid free traders in the multilateral arena. They were not. The principal multilateral forum was the GATT, and Canada's true colors showed clearly in the 1963–1967 Kennedy Round. The Kennedy Round featured conflicting objectives among the world's industrialized nations. Most sought to implement the so-called Swiss Formula of comprehensive, across-the-board tariff reductions, a radical departure from the procedure utilized in earlier GATT rounds, which had tended to constitute a series of commodity-specific bilateral accords. Canada lobbied against comprehensive reductions, insisting that because most of its exports were in low-tariff resources while the majority of its imports were in price-sensitive manufactured goods, the Kennedy Round tariff cuts would be unduly punitive and would provide few benefits.[28] Remarkably, given that the whole idea of the GATT was to reduce the sorts of high industrial tariffs that made Canada's industrial exports uncompetitive in the first place, Canada's trading partners bought this rather specious justification. Canada was spared significant tariff reductions in the Kennedy Round.

The same ploy would not work during the Tokyo Round (1973–1979), although that did not stop Canada from trying. The Canadian government was caught between a rock and a hard place during the Tokyo Round. On the one hand, Canada's commitment to multilateralism made it hard to reject mandates handed down by the GATT. On the other hand, industrial rent-seekers mobilized to pressure the government not to weaken.[29] Despite their demands, however, Canadian rent-seekers were not to be gratified. Canada's industrial tariffs were reduced significantly; reductions averaged 34 to 40 percent across industrial sectors, lowering the average import duty on manufactured goods from approximately 15 percent to roughly 9–10 percent over an eight-year period.[30] In addition, Canada accepted the six Tokyo Round codes regulating the use of so-called non-tariff barriers, means less visible than tariffs for protecting the domestic economy.[31]

On the centennial of the National Policy, the Tokyo Round effectively delivered the deathblow to industrial protectionism in Canada. Within three years of the close of the Tokyo Round, the Trudeau government had appointed the (Macdonald) Royal Commission on the Economic Union and Development Prospects for Canada,[32] which ultimately recommended that Canada undertake negotiations for a continental free trade agreement.[33] Just three weeks after the Commission reported, Prime Minister Brian Mulroney announced his government's intention to seek free trade talks with the United States.[34]

The Mulroney announcement was in some respects surprising. As late as 1983, Mulroney was on record suggesting, in colorful terms, that continental free trade was not for Canada. "Free trade with the United States is like sleeping with an elephant. It's terrific until the elephant twitches, and if the elephant rolls over, you're dead."[35] Equally surprising was who supported in Mulroney in his free trade decision. Many of the same rent-seekers who had mobilized in opposition to the Tokyo Round reductions were ardent supporters of the Canada-U.S. Free Trade Agreement.[36] Lined up against the agreement were the opposition parties (the New Democratic and Liberal), organized labor, and Canadian left nationalists.

As in 1911, this trade deal was subject to informal ratification through a general election. As in 1911, a majority of the population voted for candidates from parties that did not support free trade. However, unlike as in 1911, this time (due to the magic of the plurality electoral system) the sponsoring government was returned with a majority. By 1993, the Liberal government of Jean Chrétien, despite his party's ardent opposition to the 1988 accord, also embraced continental free trade in the form of NAFTA. In fact, in the past decade, the Liberal government has sought to expand the effects of NAFTA southward, through the proposed Free Trade Area of the Americas (FTAA), which envisions a hemispheric free trade zone that includes every country in the Americas save for communist Cuba.

In sum, Canada's trade policy has evolved, but the evolution was not gradual. In the late 1970s there was a protectionist consensus among the rent-seekers, the Progressive Conservatives, and the Liberals. In less than fifteen years, that consensus had been reversed; former rent-seekers and the two traditional major parties came wholeheartedly to support free trade. Earlier in this paper I posed two questions: what changed and why? Having answered the first, let us move on to the second and seek to understand why the three major players in the Canadian trade policy game changed their positions so radically.

WHY THE CONSERVATIVES? QUEBEC AND THE CONSTITUTION

Why did the Mulroney Conservatives get over their fear of death-by-elephant in a matter of two short years? The answer lies in politics, not ideology. Although the Mulroney Conservatives won the 1984 election in a landslide, the new Prime Minister was under no illusions as to the prospects for his party's fortunes. The election had been, pure and simple, a reaction against more than twenty-one years of (almost) uninterrupted Liberal rule. One term on the sidelines and the Liberals would be ready to assume, as they always did, the reins of power. There was no mystery surrounding the Tories' long history of electoral futility: The party was unable to make any permanent headway against the Liberal Party's total dominance in Québec. True, the PCs were very strong in Western Canada, but that strength only guaranteed the party also-ran status in most elections.

Mulroney was anxious to do more than keep the prime ministerial seat warm until the next Liberal dynasty could be established, and he was pretty sure that he knew of a way to realize his objective. The cozy relationship between the Liberal Party and Québec francophones had been severely strained a few years previously. In the dying days of the 1980 Québec Referendum campaign on sovereignty association, Trudeau went to Montreal and promised Québécois that if they voted against the Parti Québécois sovereigntist option, he would deliver meaningful constitutional change. He did. It just wasn't meaningful to the francophone Québécois who took Trudeau's promise to mean that he would advance their constitutional interests. Trudeau's constitutional initiative, which culminated in the Constitution Act (1982), was passed with the support of every province *except* Québec.

The perceived constitutional betrayal of Québec almost certainly accounts for the strength of Mulroney's 1984 landslide. Mulroney's thinking was that if the Liberals' cavalier treatment of Québec could generate this sort of electoral backlash, it stood to reason that the PCs could exploit Trudeau's misstep further by delivering on his original promise, and perhaps institutionalize political support in Québec. Such a plan might even begin to break down the prevailing electoral alignment that for so long had consigned the Tories to the Opposition benches. The result of all this thinking was, of course, the Meech Lake Constitutional Accord, signed by all ten provincial premiers and subject to ratification in Parliament and each of the provincial legislatures.

The only problem with this constitutional strategy was that pandering to Québec was not favorably received in the Conservatives' traditional stronghold of Western Canada. What grounds were there to believe that the Western premiers would agree to constitutional reform just to help the electoral fortunes of Brian Mulroney? There were none. Instead, Mulroney had to find a way to engage in what economists call selective side payments. In other words, he had to buy off potential opposition in Western Canada.

Recall the earlier discussion of the National Policy tariff structure. I suggested that the National Policy, while popular in the industrial center of the country, was not well received in the West. Things had not changed much by the 1980s. Westerners still preferred the idea of free trade with the United States to a protectionist system designed to subsidize Central Canadian industrialists at their expense. And so Mulroney devised what then seemed to be a brilliant political logroll.[37] Quebeckers would get their long-standing constitutional demands, Westerners would get their long-standing economic demands, and the Conservatives would finally realize their long-standing electoral objectives.[38] True, free trade was risky—look at what happened to Laurier in 1911. But by the 1980s, the rent-seekers were not the political menace they had been seventy years previously. In fact, most of the rent-seekers themselves were on board for free trade.

WHY THE RENT-SEEKERS? NO MORE LUMPY PROTECTIONISM

If Mulroney's change of heart on free trade was sudden, it was no more dramatic than that undertaken by Canada's industrial rent-seekers, represented most importantly by the Canadian Manufacturers' Association (CMA),[39] the Canadian Federation of Independent Business (CFIB),[40] and the Business Council on National Issues (BCNI).[41] The CMA had long been the standard-bearer for industrial rent-seeking in Canada; its forerunner helped to articulate the demands of Canadian business during the National Policy debates, and a subsidiary organization, the Ontario Manufacturers' Association, had been instrumental in defeating the free trade initiative of 1911. During the 1970s, the CMA fought against the Tokyo Round tariff cuts. In this effort it was ably supported by the CFIB. The BCNI, still in its early years, did not articulate a formal position, but its leadership appears to have been well satisfied with protectionism through the 1970s.[42]

But by 1981 it was clear that the major business confederations were *not* satisfied with the post–Tokyo Round status quo. The BCNI, soon joined by the other prominent confederations, began a quiet, although increasingly public, attempt to convince (in chronological order) the Liberal government, American business leaders, Macdonald commissioners, the new Conservative government of Brian Mulroney, Parliament, and ultimately the general public, that Canada's best interests lay in a continental free trade agreement.[43] Indeed, by 1987, it is informative to note how the trade policy preferences of many notable business organizations had changed dramatically since the 1970s. In addition to the CMA and CFIB,[44] prominent organizations that changed their trade policy preferences include the Canadian Chamber of Commerce,[45] Canadian Association of Toy Manufacturers,[46] Canadian Chemical Producers' Association,[47] Machinery and Equipment Manufacturers' Association of Canada,[48] Rubber Association of Canada,[49] and the steel industry.[50]

The apparently puzzling decisions by the rent-seekers to alter their century-long demand for import protection is best understood if we think of protectionism as what economists call a "lumpy good." Lumpy goods are those that acquire value only if there is sufficient quantity of the good. Where there is insufficient quantity, the good loses its value, or even generates negative utility—that is, it becomes a "bad." In other words, there is a quantitative threshold at which point a lumpy good generates positive utility. Below that threshold, the good is without value. Protectionism is a lumpy good, because it only generates positive utility if the level of protection is sufficiently high to restrain imports. If the level of protection is too low to restrain imports (that is, if the tariff rate will not dissuade foreign producers from importing into the domestic market), protectionism becomes a bad. Foreigners still import into your market, but since their governments are likely to retaliate with import protection of their own, you will have a harder time exporting into their markets. Quite simply, the Tokyo Round reductions were decisive in Canada because they lowered the threshold of import protection from the point at which protection was a lumpy good to a point where it became a lumpy bad. The Chairman of Dupont Canada, Ted Newell, explained it better:

> We, manufacturers, are caught in a catch-22 situation. On one hand, the tariffs in Canada are no longer high enough to offset the costs of producing solely for the Canadian market. On the other hand, even modest tariffs into the U.S. can make it difficult, if not impossible, to set up production in Canada to export into that market. . . . Unless we can negotiate increased and assured access to the U.S. market, Canadian industry will be unable to take the risks involved in making the substantial investments required to operate on a North American basis.[51]

In sum, Mulroney's political calculus to balance the constitutional interests of Quebec with Western preference for free trade was made possible by the Tokyo Round. Without the Tokyo Round reductions, the level of import protection would have remained above the lumpy good threshold. Mulroney would have faced the same opposition from rent-seeking forces that doomed Laurier so many elections before.[52]

WHY THE LIBERALS? NO ONE LEFT TO PROTECT

The trade policy shift within the Liberal Party was no less dramatic than the Conservative one. When the Chrétien government came to power in 1993, it was fresh off a campaign trail in which the new Prime Minister had threatened to tear up NAFTA.[53] His promises of stalling implementation were credible enough to worry Canada's partners significantly.[54] Such a position was not terribly surprising. As noted, the Liberal Party had long been a locus of left nationalism in Canada. Under the leadership of John

Turner, the Liberals openly and defiantly opposed the Canada-U.S. Free Trade Agreement of 1988. Chrétien, a long-time member of Trudeau's cabinet, was hardly ideologically predisposed toward free market economics. Yet, within three weeks of the 1993 election, the Chrétien government dramatically reversed its field, heading 180 degrees in the other direction and implementing the treaty.[55] Indeed, not only did the Chrétien government embrace NAFTA, but it subsequently negotiated bilateral free trade accords with Israel, Chile, and Costa Rica and has taken a leading role in the FTAA negotiations.

What accounts for the Liberals' volte-face on the issue of free trade? Political economists have long been aware of the point to which I alluded above: free trade increases a country's aggregate wealth, but skews the benefits in a politically suboptimal way. As noted, the biggest losers are the ones most able to create political unpleasantness. On the other hand, absent such political unpleasantness, politicians' incentive structures can change. Regardless of their ideologies, elected politicians have a dominant preference for strong economic performance.[56] A strong economy is permissive; it permits conservative governments to lower taxes or liberal ones to raise spending. During good economic times, voters tend to be happier and happy voters typically reward incumbent politicians with reelection.[57] As such, all things being equal, incumbent governments, even of the left, may prefer the efficiency of the marketplace over their ideological mandate to rely on the state as an instrument of resource allocation.[58]

Of course, not every incumbent government rallies to the free trade cause simply because there are economic rewards to reap. In fact, this chapter has been at pains to point out that for generations, Canadian governments have eschewed free trade in favor of protectionism. On the other hand, most Canadian governments have operated in an environment in which rent-seekers were the ultimate arbiters of appropriate foreign economic policy. When the rent-seeking community changed sides during the 1980s, they removed an enormous obstacle to liberalization of trade. Governments, both Conservative and Liberal, quickly determined that they could enjoy the benefits of increased economic performance without suffering the attendant political backlash that, even a few years previously, would have been inevitable. Indeed, one of the lessons of the Canadian experience, mirrored elsewhere, is that once rent-seekers are vanquished, free trade tends to become institutionalized. Even a change in government does not result in a reversion to the status quo ante.[59]

CONCLUSION

In this chapter, I have tried to do two things: articulate the history of the evolution of Canadian trade policy, and show why that is interesting. Pursuant to the second objective, I have demonstrated that the three major players in Canadian trade policy—the two traditional parties and the industrial rent-seekers—altered their long-standing trade policy preferences within a matter of less than fifteen years. This shift helps explain Canada's activity along a number of free trade dimensions. In addition to the FTAA, Canada is active in seeking to improve market access to Europe and Asia, as well as to liberalize trade under the auspices of the WTO. Of particular importance to Canada is the liberalization of investment rules and increased trade in services.[60]

What are some of the implications for Canadian foreign policy writ large? Ironically, while economic policy has long been a source of friction between the two large economies of North America, it may well be that for the early years of the twenty-first century, trade is what binds two long-standing allies whose worldviews increasingly appear to be in conflict. Canada has joined with many other industrialized powers in seeking to restrain what they see as the United States' exuberance to prosecute the war on terror. Canada appears to have shifted seamlessly from an insistence on multilateralism in the trade arena, to multilateralism with respect to international security, preferring a larger role for the United Nations and a lesser one for the United States. At least for the medium term, Canadians can safely assume that the political intrigue surrounding trade policy is at an end; security policy, however, is another story altogether.

Many other aspects of trade might be dealt with in a further overview of the Canadian Case. The Uruguay Round of the GATT and the role of Canada within the World Trade Organization (WTO) that has replaced the GATT, along with more specific issues such as the role of Québec in trade liberalization, are some of the most important issues that come to mind.

NOTES

1. The most famous of these was with the United States in 1988. In 1994, Mexico joined Canada and the United States in the North American Free Trade

Agreement (NAFTA). While NAFTA has a number of provisions that bind all three parties, many aspects of that agreement are dyadic. In other words, in part, NAFTA can be characterized as a series of bilateral agreements among three countries. Other hemispheric bilateral accords are with Chile (1997) and Costa Rica (2002).

2. Mercantilism entails an arrangement whereby the government grants a small number of firms exclusive rights to sell or produce a particular commodity in a given market. In exchange, the government receives a share of the monopoly profits.

3. See Harold A. Innis, *The Fur Trade in Canada* (New Haven, CT: Yale University Press, 1962); W. T. Easterbrook and Hugh G. J. Aitken, *Canadian Economic History* (Toronto: Macmillan, 1967); Michael Hart, *A Trading Nation: Canadian Trade Policy from Colonialism to Globalization* (Vancouver: University of British Columbia Press, 2002).

4. The Corn Laws were a series of acts designed to protect British agriculture from foreign competition. Although they existed for hundreds of years, the Industrial Revolution rendered them increasingly controversial in the second quarter of the nineteenth century. See Michael Lusztig, *The Limits of Protectionism: Building Coalitions for Free Trade* (Pittsburgh, PA: University of Pittsburgh Press, 2004), chapter 2.

5. Easterbrook and Aitken, *Canadian Economic History*, 352.

6. Today we call such free goods *entitlements*. We tend to think of entitlements in terms of welfare provision, but as we shall see, import protection is an even longer-standing entitlement.

7. Michael S. Cross, *Free Trade, Annexation and Reciprocity* (Toronto: Holt, Rhinehart & Winston, 1971), 6.

8. Edward Porritt, *Sixty Years of Protection in Canada, 1846–1907* (London: Macmillan, 1908), 55.

9. See F. E. Haynes, "The Reciprocity Treaty with Canada of 1854," *Publications of the American Economic Association* 7, no. 6 (November 1892): 7–70.

10. The American System of 1824 was a development strategy that erected high industrial tariffs. Although very controversial in the South, the American System provided a number of benefits. First, it fostered the growth of industrial enterprises in the Northeast. Second, industrial growth stimulated the need for greater resource extraction from the West; as such the American System provided an impetus for Western migration. Finally, increased tariffs helped fill the national coffers, an important consideration in the days before the income tax.

11. See Porritt, *Sixty Years of Protection in Canada*; V. C. Fowke, "The National Policy—Old and New," *Canadian Journal of Economics and Political Science* 18,

no. 3 (August 1952): 271–286; Easterbook and Aitken, *Canadian Economic History*; Glen Williams, *Not for Export*, 3rd ed. (Toronto: McClelland & Stewart, 1994); Hart, *A Trading Nation*.

12. Officially both parties remained open, at least in theory, to the prospect of limited reciprocity with the United States through the end of World War II. However, as detailed later, the political risks were enormous; as a result, industrial protectionism was rarely threatened.

13. See Oscar D. Skelton, *The Day of Sir Wilfrid Laurier* (Toronto: Glasgow, Brook, 1916); L. Ethan Ellis, *Reciprocity 1911: A Case Study in Canadian-American Relations* (New Haven, CT: Yale University Press, 1939); Robert Craig Brown and Ramsay Cook, *Canada, 1896–1921* (Toronto: McClelland & Stewart, 1974).

14. See Lusztig, *The Limits of Protectionism*.

15. See Gordon Tullock, "Welfare Costs of Tariffs, Monopolies and Theft," *Western Economic Journal* 5, no. 2 (June 1967): 224–32; Gary Becker, "A Theory of Competition among Pressure Groups for Political Influence," *Quarterly Journal of Economics* 98, no. 3 (August 1983): 371–400; Charles K. Rowley and Robert D. Tollison, "Rent-Seeking and Trade Protection," in *The Political Economy of Rent-Seeking*, ed. Charles K. Rowley, Robert D. Tollison, and Gordon Tullock (Boston: Kluwer Academic, 1988), 217–37.

16. Hart, *A Trading Nation*, 61.

17. A revenue tariff, in the days before the enthusiastic government taxing regimes of contemporary times, was a minimal tariff, erected not to protect domestic producers, but simply to provide operating revenue for the government.

18. O. J. McDiarmid, *Commercial Policy in the Canadian Economy* (Cambridge: Harvard University Press, 1946), 274.

19. Simon S. Reisman, "The Issue of Free Trade," in *U.S.–Canada Economic Relations: Next Steps?* ed. Edward R. Fried and Philip H. Tresize (Washington: The Brookings Institution, 1984), 39–40; Hart, *A Trading Nation*, 143.

20. The RTAA ultimately became the basis for the General Agreement on Tariffs and Trade (GATT), now known as the World Trade Organization (WTO). See Stephan Haggard, "The Institutional Foundations of Hegemony: Explaining the Reciprocal Trade Agreements Act of 1934," in *The State and American Foreign Economic Policy*, ed. G. John Ikenberry, David A. Lake, and Michael Mastanduno (Ithaca: Cornell University Press, 1988), 91–119.

21. Technically, this process is known as the unconditional most-favored-nation principle.

22. The first deal, signed in 1935, did not provide the United States with anywhere near as favorable access to the Canadian market as was enjoyed by countries of the British Commonwealth. A second, more generous agreement was signed in

1938. That deal came about largely as a by-product of U.S.–British negotiations that, given Canada's trade arrangements with Great Britain, obliged Canada to negotiate in order to protect its own interests. Hart, *A Trading Nation*, chapter 4; Frank Stone, *Canada, the GATT and the International Trade System*, 2d ed. (Montreal: The Institute for Research on Public Policy, 1992), chapter 2.

23. An important exception was the 1965 Auto Pact, which institutionalized free trade in automobiles and automotive parts. By the mid-1980s, the auto trade constituted one-third of all trade in manufactured goods between the two countries. Gilbert R. Winham, *Trading with Canada: The Canada–U.S. Free Trade Agreeement* (New York: Priority Press, 1988), 51.

24. John G. Diefenbaker, *One Canada: Memoirs of the Right Honorable John G. Diefenbaker, The Years of Achievement 1956 to 1962* (Toronto: Macmillan, 1976), 73–74.

25. Mitchell Sharp, "Canada–U.S. Relations: Options for the Future," *International Perspectives* 3 (Special Issue, Autumn 1972): 1–24. This policy is implicit in an External Affairs White Paper released two years previously. See Canada, Secretary of State for External Affairs, *Foreign Policy for Canadians* (Ottawa: Information Canada, 1970).

26. Canada, Royal Commission on the Economic Union and Development Prospects for Canada, *Report*, Vol. 1 (Ottawa: Minister of Supply and Services, 1985), 263.

27. Western alienation under the Third Option was most manifest in Trudeau's 1980 National Energy Programme (NEP). The NEP institutionalized a two-tiered pricing scheme for domestic and international consumers of Canadian oil and natural gas. The domestic pricing schedule was set unilaterally by the federal government, and served to subsidize consumers in the populous (and Liberal-supporting) markets of Central Canada. See Patrick James, "The Canadian National Energy Program and Its Aftermath," *Canadian Public Policy* 16, no. 2 (June 1990): 174–90.

28. Canada, Department of External Affairs, *A Review of Canadian Trade Policy* (Ottawa: Minister of Supply and Services, 1983), chapter 7; Colleen Hamilton and John Whalley, "The GATT and Canadian Interests: Summary of the Proceedings of a Research Symposium," in *Canada and the Multilateral Trading System*, ed. John Whalley (Toronto: University of Toronto Press, 1985), 9.

29. The extent of this pressure is clear from submissions to the interdepartmental Canadian Trade and Tariffs Committee and to the Senate Standing Committee on Foreign Affairs. See Canada, Standing Senate Committee on Foreign Affairs, *Canada–United States Relations: Canada's Trade Relations with the United States* (Ottawa: Minister of Supply and Services, 1978). For example, the following

industry associations sent written briefs to the Trade and Tariffs Committee expressing their concerns over the proposed Tokyo Round trade reforms (submission dates are in parentheses): Canadian Chemical Producers' Association (2/74); Canadian Paint Manufacturers' Association (5/74); Rubber Association of Canada (6/74); Machinery and Equipment Manufacturers' Association (6/74); Society of the Plastics Industry of Canada (6/74); Canadian Particle Board Association (7/74); Canadian Council of Furniture Manufacturers (8/74); Canadian Manufacturers' Association (8/74); Canadian Battery Manufacturers' Association (9/74); Tanners' Association of Canada (12/74); Canadian Printing Ink Manufacturers' Association (12/74); Canadian Truck Trailer Manufacturers' Association (12/74); Canadian Hardwood Bureau (1/75); Canadian Grocery Bag Manufacturers' Association (3/75); Canadian Cast Iron Soil Pipe Association (4/75); Society of the Button Industry (4/75); Boxboard Manufacturers' Association(4/75); Canadian Toy Manufacturers' Association (6/75); and Canadian Chamber of Commerce (7/78). While these briefs have not been published, they are accessible under the Freedom of Information Act.

30. Jock A. Finlayson and Stefano Bertasi, "Evolution of Canadian Postwar International Trade Policy," in *Canadian Foreign Policy and International Economic Regimes*, ed. A. Claire Cutler and Mark W. Zacher (Vancouver: University of British Columbia, 1992).

31. Canada, *Review of Canadian Trade Policy*, ch. 7.

32. Canada, *Report*, Vols. 1 and 2.

33. The Macdonald Report was extremely comprehensive. It was almost 2,000 pages in length and the commission generated 280 background studies in 72 book-length volumes.

34. See G. Bruce Doern and Brian W. Tomlin, *Faith and Fear: The Free Trade Story* (Toronto: Stoddard, 1991); Michael Hart, *Decision at Midnight: Inside the Canada-U.S. Free-Trade Negotiations* (Vancouver: University of British Columbia Press, 1994); and Gordon Ritchie, *Wrestling with the Elephant: The Inside Story of the Canada-US Trade Wars* (Toronto: Macfarlane Walter and Ross, 1997).

35. Quoted in Ritchie, *Wrestling with the Elephant*, 43.

36. Lusztig, *The Limits of Protectionism*, ch. 5.

37. Had it worked, there is every reason to believe that the Progressive Conservatives would have been the ongoing beneficiary of political loyalties that in Québec were transferred from the Liberals to the Bloc Québécois after the failure of the Meech Lake Accord in 1990.

38. For more on this implicit bargain, see Michael Lusztig, *Risking Free Trade: The Politics of Trade in Britain, Canada, Mexico and the United States* (Pittsburgh: University of Pittsburgh Press, 1996), chapter 4; and Michael Lusztig and Patrick

James, "Political Entrepreneurship and the Quest for Realignment: Constitutional Reform and the Free Trade Agreement in Canada," *International Journal of Canadian Studies* 14 (Fall 1996): 239–55.

39. Now called Canadian Manufacturers and Exporters (CME), the CMA and its forerunners have served as an advocacy group for Canadian business since 1871. Currently, the CME boasts membership that accounts for three-fourths of the country's manufacturing output and 90 percent of Canada's exports. Consisting of large, medium-sized, and small business, the CMA/CME has long served as an effective bellwether for the policy preferences of the nation's manufacturing sector. See William D. Coleman, *Business and Politics: A Study of Collective Action* (Montreal: McGill-Queen's University Press, 1988), 195–98; Canadian Manufacturers and Exports, "Canadian Manufacturers & Exporters Portal," http://www.cme-m-mec.ca/national/index-en.asp.

40. The CFIB was founded in 1970 as a means of giving small business owners in Canada some political influence. The organization has more than 100,000 members and has long been the largest (direct-member) business organization in the country. See Coleman, *Business and Politics*, 87–88; Canadian Federation of Independent Business, "CFIB Homepage," http://www.cfib.ca.

41. Now called the Canadian Council of Chief Executives, the BCNI was founded in 1976 with a mandate to permit "big business" to speak with one voice in articulating its public policy demands, to make those demands clear to government and public alike, and make sure that the business community is as informed as possible about the policy choices that affect it. It is composed of the chief executive officers of the 150 largest corporations in the country. See David Langille, "The Business Council on National Issues and the Canadian State," *Studies in Political Economy* 24 (1987): 41–85; Coleman, *Business and Politics*, especially 83–87; and Canadian Council of Chief Executives, "CCCE: Canadian Council of Chief Executives," http://www.ceocouncil.ca/en/.

42. Doern and Tomlin, *Faith and Fear*, 47.

43. See Duncan Cameron, "Introduction," in *The Free Trade Papers*, ed. Duncan Cameron (Toronto: James Lorimer, 1986), xi–xlix; Langille, "The Business Council"; and Peter C. Newman, *Titans: How the New Canadian Establishment Seized Power* (Toronto: Viking, 1998).

44. Compare the protectionist testimony of Laurent Thibault, President of the CMA during the 1980s, before the Senate Standing Committee on Foreign Affairs, November 18, 1976, to his pro-free-trade stance before the House of Commons Standing Committee on External Affairs and International Trade, November 18, 1987. Similarly, CFIB President John Bulloch's preferences changed between his testimony before the Senate Standing Committee on Foreign Affairs on May 26,

1977, and before the House of Commons Standing Committee on External Affairs and International Trade, November 3, 1987.

45. Submission to the Canadian Trade and Tariff Committee, July 20, 1978; and House Committee on External Affairs and International Trade, *Minutes of Proceedings*, November 4, 1987.

46. Submission to the Canadian Trade and Tariff Committee, June 1975; and correspondence with the author regarding the organization's position on CUFTA and NAFTA, April 6, 1994.

47. Submission to the Canadian Trade and Tariff Committee, February 14, 1974; and House Committee on External Affairs and International Trade, *Minutes of Proceedings*, November 5, 1987.

48. Submission to the Canadian Trade and Tariff Committee, June 26, 1974; and correspondence with the author regarding the organization's position on CUFTA and NAFTA, April 5, 1994.

49. Submission to the Canadian Trade and Tariff Committee, June 1974; and correspondence with the author regarding the organization's position on CUFTA and NAFTA, April 11, 1994.

50. Submission from the Canadian Steel Institute to the Canadian Trade and Tariff Committee, May 27, 1975; and testimony of the Canadian Steel Producers' Association, House Committee on External Affairs and International Trade, *Minutes of Proceedings*, November 3, 1987.

51. Speech to the Conference Board of Canada, Toronto, February 6, 1985. Quoted in Hart, *Decision at Midnight*, 77.

52. For more on this case, and on similar cases where rent-seekers changed their trade policy preferences, see Michael Lusztig, "The Limits of Rent-Seeking: Why Protectionists Become Free Traders," *Review of International Political Economy* 5, no. 1 (January 1998): 38–63; and Lusztig, *The Limits of Protectionism*.

53. Clyde H. Farnsworth, "Voting in Canada Can Affect NAFTA," *New York Times*, 23 October 1993, A(9).

54. James J. Blanchard, *Behind the Embassy Door: Canada, Clinton and Quebec* (Toronto: McClelland & Stewart , 1998)

55. Hart, *A Trading Nation*, 397.

56. Charles E. Lindblom, *Politics and Markets: The World's Political-Economic Systems* (New York: Basic Books, 1977).

57. Michael S. Lewis-Beck, "Comparative Economic Voting: Britain, France, Germany, Italy," *American Journal of Political Science* 30, no. 2 (May 1986): 315–46.

58. Eric Uslaner has argued that, in the United States, free trade is the policy of "winners." That is, the party of the president tends to be more favorable to free

trade than it is when the other party controls the executive branch. This helps to explain why Bill Clinton, for example, supported NAFTA in defiance of traditional Democratic opposition to free trade in import-competing goods with low-wage economies. See Eric M. Uslaner, "The Democratic Party and Free Trade: An Old Romance Restored," *NAFTA: Law and Business Review of the Americas* 6 (2000): 347–62.

59. See Michael Lusztig and Patrick James, "How Does Free Trade Become Institutionalized? An Expected Utility Model of the Chrétien Era" (Manuscript, 2003).

60. Canada, Department of Foreign Affairs and International Trade, *Opening Doors to the World: Canada's International Access Priorities—2004* (Ottawa: Minister of International Trade, 2004).

5

Foreign Policy by Other Means: Paradiplomacy and the Canadian Provinces

RICHARD VENGROFF AND JASON RICH

In federal states such as Canada, subnational governments can play a critical role in the foreign policy making process. While analysts tend to look to the central government in Ottawa, particularly Foreign Affairs Canada, as the prime decision-making unit, other organizations, governmental and non-governmental, the private sector, political parties, and even individual citizens are viewed as having increasing input into the process of foreign policy making. However, with full consideration given to these inputs, pressures, and demands, a single, consistent policy is perceived as the main output. The central government alone is perceived as undertaking autonomous action in the international arena. In the case of Canada, the provincial and even some municipal governments act on their own behalf, either in concert with or occasionally in conflict with Ottawa. As noted by Kim Nossal, "provinces play an important international role, operating well beyond Canada's borders."[1] As we shall see, Canada's federal structure, the lack of clarity in its constitutional arrangements, growing globalization, and diversity contribute to the emergence of the provinces as more active initiators and players in the foreign policy arena.

At annual meetings alternating between New England states and Eastern Canadian provinces, six U.S. governors and five Canadian premiers discuss issues ranging from free trade to acid rain, to transportation, to border security and tourism.[2] Beginning in November of 2001 the Pacific Northwest Economic Region (PNWER), an organization that includes the states of Alaska, Washington, Idaho, Montana, and Oregon and the Provinces of Alberta and British Columbia and the Yukon Territory, began to address regional international security issues, especially those related to infrastructure. These international contacts, discussions, and agreements occur without benefit of direct involvement by either the government of Canada or the government of the United States. Yet the states and provinces introduce new policies and regulations to conform to these agreements. Recently, France and the province of Québec launched a joint trade mission to Mexico and planned a further one to Poland. Although Québec has been a leader of the paradiplomacy movement, as of this writing all of Canada's ten provincial governments maintain either an international office or a separate international ministry to handle their external relations, here identified as "para-diplomatic" activity.[3]

Canada's provinces are not alone or even at the cutting edge in terms of paradiplomacy.[4] Belgium, following the adoption of a new federal constitution in 1995, allowed its regions of Flanders and Wallonia to sign treaties and other agreements with sovereign states and have an international role that equals and sometimes surpasses that of the Belgian State itself.[5] In Spain, Catalonia maintains a presence abroad, not only in Europe but much further afield.[6] The U.S. states have significant involvement in international economic issues and trade.[7] In other federal countries, like Australia and Germany, federal and Lander/State governments jointly participate in a variety of foreign policy decisions.[8] Even in some unitary states, particularly in Europe, the European Union (EU) recognition of subnational regions has created a new dynamic in foreign policy making. These are just a few examples of the growing international presence and action of subnational governments.

How has this situation come about? Are not international relations under the purview of central governments? Why is this type of activity becoming more prevalent and growing at a rate that far exceeds the growth of international activity by the traditional representatives of sovereign states?

A review of the growing literature on paradiplomacy suggests a number of key factors that have contributed to this trend: increasing globalization, international (including continental) trade agreements, the ongoing impact of federalism, nationalism, decentralization, existing (but often somewhat ambiguous) constitutional provisions, and the expansion of international activity into spheres heretofore reserved for subnational units are among the most commonly cited factors. Ivo Duchacek was among the first scholars to talk of various types of paradiplomacy. He labels these respectively: regional paradiplomacy (i.e., regionally confined interactions between peripheral, local, provincial, state, cantonal governments); transregional paradiplomacy (i.e., institutionalized contacts between non-central governments not neighbors but whose governments are); and global paradiplomacy (i.e., contacts with noncontiguous countries' governments).[9] Let us examine these in general and then see how they play out in the Canadian context.

First, however, it is important to define the key term for discussion, paradiplomacy. James Rosenau's perspective seems to underlie the thinking of many scholars on this issue. He argues that there is a "proliferation of relevant actors" on the world stage and an increasing "density of actors that sustain world politics."[10] "Glocalization," the simultaneous push of globalization, regionalization, and local concerns, is at the root of these changes. Paradiplomacy fits under what he calls "the other world of world politics." Hocking, making the case for the growing importance of non-central governments (NCGs), argues that NCGs have made "the boundaries demarcating state and non-state actors far more permeable than hitherto and creating ambiguities about the status and character of each."[11] Thus, he concludes that foreign affairs have been at least partially removed from the exclusive control of the central state and become the concern of many subnational governments as well, a change he regards as having positive implications. Aguirre suggests that the nation-state has become "polyvocal," that is, it speaks with more than one legitimate voice.[12] Telford makes the case that "considerable political activity is happening along the multiple frontiers between the local, provincial, federal, Aboriginal and international spheres of governance."[13] In identifying this process in Canada, Telford argues "contemporary political problems do not fit neatly into distinct jurisdictional boundaries, if they ever did, and the governments of Canada are increasingly enmeshed in a complex network of relationships."[14]

According to Stéphane Paquin, paradiplomacy comes into play when a subnational government gives its representatives a mandate to negotiate with other international actors.[15] He emphasizes the importance of ethnic and linguistic diversity. Identity paradiplomacy occurs when the main objective of these foreign policy actions is to reinforce the "construction" of the nation in the context of a multinational (ethnic) country. When the goal of the "para-diplomatic" activity becomes "independence" or the creation and recognition of a new state, he labels such activity as qualitatively different and employs the term "protodiplomacy."

Some substate actors have even developed more important networks and links than many state actors. There are hundreds of such actors in federal states alone. These units negotiate treaties and agreements with sovereign actors, participate in international forums and international organizations, and are even involved in that most sacred function of the central state, "human-security" issues. Their actions include sending economic, trade, and political missions abroad, participating in commercial fairs, regional organizations, and academic and student exchanges, promoting investments, tourism, and cultural exchanges, and even international development activities.

In sum, Robert Kaiser, drawing on the work of Hans Michelman and Panayotis Soldatos as well as Francisco Aldecoa and Michael Keating, says that paradiplomacy refers to external relations of subnational actors.[16] He goes on to say that such relations can either be coordinated with and complementary to activities of the central state or they are pursued in conflict or concurrence with traditional "macro-diplomacy." It is this broad perspective on paradiplomacy which will guide the analysis in this paper.

GLOBALIZATION, FEDERALISM, CULTURE, AND PARADIPLOMACY

Several common themes regarding the origins of paradiplomacy run throughout the literature. Most prominent among them are globalization and federalism-decentralization, the latter often complemented by the notion of subsidiarity (i.e., specialization) as practiced in the European Union—whereby the supranational organization and its member states carry out separate but complementary tasks, befitting their ability and capacity to do so. André Lecours argues that paradiplomacy gained prominence in the 1990s because of the interaction of both international (i.e., economic globalization and the construction of supranational institutions) and domestic factors (i.e., the surge in territorial politics and decentralization).[17] The core of this thinking is that paradiplomacy grew out of, or expanded directly with, increasing levels of globalization. As the world economy becomes increasingly global and increasingly integrated in a variety of ways, subnational units (regions, states, provinces, and even cities) find their functions and activities circumscribed by the global system.[18]

What were once conceived of as strictly regional or local functions, now have major international implications.[19] Treaties signed at the central government level increasingly impinge on local policy or local areas of shared or full competence. Health care, education, transportation, and taxation, for example, are all subject to trade and other agreements signed by the World Trade Organization, the European Union, and numerous other organizations. As well, global competition and dispute adjudication mechanisms are critical to regional economic development activities. Wages, environmental issues, labor conditions, and investment all are subject to external influences and in some cases control. The impact of the Chapter 11 dispute settlement procedures under the 1994 North American Free Trade Agreement (NAFTA) is one of many prominent examples.

Federalism also is a key contributor to the growth of paradiplomacy.[20] Subnational actors such as states and provinces, which have a formal legal personality, are necessarily more likely to engage in international activities designed to promote and protect local or regional interests and prerogatives.[21] In some cases, such as Mexico or Belgium, constitutional provisions pertaining to foreign affairs may clarify the matter. Mexican states are forbidden from engaging in foreign policy activity, whereas Belgian regions are allowed to do so. Both Flanders and Wallonia have signed numerous international agreements (including treaties), have many representatives abroad, and participate directly in foreign policy decision-making.[22] In Spain, Catalonia has undertaken an extensive set of international initiatives in the context of its asymmetric federal relations with the Spanish government.[23] German Landers, though less independent in this regard, still exercise considerable influence over policies directly affecting their local interests.[24] In other cases, constitutional arrangements may lack clarity and mechanisms for limiting or coordinating subnational diplomatic activity. The added legitimacy associated with elected subnational governments provides another opportunity for action. It is therefore in federal states that paradiplomatic activity finds its greatest support.

In Canada, as in Australia, lack of constitutional clarity makes paradiplomacy possible, though their respective national governments typically frown upon it and try to circumscribe it as best they can. Constitutional clarity on the division of other government functions, such as education and social policy, means that, while able to sign international treaties and agreements, the central government is dependent on the subnational governments for implementation of those very same agreements.[25] Such implementation, or lack thereof, can be quite contentious.

The Canadian case is one in which there are both a federal state and a lack of constitutional clarity regarding the distribution of authority over foreign policy. The role of the provinces is governed by provisions of the British North America (BNA) Act of 1867 and the Constitutional Act of 1982. Section 91 defines federal responsibilities, while Section 92 determines what falls under provincial jurisdiction.[26] According to Nossal, these provisions "specify the division of powers but fail to explicitly assign competence in foreign affairs to either the federal or provincial levels."[27] To promote and protect their own interests, Nossal suggests that the provinces, not being prohibited from getting involved internationally, naturally sought to do so.

Section 132 of the BNA Act states that "the Parliament of Canada shall have all Powers necessary or proper for performing the Obligation of Canada or of any Province thereof, as Part of the British Empire, towards Foreign Countries, arising under Treaties between the Empire and such Foreign Countries." Canadian courts have ruled, however, that the "federal government could not enact legislation in an area explicitly given to provinces under section 92, even if it was designed to fulfill obligations under an international treaty."[28] Furthermore, "Parliament cannot amend provincial legislation or pass a new statute in an area of provincial legislative jurisdiction. Thus a treaty or a specific section thereof whose subject matter falls within the legislative competence of the provinces cannot be implemented unless the provincial legislatures intervene with respect to the matters within their jurisdiction."[29] Based on this principle, in May 2002, Québec's National Assembly went one step further and gave itself power of ratification over international treaties "of importance" to Québec's jurisdiction. It was the first legislative body from the Westminster/Whitehall tradition to acquire such powers—usually an executive body keeps this role for itself.

Consequently, one may conclude that a division exists in many key areas between the federal power to negotiate a treaty and the provincial power to implement the treaty.[30] According to James McIlroy, "The connection between the Canadian provinces and international trade treaties, like NAFTA, has been greatly influenced by the evolving relationship between the global trade agenda and the constitutional division of powers under Canada's federal form of government."[31] For example, "in Canada the power to impose customs tariffs lay solely with the federal government, and the provincial governments had no direct authority over the implementation of Canadian tariff policy."[32] The focus of trade moved away, however, from tariffs imposed on agricultural and manufactured goods, as most economic activity in the latter part of the twentieth century shifted into the service sectors. Thus, most trade treaties now go well beyond tariffs; they focus on items such as intellectual property, trade in services, and investment. Many of these recent international trade agenda items fall squarely within provincial jurisdiction in Canada.[33] This raises the issue of the power to negotiate versus the power to implement. Canada's constitution is silent on Ottawa's power to implement treaties. NAFTA provides an excellent example of the complexity of this division of power.

When the Canadian government negotiated NAFTA, not one provincial government signed the agreement. What connects the provinces to NAFTA is the "federal-state clause." In this regard, McIlroy underlines the importance of the "list it or lose it" process of exempting certain nonconforming measures. Its intention was to create transparency on whether a province was properly implementing NAFTA and, if not, what the shortcomings are. The problem lies in the fact that the federal Parliament is left at the mercy and will of each individual province, but noncompliance would leave Canada liable. In fact, it only takes one recalcitrant province to create problems. A lack of enforceability and implementation power weakens Canada's ability to effectively negotiate treaties, and even if provincial consultation is held beforehand, Canada's "negotiating ability will be hampered if it is unable to respond quickly to the cut and thrust of negotiations."[34] It may take constitutional reform to change this, but that is probably not a viable option. The country may therefore be in a bind, as "the bottom line is that Canada's nineteenth-century division of federal and provincial powers may soon collide with the emerging global economy and the international trade agenda of the twenty-first century."[35]

The federal-state clause is introduced in most international treaties negotiated when nations do not have complete authority to implement their provisions. In the case of NAFTA and Canada, the clause is a way "of informing all the parties to the treaty, that the Canadian government may encounter difficulties in implementation because it must first secure the cooperation of the Canadian provinces."[36] By introducing the clause it reduces liability for the federal government if it does not implement the proper legislation needed within the province to comply with the international treaty. What is of interest is the way in which the federal clause is phrased. Typically it is worded in a manner that obligates Canada to "make its best effort to carry out the treaty," and to avoid any liability, all the Canadian government must do is show that it was impossible to get the cooperation of just one province.

What is unusual with the NAFTA treaty is the phrasing of this clause. The federal clause in Article 24, Section 12 of the General Agreement on Tariffs and Trade treaty states that: "Each contracting party shall take such *reasonable measures* as may be available to it to ensure observance of the provision of this Agreement by the regional and local governments and authority within its territory."[37] In contrast, Article 105 of NAFTA reads: "The Parties shall ensure that *all necessary measures* are taken in order to give effect to the provision of this Agreement, including their observance, except as otherwise provided in this Agreement by state and provincial governments."[38] This language implies that "unless the Canadian government could implement each and every provision in NAFTA, it would be in default and could be subject to an application for dispute settlement."[39]

A further challenge to the federal government of Canada comes in the form of the Gérin-Lajoie doctrine. This doctrine, first put forth in 1965, asserts that Québec has the right to get involved internationally whenever issues fall under its jurisdiction.[40] To the above-mentioned issues associated with paradiplomacy must be added the question of culture, especially issues of identity and language. To the extent that these issues impose themselves we can expect greater levels of paradiplomatic activity. This was further reinforced by Canadian Prime Minister Paul Martin who, in outlining his vision of federal-provincial relations, referred to an increased role for the provinces in international relations.[41]

WHY PARADIPLOMACY IN CANADIAN PROVINCES?

Before proceeding to an examination of the individual provinces and their activities, we identify key measures of the level of paradiplomatic activity in which the provinces are engaged. These will include economic, political, cultural, environmental, and organizational/governmental measures, both of the cross-border, close proximity variety and those more extensive international relations with noncontiguous national and subnational units of other countries. We complement these measures with other data on the level of globalization in a province, such as the level of Internet use and the percentage of the provincial population that is foreign-born. We will then use these to compare the level of activity of the ten provinces and see to what extent the variation in levels of paradiplomatic activity is attributable to the various independent factors identified above.

In the economic area, we have, in addition to measures of the importance of international trade at the provincial level, included the number of trade missions initiated by the province or in which they participated, efforts to promote foreign investment, involvement in foreign technical assistance projects, and the representation of specific economic interests abroad. We also must consider relative degrees of collaboration with and autonomy from the federal government in this regard by the provinces.

In order to get at global competitiveness we have added Richard Florida's measures of the position of Canadian urban regions (large metropolitan areas) in relation to all North American city regions on measures of ethnic diversity, creative class/talent, and technology concentration and strength measured by employment in high-tech industries, and the relative emphasis on those industries in the metropolitan region. For each province we have included the ratings of the largest city or cities as indicators of the overall strength of the province as a pole for global technology and innovation and investment.

The political variables include the number of "diplomatic" or "paradiplomatic" missions a provincial government (via ministries) maintains abroad, the number and geographic dispersion of countries to which those missions are regularly sent, memberships in international organizations composed of either sub-state or national actors, and the number and variety of international agreements to which the provincial government is formally a party. In addition, we look at whether they negotiate and ratify "quasi treaties." Also included here are the more symbolic stands that a provincial government takes on human rights, international development, and international conflicts (such as the Bosnian peace mission, Afghanistan, and the Iraq war) and regional security (such as joint missile defense with the United States).

At the organizational level, we examine the commitment of resources and personnel and the administrative homes of the units charged with "international" activity in the bureaucratic hierarchy. What are the units established by provincial-level governments to manage international, including paradiplomatic, activity? Do these have a separate ministry status, or are they offices within other ministries such as intergovernmental organizations or commerce? We also look at the size of the budgets of these organizations, the number of full-time government employees assigned to them, their growth over time, and their representation abroad.

THE IMPACT OF GLOBALIZATION

The Canadian provinces are heavily dependent on international trade for a considerable portion of their gross domestic product (GDP).

On average, exports generate better than a third of GDP for each province. On the "high end," half of Ontario's GDP stems from exports (mostly to the United States); at the "low end," the figure for Nova Scotia is still 25 percent (see table 5.1). Hence, all ten provinces have heavy com-

Table 5.1. The Importance of International Trade for the Provinces

Province	International Exports/GDP % 1992	2000	2002	Annual Growth Rate 1992–2000	Annual Growth Rate 2000–02	Int'l Exports 2002, $ Million CDN
N.L.	19	41	40	15.8	7.7	$ 6,630
P.E.I.	14	29	28	14.8	3.4	$ 1,056
N.S.	17	26	25	9.8	1.8	$ 6,654
N.B.	26	39	43	10.4	7.2	$ 9,072
Que.	21	40	35	13.6	−2.7	$ 85,739
Ont.	31	51	46	12.4	−0.8	$219,022
Man.	19	29	28	9.5	3.4	$ 10,443
Sask.	28	42	37	11.2	−4.3	$ 12,819
Alta.	27	41	35	14.7	−5.4	$ 53,231
B.C.	24	33	27	9.7	−7.7	$ 37,199
CANADA TOTAL						$441,865
CANADA AVG.	22.18	37.1	34.4	12.19	2.6	$ 44,187

Source: Craig Byrd and Pierre Généreux, Statistics Canada (2003), "The Performance of Interprovincial and International Exports by Province and Territory since 1992."

mitments of their economies to international trade and are thus motivated to engage in paradiplomatic activity to represent, expand, and protect their interests. When we add to this the level of Internet access and use, these figures place Canada's provinces among the most wired areas of the world with an average of nearly 60 percent of their residents as Internet users. The presence of the foreign born among the citizenry rises to above a quarter of the population in Ontario and British Columbia and surpasses 10 percent in three other provinces: Alberta, Manitoba, and Québec. Furthermore, Canada maintains a proactive immigration policy. Québec has direct involvement in the recruitment and selection of Francophone immigrants destined for its shores. These and other indicators of international involvement help demonstrate that all ten of the provinces are highly affected by and responsive to globalization trends.

Global competitiveness is a critical component of the motivation for a provincial role in paradiplomacy. Canada is an overwhelmingly urban country with each province having one or more major municipalities. Hence we employ the index of competitiveness for the "creative class" as a measure of the international involvement or existence of "global cities" as economic motors for Canadian provinces. In *The Rise of the Creative Class*, Richard Florida equates the economic development and future status of "city regions" in the context of globalization with the ability of these cities to attract and retain what he calls the "creative class."[42] This work, which examined U.S. "city regions," was extended to include the twenty-five largest Canadian city regions.[43] Furthermore, this measure enables us to compare Canada's cities on these measures with more than three hundred U.S. cities.

The key factor that helps to attract creative individuals and related technologically advanced industries is measured by the so-called Bohemian Index (a measure of the presence of diverse cultural opportunities in the "creative and artistic occupations"). The Bohemian Index is strongly correlated with the attraction to and growth of the "creative class" and "high tech" globally competitive industries. The correlation for Canadian "city regions" is very strong ($R^2 = 0.74$)[44] and indicative of its overall importance.

We have taken the biggest cities in each province and looked at how they rank on the key measures compared to all North American cities in their population size categories. In all ten provinces we find cities which on the Bohemian Index are highly competitive among all North American cities. Among the 49 largest cities in the United States and Canada (with populations exceeding 1 million), three Canadian city-regions—Vancouver (3rd), Toronto (4th), and Montreal (10th)—rank among the top ten. Among the 39 cities with populations 500,000–1 million, Calgary and Edmonton rate 4th and 9th. Halifax is 7th among the 68 cities in its size category (two hundred to five hundred thousand), whereas Saskatoon, Regina, and St. John's all rank in the top quarter among the smaller cities. With globally competitive cities in every Canadian province except for Prince Edward Island, one expects those cities to prod provincial governments into utilizing paradiplomatic activity to promote provincial economic development. This is in addition to the strong demands made by agricultural, fishing, forestry, and extractive industries within the ten provinces.

ORGANIZATIONAL COMMITMENT

The degree to which a province has committed itself to involvement in paradiplomatic activity is indicated by the organizational structure and the level of resources allocated to international activities. Among the ten provinces, all have international offices of some type. Usually these are departments or offices housed in Ministries of Intergovernmental Relations. The lion's share of the activities and personnel in these bureaucracies is normally allocated to relations with other provinces and the Federal Government. However, the resources dedicated to international activities are substantial and growing in most provinces. In the case of a few of the smaller provinces, like PEI and Newfoundland and Labrador, intergovernmental relations is itself an office or department rather than a ministry and has a handful of staffers assigned to international efforts. Only in Québec is there a separate fairly large ministry (more than 700 staff) dedicated primarily to international relations. In several provinces, the international functions are divided between ministries of intergovernmental affairs and ministries concerned primarily with the economy and international trade. Until recently, even the largest province in terms of population and the volume of international trade, Ontario, housed its international office within the Ministry of Economic Development and Trade.

There is considerable variation in the paradiplomatic involvement of the provinces, although they are in general highly implicated in international activity. There is no question that the most active provinces have been Alberta, Ontario, and Québec, with New Brunswick as a more recent entrant into this top category. Some provinces have clearly attempted to assert themselves more fully in the international arena than others, but the important point is that in response to globalization all ten are in some manner or other heavily implicated and generally on a trajectory to increasing their level of involvement. The most active provinces (i.e., Alberta, Ontario, Québec, and New Brunswick) have a full complement of paradiplomacy-related activities, including international trade and investment missions, memberships in cross-border associations of subnational (state-provincial) governments, and bilateral treaty-like agreements with national or subnational governments, and have their own representation abroad. These four provinces have also developed considerable bureaucratic expertise and invested in organizations (ministries, departments, or offices) to manage their international activities.

In the second category are those provinces that have broad but more limited paradiplomatic activity. These include British Columbia, Nova Scotia, Manitoba, and Saskatchewan. These provinces place heavy emphasis on economic issues associated with the production and export of agricultural, forestry, and fish products. They are also involved in cross-border associations of U.S. states and Canadian provinces, and also have signed bilateral agreements, primarily with neighboring U.S. states. They each have developed linkages with other nations, provinces, states, and cities in other world regions.

Even in the third category of provinces with moderate paradiplomatic activity—including two of the smallest provinces in terms of population (PEI and Newfoundland and Labrador)—there are still some important aspects of paradiplomacy. These take the form of regional cross-border associations like the New England Governors–Eastern Canadian Premiers. The development of the offshore petroleum industry in Newfoundland and Labrador is making it an important player in high value international trade. It is likely to increase the level of paradiplomatic activity of that province as well.

The Ontario Government has undertaken 56 international missions to some 20 countries, including Germany, Italy, South Africa, and South Korea, in order to better position itself in the global market. In addition, Ontario negotiated three Memoranda of Understanding with Ottawa so that it could have its Senior Economic Officers posted at the Canadian missions in Shanghai, New York, and Munich, all of which opened in 2002. Diplomatically, in 2001–2002, Ontario interacted on 139 occasions with foreign leaders and representatives. Recently, the province participated in separate summits with New York State and Michigan, signing memoranda to strengthen bilateral cooperation for tourism, transportation, energy, and technology. Early in 2004, the Ministry of Economic Development and Trade, which housed the Office of International Relations and Protocol (OIRP), underwent reorganization. The new OIRP, which will now be housed in the Ministry of Intergovernmental Affairs, is to focus on foreign relations and has a separate department dedicated solely to relations with the United States. The Office's status is indicated by the fact that it reports directly to Ontario's deputy premier.

Alberta has a Ministry of International and Intergovernmental Relations, the primary functions of which are domestic but with significant personnel and resources devoted to international relations. The province's primary focus is on good relations with the United States, as this is the destination for 80 percent of its exports. Alberta has in recent decades been heavily involved with Canada's international relations and has been persistent in its attempts to influence Ottawa's negotiating position on matters relating to energy policy, climate change, and agriculture trade liberalization. Even with this relatively positive relationship with the federal government, Alberta still seeks to establish its own identity and to forcefully represent its own interests on the international front. Premier Ralph Klein has gone so far as to meet with U.S. Vice President Dick Cheney as well as with several senators and representatives to discuss the cattle trade freeze resulting from the 2003 case of mad cow disease.[45]

The provincial government has negotiated formal international links through twinning relationships with eleven subnational governments. Not only do these relationships focus on economic issues, but Alberta has also (as part of Canada's foreign aid program) been exporting its governance expertise, advice, and training to a number of foreign governments, including China, South Africa, and Russia. In regard to their relations to the United States, Alberta holds a number of signed agreements with U.S. states as well as maintaining membership in trans-boundary organizations such as the Pacific Northwest Economic Region, the Rocky Mountain Trade Corridor, and the Western Interstate Energy Board. Like Québec,

Alberta is a strong advocate for a greater role for the provinces in Canadian foreign policy, treaty negotiations, and decisions regarding treaty approval and implementation.

By far, Québec has been the most active province when it comes to paradiplomatic activity. It has a fully staffed ministry solely dedicated to international relations. Since 1964, Québec has signed more than 550 international agreements, of which more than 300 are still in effect, with 79 different countries.[46] In addition, the province has a considerable presence overseas, with a network of 28 separate offices abroad in 17 countries—including the United States—in Latin America, Europe, and Asia. Québec has signed nine agreements within China, including three directly with the central government of China itself regarding education, science, and technology. Similar agreements have been negotiated out of the Québec Government Bureau in Munich, which has facilitated 35 bilateral cooperation projects.

The people and government of Québec were among the strongest supporters of and advocates for the creation of the 1988 Free Trade Agreement with the United States, NAFTA, and for free trade in general. Québec has since developed surprisingly strong ties with Mexico, which is its second leading hemispheric trade partner after the United States. Since the formation of a task force in 1982, the Québec and Mexican governments have signed ten cooperation agreements on issues such as forestry, the environment, education, vocational training, and culture.

Outside of trade and development, Québec has been an active participant in educational exchanges and culture and language promotion. Québec has been particularly astute about maintaining its French cultural heritage in the face of its openness to economic globalization. The province is a member of the Organisation Internationale de la Francophonie (see the Donaghy and Carter's chapter 6 in this volume), an organization in which it plays a role similar to that of a sovereign state.

One important but largely symbolic feature of Québec's interest in foreign relations has been its increasing push for the adoption of internationally negotiated treaties. For example, Québec has striven to incorporate the Kyoto Protocol into its international and domestic policies, coordinating those efforts with Ottawa. Also, provincial policy-makers have worked for the approval of two United Nations human rights treaties regarding children: the Optional Protocol to the Convention on the Rights of the

Child on the Sale of Children, Child Prostitution and Child Pornography and the Convention on Protection of Children and Cooperation in Respect of Inter-country Adoption.

When in power, the pro-independence Parti Québécois (PQ) has often "crossed the line" from paradiplomacy to proto-diplomacy. The latter is part of an effort to achieve international recognition, which, in turn, could provide support for the PQ's nationalist agenda. Unlike the PQ, the federalist Liberal Party of Québec has been more likely to collaborate with Ottawa when implementing Canadian foreign policy, although it, too, partakes in its fair share of paradiplomacy. According to Louis Balthazar, "the development of transnational relations and of regional transborder transactions coupled with an awareness of globalization and interdependence seems to be the main reason why Québec has created and cultivated so many relations with foreign political entities."[47] Regardless of which party governs Québec, the provincial government's overwhelming thrust of international activity is aimed at cultural identity and economic interests rather than political independence. As well, both parties assert Québec's right to participate in negotiations and approval of any treaties that impinge on areas of provincial jurisdiction. This explains why both parties unanimously adopted the bill giving the Québec National Assembly powers of ratification on important treaties and why the current Liberal government of Jean Charest does not hesitate to use such a tool crafted by its PQ predecessor.

New Brunswick might be relatively small in terms of population, but in recent years its government has become increasingly aware of and committed to an active international presence as a core part of its economic development strategy. It has aggressively sought out and quite successfully competed for outsourced service centers from U.S. and global firms. One indicator of this increased global role has been the development of the province's first global strategy White Paper, *Prospering in a Global Community*, issued in 2003. In this policy statement, the province lists fifty action items, including a China Action Plan, designed to expand New Brunswick's access to the Asian market as well as increase incoming investment from the region. New Brunswick has hosted a number of foreign trade missions and is an active participant in "Team Canada Atlantic."[48] It also maintains an active provincial presence in a number of regional organizations including the New England Governors–Eastern

Canadian Premiers Association and Council of State Governments (Eastern Region).

New Brunswick is dedicated to expanding its relationship with the United States and, as a result, actively maintains a dialogue with both the U.S. government and the northern states on areas such as trade, environment, energy, and transportation. In particular, New Brunswick has had a productive relationship with Maine, signing a number of Memoranda of Understanding on issues from the border corridor to the promotion of computers in the classroom, to the more politically sensitive subjects such as pharmaceuticals and fisheries.

As Canada's only officially bilingual province, New Brunswick has taken a leading role internationally in cultural promotion, specifically Acadian culture and the French language, through its participation in and organization of international festivals and La Francophonie. Of note, the province has negotiated bilateral agreements promoting language with the Department of Vienne in France and the U.S. State of Louisiana. As well, Moncton, New Brunswick, hosted the 1999 Francophonie Summit. Both New Brunswick and Québec attended the latest summit, held in Beirut in 2002, which brought together 55 states, representing more than 625 million people who use French as a common language. In addition to these events, New Brunswick has also hosted a number of bilateral meetings with other French-speaking nations, including Bali and Burkina Faso.

For its part, British Columbia (B.C.), because of its location, resources, large immigrant population (26.1 percent of the population), and growth, is likely to move into the upper category of paradiplomatic activity in the near future. B.C., long involved with and heavily dependent on international trade, is beginning to emerge as an important paradiplomatic player. Conflict with U.S. interests on softwood lumber and salmon fishing rights has been among the most dominant international concerns, although environmental issues also play an important role. B.C.'s Intergovernmental Relations Secretariat currently has as one of its subdivisions a small but active International Relations section. This section maintains the cooperative and economic arrangements with other subnational entities, such as the Eastern Cape in South Africa. The province also maintains membership or a relationship with a number of regional organizations such as the Pacific Northwest Economic Region, the Council of State Governments, and the Western Governors Association. The government has sponsored trade missions to Hong Kong, China, and Japan, and in 2003 hosted eight trade missions from other countries. One unique, but somewhat controversial, event clearly displaying broader provincial interests in international affairs took place in April 2004 when Premier Gordon Campbell greeted Nobel Peace Prize laureates Archbishop Desmond Tutu and His Holiness the Dalai Lama in B.C. for three days of discussions on "spirituality and international peace."

Unlike British Columbia, Nova Scotia is just beginning to become more open and active within the international community. The province even notes this fact in a 2002 trade report pointing out that on a trade openness scale measuring total trade divided by GDP, the province is considerably less open than Canada as a whole.[49] Nova Scotia has begun to rectify this by conducting more trade missions, including to both New York and Paris, as well as taking a more active role inside the New England Governors–Eastern Canadian Premiers conferences (e.g., cochairing a committee to assess trade and transportation challenges among its members). Of particular importance to the province has been the reduction of U.S. softwood tariffs and issues relating to the once rich fishing grounds and fisheries in the area, issues that Nova Scotians have also promoted in Ottawa.

As a highly productive agricultural region, Saskatchewan is heavily involved in international trade, with exports accounting for 37 percent of gross domestic product in 2002. The Provincial Government has organized and conducted trade missions to many different countries, including Japan, Korea, Brazil, Argentina, and Panama, and has been involved in many others as part of the Team Canada trade missions. As a result, the province has signed a number of memoranda for trade promotion and technology development. Due to its success, Saskatchewan has developed its own separate organization, the Saskatchewan Trade and Export Partnership, to promote provincial exports.[50] Consistent with its concern for trade, the province has been extremely active and influential in the Canada–U.S. softwood lumber dispute. At the annual Premiers' Conferences, Saskatchewan's representatives have pushed Ottawa to aggressively pursue the elimination of international trade-distorting subsidies in agriculture. They have also pushed a similar agenda at the Western Premiers' Conference and Western Governors' Association meetings.

Likewise, Saskatchewan is very assertive in the negotiation of foreign cooperative agreements. The province has negotiated the Intergovernmental Accord on cross-border relations with Montana, which applies to areas such as energy, the environment, water management, agriculture, transportation, and global economic development. In addition, the province recently implemented a cooperative initiative with Jilin, China (for an educational exchange and fishery development and diversification), and conducted missions to Russia (pertaining to synchrotron research cooperation). Saskatchewan has also been active in cultural areas, particularly where these are related to Ukrainian and other immigrant ethnic communities important to many provincial residents with ancestral ties to them. As such, it is probably only a matter of time before this cultural promotion takes on more of an international focus.

Saskatchewan's neighbor to the east, Manitoba, recognized the tremendous importance of its external relations and, as a result, reorganized in 2004 its existing offices to better respond to the demands of globalization. The province's Department of Intergovernmental Affairs and Trade now has a budget of over $110 million CDN and employs thirty-three full-time staff assigned to international trade. In addition, Manitoba has foreign trade representatives in China, Mexico, Germany, and Chile. The Provincial Government recently participated in nine trade missions and meetings with individual governors of neighboring U.S. states and with associations of governors and premiers. Manitoba currently has 68 international agreements with 18 different countries, most involving economic development and trade issues. Of note, some of the province's international efforts pertain to Manitoba's French-speaking community. With over 10 percent of its population foreign-born, moreover, it is likely that the number of international agreements will increase in the coming years.

Like the other Canadian provinces, Prince Edward Island and Newfoundland and Labrador, the two provinces exhibiting the lowest level of paradiplomatic activity, are increasingly motivated to immerse themselves in the international arena. Despite not having a fully dedicated department of international relations, PEI has been increasingly committed to augmenting its international presence. The province actively participates in New England Governors–Eastern Canadian Premiers conferences to promote and advance PEI's regional interests. As well, the Provincial Government has created "Trade Team PEI" to actively promote economic development. Trade Team PEI has conducted trade missions to countries such as Chile, Ireland, and Japan.

Newfoundland and Labrador also fits into this early stage development of a paradiplomatic presence. As a matter of fact, in response to a submission made by Canadian scholar Denis Stairs to the Royal Commission on the future of the province, in which he recommended that some attention be given to international relations, the government answered with a blunt dismissal of such endeavors.[51] The government allocates only a handful of officials to international activity, and it seems that this will be the case for still some time. Despite this official attitude, the province has been active in economic development, having participated in more than twenty trade missions since 1999 and signed a number of memoranda of understanding with countries such as China, Ireland, and Thailand. Although the province has engaged in prominent fishing disputes with EU member states, it shows promise of far greater involvement in the energy sector (i.e., hydroelectric power and newly emerging offshore oil production).

CONCLUSION

The constitutional framework under which the Canadian federation functions provides an important if somewhat ambiguous role for the ten provinces. Although the federal government maintains the right to negotiate treaties and trade relations, its ability to implement those agreements is somewhat circumscribed. The provinces legally and politically maintain the right and power to implement treaties and other international agreements in those areas of policy competence constitutionally assigned to them. As agreements such as NAFTA increasingly affect areas of provincial concern such as education, health care, social policy, labor regulation, and taxes, provincial involvement in foreign policy has grown. As a result, the provinces have increased their efforts to ensure that their international interests are represented in Ottawa as well as through their own expanding paradiplomacy.

In addition to the negotiation of new trade agreements, issues as diverse as softwood lumber, the SARS epidemic, the outbreak of mad cow disease, and security issues in the wake of the 9/11 terrorist attacks have placed ever greater demands on the provinces for international action. It is therefore not surprising to find the premier of Alberta meeting with the U.S. vice president and senators regarding the cattle industry or for the premiers of Canada's provinces to meet regularly with their U.S. state governor counterparts either bilaterally or in regional associations. International trade missions, either as part of Team Canada or involving a single province, have become standard operating procedure. Specialized provincial public agencies devoted to international trade and relations regularly advise their respective premiers and legislatures on international issues. Several provinces have gone as far as establishing permanent delegations abroad, either on their own or within Canadian embassies and consulates. As a result, hundreds of treaty-like agreements have been signed and the numbers are increasing rapidly while the scope, geographic coverage, and diversity of issues covered are undergoing rapid and profound changes.

The Council of the Federation, an organization that brings together ministerial-level personnel from all of the provinces, is making demands for an expanded role for the provinces in Canadian foreign policy making. Greater involvement by the provinces in a variety of forms of collaboration with the federal government is clearly in the offing. The impact of globalization has placed Canada's provinces in a position that makes their international interests extremely important for both economic development and global competitiveness, thereby necessitating their own paradiplomatic activity. Even Québec, although somewhat unique among the provinces because it has at varying periods looked beyond para- to protodiplomacy as a mechanism for promoting a sovereigntist agenda, has consistently emphasized its economic and trade relations over all other issues.

In the broader global context, especially in federal states, subnational governments are playing an increasing role in national foreign policy making and are engaging in broad-based paradiplomatic activity. Although Canada's provinces exercise far less power than the Wallonia and Flanders regions of Belgium, they clearly are among the leaders in this regard internationally. Overall, even though federal-provincial disputes persist,[52] the involvement of Canada's provinces has served to complement Ottawa's foreign policy rather than result in bitter intergovernmental conflict. The Canadian case thus reinforces the notion that paradiplomacy may be a necessary component of international relations in an increasingly interdependent global economy. In that sense it may serve as a model of successful interaction between levels in federal states in the pursuit of common international goals and interests.

NOTES

1. Kim Richard Nossal, *The Politics of Canadian Foreign Policy*, 3rd ed. (Scarborough, ON: Prentice-Hall Canada, 1997), 292.

2. Ulrike Rausch, *The Potential of Transborder Cooperation: Still Worth a Try: An Assessment of the Conference of New England Governors and Eastern Canadian Premiers* (Halifax: Centre for Foreign Policy Studies Dalhousie University, 1997); Martin Lubin, "Strains between Governments at the Top, Hands across the Border at the Base: The Role of Subnational Governments during the Bush-Chretien Era and Beyond," *Canadian-American Public Policy*, no. 54 (September 2003): 21–43.

3. Louis Balthazar, "Quebec's International Relations: A Response to Needs and Necessities," in *Foreign Relations and Federal States*, ed. Brian Hocking (London: Leicester University Press, 1993), 140–52; Louis Balthazar, "The Quebec Experience: Success or Failure?" in *Paradiplomacy in Action: The Foreign Relations of Subnational Governments*, ed. Francisco Aldecoa and Michael Keating (London: Frank Cass, 1999), 153–69; Louis Bélanger, "Les espaces internationaux de l'Etat québécois" (paper delivered at the annual colloquium of the Canadian Political Science Association, Carleton University, Ottawa, June 6, 1993); Luc Bernier, *De Paris à Washington: La politique internationale du Québec* (Montréal: Presses de l'Université du Québec à Montréal, 1996); Nelson Michaud, "Federalism and Foreign Policy: Comparative Answers to Globalisation," in *Handbook of Federal Countries 2002*, ed. Ann L. Griffiths (Montreal & Kingston: McGill-Queen's University Press, 2002), 389–415.

4. Ivo D. Duchacek, "Multicommunal and Bicommunal Polities and Their International Relations," in *Perforated Sovereignties and International Relations*, ed. Ivo D. Duchacek, Daniel Latouche, and Garth Stevenson (Westport, CT: Greenwood Press, 1988), 3–28; Brian Hocking, "Patrolling the 'Frontier': Globalization, Localization, and the 'Actorness' of Non-Central Governments," in *Paradiplomacy in Action*, 17–39; Brian Hocking, "Managing Foreign Relations in Federal States: Linking Central and Non-central International Interests," in *Paradiplomacy in Action*, 68–69; Michaud, "Federalism and Foreign Policy."

5. Stéphane Paquin, "Paradiplomatie identitaire et diplomatie en Belgique fédérale: le cas de la Flandre," *Canadian Journal of Political* Science 36, no. 3 (2003): 621–642.

6. Paquin, "Paradiplomatie identitaire et diplomatie en Belgique fédérale."

7. Earl Fry, "The United States and Foreign Economic Policy: Federalism in the 'New World Order,'" in *Foreign Relations and Federal States*, 122–39; Earl Fry, "The Expanding Role of State, Provincial, and Local Governments in North American Economic Relations" (paper presented at the annual conference of the International Studies Association, Montreal, 20 March 2004).

8. Greg Craven, "Federal Constitutions and External Relations," in *Foreign Relations and Federal States*, 9–26; Michaud, "Federalism and Foreign Policy"; John Ravenhill, "Federal-State Relations in Australian External Affairs: A New Co-operative Era?" in *Paradiplomacy in Action*, 134–52.

9. Inaki Aguirre, "Making Sense of Paradiplomacy? An Intertextual Inquiry about a Concept in Search of a Definition," in *Paradiplomacy in Action*, 185–209; Duchacek,. "Multicommunal and Bicommunal Polities and Their International Relations," 3–28; Ivo D. Duchacek, *The Territorial Dimension of Politics Within, Among and Across Nations* (Boulder, CO: Westview Press, 1986).

10. James N. Rosenau, *Along the Domestic-Foreign Frontier: Exploring Governance in a Turbulent World* (Cambridge: Cambridge University Press, 1997), 67.

11. Brian Hocking, "Patrolling the 'Frontier': Globalization, Localization, and the 'Actorness' of Non-Central Governments," in *Paradiplomacy in Action*, 17–39.

12. Aguirre, "Making Sense of Paradiplomacy?"

13. Hamish Telford, *Expanding the Partnership: The Proposed Council of the Federation and the Challenge of Glocalization* (Montreal: Institute for Research on Public Policy, 2003).

14. Telford, *Expanding the Partnership*, 3.

15. Paquin, "Paradiplomatie identitaire et diplomatie en Belgique fédérale"; Stéphane Paquin, *Paradiplomatie identitaire en Catalogne* (Sainte-Foy, Québec: Presses de l'Université Laval, 2003).

16. Robert Kaiser, "Subnational Governments in International Arenas—Paradiplomacy and Multi-level Governance in Europe and North America" (paper presented at the 5th Symposium of the International Political Science Association on "Globalization, Nations and Multi-level Governance: Strategies and Challenges," Montréal, 24–26 October 2002); Hans J. Michelman and Panayotis Soldatos, eds., *Federalism and International Relations: The Role of Subnational Units* (Oxford: Clarendon Press, 1990); and Aldecoa and Keating, eds., *Paradiplomacy in Action*.

17. André Lecours, "When Regions Go Abroad: Globalization, Nationalism and Federalism" (paper presented at the conference on Globalization, Multilevel Governance and Democracy: Continental, Comparative and Global Perspectives, Queen's University, May 3–4, 2002), 2.

18. Earl Fry, "The Expanding Role of State, Provincial, and Local Governments in North American Economic Relations"; Guy Gosselin and Gordon Mace, "Asymétrie et relations internationales: les provinces canadiennes, l'Europe et l'Amérique latine," *Études internationales* 35, no. 3 (1994): 523–51; Nelson Michaud, "Federalism and Foreign Policy."

19. Paul Gérin-Lajoie, *Combats d'un révolutionnaire tranquille* (Montréal: Cen-

tre éducatif et culturel, 1989); Liesbet Hooghe and Gary Marks, "Unraveling the Central State, but How? Types of Multi-level Governance," *American Political Science Review* 97, no. 2 (May 2003): 233–244; James P. McIlroy, "NAFTA and the Canadian Provinces: Two Ships Passing in the Night," *Canada-United States Law Journal* 23 (1997): 431–40.

20. Michaud, "Federalism and Foreign Policy."
21. Craven, "Federal Constitutions and External Relations."
22. Paquin, "Paradiplomatie identitaire et diplomatie en Belgique fédérale."
23. Paquin, *Paradiplomatie identitaire en Catalogne*.
24. Craven, "Federal Constitutions and External Relations;" Nelson Michaud, "Federalism and Foreign Policy."
25. McIlroy, "NAFTA and the Canadian Provinces."
26. To these, one should add Section 92A, which deals with the specific question of nonrenewable natural resources, forestry, and electrical energy; 93 with respect to education; 94 with respect to old age pensions; and 95 with respect to agriculture. The environment is not mentioned in the Canadian constitution, but the Supreme Court of Canada has determined a responsibility beyond the federal government, despite provisions within Section 91(29) that give residual powers to the federal level, contrary to the case in the United States.
27. Nossal, *The Politics of Canadian Foreign Policy*.
28. Nossal, *The Politics of Canadian Foreign Policy*.
29. Daniel Dupras, "NAFTA: Implementation and the Participation of the Provinces" (Ottawa: Parliamentary Research Branch, 1993). Provided by the office of the NAFTA Secretariat in Ontario.
30. McIlroy, "NAFTA and the Canadian Provinces."
31. McIlroy, "NAFTA and the Canadian Provinces," 432.
32. McIlroy , "NAFTA and the Canadian Provinces," 432.
33. McIlroy, "NAFTA and the Canadian Provinces," 432–33.
34. Douglas M. Brown, "The Evolving Role of the Provinces in Canada-U.S. Trade Relations," in *States and Provinces in the International Economy*, ed. Douglas M. Brown and Earl H. Fry (Berkeley: Institute of Governmental Studies, University of California Press, 2003), 93–144; Dupras, "NAFTA"; McIlroy, "NAFTA and the Canadian Provinces."
35. McIlroy, "NAFTA and the Canadian Provinces."
36. Dupras, "NAFTA," 5.
37. Dupras, "NAFTA," 6.
38. Dupras, "NAFTA," 6. Italics added.
39. Dupras, "NAFTA," 6.
40. See Louis Balthazar, Louis Bélanger, and Gordon Mace, eds., *Trente ans de*

politique extérieure du Québec (Québec: CQRI/Septentrion, 1993); Louis Bélanger, "Les espaces internationaux de l'Etat québécois"; Bernier, *De Paris à Washington*; Michaud, "Federalism and Foreign Policy."

41. Paul Martin, "Canada's Role in a Complex World" (presented at the Canadian Newspaper Association Annual Super Conference, Toronto, 30 April 2003).

42. Richard Florida, *The Rise of the Creative Class* (New York: Basic Books, 2002).

43. Meric S. Gertler, Richard Florida, Gary Gates, and Tara Vinodrai, *Competing on Creativity: Placing Ontario's Cities in North American Context* (a report prepared for the Ontario Ministry and the Institute for Competitiveness and Prosperity, November 2002).

44. R^2 is the fraction of the total variance that is explained by the model. The closer the measurement is to 1, the more explanatory power there is. In other words, here, 74 percent of the variance is explained by this factor.

45. "Cheney Sympathetic: Klein," *CBC News*, June 25, 2003, http://edmonton.cbc.ca/regional/servlet/View?filename=ed_madcow20030625.

46. A complete list is available at http://www.mri.gouv.qc.ca/fr/action_internationale/ententes/ententes.asp and can be searched by country, organization, issue area, and date. Information is available in French, English, and Spanish.

47. Louis Balthazar, "Quebec's International Relations."

48. According to the Treasury Board of Canada Secretariat's website, "Team Canada Atlantic (TCA) is a partnership of ACOA [Atlantic Canada Opportunities Agency] and the four Atlantic Provinces, with support from Agriculture and Agri-Food Canada, Industry Canada, Foreign Affairs Canada, International Trade Canada. TCA is committed to strengthening the trade and investment relationship between Atlantic Canada and the United States. Since 1999, approximately $4.1 million has been spent to date on TCA missions. The core of the TCA approach is the trade mission, which puts small and medium-sized businesses from across Atlantic Canada on the ground and face-to-face with potential buyers, agents, distributors and strategic partners in the United States. The mission format features a comprehensive, top-to-bottom program that equips private sector participants with the knowledge, contacts and advice they need to make the best of their international opportunities before, during and after their venture abroad. Missions also provide the Government of Canada and the Atlantic provincial governments with crucial opportunities to promote the region as a tremendous location for foreign investment. Other partners who contribute to the development and implementation of the trade missions are Team Canada and the Atlantic Canada World Trade Centre." Accessed at http://www.tbs-sct.gc.ca/rma/eppi-ibdrp/hrdb-rhbd/tca-eca/description_e.asp.

49. Nova Scotia Department of Finance, 2002.

50. See http://www.sasktrade.sk.ca. Given its relatively small population, it is impressive that eleven countries have permanent consular officers resident in Saskatchewan for the purposes of promoting trade and investment as well as representing their citizens or former citizens.

51. Denis Stairs, *The Conduct of Canadian Foreign Policy and the Interests of Newfoundland and Labrador* (St. John's: Royal Commission on Renewing and Strengthening Our Place in Canada, 2003); *Our Place in Canada, A Summary Report* (St. John's: Royal Commission on Renewing and Strengthening Our Place in Canada, 2003).

52. In response to Alberta's efforts to establish its own autonomous delegation in Washington, DC, a step not even Québec has dared take, Ottawa has proposed housing provincial delegations within the Canadian Embassy in that city.

II

MULTICULTURAL CHALLENGES

6

"There Are No Half-Countries": Canada, La Francophonie, and the Projection of Canadian Biculturalism, 1960–2002[1]

GREG DONAGHY AND NEAL CARTER

Prime Minister Jean Chrétien had reason to feel worried. As delegates from the 53 member countries of La Francophonie gathered in Moncton, New Brunswick, in fall 1999 for their 8th biennial summit—the second to be held in Canada—it was becoming clear that this was not to be a triumphant projection of Canadian biculturalism on the world's stage. Instead, the gathering was mired in growing controversy. In the run-up to the conference, Québec's Parti Québécois premier, Lucien Bouchard, had abruptly canceled a visit by the organization's secretary-general, Boutros Boutros-Ghali, angry at what he claimed were federal efforts to monopolize the summit and humiliate Québec.[2] Marcus Gee, the foreign affairs columnist for Canada's national newspaper, the *Globe and Mail*, derided La Francophonie as the "Seymour Milquetoast of international organizations: little known, and even less respected."[3] Still more disturbing was the organization's glaring inability to come to grips with the abhorrent human rights abuses of many of its members. During the summit, Amnesty International condemned 32 of the 53 delegations for human rights violations, as a handful of new Canadians, refugees from Rwanda, Burundi, and Zaire, protested in front of the conference center.[4]

Harried on human rights questions by journalists, protesters, and nongovernment organizations (NGOs), Chrétien pleaded for time. The organization's hortatory declarations on democracy and human rights were perhaps not very effective instruments of change, but he insisted that they were important first steps that Canada would continue to pursue in the years to come.[5] And he was right. Indeed, in 1999, La Francophonie was still taking shape, though it had made significant progress since its inaugural summit in 1986. Chrétien's vigorous defense of La Francophonie simply underlined the important place this relatively new institution already occupied in Canada's foreign policy and the sizeable expectations Ottawa was inclined to thrust upon it.

Canada's strong interest in this loose and imperfect alliance of partially or wholly French-speaking countries is hardly surprising, for it reflects several of the enduring preoccupations of Canadian diplomacy since World War II. Most important, policy-makers in Ottawa have consistently seen La Francophonie as a vital element in Canada's continuing struggle to project its bicultural and bilingual character abroad. In adding a francophone dimension to its foreign policy, Ottawa sought another means to reinforce the fragile ties that bound English and French Canada together. After all, national unity has always been, and remains, the essential prerequisite of Canadian foreign policy.

Canada's long-standing interest in La Francophonie also fit in nicely with the country's traditional multilateralist instincts. Like the United Nations or the Commonwealth, La Francophonie freed Canada from the close embrace of its North American neighbor, the United States. In La Francophonie, which brought together a variety of countries from North and South as well as East and West, Canadian prime ministers from Lester B. Pearson on were exposed to an array of viewpoints and perspectives that moderated the rigid and inflexible world view they encountered in Washington. Moreover, La Francophonie provided a forum where Canadian diplomacy mattered and where Canadian prime ministers could pursue the human rights and cultural initiatives that many Canadians see as integral to their place in the world.

This chapter explores how these themes have played out since 1960 against the backdrop of a national debate over the role of the provinces in international affairs and a series of difficult negotiations over the nature and scope of La Francophonie. It consequently addresses what the institution represents in the realm of Canadian foreign policy.

The chapter begins with a look at the emergence of La Francophonie's first formal institution, the *Agence de Coopération Culturelle et Technique* (ACCT) and discusses the lengthy and contentious talks associated with establishing a Francophone Summit. The chapter's final section explores Canadian efforts since the first summit in 1986 to bring this new multilateral agency to life, to shape its identity, and to develop its long-term work plan.

ESTABLISHING THE ACCT

For most of the two decades after World War II, Canadian foreign policy tended to emphasize Canada's relations with its traditional North Atlantic allies, the United States and Great Britain. Although Canada and France were formal allies in the North Atlantic Treaty Organization (NATO) and part of the Western bloc at the United Nations (UN), direct contacts between the two countries were few and insubstantial. Canada's relations with France were mostly sentimental, based on a common linguistic heritage and the shared experience of two world wars.[6] By the early 1960s, however, this had begun to change. With the election of Jean Lesage's Liberal government in 1960, Québec embarked on a program of economic and social modernization that led it to establish new ties with France. Québeckers were delighted and urged the government on. In July 1963, for instance, Jean-Marc Léger, a journalist for *Le Devoir*, published a series on "Québec in the Francophone World" in which he described Canada as "a country that is Anglo-Saxon in its foreign policy." As Ottawa was incapable of maintaining relations with the French-speaking world, Léger argued, French Canada must look for "vigorous, imaginative, and persistent action from the Québec government."[7]

Elected in April 1963, Canada's new prime minister, Lester B. Pearson, and his minority Liberal government were alert to these developments and aware of the challenge they represented to Ottawa's exclusive jurisdiction over the country's foreign policy. During the next few years, Pearson and Paul Martin Sr., his Secretary of State for External Affairs, worked hard to improve Ottawa's capacity to project a bilingual and bicultural foreign policy. In addition to early visits to Washington and London, Pearson made a point of visiting French President Charles de Gaulle in January 1964 in order to improve relations with France. Under Martin, the Department of External Affairs increased francophone recruitment, expanded its representation in French-speaking countries, and launched a new $250,000 (Canadian) program for cultural exchanges.[8]

Despite these efforts, Ottawa was soon on the defensive. While Marcel Cadieux, who was appointed Martin's deputy minister in January 1964, had firm ideas on how to handle Québec's demands for greater international autonomy and the French meddling that encouraged them, other key policy-makers were more restrained. Pearson had little feel for Québec or France, and was by nature inclined to avoid confrontation. Martin, already wooing the French-Canadian vote in the undeclared race to succeed Pearson, tried hard to meet Paris at least halfway on most issues. His position was reinforced by the views of Jules Léger, Canada's ambassador in Paris. Léger urged patience, confident that French meddling would disappear with the passing of the French president, Charles de Gaulle.

But, in late 1964, de Gaulle extended to the Québec delegation in Paris the kinds of privileges normally reserved for full diplomatic missions, while virtually snubbing Léger. When Québec's minister of education, Paul Gérin-Lajoie, declared in April 1965 that his government had the right to conclude autonomous international agreements in fields of provincial jurisdiction, France responded by offering Québec a Paris–Québec City cultural accord. Ottawa fought back, reaching its own cultural accord with Paris that retroactively blessed the terms of Québec's agreement.

In the context of this struggle with Québec City and Paris over who would represent French Canada on the world stage and how, Ottawa reacted cautiously to the July 1966 suggestion by Senegalese President Léopold Senghor and Tunisian President Habib Bourguiba that French-speaking states form an international association for cultural and economic purposes. Clearly, there were good reasons for Canada to join this new organization. Early Canadian participation would encourage broad membership, reduce French dominance, and exert a moderating influence on organizational questions. More important, it would respond to French-Canadian demands for closer ties with francophone countries and "open up at the international level fields of cultural cooperation in which the federal government could maintain its primary position as the central coordinating authority."[9]

Nevertheless, membership in the proposed organization was not without risk. France would clearly play a major role and might even be able to force Canada into the shadows. Participation would also complicate relations with former French colonies in Africa and Asia and with the United States and the British Commonwealth. Moreover, Ottawa might not be able to retain the initiative in the cultural field and, in losing it, provide Québec nationalists with an international forum to advance their cause. Federal officials warned that "direct involvement in 'La Francophonie' would mean a radical departure from existing Canadian habits" and cautioned Martin that "the full consequences of Canadian participation are difficult to assess." As a result, Martin decided in the fall of 1966 that Canada should proceed slowly, and for the time being, Ottawa expressed only a "sympathetic and active interest" in La Francophonie.[10]

Throughout the winter of 1966–1967, Ottawa's approach remained circumspect. In March 1967, after prompting from Pearson, Canada's foreign minister finally unveiled a proposal to set up a modest "*Association internationale de solidarité francophone*" (International Association for Francophone Solidarity), a private sector network that would cooperate with national governments to promote cultural exchanges.[11] Martin had great hopes of securing French backing for his idea, which had already attracted support from several African states, but his plans were soon overtaken by events. In the summer of 1967, de Gaulle visited Québec, where, encouraged by the enthusiastic crowds that flocked to the Chemin du Roy to cheer his motorcade, he delighted Québec nationalists with an emotional speech that ended with a rousing "*Vive le Québec libre*," a popular separatist slogan.[12] On his return home, de Gaulle mystically told his staff that he had "heard" the Québec people, and he redoubled his efforts to promote their independence.[13]

It was soon clear that France was ready to exploit the growing global interest in new forms of francophone cooperation to advance this policy. In November 1967, prompted by Paris, on whom it depended for regular doses of foreign aid, the small African state of Gabon invited Québec but not Ottawa to attend a meeting of francophone education ministers that was to be held the following February in Libreville. Ottawa was naturally alarmed, and it tried hard to persuade Québec, France, and Gabon that only the federal government was competent to represent Canada at the international level and, consequently, only Ottawa should receive an invitation to attend. Drawing a parallel with the Commonwealth experience, federal ministers explained reassuringly that provinces would be welcome to join federal delegations or even lead them when the matter under consideration—like education—fell into their jurisdiction. But these representations were fruitless, though the Gabonese admitted a few days before the conference opened that Québec's minister of education, Jean-Guy Cardinal, had been invited only in his personal capacity. This was hardly reassuring, and Pearson retaliated by suspending diplomatic relations with Gabon.

With Pearson's departure from the prime minister's post in April 1968 and the selection of Pierre Trudeau as his successor, Canada's attitude toward relations with francophone countries hardened. A committed federalist with a strong centralist bent, Trudeau identified the preservation of Canada's national unity as his central foreign policy preoccupation, and he was not about to let either France or Québec subvert that unity by carving out an independent status for Québec in the international sphere. During the leadership campaign, he made his position clear: "There exist great and small countries; there are no half-countries."[14] He was equally firm during the federal election that followed in June 1968. "[T]here is one way to keep Canada united and that is to make sure Canada speaks with one voice in the world."[15] Unlike Cadieux, Trudeau was not alone in his hard-line attitude toward France but enjoyed the support of several important like-minded allies. Marc Lalonde, a relentlessly partisan Trudeau loyalist, signed on as the new prime minister's principal secretary, and Gérard Pelletier, who had come to Ottawa with Trudeau in 1965 to rescue Canadian federalism, became secretary of state, with an informal mandate for relations with La Francophonie.

They soon had plenty to do. In January 1968, France had suggested following up the Gabon conference with a second gathering of education ministers to be held in April 1968. This was billed as a successor conference to the first Gabon affair, allowing Paris to argue that Québec alone should be invited since it was the sole representative from Canada in Libreville. Busy consolidating his hold on power, Trudeau protested but refrained from turning the conference into a major issue when France promised to keep the proceedings low-key and routine.[16] It was more difficult to respond to the next proposal for a conference of education ministers to be held in Kinshasa, Zaire, in January 1969. But this time, Ottawa was ready. Lionel Chevrier, a retired Franco-Ontarian cabinet minister, had just led a large aid mission on a tour of Africa, implicitly linking Canadian aid with support for the federal government's constitutional position.[17] Paul Martin Sr., now a senator, had also visited Africa in December 1968, successfully persuading Niger's president, Hamani Diori, and the Zairean leader, Joseph Mobutu, who had secessionist problems of his own, of the validity of the federal position.[18] When the time finally came to issue the invitations, Mobutu invited Ottawa and not Québec, prompting a protracted series of negotiations on the composition of the Canadian delegation between Marc LaLonde and Claude Morin, Québec's deputy minister of intergovernmental affairs. The two eventually agreed that there would be one Canadian delegation, composed of three distinct elements: Canada-Québec, Canada-Ontario, and Canada–New Brunswick. Morin and the French-speaking premier of New Brunswick, Louis Robichaud, would act as cochairmen.[19]

From the federal perspective the Kinshasa arrangement worked reasonably well, and Ottawa hoped that it might provide a precedent for the next international meeting, a conference called to create a permanent organization devoted to promoting economic and cultural cooperation among the partially and entirely French-speaking counties of the world. Squeezed between France, which threatened to boycott the gathering if he failed to invite Québec, and Canada, which insisted on its exclusive right to represent Canadians, the wily Diori, who was to host the conference in Niger's capital of Niamey, sent letters to both Trudeau and Québec's nationalist premier, Jean-Jacques Bertrand, inviting them to resolve the question of Canada's representation. Trudeau and Bertrand agreed to send a single Canadian delegation on the Kinshasa model. Pelletier would be leader, Québec would be represented by Marcel Masse, the minister of intergovernmental affairs, and there would be additional representatives from Ontario and New Brunswick. Decisions would be reached by consensus.

On the whole, the arrangement worked, though Masse tried hard to distance himself from the Canadian delegation, and Pauline Julien, the Québec singer, caused a small stir when she greeted a Pelletier speech with a fervent shout of *"Vive le Québec libre!"*[20] In Ottawa's view, the conference gave a strong push to the creation of an international francophone organization devoted to aid—the topic is thoroughly explored by Rioux in his chapter 9—and cultural exchanges. With Pelletier's support, the conference elected the Québec journalist and separatist, Jean-Marc Léger, as secretary-general, asking him and Diori to draft a constitution for the new organization, to be called the *Agence de Coopération Culturelle et Technique* (ACCT). Perhaps more important, the Niamey conference reinforced Canada's standing in the Francophone world and ensured that Canada with Québec (rather than Québec without Canada) would have a seat at the table.[21]

Despite some early misgivings that he might give undue weight to Québec's claims, Léger proved a fairly balanced international civil servant. During the following year, he and Diori criss-crossed the French-speaking world, crafting a draft constitution in preparation for a second Niamey conference, which would finally establish an international francophone organization. While the specter of a separate invitation to Québec was avoided with Diori's help, Ottawa and France were sharply divided over the Léger-Diori constitution. Ottawa welcomed their draft, which allotted membership to sovereign states only; Québec and France did not, insisting that membership be open to governments. Ottawa made its position clear to the French at the official and ministerial level, with Trudeau even insisting—over an open telephone line that he considered bugged by French intelligence—that he was ready to break off relations with France if it continued to interfere in Canada's internal affairs.[22] However, despite representations from Pelletier, who again headed the Canadian delegation, the French insisted that Québec must be represented in the new organization, leaving the issue unresolved when the conference opened in March 1970.

This second gathering in Niamey was dominated by the clash between France and Canada over Québec's representation. On his arrival in Niger's capital, the French delegation presented Pelletier with a revised constitution that extended membership to all francophone governments whose jurisdiction covered sectors like education or culture that were addressed by the new organization. As a small concession to the Canadian position, the French offered to add a clause requiring governments joining the organization to obtain the approval of the government normally responsible for foreign affairs. Though Pelletier rejected this position, France had the support of most of the African delegates, who were inclined to dismiss Ottawa's position as "insignificant and self-serving." Continued opposition would only upset the conference and possibly lead to the creation of a new organization with Canada excluded. After consulting Trudeau by phone, Pelletier gave in, accepted the French draft, and paved the way for Québec to join the ACCT in its own right as a participating member.[23]

Headquartered in Paris, where it remained under the suspicious gaze of the French Foreign Ministry, the ACCT was a small and truncated affair, with its initial budget set at a minuscule $300,000 (Canadian) per year.[24] Though this figure rose significantly over the next decade, reaching $15 million annually by 1979, the scope of the ACCT's activities remained limited to promoting academic, cultural, and scientific exchanges.[25] As a result, it figured only marginally in the Trudeau government's efforts to promote francophone solidarity and to encourage multilateral dialogue among French-speaking countries. In contrast to the $100 million per year in bilateral aid that Ottawa was sending to Francophone Africa by the late 1970s, Canadian support for the ACCT mostly meant encouraging eligible states to join and strengthening its institutional structures and administrative capabilities.[26] Trudeau and his foreign policy advisor, Ivan Head, were inclined to dismiss La Francophonie's central organization as a "low budget, useful, but not very influential association."[27]

THE QUEST FOR A FRANCOPHONE SUMMIT

Trudeau and Head were not alone in their skepticism. By the mid-1970s, several African leaders, leery of France's dominant role in the ACCT and desperate to find new ways of tapping into a stagnating world economy, began to press for a political summit at the heads-of-government level, modeled on the British Commonwealth. Leading the charge was the Senegalese President, Léopold Senghor, whose ambassador in Ottawa informed the Department of External Affairs in the spring of 1975 that Dakar wished to "relaunch La Francophonie in order to strengthen its political framework. Senegal hopes to reenergize the ACCT, enlarge sectoral consultations, and institute meetings at the level of heads of state and heads of government."[28]

Reaction to Senghor's proposals was mixed. E. P. Black, director general of External Affairs' European branch and a veteran of the nasty squabbles over Kinshasa and Niamey, worried about the reaction in Paris, which remained anxious to safeguard its favoured economic and political position in post-colonial Africa. A debate over a francophone summit, he cautioned, might upset Trudeau's efforts to restore some equilibrium to Canada's relations with Paris just when French support was required to negotiate an economic link with Europe.[29] Others were more positive. Certainly France was a problem; so too was Québec. However, as doing nothing risked being swept away by events if suggestions for a more political Francophonie matured, Allan MacEachen, the secretary of state for external affairs, recommended taking the initiative to sound out France and the African countries for their views.[30] Trudeau agreed, but urged his minister to proceed carefully since a Commonwealth-like summit would place Québec's foreign policy "pretensions" into their proper context and spark concern in Québec City.[31]

But Trudeau himself showed little caution when he met with Senghor in June 1976 to discuss the African's hopes for a francophone summit. Trudeau insisted that any summit must be like a Commonwealth heads-of-government meeting: informal and flexible, charged with a broad international political and economic mandate. These views reflected in part the value the prime minister increasingly attached to Commonwealth meetings as fora for greater North-South dialogue. More important, they also described an organization that left no room for Québec at the table. In such a forum with such an agenda, Trudeau repeated, only Ottawa could possibly represent Canada and speak for Canadians. If Senghor accepted this position, Trudeau would throw his support strongly behind a francophone summit.[32]

Senghor was delighted. African states would have proposed a Commonwealth-like summit long ago, he replied, but refrained lest France respond by reducing its economic aid. Pocketing Trudeau's pledge, which he repeatedly described, to Ottawa's embarrassment, as a Canadian initiative, Senghor persuaded a reluctant French president, Valéry Giscard d'Estaing, to place the issue before the Franco-African summit scheduled for April 1977.[33] Determined to avoid a repeat of the second Niamey conference, when Canada was forced to compromise by an unsupportive African majority, Trudeau was quick to court Senghor and gently advise him on the policies and tactics he should pursue at the Dakar meeting. The prime minister reiterated his strong support for the system of flexible and informal heads-of-government meetings developed in the British Commonwealth. These ought to have as their principal themes the major political and economic questions of their day. He cautioned Senghor to avoid all texts, charters, and constitutions that might predetermine the summit's structure, agenda, and guest list. Instead, Senghor should aim to create an informal working group, on which Canada would be happy to serve. More important, the Senegalese president must act quickly. Determined to deny Premier René Lévesque's recently elected Parti Québécois government the time to mount an effective opposition, Trudeau demanded a summit in the fall of 1977.[34]

Senghor agreed with Trudeau on every point, but others did not despite an extensive Canadian lobby campaign in Africa and Paris.[35] At the Franco-African gathering in Dakar, the president of the Ivory Coast, Félix Houphouët-Boigny, whom Canadian officials justifiably suspected of acting as a French stalking horse, scuttled Senghor's plans. Instead of turning the matter of a francophone summit over to a working group, he asked that French and African foreign ministers review the issue at their next meeting in the spring of 1978.[36] From Ottawa's perspective, this was an alarming development. Canada was clearly not going to be invited to either this meeting or the preparatory gatherings that would precede it, forcing it to depend on others to safeguard its position.

There was a second reason for Ottawa's growing concern. The delay provided Lévesque with an opportunity to use his first official visit to Paris in November 1977 to persuade the French to convene a heads-of-government summit within the ACCT, allowing the Québec premier to attend as the head of a participating government. In October 1977, responding to advice from the Department of External Affairs, Trudeau decided to seize the initiative and place Canada's views firmly on the public record. During a press conference with the visiting head of the Organization of African Unity (OAU), President Omar Bongo of Gabon, Trudeau made it clear that he welcomed Senghor's proposals for a "Francophone Commonwealth" that would address world issues in a flexible and informal forum.[37] Almost immediately, France shot back. In response to a planted question in the National Assembly, the French foreign minister, Louis de Guiringaud, announced that France would not attend any francophone summit that did not include Québec.[38]

The French reaction was much stronger than Ottawa had anticipated and raised the unhappy specter of a renewed Canada-France contest over Québec's international standing. A public dispute over Québec would eliminate any future flexibility in the French position and allow Paris, already sceptical of a movement that might further reduce its role in Africa, to pull back from La Francophonie. Moreover, the French-speaking states of Africa might push for a compromise modeled on the ACCT arrangement, a possibility that remained unacceptable to Ottawa. On the advice of officials in the Department of External Affairs, Trudeau decided to retreat and place the issue on the back burner until he and Giscard d'Estaing had had a chance to discuss the issue.[39] But, when the two leaders broached the subject in December 1978, it was immediately clear that "the French and Canadian positions remained distinctly incompatible." Early in the new year, Trudeau informed Senghor that Canada would have to abandon the effort to arrange a francophone summit.[40]

The prospects for a summit languished for the remainder of 1979 as Canadians found themselves swept up in domestic concerns. Trudeau's defeat in the May 1979 election, Joe Clark's short-lived Conservative government, which ended with another federal election in February 1980, and the first Québec referendum on separating from Canada in May 1980 distracted Ottawa and Québec City from developments within the francophone world.[41] Trudeau was surprised therefore to discover in June 1980 that Senghor had recently dusted off his plans for a francophone summit. At the Franco-African summit in May 1980, the Senegalese president secured a resolution that convened a meeting of foreign ministers from French-speaking states in November 1980 to prepare for an inaugural summit the following November.[42] After moving quickly to obtain Senghor's assurances that he would invite only Ottawa to the foreign ministers' meeting, Trudeau decided to await developments, reluctant to confront Lévesque so soon after the referendum.[43]

Waiting proved wise. In September, Senghor convened an experts meeting to ready material for the foreign ministers, a step that further strengthened Canada's position. The experts agreed that any new francophone organization should have a broad agenda, embracing cultural exchanges, economic relations, and questions of world peace and security. It was up to the foreign ministers to decide whether they wanted to tackle this agenda through a formal organization or some kind of informal means inspired by the Commonwealth example. Ministers would also prepare the agenda for the first summit.[44] With this report before the foreign ministers, there was no question that Canada would be represented in Dakar, whatever the likelihood of a row with Québec. Not only did a prospective francophone summit reflect Canada's long-standing interest in closer ties with French-speaking countries and the Third World, Ottawa's absence at the very moment when its ideas might carry the day would not be understood in Africa.[45]

Québec, of course, would insist on being there on the same basis as it attended the ACCT meetings. Moreover, many African states would still not understand why Québec was not there. To accommodate the legitimate interests of Québec (as well as New Brunswick and Ontario) while maintaining its own responsibility for the conduct of foreign affairs, Ottawa decided to invite senior civil servants—specifically excluding ministers—from the three provinces to join the Canadian delegation. At the same time, in order to remove any ambiguity about the Canadian position and forestall outside interference, Ottawa would inform Paris of its position (being careful not to negotiate), accept Senghor's invitation, and make it clear that Ottawa would go to Dakar even if Québec rejected its offer.[46]

Ottawa acted in the final week of October 1980, with letters to Senghor and Claude Morin, Québec's minister of intergovernmental affairs, and a demarche upon the French foreign ministry. Québec's reaction followed quickly. Morin rejected the federal offer as *"inacceptable,"* demanding a place at the table and the right to speak. However, through his deputy minister, Robert Normand, Morin informally asked for a meeting with the Canadian secretary of state for external affairs, Mark MacGuigan, and hinted at a possible compromise: Québec, it turned out, would be content if Ottawa allowed Morin, rather than a senior civil servant, to be a member of the Canadian delegation. Morin would consult Ottawa before speaking and would only speak on subjects of provincial jurisdiction.[47]

From Ottawa's perspective compromise was neither possible nor necessary. Admittedly, France made no secret of its disappointment with Ottawa. Jacques Voit of the French prime minister's office told Gérard Pelletier, then Canada's ambassador in Paris, in late October that "it would be incomprehensible for Québec to be denied representation at Dakar."[48] A few weeks later, the French foreign minister, Olivier Stirn, told MacGuigan "the federal proposition was unacceptable to Québec, and therefore unacceptable to France."[49] However, many in Ottawa doubted Paris would go very far in support of Québec. French opposition had been delivered quietly and cordially, encouraging the view that France was not interested in provoking an open conflict with Canada.

The federal position seemed secure on other fronts as well. Despite pressure from France to invite Québec directly, Senghor made it "categorically" clear that he considered provincial representation to be a "purely" domestic matter for Canada to resolve. He would not invite Québec and he would not allow anyone else to do so either.[50] To avoid any backsliding, MacGuigan arranged to meet Senghor in Madrid a few weeks later. Senghor thought Canada's position "perfectly reasonable" and he urged Ottawa not to be deterred by French posturing. For his part, the African leader declared that he would not postpone the meeting even if France threatened a boycott.[51]

It was unlikely that Ottawa would have accepted Morin's compromise even if it lacked evidence of Senegalese support and French uncertainty. Federal officials and ministers simply did not trust Morin, whose behavior on the margins of the foreign ministers meeting would be beyond their control. The Québec minister's very presence in Dakar would represent a symbolic victory over Ottawa and enhance Québec's claims to an international personality.[52] In late November, MacGuigan met with Morin and rejected the Québec counteroffer.[53]

Ottawa's hard line placed Paris firmly up against the wall. When Trudeau visited the Elysée Palace a few days later, he found Giscard d'Estaing and his prime minister, Raymond Barre, boxed in by past French policy and uncertain how to proceed. By the time the visit ended, it was clear that France would press Senghor to postpone the summit rather than carry on without Québec.[54] In early December, Senghor postponed the Dakar meeting. While Ottawa and Paris launched a loud and graceless public relations battle, blaming each other for the delay, Senghor gracefully retired from office at the end of December 1980.

The possibility of a francophone summit disappeared from the international agenda for the next eighteen months before it reemerged suddenly in June 1982. Elected president in May 1981, the socialist François Mitterrand had little time for the Gaullist mysticism that had dominated French policy toward Canada and Québec since the mid-1960s. Québec was, in his view, better off as part of Canada. The president was also reportedly distressed by the strain in France's relations with its former African colonies that followed the decision to postpone Dakar. Anxious to reassure his country's African allies that they remained important French interests, Mitterrand expressed an interest in holding a summit. To the surprise of Canadian officials at the embassy in Paris, Trudeau responded positively to this evidence of renewed French interest, using his October 1982 speech to the ACCT to warn against "remain[ing] indifferent to anything that contributes to unity or that builds bridges between people." He reiterated his support for La Francophonie when he met the French president in December 1982.[55] Within a week, Régis Debray, the Marxist intellectual and one of Mitterrand's most influential foreign policy advisors, arrived on the doorstep of Michel Dupuy, Canada's ambassador in Paris, anxious to outline France's new approach to a francophone summit.

Mitterrand wanted a summit much like the one Trudeau desired: an informal gathering of heads of government, which would address the world's major political and economic problems. Of course, this depended on Paris and Ottawa reaching an agreement over Québec's role. But that was possible, Debray now hinted, even if Québec was not entirely satisfied. Debray proposed a two-track francophone summit. First there would be a "chambre haute" (upper chamber) reserved for heads of government of the member states to confront the "major international political and economic problems." This would be followed immediately by a second summit in the same location. This "chambre basse" (lower chamber) would gather the heads of all the participating governments in the ACCT to address the cultural and developmental issues normally found on its agenda. As Paris would like to see a francophone summit up and running within six months, Debray was ready to visit Ottawa in January to thrash the matter out.[56]

Officials in Ottawa were initially very interested by Debray's proposal, but the more they thought about it, the more cautious they became. The imprecise nature of the relationship between the first (haute) and the second (basse) summits was worrying. So too was the absence of any substantial indication of what Debray might have told Québec. After a series of lengthy meetings in early January, senior officials in the Department of External Affairs agreed that they and Trudeau should meet Debray. Canada's attitude, however, would remain "prudent," and officials insisted that in any two-track summit, the second session on culture and development must take place at a separate time and place in order to emphasize the distinct nature of the two parts.[57]

Debray, whose proposal would have allowed Québec a small and undefined role on the margins of the "haute" summit, found the federal position "very tough on Québec." France, he insisted, could not simply abandon Québec after supporting it for fifteen years. However, over lunch with the prime minister, a small breakthrough emerged. Trudeau suggested inviting six representative countries—France, Canada, Tunisia, Senegal, Congo, and Vietnam—to a pre-summit that would decide how to organize the summit and whom to invite. Debray found the idea "seductive" and promised to urge Mitterrand to accept it.[58]

The arrangement was too good to last. In Ottawa's view, the pre-summit gave France the multilateral cover it needed to abandon Québec. From France's perspective, however, the pre-summit provided Ottawa with a francophone "summit" meeting without Québec, a major federal victory that ought to persuade Ottawa to be more flexible. These divergent views became obvious when Mitterrand responded to Trudeau's proposal with "a conditional yes." France would only attend the pre-summit provided Paris and Ottawa agreed beforehand that Québec would be present at the real summit, in one form or another. This seemed a discouraging return to the initial French position. In a gesture of compromise, Trudeau ceased insisting that the two summits be held in separate locations. Instead, he suggested that the federal government's position would be met if the first ("haute") politicoeconomic summit was followed by a short break—perhaps a weekend—before the second ("basse") cultural summit was convened at a head-of-government or ministerial level.[59]

In early April, French and Canadian officials agreed, subject to the approval of their political masters, on a single summit of two acts. The first part, at the level of heads of government of sovereign states, would meet for two or three days to discuss the world's most pressing political and economic issues. This would be followed by a weekend intermission, during which these heads of government would continue to meet in an informal retreat. On the following Monday, the second part, which would include the heads of all participating governments and institutions of the ACCT, would open. While there would be no permanent secretariat, and hence no institutional link between the two parts, the French negotiator insisted that Canada's prime minister attend both sessions with the French president and the Québec premier, allowing the Québec government to "claim that it had participated in 'the real summit.'"[60]

Despite the risk that most African heads of government would attend both gatherings, effectively turning the second meeting into a genuine summit, Trudeau accepted the French demand. Paris, however, hesitated.

In mid-April, a series of Gaullist-inspired articles in *Le Monde* denounced Mitterrand for caving in to Ottawa on La Francophonie. By mid-May, the Elysée Palace was beginning to express renewed concerns about the state of Québec opinion and nervousness about the reaction in Africa to the new institution. Mitterrand suggested that he and Trudeau meet at the 1983 G7 summit in Williamsburg, Virginia. But even there, the French position remained unclear. Mitterrand told the prime minister that he agreed with Debray's two-track formula but asked for an additional two weeks to consider the matter.[61] When nothing arrived by September, Canadian diplomats suggested that the prime minister "politely close out the summit discussion . . . as a subject that is getting nowhere."[62] There was little more that Trudeau could do, and his hopes for a summit quickly slipped away. Less than a year later, he too would slip away.

Conservative leader Brian Mulroney, who succeeded Trudeau in September 1984 following the brief interregnum of Liberal heir John Turner, had a very different set of priorities. A bilingual anglophone from rural Baie Comeau (on Québec's North Shore), the Montreal-based Mulroney sympathized with Québec's nationalist movement, whose leading members he courted and on whose votes he depended. Like them, he argued that Trudeau's constitutional reforms had isolated Québec and locked it out of Confederation. Mulroney swept to office determined to inaugurate a new era of national reconciliation, with obvious implications for Québec's international aspirations. When French Prime Minister Laurent Fabius visited in November 1984, Mulroney greeted him with a promise to end the "flag war." The prime minister, whose remarks were drafted in part by Québec nationalist Lucien Bouchard, went on to acknowledge Québec's claim to a special international status. "We recognize the legitimacy of the privileged, direct relations between Paris and Québec," Mulroney declared, "as long as they regard and promote matters which do not impinge on federal jurisdiction."[63]

Despite this rhetoric, there was no radical change in Ottawa's approach to Québec's participation in La Francophonie. When Lévesque raised the possibility of a francophone summit with the new prime minister in November 1984, the secretary of state for external affairs, Joe Clark, recommended pursuing the same "two-part summit with both politic-economic and cultural/economic elements" that France proposed the year before.[64] Mulroney agreed and when he discussed the matter with Lévesque on 30 November 1984, he expressed his preference for a two-track summit. He closed off the discussion by turning the matter over to Clark and Bernard Landry, Québec's minister of intergovernmental affairs.[65]

Clark's talks with Landry were not as productive as the prime minister had hoped. Though the Québec minister began his January 1985 meeting with Clark on the right note, welcoming the new tone in relations between Ottawa and Québec City, he surprised the foreign minister with his demands. Québec insisted on a single, one-track summit, with the province entitled to speak to every issue on the agenda except war and peace. Only the federal government and Québec would attend the summit, leaving out the fully bilingual New Brunswick. These proposals, Clark informed the prime minister, were "extreme," designed to test the limits of the federal position. Moreover, they challenged the prime minister's own oft-declared interest in enhancing the rights of linguistic minorities in Canada.[66] There was no give in Ottawa.

In late April 1985, with Lévesque's departure from politics looming on the horizon, Québec presented a more moderate offer. The Québec premier was ready to accept a summit with two distinct and consecutive parts. The province would attend the summit's first sessions on political and economic questions as an observer only before attending the summit's second part on cultural and technical questions as a full participant.[67] The Department of External Affairs had only begun to consider the new offer, however, when France reentered the equation. Following Lévesque's trip to Paris in May 1985, where the premier mused publicly about a possible agreement with Ottawa on Québec's participation in a francophone summit, Paris issued invitations to a fall preparatory meeting for a francophone summit to be held in early 1986. Too far committed to a summit to retreat easily, Ottawa was suddenly forced back to the negotiating table. Fearful that France might proceed with a one-track summit on cultural matters, a step that could be used to justify giving Québec an independent role, officials in the Department of External Affairs agreed to resume talks on the basis of the Québec offer.[68]

At the same time, the cautious officials in the Department of External Affairs, who had jealously guarded the federal position for two decades, were losing control of the file. During the summer of 1985 Mulroney's old friend and strong Québec nationalist, Lucien Bouchard, agreed to accept an appointment as Canada's ambassador to Paris. If Bouchard had any doubts about his mandate, they were quickly dispelled. In a conversation before his departure, Lévesque was blunt with the new ambassador: "Your mission is La Francophonie."[69] Mitterrand was just as clear when Bouchard presented his credentials in September 1985. When the ambassador spoke of his projects to develop bilateral relations, Mitterrand effectively replied: "First make sure that I can convene the summit, which neither de Gaulle, nor Pompidou, nor Giscard d'Estaing were able to do. Then we will see about the rest."[70] Bouchard quickly forced Clark and his advisors aside, assuming control of federal policy on the issue.

Accompanied by Bernard Roy, the prime minister's principal secretary, Bouchard headed to Montreal on August 30 for a make-or-break meeting with Québec's negotiators, Louis Bernard, secretary of the executive council, and Louis Martin, deputy minister of intergovernmental affairs. Armed with instructions from the prime minister and the premier to cut a deal, the two teams reached an agreement within a few weeks. There would be one summit with two distinct and separate parts. The first part would be devoted to political and economic questions; the second to cultural and development issues. Québec would be present during the politico-economic discussions as an observer only but would attend the second part as a full participant. However, if there were subjects discussed during the first part of the summit that would normally be discussed in the second part, the Québec premier could intervene with the agreement of the prime minister of Canada. Finally, Québec would have its own invitation and its own "sherpa," a high-level official responsible for pre-summit preparatory talks.[71]

The deal, which represented significant concessions by Ottawa, was presented to the Québec cabinet in mid-September. Lévesque, on the verge of leaving office, decided to hand the matter over to his successor, Pierre-Marc Johnson. The uncertain new premier was soon under strong pressure from Louise Beaudoin, Québec's delegate-general in Paris, and Bernard Landry, the minister of international relations, to reject the agreement. The two hard-line separatists insisted that the arrangement was unacceptable since it did not formally acknowledge Québec's right to act internationally in fields where it enjoyed domestic jurisdiction. Johnson agreed and presented Mulroney with a new set of demands. Completely ignoring the Bouchard-Bernard deal, Johnson implicitly returned to the notion of a single-track summit, where the premier and the prime minister would be present together at all sessions. The federal prime minister alone would be a full participant at the sessions on world politics, although federal statements would be given in advance to the Québec premier, who would attend this part of the gathering as an observer. On all other political and economic questions before the summit, the two governments would harmonize their positions, giving Québec an implicit veto over federal interventions on the international economy.

Ottawa was irritated at the sudden change in Québec's position and Roy hurried to Montreal's fabled Ritz-Carlton Hotel in late October to meet Bernard. The two men soon hammered out a new deal. The final agreement, which Mulroney made public on 7 November 1985, preserved the idea of a summit "of two distinct, consecutive parts," with the first part dedicated to international political and economic questions and the second dealing with culture and development. Nevertheless, to secure a compromise, Ottawa again retreated on several important points, blurring the distinctions between the two parts. Significantly, the agreement bound the prime minister and the premier to participate together throughout the entire summit. Similarly, "a major portion" of the first part of the summit would address cooperation and development questions, giving Québec the right to intervene. More important, Ottawa agreed that Québec could intervene in discussions on the international economic situation when its interests were affected and after consulting the prime minister. With the elements of an agreement in sight after years of wrangling, the first summit was scheduled for Paris in February 1986, ushering in a new era for La Francophonie.

THE SUMMITS: SEEKING IDENTITY AND PURPOSE

Summit meetings, at which member heads of state and heads of government formulate the general orientation and priorities of La Francophonie, have been held typically once every two years since 1987, with the exception of the Beirut Summit scheduled for the fall 2001 but postponed for a year, due to security concerns following 9/11. During this period, these high-level political meetings have helped La Francophonie change dramatically and develop an organizational structure that gives it a sustained international presence. The first summits, however, were poorly organized and lacked real focus, often becoming a source of great amusement for journalists covering the gatherings. Few believed Mitterrand when he exclaimed at the end of the Paris summit in 1986 that "La Francophonie is waking up from a slumber that has lasted too long. Its renaissance is here."[72] Instead, observers puzzled over the organization's odd membership, asking why such obvious French-speaking countries as Algeria, Cameroon, and Switzerland declined to participate, while Egypt and Vietnam, where French was now rarely heard, hastened to join.

Observers were also captivated by the continuing struggle between Ottawa and Québec as the two governments tried to stake out their roles in the new organization. This was especially true of the first summit, where Mulroney and the newly elected Liberal premier of Québec, Robert Bourassa, engaged in a very public spat over the significance of La Francophonie for Canadians.[73] Mulroney insisted that "La Francophonie is a long overdue expression of Canada's unity" and argued that federal participation enhanced the international presence of Canada's French-speaking regions and provided a counterbalance to Canada's participation in the British Commonwealth.[74] In order to facilitate Québec's full participation, Canada and France, with the agreement of the other sovereign states, engineered the category of "participant government," which was given to Québec and New Brunswick to avoid giving Québec a unique status.

Bourassa quickly tried to exploit this larger role to enhance Québec's standing. He proposed that La Francophonie create a program to redistribute food surpluses from the developed world among the poor of Africa. Mulroney reacted sharply to this encroachment on the federal government's responsibilities and warned that "it will be the first and the last time it happens. . . . [B]lind-side me once, and you've got a problem."[75] These early difficulties between Ottawa and Québec City, however, were largely set aside during the following decade, for both sides realized that they shared an interest in making the new organization work.

But this would not to be easy. At the first summit, member governments remained divided over exactly how La Francophonie should be organized and what it should do. Canada still favored the loosely organized British Commonwealth model with its wide-ranging agendas, while Québec and France wanted a more tightly organized institution, focused on cultural matters and technical assistance.[76] The leaders of the forty-one governments attending the first summit rejected the Canadian proposal, with the result that the organization was initially inclined to focus on the provision of foreign aid and cultural projects.[77] Indeed, Mitterrand used the first summit to highlight La Francophonie's vital role in the promotion and development of the French language and culture, which seemed increasingly threatened by globalization and the spread of American culture. Since then, La Francophonie has been involved in several projects designed to encourage francophone culture by supporting French language publishers, establishing international competitions for athletes from member states, and promoting francophone music. It also continued to facilitate cultural and academic exchanges.

While Canada has supported these traditional kinds of cultural initiatives, it has been particularly interested in the problematic relationship between the French language and new technologies, many of which are developed with the U.S. market in mind. Sensitive to the overwhelming presence of English-language television in the francophone regions of Canada, Ottawa was quick to throw its support behind proposals to expand TV 5, an international French-language television station with programs from several different countries. Similarly, in 1995, Ottawa, despite some foot-dragging from Paris, pushed La Francophonie to begin promoting the use of French on the Internet. At the same time, La Francophonie has funded the production of francophone databanks and technical lexicons, convinced that the French language must continue to advance in lockstep with new technologies in order to maintain its international status.

As the new organization has become more established, its linguistic interests have expanded to embrace questions of cultural diversity and intercultural dialogue. Once derided as a source of great weakness, the diverse and polyglot populations of the organization's member states have encouraged La Francophonie to incorporate multicultural perspectives into its work and welcome non-francophone partners, particularly from countries where the Romance languages dominate, in its struggle to reduce the cultural dominance of the English language. Appropriately, the theme of La Francophonie's fifth summit, held in 1993 in Grand Baie (Ile Maurice), was "unity in diversity." This multicultural approach has become a potent tool in the international effort, in which both France and Canada play leading roles, to include provisions in multilateral trade agreements to protect minority cultural industries. Both the 1999 Moncton and 2002 Beirut summits discussed this subject in considerable detail, and La Francophonie endorsed a French proposal that members seek a "cultural exception" to international free trade rules that would make it possible to protect cultural products such as films, music, and literature from unfettered competition. Member governments also agreed to establish a pressure group within the United Nations Economic, Social, and Cultural Organization (UNESCO) to promote this position.[78]

In addition to its long-standing role in promoting French culture, La Francophonie has maintained its traditional interest in economic development and foreign aid. From the start, Paris and Ottawa have used foreign assistance to enhance their status within the organization and have seized upon the summits as suitable occasions to announce new initiatives. In 1987, for instance, Canada announced that it would forgive $323 million owed by seven African member states.[79] Not to be outdone, France used the next summit to indicate that it would forgive more than $3 billion in outstanding loans.[80] More substantially, La Francophonie has established several programs to help members share new technologies and production methods in the agricultural and energy sectors. The organization has also continued to push proposals for restructuring international debt and has sponsored some work on sustainable development in order to improve the economies of its poorer member countries. But for many critics, development work hardly justified La Francophonie's existence, although Prime Minister Mulroney argued unconvincingly in 1986 that the summits at least gave him and the other leaders from the developed world an opportunity to meet the people to whom they were sending aid cheques.[81]

The early emphasis on foreign aid created a powerful incentive for poorer countries to join, however tenuous their connection with France and its culture. Moldova, Romania, and Vietnam, for instance, quickly signed up with the new organization, while Poland sought observer status. Already burdened with a narrow and uncertain mandate, the lack of clear membership criteria made it even harder for La Francophonie to develop a clear sense of its own purpose. Lucien Bouchard, Canada's ambassador to Paris from 1985 to 1988, was brutally sceptical. "Francophonie is not a very credible term," he declared in 1987. He added: "What is it? It's a lot of talk, it's a lot of speechmaking, it's nostalgia. The term itself has its folkloristic side."[82] A Canadian government background paper reflected a similar vagueness and defined La Francophonie as the "community of people who speak French or use it to various degrees, either in their own countries or internationally."[83] Even after four summits there was still no clear sense of who should belong. "La Francophonie," French spokesman Daniel Bernard explained in 1991, "is like a club which one joins if one wants."[84]

Ironically, the absence of clear standards for membership, in contrast to the British Commonwealth, where members were expected to adhere (albeit loosely) to some kind of democratic standard, has forced La Francophonie to expand its mandate beyond culture and aid. Early summits came under fierce attack for inviting governments with horrific human rights records. Most of the forty-one states attending the Québec Summit in 1987 were condemned by Amnesty International as consistent human rights violators.[85] Although protesters took to the streets in Québec and elsewhere, La Francophonie was slow to address the issue. Paris opposed any type of sanctions, claiming that they did not work and that they should be left to the United Nations. Though Canadian leaders were sensitive to the charges of human rights abuse, they too were reluctant to jeopardize the new institution by acting precipitously. La Francophonie was still a young organization, Mulroney argued in 1989, and had to approach human rights issues carefully and constructively.[86] Nevertheless, La Francophonie could not ignore popular criticism about its lack of human rights action forever, and the location of the fourth summit was changed from Zaire to France, to meet the demands of Canada and France, which were critical of Zaire's record of human rights abuses.

In November 2000, after debating the subject for almost a decade, La Francophonie adopted the Bamako Declaration as a code of conduct and statement of principles supporting human rights and democracy. The signatories committed themselves to the promotion of the rule of law, the holding of free and fair elections, the maintenance of peaceful political life, the instillation of democratic culture, and respect for human rights. According to the Bamako Declaration, the secretary-general, in coordination with the Permanent Council of La Francophonie (a committee composed of representatives from each member government and chaired by the secretary-general), is expected to monitor the political situation in all member-states and establish a system to provide early warnings of abuse. In the case of a crisis, the secretary-general may send a facilitator to investigate, publicly condemn the violations, or reduce La Francophonie's level of cooperation with that government. The declaration has no real enforcement mechanism, despite Canadian efforts at the 2002 Beirut summit to establish rules and procedures to pressure countries into compliance.

Despite its loose membership requirements and relatively narrow agenda, La Francophonie has developed an elaborate institutional structure to support its mission. In many instances, it was able to build on existing non-governmental organizations devoted to promoting the use of French in a variety of fields. While some, like an international union for francophone journalists, stretched back to the early 1950s, most dated from the 1960s and early 1970s. During those decades, organizations to support French-language universities, francophone parliamentarians, and francophone athletes were successfully established. While francophone countries thus had a well-established tradition of international cooperation, there was no strong central organization to play a broad coordinating role. That changed with the first summit in 1986, which established a committee to begin exploring how to coordinate international cooperation among francophone countries. Sensibly, the committee decided to use the ACCT, established at Niamey in 1971, as La Francophonie's main vehicle for organizational coherence.

While the ACCT gave some structure to the new organization, it was hardly strong enough to impose direction on a group whose institutional links continued to multiply steadily. During the 1987 Québec City summit, member governments agreed to establish a new multilateral university consortium to increase academic interaction among francophones. Cooperation flourished in other fields as well, including the energy sector, where the *Institut de l'énergie des pays ayant en commun l'usage du français* (IEPF) was created in 1987. In 1989, Senghor University was founded in Alexandria, Egypt, as a multilateral project. More ambitious, at the 1991 summit in Paris, which was attended by almost fifty governments, Mulroney proposed that the group set up a small information bureau to help plan free elections and democratic reforms.[87] Increasingly worried that the organization was not able to manage and effectively exploit these growing links in the intervals between summits, member governments decided in December 1995 at the sixth summit in Benin to create the position of secretary-general. The new position would help La Francophonie establish a significant international presence.[88] During the ministerial conference the following year, member governments adopted the *Charte de la Francophonie*, which acted much like a constitution. It defined the organization's objective of promoting cooperation among French-speaking countries in order to encourage their cultural, economic, and political development. The *Charte* reinforced and consolidated the institutional stature of the organization. At the same time, the ACCT was reorganized. Now known as *l'Agence intergouvernementale de la Francophonie,* it was equipped to provide La Francophonie with a strong central organization and secretariat. At the Hanoi summit in November 1997, La Francophonie formalized its new charter and elected the former head of the United Nations, Boutros Boutros-Ghali, as its first secretary-general.[89] There was some controversy over the choice of secretary-general, with France and Canada allied behind Boutros-Ghali in opposition to some of the sub-Saharan states who wanted one of their own. Institutional development has continued apace. In 1998, the organization adopted the current title of *Organisation Internationale de la Francophonie (OIF),* and in 1999, economic and finance ministers began to meet regularly to work out the implementation of summit decisions.[90]

CONCLUSION

This chapter has reviewed some of the key components of Canada's involvement in La Francophonie since the notion of an international organization of French-speaking countries was first raised in the early 1960s. From the start, Ottawa welcomed the notion of La Francophonie.

Strengthening ties with the world's French-speaking countries was seen as an important part of the federal government's efforts to project Canadian biculturalism abroad. Moreover, such ties reflected the multilateralism that had characterized Canada's foreign policy since World War II and provided a welcome forum where Canada could escape the ambiguous embrace of its American neighbor and pursue its own diplomatic initiatives. But progress toward this goal was difficult. Successive Québec governments, supported by France's president Charles de Gaulle and his successors, demanded membership in the organization, which they saw as a step toward the development of a distinct international persona for Québec. The federal government naturally opposed this challenge to its jurisdiction over Canada's foreign policy, and part of Ottawa's commitment to La Francophonie is rooted in its reluctance to leave Québec alone on this stage. The resulting deadlock persisted until 1971, when Ottawa, Québec City, and Paris finally agreed to create the ACCT and La Francophonie took its first small steps on the world stage.

Since the early 1970s, La Francophonie and Canada's commitment to it have grown significantly. With the inauguration of La Francophonie summits in 1986—a long-delayed objective that was made possible by another lengthy series of tough negotiations between Ottawa, Paris, and Québec City—the organization has begun to take on a more substantial international role. Despite some early doubts about its legitimacy, La Francophonie has continued to survive. Indeed, by embracing a multicultural approach to linguistic and cultural issues, it has successfully transformed the early ambiguity about who qualified for membership into a source of political strength. At the same time, the organization has broadened its agenda to include human rights issues and democratic development. These steps have been supported by the growth of more elaborate institutional arrangements, culminating in the appointment of a permanent secretary-general in 1998. Canada welcomed these developments, which reflected many of the liberal and multilateral values at the core of its foreign policy. But just as important, the recent maturation of La Francophonie has made it easier for Canada to project its bilingual and bicultural character on the world stage, a vital consideration for a country whose continued survival depends on its ability to nurture the ties that bind French and English Canada together.

NOTES

1. The views expressed in this chapter are the authors' alone and do not reflect the policies of the Government of Canada or Foreign Affairs Canada. Research was supported by a 2004 Faculty Research Grant from St. Bonaventure University. The authors would like to thank the Canadian Institute of International Affairs for their help with this project. In addition, SUNY Plattsburgh's Québec Summer Seminar provided useful insights for this project.

2. "A Lesson in Diplomacy for Lucien Bouchard," *Financial Post,* 12 September 1998, 18; "Boutros-Ghali's Visit to Canada Sparks Controversy in Québec," *Agence France-Presse,* 9 September 1998.

3. Marus Gee, "Fading Influence of French Dulls Event's Lustre," *Globe and Mail* (Toronto), 30 August 1999, A3.

4. David Ljunggren, "Canada, France in Vague Call for Better Human Rights," *Reuters News,* 3 September 1999.

5. Anne McIlroy, "PM Says He's Pushed for Changes to La Francophonie's Rights Rules," *Globe and Mail*, 4 September 1999, A4.

6. John Hilliker and Donald Barry, *Canada's Department of External Affairs, Volume II: Coming of Age, 1946–1968* (Kingston and Montreal: McGill-Queen's University Press, 1995), 391.

7. Quoted in Hilliker and Barry, *Canada's Department of External Affairs*, 391–92. See also Dale Thomson, *Vive le Québec Libre* (Toronto: Deneau, 1988), 106.

8. Greg Donaghy, "Domesticating NATO: Canada and the North Atlantic Alliance, 1963–68," *International Journal* 52, no. 3 (Summer 1997): 445–64.

9. "Visit of President Senghor: 'La Francophonie'—September 19–21," 13 September 1966, DFAIT File 26–1, National Archives of Canada [NAC].

10. "Visit of President Senghor: 'La Francophonie'—September 19–21," 13 September 1966, DFAIT File 26–1, National Archives of Canada [NAC].

11. Paul Martin, "Draft Memorandum for the Prime Minister," 6 March 1967, and A. E. Gotlieb, "Direction juridique à la direction d'Europe: Visite du Général de Gaulle—Notes et sujets d'entretien: La Francophonie," 17 July 1967, DFAIT File 26–1, NAC.

12. John English, *The Worldly Years: The Life of Lester B. Pearson, Volume 2, 1949–72* (Toronto: Alfred A. Knopf Canada, 1992), 342–43.

13. Robert Bothwell and J. L. Granatstein, *Pirouette: Pierre Trudeau and Canadian Foreign Policy* (Toronto: University of Toronto Press, 1990), 119; Eldon Black, *Direct Intervention: Canada-France Relations 1967–1974* (Kingston and Montreal: McGill-Queen's University Press, 1996), 12–13.

14. Marotte, *Globe and Mail*, 29 August 1987.

15. Marotte, *Globe and Mail*, 29 August 1987. Cited in George Radwanski, *Trudeau* (Macmillan: Toronto, 1978), 110.

16. Black, *Direct Intervention*, 34–37.

17. Bothwell and Granatstein, *Pirouette*, 138.

18. Paul Martin, *A Very Public Life, Volume 11: So Many Worlds* (Markham, ON: Deneau Publishing, 1985), 664–65.

19. Ivan Head and Pierre Trudeau, *The Canadian Way: Shaping Canada's Foreign Policy, 1968–1984* (Toronto: McClelland and Stewart, 1995), 289; Bothwell and Granatstein, *Pirouette*, 138–39; Black, *Direct Intervention*, 86–87.

20. Bothwell and Granatstein, *Pirouette*, 143–44.

21. Black, *Direct Intervention*, 90–91.

22. Valerie Lawton, "Trudeau Warned France to Butt Out—Threatened to Cut Ties if It Supported Québec in Talks," *Toronto Star*, 24 April 2001, A-07.

23. Black, *Direct Intervention*, 141. New Brunswick also joined as a participating government in 1977.

24. Bothwell and Granatstein, *Pirouette*, 153–54.

25. Luc Bernier, "Mulroney's International 'Beau Risque': The Golden Age of Québec's Foreign Policy," in *Diplomatic Departures: The Conservative Era in Canadian Foreign Policy, 1984–93*, ed. Nelson Michaud and Kim Richard Nossal (Vancouver: University of British Columbia Press, 2001), 136. Budget figures contained in Flora MacDonald, "Note au Premier Ministre," July 1979, DFAIT File 26–2-Canada, NAC. Canada was responsible for 35 percent of the budget divided between Ottawa (31.7%), Québec (3%), and New Brunswick (0.3%).

26. For descriptions of Canadian policy in the 1970s, see "Voyage de M. Le Ministre Chrétien au Maghreb: La Francophonie," 23 August 1977; see also Flora MacDonald, "Note au Premier Ministre," July 1979, DFAIT File 26–2-Canada, NAC.

27. Head and Trudeau, *The Canadian Way*, 290.

28. A. J. MacEachen, "Note au Premier Ministre," 30 July 1975 and Trudeau's marginalia, DFAIT File 26–1, NAC. Our translation.

29. E. P. Black, "Note à FCP," 5 June 1975, DFAIT File 26–1, NAC.

30. A. J. MacEachen, "Note au Premier Ministre," 30 July 1975 and Trudeau's marginalia, DFAIT File 26–1, NAC.

31. Mary MacDonald to Tony Malone, 14 August 1975, DFAIT File 26–1, NAC.

32. Paris to Ottawa, Telegram 2578, 25 June 1976, DFAIT File 26–4-Sommet, NAC.

33. H. B. Robinson, "Memorandum for the Minister," 9 December 1976, DFAIT File 26–4-Sommet, NAC.

34. Don Jamieson, "Note pour le Premier Ministre," 30 March 1977 and Ottawa to Dakar, Telegram FCF-0236, 5 April 1977, DFAIT File 26–1, NAC.

35. Dakar to Ottawa, Telegram 695, 12 April 1977 and Ottawa to Dakar, Telegram FCF-251, 14 April 1977, DFAIT File 26–1, NAC.

36. "Voyage de M. le Ministre J. P. Goyer en Afrique, juin 1977," 24 May 1977, DFAIT File 26–2-Canada, NAC.

37. Don Jamieson, "Note au Premier Ministre," 30 September 1977, DFAIT File 26–1, NAC.

38. *Le Devoir* (Montréal), 10 novembre 1977.

39. A. E. Gotlieb, "Memorandum for the Minister," 23 November 1977, DFAIT File 26–4-Sommet, NAC.

40. Ottawa to Dakar, Telegram FCF-60, 5 January 1979, DFAIT File 26–4-Sommet, NAC. Our translation.

41. Joe Clark's government was trying to develop a more flexible attitude to Québec's place in La Francophonie when it was defeated. See Flora Macdonald,

"Memorandum for the Prime Minister," 10 December 1979, DFAIT File 26–4-Sommet, NAC.

42. Mark McGuigan, "Note pour le Premier Ministre," 30 May 1980, DFAIT File 26–4-Sommet, NAC.

43. A. E. Gotlieb, "Memoire au Ministre," 15 July 1980, DFAIT File 26–4-Sommet, NAC.

44. Mark MacGuigan, "Memoire au Premier Ministre," 5 September 1980, DFAIT File 26–4-Sommet, NAC.

45. A. E. Gotlieb, "Memoire au Ministre," 9 October 1980 and Mark MacGuigan, "Note pour le Premier Ministre," 20 October 1980, DFAIT File 26–4-Sommet, NAC.

46. A. E. Gotlieb, "Memoire au Ministre," 9 October 1980 and Mark MacGuigan, "Note pour le Premier Ministre," 20 October 1980, DFAIT File 26–4-Sommet, NAC.

47. A. E. Gotlieb, "Memoire au Ministre," 17 November 1980, DFAIT File 26–4-Sommet, NAC.

48. Paris to Ottawa, Telegram 5569, 29 October 1980, DFAIT File 26–4-Sommet, NAC. Our translation.

49. De Montigny Marchand, "Note for Monsieur Fowler," 13 November 1980, DFAIT File 26–4-Sommet, NAC. Our translation.

50. De Montigny Marchand, "Note for Monsieur Fowler," 13 November 1980, DFAIT File 26–4-Sommet, NAC.

51. De Montigny Marchand, "Note for Monsieur Fowler," 13 November 1980, DFAIT File 26–4-Sommet, NAC. See also A. E. Gotlieb, "Memoire au Ministre," le 17 novembre 1980, DFAIT File 26–4-Sommet, NAC.

52. De Montigny Marchand, "Note for Monsieur Fowler," 13 November 1980, DFAIT File 26–4-Sommet, NAC.

53. Ottawa to Paris, Telegram MDG-90, 18 November 1980, DFAIT File 26–4-Sommet, NAC.

54. Paris to Ottawa, Telegram 6137, 28 November 1980, DFAIT File 26–4-Sommet, NAC.

55. R. B. Byers, ed., *Canadian Annual Review for 1982* (Toronto: University of Toronto Press, 1984), 165. See also, Head and Trudeau, *The Canadian Way*, 291–92; Paris to Ottawa, Telegram 3802, 8 December 1982, DFAIT File 26–4-Sommet, NAC.

56. Ottawa to Paris, Telegram 3839, 14 December 1982. See also, A. J. MacEachen, "Memoire au Premier Ministre," 7 January 1983, DFAIT File 26–4-Sommet, NAC.

57. Canada's initial interest was reflected in A. J. MacEachen, "Memoire au

Premier Ministre," 7 January 1983, DFAIT File 26-4-Sommet, NAC; for growing hesitations, see De Montigny Marchand, "Memoire au Vice-Premier Ministre et SEAE," 21 janvier 1982, DFAIT File 26-4-Sommet, NAC.

58. Ottawa to Paris, Telegram CMF-0094, 31 January 1983, DFAIT File 26-4-Sommet, NAC. Our translation.

59. A. J. MacEachen, "Memoire au Premier Ministre," 3 March 1983. DFAIT File 26-4-Sommet, NAC. Our translation.

60. "Note de Paris," 12 April 1983, DFAIT File 26-4-Sommet, NAC. Our translation.

61. Robert Fowler, "Day 3: Meeting between Prime Minister Trudeau and President François Mitterrand on May 30," DFAIT File 26-4-Sommet, NAC.

62. Michael Shenstone to De Montigny Marchand, 15 September 1983, DFAIT File 26-4-Sommet, NAC.

63. Cited in R. B. Byers, ed., *Canadian Annual Review for 1984* (Toronto: University of Toronto Press, 1986), 241.

64. Marcel Massé, "Memorandum for the Secretary of State for External Affairs," No. SFD-111, 20 November 1984 and Joe Clark, "Memoire au Premier Ministre," 29 November 1984, DFAIT File 26-4-Sommet, NAC.

65. Marcel Massé, "Memoire au Dossier," 30 December 1984, DFAIT File 26-4-Sommet, NAC.

66. Joe Clark, Draft Memorandum for the Prime Minister, March 1985, DFAIT File 26-4-Sommet, NAC.

67. Joe Clark, "Memoire au Premier Ministre," 4 July 1985, DFAIT File 26-4-Sommet, NAC.

68. Joe Clark, "Memoire au Premier Ministre," 4 July 1985, DFAIT File 26-4-Sommet, NAC.

69. Lawrence Martin, *The Antagonist: Lucien Bouchard and the Politics of Delusion* (Toronto: Viking, 1997), 108.

70. Lucien Bouchard (translated by Dominique Clift), *Lucien Bouchard: On the Record* (Toronto: Stoddart, 1994), 125.

71. Bernard Roy, "Mémoire au Premier Ministre," 9 October 1985, DFAIT File 26-4-Sommet, NAC.

72. Quoted in Graham Fraser, "Paris Summit Ends as Leaders Agree to Meet in Québec," *Globe and Mail*, 20 February 1986, A13.

73. Graham Fraser, "Paris Summit a Lesson in Political Subtleties at Home," *Globe and Mail*, 22 February 1986, A8.

74. Patrick Doyle, "Senegal Talks a Quiet Victory for PM: Budget Furor Obscured Achievement at Francophone Meeting," *Toronto Star*, 27 May 1989, A8.

75. Graham Fraser, "Paris Summit Ends as Leaders Agree to Meet in Québec," *Globe and Mail*, 20 February 1986, A13.

76. Jeffrey Simpson, "In Search of a Shape,"*Globe and Mail*, 19 February, 1986, A6.

77. Stanley Meisler, "French-Speaking Nations Decide Against Commonwealth-Style Ties," *Los Angeles Times*, 20 February 1986, 24.

78. Elizabeth Thompson, "Militant Group Causes Stir at Summit: Canada Unhappy with Presence of Hezbollah," *Edmonton Journal*, 20 October 2002, A4. See also Jody Nethery-Castro and Marc Rousseau, "Québec, Francophonie, and Globalization," *Québec Studies* 32 (Fall 2001/Winter 2002): 15–35. On the fate of this initiative, see Stephen Azzi, "Negotiating Cultural Space in the Global Economy: The United States, UNESCO, and the Convention on Cultural Diversity," *International Journal* 60 no. 3, (summer 2005): 765–84.

79. Robert McKenzie, "PM Predicts Powerful Francophone Role for Canada," *Toronto Star*, 5 September 1987, A3.

80. Patrick Doyle, "Senegal Talks a Quiet Victory for PM: Budget Furor Obscured Achievement at Francophone Meeting," *Toronto Star*, A8.

81. Graham Fraser, "Paris Summit a Lesson in Political Subtleties at Home," *Globe and Mail*, 22 February 1986, A8.

82. Bertrand Marotte, "Organizer of Francophone Summit Anxious to Avoid Treading on Toes," *Globe and Mail*, 14 August 1987, A9.

83. "The Anatomy of La Francophonie," *Globe and Mail*, 25 May 1989, A6.

84. Nicholas Kotch, "French-Speaking Summit Ends Still Undecided on Its Role," *Reuters News*, 21 November 1991.

85. "Speaking the Same Language," *Globe and Mail*, 1 September 1987, A6.

86. See, for example, Graham Fraser, "Francophone Summit Officials Finally Agree to Air Human Rights," *Globe and Mail*, 24 May 1989, A8; John Stackhouse, "Summit Dilutes Rights Position: Canada Criticized for 'Selective' Stand," *Globe and Mail*, 4 December 1995, A10; Edison Stewart, "Nations Ignoring Human Rights Will Feel Heat at Summit, PM Says—La Francophonie to Condemn 'Horrific Crimes,'" *Toronto Star*, 2 September 1999, 1.

87. Canadian Press, "Mulroney to Press Rights Campaign: PM Plans Course of Action for French-Speaking Summit Next Week in Paris," *Globe and Mail*, 13 November 1991, A6.

88. John Stackhouse, "Canada, Allies Differ on Rights: Progress Made, Chrétien Tells Summit, but Chirac Skeptical," *Globe and Mail*, 5 December 1995, A16.

89. Tu Thanh Ha, "Francophonie Still at Rights Impasse: Former UN Secretary-General Boutros Boutros-Ghali Appointed Group's Spokesman," *Globe and Mail*, 17 November, 1997, A11.

90. "Canada Proposes a Series of Initiatives to the Francophonie Economic and Finance Ministers at Their Conference in Monaco," *Canada News Wire*, 15.

7

Lending Forces: Canada's Military Peacekeeping

Kimberly Marten

Ottawa has repeatedly sent Canadian military troops to serve on peacekeeping missions, both under United Nations command and under the command of regional organizations such as the North Atlantic Treaty Organization (NATO) with U.N. Security Council authorization. Its role as a peacekeeper is a reflection of Canada's tradition of Pearsonian internationalism in foreign policy, discussed more below, and also served as one of the launching points for Canada's embracing of human security issues in the 1990s. It places Canada within a select group of regular troop-lending countries. Many states have been reluctant to contribute their armed forces to U.N. missions, which leave them under the ultimate command of a foreigner (often, one with whom their states have no alliance), deployed to locations where often no direct national interest is at stake, and put them in situations where they are likely to encounter danger and hardship and suffer casualties.

Peacekeeping has changed over the years. When Canada first became a regular troop donor in the late 1950s, it was to traditional blue-helmet missions under U.N. command. States in these missions would be asked to contribute military units to the mission by the U.N. secretary-general, and were tasked with being impartial toward the parties to the conflict (usually sovereign states that had signed a cease-fire). The goal of troops then was to build confidence between the conflicting parties that the cease-fire would actually hold, so they concentrated on monitoring and reporting the activity they witnessed on the ground, and on serving as a neutral buffer between potentially warring parties. More recently, Canada has become a major troop donor to missions that are authorized by the U.N. Security Council but led by the NATO or individual states such as the United States or Australia. These newer missions have been deployed to areas destroyed by civil war, where often some of the parties to the conflict do not welcome the peacekeeping deployment, and where consequently the tasks involved are much harder and riskier—e.g., riot control, stopping the smuggling of guns over borders, and protecting returning ethnic minorities from the actions of those who wish to harm them. Canada is one of the few states to have easily navigated this gap between traditional peacekeeping roles and more complex peace enforcement roles. Several other member states of the United Nations have approached these changing roles with hesitancy, for example, by holding to the notion of U.N. impartiality even when civilians on the ground face cruel violence from some of the parties to the conflicts.

Why did Canada decide to become a troop lender over time, and why did it remain so in the 1990s and into the twenty-first century as U.N. missions became messier, more costly, and more dangerous? This question is especially puzzling as Canada now faces the problem of trying to maintain its reputation as a peacekeeper with a constrained national military budget, amid frequent accusations of inadequate equipment for its troops in the field. (Elsewhere in this volume, Canada's neglect of its military capabilities is discussed by Andrew Richter.) In August, Ottawa was criticized by both the United States and U.N. Secretary-General Kofi Annan for its decision to withdraw most of its troops on schedule from Afghanistan in August 2004, even as the security situation there became more fragile in the face of upcoming presidential elections.[1] While around seven hundred Canadian armored reconnaissance squad troops would remain in the country, Prime Minister Paul Martin refused to extend the stay of the rest of Ottawa's 2,000-soldier presence that had been leading the ISAF peace mission in Kabul so well since February 2004. Martin reversed himself, however, and in February 2006, two thousand Canadians were scheduled to serve in Afghanistan, a commitment the newly elected Conservative government of Stephen Harper would surely not curtail given its commitment to the reinvigoration of Canada's military. Many studies have been done that raise dozens of possible explanations for the decision to lend troops.[2] Rather than merely repeat those findings, this chapter examines two common explanations for Canada's decisions and adds a third possibility to the mix.

The two most common explanations given in the existing literature for Canada's peacekeeping choices are as follows. First, from the point of view of realist analysts of international relations, Canada is a so-called middle power. Realism is the oldest and perhaps still most common view of how the international system operates, especially among policy makers themselves.[3] From this perspective, all nation-states are primarily interested in retaining or increasing their power and influence relative to other states, in order to ensure their own well-being in a world where trusting the good intentions of the powerful can be dangerous. A number of scholars argue that all medium-size states face the same set of incentives and constraints in the international system. Although not rich or powerful enough to exercise much influence on their own, these states have found peacekeeping to be a niche that brings them greater authority in international institutions, allowing them to exercise a voice in international security issues.[4] Peacekeeping is thus a tool to be used by so-called realists, who wish to influence international outcomes but lack the power to gain such influence any other way. In Canada's case, peacekeeping gives Ottawa a lever in the United Nations that can be used to constrain the United States. Second, it has been argued that some states have an ingrained national culture that is oriented toward resolving conflict peacefully and being generally helpful. From this perspective, such countries have a sense of obligation to the outside world to share their resources on behalf of peace and are particularly eager to distinguish their state's behavior from the more aggressive and militaristic actions taken by some of the great powers.[5] A form of strategic culture, validated by both the uniformed military and the general public,[6] thereby impels leaders of these states to choose the peacekeeping burden. Peacekeeping is natural and appropriate, and it would be unthinkable (as well as politically untenable) for state leaders to refuse this role.

The primary argument of this chapter is that while the middle power thesis and the strategic culture argument have merit, both provide only partial truths in the Canadian case. For a full understanding of Canada's choices, one needs to look at the complex interactions of domestic party and bureaucratic politics as well. The engine for Canada's decision over the years to repeatedly be a troop-lender has been a long-standing, internal organizational culture at Foreign Affairs Canada (FAC), formerly known as the Department of Foreign Affairs and International Trade (DFAIT). This bureaucratic culture is traceable to the impact of a powerful individual who set the course of this organization in the 1950s, Lester B. Pearson. The end of the Cold War introduced the possibility of change into this ministerial culture, but change has been slow and bumpy. External affairs minister Lloyd Axworthy, along with other politicians in the late 1990s, attempted to revolutionize DFAIT from above, using structural change and budgetary stringency to alter the legacy of Lester Pearson inside the organization. Axworthy's goal in particular was to change the focus of Canada's international peace operations efforts toward civilian tasks, so that military budgets could be cut, bringing a post–Cold War peace dividend to Canada's social programs. Yet new external pressures coming from the increasingly dangerous international environment, coupled with demands from NATO that Canada pull its share in alliance peacekeeping operations in the Balkans and Afghanistan, as well as growing U.S. unilateralism and the Canadian desire to distinguish itself from its superpower neighbor to the south, meant that there were limits to how workable this solution could be.

Over the last few years, FAC has reached out more to the uniformed Canadian Forces (C.F.), as it became clear that Canadian military troops were needed on the complex new allied missions arising in the Balkans and Afghanistan. The traditional peacekeeping culture in Canada, which saw the peacekeepers as being the impartial blue-helmeted troops of past years, is being altered to give more weight to war-fighting skills, and FAC has learned the importance of partnering with those in uniform. One example of this is the current use of Canadian troops to help U.S. forces train the new Afghan National Army, a task that is central to the overall goal of the international community in gaining stability in the country. According to Kabul contingent commander Colonel Alain Tremblay, "It took us six to eight months to . . . convince Ottawa of the strategic value and return investment of getting into that initiative."[7] But the uniformed military forces still feel overburdened and underappreciated and have a tendency to blame the lasting effects of the Liberal Party cabinets of Prime Minister Jean Chrétien, in office from 1993 through the end of 2003. Efforts by new Prime Minister Harper to seek more common security interests with the United States[8] may help the C.F. change their current circumstances.

The dominant explanations for Canadian troop-lending behavior are inadequate because they fail to take these important domestic political circumstances into account. Canada's broader national culture that supports internationalism is a permissive, rather than causal, factor in the decision to lend troops. Questions of foreign or defense policy do not motivate the voting public sufficiently to pressure state leaders to take particular decisions. And while the officers sent on peacekeeping missions value the experience quite highly, the Department of National Defence (DND) and the uniformed military as a whole are ambivalent about the expenditure of resources that peacekeeping entails, and consider peacekeeping a secondary priority after territorial defense. This gives political and bureaucratic leaders in Ottawa an opportunity to exercise significant sway over individual policy decisions. As for Canada's middle-power status, while it helps impel FAC toward United Nations activism, other more specific conditions of alliance, especially relations with the United States and NATO, have been necessary components of individual troop-lending decisions. In other words, it is not merely that Canada is a middle power that matters; instead it is Canada's unique location within NATO and in relation to the United States that matters, because of the pressures they exert on Canada's foreign and military policy bureaucracies.

CULTURE AND PUBLIC OPINION

Canadians are taught from an early age that peacekeeping is the Canadian way. When anyone in the Canadian policy elite is asked why Canada chooses to be a peacekeeper, invariably the first answer given is that it is a part of Canadian culture and distinctiveness, especially because it sets Canada apart from the more heavy-handed military policies of the United States.[9] When coupled with the fact that polling data repeatedly show broad support among Canadian citizens for sending troops on peacekeeping missions,[10] this in itself may be enough to support the argument that a national strategic culture of peacekeeping is in place.

However, three anomalies indicate that national culture is not a sufficient explanation for Canadian peacekeeping decisions. First, not all Canadian leaders have supported peacekeeping with equal enthusiasm. Prime Minister Pierre Trudeau stands out as an example of someone who wished to decrease the Canadian obligation to take care of the outside world.[11] His foreign minister, Mitchell Sharp, is famous for criticizing the notion that Canada should be "cast as the 'helpful fixer' in international affairs," and for arguing that "to be liked and to be regarded as good fellows are not ends in themselves."[12] This tendency of withdrawal from an activist military peacekeeping role reemerged in the late 1990s government of Chrétien, whose defense minister at that time, Art Eggleton, stressed the importance of putting basic Canadian defense needs ahead of peacekeeping commitments in an era when sharply lowered resources were available to the military institution.[13]

Second, Canadian leaders have not said yes to every request from the U.N.[14] In the many cases where Canada has agreed to send troops on U.N. missions, it has not necessarily sent the size of contingent that the U.N. wanted.[15] By the late 1990s Canadian participation in blue-helmet operations sometimes became almost symbolic as a result, with a few officer-observers or support personnel scattered among many peacekeeping operations as Canada concentrated on contributing to the more difficult NATO-led missions instead.[16] In fact, Canada has sometimes refused requests to renew its troop commitments in the midst of ongoing U.N. missions, for example by withdrawing from Cyprus in 1993 after participating in the U.N. mission there for almost thirty years.[17] (Indeed, it also withdrew from the NATO-led Kosovo mission in early 2000, with the goal of concentrating on NATO's Bosnian mission instead, given Ottawa's limited defense resources.)

Third, in recent years Canadian defense resources have been stretched almost to the breaking point, and yet the Canadian public has not demanded that additional budgetary resources be devoted to improving Canadian peacekeeping capability. Especially because of Canadian participation in NATO peace operations under U.N. authorization in Bosnia and Kosovo, in the U.S.-led coalition forces in Operation Enduring Freedom in Afghanistan, and more recently in the NATO-led phase of the U.N.-authorized International Security Assistance Force (ISAF) in Kabul, the C.F. are almost constantly cycling in and out of foreign deployments for six-month periods. As it became clear that the Canadian public desired a post–Cold War peace dividend, with budgetary resources targeted toward health care and social welfare rather than defense, Canadian force levels have been severely cut.[18] As a result, the reserve forces have become an important source for Canadian foreign deployments.[19] The unfortunate outcome of this combination by the late 1990s was a raft of social and morale problems in the Canadian military, ranging from increasing divorce rates to suicides, associated with the stress of constant relocation and a high tempo of dangerous and traumatic operations abroad.[20] If peacekeeping were truly an ingrained symbolic priority in Canada, then the citizenry should want to give more resources to the military to ensure that the job can be performed well. By 1999 the Canadian government budget was in surplus. After very strong pressure from then Defence Minister Eggleton, a $1.9 billion (Canadian) increase spread over four years was added to the Department of National Defence (DND) budget.[21] However, this was only a fraction of what Eggleton wanted and paled in comparison to Canada's tax cuts and social spending increases. The C.F. continue to see the budgets promised to them as being stopgap measures at best,[22] and were alarmed when Eggleton's replacement, John McCallum, offered to shave $200 million from the DND 2003/4 fiscal budget, suggesting that he could do this by increasing efficiency.[23]

Indeed, while no one really objects to the peacekeeping role in Canada, it has never been an issue that has motivated voters, who (like voters everywhere) tend to be more concerned about their pocketbooks.[24] In recent years the military has become a relatively unpopular institution in Canada, and military involvement abroad has lost its cachet, at least in part because the scandalous and criminal behavior of a few soldiers and officers in the Canadian peacekeeping contingent in Somalia ended up tarring the entire Canadian Forces in the minds of the public.[25] In March 1993, a thief who broke into a C.F. encampment in the Somali desert was tortured to death as punishment by a few apparently drunken Canadian soldiers from the Canadian Airborne Regiment (CAR) who shouted racial epitaphs as they beat him. The resulting public investigation and outcry in Canada led to the disbanding of the entire CAR regiment, as well as stinging criticism of Canadian peacekeeper training, discipline, and leadership. Ottawa's initial reaction to those events was widely seen by the public to entail a cover-up; its ultimate decision to disband the CAR was seen by the uniformed military as an unwarranted overreaction that unfairly tarred the C.F. as a whole in the public mind for the misjudgments of a few.

Certainly there is no evidence to suggest that public opinion would turn against an otherwise popular government that declined a troop-lending request from the U.N. or NATO. National culture is an enabling factor in the Canadian case as it protects the government from criticism when it chooses to send troops on missions, but culture does not appear to be the primary motivation of the peacekeeping decision. In fact there is not a great deal of public political discussion about individual Canadian peacekeeping decisions. While the Prime Minister and his Cabinet often consult the House of Commons as a deployment is being made, Parliament is unlikely to be informed by the government about any U.N. requests that the Prime Minister decides to turn down. Formal parliamentary votes on peacekeeping decisions are rare, and the "consultations" between the ruling government and the Parliament have often occurred after the government has already made its decision to accept a U.N. request, leaving Parliament no real say in the issue.[26] Since the executive needs the support of the majority in the House of Commons, a formal vote would furthermore merely reaffirm the policy of the ruling party or (on relatively rare occasions) coalition.[27] For example, in 1995 there was an emergency debate in the House of Commons because Canadian troops were coming under repeated violent attack in Bosnia. Although the official Opposition led by the Reform Party called for a unilateral withdrawal of Canadian troops, no withdrawal occurred.[28]

PEACEKEEPING IN CANADA: FAC AND MIDDLE-POWER DIPLOMACY

Although peacekeeping operations are largely military in nature and the role the Department of National Defence plays should not be neglected, it is important to understand the aspects that also involve diplomatic channels. Such an arrangement offers a fertile ground for bureaucratic politics and provides the student of these policymaking processes a lot of material to take into consideration. Usually it is the Canadian foreign ministry, FAC, that officially takes the lead role in advising the government when a peacekeeping request is received from the U.N. Secretariat or another diplomatic source such as NATO.[29]

While it is unclear from press reports what role FAC has played in more recent decisions, questions of diplomacy were apparently what drove Chrétien to agree to send C.F. troops into the NATO peacekeeping mission in Afghanistan in 2003, and his government was widely criticized by the uniformed military for not consulting with them adequately about the resources they had available for that mission.[30] One top officer, Maj. Gen. Cameron Ross, the DND official in charge of international security policy, resigned in disgust when the decision was announced, believing it would place the equipment-strapped forces, especially medical support teams, into too much danger.[31] It was widely perceived in the press that Chrétien's decision was made in order to avoid sending Canadian troops to Iraq—a deployment that the C.F. would have welcomed as an opportunity to show off its strengths, but that Chrétien avoided because it lacked U.N. approval.

While the Cabinet and the Prime Minister's Office ultimately decide which policy to pursue, it is widely perceived in Ottawa that the advice of the FAC bureaucracy usually prevails. FAC's primary concern is to ensure that the operation is compatible with Canada's overall foreign policy strategy at both a bilateral and multilateral level.[32] In practice, FAC has had three primary concerns as it faces individual peacekeeping request decisions.

First, FAC has wanted to ensure that Canada maintains a good reputation inside the United Nations. FAC is reluctant to say "no" to any U.N. request, whether for an initial troop contribution to a mission, or for maintaining Canadian troops or commanders on-site once an operation is under way.[33] A 1996 study by the Auditor General (AG) of Canada (an officer of the House of Commons independent from the government)[34] in fact criticized FAC for not informing the Cabinet sufficiently about how particular troop contributions would serve Canada's direct national interests.[35] This same focus on the importance of the U.N. as an institution has clearly continued to have an impact on Canadian government decisions regarding military deployments, as Canada has sided with those in the U.N. Security Council like France and Germany who objected to U.S. unilateralism in Iraq.

FAC's assumption that U.N. activism furthers Canadian interests can be traced to the influence of Lester B. Pearson, whose view of Canada's international role focused on its status as a middle power and its use of multilateralism in the U.N. context to further its impact in world affairs.[36] A career diplomat who was involved in United Nations activities from its founding, Pearson served as Minister of External Affairs in the Liberal government between 1948 and 1957, and later became Prime Minister. He is credited with inventing the concept of U.N. peacekeeping in order to respond to the Suez Crisis of 1956, for which he won the Nobel Peace Prize. Pearson volunteered a Canadian army battalion[37] to intercede between the forces involved in the crisis and monitor the withdrawal of the British and French from Egypt. In his memoirs, Pearson capitalized the words "Middle Power" to describe his view of Canada's role in international politics.[38] He believed that participation in U.N. activities would gain Canada influence and respect.[39]

Second, and again continuing in the path of Pearson's worldview, FAC has used peacekeeping policy as a way of simultaneously pleasing its American neighbor to the south while distancing Canada from the more assertive military policies of the United States. Pearson believed that worry about the United States gaining too much influence over Canada was something that acted as a "unifying force" for Canadians.[40] He thought Canada's relationship with the United States provided its strongest guarantee of security from outside military threat, but that Canada must be careful not to become "an echo of another's voice."[41]

Canadian officials believe that through its United Nations peacekeeping activity, Canada has distinguished its own policy stances from those of the United States, while simultaneously serving the interests of its American and NATO allies. Canada often volunteered troops to U.N. missions at least in part because the United States asked it to do so,[42] starting with Prime Minister Pearson's contribution of units from the C.F. to the Cyprus mission in 1964.[43] During the Cold War, policy-makers argued that Canada would be in the direct path of any nuclear missiles launched by either the United States or the Soviet Union at the other, and spoke of peacekeeping as a means for dampening tensions in areas of the world that might otherwise explode into superpower confrontation.[44] More recently, participation in multilateral, U.N.-authorized peacekeeping missions has been a way to distance Ottawa from American unilateralism, while helping cement a continuing role for NATO after the end of the Cold War. Canadian diplomats have seen peacekeeping as a means for Canada to fulfill its NATO obligations in spite of the fact that C.F. contributions to NATO have left its allies unsatisfied.[45] (Canada's defense spending as a percentage of GNP has been among the very lowest of the NATO members since the early 1970s, even though it is a relatively wealthy country which could arguably afford to spend more on defense burden-sharing.) Canada has been especially concerned to maintain NATO relevance as talk has proceeded about giving the European Union an independent defense arm; if the E.U. were to spawn a strong and effective defense policy that competed with NATO for influence, Canada might be stuck alone next to an increasingly unilateralist United States.

Beyond these first two focuses on relations with the U.N. and on those with NATO and the U.S., FAC in recent decades has also wanted to strengthen Canada's membership in La Francophonie,[46] an organization well described in this volume's chapter 6 by Donaghy and Carter. La Francophonie has held biennial summits since 1986, and now includes 55 members. At least in part Canada's strategy toward La Francophonie is driven by a domestic political desire to satisfy the citizens of Quebec. The Bloc Québécois in the House of Commons would tend (at least by intuition) to favor international intervention and peacekeeping when it is done to protect the security of francophones abroad, in countries such as the Central African Republic and Haiti. This domestic interest cannot be traced to Pearson's time in office; separatism did not become a major issue in Quebec until the 1970s. Nonetheless, support for La Francophonie is part of the consistent FAC strategy of building multilateral support in international institutions which are able to challenge the hegemony of the great powers—a major component of Pearson's approach to foreign policy.

Given these FAC priorities, the cases where the department has argued against sending the C.F. on particular U.N. missions are few.[47] However, the refusals tend to follow a pattern: a "no" answer is given in order to keep Canada's key bilateral commitments in primary focus, without bowing to U.S. pressure. For example, FAC successfully argued in the mid-1990s that Canada should refuse requests to send Canadian military observers on U.N. Chapter 6[48] missions to Tajikistan and Georgia. FAC believed that these missions had the potential to unnecessarily antagonize Russia, with whom Canada desired better relations in both defense and trade issues following the Cold War. In earlier years, FAC also successfully argued that Canada should refuse a request to send a battalion to the UNIFIL peacekeeping mission in the Israeli-occupied security zone in Lebanon. FAC wished to distance itself from U.S. support for Israel and emphasize its respect for recognized sovereignty—a goal which given the troubled history of Israeli relations with the U.N. General Assembly (known throughout the Cold War era as being pro-Arab on many issues) is consistent with Canada's overall multilateralist strategy.[49]

PEACEKEEPING IN CANADA: DND AND THE MILITARY PERSPECTIVE

Due to the use of diplomatic rather than security/military channels to call for Canada's participation in peacekeeping operations, DND officials often argue that FAC imposes its views on matters of peacekeeping.[50] However, it is obvious that peacekeeping operations cannot be conducted without DND's involvement in the decision-making process. In fact, DND indeed plays an important role in making decisions about peacekeeping requests. There is open and regular debate and negotiation between DND, FAC, and the Cabinet over how to define Canada's interests, although FAC usually seems to prevail.[51]

DND plays the greatest role at the operational level. The intelligence unit inside National Defence Headquarters monitors world conflict situations on an ongoing basis in order to be ready to perform analysis when an informal request comes from the United Nations for Canadian troops to be sent.[52] Communications between the Canadian U.N. Mission in New York and the government in Ottawa about peacekeeping requests are copied to the relevant sections of both FAC and DND, and there is immediate cooperation between them on pre-deployment assessment and planning.[53] In recent years this has included holding joint FAC and DND reconnaissance missions on the ground in the proposed mission area before advice is given to the Prime Minister about whether and how Canada should participate.

The primary traditional role of DND was to provide advice about the availability of personnel and resources for U.N. missions.[54] The U.N. was never a high DND priority. In the words of one Canadian lieutenant colonel, "From the perspective of the C.F., U.N. peacekeeping is seen as an accepted activity rather than a core concern. . . . Peacekeeping is a useful role, as it provides good experience and training, but it is also very much secondary to the central role of being ready to engage in conventional operations."[55] During the Cold War, DND and the C.F. preferred to concentrate on their missions in NATO and in NORAD (the joint territorial air defense of North America by Canada and the United States).[56] DND representatives now uniformly say that peacekeeping is a core activity of the C.F., but this might be easier to accept when the majority of Canadian troops deployed abroad are actually on NATO rather than U.N. peacekeeping missions, and ones where the military activities they are engaged in blend over into more traditional war-fighting roles. As mentioned above, there is currently talk of the need for a major review of Canadian defense policy, something that hasn't been done since the previous White Paper was published in 1994. One of the issues that may be highlighted if such a review takes place is in fact the "overlap" between complex peacekeeping and combat requirements, and how this might be translated into rational planning cost-savings.[57]

Peacekeeping in recent years has not been a particularly peaceful activity, and Canadian officers approach U.N. missions with the expectation that combat may ensue.[58] This has led to a change in the role that DND plays in its advising about peacekeeping activities. No longer is it only concerned about resource issues; it also pays close attention to practical concerns about how troops will be used. Once a mission has been deployed, DND is also consulted whenever the Canadian contingent is asked by the U.N. commander to make a major relocation of troops. The intelligence unit at National Defence Headquarters sends a threat assessment of the situation to DND, which in turn advises the political leadership about whether or not the relocation is sensible and provides adequate protection to troops.[59]

The understanding that peacekeeping and combat are not far removed from each other is reflected in the C.F. approach to training. There is a shared belief across the C.F. that "the best peacekeeper is a well-trained, well-disciplined combat arms soldier."[60] Until recently, no special training was given for Canadian troops sent on peacekeeping missions. This approach was challenged because of the violent behavior of some of the Canadian Airborne Regiment (CAR) troops on peacekeeping duty in Somalia, mentioned above. The CAR units were sent on the Somalia mission because they had been designated as the Canadian standby force for U.N. operations, even though they were trained as elite special force combat units and had not undergone the kind of cultural sensitivity or negotiation training which would ideally suit those serving in a humanitarian support capacity abroad.[61]

As a consequence, in the last several years more attention has been paid to cultural awareness training for C.F. peacekeepers, and to ensuring that battalions have adequate mission-specific preparation time before being sent into the field. While DND rejected many of the Somalia Inquiry's conclusions, it accepted the recommendation that core peace support training should become an integral part of the C.F. basic training program,[62] and a new peace support training center was opened in Kingston, Ontario, in summer 1996 to begin this process.[63] There is a widespread perception, including among C.F. officers, that despite the long Canadian tradition of sending troops on U.N. missions, no one paid much attention to the special training and preparation needs of peacekeepers until the Somalia tragedy came to light.[64] This provides further evidence that DND and the C.F. did not traditionally place a high institutional value on the peacekeeping mission.

Now the impact of the cultural awareness training programs on the C.F. is clear. In Afghanistan, for example, Canadian troops going out on patrol are acutely sensitive to cultural specifics. For example, they emphasize the importance of communicating with the recognized elders in any Afghan social setting, of accepting offers to sit down to tea with locals, and of being careful not to violate the country's traditional norms about gender roles.[65] Canadian General Rick Hillier, who commanded ISAF for six months in 2004, believed that showing concern and respect for the Afghan population—especially by not placing unnecessary psychological distance between patrolling troops and the locals—was one of the best ways to ensure the support of the Afghan people, and in turn the protection of the troops.[66]

CANADIAN POLITICS AND RECENT PEACEKEEPING INNOVATIONS

FAC's policy has clearly served Canada well in the United Nations. It is generally agreed, for example, that Canada won the competition for one of the rotating seats in the U.N. Security Council (UNSC) in 1998 largely because of its peacekeeping legacy, a theme that was emphasized in Canada's campaign strategy for the seat.[67] Former Minister of External Affairs Lloyd Axworthy worked to carve out a particular role for Canada in the United Nations as a defender of what he called "human security," as opposed to state security,[68] using the term "soft power" to describe Canada's strategic goal: to gain "the international influence that knowledge, information and an attractive set of values confer."[69]

Canadian diplomats used the UNSC seat to try to create a greater role for smaller powers in directing U.N. policy. They made an effort to expand the transparency of U.N. Security Council meetings and to take the agenda for international security issues out of the hands of the great powers. Some of them have argued that the U.S. and other permanent U.N. Security Council members lack the sense of "responsibility to the world electorate" felt by those whose presence on the council is beholden to votes received from General Assembly states.[70] This certainly supports the hypothesis that Canadian realists choose peacekeeping as an appropriate means for the country to gain influence as a middle power.

Yet when one looks more closely at the pattern of Canadian influence in the U.N., it is not clear what self-interested benefits Canada gains from this influence. It appears mostly to gain the ability to pursue its humanitarian activities more effectively. The major accomplishment that FAC officials cite as a result of Canada's increased U.N. role is that Canada has been able to promote its human security agenda, for example, and as Ayres has demonstrated in his chapter, by taking a leadership role in the Anti-Personnel Land Mine Treaty and in U.N. efforts to curtail the proliferation of small arms internationally. This has fed back to Canadian advantage on peacekeeping missions, since landmines are one of the greatest threats that peacekeepers face in the field,[71] and the proliferation of small arms makes humanitarian crises worse. Axworthy expressed particular pride that Canada was able to build support in the UNSC for the notion that better armed peacekeeping forces in the field can do a better job of defending innocent civilians from predatory insurgents. Such a policy served both the goal of "human security" in the host country[72] and of defending Canadian troops from possible attack.

All of these accomplishments are noble. But there is nothing here that clearly serves the cold, hard self-interests of Canada. Influence as described here is important not because it enhances territorial Canadian security or economic power abroad, but because it allows Canada to do "good things." At this point standard realist arguments about the purposes of diplomacy are left behind. It is FAC's cultural focus on the appropriateness of a U.N. role that explains Canadian policy best.

Yet the late 1990s presented new challenges on a redefined world stage where conflicts shifted from international to domestic. The Canadian government answered these new demands and, in view of doing so, tried to alter the traditional Pearsonian culture within FAC. The goal was to focus Canadian policy not on *peacekeeping*, using military forces, but instead on *peacebuilding* activities (primarily education for war prevention, and postwar societal reconstruction) by private or non-governmental civilian organizations. Beginning in 1995, a series of institutional changes were implemented within FAC to further this vision. First a new internal Global Issues Bureau was created, whose mandate focused on many of the complex and interlinked human security concerns championed by Axworthy. This bureau's prominence within the department grew after Axworthy acceded to office in 1996.[73] Tellingly for the importance of organizational culture within FAC, long-time department employees were not particularly interested in this new organization, and therefore the staffing process for it focused on hiring outsiders, including academics and representatives of non-governmental organizations (NGOs). The fact that it was supported by the political appointees at the top of the ministerial structure meant that it achieved a great deal of influence in a very short time.

The mandate of this bureau was enhanced by the creation of the Canadian Peacebuilding Program within FAC in 1997, to support what was known as the Canadian Peacebuilding Initiative. Among other achievements, this initiative created a Canadian Peacebuilding Fund to be administered not by FAC or DND, but instead by the Canadian International Development Agency (CIDA).[74] Many DND officials believe that CIDA is dominated by "leftists" associated with the NGO and academic community who dislike the military on principle.[75] CIDA officials now are consulted in a way never before seen on peacekeeping policy questions, and tend to prefer to have U.N. peacekeeping activities led by NGOs and other "private" actors, rather than by the military. In Afghanistan, for example, this meant there was a certain degree of tension between the priorities of CIDA officials at the embassy in Kabul and the CIMIC (Civil-Military Cooperation) troops out on patrol, who sought small aid and reconstruction projects that would help bolster the positive image of the C.F. among the locals.

While in some ways the new FAC sub-organizations fit the Pearsonian legacy, with their emphasis on multilateralism and Canada's unique, middle-power abilities to contribute to the solution of global problems, these initiatives are a challenge to the tradition Pearson established of using military troops as peacekeepers. Axworthy argued that Canada could exercise political leadership in peacebuilding efforts in hot spots around the world, without necessarily sending in military troops in large numbers.[76] In other words, it appeared that a sea change might have been under way in FAC culture, one that assigned the Pearsonian legacy to Cold War history and replaced it with a vision of Canada's place in the world that did not include the need for large defense expenditures. Yet this did not seem to last long, as the C.F. are still being asked to deploy on additional major peace missions without receiving adequate budgetary resources for the task.

At the November 2003 Liberal Party convention, following intra-party squabbling that led Chrétien to promise to step down as Prime Minister more than a year in advance, Paul Martin was chosen to take his place. Defence Minister McCallum announced that Canada might pull out of the NATO mission in Bosnia in late 2004 to concentrate on the NATO mission in Afghanistan instead, indicating that budgetary concerns were limiting the decision to lend troops to so many major foreign operations.[77] Many military officers hoped that the new leadership might be more sympathetic to their budgetary concerns than they had perceived the old cabinet to be. Yet after new elections were held on June 28, 2004, Martin was left with a minority government.

From a peacekeeping point of view, it is interesting to note that the new Harper government has committed itself publicly toward military readiness and supports a major enhancement of the Canadian Armed Forces. On the other hand, the New Democratic Party and Bloc Québécois advocate a more left-wing, socialist stance that openly opposes military expansion and even military interventions, especially if and when they are at the initiative of American government. Given a minority Conservative government now in Ottawa, the future direction of Canadian peacekeeping remains to be defined.

CONCLUSION

Rather than popular culture per se, it is the culture of the foreign ministry bureaucracy that has played an important role in determining the tenor of Canadian peacekeeping policy over the years. This culture seems to have been particularly emphasized in the decade tenure of Prime Minister Jean Chrétien, where FAC ideas about the importance of the U.N. and the NATO alliance as a constraint on U.S. unilateralism continued to be privileged. Peacekeeping duties are tolerated and even sometimes welcomed by military officers, but are not seen as the primary activities of the defense establishment. While the public does not typically object to the use of the military in peacekeeping operations, it does not appear that a national culture of international obligation is driving peacekeeping decisions by the government, or that the public would object if military peacekeeping activity died away.

Canada's seemingly enduring culture of peacekeeping rests not merely in public opinion or in societal expectations, but in particular bureaucracies and party visions which shape Ottawa's policy agenda. Lasting change in such a culture of national security policy can happen only when bureaucracies and governments are shaken up and restructured, so that new visions motivate the selection of personnel and the direction of project funding. It remains unclear whether such change will happen in Canada in the near future. In the meantime, the Canadian Forces continue to suffer through the combination of inadequate budgets and excessive deployments abroad.

NOTES

1. See Steven Edwards, "Canada Feels Heat for Troop Pullout," *Canada Leader-Post*, 27 June 2004.

2. A prominent example is Joseph T. Jockel, *Canada and International Peacekeeping*, Significant Issues Series 16, no. 3 (Washington, D.C.: Center for Strategic and International Studies, 1994).

3. While there are other broad theoretical perspectives that have commonly been used to explain the foreign policies of states in general, including such approaches as liberalism and socialism, they have not been commonly applied to Canadian peacekeeping behavior.

4. Larry L. Fabian, *Soldiers without Enemies: Preparing the United Nations for Peacekeeping* (Washington, DC: Brookings Institution Press, 1971); Carsten Holbraad, *Middle Powers in International Politics* (London: Macmillan, 1984); and Andrew F. Cooper, ed., *Niche Diplomacy: Middle Powers after the Cold War* (New York: St. Martin's Press, 1997). The intellectual inspiration for much of this literature is Robert O. Keohane, "Lilliputians' Dilemmas: Small States in International Politics," *International Organization* 23, no. 2 (Spring 1969): 291–310.

5. Erin Carrière, Marc O'Reilly, and Richard Vengroff, "'In the Service of Peace': Reflexive Multilateralism and the Canadian Experience in Bosnia," in

International Public Opinion and the Bosnia Crisis, ed. Richard Sobel and Eric Shiraev (Lanham, MD: Lexington Books, 2002), 1–32.

6. Alastair Iain Johnston, "Thinking about Strategic Culture," *International Security* 19, no. 4 (Spring 1995): 32–64.

7. Stephen Thorne, "Long-term Troop Training Ahead in Afghanistan," *Globe and Mail*, 28 July 2004.

8. See, for example, Paul Martin's speech at the Woodrow Wilson International Center for Scholars, Washington, DC, April 29, 2004, available at http://pm.gc.ca/eng/news.asp?id = 192.

9. J. L. Granatstein, "Peacekeeping: Did Canada Make a Difference? And What Difference Did Peacekeeping Make to Canada?" in *Making a Difference? Canada's Foreign Policy in a Changing World Order*, ed. John English and Norman Hillmer (Toronto: Lester Publishing Ltd., 1992), 231.

10. Carriere, O'Reilly and Vengroff, "In the Service of Peace." Also see Pierre Martin and Michel Fortmann, "Canadian Public Opinion and Peacekeeping in a Turbulent World," *International Journal* 50, no. 2 (Spring 1995): 370–400; and Barbara Waruszynski, "Determining the Canadian Pulse on Defence Matters," *Defence Matters* 2, no. 5 (July 1997): 12–17.

11. Rod D. Byers, "Peacekeeping and Canadian Defense Policy: Ambivalence and Uncertainty," in *Peacekeeping: Appraisals and Proposals*, ed. Henry Wiseman (New York: Pergamon, 1983), 136.

12. Mitchell Sharp, *Foreign Policy for Canadians* (Ottawa: Queen's Printer for Canada, 1970), 8. Also see Annette Baker Fox, "Canada in World Affairs," Association for Canadian Studies in the United States Papers (Washington, DC: ACSUS, 1989), 6.

13. See "Defense Minister: Peacekeeping Won't Jeopardize Canada," *AP Online*, 24 November 1999, accessed via the Lexis-Nexis Academic Universe online database.

14. D PK POL Peace Support Operations SITREP, unpublished Department of National Defence Report, unclassified version, July 19, 1999, A8.

15. Lt. Col. Ernest Reumiller, "Canadian Perspectives and Experiences with Peacekeeping: General Policy Considerations," in *Conflict Resolution and Peacemaking/Peacekeeping: The Irish and Canadian Experience*, ed. Padraig O'Gormaile and Ray Murphy (Galway, Ireland: Association for Canadian Studies in Ireland, 1997), 26.

16. D PK POL Peace Support Operations SITREP, July 19, 1999.

17. A full list of operations dates, locations, and personnel appears at http://www.dfait-maeci.gc.ca/peacekeeping/missions-en.asp.

18. Mitch Gillett, "Minister Balances Priorities," *Maple Leaf* 2, no. 1 (January 15, 1999): 1.

19. David A. Welch, "The New Multilateralism and Evolving Security Systems," in *Canada Among Nations 1992–93: A New World Order?* ed. Fen Osler Hampson and Christopher Maule (Ottawa: Carleton University Press, 1992): 84; and Alex Morrison, "Canada and Peacekeeping: A Time for Reanalysis?" in *Canada's International Security Policy*, ed. David B. Dewitt and David Leyton-Brown (Scarborough, ON: Prentice-Hall Canada, 1995), 222.

20. House of Commons Standing Committee on National Defence and Veterans Affairs Report, "Moving Forward: A Strategic Plan for Quality of Life Improvements in the Canadian Forces," October 1998, available online at www.parl.gc.ca/InfoComDoc/36/1/NDVA/Studies/Reports/ndvarp03-e.htm.

21. Edison Stewart, "Defence Money for the Military's Malaise," *Toronto Star*, 29 February 2000, accessed via Lexis-Nexis.

22. "Why the Canadian Military Isn't Ready for a War," *Maclean's*, 30 September 2002; and Scot Robertson, "The Defence Review: Attacking the Strategy-Resources Mismatch," *Canadian Military Journal* 3, no. 3 (Autumn 2002): 21–27.

23. Les Whittington, "McCallum Volunteers to Cut Defence," *Toronto Star*, 28 August 2003.

24. Senator Colin Kenny, "Parliamentary Control and National Defence: The Canadian Experience," Canadian Institute of Strategic Studies Strategic Datalink no. 70 (Toronto: CISS, 1998).

25. Jean-François Rioux and Robin Hay, "Canadian Foreign Policy: From Internationalism to Isolationism?" Norman Paterson School of International Affairs Discussion Paper no. 16 (Ottawa: Carleton University, 1997); and Acting Sub-Lt. Luc Charron, "Serving without Fanfare: The Challenges Affecting the Morale of Today's Canadian Forces," *Defence Matters* 2, no. 4 (May/June 1997): 12.

26. Kenny, "Parliamentary Control and National Defence." Confirmed in an off-the-record interview with a prominent Liberal member of the House of Commons Foreign Affairs Committee (November 1999), 4.

27. Kenny, "Parliamentary Control and National Defence," 1.

28. See Allan Thompson, "Mission Impossible? The Mythology of Canada's Blue Berets Is under Attack," *Toronto Star*, 1 July 1995.

29. *Peacekeeping Operations, Operations Land and Tactical Air* 3, B-GL-301–003/FP-001 (Ottawa: National Defence Headquarters, 1994), 1-3-2.

30. David Pugliese, "Forces Still Could Work Overseas," *Ottawa Citizen*, 2 July 2003.

31. Jason Fekete and Stephen Thorne, "General Quits Military over Proposed Afghanistan Peacekeeping Mission," *Ottawa Citizen*, 15 February 2003.

32. Reumiller, "Canadian Perspectives and Experiences with Peacekeeping," 26.

33. For an example, see David Lenarcie, "Meeting Each Other Halfway: The Departments of National Defence and External Affairs During the Congo Peacekeeping Mission, 1960–64," York University Centre for International and Strategic Studies Occasional Paper 37 (Toronto: York University, 1996), 7.

34. Rioux and Hay, "Canadian Foreign Policy," 14; and Kim Richard Nossal, "Pinchpenny Diplomacy: The Decline of 'Good International Citizenship' in Canadian Foreign Policy," *International Journal* 54, no. 1 (Winter 1998/99): 88–105, especially 93.

35. Report of the Auditor General of Canada to the House of Commons, "Peacekeeping," FA1–1996/1–6E (Ottawa: May 1996), 6–15.

36. Charlotte Gray, "New Faces in Old Places: The Making of Canadian Foreign Policy," in *Canada Among Nations, 1992–93*, 20. Also see Nossal, "Pinchpenny Diplomacy," 96.

37. Peter Stursberg, *Lester Pearson and the American Dilemma* (New York: Doubleday and Co., 1980), 153; Lester B. Pearson, *Mike: The Memoirs of the Right Honorable Lester B. Pearson, Volume 2: 1948–1957*, ed. John A. Munro and Alex I. Inglis (Toronto: University of Toronto Press, 1973), 262.

38. Pearson, *Mike, Volume 2*, 121.

39. Pearson, *Mike, Volume 2*, 123.

40. Pearson, *Mike: The Memoirs of the Right Honourable Lester B. Pearson, Volume 3: 1957–1968*, ed. John A Munro and Alex I. Inglis (Toronto: University of Toronto Press, 1975), 114.

41. Pearson, *Mike, Volume 2*, 132.

42. Ann Flanagan, "Canadian Peacekeeping: Where to Now?" *Behind the Headlines* 54, no. 4 (Summer 1997): 6, 10. This was confirmed in an off-the-record interview by the author at FAC in November 1999.

43. Pearson, *Mike, Volume 3*, 134–5.

44. Jockel, *Canada and International Peacekeeping*, 13–14.

45. Paul Buteux, "NATO and the Evolution of Canadian Defence and Foreign Policy," and Joel J. Sokolsky, "The Bilateral Defence Relationship with the United States," both in *Canada's International Security Policy*, ed. David B. Dewitt and David Leyton-Brown (Scarborough, ON: Prentice-Hall Canada, 1995), especially 155 and 176. Also see the remarks of NATO Secretary-General George Robertson reported in Jeff Sallot, "Ottawa Rejects NATO's Criticism," *Globe and Mail*, 2 November 1999.

46. "Interview with Secretary of State Ronald J. Duhamel," *Canada World View*, no. 5 (1999): 2.

47. For a list, see D PK POL Peace Support Operations SITREP, Annex A, 8–9.

48. These operations refer to peacekeeping activities under U.N. Charter Chap-

ter VI, whereby Blue Helmet forces are not allowed to fire back if fired upon or attacked. Chapter VI operations differ from Chapter VII, which imply a lack of consent by at least one of the parties to the dispute and the use of force.

49. These three examples were independently confirmed by two knowledgeable Canadian officials speaking not for attribution.

50. Off-the-record interviews by the author at the Department of National Defence in Ottawa, November 1999.

51. For one example, see the detailed study of the Canadian decision to intervene in Eastern Zaire in 1996 by John B. Hay, "Conditions of Influence: An Exploratory Study of the Canadian Government's Effect on U.S. Policy in the Case of Intervention in Eastern Zaire," Master of Arts Thesis, Normal Paterson School of International Affairs, Carleton University, May 1998. It is summarized in Gordon Smith and John Hay, "Canada and the Crisis in Eastern Zaire," in *Herding Cats: Multiparty Mediation in a Complex World*, ed. Chester A. Crocker, Fen Osler Hampson, and Pamela R. Aall (Washington, DC: US Institute of Peace Press, 1999).

52. *Peacekeeping Operations*, 4-2-1 and 4-5-1. This was confirmed in an interview by the author in Ottawa, November 1999.

53. Interviews conducted by the author at both FAC and DND, November 1999.

54. Reumiller, "Canadian Perspectives," 26.

55. Lt. Col. of Logistics Ian Malcolm, "Does the Blue Helmet Fit? The Canadian Forces and Peacekeeping," Norman Paterson School of International Affairs Occasional Paper no. 3 (Ottawa: Carleton University, 1993), 1, 3.

56. This was confirmed independently in three off-the-record interviews conducted with serving and retired Canadian officers in March 1999.

57. Robertson, "The Defence Review," 24.

58. James V. Arbuckle, "The Level Killing Fields of Yugoslavia: An Observer Returns," Pearson Papers no. 2 (Clementsport, Nova Scotia: Canadian Peacekeeping Press, 1998).

59. Off-the-record conversation with a mid-level C.F. officer who served in multiple peacekeeping operations, March 1999.

60. Reumiller, "Canadian Perspectives," 28. Also see *Peacekeeping Operations*, 11-4-1 to 11-4-9; the statement of Major-General Mike Jeffery, Commander of 1st Canadian Division, in Mitch Gillett, "The Future Is Now," *Maple Leaf* 2, no. 1 (Jan. 15, 1999): 6; and Paul Mooney, "War-fighting Remains Core of Collective Training," *Maple Leaf* 2, no. 13 (July 14, 1999): 17.

61. Malcolm, "Does the Blue Helmet Fit?" 9; Allen G. Sens, *Somalia and the Changing Nature of Peacekeeping: The Implications for Canada* (Ottawa: Commis-

sion of Inquiry into the Deployment of Canadian Forces to Somalia, 1997), 104; Winslow, *Canadian Airborne Regiment in Somalia*, 194–198; and Berel Rodal, *The Somalia Experience in Strategic Perspective: Implications for the Military in a Free and Democratic Society*, study prepared for the Commission of Inquiry into the Deployment of Canadian Forces to Somalia (Ottawa: Canadian Minister of Public Works and Government Services, 1997), 69.

62. Department of National Defence, *A Commitment to Change: Report on the Recommendations of the Somalia Commission of Inquiry* (Ottawa: October 1997), 36–7.

63. Paul LaRose-Edwards, Jack Dangerfield, and Randy Weekes, *Non-Traditional Military Training for Canadian Peacekeepers*, study prepared for the Commission of Inquiry into the Deployment of Canadian Forces to Somalia (Ottawa: Canadian Minister of Public Works and Government Services, 1997), 29–30.

64. Off-the-record interviews with a junior officer and a retired senior officer, March 1999.

65. All of these things were observed by the author when she was embedded with the Canadian Forces leading the ISAF mission in Kabul, Camp Julien, May 2004.

66. Interview conducted by the author with General Hillier, May 2004.

67. David M. Malone, "Eyes on the Prize: The Quest for Non-Permanent Seats on the UN Security Council," *Global Governance* 6, no. 1 (January-March 2000): 1–36.

68. "Human Security: Putting People First," *Canada World View* Special Edition (Ottawa: DFAIT, Fall 1999).

69. Lloyd Axworthy Address, *Report of the 1996 National Forum on Canada's International Relations* (Ottawa: Canadian Centre for Foreign Policy Development, 1997), 3.

70. Not-for-attribution interview of a high-ranking U.N. official, March 1999.

71. "Mine Warfare During Peace Support Operations," *Dispatches* (the Canadian Army's "Lessons Learned Newsletter") 2, no. 1 (April 1995).

72. "Canada Achieves Protection of Civilians in UN Resolution Establishing Peacekeeping Mission in Sierra Leone," DFAIT *News Release* no. 230 (October 22, 1999).

73. David M. Malone, "The Global Issues Biz: What Gives?" in *Canada Among Nations 1999: A Big League Player?* ed. Fen Osler Hampson, Martin Rudner, and Michael Hart (New York: Oxford University Press, 1999), 197–214.

74. FAAC, "Canada and Peacebuilding: The Canadian Peacebuilding Initiative," http://www.dfait-maeci.gc.ca/peacebuilding/cpi-e.asp.

75. Not-for-attribution interview by the author, November 1999.

76. Duane Bratt, "Rehabilitating the Military: Canadian Peacekeeping in the Post-Somalia Era" (paper presented at the 11th Annual Meeting of the Academic Council on the U.N. System (ACUNS), Nova Scotia, June 1998), 19–21.

77. Mike Blanchfield, "Canada Hints It Will Expand Afghan Role," *Ottawa Citizen*, 21 November 2003.

8

International Conflict Prevention: An Assessment of Canadian Perceptions and Policies

KOREN MARRIOTT AND DAVID CARMENT

Are we to go from crisis to crisis improvising in haste? Or can we now pool our experience and our resources, so that next time we, the governments and people whom the United Nations represents, will be ready and prepared to act?[1]

Lester B. Pearson's reminder of the importance of pooling resources and thinking strategically are as relevant today as they were in 1957. Circumstances have demanded an increased role for the international community and regional organizations in conflict prevention. In extreme cases, violent ethnic cleansing makes it no longer acceptable to wait until parties have signed a peace agreement and have negotiated a cease-fire before intervening. The conflicts of the past two decades have included mass killings that require immediate intervention by a third party. Unfortunately, the international community has not responded to these new challenges quickly enough and, as a result, we have seen horrendous situations develop, such as the massacre in Srebrenica, genocide in Rwanda, and the emergence of terrorist training camps in Afghanistan.

Thus, conflict prevention remains an important issue area in this era of globalization and terrorism.[2] The U.N. and other international and regional bodies remain active in many regions in conflict around the world, and individual countries, including Canada, remain committed to peace operations as well as international conflict prevention initiatives. Given the importance of conflict prevention work, and in preparation for the 2005 special U.N. Conference on the Role of Civil Society in Conflict Prevention, the Canadian Conflict Prevention Initiative (CCPI) was established with the support of Foreign Affairs Canada (FAC) and the Canadian International Development Agency (CIDA). One of the CCPI's key objectives was to identify the Canadian capacity to conduct conflict prevention abroad. The authors were asked by the government of Canada to conduct the survey.

This chapter analyzes the results of this survey. In the first part of this chapter we introduce the concept of conflict prevention. In the second part of the chapter, we identify Canada's approach to conflict prevention, including an overview of the creation of the CCPI and related organizations abroad. In the third part of the paper we discuss the results of the survey. The chapter concludes with policy and programming implications as they relate to our research findings.

TERMS AND CONCEPTS

Popular usage of the term *conflict prevention* can be traced to the activities of United Nations Secretary-general Dag Hammarskjöld, although its underlying logic has existed at least since the emergence of the modern state system.[3] Hammarskjöld realized that early engagement of the global organization could act to forestall the destructiveness of conflict created by external military intervention and arms transfers. The complementary concept of preventive diplomacy stems from the more general reasoning that external interventions can be avoided or tempered if a region is made more autonomous in terms of security. Preventive diplomacy aims to fill the vacuum so that it will not provoke a hostile response from any of the major parties. When crisis threatens, traditional diplomacy continues, but more urgent preventive efforts are required—through unilateral and multilateral channels—to arbitrate, mediate, or lend "good offices" to encourage dialogue and facilitate resolution.

Conflict prevention has grown in importance due to the evolving nature of conflict. The shift from interstate to intrastate conflict is well documented.[4] However, this change in itself has not been sufficient to generate a call for revised thinking on preventive action. It is the surrounding circumstances, the ability of complex conflicts to spread vertically and horizontally—in essence the potential of intrastate conflict to do harm to others, ordinary citizens, neighboring states, refugees, and minorities—that generates preventive efforts.

In the post–Cold War era, conflict prevention and preventive diplomacy became catch phrases for any activity by any actor to reduce the possibility of conflict, including development assistance, human rights activism, preventive peacekeeping activities, conflict resolution, and post-conflict peacebuilding. In his *Agenda for Peace*, former U.N. Secretary-General Boutros Boutros-Ghali offered a very general definition of conflict prevention, that is, the action to prevent disputes from arising between parties, to prevent existing disputes from escalating into conflicts, and to limit the spread of the latter when they occur.[5] He further suggested that the most desirable and efficient employment of diplomacy is to ease tensions before they result in conflict—or, if conflict breaks out, to act swiftly to contain it and resolve its underlying causes. Conflict prevention requires measures to create confidence; it needs early warning based on information gathering and informal or formal fact-finding; it may also involve preventive deployment and, in some situations, demilitarized zones. This is a very broad approach to preventive action, one that captures all perceivable stages of conflict, from prevention to resolution.

However, the question of timing, as to when the action is carried out, is important and needs to be addressed. Michael Lund differentiates between "peacetime diplomacy or politics" during eras of durable and stable peace, "conflict prevention" during eras of unstable peace, "crisis diplomacy or crisis management" during a crisis situation, and "peacemaking or conflict management" during war.[6] Lund envisions "peace enforcement or conflict mitigation" as the appropriate response to war situations and "peacekeeping or conflict termination" as a means to defuse war and conflict, followed by "post-conflict peacebuilding or conflict resolution."[7] Each of these stages requires different operational and institutional responses. For example, conflict prevention is only effective during a situation of unstable peace, that is, when the signs of an emerging conflict become obvious to the informed outside observer. Bruce Jentleson echoes this more subtle interpretation of conflict prevention by distinguishing between "normal diplomacy," "developmentalist diplomacy," "conflict prevention," and "war diplomacy," an approach which seems to explain the wide range of external involvement in zones of instability.[8]

The U.N. Secretary-General's 2001 *Report on the Prevention of Armed Conflict* adopted the distinction made by the Carnegie Commission on Preventing Deadly Conflict between operational prevention, which refers to measures applicable in the face of immediate crisis, and structural prevention, which consists of measures to ensure that crises do not arise in the first place or, if they do, that they do not recur. Here the stress is on the need to address root causes of potential conflicts through long-term, structural prevention. In recognition of the potential catchall character of the prevention agenda, however, there is a clear distinction between regular developmental and humanitarian assistance programs, on the one hand, and those implemented as a preventive response to problems that could lead to the outbreak or recurrence of violent conflict, on the other. This differentiation is echoed by the International Commission on Intervention and State Sovereignty in its report on *The Responsibility to Protect*. The report stresses international, regional, national, and local cooperation in both direct (operational) and root cause (structural) preventive efforts. Both reports emphasized the need for the U.N. and other inter-state, state, and non-state actors to move from a culture of reaction to a culture of prevention. While both reports argued that the main responsibility for preventive efforts lies with national governments and civil society, intergovernmental organizations such as the U.N. and regional organizations play leading roles in strengthening the capacity of national and local actors to create conditions that foster peace. The U.N. and regional organizations' commitment and ability to promote and practice preventive strategies are key to sustained preventive efforts at national and local levels.

Kalypso Nicolaides provides a useful conceptual framework for understanding conflict prevention. Conflict prevention is an operational response. It is premised on incentive structures provided by outside actors to change specific kinds of undesirable behavior. Conflict prevention is therefore targeted and short-term and the preventive action taken relates directly to changes in conflict escalation and conflict dynamics. In this regard outside actors can seek to influence the course of events and try to alter or induce specific behavior through coercive and operational threats and deterrents or through less coercive strategies of persuasion and inducement.

Standard definitions of conflict prevention often divide activities that respond to conflict into two types of prevention: structural, or root-cause prevention, and operational or direct prevention. Structural prevention transforms social, economic, cultural, or political sources of conflict either through general policies applied blindly to all countries, or through specific policies applied to countries at risk. Programs that focus on risk factors such as poverty, resource distribution, representation, strengthening the rule of law and governance, or security sector reform are included under this category. Structural prevention can also be further divided into activities that affect development, and those that affect governance.[9] The simple existence of social inequality or resource scarcity, however, does not necessarily mean that conflict is inevitable.[10] Behavioral and political motivations also play a role in the outbreak of violent conflict. Ultimately conflict prevention programs that address the structural causes of conflict must occur in states or regions where such problems are likely to lead to violence.

Operational prevention, on the other hand, is designed to contain or reverse the escalation of violence that has been sparked by leadership strategies or crises. Most operational prevention strategies operate at the official level and include peacekeeping missions, high-level negotiations, mediation, and other diplomatic measures. At a non-governmental level, operational techniques may include dispute resolution mechanisms or open dialogues between opposing groups.[11]

Ultimately though, outside actors can work to influence the incentives of the relevant parties engaged in conflict but they cannot change the initial conditions that led to conflict in the first place. That process has to take place within. Thus, structural approaches emphasize capacity building to provide conflict-prone societies with the means to address root causes of conflict. In this sense, structural conflict prevention strategies, such as those focusing on human security, conflict transformation, and development cast a much broader net. They tend to be long-term and are generally applied across a range of countries, issues, and actors. The goal is to transform conflicting behavior over time. This change in behavior can be dependent on institutional inducements—such as conditionality for membership in international institutions, arms control agreements, and stability pacts or on the promotion of sustainable development, support for human security, and regional confidence-building mechanisms.

The difference between operational and structural approaches is made clear through the analogy to the clinical and environmental approaches to health care. Clinical and environmental health care may both be preventively oriented; however, the former focuses on the treatment of sick individuals, whereas the latter emphasizes a public health model that aims to prevent illness by focusing on its associated environmental factors.

Nevertheless, failing to act in an escalating violent situation makes the difference between a situation that can be contained and a humanitarian disaster that can spiral beyond control and result in thousands of people being displaced or killed. A failure to act quickly, early and decisively not only leads to conflict escalation but incriminates the Western powers directly in the ensuing violence and severely damages the legitimacy of international norms. Effective conflict prevention requires an appreciation of what is at stake, imagination in designing solutions, stable institutions able to translate ideas into effective action, and above all strong leadership to mobilize the necessary will and resources. Even though prevention is a risky strategy, the alternatives are often riskier. For example, it is possible to engage in counterfactual analysis by comparing the costs of *actual* conflicts to *estimates* of what it would have cost to prevent these conflicts from taking place. The actual cost of the intervention in Bosnia was $53.7 billion (U.S.) compared to the cost of prevention, estimated at $33.3 billion (U.S.). In Haiti the actual cost of intervention was $5.0 billion (U.S.) and the cost of prevention is estimated at $2.3 billion (U.S.).[12]

CANADA AND CONFLICT PREVENTION

From its 1995 policy statement, Canadian foreign policy has been built on three key objectives: promoting prosperity; protecting security; and projecting Canadian culture and values abroad.[13] These three objectives are approached through a three-pronged approach that includes diplomatic efforts, development assistance, and defense. According to Foreign Affairs Canada (FAC), which was separated from the International Trade department in 2004, one of the central requirements to ensuring Canada's security is the promotion of global peace at a broader level. Stability and security both within Canada and internationally are closely linked to economic growth and development, environmental issues, issues of migration, globalization, and health, as well as such areas as human rights and international law.[14] Among the strategic priorities of the Canadian government are the reduction of international threats, including the war on terrorism, and the promotion of human rights, good governance, and the rule of law. It is within these priorities that the development of mechanisms for the promotion and implementation of conflict prevention initiatives can be situated.

Conflict prevention is increasingly recognized as an important and viable component of foreign policy. In this era of globalization and terrorism the prevention of large-scale deadly violence has become a more generally accepted goal of not only governments but of civil society organizations as well. While the United Nations and other international and regional governmental organizations remain active in traditional conflict prevention activities including mediation, peacekeeping, and diplomatic missions around the world, individual countries, including Canada, have begun supplementing their commitments to multilateral peace operations and diplomatic measures through a broader range of conflict prevention activities. At the same time, the strong civil society sector in Canada has also begun to embrace the idea of conflict prevention as an integrated component of existing international programs.

Conflict prevention has traditionally been defined in very specific, targeted terms, but the range of activities undertaken by Canadian non-governmental organizations and the Canadian government under the auspices of preventing conflict are challenging these traditional limits. A combination of defense, diplomacy, and development assets, or "3D," is often touted as *the* conflict prevention strategy, and to be sure, the concept looks promising on paper. However, it has yet to be fully incorporated into the decision-making and planning processes of various departments and not just FAC, DND (Department of National Defence), and CIDA (Canadian International Development Agency). A formal structure for fully integrating conflict prevention is currently lacking within the Canadian government. The British example of Conflict Prevention Pools (CPPs) is a model which Canada could use to organize itself. All relevant departments must clearly understand their objectives, their mandates, and how their capabilities correspond to those of other departments. All departments must recognize that they are working together for a common goal and that they are not competing with each other but complementing each other. Identifying lead departments at the earliest possible stage is crucial to avoid confusion and duplication of processes.[15]

The tools that Canada possesses in the areas of defense, diplomacy, and development are no panacea for all of the world's problems, and it will never be easy, as in extreme cases, to put back together a state that has fallen apart. The ultimate success resides in the leadership and commitment of the local population. Canada can help these leaders reach their goals.

To this end, in June 2001, U.N. Secretary-General Kofi Annan called for the "mainstreaming" of conflict prevention within the U.N. system, urging international and regional organizations to work more closely with civil society. The underlying premise of the Secretary-General's statement is that conflict prevention can only be successful if it rests on the coordination of activities between the U.N., regional organizations, states, and civil society, capitalizing on each group's expertise and skill.

In response to this call for more concerted action, the European Centre for Conflict Prevention (ECCP) initiated a process of transnational networking to address the challenge of more effective civil society involvement in conflict prevention. Since 2001, the ECCP has collaborated with both regional and international partners to work toward a global strategy of research, dialogue, and consultation that is leading to a major international conference scheduled for 2005. The main objective of this process is to increase the effectiveness of conflict prevention by improving coordination and interaction between civil society, the U.N., regional organizations, and governments.

As part of this process, as well as to identify and build upon civil society conflict prevention capacity within Canada, the Canadian Peacebuilding Coordinating Committee (CPCC) and its Conflict Prevention Working Group established the Canadian Conflict Prevention Initiative (CCPI). A major part of this initiative was to determine the range of actors engaged in conflict prevention in Canada and to identify the most common themes that are relevant to this work. These themes and range of interests were identified in a survey conducted by the authors in the summer of 2003.

RATIONALE, METHODOLOGY, AND QUANTITATIVE RESULTS[16]

The purpose of the survey was to provide information about the individuals and organizations involved in conflict prevention, their interests and their needs. Evidence from the survey indicates that many individuals and organizations in Canada feel that they are contributing to conflict prevention in ways ranging from protecting natural resources to supporting micro-finance initiatives. As a result, definitions of conflict prevention continue to evolve as development, environmental, and relief organizations increasingly incorporate conflict awareness into their traditional programming. These approaches are being undertaken alongside more traditional conflict prevention activities in an attempt to increase the positive impacts on conflict. Key objectives of the survey included:

1. To identify organizations and individuals in Canada who are currently involved in conflict prevention activities or who are likely to become involved in the future;
2. To provide inputs for the CPCC database of organizations and individuals;
3. To identify Canadian themes and issues in international conflict prevention work;
4. To identify the current needs of the conflict prevention community in Canada.

Respondents: Who Are They?

The *Conflict Prevention in Canada* survey targeted a wide range of actors in thirteen specific categories. Respondents self-identified in eleven of these thirteen categories, as identified in table 8.1, with only members of the media and colleges (not universities who were represented) not

Table 8.1. Institutional Affiliation

Government	5
University	13
College	0
Other Educational Institution	2
Think Tank	3
Business	2
Cooperative	0
Faith-based Organization	3
Full Service NGO	4
Specialized NGO	14
Media	0
Independent Consultant	3
Other	6

being included by name. Response rates from the federal government were somewhat lower than the rate of reply among other sectors. The response from the NGO community (comprising both specialized and full-service NGOs, as well as faith-based organizations) was particularly strong, indicating a clear interest among this stakeholder group in the area of conflict prevention: they represented over two-thirds of the respondents. The academic sector response rate was also very good, comprising one-quarter of all responses.

Also apparent in these results was the fact that more than half of respondents are, or intend to be, active in policy development, regional activities, governance and political development, peace education, and mediation and conflict management. At the same time, more than 50 percent of participants indicated little or no involvement in the areas of relief and humanitarian assistance, early warning systems, and children and armed conflict.

Although, the response total for table 8.1 was 55, the survey managed to almost reach the full spectrum of individuals engaged in conflict prevention activities. Notably, the responses from the business community and media were very low. Future efforts should be made to include these stakeholders in further conflict prevention activities as there is the potential for very important work to be carried out in this area. The links between trade in natural resources, including diamonds and oil, as well as issues related to the proliferation of small arms and light weapons, children and armed conflict, human rights, and women in armed conflict will be better addressed if governments, civil society groups, and the business community work together on solutions. By including the private sector stakeholders, negotiated solutions will be more likely to be effective. The issue of conflict diamonds, for example is being addressed from a multi-stakeholder approach through the Kimberley Process, and while progress may be slow, it is indeed being made.

Areas of Work

The work conducted by survey respondents covers a wide range of conflict prevention activities, from specific conflict-related initiatives, to broader programing designed to address the structural contributors to conflict. More than half of those surveyed indicated that policy development was an important component of their work, as was regional specificity.

Figure 8.1[17] makes it apparent that the majority of organizations in the sample are predominantly engaged in specific regions of the world rather than having a truly global focus. This suggests that organizations may be maximizing effectiveness by concentrating on smaller geographic areas, and that there may be ways in which such work among several organizations could be bonded in order to increase effectiveness and capitalize on individual expertise.

Three general geographic areas are indicated as most popular in terms of involvement (see table 8.2).

Asia, Africa, and the Americas (encompassing North America, South America, and Central America) far outpace other geographic regions; each is cited by more than half of the respondents as a focus for their work. When the responses indicating the Americas are divided into their subregions, however, Africa and Asia (including Southeast Asia) become the most active regions. This finding is not unexpected given the political, military, social, and economic factors at work in these areas. Examples such as the Democratic Republic of the Congo (DRC), Liberia, Sierra Leone, Indonesia, and Afghanistan demonstrate why these two geographic regions top the list. These are areas where there is ongoing conflict and a wide range of development activities under way. In addition, there are

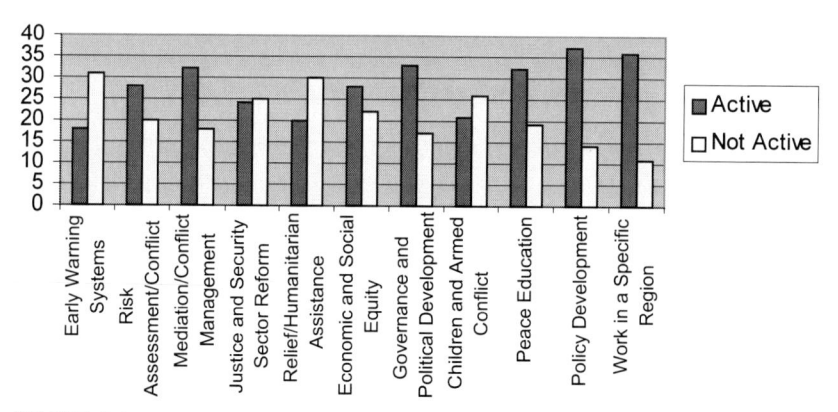

FIGURE 8.1
Areas of Work

Table 8.2. Involvement by Region by Respondent

Oceania	4
South America	8
Central America	19
North America	10
Europe	9
Africa	32
Asia	18
Southeast Asia	17
Middle East	14

places where either Canada or the greater international community is significantly involved.

This finding in favor of a regional focus was reinforced by information gathered through qualitative questions asked about specific work currently under way, including country- and region-specific initiatives. In some ways this reflects the approach of the Canadian government toward international assistance. Canadian governmental agencies are involved in many different countries and regions of the world, although there tends to be a more concerted focus on areas such as Africa, Afghanistan, and regions in which Canadian peacekeepers are involved or where Canada has a particular relationship already in place, such as through the Commonwealth and La Francophonie, as Donaghy and Carter as well as Rioux explain in their respective chapters. Opportunities for capitalizing on the convergences between government and civil society initiatives in places such as Afghanistan, Sierra Leone, Sudan, and the DRC clearly exist.

While relationships between the Canadian government and NGOs are already established to varying degrees, the potential impact of increasing the coherence and impact of conflict prevention programing on the ground is significant. Where the policy and strategic objectives of various government departments and NGOs operating overseas come together, better communication, increased coordination, and the exploitation of resources and experience can result in more effective prevention of violence. Communities that have been living under a cloud of violence for an extended period of time can benefit greatly when aid agencies, government departments, and international or regional organizations can combine or coordinate their efforts in order to more effectively address some of the issues they face.

Policy development, work in specific regions, and governance and political development are considered to be major components of current conflict prevention work in Canada, with more than half of all respondents indicating some activity in these areas. Of the responses submitted to the question of *In which of the following areas of work are you, or do you intend to be, active*, 25 individuals or groups indicated very little or no involvement in justice and security sector reform, while 23 respondents indicated that they were involved in this aspect of conflict prevention to a considerable extent. Children and armed conflict is another area where this split is also evident, with 26 respondents being involved to little or no extent and 20 being significantly engaged in related programming. This finding suggests that while certain areas are clearly a focus for many groups and organizations, some specialized issues belong to select organizations. At the same time, some approaches, such as policy development and regional-specific programing, cross institutional and organizational boundaries and involve a variety of actors. This relationship may be due to the fact that the requirements of such activities are less complex than areas such as justice and security sector reform where specialized and intensive capabilities are likely more necessary.

Additionally, the results indicate that there is relatively little concentration on early warning systems, relief and humanitarian assistance, and children and armed conflict among the respondents. Academics, for instance, were less focused on children and armed conflict than other areas, with only two of the fifteen academic respondents indicating that they are "very" or "somewhat" involved in this issue. It is difficult to conclude whether this finding is indicative of the level of involvement in these areas among all members of the conflict prevention community due to the complexity of the area or the limits of the survey. At best, it is possible to extrapolate this data to suggest that perhaps these approaches are more specialized and somewhat less common among practitioners than other areas.

Overall, the results of the survey have proved useful in influencing Canadian foreign policy. In 2004, policy development and networking opportunities between the civil society sector and the Canadian government have been established. The potential to influence official policy directions and priorities have also been identified. This is especially true given the *International Policy Review* due for release in the fall of 2004. If opportunities for direct dialogue are enhanced, there is the real potential to see some of the ideals and approaches of the non-governmental sector reflected in Canadian international policy. It is the hope of civil society practitioners to be able to feed into this process, comment on the draft review, and include a focus on conflict prevention and related activities in the new strategic plan. Some uncertainty remains, however, given Summer 2004 federal election results; interested stakeholders plan to continue to work toward an inclusionary process in which the lessons learned by civil society practitioners can be used to develop better, more effective government policy.

Qualitative Results

The qualitative component of the questionnaire addressed the identification of Canadian themes and issues in international conflict prevention and the discovery of current needs within the Canadian conflict prevention community. In order to collect this information, several open-ended questions were included in the e-mail survey and further questioning with interview subjects was used to elicit additional detail.

The range of organizations that took part in this survey hints at the breadth of activities in which Canadians are involved. Large organizations such as the CIDA claim to take part in a complete spectrum of development and conflict prevention activities, while smaller NGOs often specialize in a limited number of programming options. For instance, an organization such as One Sky focuses closely on work in Sierra Leone, particularly vocational training programs. Similarly, Peacefund Canada specializes in funding grassroots peace-related projects on such issues as alternative dispute resolution.

While individual groups and organizations are involved in a variety of projects and issue areas, certain themes recur throughout the responses. One of the most important recurring themes in the survey is the quantity of grassroots work, local-level programs, and empowering programing under way with the support of Canadian institutions and individuals. Many of these organizations also suggested that their own role is primarily one of support for "home-grown" solutions and initiatives. In essence, many respondents suggest that the solutions to ongoing conflict are more likely to be found among those involved in the conflict, and often these solutions require outside assistance to be realized. Education and development were activities that also appeared frequently in the responses and were often closely linked. Such linkages indicate that the concept of "conflict prevention," particularly for certain organizations, has broadened to include many of the structural and systemic issues relating to conflict prevention.

Several basic ideas reappeared in the responses to the question relating to the core principles that direct the work of the respondents in conflict prevention. The three most popular sentiments were *empowerment* of local actors, *education* of people in conflicted areas, and *dialogue* on conflict and violence. Additionally, democratic principles were identified as important, as were those of civil society, law and order, and human rights, including respect, accountability, and responsibility. There was also reference to documents such as the U.N. Charter and the Universal Declaration of Human Rights and the report of the International Commission on Intervention and State Sovereignty, *The Responsibility to Protect*, as physical representations of the principles at work within the organizations that responded to this survey. Interestingly, these types of principles are also the foundation of much of the Canadian government's international policy. Democratic ideals, governance, security sector reform, electoral processes, accountability, and human rights appear frequently in programing and funding initiatives announced by the federal government. Within such areas human rights, international law, and a commitment to multilateralism tend to be general overriding themes.

One current example of the application of such principles is in the Canadian approach to Iraq. Although Canada does not have military personnel on the ground, there are Canadians working with Iraqi police personnel in Jordan, assisting in training a new Iraqi police force. Similarly, Canadian organizations are working in Afghanistan on issues such as human rights education for women and microfinance enterprises. Some of the other principles identified by respondents are equity, inclusion, enabling, non-violence, and supporting, privileging, and encouraging local and/or Southern actors. The principles identified by the civil society sector in this survey clearly reflect and build upon those of the Canadian government.

The themes identified as most important in conflict prevention varied according to the type and focus of the organization responding to the survey. This institutional specificity is understandable and reflects the specializations found in the conflict prevention field. The International Development Research Centre (IDRC), for example, includes sustainable and participatory management and development as some of the most important themes,[18] while Project Ploughshares suggests that disarmament issues are integral to conflict prevention.[19] Overall, responses ranged from specific, concrete themes, such as disarmament, to more theoretical or idealistic themes, such as human rights, nonviolence, peacebuilding, and commitment at various levels of government as well as among society at large.

Among the responses from CIDA was one that mentioned the Canadian government's 3D approach which in many ways encapsulates most of the responses from other organizations and individuals. A few survey respondents even indicated that such a holistic vision should be Canada's contribution to international conflict prevention. This approach encompasses the issues regarding broadening traditional ideas relating to aid and development, commitment to international institutions and democratic processes, and peacekeeping activities, as well as issues relating to sustainability and participation.

For instance, the Youth Millennium Project (YMP) at UBC focuses on educating and empowering youth in areas where conflict has occurred or is occurring. They very eloquently summed up this important theme by saying,

> Peace is not simply the absence of war, it is the absence of fear. When communities are in need, when people don't have enough to eat, when there is a lack of clean water, people fear for their survival. The result of fear is often a power struggle that causes confusion, anxiety, and disputes over scarce resources which can lead to conflict and war.[20]

YMP has thus been working with youth to link the allocation and use of resources with fear and freedom from fear.

Another overriding theme that appeared in several of the responses was that Canada should support the work of international and regional organizations. UNICEF stated that "as a soft power, Canada is in a strong position to champion international laws and treaties through the U.N. and other regional and international bodies."[21] CUSO's response reflected similar views, stating that

Canada is respected internationally for being a promoter of peace and human security, and should continue this role. It should continue to work within multi-lateral frameworks, including the U.N., ensuring rule of law is adhered to in all its conflict prevention and interventions. Canada should support the reform of the U.N. in order to make it a more effective international body capable of effecting positive change in today's world. Canada should be more active in ensuring that people around the world share equitably in its resources. Canada should promote human rights and democratic development in all its international dealings including in trade and development.[22]

These views are fairly representative of a major portion of the responses received.

In summary, respondents believed that Canada is, or at least has the potential to be, a leader in international conflict prevention; that work by Canadians reaches every region of the globe, though Africa and Asia are of particular focus; that conflict prevention activities should include a large proportion of grassroots programs, including education, training, empowerment, and equity; and that aid and assistance are present primarily as a supporting role, and that human rights, international law, and related charters and treaties provide the framework in which such work must be conducted.

KEY FINDINGS AND DIRECTIONS FOR FURTHER RESEARCH

As noted at the outset, concepts of conflict prevention may be specific and include such things as mediation and diplomacy, or the definition can be expanded to include a range of activities designed to alleviate some of the problems that can lead to conflict, including resource allocation, corruption, ethnic or territorial disputes, and economic inequality. This duality was reflected to some extent by the range of participation in the survey. For example, organizations such as One Sky are engaged in activities that would likely not fall under traditional definitions of conflict prevention.

Another observed trend is the breadth of activities in which Canadians are involved. Programming by Canadian organizations reaches every corner of the globe and encompasses both direct conflict prevention and management activities, and involvement in initiatives that address structural, or "root," issues that have been increasingly seen to contribute to conflict. Examples of this kind of approach include aid programs as undertaken by agencies such as CIDA, training programs that teach war-affected youth specific skills, work to ensure the inclusion of women in the economic, social, and political development of a region, and natural resource and environmental management. What this indicates is that Canada and Canadians continue to be involved in the global community and that there is sustained and continuing interest in remaining involved.

A third theme that has emerged from this survey is the optimism with which the majority of organizations and individuals view the possible role of Canada and Canadians in conflict prevention. Many respondents suggested that Canada has been heading in the right direction, opting for a comprehensive and holistic approach that includes developmental as well as diplomatic, operational, and defensive work. There were also several comments on the historical traditions in Canada related to Pearson's peacekeeping initiatives, the focus on human security and Canada's support for international law and institutions such as the United Nations as being an excellent foundation upon which to build current and future conflict prevention and management activities. People seem to believe that not only are there things that can be done, but that Canada and Canadians are ready, willing, and able to do it.

While the overwhelming majority of comments seemed to be positive in nature, there were a few criticisms of Canada's work in the area, including a suggestion that foreign aid should be increased to 0.75 percent of GDP from its current level of 0.25 percent. Another comment raised the possibility that Canada restructure its military to become peacekeeping specialists, perhaps indicating a suggestion that military operations like the one currently under way in Afghanistan should not be the focus of the Canadian government in the future. The greatest need expressed by the respondents was a need to interact, share information, and offer and receive support within the rules-based international order as defined by the United Nations and international law.

With respect to Canada's involvement in conflict prevention, particular support should be offered to organizations engaged in activities such as early warning and relief and humanitarian assistance, since there appear to be fewer, but perhaps more specialized, organizations involved in this work. For example, facilitating connections between these institutions and others would be expected to be particularly beneficial by expanding awareness of early warning and relief and humanitarian assistance, as well as linking organizations which could be helpful to each other.

NOTES

1. This challenge by Canadian Prime Minister Lester B. Pearson was made in 1957 in response to the deteriorating situation in the Middle East. Despite Pearson's warning, the United Nations and its member states of today remain afflicted by a lack of cohesion, an inability to incorporate lessons learned, and an unwillingness to act preventively.

2. For a full evaluation of conflict prevention mainstreaming and new linkages, see David Carment and Schnabel Albrecht, eds., *Conflict Prevention from Rhetoric to Reality*, 2 vols. (Lanham, MD: Lexington Books, 2004); and David Carment and Schnabel Albrecht, eds., *Conflict Prevention: Path to Peace or Grand Illusion?* (Tokyo: United Nations University Press, 2003).

3. The Westphalian Treaty at its birth was an attempt to prevent the continuation of the interstate warfare of the early seventeenth century, and its rationale is deeply imbedded in such fundamentals of statecraft as deterrence, reassurance, and compellence.

4. For full data and an explanation of this shift plus an evaluation of current intrastate conflicts, see http://www.carleton.ca/cifp.

5. Boutros Boutros-Ghali, *An Agenda for Peace* (New York: UN Office of Information, 1995).

6. For full examples and explanations of these terms, see Michael Lund, *Preventing Violent Conflict* (Washington, DC: US Institute for Peace Press, 1996).

7. Lund, *Preventing Violent Conflict*.

8. See Bruce Jentleson, "The Realism of Preventive Statecraft," in *Conflict Prevention*, 2003, chapter 2.

9. Barnett R. Rubin, *Blood on the Doorstep: The Politics of Preventive Action* (New York: Century Foundation Press, 2002), 168.

10. The International Commission on Intervention and State Sovereignty, *The Responsibility to Protect: Research, Bibliography, Background* (Ottawa: International Development Research Centre, 2001), 32.

11. Rubin, *Blood on the Doorstep*, 131–132.

12. Michael E. Brown and Richard N. Rosecrance, *The Case for Conflict Prevention* (Lanham, MD: Rowman & Littlefield Publishing, 1999).

13. Department of Foreign Affairs and International Trade, "Canada in the World: Canadian Foreign Policy Review, 1995," http://www.dfait-maeci.gc.ca/foreign_policy/cnd-world/menu-en.asp.

14. More information on Canada's foreign policy priorities can be found at http://www.dfait-maeci.gc.ca.

15. The British government has created two Conflict Prevention Pools (CPPs), one for sub-Saharan Africa (ACPP) and one for outside Africa (Global CPP or GCPP) to improve department coordination and priority-setting. The CPPs are jointly funded and administered by three departments of state: the Ministry of Defence (MOD), Department for International Development (DfID), and Foreign and Commonwealth Office (FCO). The main new organizational additions were an interdepartmental steering mechanism and a process for joint priority-setting for each conflict. Once established, the CPPs brought together budgets for program spending and peacekeeping costs. Although still in development, this coordinated effort is an example of a commitment to cooperation between departments to ensure an intervening effort that includes all aspects of reconstruction, from security to economics, participation and social development.

16. The survey consisted of both an e-mail survey and follow-up interviews, which provided both quantitative, general information, and qualitative, specific data. A short e-mail questionnaire was sent to stakeholders from a variety of relevant non-governmental organizations, educational institutions, and government departments. Survey recipients included practitioners, activists, academics, businesspeople, and government officials who are actively engaged in issues of peace and conflict, either directly from a humanitarian relief, development, social/economic equity, justice, governance, educational, or other angle. The questionnaire included a range of questions encompassing both the general areas of involvement and the specific details of work being conducted in the field. Additionally, it solicited not only the institutional affiliation of the respondent, but also their core interests and activities, as well as ways in which they would be interested in participating in the Canadian Conflict Prevention Initiative.

17. Figure 8.1—For simplification purposes responses have been collapsed into Active (including "very" and "somewhat" active responses) and Not Active (comprising "hardly" and "not" active responses).

18. IDRC, Survey Response, August 2003.

19. Project Ploughshares, Survey Response, August 2003.

20. Quoted from the Youth Millennium Project, Survey Response, August 2003.

21. Quoted from the UNICEF Canada, Survey Response, August 2003.

22. From the CUSO, Survey Response, August 2003.

9

Canadian Official Development Assistance Policy: Juggling the National Interest and Humanitarian Impulses[1]

Jean-Sébastien Rioux

As the other chapters in this volume demonstrate, Canada has done its best to play an active (and sometimes activist) role in international relations ever since it came into its own during World War II and in the years that followed. Canada has a strong record of diplomatic achievement (the name Lester B. Pearson is known to most students of international politics around the world); its military once had bases in Germany during the Cold War and members of the Canadian Forces have served in almost every single peacekeeping mission approved by the United Nations since 1956; and its role in the global economy is important enough that Canadian prime ministers sit at all the major world forums, including the elite G-8 club of most developed countries. Additionally, Canada, like all developed nations attempting to promote their values and extend their influence abroad, seeks to play a role in international development by sending aid to poorer countries because development assistance is traditionally one of the cornerstones of a successful and well-rounded foreign policy, along with trade, diplomacy, and military force. An analysis of Canada's foreign aid policy thus helps us to understand one of the major pillars of its role in the world and the extent to which it "puts its money where its mouth is" in terms of helping poorer states.

Canada joined the select club of foreign aid donors in 1950, less than two decades after its foreign policy became independent from the United Kingdom in 1931. Like most other industrialized countries, Canada developed a bureaucracy to administer its foreign aid program—which is technically called "Official Development Assistance" (ODA)—and has adjusted its foreign aid on several occasions in response to domestic and international trends. The amounts of aid given by Canada have varied over time, moreover, with some periods being more generous, while in others, especially during recessions, ODA competed with more important domestic priorities. For better or worse, ODA is often perceived by the public as a luxury, to be spent when other priorities, such as education and health, have been adequately financed. As well, some critics have argued that the diminishing amounts of foreign aid that Canada has sent since the early 1990s reflects a general decline in Canada's global stature.[2] Nevertheless, foreign aid—ODA—has always been one of the key elements of Canadian foreign policy, along with its diplomatic efforts at promoting multilateralism and conflict resolution, as well as its military commitments to the North Atlantic Treaty Organization and participation in international peacekeeping.

Canadians derive much pride from their place in the international arena, and foreign aid contributes to that pride. In a fairly recent study, 86 percent of surveyed Canadians thought that the rest of the world had either "very" (44%) or "fairly" (42%) positive attitudes regarding Canada.[3] This result was attributed, by these same respondents, to two positive aspects of Canada's foreign policy: its participation in international peacekeeping (39%) and its generous foreign aid (13%).[4] Moreover, in that same survey, 82 percent of Canadians said it was important to help people from poor countries, and 74 percent believed that Canada's foreign aid spending should stay the same (51%) or increased (23%).[5] More recently and very much along those lines, David Black and Rebecca Tiessen reported Earnescliffe poll results, published by the Canadian Council for International Cooperation in May 2000, showing that "66% of Canadians thought that the government was spending either the right amount or not enough on aid, and that this percentage increased to 73% when respondents were told what the actual expenditure was."[6] In other words, Canadians generally accept the prevailing wisdom that they are a generous and important player in the international arena.[7]

Foreign aid can take several forms. There are so-called bilateral programs, which may include direct grants and loans to foreign governments, or the forgiveness of debts incurred by a poor country to one's government. There is also participation in multilateral programs such as direct cash transfers to the World Bank, humanitarian assistance to refugees in war zones, hunger prevention programs, and international action against land mines. Another form is grants to third parties such as non-governmental organizations (NGOs) to spend on specific community development for a specific project such as building a school or digging a well.

All advanced economies give development assistance in these various forms, and for government officials of any donor state, foreign aid is often seen as an important tool for making friends and gaining influence in developing states. They reason that if countries become more democratic as they develop, and if democratic countries are more peaceful and stable, then foreign aid can be used to nurture developing states whose policies please the donors. Conversely, foreign aid can be a tool to rein in governments of poorer states that displease the donor: rich states can threaten to reduce next year's ODA, for example, if the government of the recipient state does not comply with a certain issue. Obviously, these types of sanctions can harm innocent people, but they have been used against Iraq during the 1990s and, most recently, against Zimbabwe.

Canada, although less powerful and involved abroad than some of the other rich states, is not immune to the impulse to use aid to gain influence abroad; but the Canadian government (and the Canadian public, as we have seen with the survey results presented above) likes to think it gives ODA to those countries that most need it—a "humanitarian impulse" to help the poorest and neediest inhabitants of the planet. Therefore, important sums of money are spent on natural disaster relief (to help, for example, the victims of South Asian tsunamis, earthquakes in Turkey, typhoons in Bangladesh, or floods in Haiti); emergency crisis response (such as sending aid and specialists to help war refugees in the Darfur region of the Sudan); and on health crises such as HIV/AIDS in sub-Saharan Africa. Development assistance is seen as a way to reach the most helpless members of humanity.

Another impulse for governments to use ODA—including the Canadian government—is to tie foreign aid to commercial trade. For example, a donor can send foreign aid to a country which can only be used to purchase goods from the donor state. This is called "tied aid" and most donor states have used this form of ODA to boost favored economic sectors; in the recent past, Canada, for example, has encouraged aid recipients to purchase Canadian wheat with the aid money, thus helping to feed the poor in the developing country, but also helping Canadian wheat farmers in Western Canada in the process, which never hurts in an election year.

With that in mind, this chapter examines Canada's ODA program and describes some of the factors which influence it. As well, this chapter analyzes the current direction of the Canadian ODA program in light of the recent emphasis on helping Africa and, more particularly, Canada's leadership on the New Economic Partnership for Africa's Development (NEPAD). Indeed, this ambitious plan to help the poorest continent was spotlighted at the G-8 summit meeting at Kananaskis (Alberta), in June 2002. At that meeting, and after a decade of declining ODA levels, Jean Chrétien's Liberal government, in power from 1993 to 2003, promised an additional $500 million CDN for Africa which, in relative terms, represents a very large increase for Canada's ODA program. Following this trend, several questions arise regarding the coming challenges for Canadian foreign policy over the next few years. For example, in light of the stated goals of Canada's foreign aid program, how will political events in Africa affect this commitment? Will the new emphasis on Africa redress a perennial problem in Canada's ODA policy, which has been described as "a mile wide [but] an inch thick"?[8] These points, among others, are addressed in the chapter's conclusion.

THREE TYPES OF INFLUENCES ON CANADA'S OFFICIAL DEVELOPMENT ASSISTANCE PROGRAM[9]

Foreign aid generally has been studied in the context of three of the most widely adopted paradigms of international relations: realism, globalism, and pluralism.[10] These perspectives also can be considered in terms of the foreign policy motives—strategic, economic, and humanitarian—which influence states to provide ODA. While scholars have consistently demonstrated that these influences are subtle and not mutually exclusive in explaining foreign aid locations, the distinctions among them are still useful in delineating the primary political interests that sustain aid flows.

According to the realist paradigm of international relations theory, world politics and foreign policy are driven by considerations of states' geostrategic interests, and ODA is but one aspect of a state's foreign policy. One noted scholar has written that foreign assistance is "inseparable from the problem of power."[11] In the realist tradition, therefore, aid programs are expected to facilitate the strategic interests of the donor state and ODA is viewed either as minimally related to recipient economic development or, if an effect is identified, as significant solely in terms of its effect on the donor's prestige, political-military security, and economic position. For the analysis of development aid, this leads to the expectation that greater levels of aid will be directed toward recipients that are strategically important to the donor. This strategic use of foreign aid is often advanced as an explanation for the disproportionate levels of aid awarded by the United States to Israel and Egypt, for example.[12] Scholars researching patterns of ODA flows have included in their models variables representing strategic motives, such as levels of militarization or alliance ties, and have found consistent support in their analyses of aid flows.[13] For example, analyses of French ODA disbursement patterns demonstrate that aid is very much directed at its former African colonies.[14] American and British aid is heavily influenced by geostrategic considerations, such as alliances.[15]

From a realist perspective, then, Canadian government decision-makers would be expected to give larger amounts of ODA to developing states that are of strategic importance to Canada. But Canada is not a global power with worldwide military interests, so which strategic considerations would matter to decision-makers? A look at Canada's history as a colony provides some clues. Discovered in 1534 by France and first settled by French colonists starting in 1604, Canada was later "taken" by Britain at the Treaty of Paris of 1763 that marked the end of the Seven Years War.[16] To this day, Canada is still strongly linked to both founding powers and is a member of both the British Commonwealth and the Organisation internationale de la Francophonie (OIF). (See Donaghy and Carter's chapter 6 in this volume for an in-depth study of La Francophonie).

The Commonwealth, founded in 1931, consists of 53 governments and a population of 1.8 billion citizens who have a historical or colonial link to the United Kingdom, with many of these governments (including Canada's) actually owing vestigial allegiance to the British Crown. While La Francophonie is not an intergovernmental organization with strictly the same political significance as the Commonwealth, several of the OIF's 53 members are former French colonies and, in principle, all have in common usage of the French language to one degree or another. Thus, Canada is associated with two international organizations whose membership is deeply rooted in the political culture of either Britain or France. Moreover, this international duality of cultures is also found within Canada, where 7 million Canadians (about 22% of a total population of 32 million) are French-speaking, 80 percent of whom are concentrated in the province of Québec. This leads to a dual national media (where, for example, the national Canadian Broadcasting Corporation also broadcasts television and radio nationally in French through Radio-Canada) and to dual international "loyalties." Previous analyses point out that Canada's ODA is influenced by its membership in international organizations such as the Commonwealth and La Francophonie more than by its military alliances.[17] Thus, Canada would be more likely to give foreign aid to countries that are members of the Commonwealth and/or La Francophonie.

Globalist theoretical perspectives on foreign assistance are based upon neo-Marxist assumptions about the pervasive role of economic wealth in foreign policy-making. The motives driving aid programs are assumed to reflect the function of transnational capital flows, serving to preserve or even widen economic disparities between the world's rich and poor. From this perspective, aid is not given to help the recipient country or to obtain specific goals such as political cooperation, but instead to facilitate economic exploitation by elites within industrialized states. One scholar of foreign aid allocations found that world-systems analysis offers a "useful starting point" for considering the distribution of ODA.[18] From this analytical perspective, we perceive that "core states" (i.e., the capitalist center), in response to the interests of their business elites, use aid to exercise coercive influence over the development strategies of peripheral states, imposing export-oriented growth strategies that deprive developing countries of "real inward-oriented, self-reliant strategies,"[19] and enhance a dependent economic relationship between the donor and the recipient. For scholars researching international aid flows, this standpoint leads to the expectation that allocations will be directed disproportionately toward trading partners that the donor state "exploits" economically. Significant linkages may also be anticipated between aid and industrial development and raw materials production within developing countries. Specifically, variables reflecting the trade flows between recipient and donor are commonly used in analyses of bilateral aid commitments and disbursements.[20]

As a matter of fact, Canada sends more ODA to developing countries with which it has a positive trade balance. In other words, countries which are net importers of Canadian goods rather than net exporters of their goods to Canada tend to receive more Canadian ODA.[21] This point was mentioned in the introduction, with the example of the wheat farmers in Western Canada. At the same time, however, Canada's trade is overwhelmingly concentrated with the United States—more than 85 percent of all Canadian exports go to America. Thus, to claim that the remaining 15 percent would be directed to maintaining an asymmetric balance-of-trade with developing states is unrealistic, especially given the fact that a large proportion of that 15 percent in non-U.S. trade is directed at Japan, China, and Western Europe. In fact, the Least Developed Countries' share of Canada's foreign trade represents about 0.1 percent—one-tenth of one percent—of Canada's total trade.[22] Thus, one cannot realistically claim that Canadian ODA policy is directed at maintaining economic exploitation/dependency and market share in developing (periphery) states, given the small amount of trade actually conducted with developing states. Nevertheless, there are some examples of this motive, however small it may be.

Finally, the pluralist paradigm challenges both the realist and neo-Marxist assumptions and prescriptions, advancing a vision that is more positive regarding the motivations of decision-makers and other actors involved in the aid process. From this perspective, aid is conceived as being motivated by a humanitarian concern for the population in the recipient state. Donor national interests are not dismissed, but the most important influences on aid are instead said to be guided by transnational humanitarian concerns. This view has therefore challenged the realist position that foreign aid has served primarily as a vehicle for the interests of donors, with a blind eye to the developmental needs of recipient populations.[23] Values regarding social welfare and the human needs of recipient populations are argued to drive aid policies, and variables reflecting the wealth or need of the country are used in almost all models of the aid allocation decision, with per capita Gross Domestic Product (GDP) and Gross National Product (GNP) the most commonly used indicators of the level of need within the recipient country.[24] Thus, measures representing the overall wealth of the recipient country and its overall level of need, such as GDP per capita, consistently have shown a clear and substantial correlation with aid levels.

The government of Canada has, since 2002, explicitly recognized the special needs of the world's poorest continent—Africa—and modified its aid priorities accordingly: among other steps, in 2002 it produced a policy called Strengthening Aid Effectiveness, and in 2003 it created a special fund for Africa, as well as "rationalizing" the list of countries to which it sends aid by focusing on eight countries in Africa, and about 20 countries around the world (as opposed to the 100 or so countries to which Canada has given aid, thus diluting its impact, and hence the earlier comment about Canada's foreign aid being described as "a mile wide and an inch thick").

Having described general influences on Canada's ODA policy, we shall now turn to a description of the agencies that execute that policy.

CANADA'S FOREIGN AID BUREAUCRACY

Canada joined the ranks of international donor states with its participation in the Colombo Plan in 1950. In these early years, Canada's ODA program was administered by the Department of External Affairs and was very modest: it represented only 0.08% of GDP, or $13 million CDN.[25] Nowadays, while several agencies are tasked to participate in allocating foreign aid, the principal bureaucracy in charge of Canada's ODA program is the Canadian International Development Agency (CIDA), established in 1968, which oversees more than 70 percent of Canada's ODA. The agency is headed by a Minister for International Cooperation, and the senior civil servant who advises the Minister is appointed President of CIDA.[26]

Like most foreign affairs and international development bureaucracies, CIDA is structured along both regional directorates and multilateral issues/policies directorates. There are four geographical branches (the Americas, Asia, Central and Eastern Europe, and Middle East and Africa) and three multilateral/policy branches (Multilateral Programs, Canadian Partnership, and Policy).[27] There are approximately 1,600 employees working for CIDA (about 88 percent of whom are permanent while the rest work on a contractual basis). Permanent members of CIDA are eligible for diplomatic postings abroad, and most Canadian diplomatic missions to developing countries count CIDA Development Officers. The primary method of recruitment is an annual national post-secondary drive held every October by the Canadian government, which involves a full day of tests. Those individuals scoring above a predetermined threshold are invited for a second round involving personal interviews. In 2002, CIDA hired 22 "development agents" in this way (the average has been about 20 per year lately).

Other bureaucracies are part of the foreign aid disbursement process and warrant mentioning. Foreign Affairs Canada (FAC) attends to Canada's foreign policy and diplomatic representation abroad and is headed by the Minister for Foreign Affairs.[28] In the specialized circles in Ottawa, a popular saying describes the two bureaucracies' distinct roles as "Foreign Affairs handles High Politics and CIDA digs wells." While this is mostly true, FAC does administer some programs, for example, relating to human rights, education, scholarships, and humanitarian emergencies.

The other Canadian departments with a role in international development include the Department of Finance, which is in charge of transferring the funds to the International Financial Institutions (IFIs) to which Canada belongs—the World Bank and three regional banks (the Inter-American, African, and Asian Development Banks) and the International Monetary Fund (IMF). The Department of Agriculture and Agri-Foods of Canada also is an actor as it is involved in international technical assistance. However, as previously mentioned, CIDA is the main actor in Canada's ODA program.

In fiscal year 2002–2003, Canada's aid budget reached about $3 billion dollars CDN, or about $2.3 billion U.S., although in relative terms Canada's ODA spending had been on a downward trend since the end of the Cold War. Indeed, foreign aid spending reached a recent high of about 0.5 percent of GDP in 1975–1976, dropped, rose again in 1986–1987, but has been declining since and now represents only about 0.3 percent of GDP.[29] This is despite the fact that, in 1987, CIDA published a White Paper on Canada's international aid commitments called *Sharing Our Future: Canadian Assistance to International Development*, which stated that "it is the government's objective to raise the ODA/GNP ratio by gradual increments, beginning in 1991–1992, to 0.6% by 1995 and to 0.7% by 2000."[30] This would have allowed Canada to reach the United Nations' aid target for rich countries. The historical trends in Canada's ODA spending are presented in figure 9.1.

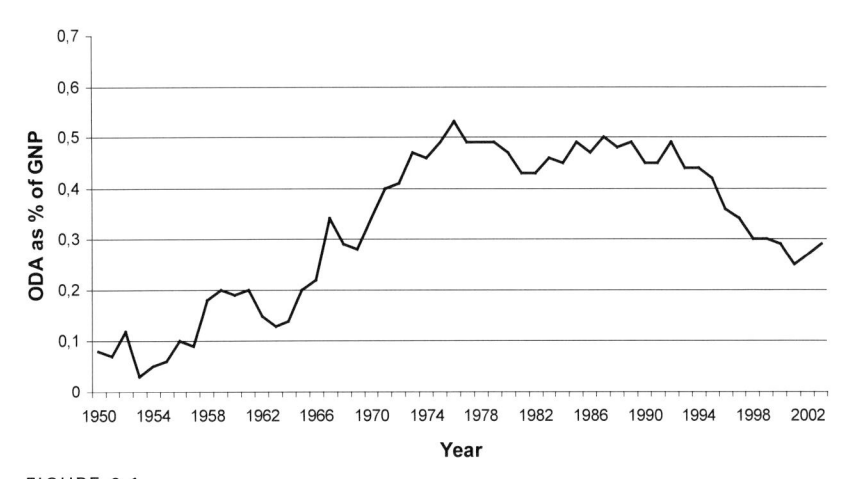

FIGURE 9.1
Canadian ODA/GNP

Source: Canadian International Development Agency (CIDA). 2003. *Statistical Report on Official Development Assistance, FY 2002–2003.* Ottawa, Statistical Analysis Section, Policy Planning and Analysis branch. Available at: http://www.acdi-cida.gc.ca/INET/IMAGES.NSF/vLUImages/stats/$file/StatRep_02...03.pdf

Therefore, there is less money going to ODA, but in terms of international presence CIDA and the other agencies of the Canadian government operate all over the world. According to CIDA's website, it "supports projects in more than 150 countries around the world." Since the United Nations has 191 members, this leaves very few areas where CIDA is not active if we leave out the 27 richer Organisation for Economic Co-operation and Development (OECD) countries[31] and countries like Liechtenstein, Andorra, and the like that are not part of OECD, but nevertheless do not need any ODA. Geographically, Canada's ODA is distributed roughly as shown in figure 9.2 (as of 2003).[32]

As previously mentioned, Canada's ODA has been said to be scattered. This generally is thought to be caused by at least three factors. First, there is a lack of a clear and strong foreign aid policy agenda in Canada. For example, CIDA does issue periodic policy papers such as the aforementioned document titled *Strengthening Aid Effectiveness* and there is an official Development section in the 2005 International Policy Statement to guide ODA.[33] However, these documents are to set priorities more than policy and they are articulated quite broadly. Thus, the lack of a focused aid policy does not set many limits on the wishes and imagination of the

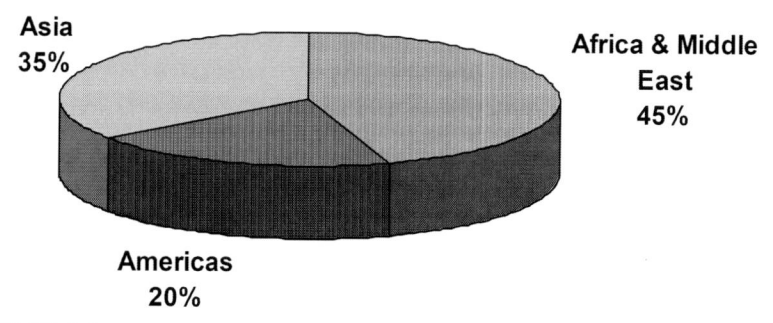

Asia 35%

Africa & Middle East 45%

Americas 20%

FIGURE 9.2
Source of the graph: Canadian International Development Agency (CIDA). 2003. *Statistical Report on Official Development Assistance, FY 2002–2003.* Ottawa, Statistical Analysis Section, Policy Planning and Analysis branch. Available at: http://www.acdi-cida.gc.ca/INET/IMAGES.NSF/vLUImages/stats/$file/StatRep_02...03.pdf

civil servants who administer aid, although the culture is changing somewhat and aid is beginning to be focused on a smaller number of countries.

Secondly, to guide its ODA policies, CIDA also takes its cues from the pronouncements of the United Nations and OECD on development needs. While FAC is concerned with Canada's interests and positions in the world, CIDA is an aid agency which is tasked with helping "people on the ground" in cooperation with the NGOs and international organizations, without necessarily having to be concerned with the foreign minister's personal agenda. Therefore, CIDA has a tendency to look for a seat at every table and to work with all NGOs, regardless of the actual size of its ODA budget.

Finally, Canada displays three different and sometimes competing impulses in the way it wants to spend ODA, which are not necessarily related to the theoretical factors described earlier. Canada displays a multilateral impulse, and it is fair to say that multilateralism is Canada's foreign policy trademark.[34] In terms of aid policy, this translates into a preference to fund development projects through multilateral forums, which is in fact the preferred method of the developing countries since that type of aid is not tied. A second impulse is bilateral, which is politically most desirable from the point of view of donor states; indeed, through CIDA, Canada can continue to be present in "over 150 countries" and thus show the flag around the world, although the government plans to concentrate two thirds of its ODA to 25 countries by 2010. Finally, there is the "third partner" approach whereby aid is subcontracted to NGOs and civil society organizations on the ground, which can be more efficient. Juggling all these interests is a challenge facing Canada as the demand for development assistance grows, while domestic priorities such as health care for an ageing baby-boomer population compete for limited funding. Other factors are at work in influencing Canada's ODA, however, and these will now be analyzed.

INFLUENCES ON CANADIAN ODA

We have discussed several factors that have been theorized to affect foreign aid allocations, and in this section some of these are examined in more detail. These factors include those which were mentioned earlier in the chapter—strategic (realist), globalist (neo-Marxist) and pluralist (humanitarian) influences on ODA. To the following analysis we will include other factors, such as culture and the impact of media coverage.

Strategic Motives for Canadian Aid

As mentioned previously, a first set of factors possibly affecting Canadian ODA levels could be related to the international ties that Canada has with other states. We hypothesized that colonial and historical ties would drive the government to invest ODA in states that share these historical ties. Indeed, previous analyses, such as a study conducted by Jean-Philippe Thérien, have pointed out that Canada's ODA disbursement is influenced by its memberships in international organizations such as the Commonwealth and La Francophonie and its predecessor, the Agence de coopération culturelle et technique.[35] This seems to be the case as we look at table 9.1, which breaks down Canadian ODA by international organization membership for the period 1950 to 1999.

Table 9.1. Comparison of Canadian ODA, 1950–1999 (in millions $US)

	Mean ODA per recipient country	Mean ODA to members of the Commonwealth	Mean ODA to members of La Francophonie
All years (1950–1999)	$5.32	$ 7.66	$4.17
Sample year: 1975	$6.46	$11.82	$3.56
Sample year: 1999	$4.30	$ 4.07	$4.34

Note that the first column represents mean aid per country per year. The first cell tells us that Canada sent, on average, about $5.32 million U.S. in ODA per country, per year. We then note that members of the Commonwealth received, on average between 1950 and 1999, $3.49 million U.S. more per year than states belonging to La Francophonie, and $2.34 million U.S. more per year than average. Surprisingly, Francophonie-member states did not receive more ODA than average; in fact they received $1.15 million U.S. less than average. To look at how the trend changed over time, we looked at two sample years: 1975 and 1999. The discrepancy in foreign aid given to members of the British Commonwealth compared to Francophonie members is accentuated in the year 1975: that year, Commonwealth members actually received $8.26 million U.S. more aid than Francophonie members and $5.36 million U.S. more than average.

Yet, the discrepancy disappears by 1999, and we see that aid is distributed more "evenly," as geostrategic ties appear to be declining. To explain the decline I introduce two additional tables that show which countries received the most aid. Table 9.2 shows the ten largest Canadian ODA recipients of all time, while table 9.3 shows the ten largest Canadian ODA recipients in the year 1999–2000. It now becomes clear why the figures for aid to Commonwealth countries were skewed: of the ten largest aid disbursements in Canadian history, nine were huge grants to two Commonwealth countries—Bangladesh and India. Recall in table 9.1 that the average aid disbursement to any one country was $5.32 million U.S.; therefore, disbursements of over $100 million U.S. represent a large portion of any given year's entire aid budget. By 1999, this bias disappears. We

Table 9.2. Canada's Ten Largest Aid Disbursements and Recipient Countries, 1950–1999

Rank	Amount (millions US$)	Year	Recipient
1	$116.98	1988	Bangladesh
2	$114.03	1996	Egypt
3	$112.56	1974	India
4	$109.30	1975	India
5	$108.87	1992	Bangladesh
6	$105.82	1970	India
7	$104.82	1971	India
8	$102.30	1990	Bangladesh
9	$101.98	1966	India
10	$101.95	1987	Bangladesh

Table 9.3. Canada's Ten Largest Aid Disbursements and Recipient Countries for FY 1999–2000

Rank	Amount (millions US$)	Year	Recipient
1	$31.42	1999	China
2	$30.31	1999	Yugoslavia, Fed. Rep.
3	$29.03	1999	Bangladesh
4	$26.31	1999	Indonesia
5	$25.83	1999	Haiti
6	$23.84	1999	Honduras
7	$18.76	1999	Côte d'Ivoire
8	$18.34	1999	Mali
9	$18.13	1999	Cameroon
10	$17.50	1999	Senegal

can see in table 9.3 that indeed, several important aid recipients—China, Yugoslavia, Indonesia, and Honduras—are members neither of the Commonwealth nor of La Francophonie. We now notice some African countries listed as top ODA recipients, which was the case only with Egypt in 1975. Finally, one also notices that no state by then receives more than $31 million U.S.; the ODA sent to China in 1999 represents 26 percent of the amount sent to Bangladesh in 1988. Indeed, the number of recipient states has increased, leading some to call Canada's aid program "scattered." However, these figures changed considerably after the September 11, 2001 attacks and the subsequent U.S.-led coalition invasions of Afghanistan in 2001 and Iraq in 2003. These two countries now represent Canada's largest individual aid recipients due to their importance in forging regional and global stability. For example, Canada pledged CDN $380 million to the Afghan Reconstruction Fund.

Humanitarianism as an Influence on Canadian Aid Levels

A second set of factors derived from the pluralist approach discussed earlier suggests that ODA will be directed at the needy. This "humanitarian motive" is logical and easily understood: given a finite foreign aid budget, the Canadian people, via the government, will send money to the poorest states; conversely, the richer the state, the less Canada will spend on ODA to that state. This hypothesis was supported by a recent study of Canadian foreign aid: it has been shown that there is a negative and statistically significant relationship between a country's wealth and ODA levels; in other words, the richer the country is, the less ODA will be sent by

Canada.[36] To give an idea of the magnitude of the relationship, that study estimated that an increase in one thousand dollars in a nation's per capita GDP correlates with a *decrease* in ODA of $800,000 CDN. Therefore, we can confidently say that the richer a country is, the less Canadian ODA it is likely to receive, and vice versa, thus lending support for a humanitarian motive for Canada's aid policy.

Cultural Values: Helping Other Democracies

A third factor pertaining to the characteristics of the recipient states that could influence the levels of aid given by Canada is the level of "good governance" present in those states. One pillar of Canadian foreign policy, as expressed in *Canada in the World*, the 1995 White Paper on Canadian foreign policy, is the "projection of Canadian values" abroad, notably "respect for democracy, the rule of law, human rights and the environment...."[37] Such a position is morally and ethically valid, and it may also be logically reasonable, for the argument can be made that the better the governance in the recipient country, the higher the probability that Canadian tax dollars will be judiciously spent; conversely, the more authoritarian the government, the higher the probability that ODA will be diverted to numbered bank accounts overseas.

Recent research has found this not to be the case. To evaluate this proposition, Van Belle, Rioux and Potter[38] measured "good governance" using Freedom House's Political Freedom Index, which publishes an annual survey of political freedom and assigns each state to one of three categories ("free," "partly free," and "not free") based their combined score on a complex checklist of 24 sets of political rights and civil liberties.[39] This organization is well-known and the data generated by Freedom House are widely used in empirical analyses. They sought to see whether the higher the level of political freedom (i.e., "democracy" or "good governance") was related to higher ODA allocations, since it forms an integral part of Canada's foreign policy articulation.

For some reason, Canada tends to give *less* ODA to politically free states than to not-free states. One possible explanation is that most aid (80%) is directed toward Africa and Asia (see Figure 1), which have a large proportion of states in the "partially free" and "not free" categories. Furthermore, recall tables 9.2 and 9.3 showing the 10 largest disbursements of foreign aid: Bangladesh scores only as "partly free," while China and

Egypt score as "not free," to mention only these three examples. Therefore, while one of the three pillars of Canadian foreign aid is allegedly to promote democracy and human rights abroad, this has not been reflected in a statistical analysis of which countries actually received Canadian ODA; furthermore, China appears on the Top 10 Aid Recipients list while it is listed by Freedom House as one of the world's 12 most repressive regimes.[40]

The Impact of the Media and on News Coverage

Finally, a last factor to be discussed as having an impact on the levels of Canadian ODA is the manifestation of a process that may be the logical link between the conditions prevailing in a developing country and the decision-making process that actually allocates levels of aid to these countries. The mechanism that informs the decision-makers in Ottawa as to the conditions mentioned previously can obviously be the Canadian embassies, consulates, and missions in those areas. But the general public is not privy to these reports. Another causal process can be imagined that links events in the foreign countries and the domestic polity—the public, legislators, NGOs, and members of the "civil society"—that have a peripheral impact on the bureaucratic decision-makers: the impact of the news media.

Previous analyses by this author and colleagues have demonstrated a positive relationship between media coverage and its effect on foreign aid bureaucracies.[41] By analyzing the net amount as well as the content of news media coverage of aid recipient states in the Canadian news media, it has been shown that media coverage does influence how much aid a recipient country receives the following year. For example, we found that each story in Toronto's *Globe and Mail*—which is as close to a national paper as there is in Canada—correlates approximately with an increase in $21,500 U.S. in foreign aid, but keep in mind that this is a very crude interpretation.

Of course, foreign aid recipients can be in the news for the "wrong reasons" and this was taken into account in the study, as the content of media coverage was examined as well. Among the types of content examined were political unrest, negative coverage, and coverage focusing on natural and humanitarian disasters (in addition, of course, to "neutral" coverage; for example, a story titled "Prime Minister to Visit Honduras" and giving information about the trip will be "neutral"). We discovered that Canada sends less ODA to unstable regimes, as each story detailing "political unrest" correlates with a decrease in almost $1 million CDN in aid.[42] Finally, and as expected, stories focusing on humanitarian need correlate positively with additional ODA.[43] In summary, there is strong evidence to suggest that media coverage affects levels of ODA, and the content of that coverage matters as well. Humanitarian disasters that are well publicized attract higher levels of Canadian aid, while political unrest appears to diminish it.

NEW TRENDS IN CANADIAN ODA

It is interesting to put these results in perspective with an analysis of what is to come in the future. One interesting challenge to Canada's foreign policy is the unveiling in June 2002 of the G-8 "Africa Action Plan" in support of the New Partnership for Africa's Development (originally called the New Africa Initiative), widely known by its acronym NEPAD. The NAI/NEPAD plan was originally articulated somewhat separately by three African presidents—Abdoulayé Wade of Senegal, Olusegun Obasanjo of Nigeria, and Thabo Mbeki of South Africa—in documents calling for a new relationship between donor countries and African states. At the core of these plans was the articulation of the heretofore taboo notion that traditional aid did not do much to help Africa and a new paradigm, based more on private investment and investment in social capital, health, and education, was needed.[44] The different plans were presented at various forums at the turn of the millennium and at the 2001 meeting of the World Economic Forum.[45] The African presidents and architects of the plans were then invited to present them at the June 2001 G-8 meeting in Genoa, Italy; the presentations were so successful that the G-8 countries urged the Organization for African Unity to propose an African development strategy to which the rich states could then respond. This was accomplished at the OAU Summit in Lusaka in July 2001, when the 53 African countries agreed on a policy and formally proposed a New Partnership for Africa's Development. Through NEPAD, developed countries were invited to "enter a new partnership based on mutual obligations and interest."[46] According to Canadian Department of Foreign Affairs and International Trade (as it was known in 2002), "the underlying objective of the Action Plan is neither to provide a massive infusion of funding nor to underwrite NEPAD projects more generally. The goal is to put in place a new partnership that will unlock greater resources, both public and private."[47]

In response to this African initiative, and at Canadian Prime Minister Chrétien's suggestion, a "sherpa" process was initiated to prepare the formal G-8 response, which was then unveiled at the Kananaskis summit of G-8 countries in June 2002.[48] This Africa Action Plan—a Canadian initiative—was thus the formal response to NEPAD and paved the way for industrialized states to work in concert with African partners to end Africa's economic marginalization, principally by promising increased funding in relation to how well the African countries stick to the goals they themselves set forth in their plan.[49]

This NEPAD process is unprecedented because, as mentioned previously, it had been approved by the 53 member states of the Organization of African Unity (now the African Union), and was intended for African states to jointly manage ODA with the industrialized states. Led by a steering committee of the five "founding states" (Algeria, Egypt, Nigeria, Sénégal, and South Africa) and an implementation committee of representatives of 15 states,[50] NEPAD is intended for Africa to manage the main elements of what would constitute durable development for Africa, which include:

- Peace and security (including conflict prevention);
- Better governance (including peer review and action against corruption);
- Fostering economic growth and private investment (including financing for development); and
- Education/Knowledge and health (including information and communications technology).

The African nations thus enunciated their own development goals and priorities, and the G-8 responded by pledging financial support and debt relief to help them in achieving those goals. It must be noted that former Prime Minister Chrétien deserves great credit for keeping Africa's development on the G-8's agenda, even after the increased priority given to security matters following the events of September 11, 2001. Moreover, in the two days prior to the G-8 meeting in June 2002, events flared up in the Middle East and President Bush proposed a plan for Palestinian statehood, which stole much of the spotlight. Nevertheless, Africa remained on the agenda, thanks also to the interest in the plan on the part of France and the United Kingdom, both former colonial powers in Africa with a remaining keen interest in the region.

One factor that will affect the direction and viability of NEPAD, in which Canada has invested a lot of political capital, concerns the willingness of the United States to participate fully in NEPAD. As a small country with a modest foreign aid budget, Canada cannot solve all the problems of Africa alone, not even in alliance with France and the United Kingdom. For such an ambitious project to work, the United States, as the most powerful country in the world and the largest single aid donor, must concur. This is a fact that will have to be dealt with by the present and future Canadian governments.

Like its predecessors, the Bush administration does not accord a great priority to economic, political, or social development in Africa. As President Bush embarks upon a second term, his foreign policy is especially concerned with international terrorism (particularly the Islamic variety), hoped-for democratic transitions in Afghanistan and Iraq, stability and democratization in the Middle East, nuclear proliferation in Iran and North Korea (considered "rogue states"), the Israeli-Palestinian conflict, and relations with China and Russia. As well, the White House, despite its Millennium Challenge Account rhetoric (i.e., its 2002 offer of development aid as a reward for good governance and responsible economic policy), may have come to the conclusion that much of Africa is not "governable" and that recent events in Zimbabwe, the poor record of governance in states such as Kenya, Malawi, Sierra Leone, and Liberia, and the continuing bloody civil wars in the Sudan and the Democratic Republic of the Congo, demonstrate that the region is a foreign policy disaster area. The 2002 election crisis in Zimbabwe, for example, could not have heartened Washington. Mugabe's illiberal behavior, the timid response from Commonwealth members generally, and the shocking attitude of many African leaders (namely Mbeki of South Africa) who seemed to support Mugabe's power grab, demonstrated to the Bush administration that the good governance issues to be championed by the NEPAD implementation committee, which includes a "peer review mechanism" to distribute ODA to deserving states, will not be taken seriously. Adding to this perception was the decision taken at the 2002 African Union Summit in Durban, South Africa, which enlarged the Implementation Committee to include two states that are among the least democratic states in Africa—Kenya and Libya (a long-time U.S. enemy until it agreed to dismantle its nuclear weapons program in December 2003).[51]

CONCLUSIONS

Prime Minister Jean Chrétien increased ODA spending (mainly for Africa) by $500 million CDN in the December 2001 budget and pledged to increased ODA by 8 percent per year (cumulatively) until Canada doubled its ODA spending. However, if Canada's sponsorship of NEPAD is to bear fruit, there are at least three challenges the country must meet in the next few years, two of which involve developments within Canada.

A first challenge is to ensure that the G-8 Action Plan for Africa, NEPAD, and the U.N. Millennium Goals not only remain on the international community's agenda, but that Canada manages to link the long-term social and economic goals espoused with these plans with broader international security objectives in an effort to secure U.S. support. This is a difficult proposition in light of the realities of American politics: U.S. presidents have domestic constituents to satisfy, and every other year is an election year. Therefore, long-term thinking on these matters has not entered the foreign policy agenda. This is coupled with the fact that American concerns right now are immediate and practical: eliminating the al-Qaeda network and securing U.S. borders. Without American financial and political support, however, NEPAD will not likely succeed. Thus, for Canada the challenge will be to keep development issues salient in light of these external factors.

The second and third challenges pertain to the Canadian foreign policy establishment. A first issue to tackle internally will be the *éparpillement* (i.e., scattering) of aid and the lack of a clear and strong foreign policy agenda in Canada. Although an International Policy Review was tabled in April 2005 which tried to improve Canada's international standing, recent domestic political events (such as two national elections in an 18-month period resulting in changes in governments) may render the plan obsolete. As for CIDA, it "takes its cues" from the pronouncements of the United Nations and OECD on development needs (the CIDA website confirms this). Furthermore, there is often a tension between Foreign Affairs Canada and CIDA that will have to be managed. While the former is concerned with Canada's interests and position in the world, the latter is an aid agency which is tasked with helping people "on the ground" in cooperation with NGOs and international organizations, without necessarily having to be concerned with the foreign minister's personal agenda.[52]

Finally, another internal challenge for Canada will be to manage the three competing agendas or ways of disbursing aid in light of the renewed commitment to double ODA spending in the next 8 years. Canada displays three different and sometimes competing impulses in international affairs and, more particularly, with respect to foreign assistance: a multilateral impulse, that is, to fund development projects through multilateral forums, the preferred method of the developing countries since that type of aid is not tied; the bilateral impulse, which is politically most desirable since Canada, through CIDA, can continue to be present in "over 150 countries" and thus show the Canadian flag; and the "third partner" approach whereby aid is subcontracted to NGOs and civil society organizations on the ground, which can be more efficient.

While Canada's ultimate impulse is to want to be liked by everybody and thus to be active in all these methods, the risk is, again, that the country's aid program will remain "a mile wide and an inch thick." This would not be new, but choices will have to be made in light of the challenges presented above. Although some observers of Canadian foreign policy, such as Andrew Cohen, have fretted about Canada's allegedly diminished role in the world, the Martin government has continued to move in the direction set by its predecessor with regard to international development and human security. For example, at the opening ceremonies of the United Nations General Assembly in September 2004, Prime Minister Martin pledged over $20 million CDN to help the situation in Darfur and urged the international community to follow suit. Canadian troops, followed by aid money, were also among the first to intervene in Haiti to restore order earlier in 2004. Finally, the Canadian government has begun adopting a more integrated framework to increase the effectiveness of its modest capacity to help rebuild war-torn countries or so-called failed states by developing a "3-D" approach in its interventions in Afghanistan. The three pillars of Canadian foreign policy—diplomacy, defense, and development (the "3Ds")—have instituted better methods for working together so that Canada's contribution can be as effective as possible.

In sum, foreign aid or ODA is one tool available to decision-makers in the foreign policy sphere to extend their influence abroad. While Canada has had an excellent reputation in the international sphere, it cannot live on its reputation alone and must continue to pursue an active role in the world to ensure that its values and interests are promoted. Although modest from a global standpoint, Canadian foreign aid will likely continue to grow as long as a Liberal government stays in power, thus reversing a decade-long decline for which the Liberals themselves were responsible. As a result, Canada's commitment to Africa will in all likelihood be maintained in the next few years, thus serving as a useful "niche" activity for a middle power perpetually in search of an international leadership role.

NOTES

1. The author thanks the Canada Research Chairs program for its important contribution to his overall research agenda, as well as Anne Kröning and Philippe Lafortune for their research assistance. The genesis of this project is to be found in a series of co-authored papers with Douglas A. Van Belle and David Potter, which culminated in a book: Douglas Van Belle, Jean-Sébastien Rioux, and David Potter, *Media, Bureaucracies, and Foreign Aid: A Comparative Analysis of United States, the United Kingdom, Canada, France and Japan* (New York: Palgrave Macmillan Press, 2004).

2. Andrew Cohen, *While Canada Slept: How We Lost Our Place in the World* (Toronto: McClelland & Stewart Ltd., 2003).

3. Insight Canada Research, *Canadian Public Opinion on Canada's Foreign Policy, Defence Policy and Foreign Aid*, Study conducted for the Department of Foreign Affairs and International Trade, the Department of National Defence, and the Canadian International Development Agency (1995), 2.

4. Insight Canada Research, *Canadian Public Opinion*, 2.

5. Insight Canada Research, *Canadian Public Opinion*, 4.

6. David Black and Rebecca Tiessen, "Canadian Aid Policy: Parameters, Pressures and Partners." Article to be published in *The Administration of Foreign Affairs: A Renewed Challenge?* Nelson Michaud and Luc Bernier, eds.

7. Evan H. Potter, "Canada and the World: Continuity and Change in Public Opinion on Aid, Trade, and International Security, 1993–2002," *Études Internationales* 33, no. 4 (December 2002): 697–722.

8. Jean-Philippe Thérien and Carolyn Lloyd, "Development Assistance on the Brink." *Third World Quarterly* 21, no. 1 (February 2000): 21–38.

9. Portions of this section are drawn from Van Belle, Rioux, and Potter, *Media, Bureaucracies, and Foreign Aid*, chapter 2.

10. This tripartite division of the theoretical literature is developed in Paul R. Viotti and Mark V. Kauppi, *International Relations Theory: Realism, Pluralism, Globalism, and Beyond*, 3rd ed. (Needham Heights, MA: Allyn and Bacon, 1999). The author understands there are many other theoretical strands of literature, but these three probably account for the majority of the "mainstream" scholarship in international politics.

11. George Liska, *The New Statecraft: Foreign Aid in American Foreign* Policy (Chicago: University of Chicago Press, 1960), 15.

12. A. F. K Organski, *The $36 Billion Bargain: Strategy and Politics in US Assistance to Israel* (New York: Columbia University Press, 1990).

13. See, for example, James Meernik, Eric L. Krueger, and Steven C. Poe, "Testing Models of US Foreign Policy: Foreign Aid During and After the Cold War," *Journal of Politics* 60, no. 1 (February 1998): 63–85.

14. Van Belle et al., *Media, Bureaucracies, and Foreign Aid*, chapter 5.

15. Van Belle et al., *Media, Bureaucracies, and Foreign Aid*.

16. Known in the United States as the "French and Indian War" and in Québec as "La Conquête" (i.e., "The Conquest").

17. Jean-Philippe Thérien, "Le Canada et le régime international de l'aide," *Études Internationales*, 20 (juin 1989): 311–340.

18. Robert E. Wood, *From Marshall Plan to Debt Crisis: Foreign Aid and Development Choices in the World Economy* (Berkeley: University of California Press, 1986), 5.

19. Wood, *From Marshall Plan to Debt Crisis*, 314.

20. See, for example, Meernik et al., "Testing Models of US Foreign Policy."

21. Van Belle et al., *Media, Bureaucracies, and Foreign Aid*, chapter 7.

22. See, for example, Industry Canada, *Monthly Trade* Bulletin 3, no. 8 (October 2001), 7, http://strategis.ic.gc.ca/pics/ra/mtboct01_e.pdf.

23. See, for example, Alain Noël and Jean-Philippe Thérien, "From Domestic to International Justice: The Welfare State and Foreign Aid," *International Organization* 49, no. 3 (Summer 1995): 523–53.

24. Meernik et al., "Testing Models of US Foreign Policy."

25. See David R. Morrison, *Aid and Ebb Tide: A History of CIDA and Canadian Development Assistance* (Waterloo, ON: Wilfrid Laurier University Press and The North-South Institution, 1998); Canadian International Development Agency (CIDA), *Statistical Report on Official Development Assistance, FY 2002–2003* (Ottawa: Statistical Analysis Section, Policy Planning and Analysis Branch, 2003), CIDA (Table A), http://www.acdi-cida.gc.ca/INET/IMAGES.NSF/vLUImages/stats/$file/StatRep_ 02 ...03.pdf. Unless otherwise stated, amounts are in Canadian dollars. Until the early 1990s, the Canadian dollar traded to within 10% of

the value of the U.S. dollar (either a little bit lower in the 1960s and 1980s, or slightly higher in the early 1970s), and is now worth approximately $0.86 US. See Bank of Canada 2004, *A History of the Canadian Dollar*, http://www.bankofcanada.ca/en/dollar_book/full_text-e.htm

26. The Web address for the Canadian International Development Agency (CIDA) is http://www.acdi-cida.gc.ca/.

27. For more information, see http://www.acdi-cida.gc.ca/organi-e.htm.

28. Foreign Affairs Canada is thus the equivalent of the U.S. State Department; CIDA is equivalent to the U.S. Agency for International Development—USAID.

29. CIDA, *Statistical Report on Official Development Assistance, FY 2002–2003*.

30. Canadian International Development Agency, *Sharing Our Future: Canadian Assistance to International Development* (Ottawa: Government of Canada, 1987).

31. The OECD has 30 members (including the European Union), and Canada gives ODA to three of them: South Korea, Mexico, and Turkey.

32. While CIDA has a Central and Eastern Europe branch, there is no direct government-to-government spending; aid is funneled through multilateral programs to strengthen democratic and economic capacity in the region.

33. See the following documents: Canadian International Development Agency (CIDA), *Strengthening Aid Effectiveness: New Approaches to Canada's International Assistance Program*, paper for consultation, 2001, http://www.acdi-cida.gc.ca/aideffectiveness; and Government of Canada, Canada's International Policy Statement, A Role of Pride and Influence in the World, available online at http://www.dfait-maeci.gc.ca/cip-pic/ips/ips-en.asp.

34. On Canada and multilateralism, see Tom Keating, *Canada and World Order*, 2nd ed. (Toronto: Oxford University Press, 2003).

35. Thérien, "Le Canada et le régime international de l'aide."

36. Van Belle et al., *Media, Bureaucracies, and Foreign Aid*, chapter 7.

37. Government of Canada, Department of Foreign Affairs and International Trade, *Canada in the World*. (Ottawa: CIDA Information Services, 1995), 11.

38. Van Belle et al., *Media, Bureaucracies, and Foreign Aid*, chapter 7.

39. Freedom House, *Annual Survey of Freedom Country Scores, 1972–1973 to 1999–2000*, http://www.freedomhouse.org/ratings/index.htm. For a discussion of the methodology, see the methodological section at http://www.freedomhouse.org/research/freeworld/2000/methodology.htm.

40. Freedom House, *The World's Most Repressive Regimes, 2002*, http://www.freedomhouse.org/research/mrr2002.pdf.

41. Van Belle et al., *Media, Bureaucracies, and Foreign Aid*, chapter 7; Rioux and Van Belle, "The Influence of Le Monde Coverage on French Foreign Aid Allo-

cations"; Van Belle et al., "A Comparative Analysis of the News Media's Influence on British, French, Japanese and US Development Aid Bureaucracies."

42. Thus, each "neutral" story adds $21,500 CDN, while one story about unrest subtracts $1 million CDN. To give the reader an example of the data, as an example I had my computer randomly select a case and here are the values for Guyana, which is a Commonwealth member and politically free, with a GDP per capita income of $3,342. In 1998, there were 15 total stories (1 unrest; 1 negative; 0 need; 13 neutral). Guyana received $3.09 million CDN in ODA that year.

43. See Van Belle, *Media, Bureaucracies, and Foreign Aid*, chapter 7.

44. The "founding documents" of NEPAD are generally regarded to be the Plan Omega (prepared by Sénégal) and the Millennium Partnership for the African Recovery (originally prepared by Nigeria, South Africa and Algeria). These documents and other information on NEPAD can be found at http://www.nepad.org/.

45. For a summary of the United Nations Millennium Goals for international development, see United Nations Development Program, *Millennium Development Goals*, http://www.undp.org/mdg/Millennium%20Development%20Goals.pdf.

46. NEPAD, http://www.nepad.org/.

47. Government of Canada, *NEPAD/G8 Africa Action Plan/APR Process Backgrounder* (Ottawa: G8 Summit Office, Department of Foreign Affairs and International Trade, 2002).

48. Sherpa refers to the Tibetan mountain guides. Before important international summits, world leaders will appoint a trusted aide—a guide—to prepare the negotiations. The "sherpas" have direct access to their government leader and full powers of negotiation.

49. New Partnership for Africa's Development (NEPAD), "About NEPAD," 2002, http://www.nepad.org/inbrief.html. See also Government of Canada, "NEPAD/G8 Africa Action Plan/APR Process Backgrounder."

50. The African Union summit of July 2002 in Durban proposed enlarging the implementation committee to 20 members.

51. Rachel L. Swarns, "African Leaders Drop Old Group for One that Has Power," *New York Times*, 8 July 2002, http://www.nytimes.com.

52. Cranford Pratt, "DFAIT's Takeover Bid of CIDA," *Canadian Foreign Policy* 5, no. 2 (Winter 1998): 1–13.

10

Canadian Foreign Policy and International Human Rights

BETHANY BARRATT

Human rights may be one of the most laudable goals of foreign policy, but it is also one of the most inconsistently pursued. There is a widespread perception among scholars and the public that Canada is at the forefront of states in the incorporation of human rights in both its domestic laws and its international policy and practice. This perception is fueled by the domestic norm of respect for human rights and the prominence of human rights rhetoric both in debates among policy-makers and in the media. In domestic policy, this has been expressed most notably in the Canadian Charter of Rights and Freedoms. In foreign policy formulation, it has led to high-profile cases of incorporation of human rights standards as a guiding principle in decision making. These include strong opposition to cases of American interventionism (in Vietnam among other locales), leadership in the international effort to sanction Apartheid-era South Africa, substantial commitment of troops and materiel by Canada to U.N. peacekeeping operations, and former Foreign Minister Lloyd Axworthy's human security agenda.

Therefore, of Western donor countries, Canada could be expected a priori to be the most likely to link aid (the foreign policy tool on which this chapter focuses) to human rights. More studies have been produced of the role of human rights in Canadian foreign policy than they have for other Commonwealth donor states.[1] Also, there is considerable evidence that both governmental orientation and public opinion contain at least a minimal basic commitment to human rights.[2] Finally, a great number of general philosophical proposals about the propriety of including human rights in foreign policy, as well as specific linkage strategies for doing so, have circulated around the highest levels of government, to a much greater extent in Canada than other Commonwealth states.[3]

This chapter focuses on aid because it is probably the most common foreign policy tool and is one of the most easily measured, as well as being comparable across donor countries. I examine the role of human rights relative to other foreign policy goals in Canadian aid patterns between 1980 and 1996, a time period that is particularly useful because it allows us to look at several years before the Cold War ended and several years after. I examine the relative roles of these various goals through both a systematic qualitative description of the incorporation of human rights into Canadian foreign policy, and pooled cross-sectional time series analyses of the determinants of aid decisions. These qualitative and quantitative approaches complement each other, with the statistical analyses allowing us to draw conclusions about robust patterns over the entire universe of Canadian foreign aid decisions, and the qualitative descriptions allowing us to infer the process behind, and causal mechanisms of, these patterns.

Are human rights, ostensibly at the heart of the democratic form of government, something for which states are willing to sacrifice gains in other arenas, or are they are only pursued when it is not costly to do so? This question is often posed about the role of human rights in foreign policy but rarely addressed systematically. It is an especially critical question in a post–Cold War world, where policy-makers and academics alike celebrate the spread of democracy—because when terms like "human rights" become hollow, so does one of the organizing principles that defines democracy. More importantly, aid generally serves to prop up whatever regime is in power in recipient states. It tends to not go to the poorest members of society, and therefore ultimately exacerbates societal inequalities.

SOME EXTANT ANSWERS TO THE QUESTION

Democracies have a long record of committing blood and treasure to the cause of political and civil rights. While realist theorists such as Waltz[4] argue that ethical concerns rarely if ever matter in foreign policy, still democratic states and multilateral organizations provide billions of dollars in aid to non-strategic countries.

There are several bodies of international relations literature that can help explain these inconsistencies.

Realism

Seldom, from a realist perspective, is the status of individual rights in another country important unless it affects state power. And realism has often given short shrift to the importance of domestic considerations to foreign policy-makers.

Whether Canada takes human rights into account in its foreign policy, therefore, has important implications for the validity of the realist assumption that the imperative to survive in an anarchic international arena subsumes all other concerns. If realist assumptions are valid, internal characteristics of states can only have the most minor impact. There has been disagreement about the extent to which Canadian foreign policy-makers have followed realist strategies. While Canada was criticized by members of the G. W. Bush administration for ignoring realist imperatives when Chrétien and then Martin declined to support the second Gulf War, Joel Sokolsky of the Royal Military College of Canada has contended that Canada *has* followed the dictates of realism by incorporating domestic concerns as the most important component in foreign policy-making. I test the role of many of these domestic concerns in the analyses below. He has also argued that Canadian foreign policy has often been sold as "liberal internationalist" at home while actually being aimed at protecting aims commensurate with realist predictions.[5]

Idealism and Legal Protections of Human Rights

Respect for civil and political human rights is at the heart of democratic governance. International legal incentives to take human rights into account are supplemented in Canada by the Canadian Charter of Rights and Freedoms and by official government rhetoric entailing a commitment to using human rights as criteria for aid disbursement.

Neoliberalism/Globalization Perspectives

Neoliberal theorists contend that trade and economic cooperation for mutual benefit between nations is a paramount concern of policy-makers.[6] Certainly during the Chrétien era, the North Star of Canadian foreign policy was its economic growth. In 1995, the government explicitly declared that employment and economic growth at home were its most essential foreign policy goals, and its emphasis on trade in its budgetary allocations reflected this prioritization.

If neoliberal assumptions are guiding government policy, one would predict that at least some trade relations may be so valuable that the donor would rather continue to generate goodwill through aid than jeopardize access to the recipient by cutting it off. These kinds of relations are likely to pertain with recipients (or potential recipients) that offer significant trade potential to the donor, provide fertile export markets, and have large or expanding economies. These countries are less likely to be punished, and if they are, punished less severely, than are other states for commensurate human rights abuses.[7]

Of major donor countries, Canada, for a number of reasons, appears a priori to be particularly likely to link aid to human rights. Policy-makers and scholars alike have produced more studies or discussions of the role of human rights in Canadian foreign policy than they have for most other major donor states (with the exception of the U.S.), such as the U.K. or Australia.[8] Also, most authors agree that both governmental orientation and public opinion contain at least a minimal basic commitment to human rights.[9] Finally, a large number of general proposals about the propriety of including human rights in foreign policy, as well as specific linkage strategies for doing so, have circulated around the highest levels of government, to a much greater extent in the Canadian case than others.

However, the question is not whether human rights is seen as important, but "what . . . is the weight [policy making] gives to human rights in contrast to other objectives and interests and [what are] the imagination, resources, and energy it devotes to the implementation of human rights."[10] Obviously, policy-making involves trade-offs. As Manzer[11] argues, "majority preference, economic efficiency, average welfare, cultural enrichment, and national security may compete with rights." Given the competition, what role do human rights play in Canadian aid policy?

RIGHTS IN THE GENERAL CONTEXT OF CANADIAN FOREIGN POLICY-MAKING

Formal Policy-Making Institutions and Structure

In spite of the fact that Canadian foreign policy has directed more rhetorical attention at human rights issues than have, for instance, the U.S. or

British foreign policy-making communities, the incorporation of human rights concerns into policy practice has been impeded by the fact that human rights issues are the nominal purview of numerous different governmental departments, depending on the proximate issue at hand. Therefore, domestically,

> Jurisdiction is determined by the constitutional division of powers: e.g. complaints involving banking, national airlines, railways, or federal government employees are in the federal jurisdiction, whereas complaints involving school boards, city government, or restaurants are in the provincial jurisdiction. In general, both federal and provincial human rights law prohibits discrimination in all aspects of employment; the leasing and sale of property; public accommodation, services and facilities; membership in labour unions and professional associations and the dissemination of hate propaganda.[12]

And internationally, human rights as a principle is incorporated into foreign policy through such diverse functional bodies as the Canadian International Development Agency (CIDA) and the Department of Foreign Affairs and International Trade. No unit perceives the need to make human rights a top priority, because each knows human rights is in part the responsibility of some other department(s). This lack of ownership by any one unit results in human rights issues becoming isolated and marginalized,[13] and means that there is an endogenous source of devaluation of human rights concerns and likely lesser degree of salience than is the case in analogous situations in other donors. And because human rights are not and have not been included in any formalized Canadian foreign policy framework, the extent to which human rights considerations are represented on policy agendas (let alone become implemented) is dependent primarily on individual officials and politicians.

Canadian institutions devoted specifically to human rights issues also are and have been temporary and ad hoc, as was the case with Parliament's appointment of a special joint committee to consider the conditions under which Canada should concern itself with human rights violations in other countries. Similarly, when there was first discussion about Canada becoming a signatory to U.N. Conventions (such as the ICCPR and ICESCR) on various rights in the 1970s, the Department of the Secretary of State was the point of contact at the federal level—but the Department of External

Affairs gradually took over responsibility for the role of human rights in foreign policy. Another example of the ad hoc nature of the development of rights policy is the formative role that individual, informal speeches have come to play in the policy process. While this ad hoc character of human rights policy-making does not in and of itself guarantee that competing priorities will win out, it opens up the door for greater influence of trade or strategic considerations if the latter policy communities are better organized than is the human rights community.

History of Human Rights in Canadian Policy-Making

The serious consideration of human rights in Canadian foreign policy began in the 1970s, when increased global attention to human rights was in part a response to Carter's inclusion of rights as an administration priority in the United States.[14] In fact, however, the first formally elucidated commitment to human rights by the government dates to 1970, in the form of a White Paper in which Pierre Trudeau's Liberal government committed to a "positive and vigorous" approach to human rights.[15]

Several other national and international trends combined in the 1970s to raise the profile of human rights discussions on policy agendas. Nationally, every Canadian province passed local antidiscrimination laws. Several members of Parliament sought to make overseas development assistance dependent on improvement in human rights conditions for the worst-violating recipients. Canada signed on to the U.N. Convention on Racial Discrimination and Covenants on Economic and Social Rights and Civil and Political Rights, and the discussion before and after these drew additional public attention to the issue of basic needs and basic rights, and whether there could be international standards thereof. The passage of the Helsinki Final Act by the Conference on Security and Cooperation in Europe enhanced the new status of human rights in the public eye. In addition, during debates over the U.N. conventions and covenants, the government established federal-provincial committees to identify and capitalize on links between domestic and international human rights issues. By 1988, Victoria Berry and Allan McChesney could note with optimism that "for over two decades the Canadian public has expressed rising interest in the place of human rights in foreign policy."[16] And throughout the 1970s and 1980s there was increasing verbal support for human rights among high-ranking Cabinet officials.

However, as human rights gained more attention internationally, activists and representatives from other governments regularly criticized Canada for its lukewarm commitment to human rights abroad, and especially its failure to put to use the development assistance tools at the government's disposal.[17] Currently, some observers note that when there is significant potential for trade with a country (in general more quickly developing states or NICs), human rights appear not to matter at all.[18] Gillies contends this discriminatory treatment of countries is a result of the extent to which an incumbent government's quest for political survival is predicated on economic growth. "This imperative is the foundation of the privileged position that business develops in the policy arena."[19] And several examples suggest this is a pattern that has been borne out in Canada's bilateral relations with several recipients.

Successive Canadian governments have had numerous rationalizations for the status of human rights as a second-tier priority in the policy-making process. For one thing, many officials are pessimistic about what can be accomplished by such actions in defense of human rights. According to some authors, "most governments have apparently concluded that unilateral initiatives are ineffective or conflict with other, more important goals."[20]

The inherent trade-offs states face in policy-making are also a consideration. As a trade-driven explanation suggests, Canada "seems to fashion human rights policies with an eye fixed firmly on commercial [and strategic] interests."[21] From the perspective of these scholars, we would expect to see these trade-offs reflected in Canadian aid patterns as well. For instance, Canada's criticisms of Eastern Bloc human rights violations during the Cold War were much more vociferous than they were for comparable problems in Western donors, much as is the case in, for instance, the U.S. and Britain.[22] As Nossal argues, "the Canadian government's interest in human rights is considerably diluted by other interests."[23]

As discussed above, two of the most critical categories of competing interests are strategic and trade considerations. Trade considerations are discussed in some detail below. Scholars of Canadian foreign policy have generally proffered two kinds of arguments about the import of strategic considerations. The first is a structural Marxist strain that emphasizes Canada's tendency to act in concert with other capitalist Western states to maintain the international politicoeconomic status quo. The second, a strategic studies variant, focuses (or focused) on the East-West conflict, Canada's interest in access to sea lanes, and its concern for key trade intersections, considerations which are measured (but receive little support) in the analyses below. Since the latter perspective was driven by Cold War concerns, it would be evidence in its favor if trade intersections and like measures had a greater effect on trade disbursements before the dissolution of the Soviet Union than was the case in the 1990s.

Nossal, for instance, believes strategic interests generally are given greater priority by foreign policy-makers, and concedes that there indeed appears to be an inverse link between Canada's perceived strategic stake in a state and the likelihood that it will take action to alleviate human rights violations in that state, though he is skeptical about the role of trade interests in trumping human rights concerns. He cites a number of cases where "strategic concerns" have been either minor or nonexistent (including Uganda, Kampuchea, and Sri Lanka), in which the government has taken a hard-line position against violations. On the other hand, he contends that "where clearly identifiable strategic interests exist, [the government] tended to play down violations," citing the cases of South Africa, East Timor, Iran and Central America.[24] Interestingly, Nossal does not define "strategic interests" in this context, a testament to the extent to which economic and security interests are inseparable. In fact, at least one other author has cited these same cases as examples of the primacy not of strategic but rather of economic interests.[25]

On the other hand, some explanations of Canada's lack of firmer commitment to human rights focus on the ineffectiveness of actions taken on behalf of such a commitment. For example, Nossal identifies four "gloomy" themes in government statements about human rights in the 1970s and 1980s. First, he says, the very terms used to describe human rights as an issue imply intractability (i.e., officials' frequent use of the terms "thorny" or "complicated"). Some of this perceived intractability stems from the second theme Nossal identifies: that because there are no universally agreed-upon definitions of human rights, dealing with such rights in an international context is particularly difficult. Third, Canadian policy-makers tend to deemphasize Canada's potential for affecting international politics unilaterally. Unlike their counterparts in the U.S., most Canadian policy-makers believe that too few recipients are dependent enough on Canada to allow it much leverage in influencing that state's domestic policy. Finally, Nossal cites the kinds of constraints on which my perspective focuses: human rights are only one of many goals that Canada pursues and often appear to be less vital to Canadian interests than are strategic or commercial concerns.[26] Therefore, though Canadian policy-makers believe citizens of other states deserve basic rights, many feel that effort in that direction would be wasted. Since there is little chance of effecting change, why not use resources in areas where they are more likely to have an impact?

Canada's perceived lack of commitment to alleviating human rights abuses abroad stands in stark contrast, as is the case with other donor nations, to apparent governmental concerns over rights violations—one of the apparent discrepancies this research attempts to explain. In what Margaret Doxey[27] has called the "rhetoric gap," there is "marked discrepancy between expression of concern and actual government behavior." In fact, "in their public statements, political leaders and departmental officials stress that they are shocked and disturbed by evidence of human rights violations by other governments, that they believe such behavior is morally wrong," and that Canada bears a responsibility to answer these violations in its foreign policy.[28] Senior policy-makers have for years adopted the stance of former Secretary of State Don Jamieson, who declared that "Canada will continue to uphold internationally the course of human rights, in the legitimate hope that we can eventually ameliorate the conditions of our fellow man."[29]

Furthermore, the commitment has been at least ostensibly bipartisan, as the Conservative governments of the late 1970s and mid 1980s (Clark and Mulroney) made public announcements to this effect as well (though possibly with greater frequency as regarded Eastern bloc states). In addition, "senior cabinet members, most notably a number of secretaries of state for external affairs, have supported a significant role for human rights in foreign policy."[30] Such pronouncements have even been formalized, especially in the area of overseas development assistance and other aid. Successive governments' commitment to linking aid to human rights is laid out in several major documents, two of which were reports to special committees in Parliament.[31] A report by the CIDA[32] claimed that these new frameworks would "help make it more feasible to take human rights under serious consideration in the formulation of our aid policy."[33]

Whether or not these kinds of commitments have been kept is examined below.

Domestic Interests

In a democracy, any foreign policy process must operate within the parameters of public opinion as expressed through polls, electoral results, and organized interests. Therefore, the last component of the foreign policy-making context that must be taken into account in predicting the role of various goals in aid decisions is the role of such interests. Two major constellations of pressure groups are especially important: human rights NGOs, and business interests.

As mentioned above, there was a major uptick in the visibility of human rights on the national political agenda in the 1970s during the debates about Canada signing the various UN conventions on human rights and racial discrimination. At that time, the first human rights NGOs gained popular notice and support (both symbolic and financial). The presence of these organized interests required that greater government attention be devoted to issues of rights both at home and abroad.

Matthews and Pratt, Nossal, and Gillies all share my assumption that commercial interests will likely mitigate a donor country's interest in pursuing human rights policy abroad. In Nossal's judgment, Canada "seems to fashion human rights policies with an eye firmly fixed on commercial interests." For instance, in examinations of Canadian foreign policy toward regimes that systematically violated human rights in Argentina, Chile, Indonesia, South Africa, South Korea, and Uganda by Keenlyside and Taylor[34], and by Scharfe[35], there was found a "general reluctance to engage in economic sanctions against violators with which Canada has substantial and growing commercial interests."[36] Gillies contends that discriminatory treatment of countries (on the basis of their human rights records) is a result of the extent to which an incumbent government's quest for political survival is predicated on economic growth. "This imperative is the foundation of the privileged position that business develops in the policy arena."[37] The veracity of these kinds of claims is tested below when the sample of recipients is divided into groups based on both the recipients' potential and actual commercial relationships with Canada.

How accurate are these claims that human rights will only be taken into account when the Canadian government perceives it will not alienate commercial interests? How likely is it that commercial or other economic relations with a violator country would actually be disrupted by Canada's imposition of some sort of economic punishment—and how important is any one of these relationships likely to be to a wealthy donor the size of Canada? While Nossal concedes that "the web of economic linkages between Canada and violators may affect human rights policy, since interruption in trade, investment, or development assistance affects some individual Canadians, and thus the Canadian economy," he objects:

> The economic argument is not as compelling as it may at first seem. Although based on rational notions of maximized self-interest, it makes little sense from a rational perspective, for it includes no assessment of the magnitude of the economic costs to Canada of measures used by Ottawa to further human rights. . . . Canada's economic links with any single state in the East or the South that violates human rights (indeed, all such violators combined) represents a tiny percentage of all external trade.[38]

One advantage of the research design I use here is that it allows one to measure not only when aid policy responds to human rights, but when both human rights records and trade relationships respond—either positively or negatively—in the wake of changes in aid policy.

As Matthews and Pratt[39] note about Canada's immigrant communities, "where there is severe denial of civil and political rights in their countries of origin, immigrants and descendants are bound to be particularly concerned." Therefore, these kinds of practical domestic politics concerns often reinforce any philosophical commitment the Canadian government might make to securing human rights within the borders of other countries. The analyses below test for their impact on the aid granting process.

REVIEW OF KEY HYPOTHESES AND DETAILS OF QUANTITATIVE RESEARCH DESIGN

Clearly, there is room for disagreement between scholars of Canadian foreign policy about the role of various goals in aid decisions. Moving from a qualitative to a quantitative approach is an important step toward resolving some of these disagreements, as it allows us to take into account *all* aid decisions during the time period in question, and also provides us with enough observations to have substantial confidence in any relationships we observe. Therefore, from the above considerations, I derive the following testable hypotheses:

The Gatekeeping Decision
1. States that are more economically valuable are more likely to receive aid.
2. States that are more economically valuable are less likely to have human rights taken into account in decisions about whether they receive aid.

The Allocation Decision
3. States that are more economically valuable will receive higher levels of aid.
4. States that are more economically valuable are less likely to have human rights taken into account in decisions about their aid amounts.

Time Period to Be Covered

The unit of analysis is the recipient-year. My analyses include the years 1980–1996, the years for which quantitative data on human rights is available. As noted above, this is a particularly useful time period to examine, for a number of reasons. It gives us more than one thousand cases in the decade before the Cold War ended, and more than seven hundred in the six years after the breakup of the Soviet Union. Finally, this time period includes aid responses of the West to genocide both in Africa and in the backyard of Europe.

DEPENDENT VARIABLE

The operational forms of the dependent variable for the gatekeeping decision are discussed above. For the allocation decision, aid is operationalized as total aid from Canada to that state in the given year. Annual aid data was obtained from the OECD (various years). If a state was a non-creditor country in a given year, it was included as a potential aid recipient.

Who receives aid from Canada? A look at table 10.1 demonstrates that it is more unusual *not* to be granted aid than to be granted aid. In 1996, 128 of the 180 potential recipients receive aid.

A look at the 60 states that did not receive aid (table 10.2) is in some ways more revealing. What sorts of potential recipients are left off the aid

Table 10.1. States That Received Aid from Canada, 1996

Afghanistan	Ghana	North Yemen
Albania	Grenada	Pakistan
Algeria	Guatemala	Palestine
Angola	Guinea	Panama
Argentina	Guinea-Bissau	Papua New Guinea
Armenia	Guyana	Paraguay
Bangladesh	Haiti	Peru
Barbados	Honduras	Philippines
Belize	Hungary	Poland
Benin	India	Romania
Bhutan	Indonesia	Russia
Bolivia	Iraq	Rwanda
Bosnia	Ivory Coast	South Africa
Botswana	Jamaica	Sao Tome and Principe
Brazil	Jordan	Senegal
Burkina Faso	Kazakhstan	Serbia
Burundi	Kenya	Seychelles
Cambodia	Korea, North	Sierra Leone
Cameroon	Kyrgyzstan	Singapore
Cape Verde	Laos	Slovakia
Central African Rep.	Lebanon	Somalia
Chad	Lesotho	Sri Lanka
Chile	Liberia	St. Exupery
China	Lithuania	Sudan
Colombia	Madagascar	Suriname
Comoros	Malawi	Swaziland
Congo	Malaysia	South Yemen
Costa Rica	Maldives	Syria
Croatia	Mali	Tajikistan
Cuba	Mauritania	Tanzania
Czech Republic	Mauritius	Thailand
Djibouti	Mexico	Togo
Dominica	Mongolia	Trinidad
Dominican Republic	Morocco	Tunisia
Ecuador	Mozambique	Turkey
Egypt	Myanmar	Uganda
El Salvador	Namibia	Ukraine
Equatorial Guinea	Nepal	Uruguay
Eritrea	Nicaragua	Venezuela
Ethiopia	Niger	Viet Nam
Gabon	Nigeria	Windward Islands
Gambia	Northern Marianas	Zaire

Source: OECD International Development Statistics Online Databases, http:/www.oecd.org/dataoecd/50/17/5037721.htm.Paris: OECD.

Table 10.2. States That Did Not Receive Aid From Canada, 1996

Anguilla (na)	Malta (na)
Antigua and Barbuda (na)	Marshall Islands (na)
Aruba (na)	Mayotte (na)
Azerbaijan (3)	Moldova (2)
Bahamas (na)	Montserrat(na)
Bahrain (2)	Nauru (na)
Belarus (2)	New Caledonia (na)
Benin (1)	Niue (na)
Bermuda (na)	Oman (2)
Bulgaria (2)	Palau (na)
Cook Islands (na)	Qatar (na)
Cyprus (1)	Saudi Arabia (2)
Estonia (2)	Slovenia (na)
Falkland Islands (na)	Solomon Islands (na)
Fiji (na)	St. Helena (na)
French Polynesia (na)	St. Kitts (na)
Georgia (3)	St. Lucia (na)
Gibraltar (na)	St. Vincent (na)
Greece(1)	Taiwan (1)
Hong Kong (na)	Timor (na)
Iran (3)	Tokelau (na)
Israel (3)	Tonga (na)
Kiribati (na)	Turkmenistan (2)
Korea, Democratic Republic of (na)	Turks and Caicos (na)
Korea, Republic of (na)	Tuvalu (na)
Kuwait (2)	United Arab Emirates (1)
Latvia (1)	Uzbekistan (2)
Libya (3)	Vanuatu (na)
Macau (na)	Virgin Islands (na)
Macedonia (1)	Wallis and Fortuna (na)
Micronesia (na)	Western Samoa (na)

Source: OECD International Development Statistics Online Databases, http://www.oecd.org/dataoecd/50/17/5037721.htm. Paris: OECD.
Numbers in parentheses indicate Political Terror Scale Score (based on U.S. State Department reports).

list? Seven (Bahrain, Kuwait, Libya, Oman, Qatar, Saudi Arabia, and UAE) are oil exporters and relatively wealthy; it is unsurprising that they would not be seen as priorities for disbursement of Canadian aid revenues. Others are island nations who receive a great deal of aid from geographically proximate donors.

Few clear patterns emerge in an examination of the human rights records of the potential recipients left off the list. The numbers in parentheses indicate the human rights scores of these states (again, higher numbers indicate worse violation levels). Forty (two-thirds) of these potential recipients were not evaluated by the U.S. State Department in 1996. Seven had the best possible human rights score at 1, and ten others had scores of 2. Clearly, human rights in itself does not explain which potential recipients are left off the aid list.

INDEPENDENT VARIABLES

Human Rights Abuses in Recipient Country

Human rights abuses, which I expect to matter only when a recipient is of little economic value to Canada, are measured using the Purdue Political Terror Index, originally compiled by Michael Stohl and including two ratings derived, respectively, from the U.S. State Department's annual country reports and those of Amnesty International. This is a five-point scale ranging from one ("Countries . . . under a secure rule of law, people are not imprisoned for their views, and torture is rare or exceptional . . . Political murders are extraordinarily rare") to five ("The violence of Level [Four] has been extended to the whole population. . . . The leaders of these societies place no limits on the means or thoroughness with which they pursue personal or ideological goals").[40] The State Department measure was chosen, though not without trepidation.[41]

Table 10.3 provides examples of the countries who received the best (1) and worst (5) human rights scores for the last year in the study (of all

Table 10.3. Best and Worst Human Rights Performers, 1996, Based on U.S. State Dept. Annual Reports

Level 5 (worst) records in 1996 (N= 12)

Afghanistan	Liberia
Algeria	Rwanda
Angola	Sierra Leone
Burundi	Somalia
Colombia	Venezuela
Iraq	Zaire

Level 1 (best) records in 1996 (N= 21)

Benin	Macedonia
Comoros	Mali
Costa Rica	Poland
Cyprus	Seychelles
Czech Republic	Singapore
Eritrea	Slovakia
Hungary	Taiwan
Jordan	UAE
Kyrgyzstan	Uruguay
Lesotho	

Source: Link for Political Terror Scale, 1980–2004, at http://www.unca.edu/politicalscience/images/Colloquium/faculty-staff/Gibney.html.

potential OECD aid recipients). This variable is lagged one year to allow for collection of data in Canada, as well as for the budgeting process to take place.[42]

Many studies of human rights treat "democracy" and "respect for human rights" as nearly synonymous.[43] However, one might also expect that democratic recipients might be less able to reciprocate aid with preferential trade agreements than are autocratic ones. This variable is included to test whether democracy is indeed a proxy for respect for human rights, and is measured as the recipient's polity score on the Polity III index.[44] However, I expect democracy to be of lesser significance in predicting aid amounts than are economic and strategic measures. Additionally, many donors are reluctant to sink aid funds into unstable regions, which are often either undemocratic or transitional.

Potential and Actual Economic Value of the Recipient State

Potential economic value of the recipient to Canada, which I expect to be positively associated with recipient aid, is measured in two ways: size of the economy of the recipient (GDP), and annual growth rate of GDP. Together, these two figures should give us some idea of how promising a trade partner the recipient looks to be. The recipient state's population is also taken into account.[45]

In addition, measurements of economic value are constructed that more specifically measure the recipient country's *trade* potential. Volume and percentage of imports and exports between Canada and each recipient are drawn from the International Monetary Fund's Direction of Trade Statistics (various years) data. Since not all trade is created equal, I also take into account whether a recipient is an oil-exporting state.

Strategic Value of the Recipient State.

Realists would predict that strategic interests trump human rights concerns. A recipient with which Canada has had recent conflict or sees possibility of future conflict should be less likely to receive aid, because that conflict would disrupt any benefit Canada would derive from its investment. However, such conflicts, at least militarized ones, are relatively rare.

The strategic value of the recipient is measured in several other ways. These measures include the geographic location of the recipient, proximity to trade intersections, location in areas of instability, and whether the recipient possesses nuclear capabilities.[46] If a state is listed as a participant in an interstate dispute, as a site of substantial civil unrest, or if it borders on such a state, it is coded as a site of instability. A state is coded as located at a key trade intersection if it contains major pipelines or key ports or is on a major shipping route.

I also take into account military commitments, measured as shared alliance membership taken from the alliance subset of the Correlates of War data set.[47] In addition, donors that are geographically proximate to a recipient have a greater stake in that recipient's fate. Geographical proximity is measured as distance in kilometers between Ottawa and the capital of each recipient.

I expect strategic value of the recipient to be taken into account to a greater extent than human rights records, but to a lesser extent than trade value.

Five other categories of variables, derived from the context of Canadian foreign policy-making discussed above, are included as controls.

Mass-Mediated Humanitarian Crises

Determining whether a recipient suffered a humanitarian crisis (that was widely publicized in the mass media) allows one to measure economically based altruism[48] as well as public awareness. This variable is a count of headlines in print news as compiled under the coding scheme used for the Kansas Events Data Set (KEDS) and its Protocol for the Assessment of Nonviolent Direct Action (PANDA) subset.[49] If states are taking into account the needs of recipients, the presence of a humanitarian crisis should be positively associated with a recipient's aid status.

Domestic Politics

Convincing policy-makers that human rights is the most important lens through which to examine a particular decision is often the goal of human rights NGOs, and I therefore include a count of all reported demonstrations in Canada in a given year regarding the human rights record of the recipient (again, taken from the PANDA data).[50] In addition, the presence of a large immigrant diaspora in Canada may facilitate success in lobbying for aid for its country of origin; therefore I also include the number of immigrants in the past ten years to Canada from the recipient country. Other measures of the impact of domestic politics are also possible.

One of the most important factors to consider is the political congruence between the donor and the recipient, as measured by similar degrees of democracy. Another is the vulnerability of the donor government. Since Kernell,[51] among others, suggests that voters pay closer attention to economic conditions than to other issues, we should see commercial concerns having an even greater impact when the ruling party in the donor has a tenuous hold on power. This is measured by the ratio of governmental to opposition seats in the government at a given time. A final measure of the impact of domestic political dynamics is the size and concentration of immigrant populations in Canada, as measured by the most recent available Canadian census data.

Former Colonial Status of Recipient

I control for whether a recipient is, like Canada, a former British colony;[52] shared colonial ties promote a tradition of financial support and account for a good deal of variation in aid amounts between recipients.[53]

End of the Cold War

Canadian policy makers might see themselves as less constrained by strategic concerns and freer to allocate aid according to either economic or human rights criteria. In addition, with the end of the Cold War, Canadian policy-makers have aspired to restore its role as a major player in world politics, using aid as one instrument. Finally, with shrinking security budgets, aid becomes a more versatile (and available) policy tool than was heretofore the case. Whether the aid year occurs during the Cold War is measured as a dummy variable—coded one before and including 1991 (when the Soviet Union finally broke apart), zero after. I expect more states to get aid, but less of it, after the Cold War ends.

Because it is probable that in the less rigid strategic atmosphere of the post–Cold War world, human rights would have a better chance of being a criterion in aid decisions, I include an interaction term to determine whether the effect of human rights considerations is greater after the Cold War.

Past Aid

Past aid is a key determinant of present aid, because appropriations are often left unchanged as a result of institutional inertia. At the gatekeeping stage, whether a state received aid in the previous year is measured as a dichotomous variable (1 if the state did receive aid, 0 if it did not). In the allocation model, past aid is measured as the overall aid amount to that state in the previous year.

RESULTS

The Gatekeeping Decision

Examining all potential recipients for the seventeen years between 1979 and 1997 results in 3,067 observations (though the number of observations for most analyses is lower, due to dividing up the data set or to missing data). The following section summarizes my findings.

I first looked at the gatekeeping decision and what factors were associated with whether aid was given. Hypothesis 1 predicts that recipients that are more economically valuable are more likely to receive aid, but Canadian policy-makers have claimed that human rights is a top foreign policy priority for them. But as discussed above, some observers of Canadian foreign policy, alternatively, have held that economic and strategic considerations, especially as dictated by the United States, are more likely than human rights to rule aid decisions.

My statistical findings demonstrate that human rights records do have a marginal impact on whether a potential recipient receives aid from Canada—but an unexpected one. Potential recipients with worse human rights records are marginally *more* likely to receive aid than are states with better human rights scores. This is a counterintuitive finding, and could possibly be due to Canada's maintenance of economic relations with these potential recipients in hopes of using that continued relationship to influence them, a strategy suggested by observers.[54]

Economically valuable potential recipients (as measured by economic growth) are indeed more likely to garner aid, as an economically driven model would suggest. However, actual trade relations have no impact. States with larger populations are more likely to receive aid, suggesting that it is larger potential recipients (which, admittedly, could be thought of as larger potential export markets) that are more likely to receive aid.

In terms of a recipient's strategic importance, it will be remembered that many scholars of Canadian foreign policy devote substantial attention to the extent to which strategic concerns take center stage in aid policy and other policy arenas.[55] As this would lead one to expect, several measures of a state's strategic importance have an impact on the likelihood it receives aid. For instance, potential recipients located at sites of instability are less likely to find themselves recipients of aid, perhaps being perceived as uncertain investments. Surprisingly, this is also the case for recipients in military alliances with Canada, but this is in part explained by the fact that most non-OECD states with which Canada has an alliance (i.e., Turkey and Greece) are also among the wealthier of potential recipients, and are not perceived as needing aid (or are not requesting it). The end of the Cold War makes a marginal negative difference in the likelihood a potential recipient receives aid in a given year. This evidence challenges the assertions of strategic studies perspectives that aid patterns were profoundly influenced by the East-West conflict, unless Canada felt the need to spread its resources more thinly *during* the Cold War to try to support regimes that were only important to it in the context of the zero-sum territorial perceptions of the 1950s–1980s.[56]

Only one measure of domestic political dynamics is significant in the decision to allocate aid to a recipient. The closer the recipient's own democracy score to Canada's highly democratic one, the more likely it is to receive aid. Domestic politics in general appear to have a negligible effect at the gatekeeping phase. Potential recipients that have experienced a widely publicized humanitarian crisis also are not more likely to receive aid, and aid patterns do not change significantly when the government is more vulnerable or when there has been significant domestic activism around a particular case of violations. Finally, as expected, states that received aid in one year are more likely to receive it in subsequent years than those that did not.

However, these results provide only the broadest perspective because they include all aid recipients for all years. Further analyses are necessary to determine in what kinds of decisions the above factors have an impact.

The Allocation Decision

When we look at only states that have received aid, and determinants of how much they received, we see some similar and some different factors than was the case at the previous decision stage.

Hypothesis 3 states that more economically viable recipients will receive higher levels of aid, but Canadian policy-makers claim that human rights is a top foreign policy priority. But at this stage again, human rights has no effect. In addition, neither potential nor actual economic value appears to matter at the allocation stage. This is especially interesting since neither the trade measures nor human rights had a significant impact on their own, and supports the expectations of this research that human rights are likely to matter only when trade volumes are not significant. In addition, more populous recipients are again more likely to receive aid. Unlike the gatekeeping decision, where several strategic variables had an impact, only one strategic variable comes into play—the end of the Cold War. At this stage, any given state is likely to receive less aid *after* the Cold War than during it. However, Canadian aid goes down overall in the 1990s—not only do recipients obtain less aid, but fewer states receive aid at all. Finally, the amount of aid a recipient received in the previous year has a highly significant positive impact on the amount of aid it receives in the subsequent year.

Variation between Categories of Recipients

I predicted that states that are more potentially economically valuable would be less likely to be "punished" for human rights violations by having aid terminated or decreased. In order to test this, one would need to choose a measure of economic importance, disaggregate the pool of recipients based on these measures, and examine whether human rights was more strongly associated with the aid fortunes of "unimportant" states than of "important" ones.

What is the best measure of economic importance of a state? Measures based on trade are in some ways the most natural choice, since they clearly capture the issue of interest for this argument, but since growth rate of a nation's economy is the most commonly used indicator of economic vibrancy and therefore potential economic value, it is the measure I use here.

Therefore, I divided recipient states into categories of importance based on economic growth and tested whether, at either stage, human rights had a greater impact on the aid fortunes of "unimportant" recipients or of "important" ones.

Gatekeeping Decision

There appear to be significant differences in the decisional calculus for states with stagnant versus expanding economies. Table 10.4 presents these results.

Table 10.4. Recipients with Growing versus Stagnant Economies, Pooled Cross-Sectional Probit Analysis of Whether a State Receives Aid

Variable	GDP Growth 0 Or Negative	GDP Growth 1st Quartile	GDP Growth 2nd Quartile	GDP Growth 3d Quartile	GDP Growth 4th Quartile
Human Rights	.169§	Outcome did not vary	Outcome did not vary	1.764	−7.118
	(.112)			(1.71[8])	(2.57[8])
Recipient GDP	.000			−.004	.054
	(.001)			(597668.400)	(.108)
Population	−5.08[−6]			−.000	−.000
	(5.67[−6])			(852.511)	(3526.373)
Canada Exports to Recip.	.000			−4.24[−6]	2.00[−6]
	(.000)			(397.667)	(783.817)
Canada Imports from Recip.	−7.93[−7]			9.69[−7]	−.009
	(3.47[−6])			(286.913)	(300225.300)
Oil Exporter	.456			.554	.244
	(1.90[7])			(1.92[7])	(8965231)
Human Rights* Imp./Exp. Ratio	−7.93[−7]			.072	11.451
	(3.47[−6])			(6.13[7])	(1.31[8])
Nuclear Capabilities	−.261			15.364	−5.780
	(.539)			(2.32[8])	(———)
Trade Intersection	−1.643**			−13.536	−19.035
	(.489)			(2.39[8])	(4.63[8])
Instability	.229			−3.160	−19.035
	(.356)			(2.07[8])	(4.63[8])
Alliance with Canada	−.712			(dropped)	(dropped)
	(.642)				
Dispute with Canada	(dropped)			(dropped)	(dropped)
End of Cold War	−.408			6.197	−163.405
	(.426)			(2.30[8])	(2.79[8])
Difference in Democ. Scores	−.042*			.054	.226
	(.020)			(2.84[7])	(.208)
Humanitarian Crises	−.002			−.048	1.142
	(.007)			(1.14[7])	(4.60[7])
Human Rights Activism in Canada	−1.047§			−1.075	−138.187
	(.577)			(1.18[8])	(5.09[8])
Immigrant Populations	.001			.000	.000
	(898.234)			(872.377)	(11204.690)
Distance	7.935			7.935	12.568
	(1.67[8])			(1.67[8])	(8.08[8])
Government Vulnerability	.146			8.002	−24.327
	(.152)			(1.00[8])	(6.93[8])
Any Aid Previous Year	.000***			.000	.000
	(.000)			(2424.700)	(1700.005)
Model Significance	.0003			1.0000	———
N	387			223	155
PPC	67.98	———	———	99.54	99.91
PRE (Lambda)	.7091	———	———	.0047	.0017

*** = significant at $p<.001$; ** = $p<.01$; * = $p<.05$; § = $p<.075$ (one-tailed).
Superscripts indicate scientific notation (that is, 5.55[−6] = 5.55 × 10[−6] = .00000555).

It will be noted that there are no results for two of the categories, because all of the recipients received aid. (When there is no variation in the dependent variable there is of course no way to analyze the determinants of the variation.) However, the results from the three other categories are striking. Considering one factor at a time, the differential impact of the human rights record of a recipient is in line with the expectations of a trade-driven approach. States with stagnant economies, which one would expect to be the least valuable economically to Canada, are the only ones in which human rights was a systematic factor in the decision whether or not to grant aid. As was the case for all recipients, the direction of the coefficient indicates that states with *worse* human rights records are more likely to receive aid. Nothing in stated Canadian aid or human rights policy would suggest this finding. Again, this result could be due to Canada's maintenance of economic relations with these recipients in hopes of using that continued relationship to influence them, a strategy suggested by, for instance, Matthews and Pratt.[57] Most importantly, though, these results demonstrate support for hypotheses 2 and 4: that human rights are more likely to be taken into account in aid decisions regarding states that are not economically important to the donor, than in those regarding states that are.

For none of the categories of recipients were either potential or actual economic relationships important in determining aid amounts, in contrast to patterns observed over the entire OECD, where aid decisions regarding states with expanding economies were conditioned on current trade relations with OECD members. This finding stands in marked contrast to the above predictions of many observers of Canadian foreign policy, who consider trade relations to be one of the most important foreign policy goals, often subsuming other competing objectives for which policy tools could be used.

The effects of measures of both strategic value of the recipient and Canadian domestic politics are mixed, but measures of either only matter for recipients with the most stagnant economies. For those states, recipients at key trade intersections are, surprisingly, less likely to receive aid, a result that seems difficult to explain. In terms of domestic politics, recipients who score low on the Polity democracy scale are less likely to receive aid from Canada. States which have been the target of human rights activism within Canada are also less likely to receive aid.

Allocation Decision

Human rights have an effect for none of the categories of recipients at the allocation stage, in stark contrast to the human rights commitments enunciated in Canadian foreign policy instruments including the Winegard report and *In Whose Interest?* The pattern matches more closely what would be predicted given the lack of institutionalization of human rights issues in the Canadian aid policy-making apparatus. The size of the recipient's GDP is inversely related to aid for the first category of states (but only for the first category), indicating that at least for recipients with the most stagnant economies, it truly is the states that need aid the most that receive it.

But, contrary to the predictions of a trade-driven model, variables measuring the current trade relationships between Canada and the recipient matter for *none* of the categories. This finding suggests that Canada truly does pursue the need-based aid policies that many scholars have advocated.

Domestic politics variables appear to have little impact. In fact the only one that matters in any category is human rights activism (for states with the slowest growth). It does, however, have the impact expected—to dampen aid amounts—and is consistent with the fact that at the gatekeeping stage, human rights activism decreases the probability that a recipient will obtain aid.

CONCLUSION

An examination of aid decisions on the part of the Canadian government yields far less support for the hypotheses at the heart of this research than is the case for other donor states such as Britain and Australia.[58] Analyses of the gatekeeping decision in the context of all potential aid recipients reveal that neither human rights concerns, nor the current economic value of the recipient, has an impact. However, potential recipients with more stagnant economies are more likely to receive aid, something that is consistent with Canada's explicit efforts to pursue need-based aid policy. This conclusion is lent further support by the fact that states with larger populations are also more likely to receive aid.

Some strategic characteristics of the recipient also make it more likely to receive aid, such as being in an area of relative stability, in part because such states are seen as being more likely to be able to put aid to good use.

Interestingly, potential recipients in military alliances with Canada are less likely to receive aid, but this is in part because they are among the wealthiest of potential recipients. Surprisingly, few domestic political factors in Canada have an impact on how much aid it receives, and in fact it is only the difference in the recipient's democracy score from that of Canada that makes it less likely to receive aid. Past aid is the single most important predictor of whether a recipient will receive aid in the current year, indicating a certain lack of flexibility. Humanitarian catastrophes make no impact on the likelihood that a state receives aid from Canada.

Analyses of the allocation stage likewise demonstrated no impact of human rights on the level of aid a recipient receives. Trade interests in and of themselves clearly do not come into play at this stage in the aid process, either—although interestingly enough, the variable measuring the interaction of the recipient's human rights record and its trade relationship with Canada *is* significant—lending support to the idea that the human rights relationship is conditioned on the extent to which the recipient is important in other ways. More populous states are once again more likely to receive aid, but the strategic variables have mixed impact. In fact, only one strategic variable has an effect—that of the end of the Cold War, which makes any given recipient likely to receive less aid. Domestic politics variables have no impact at this stage in Canadian aid patterns.

Finally, to test whether Canadian decision-making relied on a different set of factors for different kinds of states, decisions were examined for various categories of recipients based on their economic growth. At the gatekeeping stage, results provided some support for the conditional effect of human rights on the aid decision process. Analyses were impossible to conduct for the two categories of positive but slower growth, but for the other categories, human rights only mattered for the states with least potential economic value to Canada. However, neither potential nor actual economic value of the recipient to Canada had an impact on whether recipients received aid for any of the other categories. Interestingly, strategic and domestic politics variables only mattered for recipients with the most stagnant economies as well.

The allocation decision reflected similar patterns. At this stage, human rights mattered in no subset of recipients, though for the first category it was, in fact, the poorest states that received aid, in keeping with explicit Canadian commitments to need-based aid policies. This conclusion is lent additional support by the fact that, for three categories, more populous recipients receive more aid. Trade considerations have no impact for any category at the allocation stage for Canada—nor does need of the recipient, except as measured by population.

The impact of strategic variables is mixed. States in areas of instability receive less aid among the states with the most stagnant economies, while military alliances make them likely to receive more aid. The end of the Cold War also makes recipients less likely to receive aid. Contiguity of a recipient with Canada only matters for the final category, and actually makes a state less likely to receive aid. However, because the distribution of this variable is so skewed, it is likely that these results are epiphenomenal.

Domestic politics variables at this stage have little impact as well, except for human rights activism in the second category, which makes a recipient less likely to receive aid. This result stands in sharp contrast to what most scholars of Canadian aid predict, suggesting that domestic politics has less to do with aid patterns than does inherent value of the recipient or other kinds of international/external considerations.

A survey of the general context of Canadian foreign policy-making would lead one to expect an impact of human rights—at least in some decisions. These analyses reveal that human rights can play a role—but only in a very few, and very specific, cases.

Human rights abuses continue apace despite the fact that policymakers and activists in democratic states profess a firm commitment to civil and political rights. Determining when and why states take action in defense of those goals helps us understand why so many continue to be denied basic political and civil liberties, and what can be done about it by states that possess the resources to encourage change.

NOTES

1. See for instance Victoria Berry and Allan McChesney, "Human Rights and Foreign Policy-Making," in *Human Rights in Canadian Foreign Policy*, ed. Robert O. Matthews and Cranford Pratt (Kingston, ON: McGill-Queen's University Press, 1988); Rhoda E. Howard-Hassmann, *Compassionate Canadians: Civic Leaders Discuss Human Rights* (Toronto: University of Toronto Press, 2003); Ronald Manzer, "Human Rights in Domestic Politics and Policy," in *Human Rights in Canadian Foreign Policy*, ed. Matthews and Pratt (ON: McGill-Queen's University

Press, 1988); Robert Matthews and Cranford Pratt, "Introduction," in *Human Rights in Canadian Foreign Policy*, ed. Matthews and Pratt; Kim Richard Nossal, "Cabin'd, Cribb'd, Confin'd? Canada's Interest in Human Rights," in *Human Rights in Canadian Foreign Policy*, ed. Matthews and Pratt; Sharon Scharfe, *Complicity-Human Rights and Canadian Foreign Policy: The Case of East Timor* (Montreal: Black Rose Books, 1996); H. Gordon Skilling, "The Helsinki Process," in *Human Rights in Canadian Foreign Policy*, ed. Matthews and Pratt.

2. Berry and McChesney, "Human Rights and Foreign Policy-Making"; Howard-Hassman, *Compassionate Canadians*; Manzer, "Human Rights in Domestic Politics and Policy;" Matthews and Pratt, "Introduction"; Nossal "Cabin'd, Cribb'd, Confin'd? Canada's Interest In Human Rights."

3. Scharfe, *Complicity-Human Rights and Canadian Foreign Policy*.

4. Kenneth Waltz, *Theory of International Politics* (Reading, MA: Addison Wesley, 1979).

5. Woodrow Wilson Center for International Scholars, Canada Institute, "Realism Canadian Style: The Chrétien Legacy in Foreign and Defense Policy and the Lessons for Canada-U.S. Relations," http://wwics.si.edu/index.cfm?topic_id=1420&fuseaction=topics.event_summary&event_id=52644.

6. Robert O. Keohane, "Institutional Theory and the Realist Challenge After the Cold War," in *Neorealism and Neoliberalism: The Contemporary Debate*, ed. David. A. Baldwin (New York: Columbia University Press, 1993); Charles Lipson, "International Cooperation in Economic and Security Affairs," in *Neorealism and Neoliberalism*; Robert Axelrod and Robert O. Keohane, "Achieving Cooperation Under Anarchy: Strategies and Institutions," in *Neorealism and Neoliberalism*.

7. David Gillies, "Do Interest Groups Make a Difference? Domestic Influences on Canadian Development Aid Policies," in *Human Rights, Development, and Foreign Policy: Canadian Perspectives*, ed. Irving Brecher (Halifax, Nova Scotia: The Institute for Research on Public Policy, 1992) 435–465; Scharfe, *Complicity-Human Rights and Canadian Foreign Policy*.

8. Berry and McChesney "Human Rights and Foreign Policy-Making;" Manzer "Human Rights in Domestic Politics and Policy"; Matthews and Pratt "Introduction"; Nossal "Cabin'd, Cribb'd, Confin'd? Canada's Interest In Human Rights;" Scharfe *Complicity-Human Rights and Canadian Foreign Policy*; Skilling "The Helsinki Process."

9. Berry and McChesney "Human Rights and Foreign Policy-Making;" Manzer, "Human Rights in Domestic Politics and Policy"; Matthews and Pratt "Introduction"; Nossal "Cabin'd, Cribb'd, Confin'd?"

10. Matthews and Pratt "Introduction," 11.

11. Manzer, "Human Rights in Domestic Politics and Policy"; Nossal, "Cabin'd, Cribb'd, Confin'd?"

12. Canadian Human Rights Reporter, *Human Rights Law: Basics*, http://www.chrr.org (27 Dec. 2003).

13. Berry and McChesney, "Human Rights and Foreign Policy-Making," 60.

14. Matthews and Pratt, "Introduction," 13; Nossal "Cabin'd, Cribb'd, Confin'd?" 46.

15. Nossal, "Cabin'd, Cribb'd, Confin'd?" 47.

16. Berry and McChesney, "Human Rights and Foreign Policy-Making," 60.

17. Nossal, "Cabin'd, Cribb'd, Confin'd?" 47. Prior to the below-mentioned reports, discussion of the motives behind Canada's foreign aid did not even touch on human rights as a consideration. Dobell (1972) notes the following motives behind Canada's aid program to francophone Africa: finding an outlet for francophone Canadians, the desire to preempt a Québecois aid program in Africa, and the desire to outflank Québec in its attempts to heighten its international presence. He bemoans the failure of Canada to join Europe and the U.S. in involvement with "far eastern" development efforts and the economic benefits they could render (103). Even at that point, however, Dobell documents calls from, at the very least, the academy, for greater altruism in Canada's foreign policy (97).

18. Gillies, "Do Interest Groups Make a Difference?"

19. Gillies, "Do Interest Groups Make a Difference?" 455.

20. Matthews and Pratt, "Introduction," 15.

21. Nossal, "Cabin'd, Cribb'd, Confin'd?" 49.

22. Skilling, "The Helsinki Process."

23. Nossal, "Cabin'd, Cribb'd, Confin'd?" 49.

24. Nossal, "Cabin'd, Cribb'd, Confin'd?" 47.

25. Scharfe, *Complicity-Human Rights and Canadian Foreign Policy*.

26. Nossal, "Cabin'd, Cribb'd, Confin'd?" 47–48.

27. Cited in Nossal, "Cabin'd, Cribb'd, Confin'd?: Canada's Interest In Human Rights," 47.

28. Nossal, "Cabin'd, Cribb'd, Confin'd?" 47.

29. Nossal, "Cabin'd, Cribb'd, Confin'd?" 47.

30. Nossal, "Cabin'd, Cribb'd, Confin'd?" 47.

31. The 1986 Hockin-Simard Report and the 1988 Winegard Report, *For Whose Benefit?*

32. *Sharing Our Future*, 1988.

33. Quoted in Scharfe, *Complicity-Human Rights and Canadian Foreign Policy*, 15.

34. T. A. Keenleyside and Patricia Taylor, "The Impact of Human Rights Violations on the Conduct of Canadian Bilateral Relations: A Contemporary Dilemma," *Behind the Headlines* 42 (March 1990): 1–27.

35. Scharfe, *Complicity-Human Rights and Canadian Foreign Policy.*
36. Keenleyside and Taylor, "The Impact of Human Rights Violations."
37. Gillies, "Do Interest Groups Make a Difference?" 455.
38. Nossal, "Cabin'd, Cribb'd, Confin'd?" 49.
39. Matthews and Pratt, "Introduction," 9.
40. Michael Stohl, *The Purdue Political Terror Scale*, Codebook 1993.
41. Key differences between the two scales are discussed in Bethany A. Barratt, *Aiding or Abetting: The Comparative Role of Human Rights in Foreign Aid Decisions* (Ph.D. dissertation, University of California, Davis, 2002).
42. In addition, these analyses were run substituting in other proxies for the status of rights in the recipient states, such as levels of democracy and counts of internal disorder incidents (riots, demonstrations, etc.). Similar results were observed.
43. Charles R. Beitz, *Political Theory and International Relations* (Princeton, NJ: Princeton University Press 1994), 179; Thomas M. Franck, "The Emerging Right to Democratic Governance," *American Journal of International Law* 86 (1992): 46–47; James Lee Ray, *Global Politics* (Boston: Houghton Mifflin, 1998), 442–43.
44. Keith Jaggers and Ted Robert Gurr, *Polity III: Regime Change And Political Authority, 1800–1994* [computer file], 2nd ICPSR version (Ann Arbor: Inter-university Consortium for Political and Social Research, 1995).
45. Central Intelligence Agency, *CIA World Factbook* (Washington, DC: U.S. Government Printing Office, Various Years).
46. *Historical Statistics of the United States On CD-ROM: Colonial Times to 1970* . . . [computer file], Millennial Edition (New York: Cambridge University Press, 2006).
47. David J. Singer and Melvin Small, Annual Alliance Membership Data, 1815–1965 [computer file], ICPSR version (Ann Arbor: University of Michigan Mental Health Institute, Correlates of War Project, 1967).
48. This control is also included in the interest of replicabililty. It is included in many studies of U.S. aid such as David L. Cingranelli and Thomas E. Pasquarello, "Human Rights Practices and the Distribution of US Foreign Aid to Latin American Countries," *American Journal of Political Science* 29, no. 3 (September 1995): 539–563; Steven C. Poe, "Human Rights and the Allocation of US Military Assistance," *Journal of Peace Research* 28, no. 2 (1991): 205–216; Steven C. Poe, "Human Rights and Economic Aid Allocation under Ronald Reagan and Jimmy Carter," *American Journal of Political Science* 3, no. 1 (1992): 47–67.
49. See http://www.wcfia.harvard.edu/ponsacs/panda.htm.
50. Ideally, I would have obtained measures of the amount and intensity of campaigning done on behalf of particular human rights crises from the major

human rights interest groups themselves. However, both Amnesty and Human Rights Watch claim not to keep records of this kind or any other that would lend itself to systematic analysis—not even a financial audit that would contain country-specific line items.

51. Samuel Kernell, *Going Public: New Strategies of Presidential Leadership* (Washington, DC: Congressional Quarterly Press, 1993).

52. *Flags of the World*, 2003.

53. David Halbran Lumsdaine, *Moral Vision In International Politics : The Foreign Aid Regime, 1949–1989* (Princeton, NJ: Princeton University Press, 1993).

54. Such as Matthews and Pratt, "Introduction."

55. T. A. Keenleyside, "Development Assistance," in *Human Rights in Canadian Foreign Policy*, ed. Robert O. Matthews and Cranford Pratt (Kingston, ON: McGill-Queen's University Press, 1988); Matthews and Pratt, "Introduction"; Scharfe, *Complicity-Human Rights and Canadian Foreign Policy*.

56. The reverse pattern holds for many other major donors.

57. Matthews and Pratt, "Introduction."

58. See discussions in Barratt, *Aiding or Abetting: The Comparative Role of Human Rights in Foreign Aid Decisions*; Bethany A. Barratt, "Aiding or Abetting? Human Rights and British Foreign Aid Decisions," in *Human Rights in European Perspective*, ed. Steven Poe and Sabine Carey (London: Ashgate, 2004).

11

Canada and International Financial Policy: Non-Hegemonic Leadership and Systemic Stability

Duncan Wood

As a small, open economy, dependent on trade and seeking international investment opportunities, both inward and outward, Canada has always had a strong interest in the health and stability of the international economy in general and the financial system in particular. Indeed, as the country's economic interdependence with the rest of the world has intensified, systemic instability, financial turbulence, and crisis increasingly threaten Canada's economic well-being directly. Canadian financial firms are active internationally in all regions of the world and Canadian business in general is more and more outward-looking. As Canada's proclivity toward free trade has grown (see Lusztig's chapter in this volume on the evolution of Canada's trade policy), the financial health of the rest of the world matters to Canadian interests, both public and private, and the government has consistently contributed to the management of the international financial system. In recent years the Canadian government has identified financial crisis as a source of not just economic instability, but also of political instability and as a threat to human security. The need, therefore, for effective mechanisms to manage and prevent crises has been obvious to successive Canadian governments since the middle of the twentieth century.

The financial crises of the 1990s, perhaps most notably those involving currency for major Asian states, posed a fundamental challenge to both the stability of the international financial system and the international political economy as a whole. By linking together so explicitly the interests and futures of developing and developed countries through the interdependence of globalized finance, the crises forced the leading organ of global economic and financial governance, the G-8, to pursue a strategy of reforming the basic structure of the international financial system. This process demanded diverse and varied policies, but most of all it required cooperation and coordination between the world's leading economic powers to implement meaningful changes.

The argument of this chapter is that the challenges of financial architecture reform in the 1990s provided Canada with the opportunity to exhibit qualities of intellectual and moral leadership in the system, as well as supporting U.S. leadership, and that this was made possible by the nature of the G-8 itself, in particular its commitment to multilateral decision-making. Canada displayed both the will and the capability to influence the direction of the reforms, and highlighted the importance of the G-8, and later the G-20, to the projection of Canadian power and influence in the system.[1]

The chapter addresses diverse theoretical issues such as leadership (in particular institutional and situational forms of leadership), "supportership," co-optive power, institutionalized cooperation, pluri-lateralism and legitimacy. (All of the preceding terms will be explained at later points in this chapter.) The chapter describes the role played by Canada in the reform process and emphasizes the role played by the Department of Finance, ahead of Foreign Affairs Canada and International Trade Canada (formerly known as the Department of Foreign Affairs and International Trade—i.e., DFAIT) in the ongoing business of changing the structure of international finance. It shows us the possibilities for a relatively weak state such as Canada to exercise influence over the emerging structure of the global economy by working through institutions that afford it both access to the major powers (in particular the U.S.) and freedom to formulate alternative approaches to those of the dominant states. The G-8, therefore, is seen as a valuable element in giving Canada the ability to "punch above its weight"—in particular, above its military prowess—in the international system.

POWER AND LEADERSHIP IN THE INTERNATIONAL SYSTEM

In order to understand the exercise of Canadian power and leadership in the process of reform of the international financial system in the 1990s, it is necessary to explore these terms as multidimensional concepts. Canada is clearly not a country that possesses high levels of relative power, particularly with reference to its fellow G-8 states. Although resources, capacities, and the ability to project are always fundamental to the exercise of power and leadership in international politics, the challenge here, then, is to define the concepts in ways that allow us to focus on more than just the great powers.

Power

An emphasis on capabilities, resources, and relative power has traditionally meant that the exercise of power in the international system has been an issue that has been dominated by analyses of the great powers. Joseph Nye's 1991 study of power, although focusing on the diverse elements of U.S. power, provides us with alternative understandings of the concept that do not necessarily imply an exclusive focus on the major states in the system. In pondering the future of American leadership of the international system, Nye examines the various faces of power and finds two main distinct forms. The first he calls "command power," which closely resembles the established, realist definition of power familiar to most of us. This can rest on either threats or inducements, but the second face of power is more subtle. "Co-optive power" he defines as

> an indirect way to exercise power. A country may achieve the outcomes it prefers in world politics because other countries want to follow it or have agreed to a system that produces such effects. In this sense, it is just as important to set the agenda and structure the situations in world politics as it is to get others to change in particular situations. . . . Co-optive power can rest on the attraction of one's ideas or on the ability to set the political agenda in a way that shapes the preferences that others express.[2]

This understanding of power is useful for an examination of Canadian foreign policy in two ways. First, it is clear that Canada lacks significant command power resources, while relying on "indirect ways" to achieve its goals. Second, Nye's concepts show the unavoidable crossover between the issues of power and leadership, but impels us to seek understandings of leadership that do not rest exclusively on the more tangible resources of states such as military capabilities or economic size.

Susan Strange has made a similar distinction between two different types of power. Alongside the traditional, realist definition of power (i.e., as the ability of agent X to get agent Y to do something agent Y would not otherwise do) which she refers to as "relational power," Strange posits the existence of what she calls "structural power," which is "the power to shape and determine the structures of the global political economy within which other states, their political institutions, their economic enterprises, and (not least) their scientists and other professional people have to operate."[3] This means more than merely setting agendas or deciding the rules of the economic game; strange holds that structural power refers to the ability to mold the international economic and political environment and thus control the manner in which agents (be they states, international organizations [IOs], businesses, or individuals) interact with each other. Strange stresses that the extent to which one actor in a relationship holds structural power will increase or decrease its relative power over another actor.

This definition of power is clearly of great utility when both international organizations and the evolution of new rules and norms for international finance are addressed. Strange identifies the international credit or financial system as one of the four preeminent structures in the international political economy. Moreover, because structural power is the ability to shape and mold the environment in which interstate and private actor activity occurs, the exercise of such power will help to determine a host of related issues, such as economic distribution and efficiency in the system. A key element here is that not only major powers can exhibit and exercise structural power. Smaller states can do so through playing a role in the formation of new rules for the system and by providing ideas-based solutions to common problems. It is also, of course, conceivable that non-state actors can exert structural power, though there is a notable absence of research into this question. Although Canada is not a country known for shaping the structures of the global economy, it has had success in influencing the rules of the international system at key moments and is well-known for suggesting ideas-based solutions. The innovations of peacekeeping and the land-mines ban in the security sphere are notable examples.

Having questioned how control over structure might translate into political and economic power, the ability of states to convert potential power into realized power should also be questioned. Kim Nossal stresses that it is vital to question the ability of states (in this case, Canada) to convert potential power into actual power, or more accurately, results.[4] Nossal notes that by some measures Canada should qualify as a great power; but a failure or inability to convert power resources effectively has limited Canada's ability to advance its interests in the international system. Institutional membership and cooperation have been two ways of attempting to improve the success of converting potential Canadian power into results in the system. By working through institutions Canada has been able to increase the impact of its foreign policy in the system, and has been able to both form alliances with more powerful states and to oppose them without risking Canadian interests.

Leadership

Many of the same issues that were seen in the preceding examination of the concept of power can also be identified in discussions of leadership. There has been a tendency for studies of this concept to concentrate on the question of hegemony and the theory of hegemonic stability. Although hegemonic stability theory (HST) in its commonly held formulation may appear to be of little use in studying Canadian foreign policy in the contemporary era, the various formulations of hegemony, and in particular of variants that emphasize leadership, help to cast some light on the opportunities available to Canada as a second-tier power in the system.

The importance of leadership in the system is nowhere clearer than with reference to international finance. As a number of authors have noted,[5] the globalization of finance involving deregulation and rapid movements of capital around the world has made the system much more risk-prone than in earlier periods, and thus in greater need of a stabilizing influence.

Mark Brawley has argued persuasively of the need for hegemonic leadership in explaining the success and failure of the process of international financial architecture reform.[6] Basing his argument in the assumption of rationality, he shows the importance of U.S. leadership in resolving crises in the international financial system and establishes reasons for expecting future leadership in the system.

Charles Kindleberger's original formulation of HST dictated that a stable, liberal international economic system required the leadership or hegemony of one power.[7] Taking his lead from the Gold Standard and Bretton Woods systems originating in British and American leadership of the international system, respectively, Kindleberger posited that "for the world economy to be stabilized, there has to be a stabilizer, one stabilizer."[8] The theory gained currency throughout the 1970s and 1980s as it was applied to what was seen as declining U.S. hegemony. In the process, much attention was given to the concept of hegemony.

It should be noted at this point that the concept of hegemony, although it has dominated discussions in the area, represents but one manifestation of leadership. David Lake has approached the issue by adopting a novel approach that breaks HST down into its constituent parts. His recognition of two sub-theories within HST provides us with an interesting way forward.[9] Lake identifies both leadership and hegemony theories within the parameters of HST, and demands renewed investigation into the importance of leadership to the functioning of the international economy.

Leadership studies will broaden the parameters of the enquiry and eliminate needless debates over the existence or not of "true" hegemony. By focusing on leadership we may include nations not usually recognized as leading powers, we can be issue specific, and we do not have to neglect ideological or consensual elements. Looking at leadership rather than merely hegemony should broaden comprehension of the workings of international organizations and structures alike. A leading nation attempts to create institutions designed to facilitate the effective functioning of the international economy through cooperation and collective action. A useful definition of leadership, must include a recognition of this factor. Lake notes:

> It is always possible to define any state that effectively produces stability as a "leader" and any state that does not as a "non-leader." Indeed, it is a fairly common tendency in the literature. But in the end, of course, this sleight-of-hand produces not an explanation but a tautology. The task before us is to move beyond behavioral definitions of leadership and to

define the necessary and sufficient conditions for the production of the international economic infrastructure.[10]

Hegemony itself, it must be remembered, involves not just power but also ideological elements of consensus and legitimacy. The Gramscian and neo-Gramscian approaches to hegemony define it as a form of dominance that involves a more consensual understanding of power and leadership, one that incorporates ideological elements as well as the notion of legitimacy. These two elements combined help us to understand one of the less commonly considered but very basic elements of leadership. To be a leader, others must follow; to be an effective leader the others must *want* to follow.

A more specific definition of leadership comes from John Ikenberry in a 1996 article on the future of American dominance of the international system. Defining leadership as "the ability to foster cooperation and commonalty of social purpose among states,"[11] he therefore opens the possibility (although he himself does not explore the option) of leadership coming from states not possessing significant relative power resources. He outlines three manifestations of leadership: structural, institutional, and situational. Structural leadership "refers to the underlying distribution of material capabilities that gives some states the ability to direct the overall shape of world political order."[12] Institutional leadership, for Ikenberry, "refers to the rules and practices that states agree to that set in place principles and procedures that guide their relations."[13] The third kind of leadership, situational, is defined by Ikenberry as "the actions and initiatives of states that induce cooperation quite apart from the distribution of power or the array of institutions. It is more cleverness or the ability to see specific opportunities to build or reorient international political order. . . . that makes a difference."[14] While Canada lacks the resources necessary for structural leadership, it has a fine tradition in providing both institutional and situational forms. Canada has shaped rules (in multilateral settings) and seized "specific opportunities" to contribute to international order.

David Lake's discussion of international leadership in the 1990s was preceded a decade earlier by an examination of U.S. foreign economic policy in the late nineteenth and early twentieth centuries.[15] In that piece he analyzed the international sources of American foreign economic policy and concluded that the major causal factor in shifting the U.S. from a protectionist to a liberal foreign trade posture was the distribution of power and its position in the structure of the international system. But within that discussion, Lake identified four categories of states: hegemons, supporters, free riders, and spoilers. Hegemons, or hegemonic leaders, are the dominant states in the system who pay the overwhelming proportion of costs of maintaining systemic stability. Free riders are the smaller states in the system who benefit from international cooperation without having to contribute to its maintenance. Supporters are middle-sized states that, while they do not possess sufficient power to lead, can contribute to the long-term management of the system. They do so often by sharing the costs of providing public goods. Spoilers, on the other hand, are middle-sized powers that free ride and thus are highly disruptive to the process of cooperation. Canada's role as a supporter state is clear; it contributes faithfully to multilateral institutions and has a history of supporting the U.S. in both security and economic spheres.

Susan Strange has pointed out that the absence of one country with either the will or the capacity to manage the system alone pushes us to look for alternatives that involve collective leadership.[16] Describing international finance in the 1990s as a system of "mad money," she writes:

> For us in the 1990s, it seems to many experts that Kindleberger was right: the system does need management or "governance" when things start to go wrong. Yet these days, no single hegemonic leader is strong enough or rich enough to fill the role unaided. Instead, we may have to pin our hopes to the chances of a collective leadership as a substitute for the national hegemon.[17]

The G-8, then, emerges as a potential substitute for unilateral leadership and for hegemony. Within the pluri-lateral process of G-8 bargaining and decision-making, we can identify Canada as both supporter and leader, depending on the issue at hand, and we can identify examples of both institutional and situational leadership. Canada has repeatedly contributed to the provision of public goods through the G-8 and other institutions, and has provided leadership within the institution of the G-8 by proposing solutions to problems, and by suggesting and pressuring other states to embrace alternative solutions to contemporary problems. A clear example of this last point that will be explored later has been the Canadian concern with legitimacy and burden-sharing. The issue of legitimacy will also highlight Canada's recognition of the need for adopting a more consensual approach to leadership and governance in the international system.

CANADA AND INTERNATIONAL FINANCIAL MANAGEMENT IN HISTORICAL PERSPECTIVE

Canada's interest in international financial stability has been apparent since the mid-twentieth century. The international financial turbulence of the 1930s affected Canada deeply as the severe reduction in global financial flows brought currency instability and trade protectionism. The Great Depression and the Smoot-Hawley Tariff Act of 1930 in the United States demonstrated to Canada how financial instability at the level of the international system directly affected Canadian welfare and prosperity. Canadian policy-makers, therefore, shared the views of the British and American negotiators at the Bretton Woods conference in 1944, where the structure of the post-war financial system was determined, that international finance should be predominantly public, not private, and that there was an urgent need for strong, multilateral international financial institutions like the International Monetary Fund (IMF) and the International Bank for Reconstruction and Development (IBRD or World Bank).

Throughout the post-war period Canada played an active role in international financial management, joining the world's preeminent institutions and, just as importantly, voting alongside the major Western powers in key decisions. Although Canada does not command the same number of votes in the IMF as the United States, Japan, Germany, Britain, or France, it is the most important country in a group of states that represents around 5 percent of the total votes of the organization, thus giving Canada an important role in voting patterns. In the area of development financing, Canada has acquired a reputation as a major contributor, with traditionally high levels of bilateral aid coming from Ottawa, although those levels have been cut in recent years.

The Canadian private sector is also an important actor in the international financial system. Banks such as Scotiabank, Toronto Dominion, Royal Bank, and the Canadian Imperial Bank of Commerce (CIBC) are all active internationally, from Latin America to Asia to Europe. Canada's domestic financial system is also becoming more international as foreign banks such as HSBC and ING increase their market share. These ties of interdependence in the financial arena, ties that have intensified since the closing years of the twentieth century, have increased Canada's material interests in maintaining a stable international financial system.

Canada and the G-8

Canada has been a member of the G-7 since 1976, when the United States invited it, over the protests of the European members (particularly France), to join an institution that had been created the year before in Rambouillet, France. Canada has, throughout the life of the G-7 and its successor, the G-8 (after Russia became a full member of the summit process in the second half of the 1990s), been an active member that has sought to achieve broader Canadian foreign policy. In doing so Canada has sought to project Canadian values into the decisions of the G-7/G-8 and has formed a variety of coalitions with other members in an attempt to achieve its interests and preferences.

John Kirton, a leading scholar on the G-8 and on Canada's participation in the body, has characterized the Canadian government's activities within the framework of the G-8 as "the diplomacy of concert."[18] According to Kirton, Canada's approach to the G-8 has been marked by six areas of success. Canada has:

1. Participated in all areas of G-7 activity;
2. Asserted Canada's interest- and value-based priorities;
3. Used coalition diplomacy with any member to achieve its goals;
4. Influenced the outcome of the summits in this way;
5. Gained domestic political support by its actions at the summits;
6. Ranked near the top in percentage of implementation for summit decisions.

Kirton stresses that this has happened despite Canada's being the weakest member of the G-8 and shows skillful diplomacy and a close understanding. Kirton also points out the ways in which Canada has used divisions within the grouping to practice "mediatory diplomacy." This has helped to give Canada a reputation within the G-8 as an autonomous actor, relatively independent of the influence of the United States, a key concern for the Europeans when Canada first joined the group.

The combination of these factors has meant that the Canadian government continues to see the G-8 process as an invaluable element in national foreign policy. Prime Minister Chrétien recognized as much when, in the lead-up to the 1995 Halifax summit, he noted that "Canada can further its global interests better than any other country through its active membership in key international groupings, for example hosting the G7 Summit."[19] This was more than just a reference to traditional Canadian multilateralism. Chrétien went on to stress the importance of the G-7 as an organ of governance and its importance in reshaping the system.

CANADA AND THE REFORM OF THE INTERNATIONAL FINANCIAL ARCHITECTURE

Canada's position as a member of the G-7 since 1976 has been a central element both in its relations with the other major economic powers and in asserting influence over the structure of the international economy. As a G-7 and later a G-8 member, Canada has participated in decision-making at the highest level in the international system and has used the institution as a platform for promoting Canadian values at the global level.

The wave of financial crises that hit the international system during the mid- to late-1990s demonstrated to the advanced capitalist democracies that the prospect of contagion from financial turbulence and crisis in the developing states now threatened their own economic and financial interests, both directly and indirectly. This recognition of financial vulnerability pushed the major economic powers to question the stability of the international financial system itself and to look for measures that might increase certainty and predictability within it.

Canada's interests in maintaining and reinforcing international financial stability are clear: as a medium-sized, advanced, open economy that depends on foreign trade and investment to prosper, and as a country committed to the overall stability of the international system, something that is threatened by repeated financial crises. As then Finance Minister Paul Martin put it in testimony to the House of Commons in 2000:

> The stability of the international financial system is a bottom-line pocketbook issue for us all. And there's another reason as well that these issues

matter to Canadians. There is a deep and lasting relationship between security and prosperity, and it follows that if Canadians want a world free of armed conflict, as we surely do, we need to ensure the foundations for international prosperity have been established.[20]

Although other nations articulated their concern with the growing turbulence in international finance in different ways, a general consensus soon emerged that globalization had made the international financial system a boat in which both developed and developing nations found themselves, and that crisis threatened to capsize it to the detriment of all.

The first crisis to hit the system in the 1990s was, of course, the Mexican peso crisis. IMF managing director Michel Camdessus termed it the "first financial crisis of the 21st century" due to the fact that the crisis was caused by rapid and massive movements of short-term or portfolio capital. Unlike the Latin American debt crisis of the previous decade, the sheer number of creditors involved and the pace of capital flight made effective management of the crisis near impossible. Instead a massive bailout, totalling some $50 U.S. billion and organized by the Clinton administration in the United States, was necessary to stabilize Mexico's finances and prevent further contagion to both developing and developed economies.

Halifax

The first international organization to respond to the new financial instability in a meaningful way that looked beyond the immediate implications of the Mexican crisis was the G-7. At their annual summit in Halifax in June 1995, the G-7 leaders focused on the meaning of crisis in Mexico and instituted a review of the international financial institutions that sought to identify weaknesses in the structure of the system and to provide some kind of early warning mechanism for future crises. Canada, as a fellow NAFTA country and as host of the summit, placed special emphasis on the issue of financial stability in the agenda. As host, Prime Minister Chrétien argued, "Canada has a unique opportunity . . . to influence the process of the reform and reshaping of these institutions to ensure their efficiency and relevancy in the increasingly integrated world of the 21st century" and thus represented "a historic opportunity for Canadian leadership."

The issue of institutional reform was central to the Halifax meeting.

The discussions over the implications of the Mexican crisis, of course, coincided with the fiftieth anniversary of the creation of the Bretton Woods financial institutions. Canada's approach to the Halifax summit combined questions of reform and efficiency with a concern for economic justice and the needs of the developing countries. On a number of issues throughout the process of IFA reform, Canada adopted a heterodox approach, proposing non-liberal options. Though the success of these proposals varied, nonetheless they showed Canada's concern for infusing the process of reform with Canadian values as well as interests.

Another issue for Canada in the Halifax summit was that of globalization. The leading economic powers were becoming aware by the mid-1990s that a rising tide of protest against the perceived dehumanizing and highly unequal effects of globalization threatened the ability of industrialised states to push the process any further. Protests at the World Bank's annual general meeting in 1994 in Madrid had shown the major financial powers the importance of trying to secure the goodwill of civil society organizations.[21] The Chrétien government was keen to emphasize that the most effective way to proceed with globalization was to legitimize the process in the eyes of citizens in both developed and developing states, and not to neglect issues of equity and justice. Canada's insistence on these issues at the Halifax summit and beyond once again demonstrated a canny, and entirely healthy, combination of idealism and pragmatism in Canadian foreign policy.

As for the actual reform process at Halifax, Canada briefly flirted with the idea of the Tobin Tax, an international tax on investments that is aimed, in theory, at slowing down the flow of private capital. In the talks leading up to the 1995 summit, several countries, including France and Germany, had proposed the idea of such a tax as a way to reduce speculative activity in international capital markets. Both Prime Minister Chrétien and Finance Minister Paul Martin had developed doubts about the stability of an international system of liberalized capital. In 1995, Canada supported the notion of a Tobin Tax (a tax on short-term international financial flows), though not unreservedly, recognizing that in practice the tax would be near impossible to implement without universal agreement from the regulatory authorities in the world's major financial centers.

Minister Paul Martin repeatedly announced his personal liking for the idea of the Tobin Tax, arguing that, although it would not end international speculation, it would "be a source of money for the international community . . . to decrease poverty."[22] However, Martin openly recognized that the lack of a consensus among the leading financial powers on the issue negates the possibility of moving forward with a meaningful effort to implement a Tobin Tax. All it would take is for one country to refuse to comply and the remaining states would be forced to follow suit, in order to avoid a huge loss in the competitiveness of their financial markets.

Prior to the summit, Canada had hoped to push an agenda that stressed issues of equitable and sustainable development. Given the overwhelming focus on the Mexican crisis and its implications for systemic stability, little progress was made on this companion agenda. The summit in fact concluded with calls for an early warning system to identify crises before they happened, and for the creation of an Emergency Financing Mechanism (EFM) that would create a rapid and established procedure for approving credit to countries experiencing financial crisis. The Halifax summit also saw the creation of a working group, consisting of representatives from the G 10 states, which produced what came to be known as the Rey Report. This set of recommendations became an important complement to later Canadian proposals in IFA reform.

One Canadian initiative at Halifax concerned the issue of involving more states in the process of reform. Canada had argued strongly that to make the process of reform workable, the G-7 needed to gain the support of key developing countries. This emphasis on legitimacy and inclusiveness became a fundamental element in the reform process, although the immediate results of Canada's initiative were not apparent for several years. However, in the later reforms involving the IMF, the G-22 and then G-20, and the Financial Stability Forum (FSF), the issue of broader representation was institutionalized.

Despite the fact that Canadian priorities concerning development and the inequitable effects of globalization failed to produce an agenda for action at this time, the nature of Canada's contribution to the progressive reform of the IFA was set at the Halifax summit. An emphasis on both efficiency and justice, values and pragmatism was to mark Canada's contributions to the process throughout the rest of the decade. Rather than follow the process chronologically, the rest of this section will address Canadian activities and initiatives by theme. In fact, in the period between

Halifax and the 1998 summit in Birmingham, England, when the full effects of the Asian crisis began to manifest themselves, discussion of IFA reform did not top the agenda of the G-8. Many of the Canadian actions and proposals discussed below emerged out of the post-Asian reform process.

Intellectual Leadership

Finance Minister Paul Martin exhibited leadership in the late 1990s by coming up with a six-point plan for structuring the reform process. In the aftermath of the Asian and Russian crisis, it was clear that the national financial crises threatened to become a global crisis that could damage the interests of the G-7 states themselves directly. The failure of Long Term Capital Management (LTCM) in 1998 in the U.S. demonstrated the way in which even the world's dominant economy and financial system could not effectively isolate itself from the negative impact of global financial turbulence.

Minister Martin announced his plan for financial stabilization at a meeting of Commonwealth finance ministers just before the October Washington meeting of G-7 finance ministers. The plan contained distinct elements for dealing with the spreading international crisis, and as a package, clearly reflected Canadian values as well as interests:

1. Lowering interest rates to stimulate growth in the world economy.
2. Social targeting of IMF programs to diminish the use of "one size fits all" packages.
3. Applying international standards of supervision to national financial systems.
4. Moving away from unrestrained capital account liberalization, to allow states to use capital controls on a voluntary basis.
5. An Emergency Standstill Clause, to be used by debtor nations to allow them more time to negotiate debt rescheduling.
6. A call for innovative approaches to the debt problems and relief needs of the world's poorest nations.

Many of the themes included in Martin's six-point plan would come to fruition through cooperation in the G-7 and are discussed below in greater detail. However, one issue that merits attention here is the fourth item, namely, that of capital account liberalization. In opposition to both the established wisdom of the IMF and the policy preferences of the United States and Britain, Canada actively lobbied for the necessity of recognizing that many LDCs may need to impose short-term capital controls in order to maintain control over national finances. This initiative on the part of Canada showed not only an understanding of the needs of developing states; it also showed a willingness to stand up to the more powerful members of the G-7.

Financial Supervision

From the early days of the reform process, Canada had argued that a fundamental element in reinforcing the international financial system would be increased harmonization of national financial supervisory systems. The Canadian government called for an institutionalized process of peer review of national regulatory and supervisory systems. This notion took several years to come to fruition, but both the IMF and the World Bank began to include an examination of banking and financial regulation and supervision in their annual consultations with member states. Canada showed leadership here as one of the first countries to submit itself to evaluation in this way. What is more, with the creation of the Financial Stability Forum (FSF) in early 1999, the concept of peer review of financial supervisory practices was further institutionalized as a standard mechanism of cooperation. Canada found its interests and preferences coincided with Germany within the G-7, and indeed it was the German government of Gerhard Schroeder, as host of the Cologne summit that year, that put the issue of the FSF onto the agenda. The FSF was a further institutional addition to the growing network of national regulatory and supervisory officials that includes the Bank for International Settlements' Basel Committee on Banking Supervision (BCBS), the International Organisation of Securities Commissions (IOSCO) and the International Association of Insurance Supervisors (IAIS). Randall Germain has argued that the FSF has joined the G-7 as one of the principal institutions in the IFA.[23] Canada also showed situational leadership in creating the Toronto Centre for Financial Supervision, an organization designed to train developing countries' financial officials in advanced supervisory methods.

Broadening Participation in the Reform Process

The Canadian government introduced the idea of a broader consultation with developing countries over themes of globalization in the early years of the 1990s. As the IFA reform process got under way, the same notion was applied to Canadian perspectives on financial crisis management and prevention. Canada achieved considerable success from this line of argument and pressure on its G-7/G-8 colleagues. This is not to say that increased involvement by developing countries in the decision-making process in international finance was an exclusively Canadian idea; on the contrary, other states, including the United States, embraced the concept of consulting more closely with key LDCs whose financial systems were considered "significant" at the international level. But it was one of the most tangibly successful of Canada's reform priorities.

It was in fact the Clinton administration that took the first steps toward institutionalizing the involvement of the key developing financial systems in the reform process. In April 1998, at the Willard Hotel in Washington, D.C., the United States convened an ad hoc group of 22 states, including 14 representatives from emerging economies. The purpose of the G-22 was to produce a series of reports on the functioning of the international financial system and to make policy suggestions for both crisis prevention and crisis resolution.[24] Three working groups were formed, each of which produced a report on a different issue concerned with finance: transparency and accountability, strengthening financial systems, and, lastly, international financial crises. These groups were co-chaired by a developed and a developing state. The reasoning behind this close cooperation with key developing states was both to increase legitimacy and to incorporate the experience and expertise of their regulatory officials. Nonetheless, the G-22 was criticized for being merely a temporary measure and "the arbitrary way in which its membership was chosen."[25]

The G-22 concluded its work in October of 1998 but was replaced within months by a new and permanent institution in the panoply of international financial governance. Bringing together representatives from the G-7 states, Argentina, Australia, Brazil, China, India, Mexico, Russia, Saudi Arabia, South Africa, South Korea, Turkey, the European Union, the IMF, and the World Bank (with Indonesia added shortly after), the G-20 emerged as a sister institution to the G-8, with an initial focus on international financial crisis, but with a prospective mandate that potentially includes any issue related to international finance. The G-20 states represent approximately 87 percent of global GDP and around 65 percent of global population. Canada showed obvious leadership in this forum as Finance Minister Martin became the group's first chair. He has explained the importance of the G-20 in these terms: "Even the most well-intentioned programs are likely to fail unless the countries that are involved are given ownership of their own development agenda."[26] What's more, the creation of the G-20 marks a turning point in international financial governance. Not only does it increase the legitimacy of the G-7/G-8, but it also means that "it will be impossible to turn the clock back" on the issue of including developing countries in the decision-making process.[27]

BURDEN SHARING WITH THE PRIVATE SECTOR IN FINANCIAL CRISES

From the beginning of the process of IFA reform, Canada argued that it was unreasonable to expect public money from the IMF and the World Bank to be used to provide emergency financing to developing countries that ultimately helped protect the investments of private financial institutions. As Kirton has explained, Prime Minister Chrétien "retained a strong aversion . . . to privatising profits and nationalizing losses."[28] Not only did such measures protect the investments of private actors, it also contributed to a perceived moral hazard problem in the system of international finance. In part in response to these criticisms, Canada proposed two measures that sought to redistribute the burden of managing financial crises, away from the developing countries and taxpayers in developed states, and toward a sense of greater responsibility on the part of private financial actors.

First, Canada put forward the idea of collective action clauses in the wording of debt contracts. One of the problems of the financial crises of the 1990s, in comparison with the debt crisis of the 1980s, was that negotiations between debtors and creditors were greatly complicated by an absence of organization among the huge number of creditors. A collective action clause forces bondholders to appoint a single representative who is empowered to negotiate on behalf of all other debt holders. The advantage of such a clause is that negotiation between debtors and creditors, made so complicated by the enormous numbers of creditors in a system of portfolio capital and non-bank financial actors, is simplified and responsibility can be shared between the debtor nation and creditors as a group. Canada has acted as a leader in this regard by introducing collective action clauses in its foreign currency debt.

The second proposal made by Canada—with regard to burden sharing and crisis management—concerned the innovation of an emergency standstill provision to enable debtor nations to halt debt payments for a period of time to allow them to negotiate with creditors and seek rescheduling arrangements. Canada's active lobbying for such a mechanism was initially strongly opposed by the United States. However, Canada was able to convince Britain of the value of the provision, and by the end of the decade the U.S. had ceased its opposition to the idea. In April 2002, the G-7 as a group endorsed the proposal.

FINANCIAL CONTRIBUTIONS

Canada led within the context of IFA reform and crisis management throughout the 1990s by contributing a disproportionate amount of funds to the rescue packages provided to crisis-stricken states. Canada contributed indirectly, of course, through the multilateral financial institutions. But Canada also contributed to rescue packages when other G-7 states refused. For example, in April 1998 Canada offered half a billion U.S. dollars for the Thai emergency financing package, at a time when all other G-7 nations, with the exception of Japan, refused to contribute.

DEBT RELIEF

The issue of the indebtedness of the poorest countries in the system was one of direct relevance to Canada, given its traditional emphasis on poverty alleviation and commitment to overseas development assistance (ODA). Given its focus on humanizing globalization, Canada could not ignore the potential benefits of eliminating the official debt of the Highly Indebted Poorest Countries (HIPC). Canada formed a coalition behind the notion of debt relief for the most poverty-stricken states alongside Germany and Britain, against the resistance of France and Japan. The HIPC initiative involved the sale of some 10 million ounces of IMF gold at the same time as creditor governments eliminated the poorest country debt they held. Canada was also successful in ensuring that political and economic conditionality was attached to the debt relief program in an attempt to link debt relief to sustainable and equitable development. Largely due to Canada's willingness to lead on debt relief on a unilateral basis, by the end of the 1999 Cologne summit the G-7 had committed itself to reducing the debt of the HIPC states by as much as half.

CONCLUSION

The issues involved in G-7/G-8 work in the mid- to late-1990s reflected the preferences of Canada in a way that highlighted and even exaggerated the importance of Canada within the organization. This was due to the skillful use of Canada's intellectual resources and its willingness to form coalitions with any and all other member states when necessary. The issues also helped to push the ascendancy of the Department of Finance ahead of DFAIT in the making of Canadian foreign policy, and therefore of Paul Martin ahead of Lloyd Axworthy. The international agenda, dominated as it was by issues of financial turbulence, created the right conditions for this ascendancy and, in the persona of Paul Martin, the Department of Finance was able to seize the day.

Canada's activities throughout the 1990s with regard to international financial reform highlight the possibility for non-hegemonic leadership by smaller states in the system through their participation in organs of global governance. Canada certainly acted as a leader in the sense of "the ability to foster cooperation and commonalty of social purpose among states." Canada displayed two obvious forms of such leadership. First, it exhibited institutional leadership by helping to define "the rules and practices that states agree to." The call for peer review and Paul Martin's six-point plan both fit into this category. Second, it displayed situational leadership by exhibiting "cleverness or the ability to see specific opportunities to build or reorient international political order." Canada's innovative proposals for standstill and collective action clauses support an understanding of Canadian leadership in this sense.

Furthermore, Canada demonstrated a clear understanding of the need for building legitimacy and consensus. Canada's ongoing insistence on including developing states and securing their consent and involvement in the reform process showed that the Chrétien government and Paul Martin in particular recognized the dual benefits of legitimacy and efficiency to be had from such initiatives.

Lastly, we must recognize that, in addition to showing qualities of leadership, Canada also played the role of supporter. It did this predominantly through its contributions to rescue packages and to debt relief. By contributing to the costs of maintaining systemic stability, Canada refused to free ride on the financial strengths of the dominant powers.

The G-7/G-8, therefore, provided an important framework within which Canada could exercise a leadership role within the system. It has allowed Canada to "punch above its weight" and to assert its priorities and prerogatives alongside those of its more powerful coalition partners. We can expect the organization to continue to be a central element in Canadian foreign policy in the years to come. Furthermore, Canada's interest in international financial stability will not, indeed cannot, diminish in the future. As Canadian financial firms become more global in their business dealings, and as the Canadian economy in general is more affected by the forces of globalization, the country's prosperity will become ever more interdependent with the rest of the world, and the risk of financial crisis damaging Canada's national interest will increase, ensuring the commitment of the Canadian government to international financial management.

NOTES

1. Throughout this chapter a number of abbreviations will be used to refer to multilateral organizations. The G-7 is the Group of Seven: the United States, Germany, Japan, the United Kingdom, France, Italy, and Canada, with the European Union acting in a participatory but non-voting role. The G-8 is the G-7 plus Russia. The G-20 is the Group of Twenty, a meeting of finance ministers from the G-8 countries plus Argentina, Australia, Brazil, China, India, Indonesia, Mexico, Saudi Arabia, South Africa, Turkey, the International Monetary Fund, and the World Bank. The G-22 was a similar grouping that conducted studies of international financial stability and was replaced after a couple of years by the more permanent G-20.

2. Joseph S. Nye Jr., *Bound to Lead: The Changing Nature of American Power* (New York: Basic Books, 1991), 31.

3. Susan Strange, *States and Markets* (New York: Basil Blackwell Press, 1988), 25.

4. Kim Richard Nossal, *The Politics of Canadian Foreign Policy*, 3rd ed. (Scarborough, ON: Prentice-Hall Canada, 1997), 68–69.

5. See, for example, Susan Strange, *Casino Capitalism* (Oxford: Basil Blackwell Inc., 1986); Eric Helleiner, *States and the Reemergence of Global Finance* (Ithaca, NY: Cornell University Press, 1994).

6. Mark Brawley, "Global Financial Architecture and Hegemonic Leadership in the New Millennium," in *Debating the Global Financial Architecture*, ed. Leslie Elliott Armijo (Albany: State University of New York Press, 2002).

7. Charles Kindleberger, *The World in Depression: 1929–39* (Berkeley, CA: University of California Press, 1973).

8. Kindleberger, *The World in Depression*, 37.

9. David Lake, "Leadership, Hegemony, and the International Economy: Naked Emperor or Tattered Monarch with Potential?" *International Studies Quarterly* 37, no. 4 (December 1993): 459–489.

10. Lake, "Leadership, Hegemony," 466.

11. G. John Ikenberry, "The Future of International Leadership," *Political Science Quarterly* 111, no. 3 (Autumn 1996): 386.

12. Ikenberry, "Future Leadership," 389.

13. Ikenberry, "Future Leadership," 391.

14. Ikenberry, "Future Leadership," 395.

15. David A. Lake, "International Economic Structures and American Foreign Policy, 1887–1934," *World Politics* 35, no. 4 (July 1983): 517–543.

16. Susan Strange, *Mad Money: When Markets Outgrow Governments* (Ann Arbor: University of Michigan Press, 1998).

17. Strange, *Mad Money*, 55.

18. John J. Kirton, "The Diplomacy of Concert: Canada, the G7 and the Halifax Summit," *Canadian Foreign Policy* 3, no.1 (Spring 1995): 63–80.

19. Kirton, "The Diplomacy of Concert," 67.

20. Paul Martin, "Speech and Response to Questions in Evidence," Standing Committee on Foreign Affairs and International Trade, House of Parliament, Canada, May 18, 2000, http://www.parl.gc.ca.

21. Tony Porter and Duncan Wood, "Reform without Representation? The Transnational Dialogue on the Global Financial Architecture," in *Debating the Global Financial Architecture*.

22. Martin, "Speech and Response to Questions in Evidence."

23. Randall Germain, "Reforming the International Financial Architecture: the New Political Agenda," http://www.g7.utoronto.ca.

24. Peter B. Kenen, *The International Financial Architecture: What's New? What's Missing?* (Washington, DC: Institute for International Economics, 2001).

25. Porter and Wood, "Reform without Representation?"

26. Martin, "Speech and Response to Questions in Evidence."

27. Porter and Wood, "Reform without Representation?"

28. John J. Kirton, "Canada as a Principal Financial Power: G-7 and IMF Diplomacy in the Crisis of 1997–9," *International Journal* 54, no. 4 (Autumn 1999): 603–624.

III

CANADA AND WORLD REGIONS

12

Canada as a Northern Nation: Finding a Role for the Arctic Council

Douglas C. Nord

Although most of the world considers Canada to be a distinctively northern nation, many Canadians fail to acknowledge this fairly obvious condition. There is a tendency for many Canadians to cast their gaze southward rather than northward when they consider developments in the international arena. This a reflection not only of the traditional pull on their attention exerted by their immediate neighbor to the south, the United States, but also a response to a general belief that significant global happenings take place far from the Arctic. According to this popular view, important international events occur in the metropolitan capitals of Europe, the desert lands of the Middle East, or the tropical rainforests of Latin America or Southeast Asia—not near the North Pole.

Those who argue the importance of a "northern orientation" for Canadian foreign policy tend to receive only limited respect or concern. This can be seen in the coverage accorded to former Governor-General Adrienne Clarkson's 2003 state visits to some of Canada's northern neighbors, Russia, Finland, and Iceland. Not only was Ms. Clarkson's trip attacked by some as a wasteful expenditure of public funds, but the overall significance of visiting and learning from the experiences of other "northern peoples" was questioned. Speaking to reporters as she traveled through northern Russia, the former Governor-General noted that: "It is rather frustrating that people don't understand that we are a northern country."[1] She later added: "We know the North is there, it is just above our heads on the map. It is also in our heads imaginatively; it fulfills and describes that archetypal image which all Canadians have and which they respond to—or try to deny. But denial of the North is a form of self-contempt that is extremely puzzling and terribly depriving."[2]

Despite this Canadian proclivity to look south rather than north, the government of Canada over the past three decades has undertaken a concerted effort to raise the nation's profile in Arctic affairs and to establish a distinctive role for the country in circumpolar diplomacy. A centerpiece of this endeavor has been Ottawa's efforts to create an Arctic Council and to establish a meaningful agenda for its efforts. It has also worked to create a distinctive "northern dimension" to Canadian foreign policy and to familiarize both domestic and external audiences with its main features and dimensions.

THE NATURE OF THE INQUIRY

This chapter considers the growth of a distinctive northern dimension to Canadian foreign policy over the past several decades. It first discusses how Canada developed a specific set of perspectives on northern affairs during the twentieth century and how these operated within its broader national foreign policy goals. The particular imprints of concern over sovereignty and the Cold War are discussed. Note is taken of the extent to which Arctic defense initiatives within the context of the North Atlantic Treaty Organization (NATO) and the North American Air Defense Agreement (NORAD) set some basic parameters for Canadian thinking about the North then and now.

The chapter then moves on to consider the character of new Canadian approaches to northern issues following the end of the Cold War. It looks specifically at how a variety of environmental, economic, and social development concerns have been added to an established security agenda in the North over the past three decades. It examines how Ottawa sought to develop new opportunities and mechanisms for international cooperation in the North. Detailed attention is given to the establishment of the new Arctic Council and the extended and complex negotiations that took place between Canada and the United States that resulted in its creation.

The next portion of the chapter examines the distinctive roles that Canada has played in providing leadership and direction for this new regional organization. It also considers the most recent efforts of the Canadian government to create a distinctive "northern dimension" to Canadian foreign policy and to raise the consciousness of its own citizens regarding the significance of this endeavor. The rationale behind such an effort is discussed as well as the manner in which this new initiative serves as a hallmark of efforts to make external policies more reflective of domestic national values and aspirations.

The final section of the chapter raises a series of questions for further consideration regarding the ultimate significance of Canada's efforts at establishing a "northern dimension" to its foreign policy. It endeavors to make an assessment of the achievements that Ottawa has secured in promoting the idea and operation of the Arctic Council over the past three decades. It also seeks to place Canadian diplomatic initiatives within the broader context of a changing national foreign policy.

CANADIAN VIEWS OF THE NORTH PRIOR TO WORLD WAR II

Before the coming of World War II, Canada did not possess a well-defined and articulated policy toward the North.[3] To the extent that Canadian foreign policy touched upon northern matters, it was primarily focused on protecting national sovereignty and securing development opportunities in the region. A significant portion of the Canada's national territory has been formed from northern lands. These it acquired over a period of three centuries as it moved from the status of a European colony to a self-governing state. During the nineteenth century, major stretches of northern lands were transferred from the control of the British Crown and the Hudson's Bay Company to the government of Canada. Much of this vast area was opened to development and settlement by Ottawa and became a major element of the nation's expansion beyond the Maritimes and the St. Lawrence River Valley. The forest, mineral, and agricultural wealth derived from many of these lands represented a significant component of the economic foundation of the nation from the second half of the nineteenth century to the present day.[4]

Yet most Canadians had only a limited direct exposure to these northern lands. The vast majority of the population settled in the more temperate zone close to the American border. A number of young men found seasonal employment in the forest and mining camps of the various provincial norths of the country, but much of the Canadian north remained uninhabited by permanent European settlers. Its vast territory was populated primarily by native peoples—who were largely removed from the economy and society of the south. Administrative control was exercised by a small number of government agents and a fledgling police force—the Royal Canadian Mounted Police. For most Canadians, the North remained as a land of untested promise and potential.[5]

For its part, the Canadian government sought to encourage its citizens to move northward to develop the resources of the region. It sold land and distributed timber and mineral rights to Canadian citizens and new immigrants who would be willing to seek their futures in this northern frontier. Northern development initiatives became an ongoing feature of both federal and provincial government efforts throughout the first few decades of the twentieth century. It became an oft-cited "fact" that the future of Canada lay in its North.[6]

During much of this period, the Canadian government also worried about foreign encroachment—especially American—in its North. As early as the nineteenth century gold rushes in British Columbia and the Yukon, Ottawa expressed a continuing worry that its northern lands might come under the control of the United States—either by direct annexation or by more subtle alienation. The American expansionist rhetoric of "54–40 or Fight" of the mid-nineteenth century (pertaining to the Oregon Territory boundary) did nothing to lessen Canadian anxieties in this regard. Nor did the highly unsatisfactory resolution of the Alaska Boundary Dispute in 1903 (when via controversial arbitration the United States received coastal territory also claimed by Canada) calm their fears. Throughout the first few decades of the twentieth century, the Canadian government conducted an ongoing diplomatic effort to secure international recognition of its territorial claims to various Arctic lands and waters. It was able to come to a number of agreements with both the United States and several interested European states over disputed territorial claims. However, Ottawa failed to achieve its most-prized goal—international acceptance of Canadian jurisdiction and sovereignty over the Arctic waters of the Northwest Passage.[7] More serious international events taking place in Europe and Asia soon drove this concern to the background of Canadian foreign policy interests. They were not to surface again until the waning days of the Cold War.

CANADIAN INTERESTS IN THE NORTH—
COLD WAR PERSPECTIVES

The coming of World War II refocused Canadian views of the North. Before the outbreak of military conflict, the area had been seen primarily as an international backwater of little strategic significance. Suddenly, with fighting taking place in both Europe and Asia, the North became a strategic region—critical to the war effort in both theaters. Equally significant, Ottawa began to view the North no longer simply as its own backyard area—but as a true circumpolar domain.[8]

Throughout the period of World War II, Canada and especially the United States expanded their military presence in the region. The latter established military bases in Greenland and Iceland to secure these domains as part of the Allied war effort against Germany. A number of naval campaigns were undertaken against German forces from the North Atlantic. Canadian and American naval forces and merchant fleets also delivered wartime supplies to Britain and the Soviet Union through northern waters. The United States also expanded its wartime military presence in Alaska as a barrier to possible Japanese military attack upon the west coast of North America. American troops were also stationed in several northern Canadian communities to assist in the transport of military equipment to the front, the training of key personnel, and the construction of needed supply facilities and transport routes. The most significant of the latter activities was the successful effort to construct the Alaska Highway. At the height of the war, more than 50,000 Canadian and American troops were stationed at various points in the circumpolar north.[9]

The military and strategic significance of the North that had become evident in World War II became further underscored during the progress of the Cold War. By the late 1940s it was evident that the Circumpolar North was to be one of the potential zones of conflict between the NATO Alliance and the Soviet Union. From the Western allied vantage point it was to be critical to their defense effort. As early as 1949, with the initiation of NATO, both Canada and the United States saw themselves as providing critical military support and assistance to each other and their European allies from their northern territories. Military bases, troops, and equipment were stationed in northern Canada and the United States in order to respond to any military need. Similarly, plans were drawn up for the quick deployment of American and Canadian personnel and supplies in northern Europe in event of a crisis.

As the Cold War progressed and the technological means improved for delivering serious blows to the enemy, Canada and the United States expanded their defense cooperation in the North. In 1951 they agreed to build the Pinetree Radar Defense System to give warning of possible Soviet bomber attack from across the Arctic region. In 1955 this was followed up by a commitment to construct a more sophisticated Distant Early Warning (DEW Line) radar system in the High Arctic of Canada. Finally, in 1958, the two countries signed NORAD, which went a substantial way toward integrating American and Canadian defense planning for North America.[10]

Despite a number of mutual irritants that developed between Canada and the United States during this period of close defense cooperation, the two countries tended to develop similar views of the North's post-war position in international relations. From the vantage point of both Ottawa and Washington, the North was seen primarily a zone of potential conflict in a bipolar world characterized by both ideological and strategic confrontation. It was a region in which both sides deployed their most prized military forces and around which very little in the way of mutual cooperation could be expected. This latter point is highlighted by the relative dearth of international agreements that were signed by the various circumpolar states during the entire period of the Cold War. Even rather innocuous proposals to cooperate in areas of weather and environmental monitoring tended to be rejected by both sides at the height of the Cold War.

Gradually there was to be a general thawing of the Cold War environment throughout the international system during the late 1960s and 1970s. In the spirit of detente, both Canada and the United States began to initiate several forms of improved communication with the Soviet Union. Some initial discussions were undertaken between scholars and policy-makers from each side around the general need to diminish bipolar confrontation and replace it with true circumpolar cooperation. Yet progress in this direction remained relatively slow. It nearly came to a virtual halt in the early 1980s when both the United States and the Soviet Union engaged in renewed military buildups. Interestingly, at this time, the

North grew to become an area of even more strategic significance. The "Age of the Arctic" was being heralded for the first time—largely in defense terms.[11] Yet Canada still retained an optimistic view that circumpolar cooperation could win out in the longer term.

CANADIAN PERCEPTIONS OF THE NORTH AT THE END OF THE COLD WAR

By the mid-1980s, the nature of the international system was experiencing significant change. With the coming to power of Mikhail Gorbachev in the Soviet Union, it was apparent that there would be new initiatives designed to lessen the tensions that had developed between the Cold War superpowers. This had the potential of lessening potential conflict in a wide number of areas of regional discord—including the Arctic. While the area still remained a priority zone for military planners in Moscow, Ottawa, and Washington, new issues and new actors were being gradually added to the Northern agenda. The North was no longer being seen entirely as an "empty land." The needs and interests of the people, animals, and environment of the region were being discussed with growing frequency. Groups like the Inuit Circumpolar Conference, which had been formed as early as 1977, began to discuss the need to construct lines of communication and cooperation between the various peoples who resided in the separate sectors of the Circumpolar North.

Increasingly, as the decade wore on, a variety of new collaborative efforts were being proposed by scientists, researchers, and environmentalists from Canada, the United States, the Soviet Union and the Nordic countries. They were interested in working together in the North to investigate common regional concerns such as Arctic air and water pollution, atmospheric warming, and threats to species survival. They were interested in using the Arctic in a peaceful and cooperative manner and destroying the established view that it was forever to be a zone of conflict. These early initiatives were to bear substantial fruit in the next decade, being the forerunners of such initiatives as the International Arctic Science Committee and the Arctic Environmental Protection Strategy (AEPS).

The government of the United States, for its part, was fairly reluctant to abandon its established Cold War thinking regarding the North. This is clearly suggested in the policy statement that was issued by the Reagan administration in the spring of 1983. It noted, in part, that national defense issues were of priority concern in the region and that the first element of U.S. Arctic policy was to be "protecting essential security interests in the Arctic region, including preserving the principle of freedom of the high seas and superjacent airspace."[12] Washington continued with this primarily strategic view of the region well into the early 1990s, augmenting it a bit in the new decade to include elements of economic and environmental security. Even after the fall of the Berlin Wall, it was unwilling to abandon its superpower vision of the North.

Canada's response to a changing international environment was far more flexible. Canadian scholars and policy-makers were far more eager than their American counterparts to consider broadening the agenda of Northern diplomacy beyond strategic and military affairs. They were early supporters of the idea of abandoning the old bipolar framework for considering northern questions and replacing it with a broader and more inclusive circumpolar orientation. Ottawa was interested in supporting a wide variety of international initiatives that were directed at addressing problems of pollution and the environment the Arctic. It did so partly as a means to guarantee itself a place in the vanguard of reform-minded states. It also served as a means to place some of its outstanding bilateral problems with the United States—such as the Northwest Passage and acid rain—within an international arena. Canadian interest in supporting circumpolar discussion of native rights and economic development in the Arctic was also linked, in part, to important domestic political agendas within the country. These various strands of interest came together in the late 1980s in the form of Canada's proposal for the creation of an Arctic Council. Its strong push to inaugurate such an organization—and American opposition to it—clearly highlight the manner in which Canadian and American perceptions of the North have tended to diverge from one another over the past decade.[13]

THE IDEA OF AN ARCTIC COUNCIL

In has been noted by several scholars of international affairs that the end of the Cold War and the collapse of the Soviet Union set the stage for new initiatives toward international cooperation in the Circumpolar North. Mikhail Gorbachev's speech in Murmansk in October of 1987 established the foundation for expanded East-West peaceful interaction in the North. In his remarks he called for the Arctic states to set aside their historic differences and to join in "a genuine zone of peace and fruitful cooperation."[14] Such a conciliatory tone was to engender positive responses from nearly all of the Soviet Union's northern neighbors.

In the case of Canada, a simple offhand remark by Prime Minister Brian Mulroney during his November 1989 visit to the Soviet Union launched Ottawa's effort to establish an Arctic Council. Asked to respond to the theme of Gorbachev's Murmansk speech, the Canadian Prime Minister enthusiastically endorsed the idea of expanded circumpolar cooperation. He indicated to a Leningrad audience that such peaceful interaction would be a benefit to all involved and should be regularized in the coming years. He went one step further and suggested: "And why not a council of Arctic countries eventually coming into existence to co-ordinate and promote co-operation among them?"[15]

While the idea for such northern community building might have seemed revolutionary to some, it should be remembered that the concept of a circumpolar international organization had been discussed within Canadian foreign circles for some twenty years—even during the depths of the Cold War. Professor Maxwell Cohen had suggested as early as 1971 that the time had come to establish a framework for international cooperation among the nations of the Arctic region. He proposed an Arctic Basin Treaty that would foster environmental, scientific, and economic interactions among the peoples of the area.[16] This innovative idea lay dormant for more than a decade until the National Capital Branch of the Canadian Institute of International Affairs revived the proposal and brought it to the attention of the Canadian government. In 1987, a working group of established northern scholars came together under the auspices of the CBCIIA and drafted a position paper on Canadian Arctic diplomacy. One of its provisions called for the creation of an Arctic Council to coordinate international activities in this area. It was this document that caught the eye and fired the imagination of Prime Minister Mulroney and his advisors during his visit to the Soviet Union in late 1989.

Encouraged by such a positive official response, another group of Canadian scholars known as the Arctic Council Panel produced, in March of 1990, a more extensive report entitled *To Establish an Arctic Basin Council*. This report was then forwarded to the Canadian government for its consideration. It was reviewed and quickly endorsed by the Department of External Affairs—which had been avidly looking for new foreign policy initiatives to distinguish Canada's role within a rapidly changing international environment. Speaking in Ottawa on November 20, 1990, the Secretary of State for External Affairs, Joe Clark, noted that: "The Government believes that now is the time to move forward to establish that Arctic Council. Canada intends to propose an Arctic Council to the seven other Arctic countries." As a sign of the seriousness of his proposal, Clark went on to state that "Canada is willing to host a small secretariat for this Council and contribute to sustaining it from the outset."[17]

Buoyed by the Foreign Minister's statement, the Arctic Council Panel produced a more comprehensive *Framework Report* in January of 1991, which became the focus of a policy roundtable discussion in Ottawa that spring. The main features of the *Framework Report* were generally well received by both government and academic participants of the roundtable. It proposed an inclusive membership for the Arctic Council in which there would be direct representation of northern aboriginal peoples and non-governmental organizations as well as the traditional nation-states. It also suggested that the Arctic Council should have a broad agenda allowing for matters of economic, political, social, military, and environmental affairs to be addressed. In its subsequent *Second Framework Report* of May 1991, the Arctic Council Panel specifically urged that the "mandate of an Arctic Council be an open one that allows for the growth of the Council's agenda with the growth of consensus."[18]

These recommendations were again quickly seized upon by the Canadian government. It saw within them the means to establish a distinctive Canadian northern foreign policy worthy of recognition by its circumpolar partners. With this in mind, it raised the issue of the need to create such an Arctic Council in June of 1991 at the first Arctic Environmental Protection Strategy Conference in Rovaniemi, Finland. Canada's Minister of Indian Affairs and Northern Development, Tom Siddon, noted the importance of creating such an institution in remarks delivered at that time: "Achieving a permanent Arctic Council among a group of nations with widely differing geographic, economic, cultural and strategic interests will not be a simple task. But we believe it is a goal worth pursuing. . . . To move the process along, Prime Minister Mulroney will be writing to the heads of governments of the seven other nations inviting them to send representatives to Canada later this year. Together they can begin exploring how such a permanent council might be constructed and what its mandate and responsibilities might be."[19]

It became clear, however, even to the most fervent advocates of the Arctic Council that before any extensive international negotiations could be conducted a more thorough consideration of the goals and operation of the proposed institution would have to be undertaken. While the Arctic Council Panel had done an admirable job in presenting the potentialities of the organization, the specific features of the Arctic Council required considerable more development. This was undertaken as a joint effort by the responsible government departments and interested policy groups like CARC and the Capital Branch of the Canadian Institute of International Affairs (CBCIIA) during the summer and fall of 1991. Together they produced a series of discussion papers and a draft convention that further delineated the structures, goals, and functions of the proposed Arctic Council.

Within each of these documents the proponents of the Arctic Council attempted to address the promise and potential of such an innovative organization. They identified at least four major goals around which the new entity should focus its energies. These included:

1. Expanding beneficial contact between the various peoples of the Circumpolar North;
2. Improving environmental protection for the fragile ecosystems of the North;
3. Reducing the overall military presence in the region;
4. Securing broad recognition of the economic, political, and social rights of the aboriginal peoples of the area.

There seemed to be a distinct consensus among those involved that Canada was paving the way for a new era of peaceful relations in the Arctic.

Throughout these discussions, however, very little attention was paid to potential conflicting views arising from any of the other Arctic states. Only a limited effort was made to seek out the opinions of the other governments of the circumpolar region regarding the goals and objectives of the proposed Arctic Council. Buoyed by an optimistic belief that the end of the Cold War truly allowed for entirely new thinking to take place in the Arctic, Canadian policy-makers plowed ahead in their efforts to sell their new and innovative organization.[20]

SELLING THE ARCTIC COUNCIL

Once having more fully developed its Arctic Council proposal, the Canadian government began almost immediately to seek support for its initiative within the international arena. Specifically it sought the support of the seven other Arctic states that were slated to become members of the Arctic Council. Its first success was secured with the government of the new Russian Federation. As part of his visit to Ottawa in February of 1992, Russian President Boris Yeltsin signed with Prime Minister Mulroney a *Declaration of Friendship and Cooperation* in which they affirmed their support for the establishment of the Arctic Council. The Declaration stated, in part, that: "Canada and the Russian Federation as major Arctic states, affirm their support for the creation of an international Arctic Council to protect the Arctic, its peoples and its resources, while fostering prosperity in the region through enhanced cooperation among circumpolar states."[21] With this endorsement from one of the major Arctic states, the Canadian initiative seemed well on its way to fruition.

During the following early spring months of 1992, the Canadian government also pressed its initiative with the governments of the Nordic states. Most of these countries saw substantial merit in the Canadian proposal and indicated their tentative approval for the creation of such a circumpolar organization. Norway and Finland did express some reservations that the proposed Arctic Council might detract some attention and energies from environmental priorities of the AEPS. These reservations, however, were made to Ottawa largely in private. All of the Nordic states did publicly state, however, that their eventual membership in the Arctic Council would be dependent upon securing the full participation of the United States as well as Russia.[22]

Later that same spring, Ottawa sought additional support for its Arctic initiative from the leading aboriginal NGO of the region—the Inuit Circumpolar Conference. At its meeting in May of 1992, the organization considered the proposal and gave its provisional endorsement. The membership of the Inuit Circumpolar Conference was encouraged by the Canadian government's recognition that the indigenous peoples of the region should have a substantial voice in the operation and agenda setting of the proposed Arctic Council.

The one voice of discord within these diplomatic discussions was to be heard from the government of the United States. While Washington did not at any time actively oppose Canada's initiative to gain support for the creation of the Arctic Council among the other circumpolar states, it let it be known from the outset that it had significant reservations regarding the thrust and direction of Ottawa's proposal. It indicated on more than one occasion that until these concerns were adequately addressed, the United States would not become a member of the proposed circumpolar organization.

American objections to the Arctic Council took a variety of forms. Most prominent of these during the period of the first Bush Administration was a concern over how the operation of a multifaceted Arctic Council might interfere with Washington's established security and defense-oriented approach to the region. American Arctic policy had long given a priority to defense issues in the area. Even with the end of the Cold War, most Washington policy-makers were reluctant to replace their strategic vision of the region with one that gave an equal priority to environmental, economic, and social concerns.[23]

Equally significant was the unwillingness of American policy analysts to abandon their superpower vision of Arctic decision-making. Basking in the realization that the United States was the last of the global superpowers, Washington policy formulators were reluctant to accept the idea of a new model of multilateral decision-making even for a relatively remote region such as the Arctic. They also expressed concerns over surrendering too much policy-making authority to the non-state actors that were to be represented within the proposed Arctic Council.[24]

Still another area of concern expressed by Washington was the belief that the creation of an Arctic Council would establish still another "bloated international bureaucracy." The Bush Administration, sounding a fiscally conservative tone, indicated its reluctance to contribute any significant financial or staff resources to a new Arctic Council. It expressed its belief that the needs of the region could be best addressed by already existing diplomatic structures and procedures.

With this in mind, Washington officials drove home the point that, having only recently agreed to the establishment of the Arctic Environmental Strategy, they did not want to endorse the creation of any new international institution that might either duplicate or compete with this important circumpolar initiative. Policy-makers in Washington suggested that, in recognition of this fact, the Arctic Council might perhaps be better conceived as a constituent element of the AEPS rather than an autonomous entity.[25]

These competing Canadian and American visions of the Arctic Council were well represented at a conference on U.S. Arctic Policy held at the University of Alaska, Fairbanks, in August of 1992. One of the major presentations at this meeting was given by Gilles Breton, the Director of the Office of Circumpolar Affairs within the Department of Indian Affairs and Northern Development in Ottawa. In his remarks he made a strong case for the establishment of the Arctic Council. He noted, in part, that: "Such an organization would support the harmonious development of the Arctic region by providing a better, clearer and more sustained focus to the efforts of governments and organizations active in circumpolar cooperation. An Arctic Council would be an effective umbrella organization to provide a forum for these organizations on issues of interest to Arctic countries."[26] American government representatives at the conference—including the Director of the Central Intelligence Agency and the Assistant Secretary of State for Arctic Affairs—chose in their remarks to ignore the Canadian proposal and instead focused on traditional security-related concerns of the United States in the region.

This approach of ignoring Canada's Arctic Council initiative continued as a central element of American policy for the remainder of the Bush Administration. It was a "cold shoulder" which might well have been anticipated. Yet it seemed to catch many in Ottawa unprepared. In many respects, the American reluctance to join the proposed Arctic Council served as the most significant barrier to the quick realization of Ottawa's initiative. This American hesitancy was not to change much until well into the second year of the new Clinton Administration, that is, 1994.

Patiently awaiting a change of heart in Washington, Ottawa pressed forward with its fervent efforts to create the Arctic Council. In May of 1993, Canadian government officials met with representatives of indigenous peoples associations from around the Circumpolar North. These included representatives from the Sami Council and the Association of Indigenous Peoples of Northern Russia. Ottawa also conducted discussions with various northern NGOs and sub-national governmental associations including the Northern Forum. As a result of these and other discussions, Ottawa brought forth a draft declaration later that year outlining the purpose and structure of the proposed Arctic Council. This draft was circulated among all potential participants for their comments and recommendations.

SECURING ACCEPTANCE OF THE ARCTIC COUNCIL AND CANADIAN-AMERICAN RELATIONS

In early 1993, after nearly two years of solidly promoting the concept of an Arctic Council, it appeared that the Canadian government had fallen short of its final objective. While seven of the eight Arctic States had given their approval to the creation of the Arctic Council, one had not—the United States. Fortunately for the Canadian proponents of the Arctic Council, there was to be a change in government in Washington. The resistant Bush Administration was to be replaced by a seemingly more cooperative Clinton Administration. As part of its own foreign policy review, the Clinton Administration undertook a reexamination of the nation's goals and objectives in the Circumpolar North. It came away from this policy review in late 1994 more open to the idea of an Arctic Council. Specifically, the Clinton foreign policy team declared itself more supportive of multilateral negotiations in the region and more sympathetic to the need to address environmental as well as economic and social agendas in the region area.

As a consequence, a new dialogue began between Washington and Ottawa. The new Liberal government that came to power in late 1993 seized the opportunity to reemphasize the importance of moving forward to complete the Arctic Council. The Council was to be a priority concern of Canadian foreign policy. This message was repeatedly conveyed by Canadian representatives during their meetings with their American counterparts throughout all of 1994.

In an effort to further emphasize the centrality of the issue to overall Canadian foreign policy, a special conference was convened in the spring of 1994 on the theme of "A Northern Foreign Policy for Canada." At this meeting several of the leading Canadian foreign policy planners articulated the reasons why it was essential that the Arctic Council negotiations be quickly and successfully concluded. The then Minister of Foreign Affairs, André Ouellet, pointed out in his remarks that: "The interests we have in a circumpolar Arctic is to ensure that policy making is as coherent and integrated as possible. It is essential that we give ourselves the necessary means to conduct proper scientific research, to develop transportation networks and to ensure sustainable economic development that is attuned to the Arctic's unique character. A framework must be established to guarantee the full participation of the Arctic aboriginal peoples in the process. . . . The Arctic Council is the best forum in which to address issues of common concern to Arctic communities."[27]

As an additional step to heighten Washington's awareness of the significance of the Arctic Council initiative, Ottawa moved forward to appoint a Circumpolar Ambassador—a position that had been promoted at the Northern Foreign Policy Conference. Ottawa chose for this critical post Mary Simon, the former head of the Inuit Circumpolar Conference. Her international stature and background gave new impetus to Ottawa's Arctic Council effort.

Further discussions between the American and Canadian foreign policy establishments continued throughout the fall of 1994 and during the first few weeks of 1995. However, there remained several areas of sharp disagreement between the two sides as to the goals, structure, and eventual operation of the Arctic Council. The Americans made it clear to Canadian representatives that they did not believe that the Arctic Council should take on a wide area of activity. They indicated that they saw the chief contribution of the Arctic Council to be in the area of environmental protection—akin to the role of the AEPS. They did not believe that the proposed Council should involve itself in other matters, including issues related to sustainable development in the North—a favored Canadian initiative. Equally important, the American policy-makers indicated their continued reluctance to accept the Canadian call for an "open agenda" for the organization. More specifically, they declared their complete opposition to the inclusion of any security or military-related issues being discussed within the domain of the Arctic Council.

Washington also let Ottawa know quite clearly that it did not envision the Arctic Council becoming in any way a major multilateral organization with a permanent headquarters and staff. Instead it suggested that the Arctic Council should be envisioned more as a flexible forum at which likeminded states might share the ideas and views on issues related to the Arctic but not be formally bound by any collective decision. The United States continued to press its initial view that any such organization should be small in scale and should not cost too much to operate. It opposed the original Canadian idea that the Arctic Council should have its own autonomous chair, secretariat and budget. Instead, it pushed the idea that staff support should be furnished by the rotating country chair of the body and that funding should be voluntary and project based. The United States argued that individual countries should provide resources directly to specific northern initiatives that they wished to sponsor and not to a collective pot.

The United States also made it clear to the Canadians that such an entity as the Arctic Council should continue primarily as an intergovernmental association. It was not opposed to having native peoples and NGOs present to contribute their ideas to discussions of the Council, but it rejected the idea of any equality of status between such groups and the Arctic Eight nation states.

Because of these major differences in views, little headway was made in these ongoing discussions. It was clear that Canada and the United States had very different visions as to what the Arctic Council was to be. Due to the lack of progress in securing agreement on the matter, the Canadian government finally asked that the issue of American adherence to the Arctic Council placed on the agenda for discussion between President Clinton and Prime Minister Chrétien during their Ottawa Summit in February of 1995. At that time the Canadian government again asked the United States to commit itself to the idea of an Arctic Council. This, the top leadership of the American government agreed to—seemingly in the spirit of good neighborliness—and in an effort to eliminate a nagging irritant from the bilateral relationship. Most of the American delegates attending the Ottawa meeting did not consider the Arctic Council worthy of further prolonged debate and discussion. The Canadian side, for its part, breathed a sign of relief and moved forward toward the drafting of a final document.

Despite having given its provisional consent to participate in the Arctic Council, the United States foreign affairs bureaucracy still remained resistant to all Canadian entreaties to become more flexible in its views regarding the structure and function of the proposed body. Throughout the remainder of 1995 and early 1996 representatives from Ottawa met regularly with their American diplomatic counterparts in an effort to encourage them to ease their continued opposition to key elements of the Canadian plan. Most of these meetings proved to be spectacularly unsuccessful.[28]

A year after the Clinton-Chrétien summit, the discussions on the Arctic Council again appeared to be on the course toward stalemate between the two sides. The Canadian government continued to fervently entreat the American side to change their position. The American response to the matter was more direct. It authored its own draft of the founding document in early 1996. It removed most of the "objectionable" features of the Canadian plan and further diluted the authority of the Council. American officials then indicated that this was as far as they were prepared to move and suggested that Ottawa respond to their draft on a "take or leave it basis." Failure to take it implied that the proposed fall Ottawa signing ceremony would have to be indefinitely postponed.[29]

In the end, the Canadians "took it" and accepted American views on nearly all of the key areas of contention. The final draft of the Arctic Council circulated during the summer of 1996. This document looked significantly different from the original version that had been developed in Ottawa and had been announced with great enthusiasm and confidence in early 1993. It bore the clear imprint of Washington in nearly all its critical areas.

First, and perhaps most significant, the character of the Council had dramatically changed. The Canadian view of a wide-ranging, ongoing organization sponsoring dramatic change in the Arctic had been replaced by a more limited and constrained American vision. The latter portrayed the Council as a limited problem-solving forum. It was to have no permanent institutional structure or staff. Its chair would rotate among the eight Arctic nation-states. It would be "project oriented" rather than change directed. Its limited scope and status was perhaps best symbolized by the fact that the Arctic Council was created by means of a voluntary international declaration and not through a more formal and binding international treaty or covenant.

Second, the mandate and the goals of the organization were similarly attenuated. While Canadian interests in sustainable development were mentioned in the body of the document, it was clear that environmental protection issues were to be given a distinct priority position in the operation of the Arctic Council. The AEPS and most of its subsidiary bodies were incorporated into the Council and appeared to establish the initial agenda for the new body.

Third, the agenda of the Arctic Council was not to be an "open" one.

While the wording of the document allowed for some areas of broad discussion, the United States was able to secure the acceptance by Canada and the other Arctic states that issues of defense and military security would not be open for discussion. It underscored this point by insisting on the inclusion of specific wording to this effect in the draft declaration.

Finally, with regards membership and representation, the American view also ultimately prevailed. The draft declaration clearly indicated that the organization was primarily an interstate entity. While northern native peoples and concerned NGOs might participate in the discussions of the Arctic Council as "permanent participants" or "observers," the primary players were to be the governments of the Arctic Eight through their responsible ministers and Senior Arctic Officials.

In the end, the organization that came into existence in Ottawa in September of 1996 resembled, initially, only a pale shadow of the vibrant international body that had been originally proposed by the Canadian government earlier in the decade. In many respects, the new Arctic Council looked more like an American product than that of a Canadian initiative. It carried with it as many trappings of traditional multilateral diplomacy as it did specific elements of innovative design.[30]

CREATING A NORTHERN DIMENSION TO CANADIAN FOREIGN POLICY

In the seven years since the establishment of the Arctic Council, Ottawa has worked hard to both invigorate the institution it so long labored to create as well as to fashion an overall northern theme for its diplomacy within this organization and the region. Canada took the chair of the Arctic Council during its first two years of existence (1996–1998) and promoted a series of initiatives that have served as the foundation of its ongoing efforts. These included crafting and adopting the Council's rules of procedure and terms of reference; facilitating the establishment of four of the Council's working groups [the Arctic Monitoring and Assessment Program (AMAP), the Conservation of Arctic Flora and Fauna (CAFF), the Protection of Arctic Marine Environment (PAME), and Emergency and Preparedness and Response (EPPR)], and the encouragement of the active participation of international indigenous peoples as Permanent Participants within the Council.[31]

During the subsequent chairmanship of the United States (1998–2000),

Canada worked within Council and behind the scenes to ensure that many of its original initiatives for the organization continued to move forward despite the notable lack of enthusiasm evidenced by Washington. Ottawa also endorsed the establishment of a fifth working group of the Council, the Sustainable Development Working Group (SDWG) and encouraged the active participation of interested countries, international organizations, and non-governmental organizations in the efforts of the Arctic Council.[32]

Over the course of the most recent chairmanships of Finland (2000–2002) and Iceland (2002–2004) Canada has taken a similarly strong and supportive role. It has taken the lead in funding projects related to capacity building within northern communities, improving the health and well-being of children and youth in the Arctic, and protecting the environmental quality and biodiversity of the region. Ottawa has also worked on behalf of enhanced exchanges between artists and cultural leaders of the North, as in support of the creation of the University of the Arctic.[33]

Yet, perhaps, the most significant development in Canadian foreign policy with respect to the North came in 2000 when the Department of Foreign Affairs and International Trade issued its report on *The Northern Dimension of Canada's Foreign Policy*.[34] This slim document was the end product of a concerted effort on the part of Ottawa and northern scholars and advocates to place Canada's efforts on behalf of the Arctic Council into a broader context. This initiative had begun in 1997 with the House of Common's Standing Committee on Foreign Affairs and International Trade taking a new look at Canada's overall interests and role in the region and preparing a comprehensive report entitled *Canada and the Circumpolar World: Meeting the Challenges of Cooperation in the 21st Century*.[35] This was followed up by a process of extensive consultation with experts in northern affairs, northern and aboriginal stakeholders, and the general Canadian public in which issues of interest and concern were identified and prioritized. The then Foreign Minister Lloyd Axworthy and the Ambassador for Circumpolar Affairs, Mary Simon, took major roles in these consultation efforts and focused the attention of the Canadian foreign policy establishment on the need to make sure that northern issues were given proper attention within the overall framework of Canadian external relations.

As set forth in the document of the same name, the Northern Dimension of Canadian Foreign Policy was to be focused on achieving four major objectives: First, enhancing the security and prosperity of Canadians—especially northern and aboriginal peoples; second, ensuring the preservation of Canada's sovereignty in the North; and third, establishing the Circumpolar Region as a vibrant geopolitical entity in a rules-based international system. Fourth, and finally, promoting the human security of northerners and the sustainable development of the Arctic.[36] In achieving such objectives, drafters of the document felt that Canada brought "a number of important assets to the circumpolar table" including:

- experience in developing northern institutions, community building, and working with aboriginal peoples and other Northerners;
- acknowledged expertise in northern science and environmental technology;
- cutting-edge capability in telecommunications and information technology;
- an innovative approach to governance and natural resource management in the North; and
- a wealth of experience in cooperating with Russia on Arctic affairs.[37]

In addition, the authors of *The Northern Dimension of Canadian Foreign Policy* believed that three major principles should guide the implementation of such a new policy. They envisioned Canada "meeting our commitments and taking a leadership role" in all circumpolar affairs. In so doing, they argued that Canada should undertake its responsibilities through "partnerships within and beyond government." Finally, they indicated that the Canadian government's pursuit of a northern dimension to its foreign policy would be informed by "engaging in ongoing dialogue with Canadians, especially northerners."[38] The drafters of the document clearly had in mind that Canadian foreign policy in the North should take account of domestic social, economic, and cultural priorities as well as international concerns. This reality is clearly reflected in the specific type of projects and initiatives that have been funded in the name of the Northern Dimension of Canada's Foreign Policy (NDFP) since 2000.

It is no coincidence, either, that the Northern Dimension of Canadian Foreign Policy was announced at nearly the same time that the new Territory of Nunavut was established. Ottawa has long seen the NDFP as one of the means to highlight the rights and the improved status of its aboriginal peoples both at home and abroad. In advocating the inclusion of indigenous groups as permanent representatives of the Arctic Council and by sponsoring specific projects focused on the improvement of their social, economic, and health environments, the Canadian government has sought to harmonize its foreign policy goals with some of its prime domestic policy objectives. It is instructive to note that both the Department of Foreign Affairs and International Trade and the Department of Indian Affairs and Northern Development contribute to the formulation and implementation of Canada's policy toward the Circumpolar North.

ASSESSING THE SIGNIFICANCE OF A "NORTHERN DIMENSION" TO CANADIAN FOREIGN POLICY

Looking back over the period since the Arctic Council was established and the NDFP was announced, one can discern both positive and less than positive developments regarding Canada's aspirations to project itself as "northern nation" within the international community. Clearly over the past decade, Ottawa has done more than in any other period in the past to project an image of being vitally concerned with the welfare of the lands and peoples of the Circumpolar North. It has spoken at any number of international forums regarding the importance of this region to Canada and to the global community as a whole. It has allocated nearly eight million dollars of funding to provide support for such worthy endeavors as promoting sustainable economic opportunities in the region, protecting sensitive environmental landscapes, establishing a University of the Arctic, and creating a Canadian and circumpolar research network to address ongoing concerns of the area.

Yet, on the other hand, the Circumpolar North remains a bit of a backwater in the consciousness of most Canadian foreign policy planners and the general Canadian public. Despite the worthy pronouncements by officials in Ottawa, the North tends to grab neither media headlines nor the attention of Canadian society. Major political interest and financial resources tend to be focused elsewhere—on the Asia/Pacific Region, the Middle East, and, of course, on the United States. The limited attention which the Arctic receives from Ottawa—while welcomed by the people who live in the region—tends to be often sporadic in nature and sometimes even the focus of criticism by Canadians who cannot relate to northern needs and opportunities. Despite the lofty pronouncement of a "northern dimension" to Canadian foreign policy, reality suggests that such an orientation or approach rests on a less than solid foundation. It remains to be seen whether the limited progress that has been made in building northern consciousness among Canadians by their government over the past decade can survive new challenges to Canada's role in the world as well as new currents in Canadian foreign policy thinking.

Ottawa's approach to promoting of the idea of an Arctic Council and a "northern dimension" to Canadian foreign policy reflects three limitations that have been witnessed in other aspects of Canada's external relations. The first of these has been a tendency to run too quickly with an idea for policy promotion without either assessing its full costs and benefits or determining the specific means for its implementation. Clearly Canadian foreign policy planners "liked the image and sound" of an Arctic Council and a "northern dimension" to the nation's foreign policy but had only the most limited understanding of what it would cost or how it might be achieved. This approach of charging forward without a clear set of cost estimates for implementation has been in evidence over the past decade over a wide area of other Canadian foreign policy initiatives ranging from environmental protection, to peace keeping, to various trade negotiations.[39]

The second limitation seen in the promotion of the Arctic Council and the NDFP has been a certain degree of self-delusion regarding the amount of global innovation that Canada can reasonably expect to introduce by itself into the prevailing dynamics of international relations. Canadian foreign policy in recent years has been long on promises of introducing major changes to the international system and often short on results.[40] This has been very much in evidence in its promotion of "soft power" and multilateral decision-making across a number of issue areas in the international arena—including the Arctic.[41] Many statements have been made regarding how the Arctic Council would dramatically transform the character of Arctic relations. Many of these remain as promises yet to be realized.

Finally, the third limitation seen in the promotion of the Arctic Council and the "northern dimension" of Canadian foreign policy has been a tendency for Canada to underestimate the impact of the United States in influencing developments in this domain. While it is desirable that Canada should differentiate itself from the United States in foreign policy arenas where the two countries do not share common views, this does not mean that Ottawa should underestimate the political clout of its southern neighbor. No amount of simply asserting the "superiority" of one's view or approach is likely to compensate for the unequal distribution of power and influence that exists between Canada and the United States. The lesson to be learned from undertakings such as the promotion of the Arctic Council is the need for Ottawa to be more aware of the nature of opposing American viewpoints and capable of developing effective strategies to respond to them. To fail to do so is to risk being either rebuffed or ignored.[42]

Clearly the challenge for Canadians in the coming decades—for both government officials and the general public—is to become more aware of the North and its significance and importance to national goals and aspirations with respect to both domestic and foreign policies. The North needs to become more than "that map above our heads" to quote Governor-General Clarkson. It needs to be a focus of national exploration, discussion, and policy debate. It no doubt is an area where Canadian foreign policy can diversify itself with great advantage. It also is a field in which nontraditional actions are undertaken and challenge the idea of a profound neglect in foreign affairs. The North needs to be incorporated into programs of education and action that benefit the people and lands that it embraces. Such programs need to be carried out by both national and multilateral institutions and organizations. It is in this way that a truly productive role and future can be found for an institution like the Arctic Council.

NOTES

1. Mark MacKinnon, "Rolling Out the Red Carpet," *Globe and Mail*, 29 September 2003, 5.

2. Adrienne Clarkson, "Shaped by Our North," *Globe and Mail*, 1 October 2003, 19.

3. Ken S. Coates, "The Discovery of the North: Towards a Conceptual Framework for the Study of Northern/Regions," *The Northern Review*, no. 12/13 (Summer/Winter 1994): 17.

4. Kerry Abel and Ken S. Coates, eds., *Northern Visions: New Perspectives on the North in Canadian History* (Peterborough, ON: Broadview Press, 2001), 7–21.

5. Morris Zaslow, *The Northern Expansion of Canada 1914–1967* (Toronto: McClelland and Stewart, 1988), 19–22.

6. Renée Hulan, ed., *Northern Experience and the Myths of Canadian Culture* (Montreal and Kingston: McGill-Queen's Press, 2002), 3–8.

7. Nancy Fogelson, *Arctic Exploration and International Relations 1900–1932* (Fairbanks, AK: University of Alaska Press, 1992), 29–32.

8. Shelagh D. Grant, *Sovereignty or Security? Government Policy in the Canadian North, 1936–1950* (Vancouver: University of British Columbia Press, 1988), 49–69.

9. William R. Morrison, *True North: The Yukon and the Northwest Territories* (New York: Oxford University Press, 1998), 71–85.

10. Joseph T. Jockel, *Security to the North: Canada-U.S. Defense Relations in the 1990s* (East Lansing: Michigan State University Press, 1991), 3–5.

11. Oran Young, "The Age of the Arctic," *Foreign Policy*, no. 61 (Winter 1985–86): 160–79; Sverre Jervell and Kare Nyblom, eds., *The Military Buildup in the High North: American and Nordic Perspectives* (Boston: University Press of America, 1986); John Honderich, *Is Canada Losing the North?* (Toronto: University of Toronto Press, 1987).

12. United States Government, National Security Decisions Directive Number 90, *U.S. Arctic Policy*, April 14, 1983.

13. Douglas C. Nord, "Northern Foreign Policies: Tensions Between Canadian and American Visions—Past and Present," in *North European and Baltic Sea Integration*, ed. Lars Hedegaard and Bjarne Lindström (Berlin: Springer-Verlag, 2003), 291–309.

14. Mikhail Gorbachev, *The Speech in Murmansk* (Moscow: Novostoi Press Agency, 1987), 30.

15. *Notes for an Address by the Right Honourable Brian Mulroney*, November 24, 1989 (Ottawa: PMO Press, November 27, 1989), 14:12, 6.

16. Maxwell Cohen, "The Arctic and the National Interest," *International Journal* 21 (Spring 1970): 52–81.

17. Joe Clark, *The Changing Soviet Union: Implications for Canada and the World* (Ottawa: Department of External Affairs, 1990), 3–4.

18. Canadian Arctic Resources Committee, *To Establish an International Arctic Council* (Ottawa: Canadian Arctic Resources Committee, 1991), 5.

19. Alan Saunders, "Pondering the Arctic Council," *Northern Perspectives* 19 (Fall 1991): 2–3.

20. Rob Huebert, "New Directions in Circumpolar Cooperation," *Canadian Foreign Policy* 5, no. 2 (Winter 1998): 53–54.

21. Government of Canada, *Declaration of Friendship and Cooperation Between Canada and the Russian Federation* (Ottawa: Department of External Affairs, 1992), 1.

22. David Scrivener, *Environmental Cooperation in the Arctic: From Strategy to Council* (Oslo: Norwegian Atlantic Committee, 1996), 6–9.

23. Oran Young, *Arctic Politics: Conflict and Cooperation in the Circumpolar North* (Hanover, NH: University Press of New England, 1992), 24–30.

24. Oran Young and Gail Osherenko, *Polar Politics: Creating International Environmental Regimes* (Ithaca, NY: Cornell University Press, 1993), 9–20.

25. Rob Huebert, "Canadian Arctic Security Issues: Transformation in the Post-Cold War Era," *International Journal* 54, no. 2 (Spring 1999): 205–215.

26. Gilles Breton, "The Case for the Arctic Council" (conference proceedings, "Changing Roles of the United States in the Circumpolar North" conference, University of Alaska, Fairbanks, August 12–14, 1992), 28.

27. Canadian Polar Commission (conference proceedings, "A Northern Foreign Policy for Canada" conference, Ottawa, October 14–17, 1994), 56–57.

28. Paul Koring, "Foreign Policy and the Circumpolar Dimension," *Canadian Foreign Policy* 6, no. 1 (Fall 1998): 51–59.

29. David Scrivener, "Arctic Environmental Co-operation in Transition," *Polar Record* 35 (Fall 1999): 51–58; Monica Tennberg, *The Arctic Council: A Study in Governability* (Rovaniemi, Finland: University of Lapland Press, 1998), 84–89.

30. David Scrivener, "From Ottawa to Iqaluit: Towards Sustainable Arctic Cooperation?" *Environmental Politics* 7, no. 4 (Winter 1998): 136–141.

31. Arctic Council, *The Iqaluit Declaration*, September 17, 1998.

32. Arctic Council, *The Barrow Declaration*, October 13, 2000.

33. Arctic Council, *The Inari Declaration,* October 10, 2002; Arctic Council, *Program for the Icelandic Chair of the Arctic Council 2003–04.*

34. Government of Canada, *The Northern Dimension of Canada's Foreign Policy* (Ottawa: Department of Foreign Affairs and International Trade, 2000).

35. House of Commons, Standing Committee on Foreign Affairs and International Trade, *Canada and the Circumpolar North: Meeting the Challenges of Co-operation in the Twenty-First Century* (Ottawa: 1997).

36. *The Northern Dimension of Canada's Foreign Policy*, 2.

37. *The Northern Dimension of Canada's Foreign Policy*, 10.

38. *The Northern Dimension of Canada's Foreign Policy*, 10.

39. Fen Osler Hampson, Michael Hart and Martin Rudner, eds., *Canada Among Nations 1999: A Big League Player?* (Don Mills, ON: Oxford University Press, 1999), 1–23.

40. Andrew Cooper, "In Search of Niches: Saying 'Yes' and Saying 'No' in Canada's External Relations," *Canadian Foreign Policy* 3, no. 3 (Winter 1995/96): 1–14.

41. Fen Osler Hampson and Dean F. Oliver, "Pulpit Diplomacy: A Critical

Assessment of the Axworthy Doctrine," *International Journal* 53, no. 3 (Summer 1998): 379–406.

42. Andrew Cohen, "Canadian-American Relations: Does Canada Matter in Washington? Does It Matter if Canada Doesn't Matter?" in *Canada Among Nations 2002: A Fading Power*, ed. Norman Hillmer and Maureen Appel Molot (Don Mills, ON: Oxford University Press, 2002), 34–48.

13

Canada in Latin America: A Foreign Policy of Ambivalence, Pragmatism, or Inconsistency?

ATHANASIOS HRISTOULAS

Approximately ten years ago, seasoned observers of Canadian foreign policy highlighted the noteworthy attempts by the then Department of Foreign Affairs and International Trade (DFAIT) to "discover" the Americas after decades of neglect.[1] Indeed, as argued by James Rochlin in 1994, Canada's decision to enter the OAS, the signing of NAFTA, and peacekeeping in Central America were "marked by the prospect of an emerging hegemony in the Americas."[2]

The Human Security agenda, introduced by former DFAIT Minister Lloyd Axworthy, complemented this new openness toward Latin America. Given the region's political, economic, and social challenges, Latin America seemed the ideal proving ground for DFAIT's hallmark foreign policy doctrine in the 1990s.

Others went as far as to argue that Latin America—and in particular Mexico—could act as "a counterpoise to U.S. hegemony."[3] Klepak argues that Canada's decision to focus on Latin America after the Cold War is based on three factors.[4] First, Canada could benefit tremendously from the cultural diversity the region offers. Second, Canada's emphasis on multilateralism in foreign policy finds multiple allies in Latin America.

Third, and most importantly, the region has tremendous potential for economic growth and that Canada is well posed to take advantage of the situation. The region can also serve as an economic counterbalance to the overwhelming power of the United States. Klepak argues that this last reason holds particular urgency for Canadian decision-makers because it seems as though the rest of the world is not prepared to take Canada seriously in economic terms.

The sudden emphasis on Latin America in the 1990s thus stands in sharp contrast to Canada's previous foreign policy orientation. Prior to World War II, Canada's foreign policy was intimately linked to that of Great Britain and the Commonwealth. After World War II, Canada shifted its attention away from Great Britain and onto the United States. The United States became Canada's most important trade partner, and through multiple military alliances and arrangements, Canada clearly came under the protectorship of the United States.

By the 1970s, Canadian decision-makers introduced a policy intended to diversify the country's political and economic relations. An initial and unsuccessful appeal was made to Europe. Canada then started looking toward Asia. Yet, even given its proximity, Latin America was not considered as an ideal second option for Canada. Canadian decision-makers consistently argued that Latin America was the United States' "backyard" and besides, Canadian values of democracy and respect for human rights limited the ability of Ottawa to generate linkages with the dictatorial Latin American regimes.[5]

To begin, the chapter briefly examines Canada's historical relations with the American hemisphere, with special emphasis on the reasons why the region was systematically ignored for the better part of the twentieth century. Second, given the fact that Canadian foreign policy has encapsulated its perception of Latin America along Human Security dimensions, it seems relevant to outline this doctrine. Third, it looks at how Human Security has been applied to the region and its subsequent consequences. Special emphasis is placed on examining Canada's policy toward the Organization of American States (OAS) and the Summit of the Americas process. The specific instance of Canada's bilateral relationship with Mexico is examined. Mexico is chosen as a case study given its critical nature in Canada's relations with Latin America. Mexico was the first country in the region with which Canada began to have systematic diplomatic, cultural, and economic relations. The chapter concludes by arguing that Canada's "discovery" of the Americas has had a less than positive impact precisely because the country's hemispheric policy itself is not well defined.

CANADA AND LATIN AMERICA PRIOR TO THE END OF THE COLD WAR

Canada's policy toward Latin America before the end of the Cold War was—for lack of a better word—ambivalent. Different but related dynamics often led Canadian decision-makers to the conclusion that Canada simply had no real interests in the region. First, Latin America was the U.S.'s backyard, not Canada's. Moreover, Ottawa and Washington had differing interpretations of the root causes of instability in the region. Canadian decision-makers worried that if Canada increased its involvement in the hemisphere, this might ultimately hurt the bilateral Canada-U.S. relationship. Canada's relationship with the United States was considered too important to risk over Latin American policy. Second, Canada was a member of the Commonwealth with persistent cultural ties to the "motherland." Third, Canada was a country of the "North," not the "South." As such, deep relations with Latin America seemed almost nonsensical from a Canadian perspective.

This Canadian ambivalence toward the region dates back to the beginning of the century. In 1908, an institution named the Pan American Union was formed in order to deal with western hemispheric issues. Almost immediately, Latin American countries wanted Canada to join this precursor to the Organization of American States (OAS). Canadian fears about "joining" the hemisphere were proven correct according to Rochlin, because requests for Canadian participation were driven by the hope of "certain Latin American countries that Canada, through its association with Great Britain, could help balance growing U.S. power."[6]

It was also clear, however, that the United States did not want Canadian membership in the organization on the grounds that Canada was still technically controlled by Great Britain. Indeed, President Coolidge opposed Canadian membership because he did not like the idea of the British Empire being indirectly admitted into the organization.[7] In light of this U.S. resistance and also because Latin America was simply not an issue for Canada in the pre–World War II era, Canada remained at the margins of hemispheric issues.

World War II further solidified the idea that Canada was not a country of the Americas. The war completely focused Canadian attention on Europe, and Canadian decision-makers vehemently defended the idea that Canada was part of the British Commonwealth. In that respect, Canada felt greater affinity with India than with Mexico or Chile. Economic motives drove Canada closer to Europe and further away from Latin America in the Cold War period. Canada saw an excellent opportunity to participate in the reconstruction of Europe after World War II. Thus, once again, the hemisphere was ignored.

The formation of the OAS in 1948 consolidated Canada's Cold War position vis-à-vis the hemisphere. First and foremost, Canadian decision-makers viewed the organization as dominated by the United States and therefore less than useful in serving Canadian interests. Thus, for the remainder of the Cold War, Canada would remain an "outsider" from hemispheric issues.

Canada's view of Latin America began to change as the Cold War came to a close. Canada had vehemently tried to convince the Europeans (through the deployment of Canadian troops on the continent during the Cold War) that Canada was in some way a European and not an American nation. This policy failed in the face of cold, hard geographic facts as well as the powerful gravitational pull toward the U.S. along various dimensions, leaving Canada with few options. It is within this context (as well as the attempt to turn Canada into a "pacific" country during the Pierre Trudeau years) that Canada begins to discover Latin America. Almost through a process of elimination, Canadian decision-makers came to the realization in the late 1980s to early 1990s that Canada's hope for continued prosperity rested not with its European or Asian friends but with its American neighbors. The signing of the North American Free Trade Agreement (NAFTA) with the United States and Mexico signaled once and for all the recognition on the part of Canadian decision-makers that Canada is a country of the Americas.

THE HUMAN SECURITY AGENDA

Human Security as an objective of Canadian Foreign Policy was adopted in the middle of the 1990s immediately after it was mentioned in the 1994 U.N. Development Report. Foreign Affairs Canada defines the Canadian version of Human Security as "safety for people from both violent and non-violent threats. It is a condition or state of being characterized by freedom from pervasive threats to people's rights, their safety, or even their lives."[8] More precisely, Canadian foreign policy decision-makers see Human Security as an alternative way of viewing the world, in other words, "taking people as its point of reference, rather than focusing exclusively on the security of territory or governments."[9]

Human Security is linked conceptually to Canada's previous foreign policy orientation of internationalism developed immediately after World War II. The main goals of an internationalist foreign policy are the avoidance of war and instability in the international system. To achieve these related goals, an internationalist state seeks political, social, and economic engagement of other actors in the international system.[10] Only through constructive dialogue can states resolve mutual problems. With the end of the Cold War, Human Security has replaced internationalism because Canadian decision-makers believe that the predictable nature of bipolarity has disappeared and has been replaced by uncertainty.[11] More precisely, Canadian decision-makers argue that:

(1) Authority in the international system is dispersing along regional lines. Rising centers of influence in Europe (EU), Asia (Japan), and the Americas (NAFTA) characterize the new international system. Canadian decision-makers believe that cooperation between these centers is possible and necessary, but should not be assumed to be automatic;
(2) Although the state is still the dominant international actor, other actors such as supranational organizations and multinational corporations have gained significant influence;
(3) International power has become more a function of economic strength rather than military might;
(4) The concept of *security* has been redefined since the end of the Cold War. Canadian decision-makers argue that the greatest threats we face are nontraditional in nature. In general, these threats transcend political borders and affect entire regions or even the entire globe. Examples include international organized crime, civil and ethnic war, disease, and global warming;
(5) Canadian foreign policy further argues that the possibility of interstate war has almost disappeared from the international system. Thus, tra-

ditional notions *of national security* seem outdated and also potentially dangerous.[12]

As a result, Canada has identified Human Security as a key objective for the post–Cold War era. The central reason for this emphasis is the strong belief among officials at Foreign Affairs Canada that economics and security are linked closely in today's globalized world. In other words, global Human Security is a prerequisite for economic growth and development. What makes Canadian foreign policy innovative in this respect is the belief that the country's security depends on the security of others. Canadian decision-makers believe that Canada's national interest necessarily intersects and depends on the national interests of other states. Broadly defined, Canadian national security *is* global security. The idea that national interests are necessarily a function of global interests is new. Most states continue to define national interests in very narrow terms. For these states, national security interests essentially stop at the border because what happens "outside" the country is believed to have little impact "inside." Alternatively, Canadian foreign policy has evolved beyond this view. Canada has essentially become a *Post-National* state.[13]

Post-Nationalist interpretations of national interests can be viewed in a number of ways. First, as noted, *economic issues are considered security issues and security issues are economic* in nature. Canadian decision-makers believe that the fundamental causes of global security problems can be traced to economic instability. Second, much more than in the past, *international relations are a positive sum game*: *cooperation rather than competition* between states is the only way to deal with global security threats. Finally, Post-Nationalism implies a more flexible definition of sovereignty in order to allow other states and non-state actors to actively participate in the resolution of national and international problems. Canadian decision-makers even go so far as to argue that it is the right and obligation of states to interfere in another state (even violate its sovereignty) if the need arises. Such an occurrence, however, can only take place under the auspices of an international organization such as the OAS or the U.N. Indeed, Canada has identified these two institutions as key vehicles for the pursuit of its security objectives.

CANADA'S PLAN FOR THE HEMISPHERE: LINKING SECURITY TO ECONOMIC SUCCESS

Since the end of the Cold War, Canada has been attempting to become a "country of the Americas."[14] To a certain degree, Canada sees its future economic prosperity tied to Latin America.[15] However, given the fact that many Latin American countries still have a long way to go in terms of democratization (i.e., respect for human rights and the evolution of civil society), economic partnerships with these countries will continue to be questioned at a domestic political level. Moreover, the creation of economic linkages with countries that periodically experience high levels of internal instability may ultimately hurt Canada's economy.

Thus, one possible explanation for the linkage between politics and economics in Canadian foreign policy stems from the belief that in order to establish a successful economic relationship with a country, that country must be a political success as well. Hence, political pressure on themes such as human rights, electoral reform, social justice, and the emphasis on collective security themes such as peacekeeping, peacemaking and disaster relief are considered necessary in order to assist Latin American countries achieve political stability. Therefore, Canada's Plan for the Americas includes not only enhanced economic linkages, but also Human Security as a guarantee toward the future success of hemispheric integration. Canadian foreign policy decision-makers do not believe that Latin American countries will be able to succeed economically unless they can resolve their domestic political and social problems.

This position came out clearly in speech by Canada's former Minister of Foreign Affairs. Minister Axworthy highlighted that with respect to the hemisphere of the Americas, Canada seeks to reform its institutions so they can "better reflect the changing nature of threats to peace and security—especially their human dimension."[16] More specifically, "Canada is working in concert with other like-minded countries to advance regional action on human security issues and in many ways, human security concerns—and collective hemispheric responses to them—are already part of the regional agenda."[17] The speech continues to argue that the central issues that all countries of the Americas need to put collective emphasis on are "(i) strengthening democracy, justice and human rights, (ii) eradicating poverty and discrimination, (iii) improving access to education and (iv) ensuring economic prosperity." These issues are interrelated and thus the success of any one depends on the other three. Adopting an almost self-righteous position, Foreign Affairs Canada presents Human Security as the necessary condition for political and social stability, without seriously taking into account country-to-country differences.

Canada's more specific goals in its hemispheric relations in the twenty-first century center on two areas. First, Canada is attempting to build a leadership role for itself in the promotion of normative issues such as human rights protection and democratization, and it is here that Human Security finds its most obvious expression. The second area concerns the question of the economic future of the region, in particular, of free trading relations throughout the hemisphere. In this second area, Canada again sees itself as pursuing a leadership role. Canadian activities in these two areas are concentrated in two major institutions: the Organization of American States (OAS) and the Summit of the Americas.

It is undeniable that the Canadian government wants to project an image of leadership; to quote the department's own website, "Canada's active interest and role in the Americas has resulted in Canada emerging as a leader in the region."[18]

THE OAS

In addition to bilateral relations, the central focus of Canada's promotion of the concept of Human Security in the Americas since the mid-1990s has been the OAS. Since joining the organization officially in January of 1990, Canada has seen itself as taking on a "leader's" role, pushing forward consensus on issues such as land mines, institutional renewal, human rights, and drugs. Underlying the Canadian position on most issues has been the concept of Human Security, naturally enough, as it has become the dominant theme of Canadian foreign policy in general.

According to statements by Foreign Affairs Canada, Canadian priorities for the General Assembly of the OAS are founded on the principle of Human Security, and indeed there is a discernible link between the concept and eight of the ten priority areas identified by the department. The following discussion critically examines these areas before moving on to a discussion of one of the remaining priorities identified by the department, that of free trade.

The first, and clearly major, priority identified by Foreign Affairs Canada for the General Assembly is promoting the concept itself. Foreign

Affairs Canada statements repeatedly explain the importance of the concept, arguing that globalization and the changing nature of the international system necessitate a redefinition of our understanding of security. Interestingly enough, those same statements are conspicuously silent about the attitudes of other states to the notion.

The second priority area for the General Assembly from the Canadian perspective is the illicit trade in drugs. Rather than framing the issue as a challenge to legal systems and state sovereignty, as every other state in the hemisphere has done, Canada has attempted to bring the states of the region to look at the issue in light of Human Security, with Secretary of State for Latin America and Africa, David Kilgour, leading a "ministerial dialogue" session at the OAS summit in Guatemala in 1999. There was, however, no mention of Human Security in the final documents on drugs to emerge from the General Assembly.

The third and fourth priority policy issues for Canada at the OAS have been land mines and firearms. Largely due to Canadian initiatives, the organization has signed agreements to eliminate land mines in the hemisphere in the long term, and to control manufacturing and trafficking of firearms. The Canadian government argues that each of these issues has an obvious Human Security aspect, though other states in the region again associate these two areas with questions of national sovereignty and of traditional security.

Human rights and the promotion of democracy constitute the fifth and sixth priority areas for Canada in the OAS. These two issues demonstrate the truly radical nature of Canada's redefinition of security, for human rights violations and nondemocratic systems can be included under the heading of violent and nonviolent threats. The seventh priority area for Canada in the OAS is hemispheric security. As noted above, Canadian decision-makers recognize the difference between the areas of hemispheric security (state-centric) and Human Security (individual-centric). However, in the application of policy this difference is all too often forgotten.

The eighth area that reflects the influence of the Human Security paradigm is Canada's drive to strengthen civil society throughout the Americas. The influence of civil society in the Canadian foreign policy process is largely responsible for the Human Security agenda, and now Canada seems to want to bring about similar social and policy structures throughout the region.

Two areas that do not directly reflect the Human Security agenda concern institutional renewal/financial stability and trade and integration. However, as the next section of the chapter argues, there is a close, and not necessarily complementary, connection to be found between the second of these issues and Human Security.

THE SUMMIT OF THE AMERICAS
While Canada does not talk explicitly about the issue of Human Security with reference to the Free Trade Agreement of the Americas, they were inextricably connected when the nations of the hemisphere came together for the Summit of the Americas in Quebec City in 2001, and it must be remembered that the Summit of the Americas is as much a political as an economic forum. It is as yet unclear how the Canadian government will link, or distinguish between, its two main goals in the hemisphere. What is clear is that, after the growing protests against globalization and global capitalism that we have witnessed over the past few years, Canadian NGOs and civil society will not welcome Foreign Affairs Canada signing a free trade agreement with certain nations in the region whose human rights and democratic records are suspect.

This societal pressure on Foreign Affairs Canada will ensure that Canada attempts to secure agreement on both Human Security and free trade.[19] As argued earlier in this chapter, the Canadian government does not perceive any tension between the two areas: for Foreign Affairs Canada, Human Security is closely tied to the long-term prosperity of individuals throughout the region as well as Canada as a country. The interconnectedness between Human Security, stability, and economic growth is endemic to the world vision of the Canadian government.

Even if no explicit link is made between the two issue areas, Latin American governments can be expected to continue to hold a suspicious attitude toward the concept of Human Security, for reasons that will be explained below. What should be a cause for concern for Canadian policy makers, as well as political and economic commentators who want to see progress on the issue of free trade in the region, is that Latin American governments may decide that the credibility of the Canadian government as a leader in the drive for free trade has been compromised by its incessant diplomatic emphasis on Human Security. Rather than being compatible with free trade, it is conceivable, even probable, that certain national governments in the region will view Canada's insistence on Human Security as an irritation and unnecessary provocation.

HUMAN SECURITY AND LATIN AMERICA

Before examining the problems with the Human Security paradigm from the Latin American perspective, we should first make it clear that in public, and face-to-face with Canadian diplomats and decision-makers, Latin American political elites overwhelmingly agree with the principles embodied in the Human Security approach; however, out of the public eye, and in discussions with other national policy-makers, their attitude tends to be quite different. At best, many policy-makers find the apparent Canadian obsession with Human Security annoying; at worst they see it as a direct attempt to meddle in internal affairs. As a result of this, officials from Foreign Affairs Canada are anxious to distinguish between the concepts of hemispheric security and Human Security, and they are quite correct in doing so. Hemispheric security is normally used to refer to national and interstate security issues, whereas Human Security focuses not on the state as the unit of analysis, but on the individual. Human Security, it should be remembered, is "people-centered" and "means safety for people from both violent and non-violent threats."[20]

Foreign Affairs Canada tends, however, to mix the two areas together in a way that can cause confusion. In a document that was intended to explain the concept of Human Security, the Department explained that "(h)uman security does not supplant national security . . . state security and human security are mutually supportive,"[21] and suggested that the areas overlap considerably. Meanwhile, Canadian diplomats often argue within the context of the Permanent Council of the OAS that Human Security should be seen as fundamental to discussions on enhancing security in the region.[22] In effect, there is no discernible difference in the way the department uses the two concepts.

Why, though, should the issue of Human Security be so problematic for Canadian negotiators and for the relationship between Canada and the Latin American states? Several reasons can be identified for this. First, we should look at the kind of security problems and perspectives that some states in the region continue to possess. Security is still viewed by many of the most influential countries in the hemisphere (such as Brazil and the United States) in a very traditional, realist, and Cold War fashion. The threats that concern policy-makers in these countries are not threats to individuals, but rather to the integrity and survival of the state itself. Decision-makers in the security area in such states are concerned more with issues of military conflict, both within and without their territory, drugs, and even long-standing border disputes, than with the notion of protecting individual citizens from the exceedingly large array of threats included under the heading of Human Security.

Second, some states in the region continue to be concerned about the issue of foreign intervention, something that is not at all surprising given the history of U.S. and other states' activities in the hemisphere. Non-intervention remains a priority and an inviolable principle of international law for many top Latin American policy-makers, and it is something that they are not ready to relinquish. This concern has been seen time and time again in discussions over drug trafficking as well as human rights.

The third explanation is probably the most important, and it is to be found at the level of the national political system. No Latin American states have even come close to the level of public involvement in the area of national security and foreign policy decision-making, as has Canada. Political systems throughout the region continue to be based on elite control rather than including civil society in the way that FAC has succeeded in doing over the past decade. Foreign policy is still made in a rarefied atmosphere, away from public discussion. When issues are presented to the public, it is done in such a way and in such cases as will increase regime popularity. This is, of course, not unusual in the international system; indeed, it is the way in which most states continue to make their foreign policy.

Canada, though, is not a typical state, at least with regard to foreign policy. As noted above, it is a state in which civil society is very active in the foreign policy arena and is seen by the government as an ally rather than a threat. In many Latin American states the opposite is true. This may be why the Canadian government has been encouraging the growth of civil society and its involvement in the policy process in states throughout the region over the past few years. In some ways this could be viewed as an attempt to remake Latin American states in Canada's own image. This attempt is likely to be strongly resisted by Canada's Latin American partners. Ultimately, Canada risks alienating those states that view security along more traditional lines.

BEYOND CONFUSION: CANADA–MEXICO RELATIONS AFTER 9/11

September 11, 2001, served as a turning point in hemispheric relations. In the specific area of North American cooperation, it dramatically reminded leaders in both Canada and Mexico that when the U.S. worries about security, so must its closest trading partners. In the hours following the terrorist attacks, the United States shut down its borders with Canada and Mexico, essentially imposing an embargo on the North American continent in the name of national security. Border crossings into the United States that ordinarily delay travelers and commerce a few moments (or at worst, a couple of hours) were converted into vast parking lots spanning kilometers and lasting up to 15 hours. Canadian and Mexican leaders understandably panicked, not because of the terrorist attacks *per se*, but rather because of the impact that the September 11 events had had and would continue to have on their relations with the United States. The business of trilateral relations would no longer be the same.

In response to the economic threat posed by Al-qaeda's attack on U.S. interests, Canadian decision-makers began calling for the creation of a North American security perimeter or "zone of confidence." In its simplest form, perimeter security implies enhanced cooperation between North American Security institutions in order to convert the region into a "terrorist free" zone. Security and border cooperation makes good economic sense for the Canada. Early on in the debate over perimeter security (immediately following the terrorist attacks of September 11), the then Canadian Foreign Minister John Manley, highlighted this fact very clearly by stating that "Canada must be inside any such (security perimeter) because 87% of our exports (go to the U.S.)."[23] In other words, a policy where the United States inspects almost every single vehicle entering its territory from Canada would be absolutely devastating to the Canadian economy. Echoing similar concerns, the Conference Board of Canada[24] argues that "with over 1.3 billion dollars worth of goods crossing the Canada-U.S. border every day the efficient flow of goods and people between Canada and the United States is vital to (the Canadian) economy."

Yet in a sudden policy change, within weeks Canadian officials were arguing against a common continental defense. John Manley, after announcing how important it was for Canada to be inside the perimeter, later "expressed reservations telling a parliament committee that the notion that somehow or other (Canada) can solve a perceived problem by something called a perimeter is just rather simplistic."[25]

One possible (and official) explanation for this policy change has to do with the issue of Canadian sovereignty.[26] The former Jean Chrétien administration argued that a common continental defense would adversely affect the right of self-determination of Canadians and their elected officials. The government highlighted that Canada would have to modify many of its laws with respect to immigration, refugees, visas, customs, etc.

First and foremost, this emphasis on sovereignty seems odd given the context of the Human Security agenda. Second, sovereignty does not appear to be an issue with respect to Canadian voters. In a poll conducted on October the 15, 2001, by Ipsos-Reid, 70 percent of Canadians supported jointly manned border posts and 85 percent believed that Canada should make the changes that are necessary to create a joint North America Security Perimeter and 81 percent said that the two countries should adopt common entry controls in treating refugees and immigrants. The same poll found that 53 percent of Canadians supported the creation of a Canadian-U.S. security perimeter even if it meant accepting American security and immigration policies.[27] More recent polls would undoubtedly find that Canadians are less likely to support a Canada-U.S. "security perimeter." However, this initial poll does highlight that Canadians are less sovereignty-sensitive than the country's leaders. Indeed, various provincial governments (Ontario and British Columbia, for example) and the wider Canadian business community have lent strong support to the idea of shared continental and border security. Thus sovereignty, at least at first glance, does not appear to be a central concern for Canadian public opinion.

Beyond the sovereignty issue, the participation of Mexico in a continental security mechanism seems to pose problems for Canadian decision-makers.[28] Bloc Québécois Member of Parliament Stephane Bergeron in a parliamentary question period said, "What seems to bother [former Canadian Minister of Foreign Affairs, John Manley] about the idea of a security perimeter is that the discussions would involve Mexico."[29] Bergeron then went on to argue in the same speech that "Canada has everything to gain in seeing the discussions go from bilateral to multilateral. How can Canada claim to be a partner of Mexico and the U.S. in NAFTA and in the same breath exclude one of its partners from crucial discussions concerning security and trade in North America?" In response, John Manley stated that Canada and Mexico do not share any border. In this regard, the Canadian government seems to be pushing the idea that the kinds of security concerns that Canada and the U.S. face are completely different from the threats present at the Mexican-U.S. border, which again, stands in sharp contrast to the Human Security agenda.

On the other hand, the Mexican government sees continental and border security as offering multiple opportunities in the areas of trade, security, migration and even social development.[30] Similar to Canadian concerns, Mexico worries that enhanced security at the border will hurt trade between the United States and Mexico. But Mexico's interests go beyond simply trade. Mexico's strategy has been one of issue *linkage* or the attempt to trade security for other types of benefits. The first such issue linkage is in the area of law enforcement cooperation and technology transfer for proper and efficient border security, an area where Mexico desperately needs assistance with or without the existence of international terrorists. The Mexican ministry of foreign relations and the Interior Ministry see this law enforcement co-operation and technology transfer as the first and most obvious way in which the three NAFTA partners can cooperate in areas beyond trade and commerce.

A second and more important issue linkage on the part of the Mexican government directly relates to the expansion of NAFTA to include other non-trade related issues. When Mexican President Carlos Salinas signed NAFTA in the early 1990s, his administration argued that the trilateral trade agreement would result in the improvement in the standard of living of all Mexicans. Seven years later, Vicente Fox's administration is under tremendous domestic pressure to deliver on Salinas's promises. He has repeatedly argued that as long as Mexico is a place where 40 percent of the population makes less than two dollars a day, U.S. borders will never be secure. The solution is either a migration agreement whereby the U.S. *legally* absorbs a substantial number of Mexican migrant workers or a North American social cohesion program similar to that in existence in the European Union or preferably *both*. Pushing this linkage idea even further, Mexican officials have even gone as far as to argue that it is in the national security interests of the United States to legalize the 3.5 million undocumented Mexican workers because it is better to know who they actually are given the context of homeland defense.

At first glance, 9/11 should have served as an excellent opportunity for Canadian decision-makers to apply the Human Security agenda in the context of North American relations. Mexico is a trade partner of Canada and what is good for one, generally is good for the other. Along similar lines, bilateral trade has more than tripled[31] since the signing of NAFTA and this positive trend is not likely to continue if Mexico is somehow left out of the process. Third, and most importantly for the purposes of this chapter, corruption, migration, and social development are central not only to Mexico but also to Canada in that they are essentially *Human Security* issues. Vicente Fox's proposals for enhanced trilateral cooperation are precisely in those areas where Canadian officials have repeatedly argued Mexico should make changes. Therefore, at least with respect to Mexico, Canada's Human Security agenda has gone beyond the issue of confusion—which was present with the context of the OAS and the Summit process—and borders on hypocrisy.

Canada's attempts to exclude Mexico from the process of North American integration are based on a very narrow definition of national interest. Canadian decision-makers argue that issues facing Canada and the United States are essentially the efficient flow of legitimate goods and travelers within the context of heightened U.S. security concerns. On the other, the U.S.-Mexican border is far more complex, characterized not only by a high level of trade, but also by the existence of illegal migration, drug trafficking, and corruption. The negotiation of a trilateral security mechanism would therefore require much more time. Canada needs a deal as soon as possible, and the introduction of a third actor, especially Mexico, would—from a Canadian perspective—unnecessarily delay the entire process or possibly stall it completely. Moreover, "smart border" technology at the Canada-U.S. border has been in place for a while, predating the terrorist attacks by a number of years. The same is not the case along the Mexican-U.S. border.

Related to this is the idea that any deal struck between Canada, Mexico, and the United States would ultimately be less than perfect from the Canadian perspective. Given the fact that police, customs, and immigration officials in Mexico are neither well paid nor well trained, the possibility of "holes" in the southern flank of the perimeter would present a serious problem for the United States. And given the trilateral nature of border defense, these southern flank problems could migrate *politically* to the north. The U.S. could, for purely domestic political reasons, insist that the treaty establishing a NAFTA-plus North American security mechanism be based on the lowest common denominator, namely, Mexico's capacity to contribute. It is therefore quite clearly in the interests of Canada to exclude Mexico from the discussions.

Thus, Canada risks alienating its newly discovered partners with a policy that is perceived to be at best ill-conceived and at worst, a blatant violation of state sovereignty. Given the nature of the regimes in the hemisphere, it appears as though Canadian decision-makers have to choose between two seemingly exclusive foreign policy options. If economic linkages are the priority for FAC, the ministry should tone down the Human Security rhetoric. On the other hand, FAC needs to recognize that, if Canada is to continue pushing the Human Security agenda, there will be negative economic consequences.

Canada, however, may not even have a choice in the matter. To quote a September 2003 *Jane's Defense Weekly* report, "chronic under funding, over commitment and government neglect is causing irreversible damage to the Canadian forces. Politicians, academics, and serving and retired military officers are all rapidly coming to the conclusion that the CF is on a downward slope to irrelevancy."[32] This damning report suggests that the Human Security agenda, especially in areas that involve peacekeeping, peacebuilding, disaster relief, and policing will be toned down for lack of funding. Canada spends 1.1 percent of GDP on defense compared to an average of 1.9 non-U.S. NATO. In many ways, Australia has taken over where Canada has fallen behind. Even countries such as Brazil can boast that they have participated in no less than 15 peacekeeping operations since the end of the Cold War. Yet, in an almost ironic twist of fate, Canada's inability to fully implement a Human Security agenda may signal a positive shift in Canada's relations with Latin America.

NOTES

1. See for example, James Rochlin, *Discovering the Americas: The Evolution of Canadian Foreign Policy Towards Latin America* (Vancouver: UBC Press, 1994) as well as Brian Stevenson, *Canada, Latin America and the New Internationalism* (Montreal and Kingston: McGill-Queen's University Press, 2000).

2. James Rochlin, *Discovering the Americas*, 7.

3. Hal Klepak, "What's in It for us? Canada's Relationship with Latin America," *The Focal Papers*, no. 2 (1990).

4. Klepak, "What's in It for us?"

5. Vincent Massey, "Canada and the Interamerican System," *Foreign Affairs* 26 (July 1946).

6. Rochlin, *Discovering the Americas*, 12.

7. Rochlin, *Discovering the Americas*, 13.

8. *Human Security: Safety for People in a Changing World* (Ottawa: Department of Foreign Affairs and International Trade, 1999), 5.

9. *Human Security*.

10. Kim Richard Nossal, *The Politics of Canadian Foreign Policy*, 3rd edition (Scarborough, ON: Prentice-Hall, 1997).

11. See http://www.dfait-maeci.gc.ca.

12. *Human Security*.

13. For a thorough explanation of this terminology see Barry Buzan and Gerald Segal, "The Rise of Lite Powers: A Strategy for the Postmodern State," *World Policy Journal*, 13, no. 3 (July 1996): 1–10; and Gunther Hellman, "Goodbye Bismarck? The Foreign Policy of Contemporary Germany," *Mershon International Studies Review* 40 (April 1996): 1–39.

14. Nossal, *The Politics of Canadian Foreign Policy*.

15. Duncan Wood and George MacLean, "A New Partnership for the Millennium," *Canadian Foreign Policy* 7, no. 2 (Winter 1999).

16. Lloyd Axworthy, "Notes for an address by the Honourable Lloyd Axworthy, Minister of Foreign Affairs to the Permanent Council of the Organization of American States," http://www.dfait-maeci.gc.ca/oas/oas04m-e.html.

17. Axworthy. "Notes for an address by the Honourable Lloyd Axworthy."

18. See http://www.dfait-maeci.gc.ca.

19. Wood and MacLean. "A New Partnership for the Millennium."

20. *Human Security*, 5.

21. *Human Security*, 5.

22. Axworthy, "Notes for an address by the Honourable Lloyd Axworthy."

23. "Securing Our Future: Report of the Standing Committee on Finance," House of Commons Committee Reports, http://www.parl.gc.ca/InfoComDoc /37/ 1/FINA/Studies/ Reports.html.

24. "Border Choices: Balancing the Need for Trade and Security," The Conference Board of Canada, 2001, http://www.conferenceboard.ca/pubs/ borderchoices.10.01.pdf.

25. Tom Cohen, "US Ambassador Details 'No-brainer' Security Plan," *The Daily Camera*, 6 October 2001.

26. DeNeen L. Brown, "Canada Wary of U.S. Anti-Terror Plan: Some Fear a Continental Defense System Would Threaten Ottawa's Sovereignty," *Washington Post*, 24 February 2002.

27. See Ipsos-Reid at http://www.angusreid.com/media/dsp_pre_more_cdn.cfm for more information on this and other related polls.

28. Athanasios Hristoulas, "Trading Places: Canada, Mexico and North American Security," in *The Rebordering of North America: Integration and Exclusion in a New Security Context*, ed. Peter Andreas and Thomas Biersteker (New York: Routledge, 2003).

29. "Securing Our Future."

30. Hristoulas, "Trading Places."

31. According to the Department of Foreign Affairs and International Trade (DFAIT), Mexico is Canada's largest trading partner in Latin America, and Canada has become Mexico's second-largest export market after the United States. For Canada, Mexico is its third-largest source of imports. Mexico ranks as Canada's fourth largest export market. See Report of the Standing Committee on Foreign Affairs and International Trade, *Partners in North America: Advancing Canada's Relations with the United States and Mexico* (Ottawa: Department of Foreign Affairs and International Trade, December, 2002).

32. Sharon Hobson, "Canada—Readiness at a Price," *Jane's Defense Weekly*, 17 September 2003.

14

Canadian Foreign Policy in the Middle East: Reflexive Multilateralism in an Evolving World

Marc J. O'Reilly

The Middle East continues to evoke many passions, as conflict persists between Arabs and Israelis, Arabs and Persians, Turks and Kurds, Sunnis and Shi'a, radicals and conservatives, as well as Muslims and the Christian West. Until World War II, Canada refrained from involving itself in this volatile, yet critical, region for good reason. Substantial British geostrategic interests in the Middle East ensured sustained U.K. involvement, a role that did not require assistance from Ottawa. Following the end of World War II, however, Canadian diplomats began participating in Near Eastern matters as part of the country's commitment to the United Nations (U.N.), whose multilateralism Canadians approved of wholeheartedly. Whether as an observer, peacemaker, or peacekeeper, Canada worked diligently to affix the U.N. imprimatur on the region. Such a policy earned Ottawa much international admiration and kudos from Washington, which benefited from Canadian diplomatic and military contributions to Middle Eastern stability.

When the Canadian Government announced in March 2003 that it would not support the United States in its efforts to overthrow Saddam Hussein's Iraqi Government, Ottawa again sided with the United Nations.

On this occasion, though, Prime Minister Jean Chrétien's Liberal Government forfeited an opportunity to influence U.S. policy in the Middle East—a potentially disastrous decision given the paramount importance of Canada's economic and other ties to America. Although Ottawa pledged to assist in the reconstruction of a post-Saddam Iraq, Canada seemed far removed from the heady days when Foreign Minister Lester B. Pearson won the Nobel Peace Prize for his diplomacy during the 1956 Suez crisis.

As a Middle Power that could contribute political, economic, diplomatic, and military expertise selectively and appropriately, Canada took advantage of the early Cold War competition between Washington and Moscow to shape political outcomes in the Middle East and elsewhere.[1] Ottawa's reflexive multilateralism—i.e., its tendency to rely on international organizations such as the United Nations to resolve global problems—earned it plaudits, especially from developing countries suspicious of the United States, and credibility as a serious, committed problem-solver. Shifts in the international environment (e.g., the tendency starting in the 1960s for America and the Soviet Union to tackle world problems on their own, the end of the Cold War, the emergence of the United States in the 1990s as an unrivaled world power, and the aftermath of the September 11, 2001, terrorist attacks) undercut Canada's ability, however, to sustain its preferred international role. Making matters worse, Ottawa significantly reduced its defense, diplomatic service, and development assistance budgets.

The demise of Canadian foreign policy—critics referred to the country as a "fading power"[2]—culminated in Ottawa's inability to exercise meaningful and sustained global influence throughout the 2003 Iraq crisis. This example of failed Canadian statecraft involving an important Middle East matter contrasted markedly with the country's successful Suez diplomacy decades earlier. While scholars can spotlight the performance of key individuals, such as Pearson and Chrétien, to explain how one event qualifies as the apogee of post–World War II Canadian external policy while the other may rank as the nadir, the issue of human agency must be contextualized. Given the reality of international politics in the early twenty-first century, could someone such as Pearson, a highly skilled diplomat, somehow have effected Canadian success in 2003? Probably not, policy experts would likely answer.

Using the Suez and Iraq crises as case studies, this chapter analyzes Canadian security policy vis-à-vis the Middle East since World War II (for an assessment of some recent political economy issues, see Duncan Wood's chapter in this volume) and asserts that Ottawa's reflexive multilateralism succeeded only when the global context allowed Canadian diplomats to make significant contributions to conflict resolution. Systemic constraints thus limit what Middle Powers such as Canada can accomplish internationally and force them to resort to so-called niche diplomacy,[3] whereby countries develop expertise and use that scarce knowledge to remedy, for example, humanitarian issues such as anti-personnel land mines (in 1997, Canada sponsored the Ottawa treaty) and refugees.[4] Within the limits that every country must contend with, however, occasions present themselves when individuals and governments can make a contribution above what one would normally expect from that state—a point Wood makes when discussing the Canadian role in the G-8 and the G-20, which includes two Middle Eastern countries, Saudi Arabia and Turkey. In Canada's case, its moment of exponentially increased influence occurred in the final months of 1956.

WHEN OPPORTUNITY KNOCKS: THE SUEZ CRISIS

As a young journalist in London, Robert MacNeil experienced the Suez crisis the way many observers did—in utter disbelief: "The Suez crisis is very old and stale now. It is hard to remember what volcanic emotions it produced, what a decisive moment it was: a symbolic turning point in the retreat from empire of Europe's colonial powers and the consequent bursting of new nations like seeds from a ripe pod."[5] Yet MacNeil's perspective also mirrored that of many diplomats burdened with a most daunting task: defusing a crisis that splintered the Western Alliance. Solutions would not be easy to come by, however, as several *dramatis personae* turned "Suez" into memorable, if not moving, theater.

Unlike the Arab-Israeli war of 1948–1949, Israelis attacked Arabs in October 1956, with British and French approval. Invading the Sinai Peninsula on the 29th, Israel sought to expand its borders, and used Franco-U.K. intervention to carry out its expansionist policies. The French envisioned themselves resisting Egyptian President Gamal Abdel Nasser, to prevent him from supplying the Algerians trying to overthrow French colonialism. Finally, British Prime Minister Anthony Eden convinced himself that, in Cairo's fiery leader, he recognized another Adolf Hitler undermining U.K. interests in the Middle East.

To preserve his rule, Nasser summoned his people to expel the invaders. By taking on his oppressors, he stirred widespread passions. Leaders of the so-called Third World, particularly Indian Prime Minister Jawaharlal Nehru, openly supported him. Other policy-makers, however, most notably the prime ministers of Australia and New Zealand, endorsed Anglo-French policy.

Suez galvanized the superpowers, as they quickly realized the stakes involved in this new round of European imperialism. With the Soviets knee-deep in a Hungarian political crisis that could unravel their entire empire, the Eisenhower administration yearned to spotlight Moscow's perfidy. Unfortunately, Great Britain and France's October 30, 1956, ultimatum to Cairo and Tel Aviv prevented Washington from swaying world opinion. To the Soviets, Suez seemed to offer cover while they crushed the insolent Hungarians. Kremlin decision-makers also wanted to protect their client, Nasser, whose 1955 purchase of Soviet-bloc weapons had infuriated the West.

Fearing disastrous consequences should the Suez crisis not be resolved promptly and peacefully, Canada joined the diplomatic fray. The Canadian Ambassador in Washington, Arnold Heeney, wrote in his diary: "The Middle East crisis broke over our heads this week. The worst feature of it for us anyway is the shocking strain upon the Anglo-US alliance, [the North Atlantic Treaty Organization] NATO [and] the Commonwealth."[6] Canadian officials sensed that the outcome of the crisis would bear directly upon Canada's position within the international system.

Confident that Washington would do the same, Ottawa mobilized most of its diplomatic resources. When the Suez war threatened to rend the Western Alliance asunder, Canada elected not to "free ride," but instead heroically tried to prevent a transatlantic debacle. To fulfill its goal, it sided with the United States so that France and especially Great Britain could be guided back to the NATO fold.

U.S. President Dwight D. Eisenhower sought to defuse the Suez crisis quickly so that world opinion could turn its attention back to Soviet brutalities in Hungary. He searched for allies who could further U.S. Cold War interests and ensure that America's ideological imperatives superseded Great Britain's and France's resurgent imperial aspirations. In Canada, he found a neighbor whose diplomatic skill could placate outspoken neutrals such as India, impress onlookers, and strike a blow for the United Nations, whose raison d'être, collective security, Ottawa strove to promote.

The undeclared war in the Near East offered Canada the opportunity to try out its "utilitarian morality."[7] Though shocked at the news of the Anglo-French decision to intervene in Egypt, Ottawa wore its favorite diplomatic hat, that of "facilitator" or "interpreter,"[8] so that the U.S.-British political rift could mend as soon as possible. Secretary of State for External Affairs (i.e., Foreign Minister) Lester B. Pearson and Prime Minister Louis St. Laurent understood Washington's and London's divergent priorities. While the Eisenhower administration practiced Cold War diplomacy, and thus subscribed to the "rules" of bipolarity, the doctrine of anti-communism, and a "New Look" strategy of containment,[9] Her Majesty's Government, under Eden's prime ministership, sought to reverse the waning influence of a British empire in inexorable decline.[10] The Canadians recognized, moreover, that if the Americans vetoed Britain's Suez policy, then U.K. leaders could not order the Royal Navy to shell defenseless Egyptian cities.

Eden believed otherwise. He expected the Canadian Government to support his aim of deposing Nasser who, according to the British prime minister, "followed Hitler's pattern."[11] In his October 30, 1956, message to St. Laurent, he asked for Canada's support of Britain's Middle East policy.[12] The Canadian balked. The United Kingdom had circumvented the United Nations, violated that organization's charter, angered several Commonwealth countries (India in particular), and ruptured the Atlantic Alliance.[13] If Eden's efforts jeopardized Canadian security, how, then, could St. Laurent possibly cheer him on?[14]

He could not. But when the piqued prime minister refused to sanction London's daring Suez policy,[15] numerous Canadians expressed their dissatisfaction with his preference.[16] Many English Canadians, trying to bask in Canada's post-World War II prosperity and dreading more intimate Canadian-American ties, thought their government should remain loyal to Great Britain.[17] The *Toronto Telegram*, for example, endorsed Anglo-French policy, whereas the Toronto *Globe and Mail*, a Conservative newspaper, doubted the wisdom of the Liberal Party's foreign policy.[18]

The *Montreal Star* and the *Montreal Herald* even claimed to understand

London's and Paris's Suez rationale. The *Herald* told its readers, "we are, on principle, against the recourse to the use of arms, but we must be practical minded. If a small display of force by Britain and France now will prevent all-out war in the Middle East, we must, perforce, favor it."[19] Other Canadians, however, echoed St. Laurent's distress and frustration. How could the British eschew their international moral duty?, they wondered.[20]

Similarly, Pearson could not fathom Anglo-French myopia.[21] He remarked to Norman A. Robertson, the Canadian High Commissioner in London, that, since Canada's foremost European allies had neglected to inform Ottawa of their Middle East designs, "co-operation [would be] extremely difficult."[22] U.S. Secretary of State John Foster Dulles worried, moreover, that "the British and French decision undid everything."[23] World opinion, Dulles lamented, would compare Soviet tanks in Budapest to British cruisers off of Cairo and condemn both as examples of neo-colonialism. Despite the apprehensions of his American counterpart, Pearson fully expected that London and Paris would proceed with their plans to secure the Suez Canal Zone.[24] According to the future Canadian prime minister, they "found loss of [Great-Power] status difficult."[25]

After careful discussion, St. Laurent and his cabinet agreed that Canada should adopt a prudent and flexible Middle East policy.[26] They knew that the British Government resented Canada's position, which London perceived as anti-U.K.[27] Empathizing with Great Britain's predicament, but not sharing in it, Ottawa could turn its sensitive diplomatic ears to those states criticizing or supporting Eden's government.[28] Still, the Canadian Government would not condone Anglo-French aggression, nor would it promote violence in the Suez Canal Zone.

Most Canadian newspapers approved of their country's exemplar role and applauded the government's properly calibrated response.[29] Canadians also seemed to cheer President Eisenhower, whose October 31, 1956, speech, in Acting U.K. High Commissioner Neil Pritchard's view, "made a very considerable impression in Canada."[30]

Predictably, Canada sought a U.N. solution,[31] with its foreign minister, the experienced diplomat "Mike" Pearson,[32] in the forefront of Canadian efforts to resolve this particularly stressful Cold War crisis.[33] Pearson recognized that Canada could not weather a Suez storm that destroyed the two foreign-policy structures Ottawa prized most, NATO and the Commonwealth.³⁴ As a result, he proposed, at a November 1 cabinet meeting, that the United Nations establish an emergency force (UNEF). In his memoirs, Pearson explained UNEF's purpose: "to provide a substitute for British-French intervention, thus giving them a good reason to withdraw from their own stated objective of restoring peace before they could be formally condemned by the [U.N. General] Assembly."³⁵ This "compromise" could perhaps assuage London, Paris, and Tel Aviv, as well as those opposed (particularly the Asian Commonwealth countries) to the Sèvres protocol—which called for the British, French, and Israeli invasion of Egypt.³⁶

With St. Laurent and other Liberal ministers convinced of UNEF's potential usefulness, Pearson exited his nation's capital to take part in U.N. fora on the Suez and Hungary crises. Before leaving, he instructed Ambassadors Arnold Heeney and Norman Robertson (in Washington and London, respectively) to report on U.S. and British reaction to a possible UNEF.³⁷ At this juncture, his idea could hardly be called a plan. His practical idealism, moreover, would have to mesh with American *realpolitik*.

Due to UNEF's shortcomings, Eden seized upon the Canadian foreign minister's concept to cloak U.K. policy in respectability. Inadvertently, then, Pearson provided the British prime minister with a fig leaf of sorts: "Yes" to a police force in Egypt, "No" to UNEF. As Eden exclaimed at Westminster, only British and French soldiers could secure the vital Suez Canal Zone quickly and efficiently. Defiantly, he added that if a U.N. contingent could be devised, it "should eventually be associated with the Anglo-French police action."³⁸

In New York, Pearson worked arduously to convince Dulles and other foreign-policy elites that a UNEF could help end the Middle East war before it escalated into a superpower conflict. The Canadian representative understood that neither the General Assembly nor Nasser would endorse Eden's tokenism. Under no circumstances could British and French troops be used to separate the Israelis and Egyptians, the official belligerents.³⁹ Pearson also realized that Canada could not vote in favor of an American cease-fire draft resolution since it did not "provide for any steps to be taken by the United Nations for a peace settlement, without which a cease-fire [could] be only of temporary value at best."⁴⁰

As an addendum to the United States' diplomatic handiwork, the Canadian foreign minister proposed the creation of a "truly international peace and police force," a U.N. force "large enough to keep [the] borders at peace while a political settlement is being worked out."[41] Such a proposal, he reasoned, could satisfy both supporters and opponents of Anglo-French military endeavors. It would also position Canada as a peace broker that could offer diplomatic integrity and solutions, rather than biased rhetoric and brittle palliatives.[42]

Pearson's diplomatic maneuvering proved controversial. With British and French bombs killing more Egyptian civilians, the crisis intensified. Respectful of Canada's decision to criticize its two Motherlands, Britain and France, most Third World states warmed to the UNEF concept.[43] Several diplomats even asked Pearson to work out a plan whereby the United Nations could send peacekeepers to the Sinai Peninsula so that no future rerun of the events of October–November 1956 could surprise as well as polarize the international community.

For several days (November 2–3, 1956), discussion regarding a UNEF continued.[44] Numerous problems threatened to thwart Pearson's attempt at conflict resolution. Initially, Canada wanted to include British and French soldiers, who were closest to the battlefield, in its proposed U.N. operation until permanent units arrived to take over cease-fire duties.[45] But Arab states, which controlled the Arab-Asian voting bloc in the United Nations, would never invite the European aggressors to remain in the Egyptian desert. Eden rejected, moreover, the notion that the United Nations should decide who would control the Suez Canal Zone.[46] Of most concern to Pearson, prominent diplomats, including Dulles and U.N. Secretary-General Dag Hammarskjöld, voiced their skepticism.[47]

Early on in the General Assembly, Dulles rushed to second Pearson's call for a UNEF that would separate Arabs and Israelis. But now Washington stopped short of endorsing Ottawa's full proposal. While sympathetic to Pearson's idealism, Dulles nevertheless dismissed UNEF as an impractical solution. The United Nations, the secretary of state informed Ambassador Heeney, could not muster logistical support for a U.N. force in time to prevent a clash between the Egyptian and Anglo-French armies.[48] Worse for the Canadians, Hammarskjöld shared U.S. concerns.[49] With the Soviets occupying Budapest, the Americans could not coddle those generally regarded as oppressors, not even states with strong NATO ties.

Despite Dulles' pessimism, Pearson kept pushing for UNEF. Soon the St. Laurent cabinet modified its proposal to reassure the Eisenhower administration and empowered the Canadian foreign minister to present whatever plan he thought the General Assembly would approve.[50] Hammarskjöld reversed himself, moreover; locked in his office with a UNEF committee that included his friend Pearson, he worked toward a U.N. solution.[51] Within a day or so, the committee would present the Assembly with an outline for a peacekeeping force.

In devising a plan for a UNEF and a "settlement of Middle East questions," Canada could count on its solid U.N. reputation, the experience of its diplomats, its lack of partisan involvement in the events following Nasser's nationalization of the Suez Canal in July 1956, and NATO support.[52] Most Canadian radio and press, as well, supported Pearson's "initiative."[53] The *Ottawa Citizen*, for example, said that Canada "has a policy to seek a U.N. solution."[54] Though some newspapers, including the *Toronto Star* and the respected *Financial Post*, reconsidered earlier opinions with respect to the Anglo-French intervention, most counseled, as the *Montreal Star* did, that "[t]he sooner now that the whole problem is turned back to the United Nations the better."[55]

On November 3, 1956, Eden, in a surprising yet understandable about-face, informed the Canadian Government that London would not oppose a UNEF resolution, if one were tabled in New York.[56] The British prime minister could not steel himself to carry on his Suez policy in view of world protestation and cries of revolt from U.K. voters.[57] Better to give in, salvage some national pride, and keep Number 10 Conservative, Eden reckoned. Pearson welcomed the decision. He asked Heeney to convey the information to the Americans, so that Washington could join Ottawa in writing up a U.N. document that would curtail the hostilities.[58]

The Eisenhower administration heeded Pearson's call for assistance. Though lacking U.N. experts, the State Department completed a UNEF draft resolution that day.[59] Preparing for a presidential election and anxious to remove the Suez irritant so that it could concentrate on the Hungarian crisis, the White House, according to one scholar, "saw Mike [Pearson]'s plan, under Hammarskjöld's rather than the [Canadian-] proposed Committee of Five's control, as the best option among many bad ones."[60] As instructed, U.N. Ambassador Henry Cabot Lodge passed the U.S. proposal to Canada. He was convinced that if Pearson presented it, the Assembly would accept it.[61] The Canadian foreign minister took the

American draft, now somewhat amended following some Pearson-Lodge modifications, and asked the United Nations to consider it.

The General Assembly voted in favor of the Canadian draft resolution (U.N. Document A/3276), which called upon the secretary-general to create the first-ever peacekeeping operation. Hammarskjöld presented his report to the Assembly, which overwhelmingly adopted Mike Pearson's UNEF plan (U.N. Resolution 1000 (ES-I)) on November 5, 1956.[62] Several countries, including Canada, then volunteered their soldiers for peacekeeping duty in Sinai; such a mission would commence as soon as a cease-fire could be secured.[63]

The endgame occurred soon after the Soviet Union issued its threat to use rockets.[64] On November 6, 1956, in response to allied (mostly American) not Soviet pressure, the British and French decided that it would be wiser to call off their invasion of Egypt and accept a cease-fire.[65] The Israelis also abided by U.N. terms, but rejected the UNEF. Nasser, nevertheless, asked the U.N. force to occupy a demilitarized zone on Egyptian soil and thus prevent yet another Arab-Israeli war.

Canada's U.N. diplomacy, coupled with U.S. economic pressure, pushed the British and the French to the edge of an international precipice normally reserved for pariah states.[66] The Soviet Union, already trying to climb out of the canyon known as Hungary 1956, thought it could hurl London and Paris into a political abyss. Eden knew better; the French likewise.

Such a bow to common sense could not restore past grandeur, however. Once a stupefied Eden discovered that a whimper now replaced the roar of empire, the antiquated era of European gunboat diplomacy gave way to Soviet-American coercive diplomacy. Ironically, in the aftermath of the Suez crisis, London cozied up to Washington and, more often than not, whistled a U.S. tune. Such sweet Anglo-American music failed to hypnotize Conservative John G. Diefenbaker—St. Laurent's successor—but it pleased Mike Pearson, whose brio and relentless pursuit of peace at the United Nations in late 1956 epitomized Canada's "can-do" North Atlantic diplomacy.[67]

Perhaps the *Winnipeg Free Press* best summarized Canada's Suez experience, and Ottawa's penchant for collective security, when it editorialized that "[t]he position taken by Mr. Pearson is exactly the right one for the Canadian Government."[68] By pushing for a U.N. cease-fire, Canada won over most neutralist states and provided the United Kingdom with succor and an excuse to leave Egypt before the United States tightened the financial screws. The UNEF, moreover, vaulted Pearson and his country into international prominence, a position Canada welcomed. Suez symbolized Canada's crowning diplomatic achievement; it would be impossible to surpass it.

To solve its Suez problem, Ottawa specialized, as did Washington.[69] Canada capitalized upon its past success at the United Nations as it worked to pass a General Assembly resolution. The United States, while allowing the Canadians to play to their strength, applied intense financial pressure on London.[70] This "carrot-and-stick" diplomacy proved successful: Canadian-American cooperation resulted in an Anglo-French ceasefire; the UNEF averted NATO's demise; and U.S. economic diplomacy reminded Great Britain and France that the West's enemy, the Soviet Bear, did not prowl the back alleys of Cairo but lumbered instead through the streets of Budapest.

Short on "sticks," the Canadians made what they considered an appropriate contribution to NATO security. In maximizing its "political comparative advantage,"[71] Ottawa showed that a smaller power could play an important role in securing a peaceful dénouement to a crisis that threatened to involve the superpowers directly. By making the most of an opportunity to show the world that it could contribute to international peace as well as anyone, Canada earned a reputation: peacemaker. In earning the respect of the global community, Canadian diplomats seemed poised to continue extinguishing Cold War fires.

Surprisingly to its citizens and policy-makers, Canada never achieved a similar diplomatic tour de force throughout the remainder of the Cold War. Canadian foreign ministers continued to craft and push for bold initiatives at the United Nations and elsewhere. All probably reached for the Nobel Peace Prize, awarded to Mike Pearson for his Suez diplomacy. Unfortunately for them, the international context underwent a profound transformation. NATO survived the French withdrawal and united to confront the Soviet menace, thereby avoiding a repeat of Suez. Alarmed at how British-French recklessness could have undone its containment strategy vis-à-vis Moscow, Washington henceforth insisted on "managing" most Cold War crises by itself. Other Middle Powers, such as Norway and

Sweden, increased their involvement in U.N. conflict-resolution efforts. Finally, the U.N. General Assembly became stridently anti-American.

A systemic-level opportunity thus never presented itself to Ottawa once the Suez War ceased. Canada supported several U.N. peacekeeping missions, but those failed to compare to the UNEF. The Canadian Government dithered, moreover, when it came to selecting what kind of a role it would play in an increasingly unstable world. A decade removed from his Suez triumph, not even *Prime Minister* Lester Pearson could infuse Canadian foreign policy with the worldwide influence and relevance it enjoyed while he served as minister of external affairs.

This trend continued. Liberal and Conservative prime ministers tried out different strategies, yet Ottawa could not reprise its Suez exploit—not that it always explicitly sought to do so.[72] In the 1970s, Liberal Pierre Trudeau parlayed his skeptical attitude toward U.S. foreign policy and American market capitalism into a Canadian policy known more for its moralizing than its ability to achieve global solutions. In the following decade, Conservative Brian Mulroney befriended Republican White Houses, thus solidifying the U.S.-Canadian partnership, so crucial to Canada's economic success following the signing of the 1988 Free Trade Agreement. In the 1990s, Liberal Jean Chrétien mostly eschewed foreign policy—though Canadian peacekeepers went to Bosnia[73]—in favor of trade and domestic policy. His palpable disdain for George W. Bush's administration undermined the amicable Canadian-American relations of the Clinton years. The Ottawa-Washington rift, exacerbated by the Chrétien Government's somewhat tepid support for the United States following the events of 9/11, only worsened when, unlike the United Kingdom and Australia, both staunch Canadian allies, Canada refused to join the U.S. coalition intent on eliminating Saddam Hussein and Iraq's supposed weapons of mass destruction (WMD).

Previous to the 2003 Iraq crisis, Ottawa's post-Suez policy in the Middle East had followed a predictable pattern. Canada worked consistently to achieve multilateral, mostly U.N., solutions. It sent peacekeepers to Lebanon and the Golan Heights, supported Israel while offering assistance to Palestinian refugees, and enthusiastically participated in *Operation Desert Storm*—an event that allowed Canada to support both the United States and the United Nations, the best possible scenario for Ottawa. Setbacks occurred, such as when Nasser asked UNEF soldiers to exit Egypt on the eve of the 1967 Six-Day War, but Canadians kept trying to make a helpful contribution to end or attenuate the region's many political, economic, and other problems. For example, following the 1991 Madrid Conference that called for direct negotiations between Israel and its Arab neighbors, Canada agreed to host talks on refugees. Unsurprisingly, then, as the Bush administration threatened to invade Iraq starting in the fall of 2002, Canada referred to its doctrine of reflexive multilateralism—which typically incarnated important Canadian foreign-policy priorities such as "working for international peace"[74]—to assess how it would respond.[75]

DESPERATE FOR COMPROMISE: THE 2003 IRAQ CRISIS

When the Bush administration tried to convince the international community that Saddam Hussein should be ousted as leader of Iraq, the Chrétien Government opined that only the United Nations could authorize such a removal.[76] Persuaded by Secretary of State Colin Powell, President Bush opted for U.N. approval, much to Canada's satisfaction, instead of proceeding unilaterally. Objections to U.S. policy complicated the matter, however, as France, Russia, and the People's Republic of China, three permanent members of the Security Council, as well as Germany—then a rotating Council member—opposed an invasion of Iraq. The approval of Resolution 1441 in November 2002 temporarily satisfied everyone, but the document's ambiguous wording soon prompted disagreement. Washington and its Council supporters, the United Kingdom and Spain, stated that if Iraq failed to comply with the provisions of the resolution, then they could use military intervention to enforce U.N. will. France, Germany, Russia, and China disagreed; only a second resolution could authorize such recourse.

As the Security Council bickered, Ottawa equivocated. Publicly, it refused to side with either camp or commit to a specific course of action. When Defence Minister John McCallum hinted that Canada might join a U.S.-led effort to unseat Hussein that lacked U.N. approval, Prime Minister Chrétien dispelled such a notion.[77] Chrétien knew that a majority of Canadians objected to the country's involvement in that kind of war. According to a mid-January 2003 Ipsos-Reid poll, 18 percent of Canadians opposed any involvement by their country in an Iraq war, 62 percent supported Canadian participation in such a conflict if the United Nations authorized the use of force, and 15 percent supported an American-led invasion sans U.N. approval. A Decima poll reported, moreover, that 61 percent of Canadians objected to an attack spearheaded by the United States. Residents of francophone Québec, the prime minister's native province, objected most vociferously to the possibility of military conflict.[78]

In any event, with Canadian soldiers already performing hazardous duty in post-Taliban Afghanistan and with Canada's military in tatters following years of neglect and budget cuts (see Andrew Richter's chapter in this volume), Ottawa could not contribute much to an operation in Iraq. Despite its deficiencies, Canada sent three ships, some aircraft, and 1,200 or so military personnel to the Persian Gulf to assist with the U.S.-led war against international terrorism. Some Canadians considered such a contribution inappropriate since it could be used in an invasion of Iraq. The Chrétien Government dismissed such concerns, as it considered what policy to adopt.[79]

Although Canadian officers conferred with their U.S. counterparts at Central Command in Florida, indicating that Canada might well participate in an Iraqi war, several journalists and politicians such as Stephen Harper, the leader of the Canadian Alliance Party, the Official Opposition, relentlessly criticized Ottawa for not supporting Washington wholeheartedly. These elites thought it nonsensical and even foolish for Canada to trust the judgment of the Security Council, a notoriously capricious institution that routinely underplayed or ignored threats to world peace and security. Better to align with the United States (a reliable ally that bought most of Canada's exports and insured the country's defense), the United Kingdom (to whom Canadians owed their independence and Parliamentary democracy), and Australia (a fellow member of the Commonwealth).[80]

As the standoff at the Security Council intensified in early 2003 and threatened to wreck the United Nations, and as Joe Clark, leader of the Progressive Conservative Party and ex-foreign minister, referred to Canada as the "invisible country,"[81] the Chrétien Government, despite dissent within the Cabinet,[82] finally responded with something more than evasive or ambivalent rhetoric. Similar to what Pearson had done during the Suez crisis, Canada's U.N. Ambassador, Paul Heinbecker, secretly presented members of the Security Council, in the final week of February, with a compromise that could avert yet another round of hostilities in the Middle

East. Heinbecker proposed a March 28 deadline for U.N. and International Atomic Energy Agency inspections of Iraqi WMD programs. At that point, the Security Council could evaluate Iraq's compliance with U.N. demands and proceed accordingly. This plan sought to reconcile the U.S.-U.K.-Spanish position, calling for immediate military intervention via a second Security Council resolution, with that of France, Germany, and Russia, which favored continuous inspections without threat of invasion.[83]

Without a seat on the Security Council, however, Canada lacked clout within that body. Neither of the bitterly opposed camps endorsed the Canadian proposal and, more importantly, neither needed Canada's vote when it came to the contentious second resolution. Thus, Ottawa turned to Mexico and the others on the Council still uncommitted—Chile, Cameroon, Angola, Guinea, and Pakistan. These countries expressed an interest in the Canadian solution, as did U.N. Secretary-General Kofi Annan, but the effort—Canada offered four versions of its plan—proved in vain when the United States, United Kingdom, and Spain withdrew their resolution in mid-March and attacked Iraq on the 19th.[84]

As the U.S.-led "coalition of the willing" initiated Operation Iraqi Freedom, Canadians watched their closest allies invade a sovereign country without U.N. sanction. Unlike in 1999, when Canada participated in the NATO attack that expelled Serb soldiers from Kosovo, Ottawa thought it unwise on this occasion to proceed sans Security Council approbation.[85] In explaining his government's decision, the prime minister said, "If it [i.e., the attack on Iraq] was justified and approved in a resolution by the Security Council, we would have said yes."[86] Domestic imperative seemed to explain the decision to snub the United States. Though the Canadian Alliance and other conservatives, such as Alberta Premier Ralph Klein, strongly favored Canada joining the U.S.-led invasion of Iraq, a majority of Canadians, including members of the socialist New Democratic Party and the separatist Bloc Québécois, remained steadfastly opposed to an invasion without U.N. approval.[87] Such sentiments permeated Québec, the French-speaking province where impassioned pre-war protests rekindled pacifist instincts dating back to the conscription crises of World War I and II—such political stirrings, which always risked reviving separatist aspirations, regularly worried Canadian prime ministers. Similar opposition reverberated throughout the United Kingdom, Spain, and Australia, yet Prime Ministers Tony Blair, Jose Maria Aznar, and John Howard followed

President Bush into war. U.S. Ambassador to Canada Paul Cellucci chastised Ottawa for its choice, prompting angry rebuttals from many outraged Canadians and the Chrétien Government, though not Deputy Prime Minister John Manley, who thought Canada should have unashamedly condoned the U.S.-led attack.[88] Critics of Canadian policy, both in Canada and the United States, then vented their frustration, thereby further polarizing public debate in Canada and straining U.S.-Canadian relations even more.[89]

Despite the acrimony engendered by the Iraq crisis, Ottawa vowed to help with the reconstruction of post-war Iraq. This more familiar task would allow Canada to rehabilitate its ties with its southern neighbor and contribute to international peace and security. Yet, following the official end of hostilities (which President Bush declared on May 1, 2003), the White House initially disallowed Canada from bidding on U.S. Government contracts in Iraq, bruising Canadian feelings once more. Only when Paul Martin, Chrétien's longtime heir apparent, became prime minister in December 2003 did Canadian-American relations improve. Martin reassured Bush of Canada's commitment to the U.S.-led War on Terror and, in turn, Washington allowed Canadian firms to partake in the rebuilding of Iraq's shattered or dilapidated infrastructure.

CONCLUSION

The Economist may consider Canada rejuvenated and "cool" these days,[90] but Canadian foreign policy rarely draws such rave reviews. Nostalgia for Foreign Minister Lester Pearson and his bygone era continues to suffuse many policy discussions, as Canada tries to make its views relevant in a world vastly different from that of 1956. With a post-9/11 United States fixated on international terrorism and intent on thwarting—unilaterally and preventively, if need be—any threats to its security, Ottawa must adjust its diplomacy or else risk irrelevance.

In 2003, the Chrétien Government sought the same outcome, peace courtesy of the United Nations, as Pearson nearly fifty years ago. Unlike the Suez crisis, when the Eisenhower administration made effective use of the United Nations thanks to Canadian efforts, George W. Bush could not persuade the Security Council to condone an invasion of Iraq that would penalize Saddam Hussein for his continued infractions of international law. Ottawa relied on Pearsonian tactics—i.e., U.N. resolutions that sought to reconcile differences between the antagonists—yet its diplomacy failed. While certain Canadian elites ridiculed their country's impartial stance, just as some journalists and Conservative politicians condemned the St. Laurent Government for not supporting the British during Suez, most Canadians agreed with their government's pursuit of a U.N. solution, just like in 1956.

Pearson achieved success due to American acquiescence. If Washington had opposed Ottawa's diplomatic handiwork at the United Nations, then the Suez crisis would not have ended with the creation of the UNEF. The confluence of U.S. and Canadian positions enabled the St. Laurent Government to surpass its usual capacity for political influence. Without that kind of synergy, however, Canada will typically offer only modest contributions to international peace and security. Historically, Great Powers, whether by themselves or in concert, have monitored and contributed the most to such matters, albeit sometimes with awful results.

Despite their frequent marginalization, Middle Powers can extend valuable assistance, especially in a volatile region such as the Middle East. But the positive result can be ephemeral. For example, Norway brokered the 1993 Oslo accords, considered an important breakthrough in the Israeli-Palestinian conflict. Yet by September 2000 hostilities had resumed. Currently, peace and coexistence remain elusive, even quixotic, despite American endorsement of the Oslo agreements and the U.N.-approved Road Map, as well as continued involvement in the so-called peace process—which many Palestinians and Israelis considered moribund in 2005 despite the January election of Mahmoud Abbas as president of the Palestinian Authority following the death of Yasir Arafat and Israel's withdrawal from Gaza.

Like Norway's Middle East coup a decade ago, Canada's exploit during the Suez crisis merely confirmed the axiom that only Great Powers can ensure international peace and security, although they often fail. While Great-Power involvement seems necessary, Middle-Power assistance should be considered optional, though sometimes crucial. The Canadian role in resolving Suez, a major world conflict, proved exceptional, something the country's policy-makers should have kept in mind when they tried to reprise that modus operandi in the crises that followed.

Ottawa's inability in 2003 to sway the Security Council, especially the Great Powers on it, should thus be considered understandable, even easily predictable, especially given Washington's insistence on ousting Saddam Hussein. The more determined and capable the Great Power, the less likely a Middle Power, especially one considered marginal to the politics of a given issue, can affect the dénouement. As a country with minimal influence within the Middle East, Canada should not have expected to convert the Security Council to its position; the polarized views within that institution and the geopolitical stakes involved made any compromise unlikely. Still, true to its diplomatic tradition, Canada tried. Had it succeeded, its prestige in the short term might have approximated that of the 1950s and its withered reputation as a facilitator might have recovered somewhat.

Knowing that it probably could not effect its preferred outcome, Ottawa perhaps should have followed Tony Blair's example and endorsed the U.S. position. Canada's national interest seemed to call for exactly that kind of policy. Yet the Chrétien Government preferred to irk the Bush administration by instinctively, or so it seemed, turning to the United Nations, an institution that routinely sacrificed moral imperative on the alter of geopolitical expediency. While the prime minister could have justified Canadian support for a U.S.-led invasion of Iraq by invoking Saddam Hussein's countless violations of international human-rights law, Chrétien refused to commit his country to a humanitarian intervention unless the United Nations sanctioned such recourse. His preference for reflexive multilateralism may have enraged the White House, but the decision accorded with Canadian tradition.

Ottawa's penchant for reflexive multilateralism may strike critics as myopic, if not irrational, given American policy since 9/11. Obviously, Canada cannot defy the United States incessantly simply to uphold its favorite foreign-policy doctrine. Notwithstanding the bitter Canadian-U.S. disagreement over Iraq and contentious trade matters, Canadians should continue to express solidarity with Americans on most issues. Both countries share similar political, economic, and social values, even if important differences exist and some Canadian sociocultural views mirror those of western Europe. Ottawa will continue to embrace multilateralism—Canadian identity requires it—but should reconsider whether it always, or even mostly, resorts to that kind of policy. Diplomats, even those as skilled as Lester Pearson, cannot overcome an international system, or a Middle East subsystem, that allows Washington opportunities to impose its will unilaterally or with "coalitions of the willing." With America militarily preponderant, Canada must carefully consider its interests, particularly its trade and security ties to its neighbor, and calculate the worth of standing with the United Nations when that organization's policy contravenes Washington's. Canadians may think of themselves as morally superior to Americans—explaining the anti-Americanism exhibited during the Iraq crisis—but Ottawa's occasionally condescending attitude will not translate into a better foreign policy, something Canada sorely needs if it wants to regain its former status as a Middle Power that matters.

NOTES

1. J. L. Granatstein, *The Ottawa Men: The Civil Service Mandarins, 1935–1957* (Toronto: Oxford University Press, 1982); Denis Smith, *Diplomacy of Fear: Canada and the Cold War 1941–1948* (Toronto: University of Toronto Press, 1988).

2. Norman Hillmer and Maureen Appel Molot, "Preface," in *Canada Among Nations 2002: A Fading Power* (Don Mills, ON: Oxford University Press, 2002), xi-xii; Molot and Hillmer, "The Diplomacy of Decline," in *Canada Among Nations 2002*, 1–33. See also Andrew Cohen, *While Canada Slept: How We Lost Our Place in the World* (Toronto: McClelland & Stewart, 2003).

3. On niche diplomacy, see Andrew F. Cooper, "Niche Diplomacy: A Conceptual Overview," in *Niche Diplomacy: Middle Powers after the Cold War*, ed. Andrew F. Cooper (London: Macmillan Press, 1997), 1–24.

4. Foreigners often characterize Canadians as "do-gooders." Evan H. Potter, "Niche Diplomacy as Canadian Foreign Policy," *International Journal* 52, no. 1 (Winter 1996–1997): 31.

5. Robert MacNeil, *The Right Place at the Right Time* (New York: Penguin Books, 1990), 30.

6. Heeney Diary #4 (1956, 1957), Entry for Nov. 4–10, 23 [1956], *Papers of Arnold Heeney*, MG 30, E 144, Volume 2, National Archives of Canada (Ottawa) [hereafter NAC].

7. For the term, see Denis Stairs, "Canada and the Korean War: The Boundaries of Diplomacy," in *Partners Nevertheless: Canadian-American Relations in the Twentieth Century*, ed. Norman Hillmer (Toronto: Copp Clark Pitman Ltd., 1989), 220.

8. On these concepts, see Lester B. Pearson, *Mike: The Memoirs of the Right Honourable Lester B. Pearson, Volume 1: 1897–1948* (Toronto: University of Toronto Press, 1972), 212.

9. John Lewis Gaddis, *Strategies of Containment: A Critical Appraisal of Postwar American National Security Policy* (New York: Oxford University Press, 1982), chapters 5 and 6.

10. See "Greatness," *London Observer,* December 9, 1956, in DO 35/5422, Public Record Office (London) [hereafter PRO]. Nota: DO refers to Commonwealth Relations Office (CRO) files.

11. Anthony Eden, *Full Circle* (Boston: Houghton Mifflin Company, 1960), 481.

12. Personal Message [Anthony] Eden to [Louis] St. Laurent, in CRO to Acting U.K. High Commissioner [Neil Pritchard] in Canada, October 30, 1956, PREM 11/1096, PRO. Nota: PREM refers to the British prime minister's files.

13. Lord Home [U.K. Minister of Commonwealth Relations] (CRO) to Pritchard, October 30, 1956, PREM 11/1096, PRO; Dale C. Thomson, *Louis St. Laurent: Canadian* (New York: St. Martin's Press, 1968), 468; Escott Reid to [Canadian] Department of External Affairs [DEA], November 1, 1956, RG 25, Series 50372–40, Box 175, Volume 9, NAC; James Eayrs, *Canada in World Affairs: October 1955 to June 1957,* Volume 9 (Toronto: Oxford University Press, 1959), 183–185.

14. For an excellent summary of Canada's reaction to Britain's apparent folly, see Pritchard to Lord Home (CRO), Canada Fortnightly Summary, Part 1, 28th October-10th November, 1956, November 14, 1956, DO 35/5422, PRO.

15. J. W. Pickersgill, *My Years with Louis St Laurent: A Political Memoir* (Toronto: University of Toronto Press, 1975), 314.

16. That many Canadians knew about the Suez crisis is remarkable. Unlike most foreign policy issues, events in the Middle East sparked tremendous public interest. See Eayrs, *Canada in World Affairs,* 182–183.

17. See, for example, L. B. Pearson to Mrs. K. W. Biglow, November 24, 1956, *Papers of Lester B. Pearson,* Pre 1958 Series Correspondence, MG 26, N 1, Volume 38, NAC. Canadians, especially those who carried Conservative Party membership cards, reminded their government leaders that the prime ministers of Australia and New Zealand stood behind Her Majesty's government. Since Canada (like Australia and New Zealand) had supported the United Kingdom in 1939, why would Ottawa not back British policy now? On Canberra's and Wellington's endorsement of Eden, see R. G. Menzies [Prime Minister of Australia] to Eden, November 1, 1956, PREM 11/1096, PRO; and S.G. Holland [Prime Minister of New Zealand] to Eden, November 1, 1956, PREM 11/1096, PRO.

18. Pritchard to Lord Home (CRO), October 31, 1956, No. 1031, DO 35/6334, PRO; and Pritchard to Lord Home (CRO), November 1, 1956, No. 1038, DO 35/6334, PRO.

19. Pritchard to Lord Home (CRO), October 31, 1956, No. 1036, DO 35/6334, PRO.

20. Pritchard to Lord Home (CRO), October 31, 1956, PREM 11/1096, PRO; "Shock and Distress in Ottawa," *Economist*, November 10, 1956, 516, in DO 35/5422, PRO. The *Ottawa Citizen* called the British-French ultimatum "a desperate gamble." Pritchard to Lord Home (CRO), October 31, 1956, PREM 11/1096, PRO [nota: this is a different document from the one cited above].

21. Pearson to Norman A. Robertson [Canadian High Commissioner in London], October 30, 1956, DO 35/6334, PRO. Still, Pearson did realize that, in issuing their surprise ultimatum, the United Kingdom and France lacked the time needed to consult with their allies. See Pritchard to Lord Home (CRO), October 31, 1956, No. 1031, DO 35/6334, PRO. But Canada had informed Great Britain on several occasions that it would not support any use of force directed at Egypt and its leader, Nasser. See J. L. Granatstein, *A Man of Influence: Norman A. Robertson and Canadian Statecraft, 1929–68* (Toronto: Deneau Publishers, 1981), 299–300, 308.

22. Pearson to N.A. Robertson, October 30, 1956.

23. Pearson to Robertson, October 30.

24. Terence Robertson, *Crisis: The Inside Story of the Suez Conspiracy* (New York: Atheneum, 1965), 172.

25. John English, *The Worldly Years: The Life of Lester Pearson, Volume II: 1949–1972* (Toronto: Vintage Books, 1993), 117.

26. Government of Canada, Cabinet Conclusions, October 31, 1956, RG 2, Series A-5-a, Volume 5775, NAC.

27. N.A. Robertson to Pearson, November 1, 1956, *Papers of Lester B. Pearson*, MG 26, N 1, Volume 39, NAC.

28. Robertson to Pearson, Nov. 1; Pritchard to Lord Home (CRO), October 31, 1956, No. 1028, DO 35/6334, PRO. The United States, India, Pakistan, and Ceylon (now Sri Lanka) disapproved of British policy, while Australia and New Zealand approved. Pearson later recounted that "Canada would have had no influence [during the crisis] if . . . she had given automatic support to the United Kingdom." Pritchard to Lord Home (CRO), November 27, 1956, DO 35/5422. Norman Robertson told Pearson that he did not know how Canada could be of help to Great Britain. N. A. Robertson to Pearson, November 1, 1956, *Papers of Lester B. Pearson*, DEA—Selected Documents—1956—No. 42 "Middle East Crisis," MG 26, N 1, Volume 39, NAC. Canadian diplomats in London insisted, though, that Ottawa should do its "best to assure that the British and French intervention in Egypt [was] not examined under a spotlight narrowly focussed [sic] only on the recent events." Canadian Embassy in London to DEA, November 1, 1956, RG 25, Series 50372–40, NAC.

29. Pritchard to Lord Home (CRO), November 1, 1956, No. 1038, DO 35/6334, PRO.

30. Pritchard to Sir Gilbert Laithwaite (CRO), November 1, 1956, No. 1039, DO 35/6334, PRO.

31. Lester B. Pearson, *Mike: The Memoirs of the Right Honourable Lester B. Pearson, Volume 2: 1948–1957*, with ed. John A. Munro and Alex I. Inglis (Toronto: University of Toronto Press, 1973), 238–239, 243; *Papers of Louis St. Laurent*, "L. B. Pearson Statements on Middle East Crisis 1956–57" File, MG 26, L, Volume 239, NAC. See also Lester B. Pearson, "The Development of Canadian Foreign Policy," *Foreign Affairs* 30, no. 1 (October 1951): 17–30.

32. On Pearson's background, diplomatic and otherwise, see John English, *Shadow of Heaven: The Life of Lester Pearson, Volume 1: 1897–1948* (Toronto: Lester & Orpen Dennys, 1989); English, *The Worldly Years*; Bruce Thordarson, *Lester Pearson: Diplomat and Politician* (Toronto: Oxford University Press, 1974). For an informative article on the Pearson diplomatic style, see Denis Stairs, "Present in Moderation: Lester Pearson and the Craft of Diplomacy," *International Journal* 39, no. 1 (Winter 1973–4): 143–153. But see also Peter Gellman, "Lester B. Pearson, Collective Security, and the World Order Tradition," *International Journal* 44, no. 1 (Winter 1988–89): 68–101.

33. John W. Holmes, *The Shaping of Peace: Canada and the Search for World Order 1943–1957, Volume 2* (Toronto: University of Toronto Press, 1982), 356–57.

34. On the Commonwealth's polarization, see "Commonwealth Reactions," in Lord Home (CRO) to Pritchard, November 5, 1956, W. No. 462, DO 35/6342, PRO.

35. Pearson, *Mike, Volume 2: 1948–1957*, 244.

36. Gabriella Rosner, the expert on the UNEF, argues that the force "entailed compromise between use of strong, condemnatory methods to achieve peaceful settlement and mild policies of pacification and conciliation." Gabriella Rosner, *The United Nations Emergency Force* (New York: Columbia University Press, 1963), 2. In her book, she points out that only the Saar Force of the 1930s preceded the UNEF and labels the latter "a distinct pioneering effort." Rosner, *The United Nations Emergency Force*, 211–217, 222. Quote is on 222. See also Lester B. Pearson, "Force for U.N.," *Foreign Affairs* 35, no. 3 (April 1957): 395–404.

37. Pritchard to Lord Home (CRO), November 1, 1956, No. 1041, DO 35/6334, PRO.

38. See Eden, *Full Circle*, 598–9. Eden called Anglo-French policy a "police action," a term the United Nations used to describe its intervention in Korea in 1950. The British prime minister desperately tried to equate Suez 1956 with Korea 1950 and the U.S. intervention in Guatemala in 1954 to justify his course of action.

39. Pritchard to Lord Home (CRO), November 3, 1956, PREM 11/1096, PRO.

40. Canada abstained. On the draft resolution, see Pearson, *Mike, Volume 2: 1948–1957*, 245; Michael G. Fry, "Canada, the North Atlantic Triangle, and the United Nations," in *Suez 1956: The Crisis and Its Consequences*, ed. W. M. Roger Louis and Roger Owen (Oxford: Clarendon Press, 1989), 308; A. D. P. Heeney to DEA, November 1, 1956, RG 25, Series 50372–40, NAC. See also Lester B. Pearson, *Words and Occasions* (Cambridge, MA: Harvard University Press, 1970), 149–50.

41. Pearson, *Words and Occasions*, 149–50.

42. Pearson, *Mike, Volume 2: 1948–1957*, 246–247; English, *The Worldly Years*, 138.

43. Keith Kyle, *Suez* (New York: St. Martin's Press, 1991), 436. But, on November 2, 1956, a Canadian U.N. correspondent, Charles Lynch, reported that Arab countries fumed over Canada's refusal to endorse the American draft resolution calling for a cease-fire. *Canada on Record: Part Eight (8), Suez Crisis and Pearson the Peacemaker*, Canadian Broadcasting Corporation (C.B.C.) Radio Broadcast, September 28, 1979, C.B.C. Archives, NAC.

44. On Canada's role in the U.N. debate, see Rosner, *The United Nations Emergency Force*; Graham Spry, "Canada, the United Nations Emergency Force, and the Commonwealth," *International Affairs* 33, no. 3 (July 1957): 289–300; S. Mack Eastman, "Canada and World Police," *The Canadian Forum* (January 1957): 217, 240.

45. Pearson, *Mike, Volume 2: 1948–1957*, 249.

46. English, *The Worldly Years*, 129.

47. On Hammarskjöld's reaction to Canada's plan, see Pearson, *Mike, Volume 2: 1948–1957*, 247. See also Kyle, *Suez*, 436.

48. C. Burke Elbrick Memorandum, Department of State, Washington, November 2, 1956, *Foreign Relations of the United States [hereafter FRUS]*, 1955–1957, XVI (Washington, D.C.: Government Printing Office, 1990), 941–942.

49. Geoffrey A. H. Pearson, *Seize the Day: Lester B. Pearson and Crisis Diplomacy* (Ottawa: Carleton University Press, 1993), 148.

50. Pearson, *Mike, Volume 2: 1948–1957*, 249–50; English, *The Worldly Years*, 139.

51. On the Pearson-Hammarskjöld relationship, see G. Pearson, *Seize the Day*, 151. Geoffrey Pearson, Mike's son, writes that "[b]oth men were pragmatists about means and idealists about ends." G. Pearson, *Seize the Day*, 151.

52. Pritchard to Lord Home (CRO), November 2, 1956, PREM 11/1096, PRO. On how the British Government tried to influence the Canadians, see Pritchard to Lord Home, November 2.

53. Pritchard to Lord Home (CRO), November 2, 1956, DO 35/6334, PRO.

According to *Canada on Record*, most Canadians considered Pearson the "master diplomat" throughout the Suez crisis.

54. Pritchard to Lord Home (CRO), November 3, 1956, DO 35/6334, PRO.

55. Pritchard to Lord Home (CRO), November 2, 1956, DO 35/6334.

56. Pearson, *Mike, Volume 2: 1948–1957*, 250. Eden did think, however, that the UNEF proposal necessitated "a few minor changes."

57. Even Eden's friends begged him to reevaluate his policy. See, for example, Holland to U.K. Government, November 3, 1956, PREM 11/1096, PRO.

58. Pritchard to Lord Home (CRO), November 3, 1956, No. 1057, DO 35/6334, PRO; and Heeney Diary #4 (1956, 1957).

59. Lincoln P. Bloomfield, "American Policy toward the UN—Some Bureaucratic Reflections," *International Organization* 12 (1958): 13, 15.

60. English, *The Worldly Years*, 139.

61. Pearson, *Mike, Volume 2: 1948–1957*, 251; [Henry Cabot] Lodge Memorandum for the Record, November 3, 1956, *FRUS*, 957n. According to Canadian diplomat John Holmes, "An American initiative could [have] conceivably provoke[d] Cold War divisions of opposition and abstention." Holmes, *The Shaping of Peace*, 361.

62. Pearson, *Mike, Volume 2: 1948–1957*, 252–4; Pritchard to Lord Home (CRO), November 4, 1956, PREM 11/1096, PRO; Excerpts L. B. Pearson Speech, [Canadian] House of Commons, March 15, 1957, *Papers of Louis St. Laurent*, NAC.

63. Rosner, *The United Nations Emergency Force*, 31.

64. John Lewis Gaddis, *We Now Know: Rethinking Cold War History* (New York: Oxford University Press, 1997), 234–239. On Eisenhower's and St. Laurent's reaction to Soviet bluster, see Dwight D. Eisenhower, *Waging Peace 1956–1961* (New York: Doubleday & Company, 1965), 89–90; Pritchard to Lord Home (CRO), November 6, 1956, No. 1076, DO 35/6334, PRO.

65. Gaddis, *We Now Know*, 236.

66. According to one scholar, "[l]andings in Suez went ahead on November 5, but pressure from the United States and the UN was such that a cease-fire had to be ordered almost immediately." Martin Kitchen, "From the Korean War to Suez: Anglo-American-Canadian Relations, 1950–1956," in *The North Atlantic Triangle in a Changing World*, ed. B.J.C. McKercher and Lawrence Aronsen (Toronto: University of Toronto Press, 1996), 251.

67. In the end, however, the Canadian public's reaction to the Suez crisis proved mixed. See, for example, Pritchard to Lord Home (CRO), November 5, 1956, No. 1072, DO 35/6334, PRO.

68. Pritchard to Lord Home, November 5.

69. On the American role, see Marc J. O'Reilly, "Following Ike? Explaining Canadian-US Co-operation during the 1956 Suez Crisis," *The Journal of Commonwealth & Comparative Politics* 35, no. 3 (November 1997): 81–86.

70. Diane B. Kunz, "The Importance of Having Money: The Economic Diplomacy of the Suez Crisis," in *Suez 1956*, 215–232.

71. Mark A. Boyer, *International Cooperation and Public Goods: Opportunities for the Western Alliance* (Baltimore: Johns Hopkins University Press, 1993), chapters 3 and 4.

72. Erin Carrière, Marc O'Reilly, and Richard Vengroff, "'In the Service of Peace': Reflexive Multilateralism and the Canadian Experience in Bosnia," in *International Public Opinion and the Bosnia Crisis*, ed. Eric Shiraev and Richard Sobel (Lanham, MD: Lexington Books, 2003), 14–17.

73. Carrière, O'Reilly, and Vengroff, "In the Service of Peace," 1–32.

74. On Canada's political culture and foreign-policy priorities, see Carrière, O'Reilly, and Vengroff, "In the Service of Peace," 17–25.

75. For an overview of Canada's Middle East policy, see Tareq Y. Ismael, *Canada and the Middle East: The Foreign Policy of a Client State* (Calgary, Alberta: Detselig Enterprises Ltd., 1994).

76. Haroon Siddiqui, "Canada Clearly Draws the Line on Iraq," *Toronto Star*, 6 October 2002, EBSCOhost, http://www.epnet.com.

77. The Canadian Press, "PM Repeats Support for UN on Iraq; Chretien Contradicts Defence Minister's Assertion that Canada Would Join Unilateral U.S. Military Action," *Windsor Star*, 16 January 2003, LexisNexis Academic, http://www.lexis-nexis.com/universe; Richard Gwyn, "A Morally Inert Foreign Policy," *Toronto Star*, 12 January 2003, EBSCOhost.

78. Bruce Cheadle, "Chretien's Fence-sitting on War against Iraq Irks Both Hawks and Doves," *Canadian Business and Current Affairs*, 30 January 2003, LexisNexis Academic.

79. Don Munton, "The Limits of American Hegemony and the Impact of Norms: Canada and the Invasion of Iraq" (paper presented at the annual conference of the International Studies Association, 16–20 March 2004, Montreal, Canada), 1; Canadian Press, "Foreign Affairs Minister Defends Presence in Persian Gulf," *Portage Daily Graphic* (Manitoba), 5 March 2003, LexisNexis Academic.

80. Andrew Cohen, "Canada Must Ante Up If It Wants a Seat at the Foreign-Policy Table," *Ottawa Citizen*, 18 February 2003, LexisNexis Academic; Barbara Amiel, "Afraid to Take a Stand," *Maclean's*, 17 February 2003, LexisNexis Academic; Barbara Yaffe, "U.S. Hardly Notices Our Position on Iraq: We Get the Message—We Don't Count Much When It Comes to the Execution of U.S. Foreign Policy," *Guardian* (Charlottetown), 31 January 2003, LexisNexis Academic;

Chris Wattie, "PM's War Message a 'Confused Muddle': Is He For or Against? Media Not Sure Where Chretien Stands," *National Post* (Toronto), 25 January 2003, LexisNexis Academic; Howard Gerson and Harold Waller, "Canada Should Get Off Fence: The United States Has Changed Its Mideast Policy of Trying to Appease So-Called Moderate Arab Regimes, and Canada Should Follow the Lead," *Gazette* (Montreal), 23 January 2003, LexisNexis Academic; Gordon Gibson, "The Story of Our Shabby Foreign Policy," *National Post*, 22 January 2003, LexisNexis Academic.

81. Robert Fife, "Chretien Accused of 'Hiding' from Issue: Assailed by Opposition: Canada 'Has Become the Invisible Country on These Issues,'" *National Post*, 28 January 2003, LexisNexis Academic.

82. Mike Blanchfield, "Chretien Shows Signs of Backing U.S.: But There's Fresh Evidence of Cabinet Split over Iraq," *Standard* (St. Catharines), 11 February 2003, LexisNexis Academic.

83. Steven Edwards, "Nations Brace for UN Showdown: U.S. Resolution Faces a Rival; Canada Proposes Middle Course; Saddam Defies Inspectors," *National Post*, 25 February 2003, LexisNexis Academic; Steven Edwards, "Canada's Plan Threatens Iraq War: Secret Document Chooses March 31 as Decision Day: Proposal to Security Council Suggests 'All Necessary Means' Be Used if Iraq Balks," *National Post*, 26 February 2003, LexisNexis Academic.

84. April Lindgren and Mike Trickey, "Indifference Greets Canadian Compromise: Canada Pushes Ahead Despite Rejection by U.S., France, Germany," *Ottawa Citizen*, 27 February 2003, LexisNexis Academic; Steven Edwards, "Bush Rejects Canada's Compromise on Iraq: Washington Gains Support in UN Security Council," *National Post*, 27 February 2003, LexisNexis Academic; Steven Edwards and April Lindgren, "Mexico and Chile Sign Up for Canada's Compromise: Attempt to End UN Deadlock Proves 'Useful at This Time,'" *National Post*, 28 February 2003, LexisNexis Academic; Steven Edwards, "Canadian Peace Plan May Depend on Guinea: New Security Council Head: Impoverished State Unlikely to Adopt Ideological Stand on Dictatorship in Iraq," *National Post*, 1 March 2003, LexisNexis Academic; Spectator Wire Services, "Canada's Pitch for Peace; Kofi Annan Accepts Canadian Plan for UN Debate," *Hamilton Spectator*, 5 March 2003, LexisNexis Academic; Mike Trickey, "Canada Faces Tough Choice Over UN Vote: The U.S. Will Fight Iraq If It Loses the Vote at the Security Council—but Will Canada?" *Ottawa Citizen*, 11 March 2003, LexisNexis Academic. For an overview of Canadian efforts, see Munton, "The Limits of American Hegemony and the Impact of Norms," 6–7.

85. "The Wrong Way: Canada Should Have Stood with Its Allies against Iraq," *Ottawa Citizen*, 18 March 2003, LexisNexis Academic.

86. Quoted in "Munton, "The Limits of American Hegemony and the Impact of Norms," 7.

87. Munton, "The Limits of American Hegemony and the Impact of Norms," 7–9; Robin Summerfield, "Canadians Seek UN Backing for Conflict: Poll," *Windsor Star*, 10 March 2003, LexisNexis Academic.

88. Munton, "The Limits of American Hegemony and the Impact of Norms," 10–12; Richard Gwyn, "Embracing a Self-Indulgent Anti-Americanism Would Be As Stupid a Collective Act As We've Committed in a Long Time," *Toronto Star*, 30 March 2003, LexisNexis Academic.

89. Steven Edwards, "Failure of the Security Council a Blow to Chretien Government: Tried for a Compromise: Canada Too Reliant on the International Body to Set Foreign Policy, Analysts Say," *National Post*, 19 March 2003, LexisNexis Academic; Andrew Richter, "Canada Will Pay for Stand on Iraq," *Windsor Star*, 19 March 2003, LexisNexis Academic.

90. "Canada's New Spirit," *Economist*, 25 September 2003, http://www.economist.com.

15

The Political Economy of Canada's Relations with the European Union[1]

AXEL HÜLSEMEYER

INTRODUCTION

Other chapters of this book have concerned themselves with Canada's foreign policy toward either the U.S., individual countries with a unique importance to Canada, or regions per se, such as Latin America. While Canada also has direct diplomatic relations with all European states, the concern of this chapter is with the European Union (E.U.) as a whole. The E.U. has an embassy separate from its member states in Ottawa; likewise, Canada maintains one in Brussels just for E.U. matters.[2]

The European Union stands apart from other regions because it is involved in certain aspects of foreign policy, especially in the economic realm, as a *bloc*. In other words, negotiations do not take place with France, Italy, or Poland but with an E.U. delegation representing its now 480 million citizens. This has profound implications for the leverage of sovereign states in general, and for Canada as a "middle power" in particular, vis-à-vis the European Union. Canada's relationship with the E.U. focuses on *economic* ties, notwithstanding the cultural bonds due to the large number of Europeans who immigrated into Canada. Indeed, after the United States, the European Union is Canada's second largest trading partner.

The economic interaction between Canada and the E.U. takes place on a "bilateral" basis as well as in multilateral forums like the General Agreement on Tariffs and Trade (G.A.T.T.), since 1995 the World Trade Organization (W.T.O.). On either level, the regulation of trade and financial cooperation is inherently political, for the rules of arbitration, technical, labor, or environmental standards, to name just a few, always have distributional effects; not all parties benefit evenly from the same set of policies. The academic discipline that specifically deals with this type of interaction is called International Political Economy (IPE). It holds that one cannot meaningfully discuss political developments without taking economic aspects into account and vice versa. Put differently, IPE concerns itself with the interface between the two most dominant forms of social organization, "the state" and "the market."[3] It is the role of the former to regulate the latter, i.e., to enable the functioning of the market in the first place (e.g., through ensuring private property and establishing a common currency).[4] Given the primary nature of Canada's relations with the E.U., the political economy perspective is indispensable for this chapter.

To provide an idea of the importance of the E.U., a few numbers will suffice. With the accession of ten new member states in May 2004, the E.U. is one of the largest markets in the world. It includes 480 million consumers and a combined Gross Domestic Product (G.D.P.) of $13.7 trillion CDN—comparable to the North American Free Trade Agreement (N.A.F.T.A.), which encompasses about 412 million inhabitants and a joint G.D.P. of $15.7 trillion CDN. In 2001, the European Union's share of world G.D.P. was 25.2 percent and it was the destination of 38.1 percent of Canada's goods that went to places other than the United States.

In order to understand how European integration affects Canadian foreign policy, we will proceed in three steps: first, we systematize the various degrees to which countries integrate regionally, for it matters tremendously whether one deals with a free trade area like N.A.F.T.A. or a large group of states using the same currency and having common social policies (like the E.U.). Second, we discuss the relevance of the main European institutions and the extent of E.U. economic integration, concentrating on the time from the mid-1980s to the mid-1990s because of the transformative effects of the Common Market initiative in 1986 and the Maastricht treaty in 1993. Third, we detail how the single largest budgetary position of the E.U., its agricultural subsidies, compromised the Canadian negotiating position toward the end of the so-called Uruguay Round of the G.A.T.T. in 1993.

GENERALIZING ABOUT REGIONAL INTEGRATION

We at least intuitively seem to know that, say, N.A.F.T.A., MERCOSUR (Common Market of the South), and the E.U. are all instances of regional integration, but that they look quite different; yet, what exactly are the differences and how can we systematize them? The variation exists on the so-called institutional density, i.e., the degree to which the respective member states voluntarily transfer formerly national policy domains to supranational institutions.[5] Regional integration schemes, regardless of their precise institutional setup, are commonly referred to as "preferential trading arrangements" (P.T.A.'s).[6] As the name suggests, P.T.A.'s all somehow discriminate economically between *insiders*, i.e. the member states, and *outsiders*.[7] As such, they appear to violate the commitment of the World Trade Organization to the principle of nondiscrimination. This principle is embodied in the so-called most-favored nation (M.F.N.) status, which means that any tariff concession granted by a member state to any one country ought to be granted to *all* W.T.O. members. The exception specifically allowed for in Article XXIV is the conclusion of P.T.A.'s, provided that they do not, *as a group*, increase their level of protection vis-à-vis non-members of the regional integration scheme. Among P.T.A.'s, we can distinguish five categories of commitment among the member states; we discuss them from the lowest level to the highest.

The first stage of regional integration is a free trade area (F.T.A.), in which tariffs and other barriers between its members are largely abolished, while they all retain *different* customs duties toward third countries. The consequence is that outsiders have an incentive to export their goods via the P.T.A. member state with the lowest tariff for a given product and then transship freely within the free trade area to the countries with a higher external tariff structure, particularly if they comprise large markets (like the United States). To prevent precisely this from happening, F.T.A.'s necessitate the development of elaborate, so-called rules of origin (R.O.O.'s) that specify for every product group the content requirements that allow it to qualify as an F.T.A. good. If such a prerequisite is met, then the good moves freely within the free trade area. Conversely, in case this condition is *not* fulfilled, as in the case of products that are entirely or substantially produced in outsider countries, they are still subject to customs duties *within* the F.T.A.

In the North American Free Trade Agreement, which is the most prominent F.T.A., the rules of origin encompass about 200 pages. For instance, the content requirement for motor vehicles is set at 62.5 percent to qualify as a N.A.F.T.A. product, while the garment industry is based on a so-called thread-forward rule. Thus, only textiles made from N.A.F.T.A.-produced thread are not subject to duties among its members. These R.O.O.'s are different for each sector because domestic producers in the member states lobbied their respective trade representatives in that respect. Therefore, they are very detailed and impose costs *administratively* in terms of their negotiation and enforcement, as well as on *businesses* to provide formal evidence to customs authorities that a given product meets the "N.A.F.T.A. test."

Canada has experience with two free trade areas: a bilateral free trade agreement with the United States and N.A.F.T.A. In 1988, President Ronald Reagan and Prime Minister Brian Mulroney signed the Canada-U.S. free trade agreement (C.U.S.F.T.A.). The goal for Canadian foreign economic policy was not free trade in the traditional sense (in fact, prior to the agreement, 80 percent of Canadian exports to the U.S. were already duty free) but to obtain more secure access to the U.S. market than was hitherto the case. This became important because in 1986 the twelve member states of the then European Community (E.C.) had concluded the Common Market initiative (for detail, see below). Subsequent fears of a "fortress Europe" prompted the Canadian government to concentrate on better access to the U.S. economy. Further, with the United States already being the most important market, sporadic tendencies of American protectionism have a ripple effect for Canadian trade and investment.[8]

The C.U.S.F.T.A. became the blueprint for the North American Free Trade Agreement. The primary concern of the Canadian trade representatives in these negotiations was defensive, i.e., to avert a scenario in which Mexico obtained better access to the American market than Canada had achieved under the C.U.S.F.T.A. Yet, European integration again served as the instigator for the N.A.F.T.A. talks to occur in the first place. There were two reasons for this: first, the Mexican government had unsuccessfully sought to solicit funds for its market reforms because the opening of Eastern Europe meant that E.C. member states directed all their financial attention to the countries that in 2004 became E.U. member states. Like Canada since the C.U.S.F.T.A., Mexico now concentrated on the U.S. economy. Second, both Canadian and American foreign policy makers were deeply concerned with the signing of the Maastricht treaty which, among other aspects, established the timetable for the introduction of a single European currency.[9] In the eyes of one participant in the N.A.F.T.A. negotiations: "Arguably we would not have a NAFTA (and before that a Canada-U.S. free trade agreement [C.U.F.T.A.]) had the Europeans not moved to create the European Union (EU)."[10]

The second stage in the degree of regional integration is a Customs Union (C.U.). In contrast to an F.T.A., members also adopt common external tariffs toward the outside world. Hence, since there no longer is an incentive for transshipment, a C.U. does not need rules of origin. This requires a higher degree of policy coordination among the P.T.A.'s member states than is the case in an F.T.A. Specifically, setting a common external tariff demands consensus in two areas: first, the exact level at which the common customs duty should be set. This task becomes easier, the closer the tariff rates among the member states concerned already are *before* taking this step. Second, the apportionment of the now commonly collected customs revenue among the P.T.A. countries needs to be agreed upon. In an F.T.A. with *different* external tariffs, each member individually gathers these revenues, but a C.U. by definition removes the incentive for nonmembers to seek entry via a particular country into the P.T.A. Thus, given the extent of policy coordination required to move from an F.T.A. to a Customs Union, C.U.'s themselves can vary from common external tariffs only for particular sectors to a full-fledged joint customs structure. MERCOSUR, the Andean Community, and CARICOM (Caribbean Common Market) are current examples of limited customs unions, while European integration as commenced in the late 1950s already had a broader scope.

Within Canada, aided by progressive European integration, a public as well as an academic debate has surfaced in the last few years about the benefits and costs of furthering *bilateral* integration from an F.T.A. to a Customs Union. A number of officials, among them former International Trade Minister and now Foreign Minister Pierre Pettigrew, as well as Bank of Canada Governor David Dodge, have publicly spoken in favor of deeper North American integration in 2003, fueled largely by arguments advanced through the C. D. Howe Institute, a business-friendly academic think tank.[11] Notably, proposals for a North American Customs Union (N.A.C.U.) concentrate solely on the economic relationship between Canada and the United States; i.e., the designation "North American" relates to the C.U.S.F.T.A., not the N.A.F.T.A. Yet, there are formidable difficulties in deciding on the exact height of a joint tariff for all product groups, on how to share the customs revenues among the member countries, and on the supranational institutions required to oversee and to enforce the common regulations. Hence, only a very limited N.A.C.U. would appear realistic at the beginning where only those sectors are incorporated in which tariffs vis-à-vis third parties are already similar between the two countries (i.e., within one or two percentage points of each other), and in which the rules of origin costs are high.[12]

The third step of regional integration is a Common Market, which includes the free movement not only of goods, but also of services, financial capital, and labor within the P.T.A.; these are the so-called four freedoms. A Common Market is based on a high degree of coordination among its member countries, since it is almost a de facto extension of domestic economies to the regional level, absent a common currency and joint taxation. This means that customs procedures *within* the common market become superfluous. The Single European Act (S.E.A.), concluded by the E.C. member states in 1986 to establish a common market by the end of 1992, is to date the only empirical example of this degree of integration. By its very nature, a common market favors all goods, services, and financial capital originating *within* the members, since all third country products are made relatively more expensive by being subject to tariffs to enter the common market.[13]

The degree of market and policy coordination embodied in a Common Market provides the rationale for the fourth step in deepening regional integration, namely, an Economic Union. Monetary autonomy of the member states is transferred to a common central bank. The economic rationale for this move is based on the so-called Mundell-Fleming theorem, which stipulates that a country can maximally achieve two of three of the following goals at the same time: exchange rate stability; monetary autonomy; and capital mobility. Since the mobility of financial capital is often considered as part and parcel of economic globalization and therefore now as externally given,[14] countries face a trade-off between exchange rate stability and monetary autonomy.[15] Which of the two goals takes precedence is a *political* decision and crucially depends upon the socioeconomic benefactors and losers of either one. A single currency signifies a decision for exchange rate stability, since abandoning the very existence of different currencies altogether of course leads to the highest degree of exchange rate "stability" possible. Monetary autonomy is therefore lost at the national level, but regained at the P.T.A. level through a supranational Central Bank. A single currency makes the economic union so integrated that only a common government is missing to make the regional integration scheme look like a "normal" country.

The adoption of the single currency by twelve E.U. member states has led, parallel to the debate over a customs union with the United States following the Single European Act, to Canadian proposals for a North American Monetary Union (N.A.M.U.). Given the importance of the American market for the Canadian economy, the argument is that the floating exchange rate between the two currencies is hurting both Canadian exporters and reducing U.S. foreign investment in Canada because of planning insecurity. The Canadian dollar fluctuated relative to the U.S. dollar between 89¢ in the early 1980s to a low of 63¢ in the early 1990s, followed by a rise to 77¢ by 2004.[16] Mirroring the rationale for the euro, a currency union with the United States is considered the means to alleviate these irritants. To be sure, N.A.M.U. proponents recognize that at issue would not be a new and decidedly neutral currency like the euro, but simply the adoption of the U.S. dollar by Canada.[17]

The fifth and last step of P.T.A. integration is a political union in which macro-regional governmental institutions fully, or at least partially, replace the individual member governments. It entails the existence of supranational political institutions, as well as the adoption of common symbols like a flag and an anthem, intended to lead to a gradual identity shift among the populations. In other words, as the degree of economic integration within a P.T.A. increases with every stage outlined above, so does the extent of national sovereignty to be relinquished to macro-regional bodies. The European Union is the only P.T.A. to date that exhibits elements of a political union; this is the case with respect to two truly supranational institutions (the European Commission and the European Court of Justice) as well as the policy mandates carried out by them. They fundamentally affect Canadian foreign policy making, and we therefore discuss them in some detail in the next section.

This five-stage depiction of the different degrees of regional integration does *not* imply a deterministic process through all stages. In other words, a free trade area does not by some inner logic of regional integration ultimately have to evolve into an economic, let alone a political, union. What this delineation *does* stand for, however, is that there is an economic, and concomitant political, logic behind the *sequence* of integration steps. Put differently, a free trade area does not progress to an economic union directly, bypassing the intermediate stages of a customs union and a common market. This would neither make economic sense nor be politically feasible.

EUROPEAN INTEGRATION AND ITS INSTITUTIONS

E.U. Institutions

We are used to differentiating between political institutions according to their functions as executive, legislative, and jurisdictional branches. A particular feature of the E.U. is that it has *two* types of executives. The Council of the European Union is the main decision-making body and represents the individual portfolios of the member states, i.e., the ministers of, say, finance or the environment; its various configurations meet continuously. Concretely, this means that when the Council tackles environmental issues, for instance, its membership is made up of the ministers of environment from the member countries. And the same Council will have a different configuration when it meets on matters of domestic security, that is, the ministers of the interior and their counterparts. Decisions in the Council are voted on, and the larger a member state's population, the more votes it has. For instance, since November 1, 2004, Germany, France, Italy, and the United Kingdom have 29 votes, whereas Malta has 3. Since the adoption of the Single European Act in 1986, most decisions are taken by qualified majority voting (Q.M.V.), which means that a policy is adopted if a majority (sometimes two-thirds) of member states approve *and* the number of votes cast in favor exceeds two-thirds of the 121 total. In addition, the Heads of State and Government meet usually twice a year toward the end of a member state's presidency. The presidency of the E.U. rotates every six months between the member states in alphabetical order.[18] The point here is that the power of the member states is curbed through Q.M.V.; while the Heads of State and Government still decide unanimously, individual countries cannot block E.U. decisions in the Council of Ministers anymore. Therefore, for third countries like Canada, joint E.U. policies increasingly matter more than the opinions of its members—save the Franco-German foreign policy stance, which frequently still is a good indication of ensuing E.U. positions.[19]

The relevance of the *joint* foreign economic policy becomes even more pronounced with the second executive in the E.U. institutional structure, the European Commission, which represents the supranational arm. Members of the Commission usually are senior or former politicians from the member countries. They are nominated by their national governments, but are expected to act in the larger interest of the E.U. In fact, they cannot receive instructions from their national governments. Their nomination has to be ratified, not on an individual basis, but as a bloc, by the European Parliament.

Until October 31, 2004, the smaller countries nominated one, the larger ones two commissioners, a situation being reconsidered in view of an enlargement that is not as yet completed. Since November 1, 2004, when the Commission inaugurated its new mandate (2004–2009), there is only one commissioner per country. Once the E.U. reaches 27 or 28 members—with the admission of Bulgaria, Romania, and (hypothetically) Turkey—the Commission will grow neither at the same rate nor ad infinitum. Discussions are held to identify how countries will be represented on a fair, but rotational basis. Several scenarios are therefore taken into consideration for establishing a smaller Commission, and the decision will be reached by unanimous consent of the members. The Commission is headed by a President, chosen by consensus between the member states in the European Council. The President assigns Commissioners to particular governmental portfolios at the E.U. level, but the pool of individuals from which to choose also is predetermined by the member states because they are the ones who delegate their national commissioner. Through the Commission, the European Union as a whole is represented with one voice at international trade negations, whether bilaterally in Canada-E.U. relations or under the auspices of the G.A.T.T./W.T.O.

The European Parliament (E.P.), which is elected directly by the citizens in the member states since 1979, constitutes the second branch, the legislature. Its "political groups" closely mirror the makeup of its national parties. Members are organized into the European People's Party (Christian Democrats) and European Democrats, the Socialist Group in the European Parliament (P.S.E.), the Group of the Alliance of Liberals and Democrats for Europe (A.L.D.E.), the Confederal Group of the European United Left—Nordic Green Left (G.U.E./N.G.L.), the Group of Greens/ European Free Alliance (Verts/A.L.E.), the Independence/Democracy Group (IND/DEM), and the Union for Europe of the Nations Group (U.E.N.). There also are "non-attached" members who represent 4–5 percent of the members of the European parliament. Such belonging to European political families helps to build a binding that is avowedly stronger towards European institutions than national concerns. While they cannot completely forget their roots, members of the European Parliament are expected to act and think first about Europe and then about their home government's concerns. However, there is still, admittedly, some work to be done to reach such *détachement*.

The E.P.'s competencies have increased markedly with the Maastricht treaty. Parliamentarians must now approve the E.U. budget, they can reject the Commission built by its President as a whole (i.e., the E.P. cannot single out individual commissioners), and they are consulted about the selection of the president of the European Central Bank. Nonetheless, the E.P. does not yet hold the same powers that we tend to associate with the legislative process at the domestic level. Until a further marked increase in the European Parliament's competencies occurs, foreign policymakers of third countries like Canada need not concern themselves too much with the E.P.'s decisions.

This is different with the Union's jurisdictional branch, which is filled by the European Court of Justice (E.C.J.). Already created as part of the original institutions, its principal mandate is to uphold the treaties and guarantee that E.U. legislation, the so-called Community law, is interpreted and applied uniformly in all member states. In doing so, the E.C.J. has jurisdiction in disputes involving E.U. institutions, member states, businesses, and individuals. It is composed of one judge from each member state to ensure that all the E.U.'s national legal systems are represented.[20] The Court hears cases referred to it by the Commission, individual member states, and national courts needing a ruling on the application of E.U. law. In other words, the important feature of European legal integration is that community law *always* takes precedence over national law in the member states.[21] The role of the Commission in E.U. foreign policy is matched by the necessary legal integration. Trade treaties signed on behalf of the Union as a whole are then also implemented and enforced in all member states.[22]

The institutional structure of the E.U. has led some observers to conclude that its intergovernmental component (i.e., the European Council and the Council of Ministers[23]) is the only decisive aspect of European politics.[24] Critics have pointed out that the role of the Commission and its President are widely underestimated because the "big bargains" between the member states do not take place in a vacuum.[25] Instead, the Commission, through its running of day-to-day European politics, has the *ability* to set or, at a minimum, influence the very agenda that the European Council takes up.[26] In much the same way, the E.C.J. is a motor of deepening European integration "from within."[27]

The Single European Act and the Maastricht Treaty

In order to facilitate Franco-German reconciliation after World War II through tangible economic incentives, the Treaty of Rome in 1957 established the then European Economic Community (E.E.C.) from the outset as a full-fledged customs union, positing the development of a common market as its goal.[28] This was aided by the fact that the original six member states were—and continue to be—marked by a similarly high level of economic development, which resulted in considerable cross-border economic exchange.[29] A common European market proved elusive in the first three decades because countries were not prepared to give up national regulations that were the cornerstone of the national welfare state. Yet, the desire to move from a customs union to a common market came to the fore again in the early 1980s, but this time pushed by some of the largest European businesses, organized in the European Roundtable of Industrialists (E.R.T.).

The proposal for a European common market emerged against the backdrop of "Eurosclerosis," a term coined in the late 1970s to describe two related phenomena: first the political stagnation in E.C. integration; and second the poor competitiveness of most European economies vis-à-vis those of the U.S. and Japan. Different technical regulations and product standards made inner E.C. trade, in which large European companies were significantly engaged, artificially costly. The E.R.T. worked in close cooperation with the European Commission under the leadership of its then President Jacques Delors. Under the threat of E.R.T. members to otherwise relocate outside the E.C., the Single European Act (S.E.A.) was ultimately adopted on 26 February 1986 by the then twelve member states; its core was the development of a single European market (S.E.M.) by 1992, based on the assessment that non-tariff barriers to trade between member states were the major cause of the economic component of Eurosclerosis.[30] The single market is defined in the S.E.A. as "an area without internal frontiers in which the free movement of goods, persons, services, and capital is ensured." Clarifying these so-called *four freedoms*, the S.E.M. encompasses eight different aspects.

First, the elimination of *technical barriers* was to be achieved through two components: mutual recognition of national standards, and approximation through the stipulation of Community-wide "essential requirements" such as minimum safety and health standards. The intended effect of these principles was to prevent national standards from being used as impediments to cross-border trade.

Second, the reduction of *fiscal barriers* was deemed necessary, as differences in indirect taxes, in particular the value- added tax and excise duties, were also regarded as major obstacles to cross-border trade. Given the wide disparities in tax systems within the E.C., the aim was to approximate rather than to fully harmonize indirect taxes.

Third, the removal of *physical barriers* concerns especially the abolition of customs forms and formalities. While over 150 previous documents in use for the transport of goods across E.C. internal borders were replaced by a single one by January 1988, even this was abrogated by January 1993. The liberalization of transport services has been a key element in the program, particularly regarding the elimination of quota restrictions on road shipments.

Fourth, nationals of any member state have the right to seek and obtain *employment* anywhere in the Community. They also mostly enjoy the same treatment as nationals of the respective host states in matters of payment, working conditions, and trade union rights.

Fifth, professionals in many *occupations* now have the right to have their qualifications recognized in other member states.

Sixth, *financial services* have been opened, that is, cross-border restrictions on the operation of businesses in the services sector, such as banking and insurance, were largely eliminated.

Seventh, arrangements for the free *movement of capital* now apply throughout the Community.

Eighth, various directives have been introduced to open *public procurement* markets. According to the European Commission public purchasing has reached up to 15 percent of G.D.P., while in the mid-1980s only 2 percent of all government contracts went to suppliers from other E.C. countries.[31]

The European Commission was charged by the member states to institute the regulatory changes for the completion of the common market. It determined that 279 directives (regulations that legally mandate the member states to comply) needed to be put in place by the end of 1992.[32] This was accomplished primarily through the principle of "mutual recognition," whereby products approved in one of the member states were automatically deemed acceptable for consumption throughout what was then still the European Community. For instance, in the field of services, government procurement procedures varied tremendously and required harmonization. Also, the free movement of labor demanded that academic and non-academic qualifications, as well as minimum labor standards (e.g., working hours and social security) had to be standardized. In this vein, member state and E.U. redistributive policies and social and environmental regulations have grown as well.[33]

Canadian foreign policy makers feared that the S.E.A. would ultimately amount to the creation of a "fortress Europe," in which the free movement of goods, services, and capital among the member states is designed to keep competitive products from third countries out.[34] Therefore, they concentrated all their efforts toward securing Canadian market access to the U.S. market, proposing the establishment of the C.U.S.F.T.A. as a "counter-P.T.A." (see above).

Once the four freedoms are in place, businesses and travelers alike nonetheless still have to deal with different currencies in cross-border exchange. These involve a certain amount of risk for the former due to exchange rate fluctuations, and they are costly for the latter because of the bank fees incurred for currency conversions. Partly in order to alleviate this concern, the Treaty on European Union (T.E.U.), commonly referred to as the Maastricht treaty after the Dutch town in which it was signed, came into effect in 1993. It consists of three so-called pillars: (i) Economic and Monetary Union (E.M.U.); (ii) Common and Foreign Security Policy (C.F.S.P.); and (iii) Justice and Home Affairs (J.H.A.). Among them, the first pillar on the provisions and protocols relating to E.M.U., and the concomitant considerable extensions of social and economic cohesion, is probably best known. The move toward a single currency was seen as a logical consequence of the single market program adopted with the S.E.A. The free movement of goods, services, capital, and labor proved to be clearly curtailed by the vagaries of exchange rate fluctuations. In addition, a common currency would effectively prevent states with such an extraordinarily high degree of cross-border trade from using their currencies as instruments of economic policy, i.e., for competitive devaluations to promote their respective export industries.[35]

Twelve of the 25 (fifteen before May 1, 2004) member states are currently part of the euro zone, all represented with one voice by the heads of their national banks on the main decision-making body of the European Central Bank (E.C.B.), the Governing Council. The E.C.B. began operating by the end of the last century, and the euro became legal tender in 2002.[36] A single currency not only deprives a country of the symbolic value of its own legal tender (which might be important to citizens, as the British public's resistance to euro accession demonstrates), results in the loss of seignorage revenues, and leads to the abolition of autonomous national monetary policies, but it also demands increasing de facto convergence of fiscal policies among the member governments of the P.T.A. This is so because achieving the goal of monetary stability, as manifested in the E.C.B.'s mandate, depends upon the prevention of long-standing budgetary deficits among the member states. Hence, monetary and fiscal policies need to be complementary within a monetary union. While the former is centralized, the latter still belongs to the portfolio of the individual P.T.A. signatories. The ideal, therefore, would be the adoption of a monetary and fiscal union, where the latter policies are set centrally by an E.U. body. Attempts to do this failed because of resistance among the member states who jealously regard fiscal policy as one of their important prerogatives. This being said, the member states' finance ministers are de facto moving toward similar tax rates in the Council of Ministers, so that national tax policy independent from the policies in the other E.U. countries is merely symbolic.[37]

The potential implications of the euro for Canadian foreign economic policy could come in two forms: first, the advantages of the free movement of goods and services, as well as capital and labor across inner-E.U. borders become more "transparent," since prices are denominated in the same currency. The trade-diverting effect of the S.E.A. away from third-country products could thus be strengthened. By the same token, Canadian exporters who service the markets of several euro-zone countries *themselves* no longer experience the exchange rate risks associated with trade in several different currencies with varying degrees of monetary stability. The second effect of the single European currency for Canadian foreign economic policy is *indirect*, i.e., it does not concern Canada-E.U. but Canada-U.S. relations. The economic prowess of the United States manifests itself in the use of the U.S. dollar as the world's so-called reserve currency. The majority of internationally traded goods, from grain to oil, are priced in U.S. dollars. If an American administration experiences a budget deficit, lenders are less likely to call in their loans because the U.S. currency is in such wide use.

American concern with the euro is that it is likely to become the second reserve currency, thereby putting pressure on the U.S. dollar and budgetary constraints on American administrations.[38] If the euro leads to a weakening of the U.S. dollar, then the strength of the Canadian dollar relative to the U.S. currency increases. Thus, Canadian exports become comparatively more expensive in the U.S. market than before the advent of the euro. (At the time of writing this chapter, both the euro/US$ and CDN$/US$ relationships are observable in the described fashion.)

The desire to forge a Common Foreign and Security Policy for the Union is the second pillar of the T.E.U. Foreign policy was no longer to be about simple interstate cooperation through meetings of foreign ministers; rather, it focused on its Europeanization. This effort is also visible in the creation, with the 1997 Treaty of Amsterdam, of a High Representative for the C.F.S.P. This second pillar has been much maligned for yielding few concrete results. For example, the E.U. was initially unable to deal coherently and productively with the violent disintegration of Yugoslavia. The C.F.S.P. describes an *objective* rather than a current practice. However, there is no denying that despite the tremendous obstacles for integrating the foreign policies of initially 12, now 25, states, the international dimension is not escaping the logic of integration. Since the Maastricht treaty, the E.U. has its own defense organization, the West European Union (W.E.U.), and the so-called Eurocorps as the integrated military nucleus comprising several member states is currently stationed in the Balkans and Afghanistan.

The C.F.S.P. itself lies outside the scope of this chapter. However, Europe's new military engagement has a clear fiscal implication for Canadian foreign policy, and the Canadian troop commitment in Bosnia and Afghanistan has already been significantly reduced as a result. In Bosnia, the so-called S.F.O.R. (Stabilization Force) mission, which included a substantial Canadian contingent, has been replaced after its completion by a new E.U.-led force called E.U.F.O.R. In Afghanistan, the Eurocorps has taken over ISAF (International Security Assistance Force) from Canada.

Finally, the third pillar bears the title of Justice and Home Affairs, which was further built up in the 1997 Treaty of Amsterdam. With this pillar, the E.U. crafted a policy agenda in the areas of immigration, asylum, policing, and judicial cooperation. At the broadest level, the objective of J.H.A. is to create an area of "Freedom, Security, and Justice" in Europe. It is in the areas of immigration and asylum, a logical implication of the S.E.A., where there has been the strongest move toward Europeanization, codified separately under the so-called Schengen Agreement[39]. With respect to justice, the J.H.A. has produced a European law enforcement organization (Europol), police college, and task force of police chiefs, along with a Common European Warrant. As such, J.H.A. is primarily an E.U.-internal matter; its relevance for Canadian foreign policy lies in slightly easier judicial cooperation, since fewer channels are involved. Although this had not been identified as a Canadian concern when dealing solely with the individual member states, the incorporation of the new Central and Eastern European countries under the E.U.'s legal structure can be expected to benefit third parties.

EU Commercial Policies

It is important to note that the European Union does not have its own budget; i.e., the E.U. does not collect taxes itself. Instead, it finances its expenses exclusively through the contributions of the member states. More than two-thirds of its financial resources the European Union devotes to redistributive policies among member states; the Common Agricultural Policy (C.A.P.) alone accounts for about 50 percent of the overall budget.[40] Since the mid-1980s, the C.A.P. significantly concerns Canadian foreign economic policy within the G.A.T.T./W.T.O.

The C.A.P. was initially developed on French insistence in the 1950s to support its small farmers, but today there are producers in virtually every member state that receive some degree of assistance. For the longest time, the C.A.P. subsidized agricultural production down to the world market price on the basis of *output*; in other words, the more a farmer produced the more financial assistance he received; the inevitable consequences were the proverbial milk lakes and butter mountains. The financial assistance did not benefit the small farmers for which it was intended but rather those who were large-scale producers. Since the so-called Agenda 2000 of agricultural reform, the criteria for assistance include enticing farmers to actually *stop* producing and instead act as caretakers of the land in an environmental sense of the term. In other words, the term "agriculture" has been broadened considerably within C.A.P.

A group of industrialized countries, the so-called Cairns Group, criticizes the C.A.P. as a subsidy (in both the old and the new forms) designed to keep otherwise competitive agricultural products from third countries out of the E.U. market.[41] Canada is a member of the Cairns Group, which comprises 14 agricultural exporters (including the U.S., Australia, and New Zealand) that are committed to the promotion of free trade in the sector.

The various negotiating rounds on tariff reductions under the auspices of the G.A.T.T. for the longest time exempted discussing agriculture because of its contentiousness. Only the so-called Uruguay Round of the G.A.T.T., which lasted from 1986 to 1993, for the first time attempted to tackle European and North American subsidies in this sector. The topic single-handedly was responsible for the extraordinary length of the negotiations and the Round as a whole nearly failed on this account.[42]

The E.U. projects its economic power in trade talks through a single negotiating team representing its member states, and therefore several hundred million consumers. Therefore, its necessity for compromise is limited. A current illustration is the E.U.'s refusal to allow genetically modified produce from the U.S. and Canada onto the European market, unless it is clearly labeled as such. The differences in agricultural support programs between the United States and the E.U. dominated the debate in the Uruguay Round, and they continue to do so in the current so-called

Doha Round. Canada, due to the export dependency of its grain, is relegated to the position of decision *taker* in G.A.T.T./W.T.O. agricultural disputes between the E.U. and the United States.

Hence, while Canada's close trade and investment ties with the United States are overwhelming (having increased by over 170 percent since the inception of N.A.F.T.A. in 1994—compared to 60 percent with the E.U.), the dependence on exports to its southern neighbor "has made diversification of export destinations an objective of the Canadian Government."[43] (Such diversification is not only a geographical matter but by implication of Canada's economy also, and perhaps more importantly, a sectoral one. Canada's exports of oil, gas, and hydro electricity to the United States, as well as its assembly of U.S. vehicles, are naturally irrelevant in transatlantic trade.) This is true especially as Canada–E.U. trade accounts for only 6.6 percent of Canada's total goods and services trade, and it has been declining over the past decade when it was not growing as fast as the economic interaction with other regions.[44]

This prompted Canada's Prime Minister Paul Martin and then E.U. Commission President Romano Prodi to launch a Trade and Investment Enhancement Agreement (T.I.E.A.) in March 2004. This was not an extraordinarily new occurrence in itself, since the first formalization of Canada-E.U. trade dates back to the 1976 Framework Agreement for Commercial and Economic Cooperation, followed by further initiatives in the second half of the 1990s.[45] The new aspect about the T.I.E.A. is that it identifies *regulatory* barriers between Canada and the E.U. as the main obstacle to an improved trading relationship; this includes, among others, the domestic regulation of services, the mutual recognition of professional qualifications, government procurement, and investment.[46] The parallels to the 1986 Single European Act, however unintentional, are striking. The drama associated with "Eurosclerosis" can certainly not be detected in stagnant Canada-E.U. economic exchange, but the emphasis on regulatory cooperation with the specific reference to procurement, professional qualifications, and "mutual recognition" is certainly revealing.

The difference is just as clear, however. While large European businesses virtually demanded the dismantling of regulatory barriers within the then European Community and threatened exit in case the S.E.A. had not come about, an active promotion cannot be discerned here. The stakes of expected "bilateral" trade appear too low when viewed in relation to inner-European and Canada-U.S. economic exchange. Whether the strictly "voluntary framework"[47] of the T.I.E.A. is sufficient to enhance transatlantic trade and investment is at best an open question.

CONCLUSION

The E.U. currently encompasses 25 member states, a joint trade policy spanning its more than 480 million inhabitants, and a single currency for twelve of its most advanced economies. With the European Commission and the European Court of Justice (through which supranational law overrides national law, and in which individual citizens are permitted to litigate against their own governments), it already entails some *institutional* features of a political union. In terms of *policies*, the Union exhibits aspects of redistribution and is developing a joint foreign and security policy as well as a common approach to immigration and justice. Apart from the single currency, it also displays two other *symbols* traditionally associated with the rallying of citizens behind their nation states: a flag and an anthem. The text of a treaty that will be the basis for a European constitution, foreseeing, among other aspects, the creation of an E.U. president and a European foreign minister, was adopted by the heads of state and government at their summit under Irish presidency in June 2004.

Against this backdrop, it seems difficult to overestimate the increasing relevance of the European Union for third countries. Of course, in matters of foreign and security policy, the E.U. is partly still struggling to find a common approach. The creation of the position of High Representative for Foreign Policy could not alleviate the differences that initially emerged between member states with respect to the U.S.-led invasion of Iraq. Conversely, a joint policy has by now succeeded on the Balkans as well as in Afghanistan. In short, Canada's foreign policy vis-à-vis the E.U. is in the coming years likely to move beyond the economic realm, on which relations will continue to concentrate. At issue is not a diversion from Canada's primary occupation with the United States, but a gradual shift in focus from the European Union's individual member states to Brussels.

NOTES

1. I am indebted to Sarah Tarry for her assistance in finalizing this chapter.
2. Canada possesses three embassies in Brussels: one for Belgium and Luxembourg, one for the North Atlantic Treaty Organization, and one for the E.U.

3. For a more detailed overview of IPE and its development, see Axel Hülsemeyer and Julian Schofield, *Introduction to International Relations: A Reader* (Boston: Pearson Custom Publishing, 2004), Part IV.

4. While the principal function of political authority in the economy is undisputed, disagreement exists about the degree to which this should go, and who decides on behalf of "the state." The three main theoretical approaches in IPE (mercantilism, liberalism, and Marxism) and their respective twentieth-century variants have different positions on this matter.

5. It is as yet unclear what factors explain this institutional variation. For a comparison of the E.U. and N.A.F.T.A. that probes into different "cultures" of the state's function in the economy, see Axel Hülsemeyer, *Globalization and Institutional Adjustment: Federalism as an Obstacle?* (Aldershot, UK: Ashgate, 2004).

6. Edward D. Mansfield and Helen V. Milner, "The New Wave of Regionalism," *International Organization* 53, no. 3 (Summer 1999): 589–627.

7. Mattli addresses the conditions under which insiders accept new countries into "their" integration scheme, and when outsiders are more likely to form a counter-union. See Walter Mattli, *The Logic of Regional Integration: Europe and Beyond* (New York: Cambridge University Press, 1999).

8. Therefore, the core of the C.U.S.F.T.A. for Canadian negotiators was the dispute settlement mechanism of Chapter XIX. Through it, trade disputes between the two countries are no longer a matter of national law; instead, the C.U.S.F.T.A. replaces domestic judicial review procedures with a bilateral one. This means, for instance, that Canadians sit on panels that ascertain whether or not U.S. law was properly followed when imposing protectionist measures against Canadian products.

9. The Maastricht treaty is officially called Treaty on European Union (T.E.U.). With it, the European Community became, as the name suggests, the European Union.

10. Frederick W. Mayer, *Interpreting NAFTA: The Science and Art of Political Analysis* (New York: Columbia University Press, 1998), 39.

11. For public pronouncements, see David Dodge, "Check against Delivery" (remarks by David Dodge, Governor of the Bank of Canada, to the Couchiching Institute on Public Affairs, Geneva Park, Ontario, August 7, 2003), http://www.-bankofcanada.ca/en/speeches/2003/sp03–11.htm; and Pierre Pettigrew, "Dancing with the Elephant: Contending with an Assertive Super Power in Trade and Global Diplomacy" (address to the Empire Club, Toronto, September 25, 2003), http://webapps.dfait-maeci.ca/minpub/Publication.asp.

12. See Danielle Goldfarb, *The Road to a Canada-U.S. Customs Union: Step by Step or in a Single Bound?* (Toronto: C. D. Howe Institute, 2003); and Rolf Mirus

and Nataliya Rylska, "Should NAFTA Become a Customs Union?" in *NAFTA in the New Millennium*, ed. Edward D. Chambers and Peter H. Smith (Edmonton: The University of Alberta Press, 2002), 359–76.

13. In IPE, this is referred to as a "trade diversion" (i.e., goods and services from third countries are made artificially more expensive through the joint tariffs to insulate more expensive producers within the common market against foreign competition).

14. The very term *globalization* means different things to different people and is frequently employed with an ideological agenda in mind; as such, it poses sizable analytical problems. For a systematic analytical discussion of the phenomenon, see Axel Hülsemeyer, ed., *Globalization in the Twenty-First Century: Convergence or Divergence?* (Basingstoke, UK: Palgrave Macmillan, 2003).

15. Jeffrey A. Frieden, "Invested Interests: The Politics of National Economic Policies in a World of Global Finance," *International Organization* 45, no. 1 (Winter 1991): 19–56.

16. See Thomas J. Courchene and Richard G. Harris, *From Fixing to Monetary Union: Options for North American Currency Integration* (Toronto: C. D. Howe Institute, 1999). For a critical assessment of the Courchene/Harris proposal, see William B. P. Robson and David Laidler, *No Small Change: The Awkward Economics and Politics of North American Monetary Integration* (Toronto: C. D. Howe Institute, 2002). For an overview of the arguments, see Constance Smith, "Dollarization and Its Alternatives: Currency Arrangements under NAFTA," in *NAFTA in the New Millennium*, 377–96.

17. Yet, even *if* this, hypothetically, were acceptable to the Canadian public, institutional incompatibility between the American and Canadian central banks could still be a stumbling block. N.A.M.U. proponents maintain that the Bank of Canada would become the 13th district of the U.S. Federal Reserve System. However, while the former has a public mandate, the latter is in the majority owned by the commercial banks of the 12 districts. See Eric Helleiner, "What Political Architecture for North American Monetary Union? The Canadian Debate" (paper presented at the annual convention of the International Studies Association, Portland, OR, February 2003).

18. For instance, Germany is denoted by the letter "D" (Deutschland) and Greece by the letter "H" (Hellas). The delegates of the member states also sit around the table at meetings in this alphabetical order.

19. One qualification should be offered. In an overall sense, a common foreign and security policy remains deadlocked. However, this does not change the fact that many specific issues now are decided effectively at the level of the Council of Ministers rather than the individual state.

20. For the sake of efficiency, the Court is able to sit as a "Grand Chamber" of just eleven judges instead of always having to meet in a plenary session attended by all twenty-five.

21. The E.C.J.'s mandate has increased over the course of deepened European integration, particularly with the S.E.A. and the Maastricht treaty. Most significantly, private individuals, provided they have legal representation, can now bring proceedings to the Court; they are allowed to do so *directly* (i.e., they do not have to first exercise all domestic legal options).

22. Through the E.C.J., the degree of legal integration is far higher throughout the twenty-five member states of the European Union than it is in Canada. When policy areas fall primarily within provincial jurisdiction, the federal government cannot ensure to the other contracting parties the implementation of a trade treaty it signed. Precisely this dilemma materialized with the N.A.F.T.A. side agreements on labor and the environment. See Axel Hülsemeyer, *Globalization and Institutional Adjustment*.

23. The European Council is composed of the heads of government, while the Council of Ministers' composition changes according to the topic discussed, regrouping national ministers in charge of the given portfolio.

24. Andrew Moravcsik, "Negotiating the Single European Act: National Interest and Conventional Statecraft in the European Community," *International Organization* 45, no. 1 (Winter 1991): 19–56.

25. Paul Pierson, "The Path to European Integration: A Historical Institutionalist Analysis," *Comparative Political Studies* 29, no. 2 (April 1996): 123–163.

26. As we will see below, then Commission President Jacques Delors used this ability skillfully to set the stage for the adoption of the Single European Act and the Maastricht treaty by the heads of state and government.

27. The European Union has more institutions than the ones we cover here, although the others are clearly secondary (for instance, the Committee of the Regions—CoR). For a comprehensive look at the Union's institutional structure and its policies, visit the E.U.'s official webpage at http://europa.eu.int.

28. In other words, European integration had "skipped" the first stage of regional integration outlined above (i.e., the free trade area).

29. The "inner six," as they are commonly referred to, consist of France, (West) Germany, Italy, and the so-called Benelux countries (Belgium, the Netherlands, and Luxembourg).

30. The expected benefits of the S.E.M. were exhaustively elaborated in the officially commissioned Cecchini Report on the "costs of non-Europe," which was based on a survey of 11,000 firms and published in 1988. The report was criticized, inter alia, for having given insufficient weight to the strong possibility that the

benefits would be distributed very unevenly among member states, regions, and industries. See Robert A. Jones, *The Politics and Economics of the European Union: An Introductory Text* (Cheltenham, UK: Edward Elgar, 1996), 173.

31. These measures were to be enacted through the concept of "mutual recognition," breaking with the traditional arduous and time-consuming E.C. concept of a "harmonization" (i.e., a convergence of national standards around a new European one).

32. Axel Hülsemeyer, "Changing 'Political Economies of Scale' and Public Sector Adjustment: Insights from Fiscal Federalism," *Review of International Political Economy* 7, no. 1 (Spring 2000): 72–100.

33. See Martin Rhodes, "The Future of the 'Social Dimension': Labour Market Regulation in Post-1992 Europe," *Journal of Common Market Studies* 30, no. 1 (March 1992): 23–51; Giandomenico Majone, "The European Community between Social Policy and Social Regulation," *Journal of Common Market Studies* 31, no. 2 (June 1993): 153–170.

34. According to one observer, the building of such a "fortress" was indeed the purpose of the S.E.A., but due to unintended consequences of single market policies, this was unsuccessful. See Brian T. Hanson, "What Happened to Fortress Europe? External Trade Policy Liberalization in the European Union," *International Organization* 52, no. 1 (Winter 1998): 55–85.

35. In general terms, the so-called Mundell-Fleming theorem posits that under conditions of capital mobility, states are faced with a trade-off between exchange rate stability and monetary autonomy. If the exchange rate is held constant, monetary policy cannot deviate from that of other countries. See Jeffrey A. Frieden, "Invested Interests." Within the E.U., the national "room for maneuver" had already been limited through the Exchange Rate Mechanism. However, its crisis in 1992–1993 changed the band to 15% (that is, it de facto gave plenty of room for maneuver), and enabled the United Kingdom to devalue its currency and gain economic advantage as a result.

36. The three member states currently not part of the euro zone are the United Kingdom, Denmark, and Sweden. In the latter two, referenda on accession to the single currency failed in 2002 and 2003, respectively.

37. Upon establishing the single currency, the question of macro indicators that the member states would have to abide by to ensure the stability of the euro was settled with the establishment of three so-called convergence criteria, known as the "Maastricht criteria." They required an inflation rate of no more than 1.5% above the inflation rate of the three most stable economies; a national debt of no higher than 60% of G.D.P.; and a budget deficit no more than 3% of G.D.P. These criteria were supposed to be enforced through the so-called Growth and Stability

Pact. It was meant to levy financial penalties against members of the euro zone that consistently violated the Maastricht criteria. However, since several member states have repeatedly failed to fulfill the 3% deficit criterion, as of September 2004, the E.U. Commission effectively abandoned the Growth and Stability Pact, claiming that the latter had set arbitrary fiscal standards.

38. This is particularly the case the more internationally traded goods and services are priced in euros instead of U.S. dollars. Most E.U. countries that are not part of the euro zone as well as a significant number of African and Middle Eastern countries have already switched, or are in the process of switching, to the euro as their reserve currency.

39. From the Luxembourg town where they were signed.

40. The other redistributive policies are the European Regional Development Fund (E.R.D.F.) and the Cohesion Fund, which are directed to regions and member states, respectively, with a G.D.P. lower than the E.U. average.

41. Hence, the differences in opinion over agriculture are not merely a "simple" trade topic. Instead, they also reflect fundamentally different perspectives on the *role* of this sector—i.e., whether agriculture is in principle like any other sector of an economy (the perspective of the Cairns Group) or whether it is a cornerstone of the social fabric of society.

42. Note that the Uruguay Round talks occurred while negotiators worked out the S.E.A. and the Maastricht treaty in Europe, as well as the C.U.S.F.T.A. and the N.A.F.T.A. in North America. Frustration about the lack of progress at the multilateral level for both the E.U. and Canada provided additional impetus for the negotiation of the four P.T.A.s.

43. EU, "EU-Canada Summit Set to Make Relations Deeper, More Action Oriented," 2004, http://europa.eu.int/comm./trade/issues/bilateral/countries/Canada/pr_en.htm .

44. DFAIT, "Canada-European Union Economic Relations," 2004, http://webapps.dfait-maeci.gc.ca/minpub/Publication.asp.

45. EU, "EU-Canada Summit Set to Make Relations Deeper, More Action Oriented."

46. DFAIT, "Canada-European Union—Trade and Investment Enhancement Agreement," 2004, http://www.dfait-maeci.gc.ca/tna-nac/rb/tiea-en.asp.

47. DFAIT, "Canada-European Union—Trade and Investment Enhancement Agreement."

16

Canada-U.S. Relations: Personality, Pattern, and Domestic Politics

CHARLES F. DORAN

During a century and a half of historical experience, Canada-U.S. relations have been remarkably tranquil, certainly in comparison with any other pair of countries within the international system. Canadian-American relations are inescapably the centerpiece of Canadian foreign policy. Some 95 percent of all Canada-U.S. trade, the world's largest trading relationship, passes across the Canada-U.S. border undisturbed. The bulk of foreign investment in Canada is owned by U.S. corporations, and a similar amount of investment in the United States is owned by Canadian citizens, suggesting that investors on both sides of the border view border risk as minimal. Every United Nations poll regarding where Canadians or Americans would like to live puts the opposite country at the top of the list of alternate choices. Moreover, Canadians and Americans, when questioned in polls, always put the opposite country near or at the top of the roster of countries with which they identify most closely across the entire international system.[1]

Periodically, however, disturbances do mar the tranquility of Canada-U.S. relations. The timing and nature of these disturbances bears reflection.

Why should shows of bad feeling or irritants or ill-will periodically descend on this relationship, a relationship which otherwise displays so much benevolence and comity? That great democracies in dealing with each other have been shown to adopt benign tactics is scarcely the point. This format, in which force is expressly not used among the democracies, is known today as the democratic peace.[2] Canada-U.S. relations perhaps epitomized the paradigm of the democratic peace long before that paradigm became articulated, and surely before it became applicable in Europe where Germany and France, for example, will presumably never again take up arms against each other. The problem is not that either Canada or the United States would ever think of using arms against the other, for they would not, even during the wildest moments of a confrontation such as the so-called Cod War fought by a single Canadian gunboat and a Spanish fishing trawler. Ever since the early nineteenth century, after which the Great Lakes were neutralized and closed to warships of any kind, even displays of force are unacceptable dialogue in the relationship.

Rather, the problem is of a quite different nature. The problem is that periodic crankiness or coldness seems to enshroud Canada-U.S. relations in a fashion that then inhibits the bureaucratic capacity to undertake the normal business of the day.[3] Newspapers are filled with the acrimony of tired policy-makers who seem unable to find the conventional levers of diplomacy to ease differences around the rough spots of temporary impasse. In the traditional language of social science, the dependent variable—that which we try to explain—is the inability to resolve differences of approach and initiative that perhaps inevitably beset the relations between democracies, but that here are unusually associated with apparent shortcomings of imagination and statecraft. Acrimony thus results. These differences of approach and initiative that appear so implacable are marked eventually by displays of bad feeling at all levels of government.

Set against these periodic displays of dyspepsia is a mode of cross-border diplomacy known as interdependence. Interdependence is involuntary cooperation. Interdependence assumes that power cannot be substituted across issue-areas and is specific to each issue-area. Cooperation results from the awareness of the parties that, in the absence of cooperation, neither party will be able to achieve its goal. Cooperation at the border against terrorism is of this type. Were Canada and the United States not to cooperate in building a border with sophisticated technological security measures, neither country could cope with external terrorist threats, much less get commerce to move across the bridges at Fort-Erie/Buffalo and

Windsor/Detroit. According to the original derivation of the interdependence notion by Robert Keohane and Joseph Nye, power is absent from interdependence.[4] In an earlier assessment, Joseph Nye observed, however, that what distinguishes the Canada-U.S. relationship is the absence of force, not necessarily the absence of all aspects of power.[5] Regarding most policy formulation, the United States has learned that the wisest course is to take the long view rather than to try to maximize leverage in the short term.

The interdependence notion that issues are truly separate, and that power is not substitutable across issue areas, is challenged by two versions of realism. An American view, theorized by John Mearsheimer and expressed by U.S. Ambassador to Canada Paul Cellucci, is that security trumps economics.[6] In contrast, Joel Sokolsky has offered what he calls a Canadian view of realism. Security, in Sokolsky's conception of realism, does not trump economics.[7] Instead, the two are intertwined. In contrast to the Cellucci conception, security as a value is not superior to economics. Rather economics and security are intertwined such that economics is impossible without security, and security is impossible without economics. These notions of realism challenge the assumptions of interdependence that issues remain separate, as does the means to put these issues into practice.

However, the idea that economics and security are intertwined trips over the problem of linkage. How is intertwining different from linkage? If no difference exists, then treating Canada-U.S. relations as though economics and security are intertwined means that the governments will link issues.[8] Because the bigger partner possesses more resources and levers, and because the U.S. Congress loves to tie up treaties and legislation through linkage and log-rolling, Canada is not likely to fare very well in bilateral terms once linkage is admitted as a viable strategy and once interdependence with its explicit assumption that issues are separate is tossed out.

Perhaps the key to optimum discourse between Canada and the United States is reconciliation between the assumptions of realism and of interdependence. Until that happens, we may have to settle for second-best, that is, for some version of muddling through. Unevenness of cooperation is the likely result.

Cooperation is the predominant mode of discourse between Canada and the United States. First, the standard is set higher in North America than in virtually any other bilateral relationship in the international system. Breakdowns of cooperation are the exception. Second, because there is so much at stake in this relationship, breakdowns are costly for both parties. Over time, prolonged difficulties could damage the institutional fabric of the relationship itself. Third, forward movement regarding a deeper bilateral relationship, an enhanced North American Free Trade Agreement (NAFTA), an enlarged Free Trade Agreement of the Americas, and many other policy initiatives—all will require very positive and close coordination between Canada and the United States. Breakdowns of communication and resourcefulness can impede this progress.

Thus spending a bit of time assessing the periodic trouble spots in the relationship may well be worthwhile, both for analyst and for policymaker. Starting with a well-known argument explaining the episodic appearance of trouble spots in the relationship, we will also explore two further explanations that may be less familiar but that perhaps go deeper into the dynamic of societal and governmental interaction.

ACTORS AT THE TOP FAIL TO COMMUNICATE AND COORDINATE

One argument accounting for dissonance in Canada-U.S. relations that is taken by Michaud in his chapter is that the head of government and head of state do not get along and therefore are unable to conduct the business of state effectively. On the eve of the inauguration of Paul Martin as the new Prime Minister of Canada, former Canadian Ambassador to the United States Allan Gotlieb stressed the importance of good personal relations between president and prime minister.[9] The argument is especially telling for those who have been involved in policy and have observed how top decision-makers interact in political situations, not just before TV cameras, but behind closed doors. The argument has two variants.

The first variant is that a personality conflict exists between the leaders; in a word, they do not like each other. The quintessential example of this personal antipathy is between Prime Minister John Diefenbaker and President John F. Kennedy.[10] The supposedly populist, somewhat paranoid style of the Canadian prairie rhetorician is contrasted with the assertive Ivy League, Eastern, wealthy, made-for-TV style of the American President. It was not so much that their political values differed. The source of the disputation was that neither man really liked or respected the other. This lack of respect grated. Rather than restrain this personal animosity, the two leaders allowed it to spill over into their discourse. By not concealing the ill-will from the press, it was amplified and diffused. Television is a medium that invariably picks up miscues in body language communication.

But the bad deportment got entangled in issues, making issue differences appear even more intractable than was true originally. Each lacking a personal desire to get on the phone to settle some of the differences immediately, the two men allowed the issue disparities to fester. Suddenly, the differences became much larger than initially they had been, involving matters of face and comportment. As policy assistants looked on helplessly, issue molehills became mountains.

A second variant of the argument that discord ensues when policy-makers fail to empathize is that ideological and party differences may intrude. If the Liberals are in power in Ottawa and the Republicans are in power in Washington, Canadians anticipate discord. Since most Canadians are more liberal politically than their U.S. counterparts, having parties in power with differing governing agendas makes the split in the political attitudes of the electorates even more visible.[11]

Canada is concerned not just about lack of progress in policy-making but of falling back, especially in social legislation. In foreign policy, Canada seeks to mute differences with a conservative U.S. government through multilateral affiliation with other like-minded governments in Europe. Bilateral projects would, in Ottawa's way of thinking, not hold much prospect of success, given the split in party and ideology.[12] Washington ponders less over these matters than Canada does.

Thus each of the two variants of policy division between Ottawa and Washington is clear. If the differences between a Republican administration in Washington and a Liberal government in Ottawa—or conversely by a Conservative/Democrat tandem as it was with the Kennedy-Diefenbaker epoch—is worsened by the reality that neither occupant of the top political office likes the other, the result is from the Canadian perspective worsened.

Is there any validity to the interpretation of ideological and party difference affecting the tone of Canada-U.S. relations? Referring to the Diefenbaker/Kennedy years from a trade perspective, for example, Michael Hart opines that in the final year and a half of Diefenbaker's watch, the antipathy between him and President Kennedy, occasioned by both clashes of personality and matters of policy, reached such a height that Canadian officials could not use their own personal relationships to overcome it.[13] When the natural cement of a common political party outlook and common ideological base, combined with a good working relationship at the top, is not present to smooth and accommodate interstate relations, the bureaucracies on either side of the border also fail to interact effectively.

Yet with both of these variants of the notion that politics is likely to go awry when differences at the top seem insurmountable, the central question is How debilitating are the differences of personality, party, and ideology to statecraft? If we consider one of the most turbulent moments in the post–Cold War interval, the Anglo-American intervention into Iraq, we see the limits of the generalizations about debilitation. French President Jacques Chirac and President George W. Bush were both conservatives, and leaders of conservative parties, yet they clashed profoundly over Iraq policy and over international relations more generally. British Prime Minister Blair and President Bush, leaders of the leftist Labour Party and the rightist Republican Party, respectively, closely interacted on matters of world politics in a fashion that required significant trust and political resilience.[14]

We thus conclude the following. Similarity of ideological outlook and political party and personal friendship are not enough to safeguard foreign policy conduct between democracies in troubled times. Differences of party, ideology, and personality, though visible and strongly felt, are not necessarily sufficient to derail close policy coordination between democracies. To unsnarl the puzzle of the episodic deterioration of U.S.-Canada relations, we need to dig deeper for explanation.

THE U.S.-CANADA FOREIGN POLICY COOPERATION CYCLE

According to this interpretation, the explanation for the episodic deterioration of U.S.-Canada relations is not merely a problem of leaders not getting along with each other. The explanation is deeper within the evolution of policy and the societal support for that policy. According to this interpretation, a cyclical dynamic exists within the bilateral relationship that yields high points and low points in a pattern of change that is organic and repeated.[15] Two sets of forces are interlinked.

The first involves the divergence and convergence of Canadian and U.S.

policy.[16] This divergence versus convergence theme may be found in domestic legislation or foreign policy conduct.[17] Decriminalization of marijuana in Canada, at a time when the policy is generally not accepted in the United States, for example, epitomizes policy divergence. Support for the Canada-U.S. Trade Agreement, for example, indicates policy convergence.[18] Policy divergence eventually leads to intense lack of cooperation.[19] Policy convergence eventually leads to quite full cooperation. Thus cooperation in the bilateral relationship can be indexed in terms of apexes and nadirs. What "drives" the organic change in cooperation is policy divergence/convergence and the politics that underlie the respective preferences.

The question may arise as to which set of forces is dependent, and which is independent. In other words, which set of forces does the pushing? Does the divergence of issues cause lack of cooperation, or does lack of cooperation cause policy divergence? Some causation may go in the opposite direction among secondary forces that move against the predominant trend. Lack of cooperation may, out of frustration, for instance, lead through opposite causation to some additional divergence on issues. But the primary path of interaction is from divergence on issues to lack of cooperation, as cooperation is seen to be increasingly futile or unworkable. What turns this around is the eventual realization in Canada that the cost of deteriorating relations is too high and that divergence must be curbed. Regardless of the party in power in Ottawa, the Canadian private sector, the press, party strategists—looking at the prospects for the next election—and some intellectuals quietly play a large role in transforming sharply divergent policy into something more compatible with the North American norm.

Conversely, the most common pattern is that convergence on issues encourages additional cooperation. The more convergence that occurs, the more cooperation takes place. Eventually, however, convergence is seen by elites in Canada as having gone too far. On the Canadian side, the situation is sometimes described as buckling under to the Americans.[20] Americans may see that response as the rise of nascent anti-Americanism.[21]

However this change in trajectory is characterized, an apex of cooperation is reached. After that point issues begin to diverge once again and the degree of cooperation between the two governments begins decidedly to fall off. The cycle then repeats itself, though not with any predetermined amplitude or periodicity. Indeed, some of the periods involved are very short, others are measured in terms of a decade or more.

A useful starting place to illustrate the historical dynamic of the cooperation cycle is with the Diefenbaker/Kennedy relationship, for it is so obviously a nadir in cooperation between Canada and the United States.[22] The substantive difference over policy concerned the Bomarc missiles and the Canadian refusal to arm these missiles with nuclear warheads in order to help safeguard the Arctic regions of entry to the North American continent. But the lack of responsiveness spread to other areas of policy, including economic policy. Since the principal decision-makers would not talk to each other, the tone of the relationship became cold and unproductive.

In a turnaround that was presaged by informal communication between the Kennedy Administration and the opposition Liberals, the relationship underwent a rapid and extraordinary change in tone with the fall of the Conservative government in 1963 and the assumption of power by Prime Minister Lester B. Pearson. Pearson's new, more international policy and Kennedy's liberalism seemed congruent. This cooperation appeared to continue under President Lyndon B. Johnson and Prime Minister Pearson, but eventually the pressures of Vietnam policy, the effort of Canada to distinguish its opposed policy, and the American counter-response led to a gradual downturn in relations. The advent of the first Trudeau government, subsequent relations with the Nixon Administration over the financial impact on Canada of the U.S. decision to leave the fixed–exchange rate regime, and the Nixon address to the joint session of Parliament, all tempered cooperation. The publication of the Canadian foreign policy review entitled "Foreign Policy for Canadians" symbolized a slow cooling of the relationship. The nadir of cooperation between the United States and Canada did not occur until the last Trudeau government announced its National Energy Policy.[23] This policy guaranteed that relations between the new Reagan administration and the last Trudeau government would be icy.

Undoubtedly, the next high point of cooperation was between the Mulroney government and the Reagan and George H.W. Bush administrations. Free trade, first in the form of the 1988 Canada-U.S. Free Trade Agreement and then in the form of NAFTA, signified close and strong ties. The capacity of the Mulroney government to extract the Acid Rain

Abatement treaty from a reluctant Bush administration was a measure of the leverage Canada had obtained in Washington. But the warning bells were ringing in Canada. Mulroney was perceived to be too close to the United States.[24] By 1993, only 18 percent of Canadian respondents supported Mulroney for reelection. Kim Campbell, Mulroney's appointed successor, could not reverse the anti-conservative trend of Canadian opinion. Jean Chrétien and the Liberals won in 1993 by promising Canadians a new, "less cozy" relationship with the United States.[25]

Relations did not immediately sour. Even though the degree of cooperation between Washington and Ottawa witnessed in the previous decade did not recur, the behind-the-scenes relations between Chrétien and Clinton were warm. A measure of the kind of foreign policy cooperation that was possible was indexed by the coordinated efforts of the Canadian and U.S. air forces in Kosovo.[26] On the other hand, Foreign Minister Lloyd Axworthy's "human security policy" portended divergence in foreign affairs and was meant to do so. Not just the 1994 U.S. Helms-Burton legislation on Cuba, but the 1997 anti-personnel land mines treaty (known as the Ottawa treaty) and other initiatives, such as the Kyoto protocol or the economic front, spattered by disputes on softwood, steel, wheat, or beef, reflected increasing divergence between different aspects of each country's foreign policies. From the U.S. perspective, the problem was not as much that human security diverged a lot from other kinds of security (witness the ultimate justification of the Iraq intervention), but the deep suspicion that Canada was using rhetoric to cover up irresponsible neglect, a quite cynical neglect of its actual security and peacekeeping capability, a topic Andrew Richter and Kimberly Marten have covered in their chapters in this volume.[27] The Americans well knew how much material capability (or how little) Canada possessed to put peacekeepers on the ground.[28]

The nadir of cooperation occurred in the Chrétien-George W. Bush years. Many indicators both on the domestic and foreign side indicated that the relationship had cooled immensely. The pre-9/11 advent of Mexico as an important rival for attention in Washington exacerbated the problems for Canada. But in 2003 virtually nothing could be accomplished jointly.[29] The U.S.-led intervention in Iraq, the Canadian decision to say no, the increasingly warm relations between Paris and Ottawa, and anti–Bush administration remarks by Chrétien government officials—all spelled trouble. Once again, intra-party politics and elections were relied upon as the vehicles to solve foreign policy problems that policy divergence domestically and in foreign affairs had created for the Canada-U.S. relationship.

In sum, causation on this cycle moves from policy (interchangeably domestic or foreign depending upon situation and time) to degree of cooperation. The primary direction of causation is either divergence, in which the prospect of less cooperation between the United States and Canada is in the offing, or convergence, in which the prospect of cooperation increases. Existence of either divergence or convergence presupposes that attitudes and behaviors exist to reinforce that divergence or convergence on each side of the border.

The bigger actor, the United States, possesses more inertia and more momentum in its policy than the smaller actor, Canada. Canada also is capable of changing its policy much more quickly than the United States. Three reasons explain this greater flexibility. First, the prime ministership centralizes policy authority more than does the presidency and hence Canada can act more quickly than the United States on issues if Canada wants to do so. Second, the U.S. Congress is a much more independent force in foreign policy matters than is the Canadian House of Commons. Third, the United States because of its relatively greater power has more of an impact on multilateral relations than does Canada. The U.S.-Canada foreign policy cycle contains elements of asymmetry that ought to be kept in mind when the cycle is being interpreted.

Clearly the impact of foreign policy on domestic policy, and vice-versa, in each country is an important part of the larger puzzle regarding episodic change in the tone and quality of Canada-U.S. relations. But this impact of foreign policy on domestic policy (or its opposite) is not merely a matter of isolating a few variables and testing them in a statistical model. A behavioral pattern exists in the relationship between the foreign and domestic spheres that must be captured at the theoretical level if this analysis is to hold the proper interpretive value for bilateral relations in North America.

THE USE OF FOREIGN POLICY FOR DOMESTIC PURPOSE AND ITS CONSEQUENCE

The third explanation for periodic downturn in Canada-U.S. relations focuses on the propensity to use foreign policy for domestic purpose and the result that foreign policy interests become hostage to domestic needs, thus aggravating relations with other governments. Although this propensity is characteristic of contemporary Canada, it is not limited to Canada. In the aftermath of the Cold War, all of the democracies seem to be getting into the habit of mortgaging their foreign policies for some alleged domestic political benefit. Thus where this approach to politics will lead, how it will affect the democratic peace if at all, and whether the trend will worsen the capacity of the democracies to coordinate their policies to some useful end is worth some speculation.

What is the ethos of this particular explanation for the periodic worsening of Canada-U.S. relations? The ethos is that foreign policy can be used to solve domestic political problems. But when foreign policy is used in this way, it tends to worsen foreign policy relations with other governments because their interests and their concerns have been sacrificed to the furthering of one state's domestic political objectives. Whether the domestic political aims are achieved through this application of foreign policy for domestic purpose is beside the point. The government so employing foreign policy thinks that its domestic political objectives will be furthered. Although seldom admitting this trade-off of foreign for domestic political advantage, the government in its own thinking claims that it has no choice. Its domestic political imperatives are too important.[30] In reality, it is saying that it can get away with sacrificing its foreign policy objectives to its domestic political purpose because it thinks it will not have to pay much of a price for its actions in international terms. In short, it believes that by using foreign policy for domestic purpose, it will not pay a high price in the foreign realm for its actions and at home it will be able to obtain tangible gains politically.

A recent example will perhaps illustrate how foreign policy for domestic purpose works. The Chrétien government carefully listened to the arguments the George W. Bush and the Tony Blair governments made regarding the necessity of intervening militarily in Iraq. The latter governments offered three justifications: (1) possession of weapons of mass destruction that after 9/11 have demonstrated their terror potential;[31] (2) Saddam Hussein's possible possession of a nuclear weapon to raise the stakes in any future struggle over disruption of oil markets; and (3) the potential for Iraq with outside help to become a democracy and thereby bring the Arab world closer toward political modernity with all the implications this might bear for enhanced peace in the Middle East. Prophetically, Prime Minister Chrétien expressed doubt on television that Hussein possessed weapons of mass destruction. In the end, with the Canadian public mostly against war in Iraq, Ottawa's condition for joining the anti-Saddam coalition was that the U.N. Security Council had to support intervention (see Marc O'Reilly's chapter in this volume).

U.S. Secretary of State Colin Powell indicated, however, that a number of governments, often in defiance of public opinion in their own countries, supported the intervention, including Spain, Italy, Poland, Australia, South Korea, and quite a number of others. Facing a defection on the part of several prominent European countries, and a tough choice regarding whether he favored the European Union (read Germany) or the Atlantic Alliance (read the United States), President Chirac predictably chose the former, "upping the ante" for all remaining members of the alliance, especially Canada. To join the vociferous anti-intervention coalition composed of France, Germany, Russia, and others meant that Canada would openly be obliged to break on this issue with its two great alliance partners, Britain and the United States. It could do this quietly and with seeming hesitation or assertively, even boisterously. Canada chose the latter route, as the television coverage of the prime minister's speech, and the joyous applause of Liberal Party Members of Parliament, made clear to anyone interested south of the border.

The government of Canada justified its position not to support Britain and the United States chiefly on the basis of domestic political opinion; troops were not at issue, as was known, since Canada had virtually no additional peacekeepers available. But, of course, this was not a sufficient reason in the eyes of Blair and Bush since each faced very large factions of their own publics opposed to military intervention in Iraq. Former U.S. Secretary of State Henry Kissinger even mischievously pointed out that, in the 1930s, British Prime Minister Neville Chamberlain had 80 percent backing on appeasement as well. In the Canadian case, however, one further domestic political reason was found to be compelling. A large majority of francophone Québécois, like the governments of France and Germany, vehemently opposed the intervention.[32] By this time, the clash inside the Atlantic Alliance and inside the EU had all but overshadowed the original issue regarding whether the Iraq intervention itself was justified, strategically or politically.

No clearer example of the use of a foreign policy issue for domestic ends could have been imagined than this. Opposition to U.S. foreign policy was very popular in Québec. Ottawa was seen to have acted in the interest of all Canadians. Internal Québec politics were involved. The very public rebuke to Britain and the United States, and the subsequent highly cordial interaction with France, Germany, and Russia, highlighted the multilateral character of Canadian foreign policy, all of which was well understood in Québec. With the possible exception of the Canada-U.S. free trade debate in 1988, not since the much quieter recalcitrance of Prime Minister Mackenzie King in the face of British overtures to Canada to instate conscription during World War II was foreign policy used with such skill to demonstrate solidarity with political preference in Québec.[33]

The unofficial U.S. view was that Prime Minister Chrétien did not try hard enough to sway public opinion in favor of the Anglo-American position.[34] These spokesmen grumbled about a lack of leadership. In fairness to political reality, however, the United States too wanted Canadian unity.[35] The difference of viewpoint came down to this: the American judgment was that matters could have been handled differently in Ottawa if perhaps with the same ultimate result. In politics, process is as important as outcome. There seems little doubt that this latter judgment is correct regarding the salience of process. It has been understood to be so, by subsequent Canadian government strategists and advisors. But the reason process was not at the time taken into account was that, to extract the ultimate political benefit of siding with France, Russia, and Germany and of opposing the United States, Britain, and Australia, Ottawa had to be seen in Québec (and indeed elsewhere in Canada) as having acted emphatically.

With respect to the larger matter of whether this source of foreign policy difficulty is important, based on the propensity to ignore foreign policy costs and to attempt to exploit domestic political (often electoral) advantage, the answer must be in the affirmative. Indeed, the prospect is that foreign policy for domestic purpose will be used again and again with the same kind of enervating impact on the quality of relations among the democracies. For Canada and the United States, this forecast is even more worrisome, because the stakes are so high in the bilateral relationship and because the political, geographic, and economic proximity is so close. Should the United States begin to employ the same technique, with the same enthusiasm and decorum, the effect could be consequential. Many applications exist. It is easy to use foreign policy for domestic purpose when the technique can be assumed to be cost-free in terms of foreign policy. But what must be concluded is this: if the democracies continue to assume, not only that economics trumps security, but that domestic politics trumps security, the twenty-first century promises to become quite a turbulent epoch of statecraft indeed.

CONCLUSION

This chapter began with a simple question. Why does the quality of Canada-U.S. relations periodically experience a serious downturn? The answer provided is threefold. First, the familiar argument in policy circles was examined, namely, that the prime minister and president do not get along. This explanation subdivided into two variants, with the former stressing the problem of personality conflict between the principal decision-makers, the latter stressing different ideologies and party orientations on each side of the border. Basically, Canadians anticipate discord (without consistent historical evidence) when the Republicans are in office, especially when their own Liberal Party is in office at the same time. The worst problem emerges when each of these variants of the argument reinforces the other: when the top policy-makers dislike each other personally; when the ideologies of the governments are at odds; and when a governing Republican Party faces a governing Liberal Party on a host of tough foreign policy issues.

A second explanation for episodic foreign policy irritation is dynamic. Canada-U.S. relations go through a cycle of good times and bad. What seems to drive this cycle of cooperation—or lack thereof—is divergence and convergence on policy issues, both domestic and foreign. Assumed is that the origin of these issues is for the most part exogenous to the bilateral relationship per se between the governments. That means divergence or convergence emerges either from external shocks in multilateral international politics, or it stems from internal societal preferences and party politics. Complete convergence or complete divergence on the bilateral agenda probably never occurs. But, in general, convergence facilitates cooperation, and, in general, divergence reduces the level of cooperation. At some level of diminished cooperation Canada-U.S. relations show signs of distress. No determinism exists in this dynamic. Only in the widest strategic terms, and in the broader stretches of history, does the cyclical process repeat itself.

Thirdly, distress emerges in the relationship between the United States and Canada when one or other government attempts to use foreign affairs for domestic political purpose, thus sacrificing the quality of the external relationship for internal ends. Although this internal temptation is exemplified in Canada-U.S. relations, the temptation is common throughout the democratic world in the aftermath of the Cold War. The discipline imposed on the democracies by the Cold War is gone.[36] Internal political priorities loom as more important to electorates than security issues. Governments are tempted to sacrifice foreign policy matters to the ever-present imperative of reelection and the issues that seem to figure most decisively in winning those elections.

Another way of looking at this propensity to sacrifice foreign policy coordination for domestic ends is the widespread presupposition that security is taken care of and therefore more attention can be shifted to domestic issues. Although preponderant but not dictatorial, the United States is considered to be the watchdog that does and should give primary attention to security. The other democracies become free riders in such a situation, though not passive free riders, since they would like to determine the rules whereby the United States exercises its resources and makes its security decisions. Once again, for most democracies today, this situation results when a substitution of resources has occurred from the foreign field to the domestic. Under such circumstances, bad feeling thereby arises in many bilateral relationships, including between Canada and the United States.[37]

None of these explanations for the episodic re-emergence of bad feeling in the Canada-U.S. relationship is complete. Together, they provide a matrix of explanation that pushes understanding a bit deeper. The foreign policy cycle explanation is both encompassing and dynamic, but policy analysts are surely correct that the nature of personal interaction and the ideological and party orientations of each government figure strongly in the dialogue. Together these explanations avoid oversimplification in terms of personality. An old realist saying is that governments must learn to deal with other governments they do not like if peace is to be preserved and the imperatives of interest and capability are to be acted upon.

Perhaps the most rapidly increasing source of disagreement is the temptation to substitute domestic political priority for foreign policy priority, especially involving matters of security. When combined with the other sources of disorder in Canada-U.S. relations, this temptation is quite troubling.

In response to the question of whether the Canadian and U.S. governments will learn from their past mistakes and modify their behavior so as to smooth out the foreign policy cycle, the Lockean argument contends that such learning can and will take place. The Hobbesian argument insists, however, that each new generation of policy-makers must relearn the fundamentals of one of the most prized intergovernmental relationships in the contemporary world. Given recent events involving Canada-U.S. relations, the latter is likely to apply.[38]

NOTES

1. John E. Reilly, *American Public Opinion and U.S. Foreign Policy* (Chicago: Chicago Council on Foreign Relations, 1999).

2. Michael Doyle, "Liberalism and World Politics," *American Political Science Review* 80, no. 4 (December 1986): 1151–1169; Bruce Russett, *Grasping the Democratic Peace: Principles for a Post–Cold War World* (Princeton: Princeton University Press, 1993).

3. The tone in Canada-U.S. relations can change rather quickly. In 2003, only a few years after a top commentator on the relationship noted its calmness, Ottawa and Washington were barely talking to each other. See Joseph T. Jockel, "Canada and the United States: Still Calm in the Remarkable Relationship," in *Canada Among Nations 1996: Big Enough To Be Heard*, ed. Fen Osler Hampson and Maureen Appel Molot (Ottawa: Carleton University Press), 111–131.

4. Robert O. Keohane and Joseph S. Nye, *Power and Interdependence: World Politics in Transition* (Boston: Little, Brown, 1977).

5. Joseph S. Nye, "Transnational Relations and Interstate Conflicts," in *Canada and the United States: Transnational and Transgovernmental Relations*, ed. A.B. Fox et al. (New York: Columbia University Press, 1976), 367–402.

6. In fairness, later commentators have taken these cryptic words out of their original context. In the original formulation, the phrase meant that Canada and the United States could not allow anxiety about interference with commerce to prevent steps toward bolstering threats against security. As the U.S. government surely knows, both increased security and improved commerce are possible, simultaneously, with the correct application of resources and technology. See, for example, the argument in John J. Mearsheimer, *The Tragedy of Great Power Politics* (New York: W. W. Norton & Company, 2001).

7. Joel Sokolsky, "Realism Canadian Style: The Chrétien Legacy in Foreign and Defense Policy and the Lessons for Canada-U.S. Relations" (lecture given at the Woodrow Wilson International Center for Scholars, Washington, DC, January 15, 2004).

8. Fen Osler Hampson and Maureen Appel Molot raise the question whether issue linkage will now replace the traditional issue-by-issue diplomacy "Does the 49th Parallel Matter Any More," in *Canada Among Nations 2000: Vanishing Borders*, ed. Fen Osler Hampson and Maureen Appel Molot (Oxford: Oxford University Press, 2000), 1–23, 20. Were this switch to occur (which I doubt), Canada would be the decided loser. See my *Forgotten Partnership: U.S.-Canada Relations Today* (Baltimore: Johns Hopkins University Press, 1984), 66–69, for the reasons. What occurs in bad times is not issue linkage per se, but a drawing down of the reservoir of goodwill that is used generally to expedite bargaining in the relationship, especially on the U.S. side.

9. Discussion of Canada-U.S. relations between Ambassador Gotlieb and Charles Doran on *The News Hour with Jim Lehrer*, aired on PBS, 12 December, 2003. This argument of personality conflict as central is shared by Martin Lubin, "Strains between Governments at the Top, Hands across the Border at the Base," *Canadian-American Public Policy*, no. 54 (September 2003): 22–23.

10. On the relationship, see Knowlton Nash, *Kennedy and Diefenbaker: Fear and Loathing across the Undefended Border* (Toronto: McClelland & Stewart, 1990).

11. Two estimable treatments of Canadian foreign policy written from somewhat different ideological perspectives illustrate the sensitivity in Ottawa to this value dimension. Andrew F. Cooper, *Canadian Foreign Policy: Old Habits and New Directions* (Scarborough, ON: Prentice-Hall, 1997); Kim Richard Nossal, *The Politics of Canadian Foreign Policy*, 3rd ed. (Scarborough, ON.: Prentice-Hall, 1997).

12. Progress in the resolution of the softwood lumber talks is a case in point. Greg Anderson, "The Compromise of Embedded Liberalism, American Trade Remedy Law, and Canadian Softwood Lumber: Can't We All Just Get Along?" *Canadian Foreign Policy* 10, no. 2 (Winter 2003): 87–108; Charles F. Doran and Timothy J. Naftali, *U.S.-Canadian Softwood Lumber: Trade Dispute Negotiations*, Foreign Policy Institute Case Studies, no. 8, Georgetown University, 1987.

13. Michael Hart, *A Trading Nation: Canadian Trade Policy from Colonialism to Globalization* (Vancouver: University of British Columbia Press, 2002), 217.

14. Tony Blair, "Speech Delivered at King's College, London," 5 December 2001.

15. The Canada-U.S. foreign policy cycle is not to be confused with other social

scientific cycles such as the economic business cycle, or the state cycle of power and role. For an extensive discussion of the latter and its applications to contemporary international relations, see Charles F. Doran, ed., "Power Cycle Theory and Global Politics," *International Political Science Review* 24, no. 1 (January 2003).

16. When policies such as those in health care really are separate because separately conceived and administered, and therefore not formally interdependent, divergence and convergence in North America are not so problematic regarding foreign policy cooperation. See Antonia Maioni, "Divergent Pasts, Converging Futures? The Politics of Health Care Reform in Canada and the United States," *Canadian-American Public Policy*, no. 18 (1994): 1–34. Even though processes in each country seem to be moving in the same direction—say toward convergence—the underlying dynamic of convergence is virtually self-contained within the polity. But where interdependence strongly exists, such as in U.S. and Canadian monetary policy, with mutual flows of money crossing the border, divergence and convergence are not only reciprocal, but most of the pushing may come from one side, such as from the actor that is many times larger.

17. For analysis that emphasizes the elements of convergence, see John Kirton, "Promoting Plurilateral Partnership: Managing United States–Canada Relations in the Post–Cold War World," *American Review of Canadian Studies* 24, no. 4 (Winter 1994): 453–472. For analysis that stresses the elements of divergence see John Herd Thompson, "Playing by the Washington Rules: The U.S.-Canada Relationship, 1994–2003," *American Review of Canadian Studies* 33, no. 1 (Spring 2003): 5–26.

18. Robert A. Pastor, "North America's Second Decade," *Foreign Affairs* 83, no. 1 (January/February 2004): 124–135; Thomas D. Aquino, "Reinvent the Border," *Financial Post*, 17 January 2003; Wendy Dobson, *Shaping the Future of the North American Economic Space: A Framework for Action*, C. D. Howe Institute Commentary 162 (April 2002); Leonard Waverman, "Post-NAFTA: Can the United States, Canada, and Mexico Deepen Their Economic Relationship?" in *Beyond Mexico*, ed. Jean Daudelin and Edgar J. Dosman (Ottawa: Carleton University Press and Canadian Foundation for the Americas, 1995), 55–79.

19. Alistair D. Edgar, "Growth Pains or Growing Strains? The Limits of Neighbourliness and the Politicization of Canada-U.S. Defense Industry Integration," *Canadian Foreign Policy* 8, no. 2 (Winter 2001): 1–22.

20. Alan Toulin, "Canada Won't Buckle to Kyoto Pressure: Minister," *Financial Post*, March 30, 2002, 8.

21. Jeffrey G. Reitz and Raymond Breton, *The Illusion of Difference: Realities of Ethnicity in Canada and the United States* (Toronto: C. D. Howe Institute, 1994);

J. L. Granatstein, *Yankee Go Home? Canadians and Anti-Americanism* (Toronto: HarperCollins, 1996).

22. Lawrence Martin, *The Diefenbaker-Kennedy Schism, The Presidents and Prime Ministers: Washington and Ottawa Face to Face: The Myth of Bilateral Bliss 1867–1982* (Toronto: Doubleday Canada, 1982), 181–211.

23. For a contrast in energy policy, see Joseph M. Dukert, "The Evolution of the North American Energy Market: Implications of Continentalization for a Strategic Sector of the Canadian Economy," *American Review of Canadian Studies* 30, no. 3 (2000): 349–359.

24. D. K. Alper, "Trans-boundary Environmental Relations in British Columbia and the Pacific Northwest," *American Review of Canadian Studies* 27, no. 3 (Autumn 1997): 359–383; J. E. Carroll, *Environmental Diplomacy: An Examination and a Prospective of Canadian-U.S. Transboundary Environmental Relations* (Ann Arbor: University of Michigan Press, 1983).

25. The foreign policy section of the Liberals' platform, the so-called Red Book, has been written under the influence of Lloyd Axworthy and clearly referred to the distance Canada should put between 24 Sussex Drive and 1600 Pennsylvania Avenue.

26. Dwight Mason, "The Future of Canada-U.S. Defense Relations," *American Journal of Canadian Studies* 33, no. 1 (Spring 2003): 63–91; Danford W. Middlemiss and Denis Stairs, *The Canadian Forces and the Doctrine of Interoperability: The Issues, Policy Matters* (Montreal: Institute for Research on Public Policy, April 2002); Stéphane Roussel, "Fortress North America," in *Fortress North America? What Continental Security Means for Canada*, ed. David Rudd and Nicholas Furneaux (Toronto: The Canadian Institute of Strategic Studies, 2002), 13–14.

27. See also Fen Osler Hampson and Dean F. Oliver, "Pulpit Diplomacy: A Critical Assessment of the Axworthy Doctrine," *International Journal* 53, no. 3 (Summer 1998): 379–407; Anthony DePalma, *Here: A Biography of the New American Continent* (New York: Public Affairs, 2000); Earl Fry, "An Assessment of the U.S. Contribution to Global Human Security," in *Canada Among Nations 2001: The Axworthy Legacy*, eds. Fen Osler Hampson, Normal Hillmer, and Maureen Appel Molot (Oxford: Oxford University Press, 2001), 108–127.

28. Kim Richard Nossal, "Pinchpenny Diplomacy: The Decline of Good International Citizenship in Canadian Foreign Policy," *International Journal* 54, no.1 (Winter 1998–99): 88–105.

29. Maxwell Cameron and Brian Tomlin, *The Making of NAFTA: How the Deal Was Done* (Ithaca, NY: Cornell University Press, 2000). For a discussion of these new complexities from the commercial side, see Isabel Studer-Noguez, *Ford and the Global Strategies of Multinationals: The North American Auto Industry* (New York: Routledge, 2002).

30. For a sensitive analysis of how Canadian domestic politics and U.S. relations have become intermingled, see Christopher Sands, "How Canada Policy Is Made in the U.S.," in *Canada Among Nations 2000: Vanishing Borders*, ed. Maureen Appel Molot and Fen Osler Hampson (Oxford: Oxford University Press, 2000), 66.

31. Thomas Homer-Dixon, "The Rise of Complex Terrorism," *Foreign Policy*, no. 128 (January-February 2002): 52–62.

32. Anne Legaré, *Le Quebec otage de ses alliés* (Montréal: VLB, 2003); Louis Balthazar, Louis Bélanger, Gordon Mace, *Trente ans de politique extérieure du Québec 1960–1990* (Sillery, Québec: Septentrion et Centre québécois de relations internationales, 1993).

33. David Haglund, 'The North Atlantic Triangle Revisited: Canadian Grand Strategy at Century's End," *Contemporary Affairs* no. 4 (Toronto: Irwin Publishing with Canadian Institute of International Affairs, 2000).

34. More than 70 percent of the Canadian respondents to a poll thought that Canada should join the United States and should declare war on terrorism, thus indicating a strong underlying communality with the United States. Ipsos-Reid poll, 17–20 September 2001, published in *Globe and Mail* (Toronto), 22 September 2001.

35. Charles F. Doran, *Why Canadian Unity Matters and Why Americans Care: Democratic Pluralism at Risk* (Toronto: University of Toronto Press, 2001). It is interesting to contrast three reviews of my book: Stephen Clarkson, "An American de Tocqueville in Canada: Why Quebec Separation Would Really, Really Matter," *LRC: Literary Review of Canada* (September 2002):12–13; Alfred O. Hero Jr., *American Review of Canadian Studies* 33, no. 2 (June 2003): 273–277; Alan Bowker, *Bout de Papier* 19, no. 4: 23–25.

36. Hence, the issue of governance, especially in trade matters, becomes more central. Louis Belanger, Erick Duchesne, and Jonathan Paquin, "Foreign Interventions and Secessionist Movements: The Democratic Factor," *Canadian Journal of Political Science* 38, no. 2 (June 2005): 435–462; Louis W. Pauly, *Who Elected the Bankers? Surveillance and Control in the World Economy* (Ithaca, NY: Cornell University Press, 1997); Denis Stairs, "Liberalism and the Triumph of Efficiency in Canada-U.S. Relations," *ISUMA* 1, no. 1 (Spring 2000): 11–16.

37. Robert Bothwell, *Canada and the United States: The Politics of Partnership* (Toronto: Twayne Publishers, 1992).

38. For an excellent guide through the conceptual landscape of these distinctions, see Patrick James, *International Relations and Scientific Progress: Structural Realism Reconsidered* (Columbus: Ohio State University Press, 2002).

IV
EXTERNAL VIEWPOINTS INTO CANADA

17

Canada's Military Capability and Sovereignty at the Dawn of the New Century

THOMAS G. BARNES

War, like the imminence of hanging, marvelously concentrates the mind. In the immediate aftermath of 9/11 most of the usual—truly quotidian—pressing and shrill concerns between Canada and the United States faded into background noise: tensions induced by market volatility and economic slowdown, Western softwood lumber, split-issues of American magazines, etc. New issues arose to take their place, principally centering on common concerns about internal and external security, cross-border accessibility, immigration policy, military action against terrorist regimes and terrorist organizations, etc. Most of these in fact raise far less disagreement and dispute than the older issues, and that despite the fact that while Canada made an immediate and significant contribution to bringing down the Taliban in Afghanistan it withheld support for the war against Saddam Hussein's Iraq. The former was a contribution gratefully received by the United States. The latter, while a source of considerable disappointment and some anger in Washington, has had mostly a temporary and superficial effect on American-Canadian defense relations. However, the new concerns, especially those involving military operations overseas, have potentially large effects on national sovereignty—not merely on Canadian sovereignty but also on American sovereignty.

The immediate impact of the alarums and excursions following 9/11

411

was to redirect Canadian Government attention to defense and Canadians' thoughts toward defining and maintaining Canadian sovereignty in the face of new threats. Both concerns are, of course, intimately, particularly, and just short of singularly connected with the United States. The complete defense of both countries depends on the other's commitment. While the United States provides Canada with its macro-defense directed against the threat of major external powers, Canada provides the United States with the micro-defense of perimeter security, which in the age of terrorism has taken on an importance without parallel in American history.

Canada's newfound interest in the protection of its sovereignty in the face of a violent threat is a good thing. For three decades Canadians concerned about Canada's national integrity have defined sovereignty almost entirely in cultural terms. The only concrete exception has been territorial integrity. From Prime Minister Mulroney's memorable declaration in the aftermath of the transit of a U.S. Coast Guard cutter through the Northwest Passage in 1985 that the Passage belonged to Canada, "lock, stock, and iceberg," through the continuing quietly tenacious dispute over Dixon Entrance between British Columbia and the Alaska panhandle, the International Court of Justice settlement of the boundary in the Gulf of Maine in 1984, to the microscopic-to-modest summer Canadian Armed Forces' "Narwhal" exercises in the Arctic since 2002 is a reminder of how determined Canada is about its territorial sovereignty.[1] If culture defined sovereignty, Québec would have been sovereign long ago. So too would thirteen Southern states one and one-half centuries ago. Sovereignty is simply a state construct, founded upon the internal cohesion of a people centered in governing institutions and recognized either *de jure* or *de facto* by other sovereign states. Both the concept and the reality of sovereignty are products of the New Monarchies of the fifteenth–sixteenth centuries, given final form and dynamic by the "First and Second World Wars," alternately hot and cold, fought between 1494 and 1648, involving at one time or another all of the new European states and their growing empires.[2] The sure, clear, unarguable attribute of sovereignty was military capacity, the ability to project power in order to protect the state's vital interests rather than merely to acquire and hold territory. The successor states to the empires of the early modern New Monarchies—including the United States of America and ultimately British North America joined together as

Canada—were no less than the European imperial powers bound to the criterion of military capacity to project power as the necessary attribute of sovereignty: not because they chose it to be, but because the foreign recognition that alone provides the cachet of sovereignty demanded it.

Admittedly, Canada did not achieve sovereignty as defined by military capacity until a half-century after its confederation and institutionalization as a nation state. Only in 1907 did Canada take responsibility for its own defense, and even then under British auspices providing heavy armament, staff, and doctrine.[3] Its navy dates from the acquisition of the two obsolete British cruisers, *Niobe* and *Rainbow*, in 1910. A real measure of field command autonomy came only with the appointment of Major General (shortly afterward promoted to Lieutenant General) Arthur Currie as the commander of the Canadian Corps in replacement of a British general on June 9, 1917, exactly two months after Canadians accomplished on Vimy Ridge what none had been able to do before and just short of Confederation's fiftieth anniversary.[4] No sooner the armistice—two minutes after the last Imperial soldier killed in action, Private George Lawrence Price of Port William, Nova Scotia, died at Ville-sur-Haine near Mons, 3 kilometres east of where the first Imperial soldier had been killed 23 August 1914[5]—the Canadian military evaporated. Between the wars, its entire Permanent Force numbered less than the number of Canadians killed in action in the fortnight it took four Canadian divisions to take Passchendaele Ridge, October–November 1917.

Canadians came away from those horrors with a new sense of nationhood and genuine nationalist sentiments and the muted satisfaction of the ultimate cliché that Canada's share of the 1931 Statute of Westminster recognizing the old dominions' *de jure* sovereignty had been bought by 60,000 Canadian dead. But Canada was still not capable of projecting force in its own national interests. Arguably, it never has been. Desmond Morton's recent survey of Canadian military history, *Understanding Canadian Defence*, is categorical about the dependence of Canada for its defense in the twentieth century, first on Britain and latterly the United States.[6] Before the meeting between Prime Minister William Lyon MacKenzie King and President Franklin Delano Roosevelt at Ogdensburg in August 1940 to deal with the Axis threat against North America, Canada's defense depended upon British power, particularly naval power, and America's relative benignity and isolationist predilections in the early twentieth century, and afterward on active American military might, land, sea, and air by the greatest armaments, strategic and tactical, in history. In essence, Canada served as an auxiliary-in-arms of Britain for a half-century, and of the United States for a half-century since.

When Canadian forces joined United States forces in Afghanistan in the winter of 2001, Desmond Morton asked whether or not there was a problem with the fact that

> future Canadian wars will be American wars. Armed forces as expressions of national sovereignty may well be obsolete. Canadian commanders have so little experience of independence that new generals get only a few months of high-level training. Canadian Forces now define themselves by U.S. standards. George W. Bush is not their commander-in-chief, but they are more likely to serve under his authority than Governor-General Adrienne Clarkson's.[7]

Armed forces as an expression of national sovereignty are only obsolete if you have no armed forces because (1) your sovereignty is protected by others, (2) you feel no obligation to assist in that protection, and (3) you do not aspire to a substantial role in international affairs. Canada does have armed forces, it has readily, repeatedly, and at times at great cost in the past century assisted in maintaining its own defense, and it has always aspired to a substantial—and not necessarily merely irenic—role in international affairs. The issue for Canada is not whether national sovereignty demands armed forces, but how much armed force, to what ends, and under what auspices is it required to assure Canada a place as a genuinely sovereign player among sovereign states.

The problem is that Canada has been attempting to maintain a power role—albeit a "middle power" role, whatever that means—for the past decade on the cheap. Its military presence in the North Atlantic Treaty Organization (NATO) is now negligible, primarily air and secondarily naval, and consequently its political and diplomatic influence in European defense slight. In the Balkans, in the 1990s, Canadian air components were mission-capable on a par with the United States Air Force, but it is not clear that that would be true now.

Continuously since the beginning of the First Gulf War the Canadian Navy has been doing extraordinarily well what it undertook at the outset of the Gulf War: controlling the Arabian Sea and adjacent waters to interdict hostile shipping, contraband, and terrorists. This it manages with small ships—frigates, destroyers, a supply ship—with one of the frigates since 1998 routinely integrated into a U.S. carrier battle group in the region.[8] And while Canada has not been among the "coalition of the willing" in the Iraq War, its naval role has gone on apace facilitating the closure of one dangerous entrance into the military theater.

In Afghanistan, Canadian ground forces proved willing but weak for want of numbers and adequate gear. They were too few because Canadian soldiers have been too long tied down in the Balkans to make more than very modest undertakings either for effective peacekeeping or combat. The 3rd battalion of the Princess Patricia's Canadian Light Infantry (3/PPCLI), of enlarged battalion-strength, was the largest unit that Canada could rotate into Afghanistan, and once out could not be replaced without placing an onerous burden on existing ground capacity.

Canadian commanders at Kandahar in 2002 were the first to admit the force's weaknesses.[9] It had to use U.S.-supplied Humvees because the Canadian equivalent (a woefully underpowered, unarmed, and less than reliable German vehicle a quarter-century old, the "Iltis") unlike every other military vehicle in theater was gas fueled, not diesel. A number of Canadian operations were canceled because of insufficient transport capacity, especially fixed-wing, and the Canadians were almost entirely dependent upon American choppers for rotary lift and entirely so for gunship helicopter support. Their most significant hardware contribution was the light armored vehicles, LAV III, of Lord Strathcona's Horse, a trackless vehicle of the sort the U.S. Army was still in early stages of adopting and which were not fully deployed (initially using Canadian-made vehicles) until Iraq.

While American commanders spoke glowingly of the Canadians' contribution, the 3/PPCLIs were relegated largely to perimeter control at Kandahar. In the four years since the defeat of the Taliban and containment of al-Qaeda, patrolling has continued to be the function of the Canadian army in and around Kabul. The last Canadian combat unit, latterly under NATO auspices, the famous 22nd Regiment from Quebec, rotated out of this duty in August 2004, leaving only some 700 troops and light vehicles for what is largely Afghan military training duties and a conventional peacekeeping role.[10] The Canadian army's routine field contribution was dedicated and soldierly in execution, meeting the highest standards. However, there was nothing particularly distinguished about it in part because the Canadian troops were neither numerous enough nor especially skilled to be tasked with major combat responsibilities. Canadian Special Operations Forces (about which not much has been or *should* be said) on the other hand were involved in some of the most demanding, dangerous, and important missions—including long-range sniping—so adding potency to the single most important combat element in the Afghan war.[11]

There is no disagreement about the current parlous shape of the Canadian military: Andrew Richter's contribution to this volume makes that clear and compelling. There is something approaching a consensus that whatever Canada does to restore and to reform its military, a principal objective must be to make it interoperable with American forces in all elements and functions, not least on the field of battle. This was the thrust of the Department of National Defence's top leadership in their strategic framework published in June 1999.[12] A collection of essays edited by David Haglund and published in 2000 established the framework for considering the issue and advanced eloquent arguments for furthering the process.[13]

A couple of observations on interoperability can be made from looking at the Afghan campaign. At the *operations* level, with a few glitches caused by disparities in gear, a high degree of interoperability in routine patrol and reconnaissance duties between Canadian and U.S. ground forces was achieved despite the decade which had intervened since those forces had served together in war. There appear to have been very few command problems, obviated by the subordination of the Canadian role, evidenced by the absence of a Canadian general officer in the operation's chain of command, being tacitly accepted by both forces. Interoperability was less evident at the level of *doctrine*. American commanders were not sure Canadian troops fully appreciated the way their American counterparts would fight. That translated into American lack of confidence in Canadian capabilities and consequent underutilization of Canadian troops. In great part that grew from the simple fact that American land-warfare doctrine has been undergoing rapid and radical change in the past decade, evident in the difference between operations in the Gulf War 1991 and the Iraq War 2003.[14]

For the future, there is one remedy for this, and a simple one at that. There should be many more student exchanges as well as faculty secondments between Canadian Land Force Command and Staff College, Kingston, and the U.S. Army Command and General Staff College, Fort Leavenworth. In fairly short order this would provide an almost seamless doctrinal fit at the critical level of field-grade officers—the majors, lieutenant colonels, and colonels who bear the brunt of command in the new, "lite" (less "salt" and "fat" and more "vinegar") warfare essayed in Afghanistan and perfected in Iraq. But that fit must be inculcated and tested by routine Canadian Land Forces–U.S. Army exercises at the three major American tactical training centers.[15] In Afghanistan, Canadian troops sensed that the Americans lacked faith in their abilities—the Canadian commanding officer, Lieutenant-Colonel Pat Stogran, noted that "We were an unfamiliar quantity to them that had gained a reputation as a peacekeeping army and nothing more."[16] Clearly, given the limited nature of the command's assignments to the Canadian forces, the skepticism about them never entirely disappeared, especially at the higher levels. More doctrinal integration and joint exercises would dispel that misapprehension and demonstrate the capacity and confidence of Canadian soldiers, as well as making them a better prepared and more effective fighting force.

Should Canada go so far along the road of interoperability that the Canadian military becomes wholly interdependent with the American military? Realistically, for all the talk of sovereignty, that interdependence is already clear and irrevocable. The 1994 White Paper on Defense, the last full review by a Canadian government of policy and purpose for the military, did not doubt the existence—or recoil from the extent—of that interdependency. After stating the existing arrangements under the heading "Bilateral Defence," it concluded:

> First, Canada-U.S. defense cooperation continues to serve this country's fundamental interests extremely well. Second, the Government wants the Canadian Forces to maintain the ability to work closely with their U.S. counterparts in a variety of situations. Third, even if the Government decided to reduce significantly the level of defence cooperation with the United States, Canada would still be obliged to rely on the U.S. for help in protecting its territory and approaches—and this assistance would then come on strictly American terms, unmitigated by the influence Canada enjoys as a result of its defence partnership with the United States and with

our other NATO allies. Finally, while some aspects of the relationship will remain largely unchanged, certain arrangements require updating.[17]

Canada simply did not then, and even more so does not now, have a military capable of any independent projection of force in defense of its national interests overseas against any enemy actual or potential. Stretched to its maximum, and far beyond its logistical capacity, especially in airlift (five squadrons), Canada is unable to undertake independent military combat operations—everyone deployed—at a level higher than two infantry brigades on land, four fighter squadrons and eight helicopter squadrons in the air, and four light naval task forces each consisting of one destroyer, three frigates, and a conventional submarine (when the navy finally manages to get the four "Victorias" on station) without adequate air protection or supply-lift assets and probably in fact limited to two task forces since HMCSS *Protecteur* and *Preserver* alone can provide long-distance support.[18] In 2002, projected defense expenditure for FY 2005/2006 was to be only three-quarters of $1 billion more than expenditures for FY 1994/1995.[19] In the 2003 budget, $1.6 billion in new funding was provided for the next two fiscal years with $800 million per annum for the (indeterminate) future.[20]

The new prime minister, Paul Martin, having been out of government for some time and not carrying Jean Chrétien's baggage, has gone even further in promising a full review of defense and sizable additional funds to pay for new support ships, a mobile gun system, new light vehicles (retiring the Iltis), and new helicopters to replace its aged Sea Kings; he has already begun delivering on the light vehicles and the helicopters.[21] Even with this welcome, albeit still modest, increase—the largest single increase in defense spending in a decade—Canada might still be near the bottom among its NATO allies in the defense allocation of its annual budget.[22] With present assets and a total personnel under 60,000, Canadian Forces provide the semblance of a military, but precious little of substance. It will take more bodies as well as much new gear to work a measurable improvement in Canadian Forces capabilities.

Denis Stairs and Dan Middlemiss at Dalhousie addressed the politics of Canada's "non-defense" predicament in a paper published in June 2002 by the Institute for Research on Public Policy. They concluded:

In summary, as their views are manifested in their politics, Canadians appear to want their country to be an active and contributive player in a wide variety of contexts around the world. On the other hand, they also appear reluctant to allocate the resources that are appropriate to that aspiration. The consequence, as interpreted thus far by a policy community that is attempting to respond to both these preferences, is uncomfortably clear: In order to play a significant role on the world stage, Canada has to get into bed with the United States. For some, this may be a sobering thought. Others may not mind at all. But whatever the reaction, surely no one should think that the process itself should proceed by stealth, or even by osmosis. It warrants a closer public look.[23]

Agreed. But no matter how closely Canadians look at the process, its outcome is ineluctable. As the authors point out, six decades of common defense necessity and increasing interdependence diplomatically and militarily in world affairs has dictated that there can be no divorce in that bed.

The fervent hope of a succession of Canadian politicians that Canada could somehow act as interlocutor between the United States and an emerging, increasingly unitary, European State has been washed out by German and French conviction that Canada and the U.S. are too interdependent in every endeavor to give Canada an identity distinctive enough for Europe to trust. A much more ambitious enterprise, with Canada acting in a global role to do good by almost prodigal treaty-making, came with Chrétien's second government.

From 1996 to his retirement from government in 2000, Lloyd Axworthy as minister of foreign affairs made the most strenuous attempt since Prime Minister Diefenbaker (1957–1963) to effect an obvious, even raucous, disengagement of Canadian foreign and defense policy from that of the United States. From the American perspective, "Axworthyism" was a quixotic attempt that succeeded primarily in providing European Yankee-bashers a frisson of pleasure at seeing division between Canada and the United States. American refusal to sign on to Axworthy's "touchy-feely" treaties, particularly those banning anti-personnel mines and establishing a permanent supranational tribunal for trial of war criminals with potentially pernicious consequences for the exercise of American military power, effectively thwarted these grand gestures. Axworthy has the strength of his convictions: his 2002 Keith Davey Lecture, entitled "Liberals at the Border: We Stand on Guard for Whom?" clearly identifies that the threat to all that is liberal, humane, and good comes from due South.[24]

Canada can neither afford nor does it have the stomach to cut a big swath in international security matters requiring major military operations, as Stairs and Middlemiss accepted. They also recognized that peacekeeping *as a career for Canada's military* has both outlived its usefulness in international security and is at least as well, if not better, done by a number of other nations which make no pretence to "middle power" status.[25] Indeed, a Canadian military that remains tantamount to being Mounties in battledress would continue to send the signal that Canada is a small, not a "middle," power in world affairs.

Perhaps Canada really is adrift in a violent world with a radically reduced mission to improve the prospects for peace growing from its relative powerlessness, not least that of its military. But the situation is grim only if Canadians are convinced of the malevolence, blind arrogance, and stupidity of the United States. To read Canadian polls over the past three or four decades, one might—wrongly—conclude that they are. Consistently, year after year, polls of the 1970s and 1980s, when the U.S.S.R. was alive and apparently well, showed that a solid majority of Canadians believed the United States was a greater threat to international security and peace than the Soviet Union. It was rather reassuring, because it was so conventional, to learn from a Toronto *Globe & Mail* poll in the summer of 2002 that 84 percent of Canadians think that the U.S. "because of its policies and actions bears some responsibility" for 9/11.[26] I am less reassured by the fact that then Prime Minister Jean Chrétien seemed to have been among them.[27]

The prime minister having shown the way, it is not surprising either that a poll of Canadian youth, aged 14–18, in June 2004 found 40 percent described the United States as being "evil."[28] However, the one advantage that an historian of Canada has in facing such an icy wash from "friends, neighbours, family" (as Chrétien described the relationship on Parliament Hill a day or so after 9/11) is the realization that this kinder, gentler people maintains in act if not always in rhetoric a much more balanced view of its relationship with the Meridional Monster than the ephemera of polls, "pols," and public intellectuals—especially in an election year—indicate. The rhetoric rises when Canadians feel marginalized in the ongoing political discourse centered south of the border, and then their frustration spawns an exasperation bordering on desperation that clouds realities and bars clear thinking.

That is what occurred in the long, tense, international contention over what should be done about Saddam Hussein and the threat posed by his possession of weapons of mass destruction, a threat generally accepted to be a reality by all nations and by the United Nations (U.N.) staff responsible for overseeing Iraq's disarmament pursuant to the 1991 armistice ending hostilities in the Gulf, coupled with Saddam's refusal to cooperate fully with U.N. investigation to determine whether he did have such weapons. Washington signaled clearly in September 2002 that if it perceived an "imminent" threat against the United States, it was prepared to take military action "preemptively" to neutralize the threat.[29]

The Bush administration was persuaded to seek final U.N. support for the enforcement of sanctions by action that conceivably would be military. After six months of intense continuous maneuvering that revealed clearly that Saddam would not cooperate with inspections and that a resolution in the U.N. Security Council to take military action against Iraq could not be secured principally because of French and Russian intransigence, the U.S. acted with a "coalition of the willing" including Britain on March 20, 2003.

After much ambiguity and more mixed-signaling on the part of the Chrétien government and without anything approaching a real debate, parliamentary or media, Canada decided not to join the coalition. Chrétien's recalcitrance had been presaged by a less than committed show of the old Canadian honest-broker-between-the-U.S.-and-Europe role at the end-stage of the U.N. Security Council negotiations, when Canada suggested giving the weapons inspectors another month before using military force even though it was clear that the U.N. would not under any circumstances act with military force against Iraq. The final decision by Chrétien not to join the coalition was made more by default than with conviction, and the manner of it was more reprehended by the United States than the result. Canadian public opinion was in fact considerably divided on whether or not to join the coalition, and there was no attempt to fashion a parliamentary consensus on the course of inaction taken, leaving the decision entirely to the prime minister.

The immediate effect was chilling on U.S.-Canadian relations for a season. The most significant impact, though, was the raising of Canadian fears that America's action without Canadian involvement robbed Canada of any role in what was the single most important international undertaking since the end of the Cold War. Whether Canadians approved or disapproved of the invasion of Iraq and the overthrow of Saddam, whether they thought it was a legitimate use of force or illegal under international law, whether they thought the results were or were not worth the costs and the risks, Canada and Canadians found themselves marginalized. They reacted accordingly, with more than usual expressions of anti-Americanism and anger at all U.S. policy, foreign and domestic.

One need not catalog the slights and injuries patriotic Canadians felt they had suffered at American hands in the events beginning on 9/11. Some, though, are illustrative of how Canada's sense of marginalization was able to fester. President George Bush's delay in rendering full acknowledgment to Canada for its immediate aid and assistance on 9/11 and in the weeks following, appearing indeed to have been warmer toward the help of others whose sympathy did not translate into extending hospitality to thousands of airline passengers prevented from landing in the United States, was a poor start.

The American friendly-fire incident in Afghanistan in April 2002 which killed four Canadian soldiers and wounded others may have been blown out of proportion, but it was real and it rankled, and increasingly the Canadian public with the press leading became obsessed with the question of how the two American pilots should be punished.[30] When the matter was finally disposed of without judicial action but only administrative punishment in summer 2004, the Canadian press reacted with almost universal outrage. A profound visceral hatred for George Bush, attacks on his advisors and cabinet members, including even the hitherto idolized Colin Powell, acceptance of the wildest of conspiracy theories, and the almost hysterically expressed fears that the United States was launched on a new imperialism or world hegemony became daily fare in letters-to-the-editor and on op/ed pages of Canadian papers. It lapped over into serious academic commentary: a collection of thirty-eight essays, entitled *Independence in an Age of Empire: Assessing Unilateralism and Multilateralism*, maintained balance only with difficulty, and some pieces verged on real animus.[31]

Polls in the summer of 2004 showed that three out of five Canadians would vote for John Kerry against George Bush if they had the vote.[32]

Indeed, a significant contribution to the new Liberal Prime Minister Paul Martin's quasi-success in the June 2004 general elections, by which his party managed to hold on to enough seats in Parliament to form a minority government, was furnished by the Liberals characterizing the leader of the Conservative opposition, Stephen Harper, as a clone of George Bush. John Kerry may have proven unable to beat Bush, but Paul Martin appeared to have managed to do so!

The more profound problem is that Canadians have not fully accepted, or cannot yet manage other than intellectually to understand, how 9/11 changed the individual American's view of the world and his place in it. The American feels vulnerable—it is not a figment of his imagination. He sees enemies both without and within his country—these are not phantoms. He understands that he is at war, and he knows that the war is going to be a hard one and a long one—his belief that he must win it or perish is not fantasy. He also knows that the war is worldwide—every news report demonstrates the fact every day. He knows that there are no "allies" in the comfortable, continuing, and amicable way of traditional nation-state relations among friends—there are only those otherwise decent well-disposed people(s), states, nations either prepared to help win this war or which would by passivity if not active animus impede his efforts to win it. The United States at war presents a fearsome predicament to everyone else. But that predicament is not going to go away, and it will only begin to lessen as victory becomes apparent and even palpable. In the meantime, one sympathizes with the discomfort of those who face the world's hyperpower bearing down on them proclaiming Lee Iaccoca's famous dictum, "Either lead, follow, or get out of the way."

What the United States at war does not pose is a genuine threat to national sovereignty so long as other sovereign nations do not pose a threat to the United States. This is not because the United States is particularly benign but because the United States more than any other nation today believes in the value of sovereignty in ordering international relations, with its corollary that supranational authorities impinging on national sovereignty are the primary threat to the political, social, and economic structures which the nation-states have created and maintained over the past half-millennium. Marginalization is the reflection of the crippling of sovereignty.

Healthy sovereign nations cannot be marginalized, however, because they are needed to maintain the ornate, almost architectonic, structure of sovereign nation-states which in its evolution and thanks to its continuous preservation often at enormous cost has resulted in a degree of human progress under humane institutions hitherto unattainable. This is decidedly *not* a post-Westphalian world. It is a larger, more numerously "nationed," and more complex, very-Westphalian world, under stress from a sudden large surge of pre-Westphalian tribal brigandage marching under a theo-ideological banner.

Non-nation terrorist threats are nothing new: the Barbary Pirates are only two centuries back, but antiquity also knew the type. Current terrorists achieve the definition of pirates under international law: "the enemies of the human race, and the most atrocious violators of the universal law of society."[33] It is in the immediate interest of all sovereign nation-states to deal with such threats and with those nation-states that support and maintain them or that become in essence terrorist regimes themselves. Kofi Annan's glowing encomium of the peculiar legitimacy of the United Nations is touching, but misfounded and potentially pernicious, for that conglomeration of nation-states attains no more legitimacy or exercises any more power than its institutionally strongest sovereign nation-states acting in their defense and maintenance of the "universal law of society."

How can Canada avoid marginalization? By bringing more assets to the table: the U.N. table, the NATO table, the Commonwealth table, and finally—most importantly—the North American table with which its fortunes are most inextricably tied and where its influence when exercised from the inside is the greatest. There is a "special relationship" between Canada and the United States of a sort, a strength, and an intimacy that exists between no other nation-states, not even Britain and the United States. This is solid foundation for the most intimate defense relationship even while Canada maintains autonomy to decide how far it wishes to support a particular American undertaking. Stairs and Middlemiss point out that "a fully funded interoperability arrangement might still leave Canadian decision-makers with at least some military options of their own because it would not deprive them of the capacity independently of their larger partner."[34]

Jack Granatstein made the sage observation: "Steadfast small allies are important. They inspire other small nations to do their part, and groups of allies can and do sway the decisions of their superpower leaders."[35] The threat of withdrawal of Canadian assets under that arrangement in pursuit of a policy to which Canada could not lend itself would have influence in American councils. Perhaps not determinative influence. Yet, just how uninfluential Canada was in American deliberations, because of its weakness at the point at which the United States made the decision to go to war against Saddam, is clear and cautionary.

An astute scholar of Canadian defense matters at the Royal Military College, Joel Sokolsky, has suggested that, given its limited resources, Canada should be highly selective in the projection of military force overseas, while still being "prepared to support and to contribute to American-led operations in the war on terrorism," not to purchase influence in Washington, but because "American unilateralism, however it might be dressed up as multilateralism, offers the best chance for victory in the war on terror and world order." Canada can most favorably impress American opinion, political and public, by

> Contributing to the security of the United States [and not least Canada] through its military and non-military efforts to secure the American homeland. A Canadian approach to national security and defence that has as its focus, in both policy and posture, the defence of the Canadian homeland—and by extension of North America—will best serve the vital interests of not only Canada but also the United States.[36]

This prescription Canada is following now.

Coastal surveillance to maintain perimeter control justifies greater expenditure on naval assets, perhaps even the expensive four ex-British conventional submarines of limited usefulness when at long last they go on station. Showing the flag in the Arctic to maintain Canadian "sovereignty" over its unique sectoral claim ending only at the North Pole also stands guard on a frontier (even if the gravest "threat" might be a U.S. Coast Guard cutter transiting the Northwest Passage). Increased air capacity is essential to covering the landmass—most of it environmentally hostile and remote—of the largest nation in the world. Continuing cooperation under NORAD for continental defense will reach its next step—and face its next test—with the deployment of ballistic missile defense in the immediate future. The necessary preliminary step for Canada to keep that option open was taken in August 2004, and the likelihood of Canada ultimately signing on to Strategic Defense Initiative is very strong, albeit the Canadian debate will be vigorous.[37]

NORAD was the original instrument of Canadian-American interoperability. It is the perfect example of "niche interoperability," though on such a grand scale that the specificity of its objective and the limitations of its function are easily overlooked. If Sokolsky's agenda was to be followed, much of the Canadian contribution to homeland defense would constitute "niche interoperability." Especially in those instances when Canada did project military force overseas in conjunction with American forces, it would almost inevitably be in a "niche" role, neither miniscule nor subservient but sufficient and autonomous in command, carefully targeted to achieve agreed-upon results.

Though interoperability per se enjoys consensus, "niche interoperability" is less than universally attractive among Canadian defense analysts. Stairs and Middlemiss are dismissive of Canadian Forces finding a niche role in interoperability. Perhaps they accept too readily the argument of Kenneth Calder, Canada's chief defense policy bureaucrat, that the difficulty of predicting exactly what niche would fit future needs makes this policy "very bad."[38] On the contrary. This is where attaining a high degree of interoperability in *doctrine* with both the larger resources and the doctrinally "bigger picture" of the American military would increase the accuracy of prediction, provide a singular if not unique role for Canadian forces, and strengthen the capacity of both countries to extend force in advancing national interests.

At sea, Canada has brilliantly exercised a "niche operation" since 1990. In Desert Shield/Desert Storm, 27 percent of all search stops in the Persian Gulf were effected by two Canadian destroyers and one supply ship. Canadian Maritime Force did the same thing on a much larger scale—with a Canadian flag officer in command of up to a score of allied (including U.S.) warships in the North Arabian Sea from October 2001 to November 2003, and Canadian ships made 600 of the 1,300 boardings of suspect vessels in those waters in support of the Afghanistan operation. This was only possible because of established "niche operability" experience between Canadian and American naval vessels.[39] Canada didn't need an aircraft carrier to cooperate interoperably—its frigates and destroyers and supply vessel, and the experienced men and women who sailed them, were all that was necessary. In Afghanistan, Canadian special operations forces were the elite of an elite which, predictably, the free world will need a lot more of and use more extensively for a very long time in the war on terror. Special operations forces require a few extraordinarily well-trained, versatile, and courageous soldiers deployed in supple organizations, not brigades, divisions, corps, or armies.

The new Martin government undertook in 2005 the first comprehensive look at defense objectives and policy since 1994. A close election and the minority status of Martin's Liberal government have made the undertaking onerous and argumentative because there is no consensus in Canada of what defense should do and how it should be undertaken. One way to measure the innovative and reforming impact of the new policy will be to see how far it is prepared to go with interoperability toward something more substantial than merely a "further look."[40]

If interoperability "warrants a further look" and increased implementation, niche interoperability warrants the closest attention. Canada's sovereignty was raised on the Canadian reputation for niche warfare—as shock troops at Paardeberg, Courcellette, Vimy, Passchendaele, Dieppe, Ortona, Caen, and Pusan, as sailors in small ships braving great and perilous seas on the North Atlantic, and as a third of the airmen of Bomber Command over flak alley into the Ruhr and beyond. No other "middle power" can claim such a tradition of courageousness, prowess, and achievement in battle. On that tradition really does rest the maintenance of Canada's sovereignty.

NOTES

1. *Conference on Canadian and United States Strategic Concerns in the Arctic*, Canadian Studies Program, UC Berkeley, 23–24 March 1999, 2; "The Question of Sovereignty," from *Independence and Internationalism*, ch.10, http://www.carc.org/pubs/v14no4/6.htm; Gerry Deiter, "Subs Allowed in Dixon Entrance," *Peace and Environment News*, Dec. 1991–Jan. 1992; *Case Concerning Delimitation of the Maritime Boundary in the Gulf of Maine Area*, International Court of Justice, Judgement 12 Oct. 1984 [www.dal.ca/~wwwlaw/kindred.intllaw/gulfofmaine.-htm]; Miriam Hill, "Operation Polar Bear," *Nunatsiaq News* 16 (August 2002); "Rangers Trek to Confirm Canada's Arctic Claim, *North.CBC.CA News*, 30 Mar 2004, north.cbc.ca/regional/ servlet/Print Story?filename = nun-sovereignty-ranger30032004&re . . .

2. Explored, but the fundamental question not settled, in Gene M. Lyons & Michael Mastanduno, eds., *Beyond Westphalia? State Sovereignty and International Intervention* (Baltimore: Johns Hopkins University Press, 1995).

3. J. L. Granatstein, *Canada's Army Waging War and Keeping the Peace* (Toronto: University of Toronto Press, 2002), 45–52.

4. A. M. J. Hyatt, *General Sir Arthur Currie: A Military Biography* (Toronto: University of Toronto Press/Canadian War Museum, 1987), 68–89.

5. Price was killed at 1058h, 11 Nov. 1918; Pte. J. Parr (4 Middlesex Regt.) KIA 1914 and Price are buried 40m apart in the CWGC Cemetery at St. Symphorien.

6. Desmond Morton, *Understanding Canadian Defence* (Toronto: Penguin/McGill Institute, 2003).

7. Desmond Morton, "Who Stands on Guard for Us?" *Globe and Mail* (Toronto), 31 December 2001.

8. "Op APPOLO, Canada's Military Contribution to the Internation Campaign Against Terrorism," http://www.navy.forces.gc.ca/mspa_operations/operations_e.asp?x=1&id=5.

9. Stephen Thorne on Afghanistan operation, *Halifax Chronicle Herald*, 20 July 2002.

10. Stephen Thorne, "Canadian Soldiers Frustrated," *CNEWS*, 12 August 2004 http://cnews.canoe.ca/CNEWS/Canada/2004/08/12/pf-579715.html.

11. A Canadian sniper made a record-setting kill at 2,430 meters—1.51 miles—with a Tac-50 rifle, with total Canadian kills unofficially set at 20. See Stephen Thorne, "Killing Shot Made at Distance of 2,430 Metres," www.snipercountry.com/Articles/KillingShot _2430Metres.asp; Stephen Thorne, "Crack Shots Prove Worth in Rugged Hills," *Windsor Star*, 19 March 2002, 12.

12. Department of National Defence, *Shaping the Future of Canadian Defence: A Strategy for 2020* (Ottawa: Department of National Defence, 1999).

13. David G. Haglund, ed., "Over Here and Over There: Canada-US Defence Cooperation in an Era of Interoperability," *Queen's Quarterly* (2001). Eleven essays by eleven scholars, and all to the point. See also Joseph Jockel, *The Canadian Forces: Hard Choices, Soft Power* (Toronto: Canadian Institute of Strategic Studies, 1999) and *The Canadian Forces and Interoperability: Panacea or Perdition?* (Halifax: Centre for Foreign Policy Studies, Dalhousie University, 2002).

14. The ultimate assessment of U.S. military doctrine before 9/11 is summarized in *Army Transformation Wargame 2001*, published by US Army TRADOC, that took place at the U.S. Army War College, 22–27 April 2001, http://www.tradoc.army.mil/tpubs/misc/ArmyTransformationBooklet.pdf. Canadian officers were involved in this war game. Afghanistan and Iraq have rendered it as obsolete as it had rendered doctrine obtaining in 1991.

15. Fort Irwin, California, National Training Center, armor desert warfare; Fort Chafee, Arkansas, Joint Readiness Training Center, joint training light forces; Fort Bragg, North Carolina, John F. Kennedy Special Warfare Center and School, special operations.

16. Stephen Thorne on Afghanistan operation, *Halifax Chronicle Herald*, 20 July 2002. In May 2004, Stogran, now a full colonel, took command of the Canadian Forces Operations Group, responsible for army/navy/air forces command and control expertise—the right man for the right job at the right time (thanks to Afghanistan).

17. Department of National Defence, *1994 Defence White Paper* (Ottawa: Department of National Defence, 1994), ch.5.

18. The four subs, Royal Navy "Upholder" class, were purchased from the British, and have had a troubled refitting, workup, and sea-trials history. Fundamentally obsolete for offensive operations, they are diesel-electric powered, anti-ship/anti-sub torpedo weaponed. It is hard to see what they add to Canada's defensive capacity, either at home or projected overseas. The sharpest criticism is from Scott Taylor, "Navy's Defence of Sub Program as Leaky as the Boats Are," *Halifax Chronicle-Herald*, 4 August 2003).

19. Department of National Defence, *Defence Planning & Management Financial Resources, FY02/03 Final* projected for 2005/2006 was $12.5 billion; 1995/1996 expenditure was $11.5 billion.

20. Department of National Defence, *Budget 2003—Building the Canada We Want*, http://www.forces.gc.ca/site/Reports/budget03/highlights03_e.htm.

21. The Iltis is rapidly being replaced by the Mercedes-Benz G Wagon (some with light armor kits), and in July 2004 the Government announced the purchase of 28 Sikorsky H-92 multi-mission helicopters—at a cost of $32 billion.

22. "First Among Allies," *New York Times*, 16 March 2002.

23. Danford W. Middlemiss and Denis Stairs, "The Canadian Forces and the Doctrine of Interoperability: The Issues," *Policy Matters* 3, no. 7 (Montréal: Institute for Research on Public Policy, 2002): 33.

24. Lloyd Axworthy, *Liberals at the Border: We Stand on Guard for Whom?* (Toronto: University of Toronto Press, 2004). His latest book, *Navigating a New World: Canada's Global Future* (Toronto: Vintage Books Canada, 2004), sets a course from comfortable though untenable Canadian "middle power" illusions to leading the world to embracing "global citizenship" without a military—not even Canadian peacekeepers—to protect it.

25. This point was made by the quintessential Canadian peacekeeper, Major General Lewis MacKenzie (ret.), in May 2002, "Our Departure from Bosnia is Long Overdue," *National Post* (Toronto), 21 May 2002.

26. Andrew Coyne, "Which Side Are We On?" *National Post*, 11 September 2002.

27. "PM slammed, defended for 9/11 remarks," *CBC News*, 13 September 2002, www.cbc.ca/stories/2002/09/12/pm_reax020912.

28. Arthur Weinreb, "Poll: Over 40% of Canadian Teens Think America is 'evil,'" *Canadafreepress.com—Politically Incorrect*, 30 June 2004, http://www

.torontofreepress.com/2004/weinreb063004.htm; "Teens See United States as Evil Global Force," *CanWest News Service*, 25 June 2004, http://www.canada.com/national/features/youthvote2004/story,html?id=26d.

29. President George W. Bush, *The National Security Strategy of the United States of America*, 20 September 2002, http://www.whitehouse.gov/nsc/print/nssall.html.

30. Between 18 April 2002 and 22 Jan 2003—from the incident to the preliminary criminal hearing for the two U.S. Air National Guard pilots charged—CBC radio and TV broadcast 93 segments totaling 7.66 hours, of which 63 (4.40 hours) were in the last three weeks of April 2002 alone. Only 8 segments were more than 10 minutes long. All but a few were interviews ranging from Canadian and American military to relatives of the casualties. See "Afghanistan: Friendly Fire," *CBC News*, http://www.cbc.ca/news/indepth/cdn-casualties/media.html.

31. Graham F. Walker, ed., *Independence in an Age of Empire: Assessing Unilateralism and Multilateralism* (Halifax: Centre for Foreign Policy Studies, Dalhousie University, 2004).

32. Canadian Ipsos-Reid Express poll, 27 June 2004, http://www.ipsos-na.com/new/pressrelease.cfm?id=2322.

33. James Kent, *Commentaries on American Law* 1 (New York: O. Halsted, 1826), 171–172.

34. Middlemiss and Stairs, "The Canadian Forces and the Doctrine of Interoperability," 30.

35. J. L. Granatstein, *Who Killed the Canadian Military?* (Toronto: Harper Flamingo Canada, 2004), 123.

36. Joel J. Sokolsky, "Realism Canadian Style: National Security Policy and the Chrétien Legacy, *Policy Matters* 5, no. 2 (Montréal: Institute for Research on Public Policy, 2004), 37–38.

37. Department of National Defence, "Canada and United States Amend NORAD Agreement," 5 Aug. 2004, http://www.forces.gc.ca/site/Newsroom/view_news_e.asp?id=1422. In March 2005, Martin declined further discussion without slamming the door on SDI.

38. Middlemiss and Stairs, "The Canadian Forces and the Doctrine of Interoperability," 33, quoting Calder. 2001.

39. Richard Gimblett, "The Navy's Marathon War on Terrorism," Department of National Defence, *Issues and Challenges*, 12 January 2004, http://www.navy.forces.gc.ca/mspa_news/news_issues_e.asp?category=2&title; "Canadian to Command Allied Warships in the Gulf," *CTV.ca*, 11 Feb. 2003, http://www.ctv.ca/servlet/ArticleNews/story/CTVNes/1044964458943_10.

40. The defense part of *A Role of Pride and Influence in the World* can be accessed at http://www.forces.gc.ca/site/reports/dps/main/toc_e.asp.

18

The Foundations of Canadian Foreign Policy: Federalism, Confederalism, International Law, and the Quebec Precedent

JAMES McHUGH

Quebec's search for an expression of its national identity continues to pose an irritation, if not an outright problem, for Canadian foreign policy. Although explicit attempts to gain recognition for the legal validity of claims to a unilateral right to self-determination appear to have been muted since the end of the 1990s, the desire to establish a more independent status within the international community continues to influence the tone, if not always the substance, of many aspects of Quebec's governmental policy, especially in the areas of trade and culture. Any lingering ambiguity regarding Quebec's sovereign status within Canada could contribute to continued difficulties (including potential embarrassments) in its foreign policy.

Therefore, the issue raised by the Supreme Court challenge of Quebec within the *Quebec Reference case* of 1998 regarding the legal authority of Quebec to withdraw from the Canadian federal union was a crucial one, not just domestically but, also, for Canadian foreign policy. It helped to establish more clearly the nature of Canada's sovereign union and the status of its provinces under international law, including the continued monopoly of the federal government in Ottawa regarding foreign policy and international institutions.[1] It also offers a potentially useful precedent for other international actors (especially the European Union) in addressing their own sovereign status, the implications for their respective component subunits, and the effect it could have upon their foreign relations and the international status of those subunits. Any claim to self-determination, based upon a unilateral right to withdraw from a federal union as part of a previously established sovereign identity (as Quebec claimed within the *Quebec Reference case*), presents potentially severe consequences for a federal state's foreign policy. Even if full sovereignty is not attained (as in a relationship such as "sovereignty association" would have represented), any attempt to claim an enhanced sovereign identity for the purpose of establishing the status of a "state" under international law, represents a difficulty quandary.

The authority to engage in foreign policy is one of the benchmarks of sovereign status under international law. The claim to a right of unilateral withdrawal also represents, indirectly, a further claim to this enhanced sovereign status. For example, member states of the European Union have delegated, by treaty, certain areas of sovereign authority to the union. However, these member states may withdraw from the union, unilaterally. Therefore, ultimate control over their sovereign status remains with them and, so, individual states may dissent from, and contradict, the consensus foreign policy of the European Union and engage in their own foreign policy, even at the potential expense of undermining the union.[2]

The Canadian union, however, has never tolerated (as Kim Nossal has emphatically noted) any such claim among its subunits, even when one province and/or its people have disagreed, strongly, with Canadian foreign policy.[3] However, as Vengroff and Rich demonstrate in their chapter, Canadian provinces (particularly Quebec) have asserted themselves abroad, including in the promotion of trade and culture but, also (in the case of Quebec), in terms of a more overtly political agenda regarding claims to enhanced sovereign status within Canada and the international community.[4] Therefore, the precise nature of Quebec's status within the Canadian federal system has implications beyond Canadian constitutional law, extending into international law and, subsequently, the status of Canadian foreign policy.

Sovereignty has been, and continues to be, a foundational principle of international politics and foreign policy. It also remains, especially under international law, one of the most difficult political principles to articulate.[5] The rise in popularity of various forms of shared sovereignty has exacerbated this ambiguity. Canada has assumed a potentially pivotal role in this ongoing international political and legal development. Canada's historically dominant preoccupation with sovereign relationships within its federal system and its struggles with Quebec over that province's sense of a distinct national identity have been a source of tremendous stress for Canadian society and its political system.[6] Different themes have arisen in terms of this relationship, including the internal struggle of a self-perceived "inferior colony," the desire for self-determination, and the strategy of seeking expression through formal international relationships.[7] These experiences have provided an internationally relevant model (especially as they apply to the difficult themes of sovereignty and self-determination) that will continue to be crucial to international politics throughout the twenty-first century. Therefore, the international political and legal precedents that Canada offers should be examined and considered, very carefully.

During the late 1990s, the ongoing saga of Canadian federal unity and Quebec separatism entered a new phase, with implications for Canadian federalism that would affect the country, greatly, throughout the twenty-first century. Developments that included the near success of the Quebec government's attempt to receive approval for its separatist agenda from the Quebec electorate, during the 1995 referendum, and the declared intention of the governing *Parti Québécois* to continue to pursue this agenda, aggressively, prompted a constitutional referral to the Supreme Court of Canada. This reference case was intended, partly, to provide political guidance in response to a hypothetical attempt of the Quebec government to effect some sort of separation from Canada. The decision to bring this reference case before the high court, as well as the court's opinion, added further controversy to this persistently divisive issue. It also provided a forum for contemplating some of the most fundamental conundrums of the Canadian political system from a particularly intellectual perspective, including the essence of federalism as a theory of government and its relationship to the crucial concepts of political unity, democratic polity, and self-determination.[8]

One fundamental controversy was addressed, indirectly, within the Supreme Court of Canada's *per curiam* opinion, even though the question was not actually asked: whether or not Canada possesses, truly, a federal, or a confederal, system of government. This topic is difficult, because the distinctions between the two systems generally have not been clarified or, even, broached, either by scholars, politicians, or jurists. However, its determination carries potentially crucial consequences, especially in terms of controversies over sovereignty, nationalism, and political identity. It seems remarkable, therefore, that the distinction between these two systems have not been identified more precisely than the evidence suggests.

Federalism has been identified as one of the most important themes in political science. It also has been considered, arguably, the pivotal theme of both Canadian and American politics. Therefore, the academic literature devoted to the subject by scholars from the United States, Canada, and other countries is considerable. Interestingly, though, that literature often contains a paucity of critical references to, or precise definitions of, the concept of confederalism.[9] Possibly, that structure was not judged to be a viable option for Canada; the "Fathers of Confederation" seemed to prefer a relatively centralized system, yet one that maintained a degree of political autonomy for each of the provinces.[10] Since that time, Canadian politicians, jurists, and scholars have emphasized this theme more frequently, arguably, than any other concern.[11]

Federalism is primarily grounded upon a concept of shared sovereignty.[12] Distinctions regarding the degree of relative sovereignty enjoyed by each level of government often dominate discourses upon this issue,[13] while matters of institutional expression, relationships among various participating governments, and shared resources also are quite prominent.[14] Ultimately, though, the central theme remains sovereignty and its division among different levels of authority, within an overarching political system.[15] The development of the federal principle originated with this preoccupation, as the musings surrounding the emergence of medieval associations demonstrate. It was considered, further, in relation to the broader concept of a separation of sovereign powers, especially among political theorists of the sixteenth and seventeenth centuries.[16] This consideration has been a crucial theme of international relations and foreign policy, even though it has been, generally, grossly underemphasized. Scholarly and political treatments of sovereign relations among states conventionally are grounded upon a treatment of all states, within the international community, as though they are uniform regarding their sovereign expression. Of course, all federal systems delegate exclusive sovereign authority over external relations to the central level of government. But the broader implications of shared sovereign arrangements have become increasingly relevant to international, as well as domestic, politics.[17]

By the late eighteenth century, concerns over reconciling the advantages of small sovereign states, with their emphasis upon popular control and individual rights, and larger sovereign unions, with their emphasis upon security, efficiency, and pooled resources, prompted the advent of modern federalism, as it has come to be understood in the twenty-first century, as a combining of different expressions of smaller and, thus, more politically cohesive units of sovereign authority.[18] Nonetheless, federalism often is represented simply in terms of institutions and methods, rather than in terms of the ultimate source of its theoretical identity. Prominent Canadian treatments of this subject frequently approach this subject in terms of its varied institutional manifestations, such as Edwin R. Black's authoritative theoretical definition:

1. A written constitutional document which distributes significant powers between two sets of territorial governments, co-equal in the exercise of their executive jurisdictions;
2. A method of authoritative interpretation of the constitutional division of powers;
3. Dual citizenship, which implies that both sets of government have dealings with the people in respect of some important areas of life;
4. Some representation of the provinces *as* provinces in the central legislature;
5. A federalized executive, either in composition or in appointment.[19]

Confederal government, properly understood, also is based upon an idea of shared sovereignty. Unfortunately, a general assumption regarding the essential difference between federal and confederal systems occasionally seems to dwell, mistakenly, upon a measurement of the degree of political centralization within the system.[20] A confederal system is represented, under that assumption, as a government in which the component units retain the bulk of sovereign authority, except in areas in which central power is necessary to address shared responsibilities, particularly in terms of a common defense.[21] Consequently, the emphasis of this approach to the concept of confederal government remains upon the component units, rather than the central authority they create. Therefore, thoughtful attempts to address this concept (when offered at all) will acknowledge this fundamental factor, as Ronald Watts has provided:

> [Confederations] occur where several pre-existing polities join together to form a common government for certain limited purposes (for foreign affairs, defence or economic purposes), but the common government is dependent upon the constituent governments, being composed of delegates from the constituent governments and therefore having only an indirect electoral and fiscal base.[22]

But a political system can be very decentralized and still be legitimately classified as federal. Indeed, a system can be highly decentralized and even be classified as unitary. The creation of legislative assemblies for both Scotland and Wales, within the United Kingdom, could be extended, considerably, without surrendering ultimate sovereign authority from the British Parliament at Westminster.[23] Again, the rudimentary condition for classifying a system must be found in terms of its ultimate source of sovereign authority.[24] That fact has been acknowledged in practice, if not always in theory. A confederal system differs from a federal system, in this respect, because the central government's sovereign authority remains a grant of the separate units that comprise it, and those units retain the option of individually withdrawing from, or collectively dissolving, the confederal union.[25]

The implications of this distinction for international law and foreign policy are profound. Under a confederal system, component states generally are free to conduct their own foreign policy. They may join together to present a unified foreign policy under the central government but they also frequently remain free to abstain from that foreign policy and develop one that differs from the unified one. Ultimately, if the nature of the constitutional arrangements that created this confederal union compels acquiescence in a unified foreign policy to which a component state objects, that state retains the sovereign authority to withdraw from that union, entirely, in order to pursue its own foreign policy objectives, although the economic and political consequences of such action might, as a practical matter, deter such a severe action.[26]

Consequently, the challenge posed to the interpretation of the nature of the Canadian union and Quebec's sovereign status within it had profound implications, both domestically and internationally. Furthermore, it presents additional challenges to Canada's adherence to principles of international law that have been enshrined by the United Nations Charter and widely accepted during the twentieth century. For example, one way the issue of Quebec separatism has been expressed has been in terms of a claim for self-determination. This concept was popularized after World War I and codified, under international law, after World War II.[27] Self-determination has been used to advance the cause of nationalism and political independence of many peoples and states. However, the conclusion that a people are entitled to self-determination is not synonymous with recognition of an entitlement to full sovereignty and equal status among the international community of states that engage in foreign policy with each other.[28] A political forum for the expression of a social, cultural, or national identity can be achieved by means that fall short of outright independence, and the degree of sovereignty that a genuine federal system provides such a community certainly meets those criteria of international law.[29] That condition is given legal sanction under United Nations conventions:

> "By virtue of the principle of equal rights and self-determination of peoples enshrined in the Charter of the United Nations, all peoples have the right freely to determine, without external interference, their political status and to pursue their economic, social and cultural development, and every state has the duty to respect this right in accordance with the provisions of the Charter...."
>
> Nothing in the foregoing paragraphs shall be construed as authorizing or encouraging any action which would dismember or impair, totally or in part, the territorial integrity or political unity of sovereign and independent states conducting themselves in compliance with the principle of equal rights and self-determination of peoples as described above and thus possessed of a government representing the whole people belonging to the territory without distinction as to race, creed or color.[30]

The popular will of Quebec may indicate a national identity that merits recognition under the principle of self-determination. Nonetheless, that recognition does not automatically result in an entitlement to political independence. It also does not result in an entitlement to a level of sovereign authority, under a confederal arrangement, beyond the degree already enjoyed under a true federal arrangement, including the lack of authority to conduct independent foreign policy with other states.[31]

That last point is especially important, since the transition to a confederal system would place the initiative for further sovereign development within the purview of the provincial government, rather than the central government or the authority of both federal and provincial governments, collectively.[32] The Supreme Court of Canada made explicit reference to this basic principle of international law. In acknowledging this point, it undermined arguments, advanced by the Quebec government, that Canada should be compelled to grant either independence or a fundamental change in the sovereign relationship between Quebec and the rest of Canada in the event of a favorable referendum result on the subject of political separation. Under those circumstances, according to the high court, secession would be sought under conditions that are not sanctioned by international law. Furthermore, the *actual* nature of the Canadian union would require a multilateral change of the terms of that current union before it could be considered legally and politically legitimate. Thus the principle that a federal union imposes, once it is made, a *permanent* abdication of the authority of component units to withdraw from that union (as asserted by the United States government, through armed might, during the American Civil War[33]), and the further conclusion that Canada is a federal, and not a confederal, union, was declared, definitively, within the *Quebec Reference case*:

> The secession of a province from Canada must be considered, in legal terms, to require an amendment to the Constitution, which perforce requires negotiation. The amendments necessary to achieve secession could be radical and extensive. Some commentators have suggested that secession could be a change of such a magnitude that it could not be considered to be merely an amendment to the Constitution. We are not persuaded by this contention. It is of course true that the Constitution is silent as to the ability of a province to secede from Confederation but, although the Constitution neither expressly authorizes nor prohibits secession, an act of secession would purport to alter the governance of Canadian territory in a manner which undoubtedly is inconsistent with our current constitutional arrangements. The fact that those changes would be profound, or that they would

purport to have a significance with respect to international law, does not negate their nature as amendments to the Constitution of Canada.[34]

Two North American precedents have served as models of confederal government: the United States, under the Articles of Confederation, and the Confederate States of America. The issue of retained sovereignty formed a central principle of the Articles of Confederation, which served as the legal basis for the inceptive United States of America during, and just after, the period of the American Revolution. The emphasis upon the identity of each of these former colonies as independent states is suggested strongly within the text of this document:

> *Article II.* Each state retains its sovereignty, freedom, and independence, and every power, jurisdiction, and right, which is not by this confederation expressly delegated to the United States in Congress assembled.
> *Article III.* The said States hereby severally enter into a firm league of friendship with each other for their common defence, the security of their liberties, and their mutual and general welfare; binding themselves to assist each other against all force offered to, or attacks made upon them, or any of them, on account of religion, sovereignty, trade, or any other pretence whatever.[35]

The Confederate States of America were created as a result of this claim. The concept of "states rights" stimulated the antagonism between Southern and Northern states, with the former polities claiming not only pre-eminent authority over their own cultural and economic status, beliefs, and practices, but also the exclusive authority to reclaim their complete sovereignty from the central government, unilaterally, at any time, including the authority to negotiate their own, separate policies with foreign states.[36] The republican values supporting these political assertions were expounded eloquently by statesmen such as John C. Calhoun, especially in terms of his emphasis upon the desire for sovereign expression by a coherent community, without loss of that sovereign expression to another, intrusive level of government.[37]

The constitutional and political arrangements of this union of secessionist American states resulted from, and emphasized, this concept of sovereignty. Even during the American Civil War, some Southern states insisted that their governments also retained the authority to secede from the Confederate union.[38] The preamble of the Confederate Constitution underscored this belief, especially in terms of its reference to the origin of this union emanating from "each State acting in its sovereign and independent character."[39]

Another international example of a confederal system is the Swiss union prior to 1848. The Swiss cantons united, over time, initially as part of a defensive arrangement, yet they remained jealous of their sovereignty and refused to make their union permanently binding, including in terms of the ultimate (though ambiguous) authority retained by the canton to pursue certain foreign relationships, provided that these relationships did not threaten the defense of the other Swiss cantons. But the turmoil and uncertainty of European politics and society culminated in the decision of these cantons to abandon their confederal arrangement in exchange for a federal constitutional system.[40]

A better model of confederal government, especially for the international community and states that are contending with sovereign challenges, has been the current European Union. Some authors have referred to this political entity as a "supranational" organization, rather than a confederal union. This former label may seem more appropriate, because the members of this union are traditionally recognized states that conduct their own foreign policy relations with each other and the rest of the world, and most of them have long histories in that capacity. Furthermore, the union has been formed, developed, and expanded as the result of treaties among sovereign states, rather than as part of a conventional process of constitution making.[41]

But these states have, in fact, surrendered some of their sovereign authority to a central governing body they have created. Those concerns have been pivotal for expressions (particularly within countries like Great Britain) of political resistance toward further integration, especially regarding the adoption of a common currency and the development of a new European constitution. Nonetheless, despite the expansion of the sovereign powers these states have delegated to the governing bodies of the European Union, they continue to retain one crucial source of sovereignty: the authority to withdraw from the union and reclaim all sovereign control.[42] In this way, the European Community most closely reflects the principles of a confederal system.[43] It also may offer the model that Quebec had hoped to emulate through its constitutional challenge in the *Que-*

bec Reference case, including in terms of establishing a sovereign authority to pursue its own, separate foreign policy objectives.

The impressive array of legislative, executive, judicial, and administrative institutions, exercising delegated sovereign powers, provided a model for many Quebec separatists, who wanted to claim ultimate sovereign control, including in the area of foreign policy, while continuing to enjoy the infrastructural advantages of maintaining a link with Canada. Quebec separatists often cited the European example as a model for their own sovereign future. This model, for this purpose, assumed the guise, therefore, not of an international association, arranged by treaty, but as an initially internal accommodation, originally prompted by constitutional fiat.[44] This arrangement was based upon the assumption that Quebec already possessed the authority to withdraw from Canada, once the people of this community indicated such a sovereign will to pursue this goal. Quebec separatism became articulated in terms of a transformation from a federal to a confederal arrangement, particularly under Premier René Lévesque.[45]

This consideration may appear to be restricted to the theoretical intricacies of non-unitary governmental systems. However, it is essential, in order to understand and appreciate the scope of foreign policy within such systems, to understand and appreciate the ultimate foundation, including the constitutional foundation, of that sovereign authority upon which a government makes its claim to conduct foreign policy. This capacity absolutely depends upon the willingness of the international community to recognize this claim to sovereign authority and, thus, the status of a "state" under international law;[46] Quebec's attempt to gain constitutional recognition of its claim to be able to withdraw from the Canadian union, unilaterally, was a step in the process of further claiming additional sovereign powers (even if it remained within the Canadian union) that the concept of "sovereignty-association" also has represented. That demand for "sovereignty-association" that was the purpose of the 1980 referendum reflected, exactly, the basis of a true confederation:

> The term *sovereignty-association* binds together the goal of political independence (or sovereignty) for Quebec with both a recognition and acceptance of Quebec's economic integration with the rest of Canada. Its closest model comes from the European Economic Community, wherein still-sovereign states pursue coordinated and integrated economic policies.

The proposal for sovereignty-association calls for Quebec and Canada-minus-Quebec to negotiate a series of agreements designed to preserve the existing benefits of economic association. These agreements, however, would take the form of treaties between sovereign states, and hence would be flexible and adaptable rather than constitutional in character. The government of Quebec would be the only national government for Quebecers. Quebec residents would not elect representatives to Parliament, but instead would be represented in Ottawa by the Quebec government.

Sovereignty-association would provide an equal partnership between Quebec and the rest of Canada, a partnership based on diplomatic norms of equality between sovereign states. In essence, then, sovereignty-association would preserve economic linkages while creating a new form of political association.[47]

Thus, clarifying the precise constitutional nature of the Canadian union and the precise status of its component states is an essential part of identifying the source of sovereign authority within that union in the area of foreign policy. Constitutional controversies regarding federal status and self-determination might not seem to be directly applicable to foreign policy. But the legitimization of foreign policy authority absolutely depends upon constitutional sanction.[48] Therefore, the Supreme Court's ruling in the *Quebec Reference case* had profound implication for the way that Quebec often wishes to present itself to the world and its ongoing efforts for developing international ties and a foreign policy agenda of its own.[49]

Canada's political union has been labeled a "confederation." However, references to its theoretical structure and values always have been articulated in terms of the principles of federalism, both in name and description. The relative lack of integration that a true confederation conventionally provides, along with the perceived failings of both the American and Confederate States examples, provided an incentive to develop a more centralized system,[50] although some leaders challenged the need for any such system that would tie the separate provinces to each other and their respective, varying fortunes.[51] However, political leaders wanted to assuage the fears of the separate provinces regarding their future autonomy. "The term 'Confederation,' when applied to the Canadian union of 1867, is a misnomer, for the form of government set up by the BNA Act is definitely not 'confederal.' 'Confederation,' a word normally associated with the absence of a strong federal government, was deliberately misused by those who, in fact, intended to create one in an effort to confuse those who might find such a project alarming."[52]

The Supreme Court of Canada did not address this distinction, directly, as part of its opinion in the *Quebec Reference case*. However, its examination of the fundamental nature of federalism, its application to Canada, and its implications for any future aspirations of Quebec independence, indirectly depends upon the ability to appreciate that fundamental difference between federal and confederal systems of government. British colonial authorities understood that difference when they were presented with the attempt of Nova Scotia's government, soon after the enactment of the British North America Act (now the Constitution Act) of 1867, to withdraw from the new union. The colonial secretary's response to Premier Joseph Howe's petition to rescind this arrangement indicated its fundamental permanence:

> The neighboring province of New Brunswick has entered into the union in reliance on having with it the sister province of Nova Scotia, and vast obligations, political and commercial, have already been contracted on the faith of a measure so long discussed and so solemnly adopted. . . . I trust that the Assembly and the people of Nova Scotia will not be surprised that the Queen's government feel that they would not be warranted in advising the reversal of a great measure of state, attended by so many extensive consequences already in operation.[53]

The Supreme Court of Canada's summation of the federal principle ultimately echoed this sentiment:

> The federalism principle, in conjunction with the democratic principle, dictates that the clear repudiation of the existing constitutional order and the clear expression of the desire to pursue secession by the population of a province would give rise to a reciprocal obligation on all parties to Confederation to negotiate constitutional changes to respond to that desire. The amendment of the Constitution begins with a political process undertaken pursuant to the Constitution itself. . . . The corollary of a legitimate attempt by one of the participants in Confederation to seek an amendment to the Constitution is an obligation on all parties to come to the negotiating table. . . .
>
> [But] we hold that Quebec could not purport to invoke a right of self-

determination such as to dictate the terms of a proposed secession to the other parties: that would not be negotiation at all. . . . The democracy principle, as we have emphasized, cannot be invoked to trump the principles of federalism and the rule of law, the rights of individuals and minorities, or the operation of democracy in the other provinces or in Canada as a whole. No negotiations could be effective if their ultimate outcome, secession, is cast as an absolute legal entitlement based upon an obligation to give effect to that act of secession in the Constitution.[54]

An important element of this analysis was the high court's acknowledgement that the principle of self-determination, under international law, does not require a people to achieve full sovereignty in order to enjoy that condition:

As will be seen, international law expects that the right to self-determination will be exercised by peoples within the framework of existing sovereign states and consistently with the maintenance of the territorial integrity of those states. Where this is not possible, in the exceptional circumstances discussed below, a right of secession may arise.[55]

The Supreme Court's ultimate opinion appears strongly to have concluded that Canada's federal system precludes Quebec's unilateral withdrawal from the union.[56] Therefore, it also might seem to preclude other powers associated with that claim, including the power to conduct a separate foreign policy. The latter is a complex matter, of course, because it is not completely clear that it is necessary to be sovereign in order to entertain foreign relations. Various municipalities, along with Flanders, Bavaria, New South Wales, and in the present context, Quebec, show significant activities that resemble a foreign policy.

Even while seeming to discourage implicitly the notion of a separate foreign policy for Quebec, the court also concluded that a clear, democratically derived indication of the desire of the people of Quebec to secede from Canada should be met by the federal government with sincere negotiations, presumably directed toward achieving that end, in some fashion.[57] But that portion of the court's advisory opinion rests upon a political analysis, derived from its interpretation of Canada's history, political culture, and fundamental values. The conclusion that Quebec cannot secede unilaterally is based upon a more parochial *legal* analysis, derived from a constitutional comprehension of the principles of federalism.[58]

The evolution of Canada's sovereignty, within the British imperial system, may have contributed to some confusion over its federal identity. This innovation of imperial governance had been designed, during the latter nineteenth and early twentieth centuries, as a means for alleviating many of the burdens of empire while continuing to enjoy both effective control and benefits, especially from an economic perspective. This aspect of Britain's imperial system was based upon an assumption of mutual self-interest among political societies that shared similar characteristics. The arrangement provided the appearance of a federal sharing of sovereign powers: one level of government controlling internal matters, another level of government controlling external matters, and both levels of government exercising "concurrent powers" over certain shared areas of policy and administrative authority. The concept of the self-governing "dominion" (a term that was first applied to Canada) within the British Empire was limited to the "white" colonies that were dominated by populations of European descent and Eurocentric proclivities. Therefore, these colonies could be "trusted" with a measure of sovereign control, under the supervision and ultimate control of imperial authorities, which would not be exploited as a source for advancing (at least not "prematurely") unilateral independence on the part of these particular colonial populations.[59]

This arrangement served as the basis for the gradual transformation of these colonies into fully sovereign states. However, this modified version of the British Empire did not constitute a federal system, for ultimate control remained with the imperial government until these colonies were in an effective position to demand sovereign recognition. This historic example of the British imperial system offers a model for gaining an alternative appreciation of the relationship of unitary, federal, and confederal systems to the issue of sovereignty and its role within a broader international system. More importantly, it offers additional lessons regarding the difficulties of gauging international sovereign status, both legally and politically. Quebec, for example, has been established as part of a federal system as a result of the initial creation of the Dominion of Canada through the union of various colonies of British North America. Once Canada's independence was established and formally recognized, that federal arrangement persisted.

Unlike the status of colonies under the unitary authority of an imperial system, or the authority of any other unitary state, Quebec *does* possess absolute claims to a limited sovereign authority that cannot, rightfully, be denied or diminished. However, unlike the confederal authority of a European Union, these sovereign powers cannot be altered, unilaterally (especially in terms of external relationships, including in the area of foreign policy), nor can full sovereign status be achieved through a legally sanctioned separation from the federal system. Unless Canada's federal government agrees to any such alteration in the terms of this constitutional arrangement, Quebec's government cannot legally assert such a claim in a manner that would be recognizable under the principles of either municipal or international law. The same condition is true for the other provinces.

Therefore, a political subunit of a federal system, like Quebec, enjoys a limited, yet absolute, sovereign status. Ironically, though, one consequence of the terms of that limited sovereignty is the effective denial of a legal claim (under either municipal or international law) to assert full independence. Arguably, and ironically, the political representatives of an administrative region of a unitary state might be able to assert, before the international community, a stronger claim to full sovereign status than the government of a federal subunit, since the population of that region of a unitary system never agreed to the permanent settlement of shared sovereignty that is imposed by the terms of the sort of federal constitutional arrangement that Canada, in theory and practice, represents.

However, these examples are reminders of the ongoing demands of regions within unitary systems and states within federal systems to gain international recognition of their sovereign aspirations (including the authority to conduct foreign policy and relations with other states) through means that do not seek the sanction of current legal and constitutional systems.[60] Under international law, the status of statehood and the conduct of a state's foreign policy is achieved, ultimately, through diplomatic recognition, although it is possible to enunciate and implement a policy without having a recognized diplomatic status. Yet that standard also can be ambiguous, depending upon the number of states that are willing to extend that recognition and the legitimacy or, even, the actual existence of a functional government that can be diplomatically recognized and possesses the capacity for conducting foreign policy. Such an anomaly occurred in terms of the activities of diplomatic representatives of Estonia, Latvia, and Lithuania, who were recognized by certain Western countries during the Cold War period, despite the fact that those three countries had been annexed by the Soviet Union and did not even have governments-in-exile (and, consequently, no instrument for creating a specific foreign policy) to support them, adding another historical example to the confusing array of inconsistent precedents in this difficult area of sovereign status and international law.[61]

Quebec's action in bringing this reference case before the Supreme Court of Canada suggests that a unilateral option is one that Quebec currently is not inclined to pursue, including in terms of advancing a distinct Quebec foreign policy, despite certain quasi-diplomatic efforts to enhance its sovereign status, abroad.[62] The *Quebec Reference case* is extremely significant, therefore, in providing a clarification of this difficult, and increasingly relevant, aspect of international law, especially in the area of sovereignty and the sovereign status necessary for conducting a recognizable foreign policy. The international community should take advantage of this precedent and use it as a useful model for addressing these sorts of controversies, especially as they become more frequently experienced. While the question of whether Quebec can conduct international relations is not fully answered by the *Reference*, it nevertheless provides a potentially significant contribution for international law and foreign policy relations, in theory and practice, on the part of Canada and Quebec.

NOTES

1. That monopoly, and those institutions, are described in Kim Richard Nossal, *The Politics of Canadian Foreign Policy*, 3rd edition (Scarborough, ON: Prentice-Hall Canada, 1997), 174–189.

2. This historical development of the confederal arrangements of the European Community is analyzed in Michael J. Baun, *An Imperfect Union: The Maastricht Treaty and the New Politics of European Integration* (Boulder, CO: Westview Press, 1996), 11–29.

3. An excellent example, involving provinces other than Quebec, occurred during the negotiation of the Canada–United States Free Trade Accord under the government of Brian Mulroney. See Nossal, *The Politics of Canadian Foreign Policy*, 308.

4. André Donneur, *Politique Étrangère Canadienne* (Montréal: Guérin Universitaire, 1994), 43; Gordon Mace, Louis Bélanger, and Ivan Bernier, "Canadian Foreign Policy and Quebec," in *Canada Among Nations, 1995: Democracy and Foreign Policy*, ed. Maxwell A. Cameron and Maureen Appel Molot (Ottawa: Carleton University Press, 1995), 127; Nossal, *The Politics of Canadian Foreign Policy*, 292–310.

5. This difficulty is addressed specifically in F. H. Hinsley, *Sovereignty* (New York: Cambridge University Press, 1986), 214–235. Other sources that address this general theme include Patricia Carley, *Self-Determination: Sovereignty, Territorial Integrity, and the Right to Secession* (Washington, DC: United States Institute of Peace, 1996); Marlene Wind, *Sovereignty and European Integration: Toward a Post-Hobbesian Order* (New York: Palgrave, 2001); and R. Bellamy and D. Castiglione, "Building the Union: The Nature of Sovereignty in the Political Architecture of Europe, *Law and Philosophy* 16, no. 4 (July 1997), 421–445.

6. The literature on Canada's relationship with Quebec is extensive. Some of the more prominent treatments of this conflict (including in terms of federalism and nationalism) include Sylvia Bashevkin, *True Patriot Love: The Politics of Canadian Nationalism* (Oxford: Oxford University Press, 1991); Louis Balthazar, Guy Laforest, and Vincent Lemieux, eds., *Le Québec et la restructuration du Canada, 1980–1992: enjeux et perspectives* (Québec: Septentrion, 1991); Dominique Clift, *Quebec Nationalism in Crisis* (Montréal and Kingston, ON: Queen's University Press, 1989); W. D. Coleman, *The Independence Movement in Quebec, 1945–1980* (Toronto: University of Toronto Press, 1984); Léon Dion, *Le duel constitutionnel Québec-Canada* (Montréal: Boréal, 1995); Kenneth McRoberts, *Misconceiving Canada: The Struggle for National Unity* (Toronto: Oxford University Press, 1997); and Christopher Edward Taucar, *Canadian Federalism and Quebec Sovereignty* (New York, Peter Lang, 2000).

7. Kenneth McRoberts, "La question nationale québécoise," in *La Révolution Tranquille, 40 ans plus tards: un bilan*, ed. Yves Bélanger, Robert Comeau, Céline Métivier (Montréal: VLB Éditeur, 2000), 123–137.

8. Critical analyses of this case, especially in terms of these themes, can be found in Jean François Gaudreault-DesBien, "The Quebec Secession Reference and the Judicial Arbitration of Conflicting Narratives about Law, Democracy, and Identity," *Vermont Law Review* 23, no. 4 (Summer 1999): 793–844; James T. McHugh, "Making Public Law 'Public': An Analysis of the Quebec Reference Case and Its Significance for Comparative Constitutional Analysis," *International and Comparative Law Quarterly* 49, no. 2 (April 2000): 445–462; and Rosemary Rayfuse, "*Reference re Secession of Quebec from Canada*: Breaking Up Is Hard to Do," *University of New South Wales Law Journal* 21, no. 3 (1998): 834–844.

9. A few of the most prominent texts in this respect include C. F. Beckton and A. W. MacKay, eds., *Recurring Issues in Canadian Federalism* (Toronto: University of Toronto Press, 1986); Samuel H. Beer, *To Make a Nation: The Rediscovery of American Federalism* (Cambridge, MA: Belknap Press, 1993); Ivo D. Duchacek, *Comparative Federalism: The Territorial Dimensions of Politics* (Lanham, MD: University Press of America, 1987); Thomas R. Dye, *American Federalism: Competition among Governments* (Lexington, MA: Lexington Books, 1990); Daniel J. Elazar, *American Federalism: A View from the States* (New York: Harper & Row, 1984); Alain-G Gagnon, *Développement régional: État et groupes populaires* (Montréal: Éditions Asticou, 1986); G. Alan Tarr and Ellis Katz, eds., *Federalism and Rights* (Lanham, MD: Rowman & Littlefield, 1996); and M. J. C. Vile, "Federal Theory and the 'New Federalism,'" in *The Politics of "New Federalism,"* ed. D. Jaensch (Adelaide: University of Victoria Press, 1977).

10. One possible exception may be the seminal text that attempted to explain part of this ambiguity, regarding Canada's political system, by describing it as a "quasi-federal" structure, K. C. Wheare, *Federal Government* (London: Oxford University Press, 1953), 19–21.

11. This concern about the federal nature of the proposed dominion and its consequences for the sovereign status of its component parts was, understandably, a central theme of the political dialogue that led to the adoption of the British North America Act in 1867, as demonstrated by, among many other examples, the debates of the provincial legislature of United Canada in *The Confederation Debates in the Provinces of Canada, 1867*, ed. P. B. Waite (Toronto: McClelland & Stewart, 1963), 58–79.

12. This idea is expressed by many authorities, including Katharine F. Braid and Robert V. Horte, "Sovereignty and Federalism: The Canadian Perspective," *Canada–United States Law Journal* 20 (1994): 319–332; Earl H. Fry, "Sovereignty and Federalism: U. S. and Canadian Perspectives and Challenges to Sovereignty and Governance," *Canada–United States Law Journal* 20 (1994): 303–318; and L. Kinvin Wroth, "Notes for a Comparative Study of the Origins of Federalism in the United States and Canada," *Arizona Journal of International and Comparative Law* 15, no. 1 (Winter 1998): 33–56.

13. One of the most prominent scholars in this field offers an excellent example of this preoccupation, Daniel J. Elazar, *Exploring Federalism* (Birmingham, AL: University of Alabama Press, 1987), 223–231.

14. This sort of emphasis has been expressed in terms of themes such as the "new federalism" (an American movement that promotes the increased delegation of institutional responsibility to the state level), which is analyzed in Burke Marshall, *A Workable Government? The Constitution after 200 Years* (New York: W.W. Norton, 1987), 103–143.

15. A good example of this central focus is provided in Geoffrey Sawer, *Modern Federalism* (London: C. A. Watts and Co., 1969), 106–116.

16. S. Rufus Davis, *The Federal Principle: A Journey through Time in Quest of a Meaning* (Berkeley: University of California Press, 1978), 54–73.

17. This tendency to treat all states as though they are unitary under international law and practice is addressed in John Hoffman, *Sovereignty* (Minneapolis: University of Minnesota Press, 1999), 56–58. This concern about the identity of a unified sovereign within a polyarchy also is addressed within the seminal political science text of Robert Dahl, *Who Governs?* (New Haven, CT: Yale University Press, 1965), 19–21.

18. Thomas Jefferson was especially enamored of this approach to federalism, as revealed in his support for the "ward system" of especially small units of sovereign governance. This emphasis upon democratic participation at the community level was promoted by John Dewey, *The Public and Its Problems* (New York: Henry Holt, 1927), 212–214.

19. Edwin R. Black, *Divided Loyalties* (Montreal and Kingston, ON: McGill-Queen's University Press, 1975), 9–10.

20. A discussion of that tendency to classify federal and confederal systems according to their relative centralization of authority is found in Michael Burgess, *Federalism and European Union: The Building of Europe, 1950–2000* (London: Routledge, 2000), 259–265.

21. Some initial interpretations of the structure of the Commonwealth of Independent States (the loose organization that emerged, in 1992, following the dissolution of the Soviet Union) underscored the perceived confederal features of this arrangement, Gennady M. Danilenko, "The Confederate Model of the Commonwealth of Independent States: The New Russian Federalism," *New Europe Law Review* 1, no. 2 (Spring 1993): 367–386; and Stephan Kux, "Confederalism and Stability in the Commonwealth of Independent States," *New Europe Law Review* 1, no. 2 (Spring 1993): 387–420. An analysis of Russia's emerging federal system is provided in Graham Smith, "Federation, Defederation and Refederation: from the Soviet Union to Russian Statehood," in *Federalism: The Multiethnic Challenge*, ed. Graham Smith (London: Longman, 1995), 157–173.

22. Ronald L. Watts, *Comparing Federal Systems in the 1990s* (Kingston, ON: Institute of Intergovernmental Relations, 1996), 8.

23. Nonetheless, that fundamental mistake of confusing a unitary devolution of administrative and policy *authority* to Scottish and Welsh assemblies for the creation of a federal system of shared *sovereignty* continues to be made, as evidenced by the examples cited in A. Dawisha and K. Dawisha, "How to Build a Democratic Iraq," *Foreign Affairs* 82, no. 3 (Spring 2003): 36–50.

24. Michael O'Neill, "Great Britain: From Dicey to Devolution," *Parliamentary Affairs* 53, no. 1 (January 2000): 69–95.

25. That distinctive feature of confederal government seems to remain widely unappreciated. It is recognized (usually only in passing) by some authorities, such as Duchacek, *Comparative Federalism*, 163, 165. That same author also contends that the establishment of a federal system entails an "immunity against secession." Duchacek, *Comparative Federalism*, 217–222.

26. This approach was the basis of the Westphalian state system that has emphasized the sovereignty of individual states. Its problem is the ambiguity that results from negotiations that involve the component units of both federal and confederal systems. Economic globalization further has exacerbated this ambiguity, especially when component states negotiate across international boundaries. This problem is addressed in detail in Daniel J. Elazar, *Constitutionalizing Globalization: The Postmodern Revival of Confederal Arrangements* (Lanham, MD: Rowman & Littlefield, 1998), 13–15, 29–35.

27. International Covenant on Civil and Political Rights, December 16, 1966.

28. This point is addressed in Louis Henkin, Richard C. Pugh, Oscar Schachter, and Hans Smit, *International Law* (St. Paul, MN: West, 1980), 211–213.

29. Jack Donnelly, *Universal Human Rights in Theory and Practice* (Ithaca, NY: Cornell University Press, 1989), 147–149.

30. United Nations Declaration of Principles of International Law Concerning Friendly Relations among States in Accordance with the Charter of the United Nations, G.A.Res. 2625, 25 GAOR, Supp. 28 (A/8028), at 121.

31. Claims to independence are easier to assert in relation to colonial territories, Suzuki, "Self-Determination and World Public Order," *Virginia Journal of International Law* 16 (1976): 779–862. Therefore, the international community generally has refrained from supporting secessionist movements, even when upholding a territory's claim to self-determination, Boutros Boutros-Ghali, "The Addis Ababa Charter, *International Conciliation*, no. 546 (January 1964): 54–55.

32. Even relatively "radical" interpretations of this principle acknowledge, nonetheless, the belief that self-determination may warrant self-government, but it does not mandate complete sovereignty, Rosenstock, "The Declaration of Principles of International Law Concerning Friendly Relations: A Survey," *American Journal of International Law* 65 (1971): 731–733.

33. The theoretical background of that debate is considered in C. Lloyd Brown-Joh, "Self-Determination, Autonomy, and State Secession in Federal Constitutional and International Law," *South Texas Law Review* 40, no. 3 (Summer 1999): 567–602.

34. [1998] 2 S.C.R. 217, at 263–264.

35. Articles of Confederation (1777), art. II-III.

36. This belief is examined in Henry James Walker, "Henry Clayton and the Secession Movement in Alabama," *Southern Studies* 4, no. 4 (Winter 1993): 341–360.

37. John C. Calhoun, "A Disquisition on Government," in *Union and Liberty: The Political Philosophy of John Calhoun*, ed. Ross M. Lence (Indianapolis: Liberty Fund, 1992), 22–23.

38. These provisions, and their significance, are considered in Jeffrey A. Jenkins, "Partnership and Confederate Constitution-Making Reconsidered," *Studies in American Political Development* 13, no. 2 (Fall 1999): 279–301.

39. C. S. Const. preamble (1861).

40. Walter S. G. Kohn, *Governments and Politics of the German-Speaking Countries* (Chicago: Nelson-Hall, 1980), 31–39; Watts, *Comparing Federal Systems in the 1990s*, 20–21.

41. Thomas Buergenthal and Harold G. Maier, *Public International Law in a Nutshell* (St. Paul, MN: West, 1990), 51–53.

42. The converse identification of states that are, in a federal system, barred from unilaterally reclaiming their sovereign authority is indirectly affirmed in the general characterization of a federal system as being immune from unilateral amendment, as noted in Elazar, *Exploring Federalism*, 174–178; and Preston King, *Federalism and Federation* (Baltimore: Johns Hopkins University Press, 1982), 91–93.

43. This general theme is addressed in Michael Burgess, "Federalism and Federation in Western Europe," in *Federalism and Federation in Western Europe*, ed. Michael Burgess, (London: Croom Helm, 1986), 15–29; and Peter E. Herzog, *The Law of the European Community*, ed. Peter E. Herzog and Hans Smit (New York: Matthew Bender, 1999).

44. This inspiration was cited, periodically, including as part of the official Parti Québécois declaration to l'Assemblée nationale of its proposal for sovereignty-association, "Quebec-Canada: A New Deal—the Quebec Government Proposal for a New Partnership between Equals: Sovereignty-Association," November 1, 1979.

45. This concept of sovereignty-association left many observers unclear, particularly since it was based upon an allegedly confusing mixture of "connectors and independence." See Jane Jacobs, *The Question of Separatism* (New York: Random House, 1980), 90–106.

46. This situation has been exacerbated by the rapid expansion of multilateral arrangements during the late twentieth and early twenty-first centuries and the subsequent challenge to the Westphalian model that these changes have presented,

as discussed in Stephen Krasner, ed., *International Regimes* (Ithaca, NY: Cornell University Press, 1983), 195–232.

47. Quoted in Roger Gibbins, *Conflict and Unity* (Toronto: Nelson, 1988), 56–57.

48. Nossal, 174–176.

49. Andre Bernard, *La Vie Politique au Quebec et au Canada* (Sainte-Foy, QC: Presses de l'Université du Quebec, 1996), 20–25; Andre Donneur, *Politique Étrangère Canadienne* (Montréal: Guérin Universitaire, 1994), 43–59.

50. Peter J. Smith, "The Dream of Political Union: Loyalism, Toryism, and the Federal Ideal in Pre-Confederation Canada," in *The Causes of Canadian Confederation*, ed. Ged Martin (Fredericton, NB: Acadiensis Press, 1990), 148–171.

51. Ged Martin, "The Case against Canadian Confederation, 1864–1867," in *The Causes of Canadian Confederation*, ed. Martin, 19–49.

52. Garth Stevenson, *Unfulfilled Union* (Toronto: Macmillan, 1982), 9.

53. Quoted in H. Wade MacLauclan, "Accounting for Democracy and the Rule of Law in the Quebec Reference," *Canadian Bar Review* (1997): 168.

54. [1998] 2 S.C.R. 217, at 265–267.

55. [1998] 2 S.C.R. 217, at 280–281.

56. Some commentators have suggested that Quebec's right to secede is not legally based, but morally based, Pierre De Bané and Martial Asselin, "Quebec's Right to Secede," in *Canadian Federalism: Myth or Reality?* ed. J. P. Meekison, (Toronto: Methuen, 1977), 497–507.

57. This obligation was acknowledged in the Report of the Special Joint Committee of the Senate and House of Commons on the Constitution of Canada, 4th Session, 28th Parliament, 1972, 13–14.

58. A more broadly theoretical analysis of the legal limitation of secession, within a federal system, is provided in King, *Federalism and Federation*, 108–120.

59. This experiment in British colonial shared sovereignty is addressed in William Ranulf Block, *Britain and the Dominions* (Cambridge: Cambridge University Press, 1951); Hugh Edward Egerton, *Federations and Unions within the British Empire* (Oxford: Clarendon Press, 1911); and A. B. Keith, *Constitutional Law of the British Dominions* (London: Macmillan, 1933).

60. Examples of other attempts at achieving self-determination through similar appeals to the international community are documented in Donald P. Doumitt, *Conflict in Northern Ireland: The History, the Problem, and the Challenge* (New York: Peter Lang, 1985), 25–36; M. Gammer, *Muslim Resistance to the Tsar: Shamil and the Conquest of Chechnia and Daghestan* (London: F. Cass, 1994), 113–121; Christopher T. Harvie, *Scotland and Nationalism: Scottish Society and Politics, 1707–1994* (London: Routledge, 1994), 198–219; Rashid Khalidi, "The PLO as

Representative of the Palestinian People," in *The International Relations of the Palestine Liberation Organization*, ed. Augustus R. Norton and Martin H. Greenberg (Carbondale, IL: Southern Illinois University Press, 1989), 59–73; Jehuda Reinharz, "Chaim Weizmann as Political Strategist: The Initial Years, 1918–1920," in *Essays in Modern Jewish History*, ed. Frances Malino and Phyllis Cohen Albert (East Brunswick, NJ: Association of University Presses, 1982), 271–294; Gwyn A. Williams, *The Search for Beulah Land: The Welsh and the Atlantic Revolution* (New York: Holmes & Meier, 1980), 7–26; and Cyrus Ernesto Zirakzadeh, *A Rebellious People: Basques, Protests, and Politics* (Reno: University of Nevada Press, 1991), 1–16.

61. This unusual situation, including its international legal repercussions, is addressed in James T. McHugh and James S. Pacy, *Diplomats without a Country: Baltic Diplomacy, International Law, and the Cold War* (Westport, CT: Greenwood Press, 2001).

62. This activity includes the establishment of "quasi-diplomatic" delegations in various foreign countries (including missions, called *les Maisons Québec*, that conduct activities that resemble the traditional roles of foreign embassies), separate participation in international organizations (most notably, but not confined to, La Francophonie), cooperative ventures between Quebec ministries and counterparts in various foreign countries, and the more broadly international mandate that was established for the Québec Ministère des Affaires Intergouvernementales, which succeeded the former Québec Ministère des Affaires Federal-Provincials. These developments are noted in Louise Beaudoin, "Origines et développement du rôle international du Gouvernement du Québec," in *Le Canada et le Québec sur la scène internationale*, ed. Paul Painchaud (Montréal: Les Presses de l'Université du Québec, 1977), 458–461; Andre Bernard, *Problèmes politiques: Canada et Québec* (Ste. Foy: Les Presses de l'Université du Québec, 1993), 141–170; and Thomas Allen Levy, "Le rôle des provinces," in *Le Canada et le Québec sur la scène internationale*, 141–144.

V

INTERNAL PERSPECTIVES

19

Civil-Military Relations and Canadian Foreign Policy: The Case of Gender Integration and the Canadian Navy[1]

CAROLYN C. JAMES

Much of a state's foreign policy capability rests on its ability to project power. Canada has chosen to rest much of its foreign policy reputation on the protection of "human security" through an international peacekeeping role. Geostrategic realities also affect a state's international reputation. In the 2004 elections, Conservative candidate Stephen Harper asserted that for Canada's foreign policy to remain independent, it also must maintain an armed force capable of acting independently of the United States. With years of severe budget cuts, this capability has been severely undermined.

One of Canada's realities is its coastline—the longest in the world, resulting in over 11 million square kilometers of responsibility for the Navy. There is no foreseeable scenario of attack to the homeland from the sea, yet joint policies with other states often include naval forces. For example, to regulate immigration and play a key role in stopping international drug trafficking requires the ability to control Canadian coastal water. The practical result is that Canada's naval forces are, and will remain, a necessary component to its image both at home and abroad. Foreign policy implications cannot be avoided.

The most important resource for any military organization is its human resource. Canada has found, as many other states have found, that when resources are lean, change becomes necessary. Canada seeks the best possible personnel for its armed forces. Military occupations have a variety of physical requirements. For the vast majority, gender is not one of them. As more jobs and occupations in the Canadian armed forces are open to women, the pool of qualified candidates increases. Still, achieving integrated armed forces presents many challenges.

What exactly is the gender integration issue for the Canadian Navy? Three primary areas need to be analyzed in order to answer this question: civil rights, societal expectations, and civilian control. By civil rights, I refer to the legal ability for any qualified woman to enjoy the privilege of serving her country in the armed forces, including combat situations, if she so chooses. Societal expectations refer to the relationship between the military and the society it protects. The civilian control question concerns a hierarchical relationship between the armed forces and their civilian leadership. Each of these topics will be discussed and areas requiring further investigation identified. This is followed by a review of gender integration measures and successes in the Maritime Command (MARCOM) with comparisons vis-à-vis the United States Navy (USN) augmented by a timeline summary in appendix II. Canada's success then is presented comparatively with other states. An assessment of the findings is provided in the conclusion.

CIVIL RIGHTS

The status of women in the military evolved slowly over the years and has included a series of commissions and reports. The modern legal story begins with the Minister of National Defense's Manpower Study in 1965, which indicated that the number of women in Canada's workforce was increasing at a greater rate than men, and, therefore, "the privilege of serving their country in the armed forces should not be denied on the grounds of sex alone."[2] Working against the report's findings was the fact that women's attrition rates in the military were higher than for men, meaning recruitment and training per person was more costly for women. As a result, women were barred from occupations that required lengthy and expensive training.

In 1971, the Royal Commission on the Status of Women issued a report that had specific recommendations for the Canadian Forces (C.F.):

(1) Standardized enlistment criteria and pension benefits;
(2) Inclusion of married women;
(3) Not forcing pregnant women to resign;
(4) Entrance to military colleges; and
(5) Entrance to all trades and classifications.

Defence Council employment policies accepted the first four criteria. The obstacle to implementation of the fifth criterion was threefold. First, it was argued that women should not serve in positions that men required for career development. Second, a woman's posting should not result in a man's increased ratio of sea versus land duty. Third, and perhaps most significant, was the issue of women serving in combat, then deemed by the Council to be against the norms of Canadian society. The changes that did achieve implementation, however, were effective, in that the number of women in C.F. increased significantly in the 1970s.

The Canadian Human Rights Act of 1978 prohibited gender-based discrimination, unless there existed a "bona fide occupational requirement" to consider gender. In order to determine what these occupations were, the C.F. initiated the Service Women in Non-Traditional Environments and Roles, or SWINTER, trials. Even before these trials were completed, in 1980 military schools began to open their doors to female cadets.

The Canadian Charter of Rights and Freedoms (1982) included an "Equality Rights" section that came into force in 1985. As a result, the Parliamentary Sub-Committee on Equality Rights advocated that all trade and occupation decisions based upon gender be eliminated. A Charter Task Force was formed in 1986 to determine any possible adverse effects on mission readiness. Another set of trials was proposed in 1987, the Combat-Related Employment of Women, or CREW. Women began to be posted into combat units that same year.

In 1989, the Canadian Human Rights Tribunal gave the Canadian Forces the following instructions:

> Full integration is to take place with all due speed, as a matter of principle and as a matter of practice, for both active and reserve forces.

> The implementation of the principle requires the removal of all restrictions from both operational and personal considerations; the minimum male requirement should be phased out; new occupational personnel selection standards should be imposed immediately.
>
> There must be internal and external monitoring of the policy with appropriate modifications being made immediately.[3]

The 1994 MINERVA, a nine-point plan intended to expand the role of women in the military by targeting primarily cultural barriers, augmented these policies. Complete gender integration was to take place by 1999.

The subsequent Employment Equity Act of 1996 clearly is intended to apply to the C.F. It is meant to provide equal treatment in the workplace and remove disadvantages for four targeted groups: women, Aboriginal Peoples, members of visible minorities, and persons with disabilities. To reach this goal, there is a diversity office in the personnel group at National Defense Headquarters with the task of developing overall C.F. policies. All groups and commands are required to submit an annual report about their employment equity plans.

In June of 1998 (revised November 1998), the Chief Review Services released its "Evaluation: Gender Integration in the C.F." report. The tenor of this report offered little that was new in terms of goals and recommendations. A couple of points worth noting include the assertion by the Chief of Maritime Staff (CMS) about culture and attitudes in the C.F., in that, regardless of rank, it would take more than ten years to expect the kind of changes required.[4] The report also criticized the "uncoordinated" and "piecemeal" way integration had been implemented and monitored.[5]

Another government report, released in March 2000, is the Minister's Advisory Board on Canadian Forces "Gender Integration, Employment and Equity: Successes and Opportunities: 1999 Annual Report." The Board, in addition to providing an annual report, is to:

(1) Review and evaluate employment equity activities of the C.F.;
(2) Identify major issues to be addressed;
(3) Inform the C.F. on the roles and functions of the Board; and
(4) Act as impartial external spokespersons about C.F. gender integration and employment equity.

Aside from general recommendations (see appendix I), the Navy fared rather well, with specific recommendations centering around the issue of women on submarines. The report stated that the Naval Reserves had perhaps the best record of gender integration in the C.F. in 1998, with 20 percent females in the Regular Navy and 35 percent in the Reserves. As of the Minister's 2001 report, the overall goal for recruitment was to reach 28 percent women for the C.F. overall.[6]

While MARCOM strives to guarantee a woman's "civil right" to serve in any trade or occupation, it is necessary to recall that active duty military personnel, by virtue of their profession and the realities of protecting national security, must continue to sacrifice certain rights enjoyed by the general public. For example, full freedom of speech could never be feasible for the armed forces of any nation. Yet Canadian society and, more importantly, civilian decision-makers, have demanded that one particular right be enforced, breaking the long-held tradition of placing only men intentionally into the line of fire. Peacekeeping or otherwise, the military remains a component of Canadian foreign policy.

CIVILIAN CONTROL AND REFLECTIONS OF SOCIETY

Canada's civil-military relationship, as is true in most democracies, is one of civilian control. This is a key feature of foreign policy decision-making in all aspects. In other words, civilian authorities have the final say on whether or not, where and when, women will serve in MARCOM. The military is expected to provide advice, but ultimately must obey. What may appear on the surface as a rather simple formula of authority has been the subject of much research and discussion.

Whether elite or general in nature, civil-military relations in democratic societies are intrinsically complicated by the coexistence of fundamentally different worldviews. According to Samuel Huntington, military professionals hold an inherently pessimistic view toward human nature; their attitudes tend to reflect what he refers to as "conservative realism." According to conservative realism, society is more important than the individual, who will tend to be irrational and weak unless provided with guidance. This view of human nature assumes that people tend to be greedy and combative when competing for scarce resources. Combined with the state's search for power, the permanence of human frailty ensures that conflict will be a constant element in international relations.[7]

Conservative realism, however, also includes the awareness that war is quite costly. Armed conflict should be avoided if it is not in the state's ultimate best interest. The military is the servant of civilian leadership; conflict is part of politics but should be considered quite carefully. According to this school of thought, the human tendency toward competition, raised to the level of the state, means that military power will remain the most important national security asset.

Many members of the civilian policy-making community, however, adhere to the more optimistic worldview associated with liberal democratic societies: people are inherently rational and good and humanity enjoys a linear progression toward an enlightened, peaceful society. At the state level, the assumption is that a world filled with liberal democracies would not resort to armed conflict.[8] When war becomes a crusade—for instance, fighting to protect liberal democratic principles—the individuals who participate come from all walks of life. They are citizen-soldiers. By contrast, a full-time, war-waging professional appears to be a "sellout" of democratic ideals. Civilians are civilized, while those who engage in the use of force as a profession, regardless of cause or goals, represent an inherent failure in human conduct. In other words, good professional soldiers do not make good liberal democrats, and vice versa.

While there are reserve forces, Canada also maintains a professional standing military. Military or otherwise, all professions possess common characteristics. Compiled by Sam C. Sarkesian, John Allen Williams, and Fred B. Bryant, the most prominent of those traits are listed in table 19.1. The military is one such profession and, in most Western-style democratic systems, the traits listed in the table are very much in evidence. With regard to corporate-bureaucratic structure, the military establishment has a clear chain of command, acting as necessary to update rules and regulations and performance standards, especially when it becomes necessary to interpret and implement directives from the civilian government. The requirement for special education and knowledge is embodied in the tradition of the military schools. If anything, this characteristic is becoming even more in evidence with time, given the expanded needs of society for a military with expertise in the operation of technologically advanced weapons systems. Professional self-regulation and disciplinary procedures also are firmly established through military codes and a system of justice.

Table 19.1. Common Characteristics of Professions

corporate-bureaucratic structure	among other things, this structure establishes a system of rules and regulations for the behavior of those in the profession and sets performance standards.
requirement for special education/knowledge	this demands certain expertise in those skills needed by society not readily available to non-professionals and includes the need for continuing education unique to the profession.
professional self-regulation	members at the top of the professional ladder and those selected to be the regulating agency determine entrance and promotion requirements and the status of various ranks within the profession.
	additionally, professionals expect loyalty from their members and adherence to professional standards; thus, the profession also serves as a disciplinary agency for its members.
sense of professional calling/ commitment	most professionals believe that their work is not simply an occupation
	it demands more than job skills and financial motivation.
	commitment to a profession comes primarily from the inner self, leading to a commitment to serve society regardless of financial remuneration.
	professionals are motivated by a sense of service and responsibility to society.

Source: Sam C. Sarkesian, John Allen Williams and Fred B. Bryant, *Soldiers, Society, and National Security* (Boulder, CO: Lynne Rienner Publishers, 1995).

Finally, a sense of professional calling and commitment within the military is based jointly on obedience to civilian authority and patriotism.

Despite the apparent contradictions, states such as Canada and the United States maintain standing military forces without threatening their democratic forms of government. This is due to the cornerstone of Canadian and American military professionalism: civilian control. Huntington describes two types of civilian control: objective and subjective. Under objective control, the military remains separate from society. The armed forces do not participate in politics; rather, they maintain a highly militarized and hierarchical society among themselves. Subjective civilian control is the opposite. Military professionalism is secondary to fitting in and functioning within society. Huntington assumes that, under these conditions, the armed forces will become entangled in politics and may even join the pursuit of political power. According to this line of reasoning, the shift of policy-making toward greater military involvement in traditionally political decisions may hold dangers for civilian control of the government.[9]

With reference to integration, subjective civilian control has been translated into a variety of personnel requirements, most of which are intended to result in a military that reflects societal demographics. If approximately half of adult Canadians in the workforce are women, then the relatively small percentage of women in MARCOM is a matter of concern. But general representation is not the only issue. The Navy is viewed according to a myriad of occupations with elements of risk that, each on its own, also should reflect the makeup of Canadian society.

Initial resistance to gender integration in MARCOM has typically been viewed in the media as a Neanderthal-style reaction by an entrenched male military elite—an "old-boys club" that does not want to open its door to the "girls." At the other end of a very emotional spectrum rests the issue of combat readiness and ability to fulfill mission requirements. Would gender integration disrupt cohesion? Would male sailors be overly protective of female sailors, at the expense of performing their tasks efficiently? Would sexual distraction, virtually certain to occur on mixed-gender ships, weaken the overall effectiveness of MARCOM? Concerns such as these, couched as national security issues with foreign policy implications, have been given as sufficient justification by some representatives of the various military services to voice their objections. Was this inappropriate meddling in areas of exclusive civilian control? Or, instead, does it represent the kind of expert advice that practitioners of military security are expected to render?

It is all too easy to depict criticisms of some or all of the gender integration policies as antiquated thought or inappropriate resistance on the part of the armed forces. Yet, in spite of changes since the collapse of the Soviet Union, post–Cold War civil-military relations in Canada seem to provide uninterrupted support for S. E. Finer's "principle of civil supremacy."[10] Finer focuses on the specific issue of military intervention in civilian government, which at times may appear to be a professional duty. A professional military may offer three reasons to justify intervention: primary military loyalty to the national community instead of the current government, an unwillingness to be used against political opposition to incumbents, and the belief that only the military is qualified to make certain decisions. The last of these types of reasons would fit, justified, with objections to gender integration. Finer's military professionalism should not be defined by a lack of involvement in political spheres; instead, *civil* supremacy determines whether the armed forces have overstepped their boundaries.

Civil supremacy, in fact, often is explained by the conduct of the military itself. Their obedience to legitimate, recognized authority is the determining factor in civil-military relations. In other words, the military chooses, as part of its professionalism, to submit to civilian policies.[11] This remained true in Canada, with rare and relatively minor exceptions, in spite of radical change in defense-related needs that could have caused military leaders to think that they, not the civilian leaders, knew what would be best for the country. While *Seven Days in May* had great entertainment value as a movie about a military coup in the United States during the Cold War, reality supports the idea of sustained civilian supremacy in established liberal democracies under even the most difficult conditions.[12]

Contrary to much of the civil-military relations theory cited above, some recent studies have noted the potential for problems if military and civilian cultures are too far part, particularly in their value systems. This is seen more clearly in the U.S. example. Surveys conducted between 1976 and 1996 indicate that the military and civilian elites are moving apart on the political spectrum, with the military becoming increasingly conservative with respect to civilian leadership. According to Ole Holsti, this phenomenon can lead to a crisis in civil-military relations as the military becomes increasingly partisan in nature.[13] In addition, since the collapse of the Soviet Union and the end of the Cold War, there no longer exists a universal perception of a clear threat to national security that would unify the two cultures. This is a trait shared with Canadian society, in which even the danger of terrorism is subject to varying perceptions about appropriate strategy and tactics.

If military obedience to civilian authority is unaffected, what dangers could there be to the public? In this case, the power of opinion could be a significant factor. Policy might become less coherent as the two groups find themselves viewing situations through different lenses. With less of a basis for consensus, fewer policy options might appear acceptable by both groups when faced with major challenges. Finally, perceptions abroad of a division in leadership could undermine foreign policy credibility.

Holsti offers three suggestions to narrow the gap between civilian and military leadership in the United States, with implications for Canada as well. First, some kind of universal military service could be put into place. Historical evidence would indicate that this is highly unlikely, since conscription barely scraped through Congress in 1940. In Canada, the issue has always been divisive, bringing the country close to the breaking point on two occasions.[14] Second, on-base facilities such as clubs and commissaries could be reduced, forcing the military to live more heavily "on the economy." (This idea, in all likelihood, would not be met with much enthusiasm in the military community.) Third, and perhaps most palatable to the armed forces, would be a reduction in separate military education. Reserve Officer Training Corps (ROTC) could be expanded at the undergraduate level, and higher degrees earned in civilian graduate programs. Some or all of these suggestions might be applied toward reducing the cultural gap between the C.F. and Canadian society.

Officially, the C.F. openly supports the concept that the military should reflect society. The *1999–2000 Annual Report of the Chief of the Defence Staff* cites two reasons. The first addresses shortages in certain occupations, including information technology specialists, preventive medicine technicians, and construction engineers: "One method the Canadian Forces are using to improve recruiting and retention rates over the long-term is to adapt to the cultural and demographic changes that have occurred in the Canadian workforce." The other reason is less concrete: "Moreover, as a national institution, and in order to better conduct operations around the world, the Canadian Forces must adapt to change in Canadian society by continuing to build a diverse and representative military force."[15] What exactly is the connection between reflecting changes in society and mission preparedness was not made clear. In another publication, however, the methods to be used were outlined as:

(1) Revise and update harassment policies and training;
(2) Develop a comprehensive policy on the requirement to accommodate religious and cultural diversity;
(3) Validate physical fitness standards and training so they are reflective of the physical fitness needs of the Canadian Forces; and
(4) Conduct cultural awareness training for recruiters.[16]

Let us assume, therefore, that the military has an *obligation* to specify problems with gender integration policies. The basic challenge is to accomplish gender integration without adversely affecting national security or Canada's ability to implement effective foreign policy. The evidence to date undermines concerns about mission readiness. In other words, *if* women should be integrated in the C.F. is no longer an issue; instead, *when* and *how* continue to be areas of responsibility and concern for the Canadian armed forces, including the Maritime Command.

THE ROLE OF WOMEN IN MARCOM

If the Canadian and U.S. militaries are molded closer to the image of popular culture, would the armed forces find it more difficult to be true military professionals, and remain at a distance from domestic politics? Will solving one problem, or solving it too quickly, simply create others? Will the ability of the armed forces to perform their missions be compromised? The answer to the first two of these questions will not be known for a long time. What is more readily discernible is the matter of mission readiness. This is critical to Canada's foreign policy posturing, particularly if it wishes to assert itself internationally with an identity independent of the United States. The current section will approach this issue with a review of the successes and shortcomings of gender integration into the Canadian Navy and provide comparisons with the U.S. Navy.

Canada's history includes colonial and frontier chapters that have resulted in women being involved in the use of force, sometimes to protect their own homes and villages.[17] The first women to serve in the organized military were nurses. Beginning with the North-West Rebellion of 1885, women nurses also were involved in the Yukon Field Force of 1898 and the South African (Boer) war in 1899–1902. In South Africa, Canadian nurses wore uniforms for the first time and were given the rank (and pay) of lieutenant. The quality of performance in these actions resulted in the formation of the Canadian Nursing Service on August 1, 1901.[18]

World War I resulted in 1,214 Canadian women going to Europe as part of the war effort, most with the Canadian Nursing Service and some as nurses with British or American forces. The conditions were often harsh and dangerous; 43 were killed and 328 received decorations. On the home front, 1,200 women were employed by the British Royal Air Force (RAF) in Toronto, most working as mechanics.

Between the two world wars, only a few women remained in the armed forces as nurses. While women's militias and auxiliary corps had been discussed at the end of World War I, no action was taken in peacetime. It was not until 1938 that once again military opportunities for women expanded. Women's reserve and service corps were opened in several provinces. Many wore uniforms and insignia and received military-style training. At one point the DND was concerned that these groups were violating the Criminal Code of the Defence of Canada Regulations that prohibited women serving in combat.

As the national emergency rose, however, women would take on a much more formal role. Several women's organizations were formed, including the Royal Canadian Army Medical Corps Nursing Service, the Royal Canadian Air Force Medical Branch and Nursing Service, the Canadian Women in the South African Military Nursing Service, the Royal Canadian Air Force (Women's Division), and the Canadian Women's Army Corps. Under what then was called the Royal Canadian Navy (RCN), two women's groups were created: the Royal Canadian Navy Nursing Service and the Women's Royal Canadian Naval Service, or Wrens. As would become apparent with time, neither the subsequent war effort nor foreign policy in general suffered as a result of the work done by these organizations. In fact, the record suggests quite the opposite.

Change occurred gradually, even in a wartime setting. In 1941, the first naval hospitals were created. Even though they often trained male sick berth attendants, no female nurses served at sea, and there was only one overseas Canadian naval hospital, in Greenock, Scotland. The RCN Nursing Service had some opportunities for women beyond nursing. Laboratory technicians, dietitians, physiotherapists, and occupational therapists also were hired and held officer rank. There were 345 nursing officers serving, including 49 in Great Britain. Only one died, Nursing Officer Agnes W. Wilkie, when her ferry was sunk by a German submarine.

The Wrens represented a step forward for women in the Canadian Navy that initially was resisted. At an April 2, 1941, meeting of the three services to discuss women in the armed forces, the RCN did not feel that forming a women's corps was necessary. The following announcement was made on June 20, 1941:

> The government has now decided that, in view of the ever-increasing demands upon Canada's available man-power by the Armed Forces, war

industries, agriculture and other essential occupations and services, including transportation and public utilities—Canadian women should now be organized to fill these positions. Among other things this will release considerable numbers of men already in the services, for combatant duties elsewhere.[19]

The RCN did not accept this invitation from the Canadian government until May 8, 1942.[20] Wrens served as stenographers, postal clerks, stewards, coders, cooks, pay writers, motor transports drivers, teletype operators and laundry people, or those tasks that had traditionally been performed by men who otherwise could be serving in combat situations. Wrens did share much with the men who served, including the oath of allegiance, chain of command, and many veteran benefits. However, Wrens were not put into combat situations, much less allowed to serve on board warships, and earned less salary than men at the same rank. At the same time, service in the Wrens was seen as an opportunity by many women seeking higher pay than in the civilian sector while serving more directly in the war effort; 6,781 women served Canada as Wrens and 20 received decorations.

The Wrens, as well as Air Force and Army corps, did not survive the end of the war and were disbanded. The following statement by Commander William Strange, Director of Naval Information in 1945, typified the DND's overall opinion of women in the armed forces:

> [I]t seems impossible that there should be a Navy without them. So thoroughly did they become part of the Navy during the days of great emergency, that now that the emergency has passed it is going to be hard for many who have remained to realize that they were, in actual fact, an emergency force.[21]

In the Korean War period recruitment of women began again, but at a modest level, and only single women could serve. In May, 1951, the Wrens were reestablished as RCN reserve, which, at the time, meant it was not a separate organization. Women became part of the regular Navy in 1955, but the number was capped at 400 and only if they were not compromising a man's career or causing an increase in a man's ratio of service at sea. In 1955, only 55 women served in the RCN, and by 1961 there were only 140. In that year, the Wrens were reviewed. The resulting recommendations, combined with a 1962 personnel shortfall in the Communication Branch, resulted in recruitment increases. The low point for women in the RCN came in the mid-1960s. The 1964 Landymore Report recommended that women should serve only in positions unsuitable for men and which could not be filled by civilians, or temporarily in positions when there were manpower shortages.

The Wrens again were eliminated when the services were unified in 1968, but day-to-day life for women did not change. While more women served in the 1970s as a result of the Royal Commission on the Status of Women, they were not assigned aboard ship until the SWINTER trials, or Service Women in Non-Traditional Environments and Roles. Beginning in 1980, this six-year project placed women in land, sea, air, and isolated location units. In what would be deemed a successful mixed-gender crew, the HMCS *Cormorant* included servicewomen from 1980 until 1984.[22]

Until the CREW, or Combat Related to the Employment of Women trials, however, about 80 percent of postings at sea were in the destroyer fleet and were closed to women. The CREW trials were set up to introduce women into combat situations. By the end of the 1990s, women were excluded on the basis of gender only from submarine duty and as Catholic chaplains. The process of incorporating women into combat units was not welcome in all quarters, including some women themselves. Female members of MARCOM already serving had joined a navy that would not require them to face danger or long absences from home spent at sea, an arrangement that some did not want to give up. In addition, not all the women currently serving met the physical requirements for certain combat-related occupations. Men and women of the same rank often had disparate training, education, and practical experiences. Many women had to attend conversion courses in order to meld into their new responsibilities.

In spite of these initial challenges, the DND did not fall back from its commitment to gender integration. The greatest challenge would become budget cutbacks, translating into significant force downsizing from 1992 to 1996, in particular. Since more men had been serving, more men were leaving. Combined with energetic recruitment aimed at women, the ratio of women to men improved some. Gender-mixed crews, such as those serving on board the HMCS *Protecteur*, reported no adverse incidents; in fact, positive results were noted. As has been the case on USN ships, men on mixed-gender crews have noted, and often appreciated, that language and conduct aboard improved, as well as hygiene.

The *1999–2000 Annual Report of the Chief of the Defence Staff* and the Minister's Advisory Board reports noted above address the C.F. as whole. In April 1998, MARCOM published its own document, *Vision 2010–The Integrated Navy*, meant to "provide the framework for policy and practice through which women will be fully integrated within the Navy."[23] Planning is based on six "fundamental principles":

(1) The MARCOM will recruit the best, regardless of gender;
(2) The Navy will plan for future responsibilities;
(3) Progress will be judged by setting a framework to meet goals and establish a method of evaluation;
(4) The difference between policy and actual practice will be recognized;
(5) Policy will be based on solid research; and
(6) Policies will be set within the existing Divisional System.

Some successful MARCOM initiatives include the MGUs, or Mixed Gender Units, as opposed to assigning merely one or two women per unit (in 2000 the term became simply *mixed*). In this manner, integration can become incorporated practice, rather than token representation. While this policy facilitates working and living situations for women, it means that there are many men serving in the Navy who have never served aboard an integrated ship. For that reason, education and awareness must be ongoing for the foreseeable future.

Eight years after the Human Rights Tribunal, the percentages of women serving in "hard sea" trades rose more than 600 percent, but that means an increase from .9 percent to only 5.64 percent of total representation, a long way from mirroring women in the Canadian workforce. There were, at the time of the report in April 1998, no women in senior commissioned or non-commissioned ranks in hard sea occupations. That is not surprising, since women had been introduced to these occupations so recently. As time passes, eligible women will be available for promotion to these ranks, but the proportions will remain problematic unless the Navy can reverse the attrition rate for women, which stood at twice the rate of men in the years from 1989 to 1996.

Vision 2010 identified ten areas requiring action, including research, goal setting, family policy, bunking, harassment, submarine service, and clothing and equipment. Part of the research goal is to address cultural change, which the Navy views as follows:

> The military is commonly viewed as a microcosm of the society from which it is drawn, a segment that ultimately reflects the aims and values in Canadian society at large reflected in the attitudes of Navy personnel. Some changes within the CF and the Navy have occurred as a result of changing societal realities which, in turn, became prevalent within these organizations.

It is important to note that *Vision 2010* includes what many other documents have not:

> The military incorporates additional values and factors which make it in some ways unique and distinct. "Members of the Canadian Forces are expected to serve their nation . . . with (the) commitment to place the performance of their military duties and the operational effectiveness of the CF above their own concerns, for selfless acceptance of the unlimited liability of military service is the essence of a free society's defense capability" (Cotton 1981). The challenge facing the organization is to incorporate changing values within the context of the organizational culture and operational effectiveness. (quotation in original)

> Organizational culture encompasses the assumptions, norms, and values of an organization. A culture evolves over time, is difficult to manipulate, and slow to change. The integration of women in the Navy constitutes a substantial change to the culture of the organization. A review of the literature on culture change shall be undertaken to determine the most effective ways of assisting this culture change while maintaining the primacy of operational readiness and military effectiveness.

Vision 2010 goes on to note that there is a distinct advantage to changing culture in a *military* organization, as compared to a *civilian* organization, since there is greater control over the lives of C.F. members. It also is noted that attitudes underlying behavior can be difficult to detect, and therefore manipulate, since "political correctness" has resulted in hesitancy for individuals to reveal their true feelings. In an attempt to head off these kinds of problems, a reality-oriented recruitment approach by

MARCOM has been implemented. The intent is to "provide [female] applicants with fuller and more accurate expectations of a job and occupation." Better-informed recruits should translate into better retention rates.

There are two other points of interest in *Vision 2010* that many other reports also do not include. One is the recommendation for a "public forum of some kind, such as an international conference, to highlight the achievement of the Canadian Navy." Second, the problem of gender-separate bunking and filling all shipboard occupations is addressed. When a vacancy occurs, a qualified person of both the same occupation and gender often must fill it. This inevitably will cause problems, and the report raised the possibility of mixed accommodation providing, for example, privacy partitions. One solution being tried by the USN on the USS *San Antonio* is to break down the berthing compartment to smaller 24-bed units, intended to provide more flexibility in personnel selection. Other changes on the San Antonio include lowering items such as valves and electrical outlets (women on average are five inches shorter than men), providing more storage space for additional toilet paper and other toiletries, installing washing machines with a gentle cycle, and providing a sink for the ship's barber.[24]

A final item in *Vision 2010* worth mentioning is the controversy of submarine service. Only the newest Victoria class submarines provide appropriate accommodations for mixed-gender crews, yet MARCOM no longer has submarine service as voluntary duty. Therefore, the situation becomes one of reverse discrimination against men. In spite of continued impediments such as these, integration in MARCOM appears to have the admirable goal of a truly level playing field for all members, with only those unavoidable differences, such as pregnancy, differentiating men and women.

Canada's relations with other states depend to a large extent on its ability to use or threaten force offshore. Its ability to meet obligations to international agreements, either directly state-based or as part of an international organization, equally depend upon the quality of its navy. As long as force sizes remain relatively small, the quality of the people in MARCOM increasingly becomes more important. The demands of the 1982 Charter must be met as a domestic requirement without a negative impact to Canada's foreign policy options.

It might be unfair to judge gender integration in MARCOM strictly by comparing it with other sectors of Canadian society. A more valid and perhaps more rigorous test would be to compare the Canadian armed forces with other states, including those that have approached gender integration aggressively.

GENDER INTEGRATION ACROSS STATES

Relative to other states, gender integration in the C.F. is one of the better examples. As of 2003, only four states out of a sampling of 25 had a higher percentage of women in the military than Canada's 11.6 percent: Australia (12.5%), New Zealand (14.7%), South Africa (14.4%), and the U.S. (15.0%).[25] Some states are surprising; for example Jordan, a predominately Islamic nation, has about 3 percent, or 4,000 women serving in its armed forces. One, a sister of King Abdullah, is a graduate of Sandhurst and holds the rank of colonel. In 2000, France included women for the first time in its one-day call-up for service, with more than 8,000 women participating. Also in 2000 the Israeli Knesset passed a law allowing women to serve in army combat units. Lagging states include Austria, Mexico, and Italy—which allowed women to serve in the armed forces just a few years ago, and Germany—whose ban on women bearing arms was overturned by the European Court as unconstitutional in 2000.

Looking at naval services, many states in addition to Canada have women serving on combat ships: Australia, Belgium, Denmark, France, Germany, Israel, the Netherlands, New Zealand, Norway, Portugal, Singapore, South Africa, Spain, Sweden, the U.S., and the U.K. Three states have women serving on submarines—Australia, Norway, and Sweden—with Sweden having the first female submarine captain. Female captains may sound novel, but if Herodotus is to be believed, Artemisia was a naval commander during the ancient Persian Wars.

Figures 19.1 through 19.9 present recent data on women in the C.F. and U.S. Department of Defense (DOD).[26] Figure 19.1 shows C.F. Regular Force and Enrollment into the Regular Force, comparing men and women from 1989 to 1998. Due to downsizing, absolute numbers for men have been reduced, while women have remained relatively the same, increasing their overall percentage. Not surprisingly, the number of women enrolling into the Regular Force has been rising. The percentage of women, however, lags behind that of women in the USN, which was 13.3 percent for

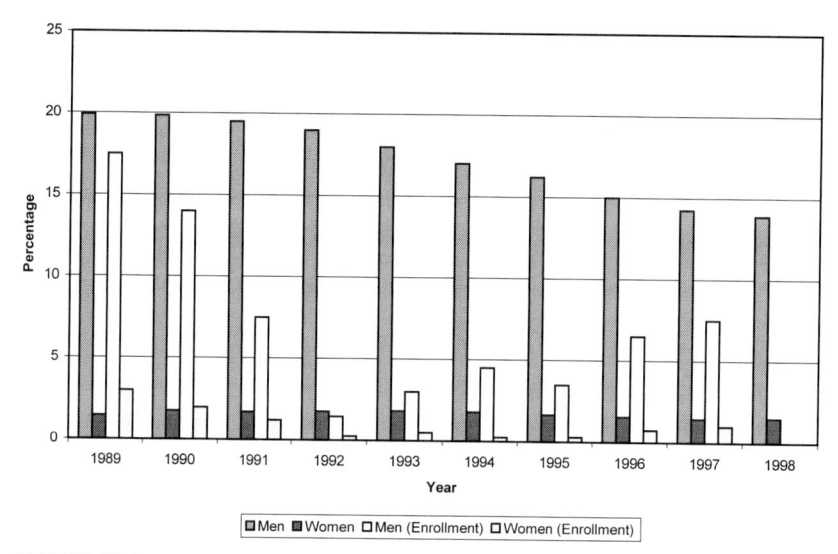

FIGURE 19.1
Total Regular Force of the CF and Enrollment into the Regular Force

enlisted and 14.4 percent for officers, increasing to 15.0 percent each by 2003.

The next four figures show differences between men and women at various ranks. In the C.F. (figure 19.2), rank distributions for officers in the C.F. show that since 1989, a greater percentage of women officers have moved from the lower ranks into the middle ranks. It can be expected that this trend will continue, with an increased percentage of women officers being represented at the highest ranks. The same trends hold for Non-Commissioned Members (NCM) (figure 19.3). The data for the U.S. are broken down by service, and represents only the highest pay grades (figures 19.4 and 19.5). The USN leads the other services for percentages of female officers, but leads only the Marines for enlisted women.

When considering occupational groups in the C.F., percentage increases of officers have exceeded non-commissioned members in three areas: combat arms, naval operational/technical, and medical/dental (figure 19.6). NCMs have the better record in air operational/technical, engineer/communications and support. In the United States (figures 19.7 and 19.8), most positions are now open to women, but not as many as in the C.F. The data for women in U.S. occupations does not compare well

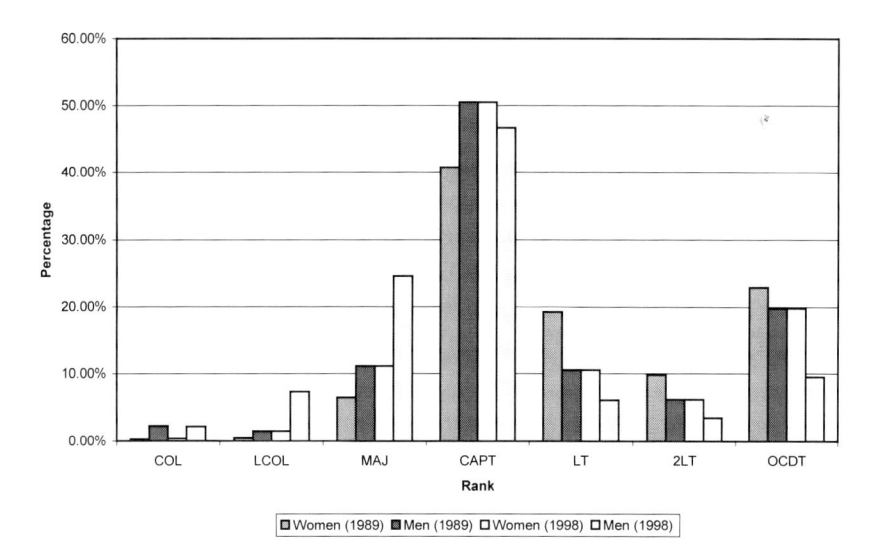

FIGURE 19.2
Rank Distribution for CF Officers

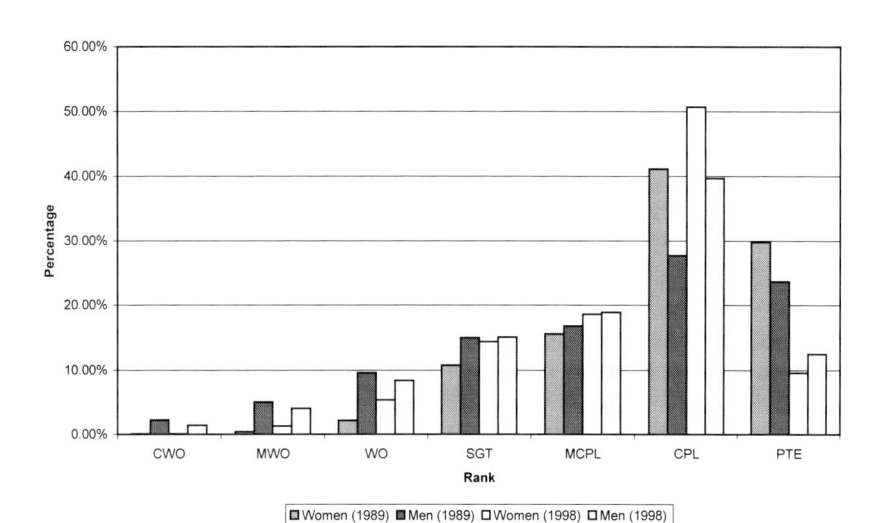

FIGURE 19.3
Rank distribution for CF Non-Commissioned Members

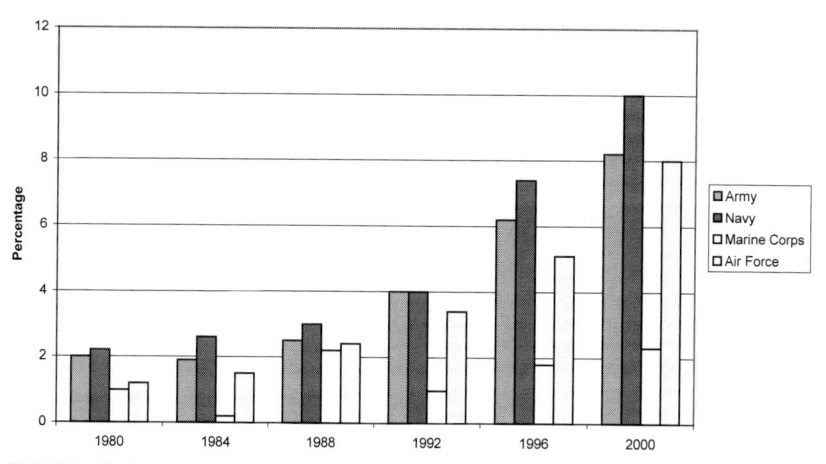

FIGURE 19.4
US Women in Senior Officer Pay Grades by Branch of Service, O6 Colonel/Navy Captain

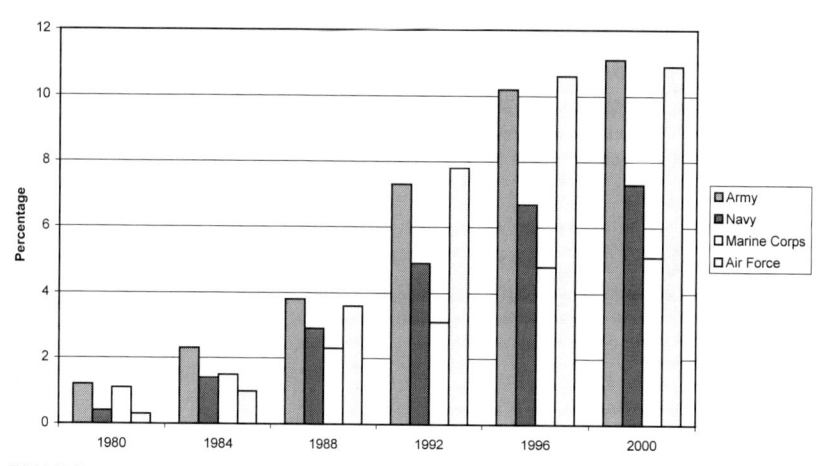

FIGURE 19.5
US Women in Senior Enlisted Pay Grades by Branch of Service, E7–E9

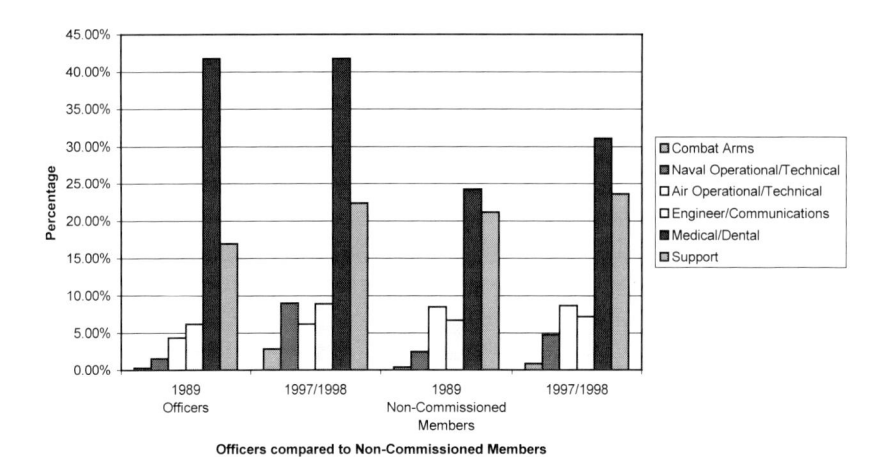

FIGURE 19.6
CP Female Representation by Occupational Group

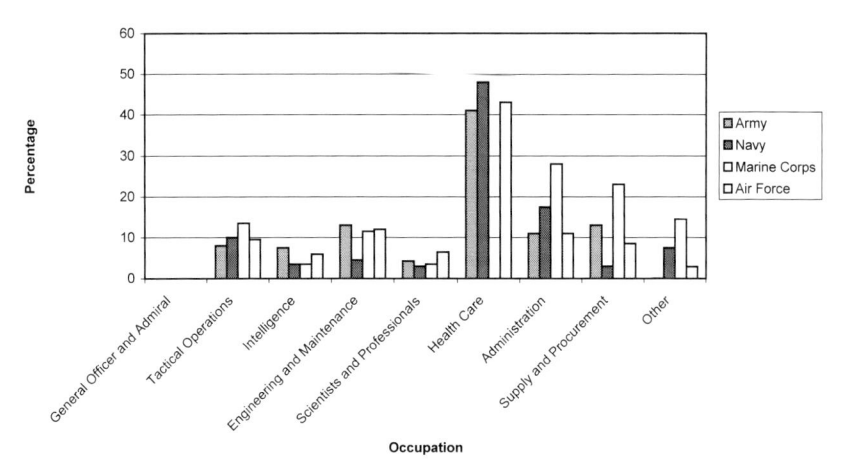

Figure 19.7*
Occupational Profile of US Active Duty Women Officers by Branch of Service, 2000
*The percentage of general officers and admirals is less than one-tenth of one percent. In the health care category, Marine Corps services are provided by the Navy.

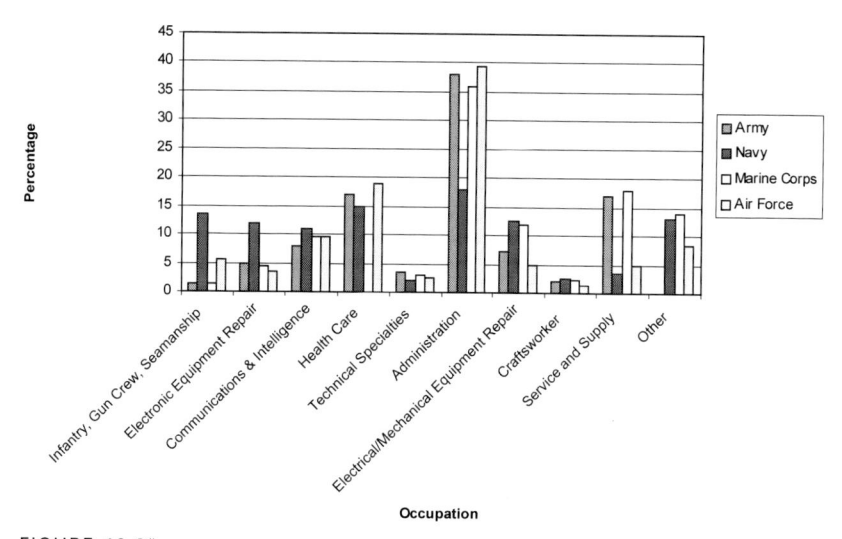

CIVIL-MILITARY RELATIONS AND CANADIAN FOREIGN POLICY 479

FIGURE 19.8*
Occupational Profile of US Active Duty Enlisted Women by Branch of Service, 2000
*Marine Corps health care services are provided by the Navy.

between officers and enlisted since different occupations are listed. Instead, the services are compared. Women officers have better percentages for the predictable occupations—health care and administration. The USN does not fare so well in the other occupations. It would appear that at the enlisted level, women in the USN are better off than the other services in many non-traditional occupations, such as seamanship, electronics, communication, and mechanical repair. Most of these occupations at sea are aboard combat ships.

Overall these figures show advances, but clearly there is room for improvement when attrition rates are considered (figure 19.9). The last figure offers data for the C.F., but MARCOM, specifically, as well as the USN, are experiencing higher attrition rates from combat arms than any other occupation.

CONCLUSION

Senator Nancy Landon Kassebaum (R-Kansas, retired) has appropriately observed that "we turn to a commission when we are afraid to say anything ourselves."[27] An effective foreign policy is difficult under the best of circumstances. Even with a peacekeeping identity, Canada is further hin-

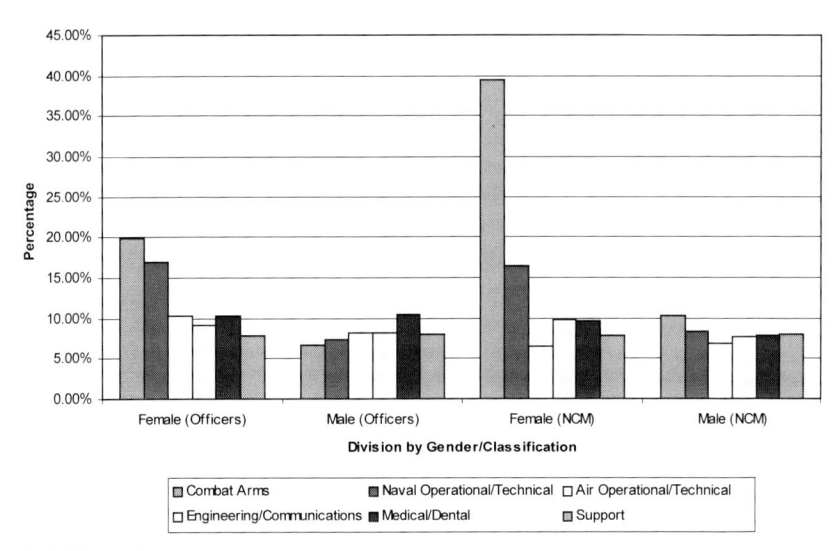

FIGURE 19.9
Average CF Attrition Rates by Occupational Group

dered by an increasingly weakened military capability. One of the ways to rebuild an armed force is to recruit the best, including both men and women. Incorporating women in combat units into the Canadian armed forces is a move to catch the military up to other sectors of society that already have begun integrating women into their professions. In the United States, gender integration often is compared to racial integration. In contrast, racial integration reforms, rather than following society's example, placed the military in the vanguard of American institutions trying to ensure equal roles for African Americans.

Racial integration of the U.S. armed forces did not, as some ill-informed politicians and political commentators claim, occur with a stroke of President Truman's pen. African Americans in World War II served in strictly segregated units. Many of these units distinguished themselves, such as the Tuskegee Airmen, which was formed in 1941. It was not until 1948 that, in true Presbyterian fashion, Truman signed Executive Order 9981, which created a committee to look into integration of the armed forces. As late as 1956, fully segregated units were serving under NATO command. This may seem too little, and much too late, but it is important to recall that racial integration in U.S. society as a whole lagged behind efforts in the military.

Racial integration in the U.S. armed services was not a smooth process. From 1968 to 1974 there were many racial disturbances on military installations, reflecting similar upheavals off base. In 1972 the Equal Opportunity Act was passed; in the same year race relations training for all Department of Defense personnel began. (In comparison, sexual harassment training did not begin until 1982, and then only in the U.S. Air Force.) Problems related to race still exist, but the military has, as whole, led American society in racial integration. This would seem to support the assertion in *Vision 2010* that culture in military organizations can be easier to change. For example, by the 1980s, interracial marriages and children were not an issue among the vast majority within the U.S. military community. When placed in terms of professional generations of, say, twenty years, then the fuller successes of racial integration policies were not realized until the professional grandchildren of the 1948 military had reached maturity. Society in Canada, and the law, requires that gender integration in the C.F. succeed much more swiftly.

By the year 2010, MARCOM hopes to have women comprise 25 percent of its personnel. To reach that goal, it is estimated that women must represent 40 percent of recruits. Getting women to join, and stay, will require a tremendous effort that is exacerbated by budgetary constraints.

Perhaps one of the main challenges to MARCOM is public relations. The media has not always been helpful. The focus tends to be on sexual relations and sexual harassment. Sexual harassment occurs in any profession, and men can be targets as well as women. This problem is not unique to the armed forces, and is being rigorously addressed. The same holds true for fraternization. MARCOM has the greatest challenge here, with the reality of men and women serving in close quarters for extended periods of time, a situation that has titillated reporters and their readers alike.[28] When the first U.S. warship, the USS *Eisenhower*, sailed in 1994 with women in the crew, the media reported that three women had to be removed due to pregnancy. Most reports neglected to mention, however, that all were married, two were pregnant when the cruise began but did not yet know, and the third became pregnant by her husband on a shore leave. It may be a matter of time before the public in states with a fully professional navy comprised of both men and women consider the situation less than newsworthy.

According to most of the literature on civil-military relations, mandating that the military base personnel decisions on societal expectations rather than military readiness undermines traditional military professionalism, and therefore the potential mission. Since the Cold War has ended, however, the majority of the Canadian public does not perceive a threat to its national security. The need for a traditional military does not exist in the minds of many Canadians. Combined with stringent policies throughout society to reduce and eliminate inequalities in professional opportunities, it is clear the military must comply with civilian leadership on the subject of integration. Yet this does not remove the responsibility among military leaders to ensure that the process does not undermine operational performance in order to execute a component of foreign policy or project a perception of military competence. It should, however, be recognized that there are inherent contradictions. This does not imply a rejection of the policy; rather it urges a better understanding. Put simply, a full comprehension of these contradictions need not challenge *if* women should be integrated, but it can inform *how* and *when* the process should occur. By providing quality advice, the C.F., or specifically MARCOM, need not violate the tenets of civilian control.

As noted at the beginning of this chapter, there have been a number of commissions and inquiries about gender integration in the C.F. as a whole and the Maritime Command specifically. The resulting reports are quite similar, in that they identify areas of concern and make recommendations to correct causes of problems and encourage successes in this critical component of Canadian foreign policy. However, there is a clear absence of quality data available. Consider, for example, the MARCOM's *Vision 2010*. More than thirty research projects are specified. It appears to be yet another new study, rather than a part of an ongoing process that builds on prior knowledge. If MARCOM is to move forward with gender integration, there needs to be a concentration on gathering quality data, rigorously analyzing and coding the data, and enabling any additional studies to be reproducible and add to a solid base of information. This needs to be accomplished without putting women in a spotlight or creating an issue that, in many cases, does not exist. By removing the "uncoordinated" and "piecemeal" aspects to these studies, a positive quality of life for MARCOM members can be guaranteed without repeated intrusion into their professional lives.

In a modern liberal democracy, the monopoly of organized military force is controlled by the state and its civilian leadership. The end of the Cold War changed much concerning Canada's foreign policy, but it did not exclude the military as a tool of foreign policy. Canada's emphasis on human security has meant that the military often has been used primarily for peacekeeping purposes such as in Bosnia or Afghanistan, both theaters of operation in which women in uniform take part. Peacekeeping operations such as Afghanistan often are situations in which traditional military training is necessary. Coupled with regional interests and responsibilities, the C.F., including MARCOM, remains a necessary component to Canada's role as a modern, sovereign state in an interdependent world.

APPENDIX I: SUMMARY OF RECOMMENDATIONS BY THE MINISTER'S ADVISORY BOARD

Recommendation 1: "The Board recommends that Land Force Command (LFC) follow the lead of the Air and Maritime Commands in clearly demonstrating that diversity is embraced and valued as an operational imperative."

Recommendation 2: "The Board recommends that all recruiting material and advertising be reviewed for its inclusiveness and lack of bias."

Recommendation 3: "The Board recommends that recruiting material be more focused on a diverse workforce and team relationships and that it show the wide variety of career opportunities available."

Recommendation 4: "The Board recommends that the C.F. partner with the community resource groups in order to develop effective, targeted outreach strategies and activities to attract members of designated groups to C.F. employment opportunities."

Recommendation 5: "The Board recommends that LFC develop and emphasize other performance standards required for excellence in soldiering in order to combat perceptions of double standards."

Recommendation 6: "The Board recommends that LFC study the development of a more task-oriented physical fitness test."

Recommendation 7: "The Board also recommends that consideration be given to developing predictive tests (like the Entrance Test for the Basic Parachutist Course) for courses requiring higher levels of physical fitness, as well as remedial programs to assist members of both sexes to meet those requirements."

Recommendation 8: "The Board recommends that the Maritime Command remove all restrictions and barriers to the service of women in submarines."

Recommendation 9: "The Board recommends that policies regarding parental leaves be endorsed in principle and in practice at both the senior and local levels."

Recommendation 10: "The Board recommends that the C.F. respond to SCONDVA's recommendations with respect to career management and develop and implement a mentoring system."

Source: http://www.forces.gc.ca/site/reports/CFGIEE/annex4-e.htm.

APPENDIX II: GENDER INTEGRATION TIMELINE

RCN/MARCOM	YEAR	United States Navy
	1812	First women at sea as nurses
Nurses serve in the Northwest Rebellion	1885	
Nurses serve in the Yukon Field Force	1898	
Nurses serve in the Boer War as uniformed lieutenants	1899	
Canadian Nursing Service formed	1901	
	1908	U.S. Navy Nurse Corps established
Nurse mobilization 18 September	1914	
	1917	Navy Department allows enrollment of women as yeomen in Naval Reserve
1,214 served in WWI, 43 fatalities	1918	
First naval hospitals; RCN Nursing Service formed	1941	
Wrens formed as legal component of RCN	1942	WAVES created (Women Accepted for Volunteer Emergency Service)
95,000 men and more than 6,000 women in RCN at war's end[a]; Wrens begin demobilization	1945	U.S.S. *Higbee*—first ship named for a woman[b]
	1947	Army-Navy Nurse Act
	1948	Women Armed Services Integration Act: women allowed to enlist, but not to comprise more than 2% of total enlisted force;

		proportion of female officers to female enlisted no more than 10%; women cannot be promoted to admiral; can serve aboard only hospital ships and certain transports; cannot command men
Wrens reestablished as RCN Reserves; women must be single	1951	Defense Advisory Committee on Women in the Services (DACOWITS) established
Women part of regular Navy but participation capped at 400, 55 serve	1955	
140 serve	1961	
Landymore Report recommends restrictions	1964	
	1967	2% cap on women in military lifted, women eligible to the rank of O6
	1972	Women allowed in ROTC; First woman promoted to admiral; Navy allows limited number of women into all enlisted ratings and allows nonmedical women to serve on U.S.S. *Sanctuary*; Women allowed into Chaplain and Civil Engineering Corps; End of restrictions on succeeding to command ashore
	1973	Women in Navy pilot training
	1976	Woman enter Annapolis and other service academies
Number of women in C.F. increases significantly; Women allowed sea duty in the Naval Reserve	1970s	
Human Rights Act passed; SWINTER trials begin	1978	Women allowed to serve on support vessels
Members of Regular Force ships company	1980	No more separate appointment, promotion, accounting, and

APPENDIX II: (Continued)

RCN/MARCOM	YEAR	United States Navy
Women enter military academies; HMCS *Cormorant* becomes mixed-gender		separation procedures; No more appointees to flag/general officer rank, now must compete with men
Charter of Rights and Freedoms	1982	
Equality Rights comes into force	1985	
Charter Task Force formed	1986	
CREW trials begin; Mixed-gender ships implemented; Removal of all gender-based restrictions	1987	
	1988	DoD Risk Rule established[c]
Canadian Human Rights Tribunal orders full integration in all CF units and occupations (except submarines), all MARCOM combat occupations open to women	1989	
	1990	Woman commands ship—USS *Opportune*
	1991	Women in forward/combat zones in the Persian Gulf as part of Operation Desert Storm
	1993	Naval Combatant Exclusion Law repealed; Women assigned to combat aircraft
MINERVA plan adopted	1994	Direct Ground Combat Exclusion Policy replaces Risk Rule[d]; USS *Eisenhower* becomes first combat ship with women on the crew; Navy submits data on standard body measurements for Navy aircraft to accommodate female pilots
Employment Equity Act	1996	First woman fires Tomahawk missile in combat
Regular Navy 20% female; Navy Reserves 35% female	1998	First woman to bomb an enemy target
	1999	Women allowed onto coastal mine

		hunters and mine counter measure ships
Vision 2010 report	2000	First warship commanded by a woman; women assigned to 155 ships—106 of them combatant; Marine troop carrier U.S.S. *San Antonio* being constructed with women crewmembers in mind; 14% in USN are women, including 12 of 220 admirals; Two women killed in terrorist attack on the destroyer USS *Cole*
Women serve in Operation Apollo in Afghanistan	2001	Six women killed in 9/11 Pentagon attack
First woman accepted into Canadian Basic Submarine Qualification Course	2002	
First warship commanded by a woman; First female clearance diving officer to command Experimental Diving Unit; 16% C.F. workforce are women	2003	14.4% naval personnel are women
	2004	Projected average 12% women per ship
Goal of 28% women's representation in C.F. workforce	2005–2006	

NOTES

1. I would like to thank the Centre for Military and Strategic Studies at the University of Calgary for its generous support of this project.

2. *National Defence: Manpower Study* (Ottawa: Department of National Defence, 1965).

3. Canadian Human Rights Tribunal, "Gauthier vs. the Canadian Forces," February 1989, 24.

4. Chief Review Services, "Evaluation: Gender Integration in the CF," 5000-1 (CRS), June 1998 (revised November 1998), iv.

5. Chief Review Services, "Evaluation: Gender Integration in the CF," 4.

6. Minister's Advisory Board on Canadian Forces Gender, Employment, Integration and Equity, "Successes and Opportunities: 1999 Annual Report," 23. Min-

ister's Advisory Board on Canadian Forces Gender, Employment, Integration and Equity, "Successes and Opportunities." The board issued another set of recommendations the next year in the "Summary of Recommendations: How to Improve the Grade, 2000 Annual Report." No specific reference was made to gender integration, only to the general category "designated group." See http://www.forces.gc.ca/site/reports/CFGIEE/annex5-e.htm; and http://www.forces.gc.ca/site/reports/CFGIEE/4a-e.htm#obj.

7. Samuel P. Huntington, *The Soldier and the State: The Theory and Politics of Civil-Military Relations* (Cambridge, MA: The Belknap Press of Harvard University Press, 1957), 59–79.

8. Put forward by Immanuel Kant centuries ago, the idea of a democratic peace recently came back into favor, although not without controversy. See Immanuel Kant, *Kant's Political Writings*, ed. Hans Reiss, trans. H. B. Nisbet (Cambridge: Cambridge University Press, 1970); Michael Doyle, "Liberalism and World Politics," *American Political Science Review* 80, no. 4 (December 1986): 1151–1169; Francis Fukuyama, "The End of History?" *The National Interest* 16 (Summer 1989), 3–18; Rudolph J. Rummel, *War, Power, and Peace* (Beverly Hills, CA: Sage, 1995); Bruce M. Russett, *Grasping the Democratic Peace* (Princeton: Princeton University Press, 1993). Some new arguments contradict the democratic peace theory. For an example based on statistical analysis, see Patrick James, Eric Solberg, and Murray Wolfson, "An Identified Systemic Model of the Democracy-Peace Nexus," *Defence and Peace Economics* 10 (1999): 1–37. Critics with historical arguments against the democratic peace now appear regularly in the pages of *International Security*.

9. Huntington, *The Soldier and the State*, 80–85.

10. S. E. Finer, *The Man on Horseback: The Role of the Military in Politics* (New York: Praeger, 1962), 23–32.

11. Finer, *The Man on Horseback*, 23–32.

12. Janowitz introduces a view of the basic nature of civil-military relations that is fundamentally different from those discussed so far. He places responsibility for civilian control with the *civilian* leadership. Janowitz emphasizes the military's permanent acceptance of civilian authority, even under conditions of dramatic change. Military involvement in politics occurs only if civilians fail to perform tasks in their sphere of responsibility. Morris Janowitz, *The Professional Soldier* (New York: The Free Press, 1971), viii, 14.

13. Ole R. Holsti, "A Widening Gap between the U.S. Military and Civilian Society? Some Evidence: 1976–1996," *International Security* 23, no. 3 (Winter 1998): 5–42. Also contributing to the gap between American military and civilian society is the fact that fewer civilians are exposed to military culture since the end of conscription in 1973.

14. When conscription was voted upon in 1917 and in 1942, French-speaking Québec and English-speaking Canada took opposite stances, the former as strongly opposed as the latter was favorable to compulsory military service.

15. *Building On a Stronger Foundation: Annual Report of the Chief of the Defence Staff 1999–2000* (Ottawa: Department of National Defence, 2000), 12–13.

16. *National Defence: Report on the Plans and Priorities—2000* (Ottawa: Department of National Defence), 31.

17. The history provided here is drawn in large part from Barbara Dundas, *A History of Women in the Canadian Military* (Ottawa: Editions Art Global and the Department of National Defence, 2000). This book includes an excellent collection of art and photographs. Additional sources include the various government reports listed above and Barbara Winters, "The Wrens of the Second World War: Their Place in the History of Canadian Servicewomen," *A Nation's Navy*, 280–296.

18. The Canadian Militia Army Medical Services had been created two years earlier.

19. As quoted in Dundas, *A History of Women in the Canadian Military*, 48.

20. The air force formed a women's corps on July 2, 1941, with the army following on August 13, 1941.

21. Dundas, *A History of Women in the Canadian Military*, 90.

22. Approval came from the shipboard commanders, the Canadian Forces Personnel Applied Research Unit (CFPARU), and ultimately the Chief of Defence Staff.

23. "Vision 2010—The Integrated Navy," Chief of the Maritime Staff, http://www.dnd.ca/navy/marcom/intro_e.htm.

24. Kathleen McGrath, "Aye, Aye, Ma'am: The Navy makes history as it sends the first U.S. warship ever commanded by a woman toward the troubled waters of the Persian Gulf," *Time*, March 27, 2000.

25. This comparative information can be found in Lory Manning and Vanessa R. Wight, *Women in the Military: Where They Stand*, 4th edition (Washington, DC: Women's Research & Education Institute, 2003).

26. The figures for Canada are for the C.F. as a whole. The C.F. figures are taken from Leesa Tanner, "Gender Integration in the Canadian Forces: A Quantitative Overview" (paper presented to the conference "Women in Uniform: Exploding the Myths; Exploring the Facts," Women's Research and Education Institute, Washington, DC, December 1998). The U.S. information is found in Manning and Wight, *Women in the Military*.

27. This quotation is from a speech delivered at Iowa State University, October 14, 1996.

28. Mark Milner wrote that concerns over fraternization often came from wives of sailors, concerned about their husbands' extended absences from home, yet serving with other women in close quarters. Mark Milner, *Canada's Navy: The First Century* (Toronto: University of Toronto Press, 1999), 286.

APPENDICES NOTES

a. Peter T. Haydon, "Sailors, Admirals, and Politicians: The Search for Identity after the War," in *A Nation's Navy: In Quest of Canadian Naval Identity*, ed. Michael L. Hadley, Rob Huebert, and Fred W. Crickard (Montreal: McGill-Queen's University Press, 1996), 231. When the war began in 1939, there were 3,843 serving in the RCN. See David Zimmerman, "The Social Background of the Wartime Navy: Some Statistical Data," *A Nation's Navy*, 256. In all, almost 50,000 Canadian women served in the military during the war. See Winters, "The Wrens of the Second World War," 281.

b. Lenah S. Higbee was the head of Navy nurses during World War II.

c. The Risk Rule states that women are barred from units and positions in which "risk of exposure to direct combat, hostile fire, or capture is equal to or greater than that experienced by associated combat units in the same theater of operations."

d. The Direct Ground Combat Exclusion Policy states the following: "Service members are eligible to be assigned to all positions for which they are qualified, except that women shall be excluded from assignment to units below brigade level whose primary mission is to engage in direct combat on the ground, defined as: 1) engaging an enemy on the ground with individual or crew served weapons, while 2) being exposed to hostile fire, and 3) to a high probability of direct physical contact with the hostile force's personnel. All three of these must be met in order to exclude women."

20

Civil Society Participation in Canadian Foreign Policy: Expanded Consultation in the Chrétien Years

JEFFREY M. AYRES[1]

EXPANDED CONSULTATION IN THE CHRÉTIEN YEARS

In the twenty-first century, foreign policy-makers increasingly have been forced to navigate through an extraordinarily more complicated international environment than did their predecessors a mere decade ago. This post–Cold War political environment of "international deregulation" has heralded new alliances, new alignments, new actors yet no new broadly accepted rules for the making and conduct of foreign policy.[2] Transnational political processes, notably the globalization of the world's economy, the explosive growth and spread of non-governmental organizations (NGOs) and the emergence of new Internet technologies, are trends inescapably affecting the more traditional hierarchical patterns of domestic foreign policy-making. As a small, historically trade-dependent and internationally-engaged state, Canada has been especially impacted by this more complex international environment.

During the 1990s, Canada's foreign policy-making establishment was forced to confront and adapt to not only these rapidly evolving transnational trends, but tremendous domestic political upheavals as well. Citizens' groups, politicians, and political observers in the media and in academic settings increasingly found fault with traditional foreign policy review processes and consultation exercises. NGOs across Canada had also become more international in approach and more adept at strategic cross-sectoral coalition-building. The late 1980s' divisive debates over the Canada-U.S. Free Trade Agreement contributed in part to a more agitated orientation and fed a groundswell of citizen unrest at established political institutions and political processes across Canada, which one political observer described as a "decline of deference."[3] Citizen groups across Canada, also increasingly politically mobilized with the introduction of the Charter of Rights and Freedoms in 1982, would by the end of the 1990s simply expect no less than ample opportunity for various forms of civil society interaction and participation within Canada's foreign policy-making process.

In part anticipating these trends, the incoming Liberal government in 1993 pledged to "democratize" Canadian foreign policy. This goal included interest in promoting greater consultation outside parliamentary chambers to link with NGOs, the holding of cross-country forums on the direction and content of Canadian foreign policy with academic, civil society, and government experts, and the creation of other new types of partnerships between Canadian citizens and the foreign policy establishment. After over a decade now of consecutive Liberal governments, this chapter will assess the progress made toward this goal of democratizing Canadian foreign policy. It will examine the impact of international and domestic-level trends, which together have shaped a Canadian political environment toward becoming if not fully democratic, at least arguably much more open to high levels of citizen participation in foreign policy-making than has ever before been experienced.

TRANSNATIONAL POLITICAL PROCESSES AND FOREIGN POLICY-MAKING

Research on transnational political processes has become an explosive and continually evolving part of the study of international relations. From early emphases on transnational economic relations,[4] the transnational politics paradigm has expanded to include, for example, humanitarian issues[5] and environmental politics.[6] Recent innovations also have embraced the increased study of transnational social movements and contentious political issues including the global justice movement against neoliberal globalization.[7] There is a general consensus that the end of the

Cold War and the globalization of the world's economy were major stimuli to the growth of the study of transnational politics. However, especially supporting this burgeoning field of study has been the explosive growth in number in recent years of NGOs, a trend particularly important for understanding concomitant changes in the process of making and conducting Canadian foreign policy.

NGOs can be defined as "private, voluntary nonprofit groups whose primary aim is to influence publicly some form of social change."[8] NGOs are but a part of domestic civil societies, the latter more broadly defined as the "arena of organized political activity between the private sphere (the household and the firm) and the formal political institutions of governance (the parliament, political parties, the army, the judiciary, etc.)"[9] The number of NGOs has grown dramatically over the past near century in both North America and the world. According to one study, in 1909 there were approximately 176 NGOs and by 1996 their numbers had increased to 5,500. Another estimate puts the number of more internationally oriented NGOs as increasing from 6,000 to 26,000 in the 1990s.[10] Most data furthermore indicate that the majority of these NGOs are based in, and draw the most membership from, the developed North.[11] The increase in number of NGOs during the late 1990s coincided with their intrusion into state policy-making processes, and with their increased penchant for transnational advocacy campaigns to promote international norms such as human rights, women's rights, environmental protection, debt relief, and reform of labor practices in the developing world.

The end of the Cold War, with its resulting democratic transitions, as well as the globalization of the world's economy, characterized in part by integrating national and regional markets and the emergence of new trade regimes, are important trends shaping not only the increased number of NGOs but their burgeoning complexity. In the effort to realize social change goals, NGOs, in addition to becoming simply more internationally oriented, have organized into structures as varied as transnational advocacy networks, transnational coalitions, or transnational social movements.[12] Generally, however, to appreciate potential NGO influence on the foreign policies of states is to recognize that international NGOs and related transnational organizations and coalitions have become enmeshed in non-hierarchical networks of relationships which facilitate greater public or civil society involvement in social change causes. Kriesberg has identified five means by which NGOs affect policies:

(1) Helping to mobilize support for particular policies
(2) Helping to widen public participation in international policy processes
(3) Helping to sustain attention on critical global problems
(4) Helping to frame issues and set the policy agenda
(5) Helping to carry out transnational policies[13]

As will be shown, NGOs increasingly would challenge the Canadian foreign policy-making process along all of these dimensions, especially regarding evolving trade and human security issues.

It is no coincidence that the proliferation and diversification of NGOs along more horizontally linked and networked models has been accompanied by revolutions in the past decade in communications technologies. Specifically, the Internet has enhanced the international influence of NGOs and increased the potential for greater citizen awareness of and involvement in social change campaigns. Much has been written about the non-hierarchical structure of the Internet, and how it has become a tool facilitating international campaigns as diverse as addressing the global AIDS crisis,[14] mobilizing support for the Zapatistas rebellion in Mexico,[15] and in buttressing opposition to neoliberal globalization trade and investment policies and institutions.[16] Through e-mail, listservs, and the proliferation of NGO websites, NGOs have been able to reach a much wider base of potential supporters and have strengthened their geographically diverse reach.

These two related trends—the proliferation and strategic innovation of NGOs, combined with the emergence of Internet technologies—would have a significant impact on the process and content of Canadian foreign policy by the mid-1990s. In the evolving new era of transnational political processes characterized in part by increasingly new horizontally linked network societies, Canadian NGOs would increasingly make the case that existing channels of civil society participation in the formation of Canadian foreign policy fell short of ideal. The more hierarchical, vertically organized and less transparent methods for civil society consultation in Canada, namely the parliamentary foreign policy review, which relied largely on expert witness testimony before parliamentary committees, would thus be challenged in favor of more open, horizontal, citizen-friendly initiatives. Continually evolving transnational innovations, along with Canada-specific domestic-level initiatives, would substantially enhance opportunities for public participation in the foreign policy consultation and formulation process.

Toward the "Democratization" of Canadian Foreign Policy

In addition to changes in the international environment, a variety of domestic-level initiatives enhanced the opportunities available for citizen participation in Canadian foreign policy-making processes. In particular, in May 1993, the Liberal Caucus Committee on External Affairs and National Defence, chaired by Lloyd Axworthy, brought forth the *Liberal Foreign Policy Handbook*, which committed the Liberal Party to the "democratization of foreign policy."[17] There are many possible reasons for the Liberal Party to have been concerned with democratizing foreign policy. In opposition, the Party had criticized the then governing Conservative Party for being too elitist in foreign policy discussions, despite their opening of the process to include public consultations through parliamentary hearings and constituency consultations at the departmental level. In fact, the Liberals also were critical of the foreign policy bureaucracy for being unresponsive to citizen interests.[18]

As well, perhaps the Liberal Party was responding to domestic political trends reflective of a more restless population affected by the 1980s debates over the Charter of Rights and Freedoms and the Canada-U.S. Free Trade Agreement. The Party may also have been considering the more populist political appeals surrounding the 1993 federal election, which criticized the then governing Progressive Conservative approach to foreign policy-making.[19] The Liberal Party may also have been reacting to the growing criticism of the limitations of parliamentary committee hearings and more broadly the traditional foreign policy review process as the central means for public input in the policy-making process.[20] Ultimately, the Liberal Party did follow up its commitment to create a more "open process for foreign policy making" in its so-called Red Book election platform in September 1993.[21] The goal, in any event, was less to undermine the decisive role played by democratically accountable ministers in the making of Canadian foreign policy, but to open up the foreign policy process by creating new mechanisms to advance civil society participation and to create a broader "menu" of ideas, options and policy advice for those ministers.[22]

New Mechanisms for Enhancing Citizen Participation

The Liberal Party followed through on its pledge to open up the foreign policy process in a number of ways.[23] As suggested in its Red Book, the government convened a National Forum on Canada's International Relations in Ottawa in March 1994. Over a hundred people broadly representative of Canadian society participated in this Forum, providing their views on the possible content and direction of the new government's foreign policy. The Forum stimulated major foreign and defense policy reviews, and these reviews were accompanied by further extensive public consultation with hundreds of additional witnesses with the Special Joint Committee of the Senate and House of Commons. The resulting government response, in particular to the 1995 foreign policy review, *Canada in the World*,[24] was both a product, then, of a diversity of citizen recommendations for Canadian foreign policy, and at the same time an instigator for further and broader public consultations to help the Canadian government grapple with global changes affecting the security of states, the protection of peoples and the increasing presence of violent civil wars.

Lloyd Axworthy, who became Foreign Minister in January 1996, would also play an important role in provoking greater openness within Canada's foreign policy process for citizen participation. Axworthy already had a reputation as a social-left Liberal, which made him more naturally inclined to support greater consultation with NGOs concerned with social change campaigns. His co-authorship of the Liberal Party pronouncements on "democratizing" foreign policy ultimately gave a clear indication of the direction he would seek for the foreign policy process. His active engagement and consultation with NGOs and academics and his support for the creation of new mechanisms to promote a more open consultation process with Canadians was instrumental in fulfilling the Liberal Party's openness pledge.

The creation of the Canadian Centre for Foreign Policy Development (CCFPD) in 1996 represented a major step toward opening up the foreign policy process to Canadian citizen participation beyond traditional parliamentary committee hearings.[25] Housed within the Department of Foreign Affairs and International Trade (DFAIT), now Foreign Affairs Canada, the

CCFPD was established directly as a result of the recommendations of the 1994 Special Joint Committee on International Relations. As the Centre's then Director, Steven Lee, noted, the Centre "has been a mechanism for engaging Canadians outside government in foreign policy-making and for promoting the value of public consultations inside the formal policy process."[26] The Centre's mandate directed it to:

- Provide policy information
- Alert citizens to opportunities for public contributions
- Facilitate and promote a policy development network across Canada
- Encourage and support policy development by civil society
- Help integrate a public dimension into foreign policy-making activities[27]

The Centre sought to fulfill its mandate in three stages: through identifying possible connections with relevant citizens and NGOs in Canada and internationally, through creating mechanisms to develop and strengthen partnerships between DFAIT and those identified actors, and developing policy drawn from this government-public partnership.

A significant part of the CCFPD's activities centered on organizing various "policy development projects."[28] These included conferences and cross-country roundtables and seminars designed to foster greater transparency and to inject a measure of public diplomacy into the foreign policy-making process. Another major responsibility for the Centre had been its hosting since 1996 of the annual National Forum on Canada's International Relations. These forums were held in over a dozen Canadian cities, and have focused each year on a subject deemed of importance to the Canadian government by the Minister of Foreign Affairs. Designed as a day-long policy discussion to gather policy recommendations, these forums attracted hundreds of people from a broad cross-section of Canadian society, from academics, to NGO representatives, to students, and members of business and labor organizations. The results of these new mechanisms, which fostered greater citizen engagement, combined with the personal interests of the then Foreign Minister Lloyd Axworthy, would set the stage for the even more ambitious and expansive consultations that marked Canadian foreign policy in the late 1990s.[29] It is interesting to note that the CCFPD is no longer in existence. It did not long survive its creator, closing its books even before the end of the Chrétien era.

Mixed Results in Expansive Consultation: The Land Mines Treaty and Trade Policy

The consultations supported by the CCFPD, on the heels of the Canadian government's *Canada in the World* report, captured the feeling that people were living in the midst of a significant change in the character of the post–Cold War international agenda. Citizens and governments alike recognized that dramatic global changes were underfoot: people were daily witnesses via the ever more ubiquitous cable television media to nationalist tensions fueling the breakup of the Soviet Union and the genocidal bloodshed in Rwanda, as well as the then still raging ethnic cleansing conflict in the former Yugoslavia.[30] This increase in civil wars helped to feed a widely accepted interpretation that Canadian foreign policy needed to reshape its agenda to address this evolving global security shift from preoccupations with the sovereignty of states to the protection of peoples.[31] These international developments, along with the clear move by the Canadian government, led by the international idealist Foreign Minister Lloyd Axworthy, set the stage for the development of the broad foreign policy themes that would characterize Axworthy's tenure at DFAIT: human security and soft power.[32]

The interpretation that the international agenda had become less hierarchical, with trade and human security issues increasingly key priorities for the Canadian government, coincided with revolutionary transformations in the available telecommunications technologies and a consistently less deferential attitude on the part of NGOs. Recognizing the public criticisms of the limits of parliamentary committee hearings as mechanisms for direct public input into foreign policy decision-making processes, and building off of the consultation initiatives set by the CCFPD, Axworthy would seek to cultivate relationships with the NGO community to build political and informational support for a new soft power agenda for Canada. Two notable cases where these efforts at expansive consultation were put into play were in the efforts to ban land mines and in the area of international trade policy. In both of these areas, government efforts shared a common thread with earlier initiatives: the goal would be to increase public participation and to develop partnerships in policy development.[33]

The Landmines Convention[34] represents arguably the clearest success story during Axworthy's tenure as Foreign Affairs Minister of expansive consultation through the construction of partnerships between government and civil society. The treaty to ban land mines was a clear reflection of Axworthy's soft power concerns. It was a product of a "coalition of the willing," as Axworthy put it, "seeking a solution to an international humanitarian crisis that ignores national boundaries."[35] During the so-called "Ottawa Process"—between the October 1996 international conference which launched the anti–land mines negotiations and the December 1997 Ottawa signing of the Convention by 122 states—the Canadian government worked in concert with Canadian and international NGOs. The resulting DFAIT-NGO consultations both created a successful negotiating process and contributed to the content of the eventual agreement.[36]

However, the Ottawa process itself was but the end result of a much longer term preceding a period of international NGO activism—a global public "consciousness raising" on the issue of anti-personnel land mines.[37] NGOs involved with various humanitarian and peacekeeping activities meeting in London in May 1993 formed a coalition called the International Campaign to Ban Landmines (ICBL). This international NGO would meet and build membership through conferences in Geneva in May 1994 and Phnom Penh in June 1995, exploiting its transnational network and the emerging Internet technologies to spread globally information about the campaign to ban land mines as well as relying upon its affiliated NGOs at the local level to exert grassroots pressure on national governments. One such local NGO coalition was the Mines Action Canada, a grouping of humanitarian, church, physician, and development NGOs across Canada, which through 1995 had engaged in a letter-writing and petition campaign to Canadian government officials to take up the anti–land mine cause.[38]

The momentum created by the ICBL campaign, in combination with the slow progress of the United Nations' Conference on Disarmament and Accompanying Convention on Certain Conventional Weapons, convinced Canada to join in January 1996 what has been described as an emerging global coalition of state and non-state actors to ban anti-personnel land mines.[39] A Canadian NGO had already been part of the Canadian government delegation during the U.N. discussions. However, the October 1996 Ottawa conference, which drew state, NGO, and other agency actors, sparked a new diplomatic approach and government-NGO partnership. From Ottawa, where NGOs and government officials participated together in workshops, through the fourteen-month period to the signing of the treaty in Ottawa in December 1997, NGOs kept in close contact with government officials. The ICBL mobilized public opinion to lobby national governments throughout the Ottawa process and NGOs played key roles in drafting the eventual treaty, maintaining daily contact with government officials, attending all preparatory meetings, and commenting on every draft throughout the process. This resulted in what one observer called an "unprecedented degree of equality achieved between state and non-state actors."[40]

The same sorts of success at NGO-government partnership through the policy process and its eventual content have not been replicated in the area of international trade policy. The trade file has become highly politicized in Canada, as civil society groups have remained in a heightened state of mobilization around trade issues since the divisive national debate over the Canada-U.S. Free Trade Agreement (CUSFTA). At that time, Canadian nationalists, coalescing in the newly formed Council of Canadians, as well as so-called popular sector civil society groups combined organizational resources to form the anti–free trade Pro-Canada Network (PCN).[41] Concerns over national identity and sovereignty, jobs and social programs prompted the PCN to launch surprisingly successful educational and lobbying efforts, working with the then opposition federal Liberal and New Democratic Parties to twist the debate over free trade into the deciding issue of the 1988 federal election campaign.

Despite the Progressive Conservative government's reelection and the implementation of the CUSFTA, Canadian civil society groups remained actively involved in trade debates and developed an increasingly international posture into the 1990s that involved the development of transnational links with civil society groups in the Americas and elsewhere.[42] Canadian groups engaged in innovative cross-border dialogue and protest actions with Mexican and U.S. civil society groups during debates and negotiations over the North American Free Trade Agreement.[43] But the protests in Vancouver in 1997 during the meeting of the Asia-Pacific Economic Forum (APEC) and the battle in 1998 over the proposed Multilateral Agreement on Investment (MAI) seem to have been the turning points in NGO-government struggles over international trade policy. Canadian government officials received but a hint of much larger challenges to follow, when groups in Vancouver protested the attendance of

Indonesia's President Suharto at the APEC meetings, where an RCMP officer's now notorious pepper-spraying of protestors was televised nationally.[44] However, the 1998 campaign against the MAI, in which the Council of Canadians played an instrumental role, marked arguably the moment when Canadian government officials recognized the need to consult more openly and transparently with NGOs over trade policy.

The MAI battle brought together all the emergent international trends pitting NGOs against government officials on trade policy. Internet technologies played a decisive role for NGOs, as they distributed copies of the MAI negotiating text over the Internet and engaged in information exchange and educational campaigns to sway public opinion against the deal.[45] NGOs had become, in part through these telecommunication advances, much more internationalist and more experienced in strategic national and transnational coalition-building around trade issues. NGOs had developed deep suspicions and criticisms of the trade policy process, labeling it hierarchical, non-transparent and unaccountable to popularly democratic pressures. Finally, NGOs in Canada and internationally had increasingly adopted a broad view of trade policy, linking trade to damaging effects on the environment, labor and human rights, consumer safety and a whole host of other social issues. This presented significant challenges to government officials in Canada, who had to grapple with the mistrust and frustration of NGOs and contemplate how if at all to integrate what from a bureaucratic standpoint appeared to be non-trade issues into the making of trade policy.[46] The collapse of the MAI negotiations in 1998, then, due to the combination of NGO pressure and growing foreign government doubts about the desirability of the accord, led Canadian trade officials to admit that they had done a poor job of consulting with Canadian NGOs, and in the future trade policy would involve engaging NGOs more directly into the policy process.[47]

Canadian government officials would be faced with two major trade preoccupations in the contentious post-MAI political climate. The multilateral World Trade Organization (WTO) negotiations were set to commence in a new so-called Millennial Round in Seattle in late 1999. At the same time, the Free Trade Area of the Americas (FTAA) trade discussions were ongoing, with critical trade ministerial meetings set to be held in Toronto in the fall of 1999 and the 3rd Summit of the Americas in Quebec City in spring 2001. Determined to be better prepared and not blindsided by an NGO backlash, but also clearly interested in developing a more transparent trade policy consultation process with NGOs, the then Canadian Trade Minister Sergio Marchi, instructed DFAIT officials to develop a more open consultation process as part of their preparations for the WTO meetings.[48]

Marchi had also instructed the House of Commons Standing Committee on Foreign Affairs and International Trade (SFAIT) to consult with Canadians during this preparatory phase about both the WTO and FTAA negotiations. Between when the Committee began its work in February 1999 until its June report, SCFAIT took oral testimony in 30 public sessions from roughly 450 witnesses and received 287 written submissions.[49] Perhaps one of the most important recommendations from the resulting SCFAIT report was for the Canadian government to provide "timely information and feedback to Parliament and citizens during all pre-negotiation, negotiation, implementation and review phases of international trade and investment agreements."[50] Thus, there was clear direction going into crucial multilateral trade negotiations for the Canadian government to create new opportunities for civil society consultation, and not just in the preparatory phase, but with more permanent mechanisms and in a more continuous fashion.

The government responded with initiatives that genuinely did create a more transparent trade policy process, keeping lines of communication open and information about the status of upcoming and ongoing negotiations readily available to civil society actors. As for the impending WTO talks in Seattle, DFAIT in May 1999 launched the "Trade Negotiations and Agreements (TNA)" website.[51] This website would provide information on the government's trade agenda as well as trade policy discussion papers, and would invite public feedback. In June and July 1999 the government would undertake cross-Canada sectoral consultations, and so-called multi-stakeholder workshops. Finally, a limited number of Canadian NGOs traveled to Seattle as part of the Canadian government's official trade delegation, while many more Canadian NGOs privately registered to attend the WTO meetings. During the subsequent and ultimately unsuccessful Seattle negotiations, all Canadian NGOs benefited from evening meetings with Canadian government representatives, while the TNA website was continuously updated.

Similar opportunities emerged for Canadian NGOs to gain greater information about the substance of the government's agenda and the status of the evolving FTAA negotiations. The apparent goal behind the FTAA was to extend the tenets of NAFTA—liberalizing rules for trade and investment—to 34 members of the Western Hemisphere, excluding Cuba. While the Canadian government supported this initiative, it also took the lead in pushing for greater civil society awareness about the FTAA process. Trade Minister Sergio Marchi, following meetings with Canadian NGOs, proposed that a Committee of Government Representatives for the Participation of Civil Society (CGR) be created as a mechanism for receiving input from NGOs on the FTAA negotiations. The proposal to create the CGR was initially resisted by a number of states across the hemisphere. The consultation process was ultimately restricted, so that civil society groups could only send written submissions via an "open invitation to civil society" initiated by the CGR in November 1998.[52] The CGR, then, was the intermediary between civil society groups and trade ministers and the FTAA negotiations. This created a situation, as one critic pointed out, where the CGR could act as a "filter," excluding non-trade-related matters, which it might deem inappropriate to the FTAA process.[53] Civil society groups were then, as they are now, forbidden to have direct access to the actual FTAA negotiations, with limited opportunities to discuss objectives or criticisms with trade ministers.

Some gains have been made since 1998 in getting trade ministers to at least meet with civil society groups outside the formal negotiation process. At the November 1999 Toronto Ministerial, the April 2001 3rd Summit of the Americas in Quebec City, and at the November 2002 Ministerial in Quito, Ecuador, trade ministers variously attended parallel civil society meetings and information exchange sessions.[54] FTAA negotiating texts have, after significant pressure from civil society groups, been released and posted on the Internet following the Quebec City Summit of the Americas and the Ministerial in Quito. And the Canadian government, parallel to its activities with the WTO, has maintained an informative section on its TNA website devoted to providing updates on the FTAA process and the Canadian government's agenda, and for receiving public feedback.[55] Multi-stakeholder information and consultation sessions also continue to be held with DFAIT officials and civil society group across Canada on the FTAA.[56]

In short, there is little doubt that over the past five years, since the collapse of the ill-fated MAI negotiations, Canadian government consultation with NGOs has dramatically expanded. The trade policy process has become much more transparent, and NGOs have been provided with what seems at time an exhaustive amount of information germane to the government's trade agenda. However, there is also no question but that the ongoing government-NGO consultation over trade policy is a pale shadow of the successful state–non-state collaboration during the Ottawa Process that produced the land mines treaty. Most notably, during the trade policy process, NGOs have had no active influence over the content of trade policy and little or no influence over the outcome of negotiations.

There are a number of reasons why the trade policy consultation process has been less agreeable for Canadian (and international) NGOs than was the case in the Ottawa process. There remains the unresolved tension between the narrow definition of trade policy accepted by most government officials, and the much broader definition embraced by civil society groups which link environmental, labor, human rights, and other social concerns to trade policy. Government and NGOs also hold quite different interpretations of what constitutes a successful consultation: NGOs continue to criticize the lack of direct civil society access to providing input into the actual writing and negotiation of trade texts, whereas the Canadian government has highlighted the latest release of the FTAA negotiating text, a move which it feels "confirms the new culture of transparency in trade negotiations, which Canada has championed."[57] Finally, many NGOs remain suspicious of the process of negotiating trade agreements, rejecting the government's underlying commitment to neoliberalism. This suspicion has helped to propel NGOs to engage in increasingly more frequent and elaborate counter-summitry, notably the so-called FTAA/WTO-parallel "People's Summits," and to develop considerable sophistication in transnational networking, as exemplified by the activity of the Hemispheric Social Alliance.[58]

EXPLOITING THE INTERNET FOR THE FOREIGN POLICY DIALOGUE 2003

One additional recent and innovative approach to expanding citizen participation in the Canadian foreign policy process emerged roughly in the first half of 2003 with the government's "Dialogue on Foreign Policy." The Dialogue was a consultation process that sought feedback and suggestions from Canadian citizens on what the goals and directions of Canadian foreign policy should be with special consideration of the new security concerns after the September 11, 2001, terrorist attacks on the United States. Minister Bill Graham's office ensured that the Dialogue was under its control, leaving CCFPD on the sidelines to conduct a parallel consultation.

Because a Liberal majority government, led by Prime Minister Jean Chrétien, still remained in place, as it had since 1993, the Dialogue process did not represent a formal new foreign policy review. However, the new Foreign Minister, Bill Graham, was following up on the September 2002 Speech from the Throne, in which the government pledged to engage Canadians in a discussion on Canada's place in the world.

Through the Dialogue process the government would especially exploit the Internet as a means of consulting Canadians for their views on foreign policy. Thus, the Dialogue would represent a continuation of the growing relevance of Internet technologies as tools for diffusing information and expanding lines of communication with citizens. The Dialogue began in January 2003 when Minister Graham posted the discussion paper, "A Dialogue on Foreign Policy," on the Internet.[59] Thematically, this Dialogue would center on the so-called three pillars of Canadian foreign policy, identified as prosperity, security, and values in the 1995 foreign policy review. The discussion paper invited Canadians to reflect on how well the Canadian foreign policy traditions of multilateralism and interdependence meshed with heightened post-September 11 security concerns and the ever-growing prominence of the Canada-U.S. relationship. In addition to a discussion built around those pillars, the discussion paper contained twelve questions, which invited an open discussion in electronic forums and requested citizen feedback, either in electronic or written form. Three major government concerns motivated the Dialogue process: the government was asking broadly and openly for advice on the appropriate direction for Canada's foreign policy, the Dialogue process was designed to show Ministerial leadership, and the consultation was designed to strengthen links between citizens and a more open foreign policy-making process.

Between January 22 and June 1, the DFAIT Dialogue website received thousands of responses from a wide spectrum of Canadian citizens.[60] DFAIT also provided weekly reports of the activity on the website, summarizing Internet responses, and revealing the number of visits to the site as well as the number of comments submitted. In addition to the electronic Dialogue process, fifteen town hall meetings were held across the country with the Minister, who also met with a session of the National Forum for Youth, while nineteen expert roundtables and meetings with provincial and territorial governments were also held. The resulting report, according to Minister Graham, "reflects the guiding impetus behind the Dialogue itself: that Canada's foreign policy must be informed by public advice fully representative of our country's diverse population and regions."[61]

ASSESSMENT AND CONCLUSION

It is apparent that the Canadian government's efforts from 1993 to 2003 have significantly expanded the opportunities for civil society participation in the foreign policy process. However, it is still much less clear whether or not these improved mechanisms for citizen consultation have contributed to the democratization of Canadian foreign policy. As one noted observer pointed out regarding the Liberal government's early promises to open up the policy process, foreign policy democratization remains an "elusive ideal" and raises difficult questions about how to define or measure such efforts.[62] Does democratization translate simply into increasing the number of people who can share their views on foreign policy? Is the democratization of foreign policy deemed a success if more opportunities exist for groups to participate in the policy process? Or as another critic has noted, what about the possible inconsistency created between consultations with civil society groups and the development and articulation of foreign policy by a democratically elected government?[63] Simply put, it is doubtful that much more consensus exists today between government officials and civil society groups than existed ten years earlier in terms of determining what is meant by the democratization of foreign policy.

Moreover, the new post–September 11 environment, burdened by heightened concerns over security and military preparedness, raises doubts about the practicality of advancing state consultations with non-state actors. The continental fears over the possibility of further terrorist attacks, the emergent "fortress North America" mentality, and the growing criticism leveled at the Chrétien government-era foreign policy[64] raise questions in some quarters more broadly about the sustainability of the

Axworthy soft-power agenda.[65] Again, as one long-time observer of Canadian foreign policy presciently commented, in the event of major crises, the NGO-state altruistic relationship is tenuous, can be easily disrupted, and can easily be placed on the backburner.[66]

Nonetheless, the Canadian government's efforts at consulting civil society groups have been at times innovative and trendsetting. Clearly NGOs and more broadly Canadian citizens have welcomed the opportunities to gain more information about the government's foreign policy agenda, and present views and perspectives sometimes at odds with established government policy. Moreover, there is little reason to think that NGOs will somehow disappear from the international scene as viable non-state actors expecting increased access to policy negotiations, or that the Internet will somehow fade as a major medium for international communication and information diffusion. In this sense the Canadian government has not merely been reactive but has been frequently proactively engaging with emerging new trends in international politics. For many Canadian and international NGOs, as well as foreign governments, then, Canada has been in the vanguard in integrating citizens and civil society groups into international policy processes.

NOTES

1. This is a revised version of a paper originally presented at the biennial meeting of the Association for Canadian Studies in the United States, Portland, Oregon, November 19–23, 2003. I want to thank Chris Kirkey, Laura Macdonald, Patrick James and Marc O'Reilly for their comments. A Saint Michael's College Faculty Research Grant helped to fund summer and fall 2003 archival and library research and interviews with personnel from the Department of Foreign Affairs and International Trade and with the NGO, the North-South Centre in the Ottawa, Canada, environs.

2. Richard N. Haass, "Paradigm Lost," *Foreign Affairs* 74, no. 1 (January/February 1995): 42–58.

3. Neil Nevitte, *The Decline of Democracy: Canadian Value Change in Cross National Perspective* (Peterborough, ON: Broadview Press, 1996).

4. Robert Keohane and Joseph Nye, eds., *Transnational Relations and World Politics* (Cambridge, MA: Harvard University Press, 1971); Robert Keohane and H. V. Milner, eds., *Internationalism and Domestic Politics* (New York: Cambridge University Press, 1976).

5. Margaret Keck and Kathryn Sikkink, *Activism beyond Borders: Advocacy Networks in International Politics* (Ithaca, NY: Cornell University Press, 1998);

Thomas Risse, Stephen C. Ropp, and Kathryn Sikkink, eds., *The Power of Human Rights: International Norms and Domestic Change* (New York/Cambridge: Cambridge University Press, 1999).

6. Paul Wapner, *Environmental Activism and World Civic Politics* (Albany, NY: SUNY Press, 1996).

7. Charles Chatfield, Ron Pagnucco, and Jackie Smith, eds., *Transnational Social Movements in Global Politics* (Syracuse: Syracuse University Press, 1997); Robert O'Brien, Anne Marie Goetz, Jan Aart Scholte, and Marc Williams, *Contesting Global Governance: Multilateral Economic Institutions and Global Social Movements* (Cambridge: Cambridge University Press, 2000); John Guidry, Michael Kenney, and Mayer N. Zald, *Globalization and Social Movements: Culture, Power and the Transnational Public Sphere* (Ann Arbor: University of Michigan Press, 2001); Hank Johnston and Jackie Smith, *Globalization and Resistance: Transnational Dimensions of Social Movements* (Lanham, MD: Rowman & Littlefield, 2002); Sanjeev Khagram, James Riker, and Kathryn Sikkink, eds., *Restructuring World Politics: Transnational Social Movements, Networks and Norms* (Minneapolis, MN: University of Minnesota Press, 2002).

8. Khagram, Riker and Sikkink, eds., *Restructuring World Politics*, 6.

9. Laura Macdonald, *Non-governmental Organizations: Agents of a 'New Development'?* as quoted in Tim Draimin and Betty Plewes, "Civil Society and the Democratization of Foreign Policy," in *Canada Among Nations 1995: Democracy and Foreign Policy*, ed. Maxwell Cameron and Maureen Appel Molot (Ottawa: Carleton University Press, 1995), 79.

10. Robert Keohane and Joseph Nye, *Globalization: What's New? What's Not (And So What?)*, Foreign Policy, no. 118 (Spring 2000): 104–119.

11. Kathryn Sikkink and Jackie Smith, "Infrastructures for Change: Transnational Organizations, 1953–93," in Khagram, Riker, and Sikkink, eds., *Restructuring World Politics*, 24–44.

12. Sidney Tarrow, "Transnational Politics: Contention and Institutions in International Politics," *Annual Review of Political Science* 4 (2001): 1–20.

13. Louis Kriesberg, "Social Movements and Global Transformation," in *Transnational Movements in Global* Politics, ed. Charles Chatfield, Ron Panucco and Jackie Smith (Syracuse, NY: Syracuse University Press,1997), 17.

14. Patricia Siplon, "Acting (Up) Globally: The Internet, AIDS and Activism" (paper presented at the annual meeting of the American Political Science Association, San Francisco, CA, September 2001).

15. Harry Cleaver, "The Zapatista Effect: The Internet and the Rise of an Alternative Political Fabric," *Journal of International Affairs* 51, no. 2 (1998): 621–640; Judith A. Hellman, "Real and Virtual Chiapas: Magic Realism and the Left," in

The Socialist Register 2000: Necessary and Unnecessary Utopias, ed. Colin Leys and Leo Panitch (London: Merlin Press, 1999), 161–186.

16. Jeffrey M. Ayres "From the Streets to the Internet: The Cyber-Diffusion of Contention," *The Annals of the American Academy of Political and Social Science* 566, no. 1 (1999): 132–143; Peter Smith and Elizabeth Smythe "Globalization, Citizenship and Technology: The MAI Meets the Internet," *Canadian Foreign Policy* 7, no. 2 (Winter 1999): 83–105.

17. Liberal Party of Canada, *Liberal Foreign Policy Handbook* (Ottawa: May 1993).

18. Maxwell A. Cameron and Maureen Appel Molot, "Introduction: Does Democracy Make a Difference?" in *Canada Among Nations 1995*, 1–25.

19. Kim Richard Nossal "The Democratization of Canadian Foreign Policy?" *Canadian Foreign Policy* 1, no. 3 (1993): 95–105.

20. Gerald Schmitz, "Democratizing Trade Agreements: Contesting the 'Corporate Millennium'?" (paper presented at the annual meeting of the Canadian Political Science Association, Québec City, July 30, 2000).

21. Liberal Party of Canada, *Creating Opportunity: The Liberal Plan for Canada* (Ottawa: October 1993).

22. Steven Lee, "Beyond Consultations: Public Contributions to Making Foreign Policy" in *Canada Among Nations 1998: Leadership and Dialogue*, ed. Fen Osler Hampson and Maureen Appel Molot (Don Mills, ON: Oxford University Press, 1998), 64.

23. As Denis Stairs has noted, foreign policy consultations with Canadian groups are not entirely new. Standing committees in the Canadian Parliament have for decades invited witnesses from outside of government, while the Trudeau government in the late 1960s consulted with academics during its review of Canadian foreign policy. See Denis Stairs, "The Policy Process and Dialogues with Demos: Liberal Pluralism with a Transnational Twist," in *Canada Among Nations 1998*, 23–54.

24. Government of Canada, Department of Foreign Affairs and International Trade, *Canada in the World: Canadian Foreign Policy Review 1995*, http://www.dfait-maeci.gc.ca/foreign_policy/cnd-world/menu-en.asp.

25. The CCFPD was recently reorganized under the Canadian International Policy website, which is managed by the Strategic Policy Branch of Foreign Affairs Canada. See http://www.dfait-maeci.gc.ca/cip-pic/about/contact-en.asp.

26. Lee, "Beyond Consultations," 55.

27. Canadian Centre for Foreign Policy Development, *Annual Report* (Ottawa: Department of Foreign Affairs and International Trade, 1998).

28. Lee, "Beyond Consultations."

29. The annual human rights consultations served as perhaps the one major example of public consultation that occurred prior to innovations under Foreign Minister Axworthy. See Alison Van Rooy, "Civil Society and the Axworthy Touch," in *Canada Among Nations 2001: the Axworthy Legacy*, ed. Fen Osler Hampson, Norman Hillmer and Maureen Appel Molot (Don Mills, ON: Oxford University Press, 2001): 253–269.

30. Several prominent academic writings that became quite popular with general readers focused on the apparent post–Cold War shift to global cultural/civilizational or nationalist conflicts and away from older political-ideological divisions. See, for example, Benjamin Barber, *Jihad vs. McWorld: How Globalism and Tribalism Are Reshaping the World* (New York: Ballantine Books, 1996); Samuel P. Huntington, "The Clash of Civilizations?" *Foreign Affairs* 72, no. 3 (Summer 1993): 22–49.

31. Stephen Clarkson, *Uncle Sam and Us: Globalization, Neoconservatism and the Canadian State* (Toronto: University of Toronto Press, 2002).

32. In an influential discussion of the limits of U.S. power in a post–Cold War world, Joseph Nye elaborated on the concept of "soft power," which he felt involved the ability to co-opt rather than coerce an actor. See Joseph S. Nye, Jr., "Soft Power." *Foreign Policy*, no. 80 (Fall 1990): 153–171.

33. For reasons primarily of space, I have focused on two of the more high-profile initiatives of expansive consultation between the Canadian government and NGOs in the late 1990s. Other initiatives, however, also bore fruit, including work on the International Criminal Court, Security Council reform, campaigns against child soldiers, and the proliferation of small arms. See the following works for more expansive treatment of these cases: Van Rooy, "Civil Society and the Axworthy Touch"; Michael Pearson, "Humanizing the UN Security Council," in *Canada Among Nations 2001*, 127–151; Greg Donaghy, "All God's Children: Lloyd Axworthy, Human Security and Canadian Foreign Policy," *Canadian Foreign Policy* 10, no. 2 (Winter 2003): 39–56.

34. Officially known as the *Convention on the Prohibition of the Use, Stockpiling, and Production and Transfer of Anti-Personnel Mines and on Their Destruction*. On this September 1997 document, see http://www.icrc.org/ihl.nsf/0/d111fff4b9c85b-0f41256585003caec3?OpenDocument.

35. Lloyd Axworthy and Sarah Taylor, "A Ban for All Seasons: The Landmine Convention and Its Implications for Canadian Diplomacy," *International Journal* 53, no. 2 (Spring 1998): 193.

36. John Hay, "Practising Democratic Foreign Policy: DFAIT's Consultation with Canadians," *Canadian Foreign Policy* 8, no. 1 (Fall 2000): 123–129.

37. Maxwell Cameron, "Democratization of Foreign Policy: The Ottawa Process as a Model," in *To Walk without Fear: The Global Movement to Ban Landmines*,

ed. Maxwell Cameron, Robert Lawson, and Brian Tomlin (Don Mills, ON: Oxford University Press, 1998), 427–447.

38. Cameron, "Democratization of Foreign Policy," 432.

39. Adam Chapnick and Norman Hillmer, "The Axworthy Revolution," in *Canada Among Nations 2001*, 76.

40. Maxwell Cameron, "Global Civil Society and the Ottawa Process: Lessons from the Movement to Ban Anti-Personnel Mines," in *Enhancing Global Governance: Towards a New Diplomacy?* ed. Andrew Cooper, John English, and Ramesh Thakur (New York: United Nations University Press, 2002), 77.

41. Jeffrey M. Ayres, *Defying Conventional Wisdom: Political Movements and Popular Contentions against North American Free Trade* (Toronto: University of Toronto Press, 1998).

42. Jeffrey M. Ayres, "Transnational Political Processes and Contention against the Global Economy," in *Globalization and Resistance: Transnational Dimensions of Social Movements*, ed. Hank Johnston and Jackie Smith (Lanham, MD: Rowman & Littlefield, 2002), 191–205.

43. Cathryn Thorup, "The Politics of Free Trade and the Dynamics of Cross-Border Coalitions in U.S.-Mexican Relations," *The Columbia Journal of World Business* 26, no. 11 (Summer 1991): 12–26; Jim Sinclair, ed., *Crossing the Line: Canada and Free Trade with Mexico* (Vancouver: New Star Books, 1992).

44. W. Wesley Pue, *Pepper in Our Eyes: The APEC Affair* (Vancouver: University of British Columbia Press, 2000).

45. Ayres, "From the Streets to the Internet," 132–143; Smith and Smythe, "Globalization, Citizenship and Technology," 83–105; Ronald J. Deibert, "International Plug 'n Play? Citizen Activism, the Internet and Global Policy," *International Studies Perspectives* 1, no. 3 (July 2000): 255–272.

46. Hay, "Practising Democratic Foreign Policy," 126.

47. Stairs, "The Policy Process and Dialogues with Demos," 23–54; Van Rooy, "Civil Society and the Axworthy Touch," 253–269.

48. Denis Stairs, "Foreign Policy Consultations in a Globalizing World," *Policy Matters* 1, no. 8 (December 2000): 1–44.

49. Stairs, "Foreign Policy Consultations in a Globalizing World," 18.

50. *Canada and the Future of the World Trade Organization—Advancing a Millennium Agenda in the Public Interest: Report of the Standing Committee on Foreign Affairs and International Trade* (Ottawa: June 1999). For more information and reports from SFAIT on the WTO and the FTAA, along with the government's responses, see http://www.dfait-maeci.gc.ca/tna-nac/Consult3-en.asp.

51. See http://www.tradeagreements.gc.ca.

52. For a recent version of this invitation, covering the time period through the

ministerial meeting in Quito, Ecuador, in November 2002, see http://www.ftaaalca.org/SPCOMM/SOC/Invitation/SOC15r3_e.asp.

53. Yasmine Shamsie, *Engaging with Civil Society: Lessons from the OAS, FTAA and Summits of the Americas* (Ottawa: North-South Institute, 2000), 14. Available at http://www.nsi-ins.ca.

54. Roberto Patricio Korzeniewicz and William Smith, *Protest and Collaboration: Transnational Civil Society Networks and the Politics of Summitry and Free Trade in the Americas*, Agenda Papers, no. 51 (Miami, FL: University of Miami North-South Center, 2001). Available at www.Miami.edu/ns/publications/Papers&Reports/SummitryandFreeTrade.html; Marc Lortie and Sylvie Bédard, "Citizen Involvement in Canadian Foreign Policy: The Summit of the Americas Experience, Quebec City, April 2001," in *Civil Society in the Information Age*, ed. Peter Hajnal (Burlington, VT: Ashgate, 2002), 201–214.

55. See http://www.dfait-maeci.gc.ca/tna-nac/ftaa_neg-en.asp and http://www.dfait-maeci.gc.ca/tna-nac/wto-en.asp.

56. See http://www.dfait-maeci.gc.ca/tna-nac/civil_society-en.asp.

57. Government of Canada, "Free Trade Area of the Americas Take Shape," *Canada World View*, no. 19 (Spring 2003): 7.

58. Marie-Josée Massicotte, "Local Organizing and Global Struggles: Coalition-Building for Social Justice in the Americas," in *Global Civil Society and Its Limits*, ed. Gordon Laxer and Sandra Halperin (Basingstoke, UK: Palgrave, 2003), 105–125.

59. See www.foreign-policy-dialogue.ca.

60. The DFAIT *Dialogue on Foreign Policy Report to Canadians* was released in June 2003, resulting in more than 60,000 Internet website visits. It provides a summary of responses received in written, electronic form and in meetings to the questions posed in the original Dialogue paper.

61. Government of Canada, Department of Foreign Affairs and International Trade, *A Dialogue on Foreign Policy: Report to Canadians* (Ottawa: June 2003), 2. See also http://www.foreign-policy-dialogue.ca/en/final_report/index.html.

62. Kim Richard Nossal, "The Democratization of Canadian Foreign Policy: the Elusive Ideal," in *Canada Among Nations 1995*, 29–44.

63. Stairs, "Foreign Policy Consultations in a Globalizing World," 3.

64. Andrew Cohen, *While Canada Slept: How We Lost Our Place in the World* (Toronto: McClelland Stewart, 2003).

65. Some analysts might contend that in the post-9/11 environment, even greater attention needs to be paid to such "soft-power concerns" as poverty, disease, refugee displacement, and other humanitarian crises, which, arguably, may nurture the political context supportive of terrorism.

66. Stairs, "The Policy Process and Dialogues with Demos," 48.

21

Conclusion: Understanding Canada's Foreign Policy Challenges

PATRICK JAMES, NELSON MICHAUD, AND MARC J. O'REILLY

Rarely does Canadian foreign policy make headlines in the *New York Times, Washington Post, Chicago Tribune, San Francisco Chronicle,* or other major American news outlets with a following around the world. As seen throughout this book, such lack of U.S. (or international) publicity does not mean that Canada's foreign policy is unimportant or immune from global influences. Canada remains involved in world affairs, yet its recent behavior has led many scholars, including those in this volume, to ask a fundamental question: Is there a new role emerging for Canada at the dawn of the twenty-first century? Several pessimistic chapters in this collection spotlight a sharp decline in Canada's influence in the world. Most of them point directly to a lack of resources, as Ottawa drastically reduced its spending in the 1990s to eliminate its budget deficit. As a result of fiscal restraint, the Canadian government significantly weakened three important facets of its foreign policy: diplomacy, defense, and development. Dramatic shifts in both the international and domestic contexts exacerbated, moreover, the impact of such changes in Ottawa's priorities.

On the international scene, the end of the Cold War and emergence of the United States as sole superpower raised new issues, especially for its northern neighbor, Canada. In George H. W. Bush's "new world order," was there still a place for countries such as Canada, which had built their international reputation on "honest brokerage" and multilateral actions? As Canada, a trading nation dedicated to international peace since 1945, tried to alter its foreign policy to fit a different era, the events of September 11, 2001, revamped global politics dramatically once again. In George W. Bush's post-9/11 Manichean view of the world, security trumped economics. As Canada struggled to adjust to this reality, other middle or regional powers, such as Sweden, Norway, Australia, Brazil, South Africa, and India, moved ahead of Canada given their ability and willingness to carry out middle-power political, diplomatic, and military tasks.

Domestically, the decade from 1993 to 2003 was deeply marked by the populist style of Canadian Prime Minister Jean Chrétien, nicknamed "The Li'l Boy from Shawinigan"—a town northeast of Montréal known for its lumber and hydroelectric industries. This plain-speaking politician built his career on defending traditional Canadian values and promoting middle-class policies. His disinterest in international affairs translated into an incoherent, if not confused, foreign policy, which Canadians, public servants, and international observers witnessed time and again. Two other key political factors intensified this sentiment tenfold.

First, for electoral reasons, Chrétien wanted Canada to keep its political distance from the United States. Though he and Bill Clinton liked each other, George W. Bush's election in 2000 soured Canada-U.S. relations. Bush's assertive unilateral agenda irritated the Canadian prime minister, an impression other foreign leaders shared of the world's "hyperpower," as former French Foreign Minister Hubert Védrine dubbed it.

The second factor was the resurgence, in the early to mid-1990s, of separatist sentiment in Québec, following the rejection of the Meech Lake accord. This purely domestic issue gave the Chrétien government ample reasons to focus most of its energy—and much of its money—on domestic policies, leaving diminished resources available for the international domain.

Some might say that the situation was much more complex than the portrait we paint here with large brushstrokes. They probably would be right. However, it is important to understand why Canada, at the close of the twentieth century, lost its clout in the international arena. With that in mind, we can speculate about Canada's future role(s) in the world and its ensuing foreign policy.

CONCLUSION

WHITHER CANADA? AN OVERVIEW

The question of Canada's decline might seem simple and straightforward, but answers turn out to be multiple and complex. At the very least, this is what different chapters in this volume suggest. For instance, in the first part of the book, where contributors examine aggregated issue areas, the historical approach taken by each author clearly outlines the need for Canadian foreign policy to adapt itself to a rapidly evolving international environment. In chapter 3, Richter explains why a military in decay diminishes Canada's influence within North America. According to his conclusions, and contrary to what some analysts have argued, leaving to the United States the defense of the continent might very well send a negative message to the world, and thereby possibly heighten global tensions, which would be contrary to Canada's stated interest in peace and stability. Paradoxically, the need to adapt is here translated into a need for Canada to return to its formerly more active military stance.

For his part, in chapter 4, Lusztig translates this need to adapt into the abrupt changes that occurred over the last two decades in the protectionist position abandoned by the three key actors within Canadian trade policy: the two major federal political parties and the industrialists/rent seekers. This need to adapt is even more important when one considers that the pro-free-trade position brings the Canadian and U.S. executives closer to each other at a time when security policies tend to make citizens of the two countries stand apart, despite the unifying role played by globalization.

Thinking of the globalized world brings to mind countries' need to adapt at the sub-national level, especially within federal states. Canada, which lacks clear constitutional guidelines to orient its foreign policy, must reconcile its obligations as a sovereign state with its recognized responsibilities to its provinces, which implement international treaties within their spheres of jurisdiction. As Vengroff and Rich demonstrate, in chapter 5, this requirement encourages provinces to have their say in global negotiations to defend their perceived interests and influence overall Canadian foreign policy. Based on these chapters, then, we conclude that Canada must adapt to the new global context.

The adaptation called for here is not meant to be implemented across the board. Canada's lack of resources would not allow widespread action, and piecemeal efforts would not allow efficient, significant adaptation. Priorities must therefore be established. The second part of this volume provides a sense of where actions should be carried out.

By focusing on issue areas, the authors in this section spotlight where and how Canada can act in order to reorient its foreign policy effectively. By identifying and defining some of the key challenges Canada faces, they outline two important elements. First, Ottawa must continue to factor in multilateralism. In this vein, Rioux (chapter 9) examines a dilemma familiar to contemporary Canadian foreign policy-makers: Does Canada (a) work in a multilateral setting; (b) orient its efforts toward bilateral exchanges; or (c) deal with and through third parties, such as non-governmental organizations (NGOs)? Rioux's analysis applies to official development assistance, but could just as well apply to diplomacy, security, and trade.

The second consideration, to some extent, is linked to the first. It deals with a necessary differentiation between Canadian and U.S. policies. Canada has opted for multilateralism as a way to counter U.S. bilateralism or unilateralism. To give an idea of the importance of this need for Canada to differentiate itself, one need only refer to the wildly popular "I Am Canadian" television ad from a few years ago—which, in true Canadian fashion, promoted a well-known beer. In the ad, a patriotic Canadian underscores key cultural differences between Canadians and Americans. While this ad constitutes merely anecdotal evidence, its popularity (especially in English Canada) underscored a need for differentiation deeply rooted in Canadian political culture.

Although the chapters in this section highlight regional matters, they all provide insights applicable to a more general understanding of Canada's foreign policy future. In their analysis of La Francophonie, Donaghy and Carter (chapter 6) outline the need for Canada to make use of its cultural distinctiveness, such as linguistic duality, and of multilateral institutions. In chapter 7, Marten emphasizes bureaucratic as well as political culture. Her analysis helps explain why Pearsonian internationalism and similar values still permeate Canadian foreign policy-making. Similarly, Barratt's study of foreign aid reinforces the notion that past practices ought to inform future policy, though previous decisions can lead to inflexibility. Some of Barratt's conclusions coincide with Marriott and Carment's. In contrast to (but not in contradiction with) Marten, Marriott and Carment insist that, in itself, innovation in foreign policy poses a genuine challenge. Thus, Canada must honor its bureaucratic and other traditions while innovating appropriately.

These considerations no doubt apply to questions of an economic nature and contribute to our understanding of the future basis for Canadian foreign policy. In chapter 9, Rioux emphasizes the importance of bringing the United States on board with international initiatives promoted by Canada through linking economic goals with "broader international security objectives." In his case studies, Rioux refers to NEPAD and the U.N. Millennium Goals, but it would be interesting to explore whether his conclusion applies to matters such as the Kyoto protocol or the International Criminal Court. Like other analysts, Rioux makes an important distinction: Canada can differentiate itself from the United States, but cannot afford to ignore its neighbor's stance completely. Rioux's other conclusion is that a better planned foreign policy is needed. Again, he is not alone in this call for improvement, since both Nord (chapter 12) and Hristoulas (chapter 13) agree that such a need is present.

Complementing the other contributions in this section, Wood (chapter 11) indicates that challenges can come from within the government apparatus when departments like Finance take precedence over Foreign Affairs in the crafting and implementation of policies. This is the case with policies that aim to influence the international economic system. This chapter also underscores the basic dichotomy of heritage versus innovation. Involvement by departments other than Foreign Affairs allows Canada to "punch above its weight" in the G-8 ring, a positive development Ottawa should ponder as it reconsiders its foreign policy.

The diversity of challenges presented in this second section is impressive. Each helps explain how Canada can adapt to the newly defined world context—and not only from a security point of view. Challenges can be summed up as the need for Canada to (1) differentiate itself by anchoring its policies in national characteristics and values, including multilateralism; (2) base policies upon past actions and doctrine while also remaining open to a more innovative road; and (3) position itself vis-à-vis the United States.

This third challenge is present in all chapters that appear in the book's third section. Of course, Doran's chapter 16 provides the most in-depth treatment; his analysis of the factors favoring a more or less harmonious relationship between Ottawa and Washington reveals the complexity of U.S.-Canadian ties, which many observers often take for granted. For bilateral relations to prosper, notes Doran, "governments must learn to deal with other governments they do not like if peace is to be preserved and the imperatives of interest and capability are to be acted upon."

Doran's conclusion brings to light an inescapable fact: While Canada can differentiate itself from the United States in terms of general orientations (such as unilateralism), or specific policies (like the invasion of Iraq), it still must contend with U.S. policy. O'Reilly (chapter 14) sums this up: "Canada cannot defy the United States incessantly simply to uphold its favorite foreign-policy doctrine."

Nord agrees. He warns against underestimating the impact of the U.S. position in the crafting of Canadian policies. Contributing to the tradition versus innovation debate, Nord identifies this factor as an important limitation to innovation in Canada's Northern policies. As with O'Reilly, Nord brings this aspect to the fore in his evaluation of a country that tries to make its views relevant in a world vastly different from 1956, when Canada was directly instrumental to the solution of a Middle East crisis. In those days, success was achieved due to U.S. willingness to support the solution promoted by Canada. Moreover, as Hristoulas contends, the risk of a lack of staying power increases when a policy is not well articulated. Hülsemeyer (chapter 15) also takes into consideration the importance of the United States when he concludes that diversification of Canadian foreign policy toward Europe "is not a diversion from Canada's primary occupation with the United States, but a gradual shift in focus from the EU's member states to Brussels."

Taken together, the first three parts of the book create an image of the stage on which Canadian foreign policy evolves, but a roughly sketched one. It needs to be refined. Consideration of exogenous and endogenous factors in sections four and five of this volume help remedy this problem.

In part four, both Barnes (chapter 17) and McHugh (chapter 18) address the key concept of sovereignty. Rather than delve deeply into the concept, as does Stephen Krasner,[1] they make two substantive points. First, their chapters clearly reveal the need for a country such as Canada to have at its disposal the tools necessary to sustain its sovereignty, a priority also referred to by Richter. The second contribution outlines the "technical" importance of sovereignty for an actor to be recognized on the world scene and the negative consequences of this status being eroded. Above and beyond the specific conclusions reached here, these contributions outline the importance of answering the calls identified up to now—

from the need to adapt to the need to differentiate itself—with a well-defined, independent foreign policy.

The last section of the book completes the overview by analyzing endogenous factors such as societal values (James, chapter 19) and the role of civil society (Ayres, chapter 20). In both cases, it is established clearly that, although "democratization" of foreign policy might be an interesting buzzword, there are limitations to it. To some extent, the conclusions of these chapters tie into the previous tradition versus innovation debate. Both authors go one step further, however. They outline the limitations imposed by operational requirements and performances and by knowledge that goes beyond opinions. Studying the case of women's integration into the Canadian Navy, James situates well where the question rests: it is not a matter of whether women *will* be integrated, but rather *how* and *when* the process should occur. Ayres poses a similar set of questions about whether more consultation and participation in the foreign policy-making process equates with a more democratic process. In other words, what a country wants to do in terms of foreign policy—an intent often driven or at least supported by its population and its values—might be different from what the same country can in fact do. Studies of public diplomacy apply here; not only do they consider this specific dimension, but they also take into account most of the other elements outlined in the different sections of this book.

This overview of the conclusions reached by the contributors to this book provides a useful reading of where Canada stands *now* in terms of foreign policy. From these analyses, however, is the future of Canada's foreign policy knowable? Hardly so, one would have to admit. Still, these conclusions offer us clues as to where to look in order to understand and evaluate Canadian foreign policy in the new millennium.

FUTURE PATHS

As we write this conclusion, Canadians have just elected a Conservative government, the first since 1993. Prime Minister Stephen Harper and his cabinet will undoubtedly attend to Canada's military capability and readiness, issues the Conservatives spotlighted while in opposition. Although the Tories should maintain better relations with the Bush administration owing to ideological affinities, they will press Washington on softwood lumber duties and Canadian sovereignty in the Arctic. Beyond that, will the Conservatives adhere to the Liberals' April 2005 foreign policy review, which the Tories condemned? Probably not, but Canadian foreign policy under Harper should accord with the above conclusions. One should be mindful, however, of the means available to conduct foreign policy.

Foreign policy differs from the more encompassing idea of international relations in one particular way. Interstate relations and transnational networks—which can be either cooperative or conflictual and vary in duration—characterize contemporary world politics. In contrast, foreign policy typically hinges on a clearly articulated doctrine outlining specific objectives for a given state. Policy-makers devise specific means allowing their country to achieve its goals. In pursuing the so-called national interest, leaders seek to maximize their nation's influence within the global community. With this distinction as well as this book's insights in mind, where does Canada find itself?

For many years, Canada's foreign policy has rested on three pillars: the promotion of prosperity and employment, the promotion of Canada's security within a stable global framework, and the projection of Canadian values and culture. As mentioned above, the Harper government should uphold those pillars. During the campaign, the Tories had promised to "articulate Canada's values of freedom, democracy, the rule of law, human rights, free markets, and free trade—and compassion for the less fortunate—on the international stage."[2] Thus, continuity, rather than radical change, seems in the offing. That said, the Conservatives will assuredly tailor a foreign policy to their liking. As such, provincial governments will be more involved in the making of Canadian foreign policy, a decision Québec, in particular, supports. Whether Foreign Affairs Canada and other federal bureaucracies implement this and other Tory directives will decide the course of Canadian foreign policy, however.

Regardless of the outcome, it would be surprising if the basis of Canadian foreign policy changed suddenly. The importance of multilateralism is something most chapters in this book may have referred to—some explicitly, some implicity. And despite the impossibility of ignoring other ways of conducting foreign policy, one can safely assert that multilateralism will still be what characterizes Canada's international conduct for some years to come. As well, Canadian doctrine will no doubt marry so-called high and low politics (that is, traditional military-security matters involving war and peace with twenty-first century transnational issues such as human rights, HIV/AIDS, and environmental degradation). In the 1995 White Paper, security was inserted between prosperity and values, something the more power-oriented U.S. foreign policy could hardly adopt as a stance. As several chapters in this book have demonstrated, this has been the Canadian way. The Liberals' April 2005 foreign policy review underscored the primacy of military security, however, a reversal the Conservatives should also promote while in office. It will be interesting to see how a Harper government statement of Canadian foreign policy will take these elements into account and how it will reflect the questions raised by contributors to this collection.

For Canadian foreign policy to succeed, however, it will need appropriate resources. Better funding for policy instruments is a natural priority. As well, the Conservatives will likely have to address several thorny issues. Will International Trade continue as its own department? Will Foreign Affairs Canada receive its fair share of the government's budget? Will the military be revamped or will helicopters continue to fall apart and submarines catch on fire? Will Canadian troops be able to move autonomously around the globe or will they still need to "hitchhike" on board U.S. aircraft in order to reach the theater of operations? As Richter might ask: Will Canada continue to abdicate its responsibilities? Will Canada do something to get closer to the United Nations' 0.7 percent GDP target for its official development assistance or will better-targeted efforts, as Rioux reports, be enough to make Canada influential within the world of aid? Answers to these questions will come from the same source: the government's purse.

Although better-funded efforts are needed, money is not enough. Canada must take better care of foreign-policy personnel. Low morale pervades the Canadian diplomatic corps due to low wages, no accommodation of spouses who have their own careers (which may endanger a foreign officer's own professional path), and difficulty in getting promoted. Efforts must be made to satisfy and support the "artisans" of Canadian foreign policy; otherwise, they will leave government service, thereby making it more difficult for Ottawa to implement its foreign policy. The same is true for members of the Canadian armed forces, which are stretched to the limit when one counts people deployed in operations, in training for the next rotation, and recuperating from a recently completed mission.

Nevertheless, men and women enrolled for the defense of Canada and the implementation of peace in the world are among the better trained anywhere and perform superbly in difficult situations, as outlined in Barnes' (otherwise critical) chapter. This cannot go on forever, of course, given an anti-military sentiment deeply rooted in several parts of the country. James is right in observing that "since the end of the Cold War . . . , the need for traditional military does not exist in the mind of many Canadians." The Canadian Government will have to bring more people under the flag if it wants to meet international commitments essential to sustaining its clout and influence. This has little to do with responding to any American requests—Canadians on the whole would staunchly oppose such a move. But Canadians live in a world where—for good or ill—security overrides everything else. Canada can remain "on the sidelines" and let others dictate the agenda or it can get involved and exert influence as it once did within the United Nations and the North Atlantic Treaty Organization—most notably when there was a need to defuse tense situations in Suez or Cyprus.

From a foreign policy means point of view, Canada lacks human resources. Recent efforts to remedy this shortcoming no doubt reflect Canadian values, as James documents in her chapter, but more needs to be done. For, without resources, Canada will not exercise significant influence abroad. And influence is what really matters in foreign policy. In his chapter, Wood refers to the days when Canada helped shape the Bretton Woods agreements. Section 2 of the NATO charter, various UN peacekeeping missions, and more recently, the right to intervene in a country to protect democracy and human rights (as outlined in the revamped OAS charter), all served as examples of Canadian influence upon world order.

The Chrétien government clearly opted, however, for a different attitude. Canada remained inactive or silent on most diplomatic fronts, with few exceptions—e.g., the Anti-personnel Landmine treaty (or Ottawa protocol), which came into existence more as a result of the efforts of Foreign Minister Lloyd Axworthy, his followers at the Department of Foreign Affairs and International Trade, and NGOs, than due to government initiative. Under Chrétien, changes in foreign policy meant that it was more important, as Ayres aptly describes, to involve domestic constituencies in a seemingly endless process of consultations that never addressed foreign issues. The Harper government needs to avoid such bureaucratic "merry-go-rounds" if Canada wants to regain its level of influence in a world dominated by the United States and replete with countries (and NGOs) eager to achieve the level of influence Canada once enjoyed.

Prime Minister Harper has indicated that his government will be more sensitive to international issues. He has clearly stated that it was time to warm up the Canada-U.S. relationship. If Harper treats foreign policy seriously, then perhaps Canada might recover some of its lost global influence. As the contributors to this collection point out, Canada must establish and pursue priorities consonant with a globalizing and post-9/11 world order and its challenges. To do so, Canada must modify its foreign policy—or else risk international irrelevance.

A FOREIGN POLICY IN THE NEW MILLENNIUM

Although Canada will likely seek to ensure its relevance, can this middle power, as well as other practitioners of so-called niche diplomacy, succeed in the new millennium? Despite the myriad political and other obstacles that will continue to hinder Canadian efforts, Ottawa should have every opportunity to help resolve the world's most persistent and intractable problems—especially "human security" issues such as disease, refugees, human rights, democratization, economic development, and the environment. As O'Reilly states in his chapter, "[w]hile Great-Power involvement seems necessary, Middle-Power assistance should be considered optional, *though sometimes crucial*" [italics added].

Canada's role in world affairs is therefore justified in three basic ways. First, Canada is not the only middle power. Sweden, Norway, and others also qualify. There is a definite niche for such countries in world politics and, due to the anarchical character of the world system, none takes precedence. So, if Canada does not want to be subjected to an agenda set by other countries, it must defend and, most importantly, strengthen its traditional role and take full advantage of new opportunities. Otherwise, Canada will be pushed to the "sidelines," marginalized and perhaps even forgotten. Its core values and interests—including those related to the key sector of trade—would then be at risk.

Second, the United States will remain Canada's neighbor and main partner both from a security and an economic point of view. This truth cannot be wished away or ignored. Prime Minister Pierre Trudeau compared the Canadian-U.S. relationship to that of a mouse trying to sleep in the same bed with an elephant—the experience can be trying, to say the least. This remains as true today as it did thirty-five years ago. If Canada does not attend to its international profile, however, the United States will likely ignore its northern neighbor (except for trade matters) and/or infringe upon its sovereignty. Both Barnes and McHugh have alluded to the importance of the latter, an issue Michaud has also analyzed in the post-9/11 context.[3] In short, Canada cannot escape the imperatives of geopolitics and thus must act accordingly.

Despite these concerns, Canada possesses several advantages—for example, its geography and culture. In many ways, Canada's mind-set resembles that of Europe rather than the United States. In his chapter, Hülsemeyer clearly outlines the importance of the Canada-Europe relationship. Complementary to this view, Hristoulas' analysis underscores the importance of articulating a well-thought-out policy for the Americas. Canada should draw upon its ties to both regions and serve as an alternative intersection point where Latin Americans and Europeans can converge instead of always relying on the United States as a hub. Canada, then, is in a position to derive significant benefits from an increasingly interdependent world.

In sum, this book has examined multiple aspects of Canadian foreign policy. Having reviewed traditional themes, historical as well as contemporary developments, and the possibilities afforded by twenty-first century global politics, this volume offers a two-tier conclusion. On the first level, the authors in this collection have underlined the recent waning of Canadian foreign policy, which Andrew Cohen so well documented in *While Canada Slept*. At a second level, however, the contributors have outlined ways for the country to rediscover a meaningful international role for itself. Competition from other countries with a similar agenda and proximity to and influence on the United States, as well as Canada's "honest broker" heritage, can and should reinvigorate Canadian foreign policy as it seeks to balance established values and practices with new priorities within an increasingly globalized world. While Canada will probably not reprise its "Golden Age" status in the next decade, it can and should improve upon its rather woeful recent performance. Canadians and the international community expect as much. Although this book has not provided Ottawa with an easy path to redemption and respectability, it has underscored various factors that any student of Canada should keep in mind as the country crafts a foreign policy for the new millennium.

NOTES

1. Stephen Krasner, *Sovereignty: Organized Hypocrisy* (Princeton, NJ: Princeton University Press, 1999).

2. Stand up for Canada, p. 45. http://media.conservative.ca/video/20060113-Platform.pdf.

3. Nelson Michaud, "Souveraineté et sécurité: Le dilemme de la politique étrangère canadienne dans l'après 11 septembre," *Études internationales* 33, no. 4 (December 2002): 647–665.

Bibliography

ARCHIVAL MATERIALS

Canada on Record: Part Eight (8), Suez Crisis and Pearson the Peacemaker. Canadian Broadcasting Corporation (C.B.C.). C.B.C. Archives. National Archives of Canada (NAC). Ottawa. Government of Canada. *Cabinet Conclusions.* RG 2. Series A-5-a. Volume 5775. NAC.

———. Department of Foreign Affairs and International Trade. File 26. NAC.

———. Department of Foreign Affairs and International Trade. RG 25. Series 50372-40. NAC.

Government of the United Kingdom. Commonwealth Relations Office. *Files.* DO 35/5422, DO 35/6334, DO 35/6342. Public Record Office (PRO). London.

———. Prime Minister's Office. *Files.* PREM 11/1096. PRO.

Government of the United States. Department of State. *Foreign Relations of the United States.* 1955–1957. Volume XVI. Washington, DC: Government Printing Office, 1990.

Papers of Arnold Heeney. MG 30. E 144. Volume 2. NAC.

Papers of Lester B. Pearson. Pre 1958 Series Correspondence. MG 26. N 1. Volumes 38 & 39. NAC.

Papers of Louis St. Laurent. MG 26. L. Volume 239. NAC.

BOOKS AND ARTICLES

Abel, Kerry, and Ken S. Coates, eds. *Northern Visions: Perspectives on the North in Canadian History.* Peterborough, ON: Broadview Press, 2001.

Aguirre, Inaki. "Making Sense of Paradiplomacy? An Intertextual Inquiry about a Concept in Search of a Definition." Pp. 185–209 in *Paradiplomacy in Action: The Foreign Relations of Subnational Governments,* edited by Francisco Aldecoa and Michael Keating. London: Frank Cass, 1999.

Aldecoa, Francisco, and Michael Keating, eds. *Paradiplomacy in Action: The Foreign Relations of Subnational Governments.* London: Frank Cass, 1999.

Alper, D. K. "Trans-boundary Environmental Relations in British Columbia and the Pacific Northwest." *American Review of Canadian Studies* 27, no. 3 (Autumn 1997): 359–383.

A Nation at Risk: The Decline of the Canadian Forces. Ottawa: Conference of Defence Associations, 2002.

Anderson, Greg. "The Compromise of Embedded Liberalism, American Trade Remedy Law, and Canadian Softwood Lumber: Can't We All Just Get Along?" *Canadian Foreign Policy* 10, no. 2 (Winter 2003): 87–108.

Arbuckle, James V. "The Level Killing Fields of Yugoslavia: An Observer Returns." *Pearson Papers*, no. 2. Clementsport, Nova Scotia: Canadian Peacekeeping Press, 1998.

Arctic Council. *Program for the Icelandic Chair of the Arctic Council 2003–2004*.

———. *The Barrow Declaration*. 13 October 2000.

———. *The Inari Declaration*. 10 October 2002.

———. *The Iqaluit Declaration*. 17 September 1998.

Articles of Confederation. United States (1777).

Army Transformation Wargame 2001. Carlisle, PA: US Army TRADOC. www.tradoc.army.mil/tpubs/misc/ArmyTransformationBooklet.pdf.

Asselin, Martial, and Pierre De Bané. "Quebec's Right to Secede." Pp. 497–507 in *Canadian Federalism: Myth or Reality?* edited by J. P. Meekison. Toronto: Methuen, 1997.

A Wake-Up Call for Canada: The Need for a New Military. Toronto: Royal Canadian Military Institute, 2001.

Axelrod, Robert, and Robert O. Keohane. "Achieving Cooperation Under Anarchy: Strategies and Institutions." Pp. 85–115 in *Neorealism and Neoliberalism: The Contemporary Debate*, edited by David. A. Baldwin. New York: Columbia University Press, 1993.

Axworthy, Lloyd. *Navigating a New World: Canada's Global Future*. Toronto: Vintage Books Canada, 2004.

———. *Liberals at the Border: We Stand on Guard for Whom?* Toronto: University of Toronto Press, 2004.

———. "Notes for an address by the Honorable Lloyd Axworthy, Minister of Foreign Affairs to the Permanent Council of the Organization of American States." <http://www.dfait-maeci.gc.ca/oas/oas04m-e.htm>.

———. "Canada and Human Security: The Need for Leadership." *International Journal* 52, no. 2 (Spring 1997): 183–196.

Axworthy, Lloyd, and Sarah Taylor. "A Ban for All Seasons: The Landmine Convention and Its Implications for Canadian Diplomacy." *International Journal* 53, no. 2 (Spring 1998): 189–203.

Ayres, Jeffrey. "Transnational Political Processes and Contention against the Global Economy." Pp. 191–205 in *Globalization and Resistance: Transnational Dimensions of Social Movements*, edited by Hank Johnston and Jackie Smith. Lanham, MD: Rowman & Littlefield, 2002.

———. "From the Streets to the Internet: The Cyber-Diffusion of Contention." *The Annals of the American Academy of Political and Social Science* 566 (November 1999): 132–143.

———. *Defying Conventional Wisdom: Political Movements and Popular Contentions against North American Free Trade*. Toronto: University of Toronto Press, 1998.

Balthazar, Louis. "The Quebec Experience: Success or Failure?" Pp. 153–169 in *Paradiplomacy in Action: The Foreign Relations of Subnational Governments*, edited by Francisco Aldecoa and Michael Keating. London: Frank Cass, 1999.

———. "Quebec's International Relations: A Response to Needs and Necessities." Pp. 140–152 in *Foreign Relations and Federal States*, edited by Brian Hocking. London: Leicester University Press, 1993.

Balthazar, Louis, Guy Laforest, and Vincent Lemieux, eds. *Le Québec et la restructuration du Canada, 1980–1992: enjeux et perspectives*. Québec: Septentrion, 1991.

Balthazar, Louis, Louis Bélanger, and Gordon Mace. *Trente ans de politique extérieure du Québec*. Québec: CQRI/Septentrion, 1993.

Barber, Benjamin. *Jihad vs. McWorld: How Globalism and Tribalism Are Reshaping the World*. New York: Ballantine Books, 1996.

Barratt, Bethany A. "Aiding or Abetting? Human Rights and British Foreign Aid Decisions." In *Human Rights in European Perspective*, edited by Steven Poe and Sabine Carey. London: Ashgate, 2004.

———. *Aiding or Abetting: The Comparative Role of Human Rights in Foreign Aid Decisions*. Ph.D. dissertation. University of California, Davis, 2002.

Bashevkin, Sylvia. *True Patriot Love: The Politics of Canadian Nationalism*. Oxford: Oxford University Press, 1991.

Bashow, David L., Colonel Dwight Daviers, and Colonel Andre Viens. "Mission Ready: Canada's Role in the Kosovo Air Campaign." *Canadian Military Journal* (Spring 2000): 55–62.

Baun, Micheal J. *An Imperfect Union: The Maastricht Treaty and the New Politics of European Integration*. Boulder, CO: Westview Press, 1996.

Beaudoin, Louise. "Origines et développement du rôle international du Gouvernement du Québec." Pp. 458–461 in *Le Canada et Le Québec sur la scène internationale*, edited by Paul Painchaud. Montréal: Les Presses de l'Université du Québec, 1997.

Becker, Gary. "A Theory of Competition among Pressure Groups for Political Influence." *Quarterly Journal of Economics* 98, no. 3 (August 1983): 371–400.

Beckton, C. F., and A. W. Mackay, eds. *Recurring Issues in Canadian Federalism*. Toronto: University of Toronto Press, 1986.

Beer, Samuel H. *To Make a Nation: The Rediscovery of American Federalism*. Cambridge, MA: Belknap Press, 1993.

Beitz, Charles R. *Political Theory and International Relations*. Princeton, NJ: Princeton University Press, 1994.

Bélanger, Louis. "La Diplomatie Culturelle des Provinces Canadiennes." *Études Internationales* 25, no. 3 (1994): 421–452.

———. "Les espaces internationaux de l'État québécois." Paper presented at the annual colloquium of the Canadian Political Science Association, Ottawa, Carleton University, 6 June 1993.

Bélanger, Louis, Andrew Cooper, Heather Smith, Claire Turenne Sjolander, and Robert Wolfe. "Most Safely on the Fence? A Roundtable on the Possibility of a 'Canadian' Foreign Policy after 9/11." *Canadian Foreign Policy* 11, no. 1 (Spring 2004): 97–118.

Bélanger, Louis, Guy Gosselin, and Gérard Hervouet. "Les Relations Internationales du Québec: Efforts de Définition d'un Nouvel Objet d'étude." *Revue Québécoise de Science Politique*, no. 23 (1993): 143–170.

Bélanger, Louis, Ivan Bernier, and Gordan Mace. "Canadian Foreign Policy and Quebec." In *Canada Among Nations 1995: Democracy and Foreign Policy*, edited by Maxwell A. Cameron and Maureen Appel Molot. Ottawa: Carleton University Press, 1995.

Bélanger, Réal. *Wilfrid Laurier: Quand la politique devient passion*. Québec: Presses de l'Université Laval et Entreprises Radio-Canada, 1987.

Bellamy, R., and D. Castiglione. "Building the Union: The Nature of Sovereignty in the Political Architecture of Europe." *Law and Philosophy* 16, no. 4 (July 1997): 421–445.

Bercuson, David. *Significant Incident: Canada's Army, the Airborne, and the Murder in Somalia*. Toronto: McClelland & Stewart, 1996.

Bernard, André. *La Vie Politique au Québec et au Canada*. Sainte-Foy, QC: Presses de l'Université du Québec, 1996.

———. *Problèmes politiques: Canada et Québec*. Sainte-Foy, QC: Les Presses de l'Université du Québec, 1993.

Bernier, Luc. "Mulroney's International 'Beau Risque': The Golden Age of Québec's Foreign Policy." In *Diplomatic Departures: The Conservative Era in Canadian Foreign Policy, 1984–1993*, edited by Nelson Michaud and Kim Richard Nossal. Vancouver: University of British Columbia Press, 2001.

———. *De Paris à Washington: La politique internationale du Québec.* Montréal: Presses de l'Université du Québec à Montréal, 1996.

Bernier, Paul. *Ernest Lapointe: Député de Kamouraska 1904-1919.* La Pocatière, QC: Société Historique de la Côte du Sud, 1979.

Berry, Victoria, and Allan McChesney. "Human Rights and Foreign Policy-Making." In *Human Rights in Canadian Foreign Policy*, edited by Robert O. Matthews and Cranford Pratt. Kingston: McGill-Queen's University Press, 1988.

Betcherman, Lita-Rose. *Ernest Lapointe: Mackenzie King's Great Québec Lieutenant.* Toronto and Buffalo: University of Toronto Press, 2002.

Bienefeld, Manfred A. "The New World Order: Echoes of a New Imperialism." *Third World Quarterly* 15, no. 1 (March 1994): 31-48.

Black, David, and Rebecca Tiessen. "Canadian Aid Policy: Parameters, Pressures and Partners." Chapter to be published in *The Administration of Foreign Affairs: A Renewed Challenge?* edited by Nelson Michaud and Luc Bernier.

Black, Edwin R. *Divided Loyalties.* Montreal and Kingston, ON: McGill-Queen's University Press, 1975.

Black, Eldon. *Direct Intervention: Canada-France Relations 1967-1974.* Montreal and Kingston, ON: McGill-Queen's University Press, 1996.

Blair, Tony. "Speech Delivered at King's College, London." 5 December 2001.

Blanchard, James J. *Behind the Embassy Door: Canada, Clinton and Quebec.* Toronto: McClelland & Stewart, 1998.

Bland, Douglas L. "A Sow's Ear from a Silk Purse." *International Journal* 54, no. 1 (Winter 1998-1999): 143-174.

———. "Controlling the Defense Policy Process in Canada: White Papers on Defense and Bureaucratic Politics in the Department of National Defense." In *Canada's Defense: Perspectives on Policy in the Twentieth Century*, edited by B. D. Hunt and R. G. Haycock. Toronto: Copp Clark Pitman, 1993.

Bland, Douglas, ed. *Canada's National Defense: Volume 1, Defense Policy.* Kingston, ON: Queen's University School of Policy Studies, 1997.

Block, William Ranulf. *Britain and the Dominions.* Cambridge: Cambridge University Press, 1951.

Bloomfield, Lincoln P. "American Policy toward the UN—Some Bureaucratic Reflections." *International Organization* 12 (1958).

Boeckelman, Keith. "Federal Systems in the Global Economy: Research Issues." *Publius* 26 (1996): 1-10.

Borden, Robert Laird. *His Memoirs.* Toronto: McClelland and Stewart, 1969.

"Border Choices: Balancing the Need for Trade and Security." *The Conference Board of Canada.* 2001. <http://www.conferenceboard.ca/pubs/borderchoices-.10.01.pdf>.

Bothwell, Robert. *The Big Chill: Canada and the Cold War*. Contemporary Affairs no. 1. Toronto: Canadian Institute of International Affairs, 1998.

———. *Canada and the United States: The Politics of Partnership*. Toronto: Twayne, 1992.

Bothwell, Robert, and J. L. Granatstein. *Pirouette: Pierre Trudeau and Canadian Foreign Policy*. Toronto: University of Toronto Press, 1990.

Bouchard, Lucien. *Lucien Bouchard: On the Record*, translated by Dominique Clift. Toronto: Stoddart, 1994.

Boutros-Ghali, Boutros. *An Agenda for Peace*. New York: UN Office of Information, 1995.

———. *The Addis-Ababa Charter*. International Conciliation collection, no. 546. New York: Carnegie Endowment for International Peace, 1964.

Boyer, Mark A. *International Cooperation and Public Goods: Opportunities for the Western Alliance*. Baltimore, MD: Johns Hopkins University Press, 1993.

Braid, Katherine F., and Robert V. Horte. "Sovereignty and Federalism: The Canadian Perspective." *Canada–United States Law Journal* 20 (1994): 319–332.

Bratt, Duane. "Rehabilitating the Military: Canadian Peacekeeping in the Post-Somalia Era." Paper presented at the 11th Annual Meeting of the Academic Council on the UN System (ACUNS), Nova Scotia, June 1998.

Brawley, Mark. "Global Financial Architecture and Hegemonic Leadership in the New Millennium." In *Debating the Global Financial Architecture*, edited by Leslie Elliott Armijo. Albany: State University of New York Press, 2002.

Breton, Giles. "The Case for the Arctic Council." Proceedings from the Conference on "Changing Roles of the United States in the Circumpolar North," University of Alaska, Fairbanks, 12–14 August 1992.

Brown, Douglas M., "The Evolving Role of the Provinces in Canada-U.S. Trade Relations." Pp. 93–144 in *States and Provinces in the International Economy*, edited by Douglas M. Brown and Earl H. Fry. Berkeley, CA: Institute of Governmental Studies, University of California Press, 1993.

Brown, Michael E., and Richard N. Rosecrance. *The Case for Conflict Prevention*. Don Mills, ON: Rowman & Littlefield Publishing, 1999.

Brown, Robert Craig. *Robert Laird Borden. A Biography*. Volumes 1 and 2. Toronto: University of Toronto Press, 1975 & 1980.

Brown, Robert Craig, and Ramsay Cook. *Canada, 1896–1921*. Toronto: McClelland & Stewart, 1974.

Brown-Joh, C. Lloyd. "Self-Determination, Autonomy, and State Secession in Federal Constitutional and International Law." *South Texas Law Review* 40, no. 3 (Summer 1990): 567–602.

Buergenthal, Thomas, and Harold G. Maier. *Public International Law in a Nutshell*. St. Paul, MN: West, 1990.

Building on a Stronger Foundation: Annual Report of the Chief of the Defense Staff 1999–2000. Ottawa: Department of National Defence, 2000.

Burgess, Michael. *Federalism and European Union: The Building of Europe, 1950–2000*. London: Routledge, 2000.

———. "Federalism and Federation in Western Europe." Pp. 15–29 in *Federalism and Federation in Western Europe*, edited by Michael Burgess. London: Croom Helm, 1986.

Burke, Marshall. *A Workable Government? The Constitution after 200 Years*. New York: W. W. Norton, 1987.

Bush, George W. *The National Security Strategy of the United States of America*. September 2002. <www.whitehouse.gov/nsc/print/nssall.html>.

Buteux, Paul. "NATO and the Evolution of Canadian Defence and Foreign Policy." In *Canada's International Security Policy*, edited by David B. Hewitt and David Leyton-Brown. Scarborough, ON: Prentice-Hall Canada, 1995.

Buzan, Barry, and Gerald Segal. "The Rise of Lite Powers: A Strategy for the Postmodern State." *World Policy Journal* 13, no. 3 (July 1996): 1–10.

Byers, R. B. "Canada's Defense Review: Strategic Doctrine and Military Commitments." *Canadian Defense Quarterly* 14, no. 4 (Spring 1985).

———. *Canadian Security and Defense: The Legacy and the Challenges*. London: International Institute for Strategic Studies, Adelphi Paper no. 214, 1986.

Byers, R. B., ed. *Canadian Annual Review of Politics and Public Affairs for 1984*. Toronto: University of Toronto Press, 1986.

———. *Canadian Annual Review of Politics and Public Affairs for 1982*. Toronto: University of Toronto Press, 1984.

Byers, Rod D. "Peacekeeping and Canadian Defense Policy: Ambivalence and Uncertainty." In *Peacekeeping: Appraisals and Proposals*, edited by Henry Wiseman. New York: Pergamon, 1983.

Calhoun, John C. "A Disquisition on Government." Pp. 22–23 in *Union and Liberty: The Political Philosophy of John Calhoun*, edited by Ross M. Lence. Indianapolis, IN: Liberty Fund, 1992.

Cameron, Duncan. "Introduction." Pp. xi–xlix in *The Free Trade Papers*, edited by Duncan Cameron. Toronto: James Lorimer, 1986.

Cameron, Maxwell. "Global Civil Society and the Ottawa Process: Lessons from the Movement to Ban Anti-Personnel Mines." Pp. 69–89 in *Enhancing Global Governance: Towards a New Diplomacy?* edited by Andrew Cooper, John English, and Ramesh Thakur. New York: United Nations University Press, 2002.

———. "Democratization of Foreign Policy: The Ottawa Process as a Model." Pp. 424–447 in *To Walk without Fear: The Global Movement to Ban Landmines*, edited by Maxwell Cameron, Robert Lawson, and Brian Tomlin. Don Mills, ON: Oxford University Press, 1998.

Cameron, Maxwell, and Maureen Appel Molot. "Introduction: Does Democracy Make a Difference?" Pp. 1–25 in *Canada Among Nations 1995: Democracy and Foreign Policy*, edited by Maxwell Cameron and Maureen Appel Molot. Ottawa: Carleton University Press, 1995.

Cameron, Maxwell, and Brian Tomlin. *The Making of NAFTA: How the Deal Was Done*. Ithaca, NY: Cornell University Press, 2000.

Campbell, Colin. *Governments under Stress: Political Executives and Key Bureaucrats in Washington, London, and Ottawa*. Toronto and Buffalo: University of Toronto Press, 1983.

Campbell, Colin, and George J. Szablowski. *The Super-Bureaucrats: Structures & Behaviour in Central Agencies*. Toronto: Macmillan, 1979.

Canada and the Future of the World Trade Organization—Advancing a Millennium Agenda in the Public Interest: Report of the Standing Committee on Foreign Affairs and International Trade. Ottawa: June 1999.

Canada's Defense Policy: Capabilities Versus Commitments. Ottawa: Business Council on National Issues, 1984.

Canada's Maritime Forces. Ottawa: Senate Subcommittee on National Defence and the Standing Committee on Foreign Affairs, 1983.

Canada 21: Canada and Common Security in the Twenty-first Century. Toronto: University of Toronto Centre for International Studies, 1994.

Canadian Arctic Resources Committee. *To Establish an International Arctic Council*. Ottawa: Canadian Arctic Resources Committee, 1991.

"Canadian Arctic Security Issues: Transformation in the Post–Cold War Era." *Canadian Foreign Policy* 7 (Spring 1999): 205–215.

Canadian Annual Review of Politics and Public Affairs, 1984. Toronto: University of Toronto Press, 1986.

Canadian Centre for Foreign Policy Development. *Annual Report*. Ottawa: Department of Foreign Affairs and International Trade, 1998.

Canadian Council of Chief Executives. "CCCE: Canadian Council of Chief Executives." 2004. <http://www.ceocouncil.ca/en/>.

Canadian Federation of Independent Business. "CFIB: Homepage." 2004. <http://www.cfib.ca>.

Canadian Human Rights Reporter. *Human Rights Law: Basics*. 2003. <www.chrr.org>.

Canadian Human Rights Tribunal. "Gauthier vs. the Canadian Forces." February 1989.

Canadian International Development Agency (CIDA). *Statistical Report on Official*

Development Assistance, FY 2002–2003. Ottawa: Statistical Analysis Section, Policy Planning and Analysis branch, CIDA (Table A) <http://www.acdicida.gc.ca/INET/IMAGES.NSF/vLUImages/stats/$file/StatRep_02_03.pdf.2003>.

———. *Strengthening Aid Effectiveness: New Approaches to Canada's International Assistance Program. A paper for consultation*. 2002. <http://www.acdi-cida.gc.ca/aideffectiveness>.

———. *Sharing Our Future: Canadian Assistance to International Development*. Ottawa: Government of Canada, 1987.

Canadian Ipsos-Reid Express poll. 2004. <www.ipsos-na.com/new/pressrelease.cfm?id=2322>.

Canadian Manufacturers and Exporters. "Canadian Manufacturers & Exporters Portal." <http://www.cme-mec.ca/national/index-en.asp>.

Canadian Polar Commission. *Proceedings*. Conference on "A Northern Foreign Policy for Canada," Ottawa, 14–17 October 1994.

Carley, Patricia. *Self-Determination: Sovereignty, Territorial Integrity, and the Right to Secession*. Washington, DC: United States Institute of Peace, 1996.

Carment, David, and Schnabel Albrecht, eds. *From Rhetoric to Reality: Applied Conflict Prevention: Opportunities and Innovations*. Lanham, MD: Lexington Books, 2004.

———. *Conflict Prevention: Path to Peace or Grand Illusion?* Tokyo: United Nations University Press, 2003.

Carnegie Commission on Preventing Deadly Conflict. *Final Report*, Washington, DC: Carnegie Corporation of New York.

Carrière, Erin, Marc O'Reilly, and Richard Vengroff. "'In the Service of Peace': Reflexive Multilateralism and the Canadian Experience in Bosnia." Pp. 1–32 in *International Public Opinion and the Bosnia Crisis*, edited by Richard Sobel and Eric Shiraev. Lanham, MD: Lexington Books, 2003.

Carroll, J. E. *Environmental Diplomacy: An Examination and a Prospective of Canadian-U.S. Transboundary Environmental Relation*. Ann Arbor, MI: University of Michigan Press, 1983.

Case Concerning Delimitation of the Maritime Boundary in the Gulf of Maine Area. International Court of Justice, Judgment. October 1984. <www.dal.ca/~www law/kindred.intllaw/gulfofmaine.htm>.

Central Intelligence Agency. *CIA World Factbook*. Washington, DC: U.S. Government Printing Office, various years.

Center for Military and Strategic Studies. *To Secure a Nation: Canadian Defence and Security in the 21st Century*. Calgary: University of Calgary Press, 2002.

Chambers, Edward J., and Nataliya Rylska. *The Alberta and Western Canada Export Experience under the Free Trade Agreements: 1988–1999*. Vol. 59. Western Center for Economic Research. University of Alberta. <http://www.bus-.ualberta.ca/cibs-wcer/WCER/pdf/59.pdf2000>.

Chapnick, Adam. "The Canadian Middle Power Myth," *International Journal* 55, no. 2 (Spring 2000): 188–206.

Chapnick, Adam, and Norman Hillmer. "The Axworthy Revolution." Pp. 65–88 in *Canada Among Nations 2001: The Axworthy Legacy*, edited by Fen Osler Hampson, Norman Hillmer, and Maureen Appel Molot. Don Mills, ON: Oxford University Press, 2001.

Charron, Acting Sub-Lt. Luc. "Serving without Fanfare: The Challenges Affecting the Morale of Today's Canadian Forces," *Defence Matters* 2, no. 4 (May/June 1997).

Chatfield, Charles, Ron Pagnucco, and Jackie Smith, eds. *Transnational Social Movements in Global Politics*. Syracuse, NY: Syracuse University Press, 1997.

Chayes, A., and Handler Chayes A., eds. *Preventing Conflict in the Post-Communist World: Mobilizing International and Regional Organizations*. Washington, DC: Brookings Institution, 1997.

Chief Review Services, "Evaluation: Gender Integration in the CF," 5000-1 (CRS), June 1998 (revised November 1998).

Cingranelli, David L., and Thomas E. Pasquarello. "Human Rights Practices and the Distribution of US Foreign Aid to Latin American Countries." *American Journal of Political Science* 29, no. 3 (September 1995): 539–563.

Clark, Joe. *The Changing Soviet Union: Implications for Canada and the World*. Ottawa, Department of External Affairs, 1990.

Clarkson, Stephen. "Locked In? Canada's External Constitution under Global Trade Governance." *American Review of Canadian Studies* 33, no. 2 (Summer 2003): 145–172.

———. "An American de Tocqueville in Canada: Why Quebec Separation Would Really, Really Matter." *Literary Review of Canada* (September 2002).

———. *Uncle Sam and Us: Globalization, Neoconservatism and the Canadian State*. Toronto: University of Toronto Press, 2002.

Cleaver, Harry. "The Zapatista Effect: The Internet and the Rise of an Alternative Political Fabric." *Journal of International Affairs* 51, no. 2 (Spring 1998): 621–40.

Clift, Dominique. *Quebec Nationalism in Crisis*. Montreal and Kingston, ON: McGill-Queen's University Press, 1998.

Coates, Ken S. "The Discovery of the North: Towards a Conceptual Framework for the Study of Northern/Remote Regions." *The Northern Review* 12/13 (Summer/Winter 1994): 15–43.

Cohen, Andrew. *While Canada Slept: How We Lost Our Place in the World*, Toronto: McClelland & Stewart, 2003.

———. "Canadian-American Relations: Does Canada Matter in Washington? Does It Matter if Canada Doesn't Matter?" In *Canada Among Nations 2002: A Fading Power*, edited by Norman Hillmer and Maureen A. Molot. Don Mills, ON: Oxford University Press, 2002.

———. "Security and NATO." In *Canada Among Nations 1993–1994: Global Jeopardy*, edited by Christopher J. Maule and Fen Osler Hampson. Ottawa: Carleton University Press, 1993.

Cohen, Leonard J. "The Soviet Union and Eastern Europe in Transition: Trends and Implications for Canada." In *Canada Among Nations 1989: The Challenge of Change*, edited by Maureen Appel Molot and Fen Osler Hampson. Ottawa: Carleton University Press, 1990.

Cohen, Maxwell. "The Arctic and the National Interest." *International Journal* 21 (Spring 1971): 52–81.

Coleman, William D. *Business and Politics: A Study of Collective Action*. Montreal: McGill-Queen's University Press, 1988.

———. *The Independence Movement in Quebec, 1945–1980*. Toronto: University of Toronto Press, 1984.

Colletta, N., and M. Cullen. *Violent Conflict and the Transformation of Social Capital: Lessons from Cambodia, Rwanda, Guatemala, and Somalia*. Washington, DC: World Bank, 2000.

Commission of Inquiry into the Deployment of Canadian Forces to Somalia. *Dishonoured Legacy: The Lessons of the Somalia Affair*. Ottawa: Minister of Public Works and Government Services, 1997.

Cooper, Andrew F. *Canadian Foreign Policy: Old Habits and New Directions*. Scarborough, ON: Prentice-Hall Allyn and Bacon Canada, 1997.

———. "Niche Diplomacy: A Conceptual Overview." Pp. 1–24 in *Niche Diplomacy: Middle Powers after the Cold War*, edited by Andrew F. Cooper. London: Macmillan Press, 1997.

———. "In Search of Niches: Saying 'Yes' and Saying 'No' in Canada's International Relations." *Canadian Foreign Policy* 3, no. 3 (Winter 1995/96): 1–14.

Cooper, Andrew F., ed., *Niche Diplomacy: Middle Powers after the Cold War*. New York: St. Martin's Press, 1997.

Coulombe, Françoise. "The Francophone Summits: A Canadian Perspective." *Current Issue Review*. Research Branch, Library of Parliament. 8 January 1988.

Courchene, Thomas J., and Richard G. Harris. *From Fixing to Monetary Union: Options for North American Currency Integration*. Toronto: C. D. Howe Institute, 1999.

Craven, Greg. "Federal Constitutions and External Relations." Pp. 9–26 in *Foreign Relations and Federal States*, edited by Brian Hocking. London: Leicester University Press, 1993.

Creighton, Donald. *John A. Macdonald. The Old Chieftain*. Toronto: Macmillan, 1955.

Cross, Michael S. *Free Trade, Annexation and Reciprocity*. Toronto: Holt, Rhinehart and Winston, 1971.

Dahl, Robert. *Who Governs?* New Haven, CT: Yale University Press, 1965.

Dandurand, Raoul. *Raoul Dandurand: Le Sénateur Diplomate*. Québec: Presses de l'Université Laval et Institut Québécois des Hautes Études Internationales, 2000.

Danilenko, Gennady M. "The Confederate Model of the Commonwealth of Independent States: The New Russian Federalism." *New Europe Law Review* 1, no.2 (Spring 1993): 367–386.

David, Charles-Philippe, ed. "De la SDN à l'ONU: Raoul Dandurand et la vision idéaliste des relations internationales." *Études internationales* 31, no. 4 (December 2000).

Davis, S. Mathin. "Nuclear Submarines for Canada: A Technical Critique." In *The U.S.-Canada Security Relationship: The Politics, Strategy, and Technology of Defense*, edited by David G. Haglund and Joel J. Sokolsky. Boulder, CO: Westview Press, 1989.

Davis, S. Rufus. *The Federal Principle: A Journey through Time in Quest of a Meaning*. Berkeley, CA: University of California Press, 1978.

Dawisha, Adeed, and Karen Dawisha. "How to Build a Democratic Iraq." *Foreign Affairs* 82, no. 3 (Spring 2003): 36–50.

Deibert, Ronald J. "International Plug 'n Play? Citizen Activism, the Internet, and Global Public Policy." *International Studies Perspectives* 1, no. 3 (July 2000): 255–272.

DePalma, Anthony. *Here: A Biography of the New American Continent*. New York: Public Affairs, 2000.

Dewey, John. *The Public and Its Problems*. New York: Henry Holt, 1927.

Dewitt, David, and John Kirton, *Canada as a Principal Power*. Toronto: John Wiley & Sons, 1983.

Diefenbaker, John George. *One Canada*. 3 Volumes. Toronto: Macmillan, 1975.

Dion, Léon. *Le duel constitutionnel Québec-Canada*. Montréal: Boréal, 1995.

Dobell, Peter C. *Canada's Search for New Roles: Foreign Policy in the Trudeau Era*. Oxford: Oxford University Press, 1972.

Dobson, Wendy. "Shaping the Future of North American Economic Space: A Framework for Action." C. D. Howe Institute Commentary 162 (April 2002).

Dockrill, Saki. *Eisenhower's New-Look National Security Policy, 1953–1961*. (London: Macmillan, 1996.

Dodge, David. "Check against Delivery." Remarks by David Dodge, Governor of the Bank of Canada, to the Couchiching Institute on Public Affairs, Geneva Park, Ontario, 7 August 2003. <http://www.bankofcanada.ca/en/speeches/2003/sp03-11.htm>.

Doern, G. Bruce, and Brian W. Tomlin. *Faith and Fear: The Free Trade Story.* Toronto: Stoddard, 1991.

Donaghy, Greg. "All God's Children: Lloyd Axworthy, Human Security and Canadian Foreign Policy." *Canadian Foreign Policy* 10, no. 2 (2003): 39–56.

———. "Domesticating NATO: Canada and the North Atlantic Alliance, 1963–1968." *International Journal* 52, no. 3 (Summer 1997): 446–463.

Donnelly, Jack. *Universal Human Rights in Theory and Practice.* Ithaca, NY: Cornell University Press, 1989.

Donneur, André. *Politique Étrangère Canadienne.* Montréal: Guérin Universitaire, 1994.

Doran, Charles F. "Power Cycle Theory and Global Politics." *International Political Science Review* 24, no. 1 (January 2003): 13–49.

———. *Why Canadian Unity Matters and Why Americans Care: Democratic Pluralism at Risk.* Toronto: University of Toronto Press, 2001.

———. *Forgotten Partnership: U.S.-Canadian Relations Today.* Baltimore, MD.: John Hopkins University Press, 1984.

Doran, Charles F., and Timothy J. Naftali. "U.S.–Canadian Softwood Lumber: Trade Dispute Negations." *Foreign Policy Institute Case Studies,* no. 8. Washington, D.C.: Georgetown University Press, 1987.

Doumitt, Donald P. *Conflict in Northern Ireland: The History, the Problem, and the Challenge.* New York: Peter Lang, 1985.

Doyle, Michael. "Liberalism and World Politics." *American Political Science Review* 80 (December 1986): 1151–1169.

D PK POL Peace Support Operations SITREP. Unpublished Department of National Defence Report, Unclassified Version, 19 July 1999, A8.

Draimin, Tim, and Betty Plewes. "Civil Society and the Democratization of Foreign Policy." Pp. 63–82 in *Canada Among Nations 1995: Democracy and Foreign Policy,* edited by Maxwell Cameron and Maureen Appel Molot. Ottawa: Carleton University Press, 1995.

Duchacek, Ivo D. "Multicommunal and Bicommunal Polities and Their International Relations." Pp. 3–28 in *Perforated Sovereignties and International Relations,* edited by Ivo D. Duchacek, Daniel Latouche, and Garth Stevenson. Westport, CT: Greenwood Press, 1988.

———. *Comparative Federalism: The Territorial Dimensions of Politics.* Lanham, MD: University Press of America, 1987.

———. *The Territorial Dimension of Politics Within, Among and Across Nations.* Boulder, CO: Westview Press, 1986.

Dukert, Joseph M. "The Evolution of the North American Energy Market: Implications of Continentalization for a Strategic Sector of the Canadian Economy." *American Review of Canadian Studies* 30, no. 3 (2000): 349–359.

Dundas, Barbara. *A History of Women in the Canadian Military*. Ottawa: Editions Art Global and the Department of National Defence, 2000.

Dupras, Daniel. "NAFTA: Implementation and the Participation of the Provinces." Parliamentary Research Branch, Background Paper, Ottawa. Provided by the Office of the NAFTA Secretariat in Ontario, 1993.

Dye, Thomas R. *American Federalism: Competition among Governments*. Lexington, MA: Lexington Books, 1990.

Dyment, David K. M. "Substate Paradiplomacy: The Case of the Ontario Government." Pp. 153–169 in *Foreign Relations and Federal States*, edited by Brian Hocking. London: Leicester University Press 1993.

Easterbrook, W. T., and Hugh G. J. Aitken. *Canadian Economic History*. Toronto: Macmillan, 1967.

Eayrs, James, *Canada in World Affairs: October 1955 to June 1957*. Volume 9. Toronto: Oxford University Press, 1959.

Eden, Anthony, *Full Circle*. Boston: Houghton Mifflin Company, 1960.

Edgar, Alistair D. "Growth Pains and Growing Strains? The Limits of Neighbourliness and the Politicization of Canada-U.S. Defence Industry Integration." *Canadian Foreign Policy* 8, no. 2 (Winter 2001): 1–22.

Egerton, Hugh Edward. *Federations and Unions within the British Empire*. Oxford: Clarendon Press, 1911.

Eisenhower, Dwight D. *Waging Peace 1956–1961*. New York: Doubleday & Company, 1965.

Elazar, Daniel J. *Constitutionalizing Globalization: The Postmodern Revival of Confederal Arrangements*. Lanham, MD: Rowman & Littlefield, 1998.

———. *Exploring Federalism*. Birmingham, AL: University of Alabama Press, 1987.

———. *American Federalism: A View from the States*. New York: Harper & Row, 1984.

Ellis, L. Ethan. *Reciprocity 1911: A Case Study in Canadian-American Relations*. New Haven: Yale University Press, 1939.

English, John. *The Worldly Years: The Life of Lester B. Pearson*. Volume 2: 1949–1972. Toronto: Alfred A. Knopf Canada, 1992.

———. *Shadow of Heaven: The Life of Lester Pearson*. Volume 1: 1897–1948. Toronto: Lester & Orpen Dennys, 1989.

European Union. "EU–Canada Summit Set to Make Relations Deeper, More Action Oriented." 2004. <http://europa.eu.int/comm./trade/issues/bilateral/countries/Canada/pr_en. htm>.

Eustace, Marilyn. *Canada's Commitment to Europe: The European Force 1964–1971.* Kingston, ON: Queen's University Centre for International Relations National Security Series No. 1, 1979.

Fabian, Larry L. *Soldiers without Enemies: Preparing the United Nations for Peacekeeping.* Washington, DC: Brookings, 1971.

Facing Our Responsibilities: The State of Readiness of the Canadian Forces. Ottawa: Report of the Standing Committee on National Defence and Veterans Affairs, 2002.

Fergusson, James. "Time for a Decision on North American Missile Defense," *Policy Options* 23, no. 3 (April 2002): 32–37.

Finer, S. E. *The Man on Horseback: The Role of the Military in Politics.* New York: Praeger, 1962.

Finlayson, Jock A., and Stefano Bertasi. "Evolution of Canadian Postwar International Trade Policy." Pp. 19–46 in *Canadian Foreign Policy and International Economic Regimes,* edited by A. Claire Cutler and Mark W. Zacher. Vancouver: University of British Columbia Press, 1992.

Flanagan, Ann. "Canadian Peacekeeping: Where to Now?" *Behind the Headlines* 54, no. 4 (Summer 1997): 4–11.

Florida, Richard. *The Rise of the Creative Class.* New York: Basic Books, 2002.

Fogelson, Nancy. *Arctic Exploration and International Relations 1900–1932.* Fairbanks: University of Alaska Press, 1992.

For an Extra $130 Bucks: Update on Canada's Military Financial Crisis. Ottawa: Report of the Standing Committee on National Security and Defence, 2002.

Foreign Relations of the United States, 1955–1957. Volume 16. Washington, DC: Government Printing Office, 1990.

Forsey, Eugene. *The Royal Power of Dissolution of Parliament in the British Commonwealth,* Toronto: Oxford University Press, 1968.

Fowke, V. C. "The National Policy—Old and New." *Canadian Journal of Economics and Political Science* 18, no. 3 (August 1952): 271–86.

Fox, Annette Baker. "Canada in World Affairs." Association for Canadian Studies in the United States Papers. Washington, DC: ACSUS, 1989.

Franck, Thomas M. "The Emerging Right to Democratic Governance." *American Journal of International Law* 86 (January 1992): 46–91.

Freedman, Lawrence. *The Evolution of Nuclear Strategy.* London: Macmillan, 1981.

Freedom House. The World's Most Repressive Regimes, 2002. <hpp://www.freedomhouse.org/research/mrr2002.pef>.

———. *Annual Survey of Freedom Country Scores, 1972–1973 to 1999–2000.* <http://www.freedomhouse.org/ratings/index.htm>.

Frieden, Jeffrey A. "Invested Interests: The Politics of National Economic Policies in a World of Global Finance." *International Organization* 45, no. 1 (Winter 1991): 19–56.

Fry, Earl. "The Expanding Role of State, Provincial, and Local Governments in North American Economic Relations." Paper presented at the International Studies Association annual conference, Montreal, Canada, 20 March 2004.

———. "An Assessment of the U.S. Contribution to Global Human Security." Pp. 108–127 in *Canada Among Nations 2001: The Axworthy Legacy,* edited by Fen Osler Hampson, Norman Hillmer, and Maureen Appel Molot. Oxford: Oxford University Press, 2001.

———. "Sovereignty and Federalism: U.S. and Canadian Perspectives and Challenges to Sovereignty and Governance." *Canada–United States Law Journal* 20 (1994): 303–318.

———. "The US States and Foreign Economic Policy: Federalism in the 'New World Order.'" Pp. 122–139 in *Foreign Relations and Federal States,* edited by Brian Hocking. London: Leicester University Press, 1993.

Fry, Michael G. "Canada, the North Atlantic Triangle, and the United Nations." Pp. 285–316 in *Suez 1956: The Crisis and Its Consequences,* edited by W. M. Roger Louis and Roger Owen. Oxford: Clarendon Press, 1989.

Fukuyama, Francis. "The End of History?" *The National Interest,* no. 16 (Summer 1989): 3–18.

Gaddis, John Lewis. *We Now Know: Rethinking Cold War History.* New York: Oxford University Press, 1997.

———. *Strategies of Containment: A Critical Appraisal of Postwar American National Security Policy.* New York: Oxford University Press, 1982.

Gagnon, Alain-G. *Développement régional: Etat et groupes populaires.* Hull: Editions Asticou, 1986.

Gammer, Moshe. *Muslim Resistance to the Tsar: Shamil and the Conquest of Chechnia and Daghestan.* London: Frank Cass, 1994.

Gaudreault-DesBien, Jean-François. "The Quebec Secession Reference and the Judicial Arbitration of Conflicting Narratives about Law, Democracy, and Identity." *Vermont Law Review* 23, no. 4 (Summer 1999): 793–844.

Gellman, Peter. "Lester B. Pearson, Collective Security, and the World Order Tradition." *International Journal* 44, no. 1 (Winter 1988–1989): 68–101.

Gérin-Lajoie, Paul. *Combats d'un révolutionnaire tranquille.* Montréal: Centre Educatif et Culturel, 1989.

Germain, Randall. "Reforming the International Financial Architecture: The New Political Agenda." 2000. <www.g7.utoronto.ca.>.

Gertler, Meric, Richard Florida, Gary Gates, and Tara Vinodrai. *Competing on*

Creativity: Placing Ontario's Cities in North American Context. Toronto: Ministry of Enterprise, Opportunity and Innovation (Ontario) and the Institute for Competitiveness and Prosperity, 2002.

Gibbins, Roger. *Conflict and Unity*. Toronto: Nelson, 1988.

Gillies, David. "Do Interest Groups Make a Difference? Domestic Influences on Canadian Development Aid Policies." Pp. 435–465 in *Human Rights, Development, and Foreign Policy: Canadian Perspectives*, edited by Irving Brecher. Halifax: The Institute for Research on Public Policy, 1992.

Gimblett, Richard. "The Navy's Marathon War on Terrorism." *Issues and Challenges*. Ottawa: Department of National Defence. <www.navy.forces.gc.ca/mspa_news/news_issues_e.asp>.

Goldfarb, Danielle. *The Road to a Canada-U.S. Customs Union: Step by Step or in a Single Bound?* Toronto: C. D. Howe Institute, 2003.

Gorbachev, Mikhail. *The Speech in Murmansk*. Moscow: Novostoi Press Agency, 1987.

Gosselin, Guy, and Gordon Mace. "Asymétrie et relations internationales: les provinces canadiennes, l'Europe et l'Amérique latine." *Études internationales* 25, no. 3 (1994): 523–551.

Government of Canada. Department of External Affairs. *Declaration of Friendship and Cooperation Between Canada and the Russian Federation*. Ottawa: Department of External Affairs, 1992.

———. Department of Foreign Affairs and International Trade. "Canada and Peacebuilding: The Canadian Peacebuilding Initiative," <www.dfait-maeci.gc.ca/peacebuilding/cpi-e.asp>.

———. Department of Foreign Affairs and International Trade. *Canada-European Union Economic Relations*. 2004. <http://webapps.dfait-maeci.gc.ca/minpub/Publication.asp?publication_id=379993&Mode=print>.

———. Department of Foreign Affairs and International Trade. *Opening Doors to the World: Canada's International Access Priorities—2004*. Ottawa: Minister of International Trade, 2004.

———. Department of Foreign Affairs and International Trade. *Canada-European Union—Trade and Investment Enhancement Agreement*. 2004. <http://www.dfait-maeci.gc.ca/tna-nac/rb/tiea-en.asp>.

———. Department of Foreign Affairs and International Trade. *Dialogue on Foreign Policy: Report to Canadians*. Ottawa: Department of Foreign Affairs and International Trade, June 2003.

———. Department of Foreign Affairs and International Trade. *NEPAD/G8 Africa Action Plan/APR Process Backgrounder*. Ottawa: G8 Summit Office, Department of Foreign Affairs and International Trade, 2002.

———. Department of Foreign Affairs and International Trade. *The Northern Dimension of Canada's Foreign Policy*. Ottawa: Department of Foreign Affairs and International Trade, 2000.

———. Department of Foreign Affairs and International Trade. *Human Security: Safety for People in a Changing World*. Ottawa: Department of Foreign Affairs and International Trade, 1999.

———. Department of Foreign Affairs and International Trade. *Canada in the World*. Ottawa: CIDA Information Services, 1995.

———. Department of Foreign Affairs and International Trade. *Canada in the World: Canadian Foreign Policy Review 1995*. Ottawa: Department of Foreign Affairs and International Trade, 1995.

———. Department of National Defence. "Canada and United States Amend NORAD Agreement." Aug. 2004. <www.forces.gc.ca>.

———. Department of National Defence. *Budget 2003—Building the Canada We Want*. <www.forces.gc.ca/site/Reports/budget03/highlights03_e.htm>.

———. Department of National Defence. *Defence Planning & Management Financial Resources, FY02/03 Final*. Ottawa.

———. Department of National Defence. *Shaping the Future of Canadian Defence: A Strategy for 2020*. Ottawa: Minister of Supply and Services, 1999.

———. Department of National Defence. *A Commitment to Change: A Report on the Recommendations of the Somalia Commission of Inquiry*. Ottawa: October 1997.

———. Department of National Defence. "Bilateral Defense."*1994 Defence White Paper*. Ottawa: 1994.

———. Department of National Defence. *1994 Defence White Paper*. Ottawa: Minister of Supply and Services, 1994.

———. Department of National Defence. *Challenge and Commitment: A Defence Policy for Canada*. Ottawa: Supply and Services Canada, 1987.

———. Department of National Defence. *Defence in the 70s*. Ottawa: Queen's Printer, 1971.

———. Department of National Defence. *White Paper on Defence*. Ottawa: Queen's Printer, 1964.

———. *"Partners in North America: Advancing Canada's Relations with the United States and Mexico."* Government Response to the Report of the Standing Committee on Foreign Affairs and International Trade. 2002.

Graham, Roger. *Arthur Meighen*. 3 Volumes. Toronto: Clarke Irwin, 1960.

Granatstein, Jack L. *Who Killed the Canadian Military?* Toronto: HarperCollins, 2003.

———. *Canada's Army Waging War and Keeping the Peace*. Toronto: University of Toronto Press, 2002.

———. "A Friendly Agreement in Advance: Canada-U.S. Defense Relations Past, Present, and Future." *C. D. Howe Institute Commentary*, no. 166 (June 2002).

———. *Yankee Go Home: Canadians and Anti-Americanism*. Toronto: Harper Collins, 1996.

———. "Peacekeeping: Did Canada Make a Difference? And What Difference Did Peacekeeping Make to Canada?" In *Making a Difference? Canada's Foreign Policy in a Changing World Order*, edited by John English and Norman Hillmer. Toronto: Lester Publishing Ltd., 1992.

———. *Canada 1957–1967: The Years of Uncertainty and Innovation*. Toronto: McClelland & Stewart, 1986.

———. *The Ottawa Men: The Civil Service Mandarins, 1935–1957*. Toronto: Oxford University Press, 1982.

———. *A Man of Influence: Norman A. Robertson and Canadian Statecraft, 1929–68*. Toronto: Deneau Publishers, 1981.

Granatstein, Jack L., and Robert Bothwell. *Pirouette: Pierre Trudeau and Canadian Foreign Policy*. Toronto: University of Toronto Press, 1990.

Grant, Shelagh H. *Sovereignty or Security? Government Policy in the Canadian North 1936–1950*. Vancouver: University of British Columbia Press, 1988.

Gray, Charlotte. "New Faces in Old Places: The Making of Canadian Foreign Policy." In *Canada Among Nations, 1992–93: A New World Order?* edited by Fen Osler Hampson and Christopher Maule. Ottawa: Carleton University Press, 1992.

Gray, Colin. *Strategic Studies and Public Policy: The American Experience*. Lexington: University of Kentucky Press, 1982.

Guidry, John, Michael Kenney, and Mayer N. Zald, *Globalizations and Social Movements: Culture, Power, and the Transnational Public Sphere*. Ann Arbor: University of Michigan Press, 2001.

Haass, Richard N. "Paradigm Lost." *Foreign Affairs* 74, no. 1 (January/February 1995): 42–58.

Haggard, Stephan. "The Institutional Foundations of Hegemony: Explaining the Reciprocal Trade Agreements Act of 1934." Pp. 91–119 in *The State and American Foreign Economic Policy*, edited by G. John Ikenberry, David A. Lake, and Michael Mastanduno. Ithaca, NY: Cornell University Press, 1988.

Haglund, David G, ed. "Over Here and Over There: Canada-US Defense Cooperation in an Era of Interoperability." *Queen's Quarterly* (2001).

———. *The North Atlantic Triangle Revisited: Canadian Grand Strategy at Century's End*. Toronto: Canadian Institute of International Affairs/Irwin Publishing of Contemporary Affairs, 2000.

Hamilton, Colleen, and John Whalley. "The GATT and Canadian Interests: Summary of the Proceedings of a Research Symposium." In *Canada and the Multilateral Trading System*, edited by John Whalley. Toronto: University of Toronto Press, 1985.

Hampson, Fen Osler, and Dean F. Oliver. "Pulpit Diplomacy: A Critical Assessment of the Axworthy Doctrine." *International Journal* 53, no. 3 (Summer 1998): 379–406.

Hampson, Fen Osler, and Maureen Appel Molot. "Does the 49th Parallel Matter Any More?" Pp. 1–23 in *Canada Among Nations 2000: Vanishing Borders*, edited by Fen Osler Hamspon and Maureen Appel Molot. Oxford: Oxford University Press, 2000.

———, eds. *Canada Among Nations 1989: The Challenge of Change*. Ottawa: Carleton University Press, 1990.

Hampson, Fen Osler, Michael Hart, and Martin Rudner, eds. *Canada Among Nations 1999: A Big League Player?* Don Mills, ON: Oxford University Press, 1999.

Hanson, Brian T. "What Happened to Fortress Europe? External Trade Policy Liberalization in the European Union." *International Organization* 52, no. 1 (Winter 1998): 55–85.

Hart, Michael. *A Trading Nation: Canadian Trade Policy from Colonialism to Globalization*. Vancouver: University of British Columbia Press, 2002.

———. *Decision at Midnight: Inside the Canada-US Free-Trade Negotiations*. Vancouver: University of British Columbia Press, 1994.

Harvie, Christopher T. *Scotland and Nationalism: Scottish Society and Politics, 1707–1994*. London: Routledge, 1994.

Hay, John B. "Practicing Democratic Foreign Policy: DFAIT's Consultations with Canadians." *Canadian Foreign Policy* 8, no. 1 (Fall 2000): 123–129.

———. "Conditions of Influence: An Exploratory Study of the Canadian Government's Effect on U.S. Policy in the Case of Intervention in Eastern Zaire." M.A. thesis, Normal Paterson School of International Affairs, Carleton University, May 1998.

Haydon, Peter T. "Sailors, Admirals, and Politicians: The Search for Identity after the War." Pp. 221–235 in *A Nation's Navy: In Quest of Canadian Naval Identity*, edited by Michael L. Hadley, Rob Huebert, and Fred W. Crickard. Montreal: McGill-Queen's University Press, 1996.

Haynes, F.E. "The Reciprocity Treaty with Canada of 1854." *Publications of the American Economic Association* 7, no. 6 (November 1892): 7–70.

Head, Ivan, and Pierre Elliott Trudeau. *The Canadian Way: Shaping Canada's Foreign Policy, 1968–1984*. Toronto: McClelland & Stewart, 1995.

Helleiner, Eric. "What Political Architecture for North American Monetary

Union? The Canadian Debate." Paper presented at the 44th annual meeting of the International Studies Association, Portland, OR, February 2003.

———. *States and the Reemergence of Global Finance*. Ithaca, NY: Cornell University Press, 1994.

Hellman, Gunther. "Goodbye Bismarck? The Foreign Policy of Contemporary Germany." *Mershon International Studies Review* 40 (April 1996): 1–39.

Hellman, Judith A. "Real and Virtual Chiapas: Magic Realism and the Left." Pp. 161–186 in *The Socialist Register 2000*, edited by Colin Leys and Leo Panitch. London: Merlin Press, 1999.

Henkin, Louis, Richard C. Pugh, Oscar Schacter, and Hans Smit. *International Law*. St. Paul, MN: West, 1980.

Hero, Alfred O., Jr. "Review of Charles F. Doran, *Why Canadian Unity Matters and Why Americans Care: Democratic Pluralism at Risk* (Toronto: University of Toronto Press, 2001)." *American Review of Canadian Studies* 33, no. 2 (Summer 2003): 273–277.

Herzog, Peter E., and Hans Smit, eds. *The Law of the European Community*. New York: Matthew Bender, 1999.

Hilliker, John, and Donald Barry. *Canada's Department of External Affairs, Volume II: Coming of Age, 1946–1968*. Kingston and Montreal: McGill-Queen's University Press, 1995.

———. *Le ministère des affaires extérieures du Canada, Volume II: L'essor (1946–1968)*. Québec: Presses de l'Université Laval et Institut d'Administration Publique du Canada, 1995.

Hillmer, Norman, ed. *Making a Difference: Canada's Foreign Policy in a Changing World Order*. Toronto: Lester Publishing, 1993.

Hillmer, Norman, and Maureen Appel Molot. "Preface." Pp. xi–xii in *Canada Among Nations 2002: A Fading Power*, edited by Norman Hillmer and Maureen Appel Molot. Don Mills, ON: Oxford University Press, 2002.

Hinsley, F. H. *Sovereignty*. New York: Cambridge University Press, 1986.

Historical Statistics of the United States on CD-ROM: Colonial Times to 1970. [Computer File]: Millennial Edition. New York: Cambridge University Press, Forthcoming.

Hochban, Major T. J. "North American Air Defense Modernization." *Canadian Defense Quarterly* 15, no. 3 (Winter 1985/86).

Hocking, Brian. *Foreign Relations and Federal States*. London: Leicester University Press, 1993.

———. "Patrolling the 'Frontier': Globalization, Localization, and the 'Actorness' of Non-Central Governments." Pp. 17–39 in *Paradiplomacy in Action: The Foreign Relations of Subnational Governments*, edited by Francisco Aldecoa and Michael Keating. London: Frank Cass, 1999.

———. "Managing Foreign Relations in Federal States: Linking Central and Non-Central International Interests." Pp. 68–89 in *Paradiplomacy in Action: The Foreign Relations of Subnational Governments*, edited by Francisco Aldecoa and Michael Keating. London: Frank Cass, 1999.

Hoffman, John. *Sovereignty*. Minneapolis: University of Minnesota Press, 1999.

Holbraad, Carsten. *Middle Powers in International Politics*. London: Macmillan, 1984.

Hollman, D.F. *NORAD in the New Millennium*. Toronto: Canadian Institute of International Affairs, 2000.

Holmes, John. "Most Safely in the Middle." *International Journal* 39, no. 2 (1984): 366–388.

———. *The Shaping of Peace: Canada and the Search for World Order 1943–1957*. Volume 2. Toronto: University of Toronto Press, 1982.

Holsti, Ole R. "A Widening Gap between the US Military and Civilian Society? Some Evidence: 1976–1996." *International Security* 23, no. 3 (Winter 1998): 5–42.

Homer-Dixon, Thomas. "The Rise of Terrorism." *Foreign Policy*, no. 128 (January–February 2002): 52–62.

Honderich, John. *Is Canada Losing the North?* Toronto: University of Toronto Press, 1987.

Hooghe, Liesbet, and Gary Marks. "Unraveling the Central State, but How? Types of Multi-level Governance." *American Political Science Review* 97 (2003): 233–244.

House of Commons Standing Committee on Foreign Affairs and International Trade. *Canada and the Circumpolar North: Meeting the Challenges of Co-operation in the Twenty-First Century*. Ottawa: House of Commons, 1997.

House of Commons Standing Committee on National Defense and Veterans Affairs. "Moving Forward: A Strategic Plan for Quality of Life Improvements in the Canadian Forces." October 1998. <www.parl.gc.ca/InfoComDoc/36/1/NDVA/Studies/Reports/ndvarp03-e.htm>.

Howard-Hassmann, Rhoda E. *Compassionate Canadians: Civic Leaders Discuss Human Rights*. Toronto: University of Toronto Press, 2003.

Hristoulas, Athanasios. "Trading Places: Canada, Mexico, and North American Security." In *The Rebordering of North America: Integration and Exclusion in a New Security Context*, edited by Peter Andreas and Thomas Biersteker. New York: Routledge, 2003.

Huebert, Ron. "Canadian Arctic Security Issues: Transformation in the Post–Cold War Era." *International Journal* 54, no. 2 (Spring 1999): 205–215.

———. "New Directions in Circumpolar Cooperation." *Canadian Foreign Policy* 6 (Winter 1998): 49–57.

Hulan, Renée. *Northern Experience and the Myths of Canadian Culture.* Montreal: McGill-Queen's University Press, 2002.

Hülsemeyer, Axel. *Globalization and Institutional Adjustment: Federalism as an Obstacle?* Aldershot, UK: Ashgate, 2004.

———, ed. *Globalization in the Twenty-First Century: Convergence or Divergence?* Basingstoke, UK: Palgrave Macmillan, 2003.

———. "Changing 'Political Economies of Scale' and Public Sector Adjustment: Insights from Fiscal Federalism." *Review of International Political Economy* 7, no. 1 (January 2000): 72–100.

Hülsemeyer, Axel, and Julian Schofield. *Introduction to International Relations: A Reader.* Boston: Pearson Custom Publishing, 2004.

Huntington, Samuel P. "The Clash of Civilizations?" *Foreign Affairs* 72, no. 3 (Summer 1993): 22–49.

———. *The Soldier and the State: The Theory and Politics of Civil-Military Relations.* Cambridge, MA: The Belknap Press of Harvard University Press, 1957.

Hyatt, A. M. J. *General Sir Arthur Currie: A Military Biography.* Toronto: University of Toronto Press/Canadian War Museum, 1987.

Ignatieff, Michael. "Canada in the Age of Terror—Multilateralism Meets a Moment of Truth." *Policy Options* 24, no. 2 (February 2003): 14–18.

Ikenberry, G. John. "The Future of International Leadership." *Political Science Quarterly* 111, no. 3 (Autumn 1996): 385–402.

Innis, Harold A. *The Fur Trade in Canada.* New Haven, CT: Yale University Press, 1962.

Insight Canada Research, *Canadian Public Opinion on Canada's Foreign Policy, Defense Policy and Foreign Aid.* Study conducted for the Department of Foreign Affairs and International Trade, the Department of National Defence, and the Canadian International Development Agency. 1995.

International Monetary Fund. *Direction of Trade Statistics, 1948–1990.* Washington, DC: International Monetary Fund, various years.

Ismael, Tareq Y. *Canada and the Middle East: The Foreign Policy of a Client State.* Calgary, AB: Detselig Enterprises Ltd., 1994.

Jacobs, Jane. *The Question of Separatism.* New York: Random House, 1980.

Jaggers, Keith, and Ted Robert Gurr. *Polity III: Regime Change and Political Authority. 1800–1994* [Computer File]. 2nd ICPSR version. Boulder, CO: Keith Jaggers/College Park, MD: Ted Robert Gurr [producers] Ann Arbor, MI: Inter-university Consortium for Political and Social Research [distributor], 1995.

James, Patrick. *International Relations and Scientific Progress: Structural Realism Reconsidered.* Columbus: Ohio State University Press, 2002.

———. "The Canadian National Energy Program and Its Aftermath." *Canadian Public Policy* 16, no. 2 (June 1990): 174–90.

James, Patrick, Eric Solberg, and Murray Wolfson. "An Identified Systemic Model of the Democracy-Peace Nexus." *Defense and Peace Economics* 10 (1999): 1–37.

Jamieson, Don. *The Political Memoirs of Don Jamieson*, edited by Carmelita McGrath. St. John's, NL: Breakwater, 1991.

Janowitz, Morris. *The Professional Soldier*. New York: The Free Press, 1971.

Jenkins, Jeffrey A. "Partnership and Confederate Constitution-Making Reconsidered." *Studies in American Political Development* 13, no. 2 (October 1999): 279–287.

Jentleson, Bruce. "The Realism of Preventive Statecraft." In *Conflict Prevention: Path to Peace or Grand Illusion?* edited by David Carment and Schnabel Albrecht. Tokyo: United Nations University Press, 2003.

Jervell, Sverre, and Kare Nyblom, eds. *The Military Buildup in the High North: American and Nordic Perspectives*. Boston: University Press of America, 1986.

Jockel, Joseph T. *The Canadian Forces: Hard Choices, Soft Power*. Toronto: Canadian Institute of Strategic Studies, 1999.

———. "Canada and the United States: Still Calm in the Remarkable Relationship." Pp. 111–131 in *Canada Among Nations 1996: Big Enough To Be Heard*, edited by Fen Osler Hampson and Maureen Appel Molot. Ottawa: Carleton University Press 1996.

———. *Canada and International Peacekeeping*. Significant Issues Series 16, no. 3. Washington, DC: Center for Strategic and International Studies, 1994.

———. "A Seat at the Table: Canada and Its Alliances." In *Canada's Defence: Perspectives on Policy in the Twentieth Century*, edited by B. D. Hunt and R. G. Haycock. Toronto: Copp Clark Pitman, 1993.

———. *Security to the North: Canada-U.S. Defense Relations in the 1990s*. East Lansing: Michigan State University Press, 1991.

———. *No Boundaries Upstairs: Canada, the United States, and the Origins of North American Air Defense, 1945–1958*. Vancouver: UBC Press, 1987.

Jockel, Joseph T., and Joel J. Sokolsky. *Canada and Collective Security: Odd Man Out*. Washington, DC: Center for Strategic and International Studies, The Washington Papers, No. 121, 1986.

Johnston, Alastair Iain. "Thinking about Strategic Culture." *International Security* 19, no. 4 (Spring 1995): 32–64.

Johnston, Hank, and Jackie Smith, eds. *Globalization and Resistance: Transnational Dimensions of Social Movements*. Lanham, MD: Rowman & Littlefield, 2002.

Jones, Richard. *Vers une hégémonie libérale*. Québec: Presses de la Libraire des PUL, 1980.

Jones, Robert A. *The Politics and Economics of the European Union: An Introductory Text*. Cheltenham, UK: Edward Elgar, 1996.

Kaiser, Robert. "Subnational Governments in International Arenas—Paradiplomacy and Multi-level Governance in Europe and North America." Paper presented at the Fifth Symposium of the International Political Science Association on "Globalization, Nations and Multi-level Governance: Strategies and Challenges," Montréal, 24–26 October 2002.

Kant, Immanuel. *Kant's Political Writings*, edited by Hans Reiss, translated by H. B. Nisbet. Cambridge: Cambridge University Press, 1970.

Keating, Michael. "Regions and International Affairs: Motives, Opportunities, and Strategies." Pp. 1–16 in *Paradiplomacy in Action: The Foreign Relations of Subnational Governments*, edited by Francisco Aldecoa and Michael Keating. London: Frank Cass, 1999.

Keating, Tom. *Canada and World Order: The Multilateralist Tradition in Canadian Foreign Policy*. Don Mills, ON: Oxford University Press, 2002.

Keating, Tom, and Don Munton. *The Provinces and Canadian Foreign Policy*. Toronto: Canadian Institute of International Affairs, 1985.

Keating, Tom, and Larry Pratt. *Canada, NATO, and the Bomb: The Western Alliance in Crisis*. Edmonton, AB: Hurtig Publishers, 1988.

Keck, Margaret, and Kathryn Sikkink. *Activism beyond Borders: Advocacy Networks in International Politics*. Ithaca, NY: Cornell University Press, 1998.

Keenleyside, T. A. "Development Assistance." In *Human Rights in Canadian Foreign Policy*, edited by Robert O. Matthews and Cranford Pratt. Kingston, ON: McGill-Queen's University Press, 1988.

Keenleyside, T. A., and Patricia Taylor. "The Impact of Human Rights Violations on the Conduct of Canadian Bilateral Relations: A Contemporary Dilemma." *Behind the Headlines* 42 (March 1990): 1–27.

Keith A.B. *Constitutional Law of the British Dominions*. London: MacMillan, 1933.

Kenny, Senator Colin. "Parliamentary Control and National Defence: The Canadian Experience." Canadian Institute of Strategic Studies Strategic Datalink no. 70. Toronto: CISS, 1998.

Kent, James. *Commentaries on American Law*. Volume 1. New York: O. Halsted, 1826.

Keohane, Robert O. "Institutional Theory and the Realist Challenge after the Cold War." In *Neorealism and Neoliberalism: The Contemporary Debate*, edited by David. A. Baldwin. New York: Columbia University Press, 1993.

———. "Lilliputians' Dilemmas: Small States in International Politics." *International Organization* 23, no. 2 (Spring 1969): 291–310.

Keohane, Robert O., and Helen V. Milner, eds. *Internationalism and Domestic Politics*. New York: Cambridge University Press, 1996.

Keohane, Robert O., and Joseph S. Nye, Jr. "Globalization: What's New? What's Not (And So What?)." *Foreign Policy*, no. 118 (Spring 2000): 104–119.

———. *Power and Interdependence: World Politics in Transition.* Boston, MA: Little & Brown, 1977.

———. *Transnational Relations and World Politics.* (Cambridge, MA: Harvard University Press, 1971).

Kenen, Peter B. *The International Financial Architecture: What's New? What's Missing?* Washington DC: Institute for International Economics, 2001.

Kernell, Samuel. *Going Public: New Strategies of Presidential Leadership.* Washington, DC: Congressional Quarterly Press, 1993.

Khagram, Sanjeev, James Riker, and Kathryn Sikkink, eds. *Restructuring World Politics: Transnational Social Movements, Networks and Norms.* Minneapolis: University of Minnesota Press, 2002.

Khalidi, Rashid. "The PLO as Representative of the Palestinian People." Pp. 59–73 in *The International Relations of the Palestine Liberation Organization*, edited by Augustus R. Norton and Martin H. Greenberg. Carbondale: Southern Illinois University Press, 1989.

Kincaid, John. "Consumership versus Citizenship: Is There Wiggle Room for Local Regulation in the Global Economy?" Pp. 27–47 in *Foreign Relations and Federal States*, edited by Brian Hocking. London: Leicester University Press, 1993.

———. "The International Competence of US States and Their Local Governments." Pp. 111–133 in *Paradiplomacy in Action: The Foreign Relations of Sub national Governments*, edited by Francisco Aldecoa and Michael Keating. London: Frank Cass, 1999.

Kindleberger, Charles. *The World in Depression: 1929–39.* Berkeley: University of California Press, 1973.

King, Gordon, ed. *Canada's Role as a Middle Power*, Toronto: Canadian Institute of International Affairs, 1966.

King, Preston. *Federalism and Federation.* Baltimore, MD: John Hopkins University Press, 1982.

Kirton, John J. "Canada as a Principal Financial Power: G-7 and IMF Diplomacy in the Crisis of 1997–1999." *International Journal* 54, no. 4 (Autumn 1999): 603–624.

———. "The Diplomacy of Concert: Canada, the G7 and the Halifax Summit." *Canadian Foreign Policy* 3, no. 1 (Spring 1995): 63–80.

———. "Promoting Plurilateral Partnership: Managing United States–Canada Relations in the Post–Cold War World." *American Review of Canadian Studies* 24, no. 4 (Winter 1994): 453–472.

Kitchen, Martin, "From the Korean War to Suez: Anglo-American-Canadian Relations, 1950–1956." Pp. 220–255 in *The North Atlantic Triangle in a Chang-*

ing World, edited by B. J. C. McKercher and Lawrence Aronsen. Toronto: University of Toronto Press, 1996.

Klepak, Hal. "What's in It for Us? Canada's Relationship with Latin America." *The Focal Papers*, no. 2 (1990).

Kohn, Walter S. G. *Governments and Politics of the German-Speaking Countries*. Chicago: Nelson-Hall, 1980.

Koring, Paul. "Foreign Policy and the Circumpolar Dimension." *Canadian Foreign Policy* 6, no. 1 (Fall 1998).

Korzeniewicz, Roberto Patricio, and William Smith. *Protest and Collaboration: Transnational Civil Society Networks and the Politics of Summitry and Free Trade in the Americas*. Miami, FL: University of Miami North-South Center Agenda Paper Number 51, 2001. <www.Miami.edu/nsc/publications/Papers&Reports/SummitryandFreeTrade.html>.

Krasner, Stephen. *Sovereignty: Organized Hypocrisy* (Princeton, NJ: Princeton University Press, 1999).

Krasner, Stephen, ed. *International Regimes*. Ithaca, NY: Cornell University Press, 1983.

Kriesberg, Louis. "Social Movements and Global Transformation." Pp. 3–18 in *Transnational Social Movements in Global Politics*, edited by Charles Chatfield, Ron Panucco, and Jackie Smith. Syracuse, NY: Syracuse University Press, 1997.

Kunz, Diane B. "The Importance of Having Money: The Economic Diplomacy of the Suez Crisis." Pp. 215–232 in *Suez 1956: The Crisis and Its Consequences*, edited by W.M. Roger Louis and Roger Owen. Oxford: Clarendon Press, 1989.

Kux, Stephan. "Confederalism and Stability in the Commonwealth of Independent States." *New Europe Law Review* 1, no. 2 (Spring 1993): 387–420.

Kyle, Keith, *Suez*. New York: St. Martin's Press, 1991.

Lake, David A. "Leadership, Hegemony, and the International Economy: Naked Emperor or Tattered Monarch with Potential?" *International Studies Quarterly* 37, no. 4 (December 1993): 459–489.

———. "International Economic Structures and American Foreign Policy, 1887–1934." *World Politics* 35, no. 4 (July 1983): 517–543.

Langille, David. "The Business Council on National Issues and the Canadian State." *Studies in Political Economy* 24 (Autumn 1987): 41–85.

Lapierre, Laurier. *Sir Wilfrid Laurier: Portrait intime*. Montréal: Éditions de l'Homme, 1996.

LaRose-Edwards, Paul, Jack Dangerfield, and Randy Weekes. *Non-Traditional Military Training for Canadian Peacekeepers*. Study prepared for the Commission of Inquiry into the Deployment of Canadian Forces to Somalia. Ottawa: Canadian Minister of Public Works and Government Services, 1997.

Lecours, André. "When Regions Go Abroad: Globalization, Nationalism and Federalism." Paper presented at the conference on "Globalization, Multilevel Governance and Democracy: Continental, Comparative and Global Perspectives," Queen's University, 3–4 May 2002.

Lee, Steven. "Beyond Consultations: Public Contributions to Making Foreign Policy." Pp. 55–67 in *Canada Among Nations 1998: Leadership and Dialogue*, edited by Maureen Appel Molot and Fen Osler Hampson. Don Mills, ON: Oxford University Press, 1998.

Légaré, Anne. *Le Québec otage de ses alliés.* Montreal: VLB Editeur, 2003.

Léger, Jean-Marc. "Vingt-cinq ans de relations internationales: un acquis riche de promesses." *Forces*, no. 100 (1992): 129–135.

Lenarcie, David. "Meeting Each Other Halfway: The Departments of National Defence and External Affairs During the Congo Peacekeeping Mission, 1960–64." York University Centre for International and Strategic Studies Occasional Paper 37. Toronto: York University, 1996.

Levy, Thomas Allen. "Le rôle des provinces." Pp. 141–144 in *Le Canada et le Québec sur la scène internationale*, edited by Paul Painchaud. Montréal: Les Presses de l'Université du Québec, 1977.

Lewis-Beck, Michael S. "Comparative Economic Voting: Britain, France, Germany, Italy." *American Journal of Political Science* 30, no. 2 (May 1986): 315–46.

Lipson, Charles. "International Cooperation in Economic and Security Affairs." In *Neorealism and Neoliberalism: The Contemporary Debate*, edited by David. A. Baldwin. New York: Columbia University Press, 1993.

Liberal Party of Canada. *Liberal Foreign Policy Handbook.* Ottawa: May 1993.

———. *Creating Opportunity: The Liberal Plan for Canada.* Ottawa: October 1993.

Lindblom, Charles E. *Politics and Markets: The World's Political-Economic Systems.* New York: Basic Books, 1977.

Liska, George. *The New Statecraft: Foreign Aid in American Foreign Policy.* Chicago: University of Chicago Press, 1960.

Lortie, Marc, and Sylvie Bédard. "Citizen Involvement in Canadian Foreign Policy: The Summit of the Americas Experience, Québec City, April 2001." Pp. 201–214 in *Civil Society in the Information Age*, edited by Peter Hajnal. Burlington, VT: Ashgate, 2002.

Lubin, Martin. "Strains between Governments at the Top, Hands across the Border at the Base: The Role of Subnational Governments during the Bush–Chretien Era and Beyond." *Canadian-American Public Policy*, no. 54 (2003): 21–43.

Lumsdaine, David Halloran. *Moral Vision In International Politics: The Foreign Aid Regime, 1949–1989.* Princeton, NJ: Princeton University Press, 1993.

Lund, M. "Introduction and Overview." In *The Impact of Conflict Prevention Policy: Cases, Measures, Assessments: Conflict Prevention Network Yearbook.* Baden-Baden, Germany: Nomos Verlagsgesellschaft, 1999/2000.

———. "Early Warning and Conflict Prevention." In *Managing Global Chaos,* edited by C. Crocker, F. Hampson, and P. Aal. Washington, DC: USIP Press, 1996.

———. *Preventing Violent Conflict.* Washington, DC: USIP Press, 1996.

Lusztig, Michael. *The Limits of Protectionism: Building Coalitions for Free Trade.* Pittsburgh, PA: University of Pittsburgh Press, 2004.

———. "The Limits of Rent-Seeking: Why Protectionists Become Free Traders." *Review of International Political Economy* 5, no. 1 (January 1998): 38–63.

———. *Risking Free Trade: The Politics of Trade in Britain, Canada, Mexico and the United States.* Pittsburgh, PA: University of Pittsburgh Press, 1996.

Lusztig, Michael, and Patrick James. "How Does Free Trade Become Institutionalized? An Expected Utility Model of the Chrétien Era." Manuscript, 2003.

———. "Political Entrepreneurship and the Quest for Realignment: Constitutional Reform and the Free Trade Agreement in Canada." *International Journal of Canadian Studies* 14 (Fall 1996): 239–55.

Lyon, Peyton V. "The Evolution of Canadian Diplomacy since 1945." In *From Mackenzie King to Pierre Trudeau: Forty Years of Canadian Diplomacy,* edited by Paul Painchaud. Québec: Presses de l'Université of Laval, 1989.

Lyons, Gene M., and Michael Mastanduno, eds. *Beyond Westphalia? State Sovereignty and International Intervention.* Baltimore, MD: Johns Hopkins University Press, 1995.

Macdonald, Laura. "Adapting to a New Playing Field? Civil Society Inclusion in the Hemisphere's Multilateral Processes." *FOCAL Policy Paper* (2000).

Mace, Gordon, Louis Bélanger, and Ivan Bernier. "Canadian Foreign Policy and Québec." Pp. 119–143 in *Canada Among Nations 1995: Democracy and Foreign Policy,* edited by Maxwell A. Cameron and Maureen Appel Molot. Ottawa: Carleton University Press, 1995.

MacFarlane, John. *Ernest Lapointe and Québec's Influence on Canadian Foreign Policy,* Toronto and Buffalo: University of Toronto Press, 1999.

MacGuigan, Mark. *An Inside Look at External Affairs during the Trudeau Years,* edited by P. Whitney Lackenbauer. Calgary, AB: University of Calgary Press, 2002.

Mackay, R. A., ed. *Canadian Foreign Policy 1945–1954: Selected Speeches and Documents.* Toronto: McClelland & Stewart, 1970.

MacLauclan, H. Wade. "Accounting for Democracy and the Rule of Law in the Quebec Reference." *Canadian Bar Review* (1997).

MacLean, George, and Kim Richard Nossal. "Triangular Dynamics: Australian States, Canadian Provinces and Relations with China." Pp. 170–189 in *Foreign Relations and Federal States*, edited by Brian Hocking. London: Leicester University Press, 1993.

MacNeil, Robert. *The Right Place at the Right Time*. New York: Penguin Books, 1990.

Maioni, Antonia. "Divergent Pasts, Converging Futures? The Politics of Health Care Reform in Canada and the United States." *Canadian-American Public Policy*, no. 18 (1994): 1–34.

Majone, Giandomenico. "The European Community between Social Policy and Social Regulation." *Journal of Common Market Studies* 31, no. 2 (June 1993): 153–170.

Malcolm, Lt. Col. of Logistics Ian. "Does the Blue Helmet Fit? The Canadian Forces and Peacekeeping." Norman Paterson School of International Affairs Occasional Paper no. 3. Ottawa: Carleton University, 1993.

Malone, David M. "Eyes on the Prize: The Quest for Non-Permanent Seats on the UN Security Council," *Global Governance* 6, no. 1 (January–March 2000): 1–36.

———. "The Global Issues Biz: What Gives?" Pp. 197–214 in *Canada Among Nations 1999: A Big League Player?* edited by Fen Osler Hampson, Martin Rudner, and Michael Hart. New York: Oxford University Press, 1999.

Manning, Lory, and Vanessa R. Wight. *Women in the Military: Where They Stand*, 4th edition. Washington, DC: Women's Research & Education Institute, 2003.

Mansfield, Edward D., and Helen V. Milner. "The New Wave of Regionalism." *International Organization* 53, no. 3 (Summer 1999): 589–627.

Manzer, Ronald. "Human Rights in Domestic Politics and Policy." In *Human Rights in Canadian Foreign Policy*, edited by Robert O. Matthews and Cranford Pratt. Kingston, ON: McGill-Queen's University Press, 1988.

Marteinson, John. "Editorial." *Canadian Defense Quarterly* 24, no. 2 (December 1994).

Martin, Ged. "The Case against Canadian Confederation, 1864–1867." Pp. 19–49 in *The Causes of Canadian Confederation*, edited by Ged Martin. Fredericton, NB: Acadiensis Press, 1990.

Martin, Lawrence. *The Antagonist: Lucien Bouchard and the Politics of Delusion*. Toronto: Viking, 1997.

———. *The Diefenbaker-Kennedy Schism: The President and Prime Ministers: Washington and Ottawa Face to Face: The Myth of Bilateral Bliss 1867–1982*. Toronto: Doubleday Canada, 1982.

Martin, Jr., Paul. "Canada's Role in a Complex World." Presented at the Canadian Newspaper Association Annual Super Conference, Toronto, 30 April 2003.

———. "Speech and Response to Questions in Evidence." Standing Committee on Foreign Affairs and International Trade, House of Parliament, Canada, May 18, 2000. <www.parl.gc.ca>.

Martin, Sr., Paul. *A Very Public Life*. 2 volumes. Markham, ON: Deneau Publishing, 1985.

Martin, Pierre, and Michel Fortmann. "Canadian Public Opinion and Peacekeeping in a Turbulent World." *International Journal* 50, no. 2 (Spring 1995): 370–400.

Mason, Dwight N. "The Future of Canada-U.S. Defense Relations." *American Journal of Canadian Studies* 33, no. 1 (Spring 2003): 63–91.

———. "U.S.–Canada Defense Relations: A View from Washington." In *Canada Among Nations 2003: Coping with the American Colossus*, edited by David Carment, Fen Osler Hampson, and Norman Hillmer. Don Mills, ON: Oxford University Press, 2003.

Massey, Vincent. "Canada and the Interamerican System." *Foreign Affairs* 26 (July 1946).

Massicotte, Marie-Josée. "Local Organizing and Global Struggles: Coalition-Building for Social Justice in the Americas." Pp. 105–125 in *Global Civil Society and Its Limits*, edited by Gordon Laxer and Sandra Halperin. Basingstoke, UK: Palgrave, 2003.

Matthews, Robert O., and Cranford Pratt. "Introduction." In *Human Rights in Canadian Foreign Policy*, edited by Robert O. Matthews and Cranford Pratt. Kingston, ON: McGill-Queen's University Press, 1988.

Mattli, Walter. *The Logic of Regional Integration: Europe and Beyond*. New York: Cambridge University Press, 1999.

Mayer, Frederick W. *Interpreting NAFTA: The Science and Art of Political Analysis*. New York: Columbia University Press, 1998.

McDiarmid, O. J. *Commercial Policy in the Canadian Economy*. Cambridge, MA: Harvard University Press, 1946.

McHugh, James T. "Making Public Law 'Public': An Analysis of the Quebec Reference Case and Its Significance for Comparative Constitutional Analysis." *International and Comparative Law Quarterly* 49, no. 2 (April 2000): 445–462.

McHugh, James T., and James S. Pacy. *Diplomats without a Country: Baltic Diplomacy, International Law, and the Cold War*. Westport, CT: Greenwood Press, 2001.

McIlroy, James P. "NAFTA and the Canadian Provinces: Two Ships Passing in the Night." *Canada–United States Law Journal* 23 (1997): 431–440.

McKillip, Jack. *Need Analysis: Tools for the Human Services and Education.* Newbury Park, CA: Sage, 1991.

McLin, Jon B. *Canada's Changing Defense Policy, 1957–1963: The Problems of a Middle Power in Alliance.* Baltimore, MD: Johns Hopkins University Press, 1967.

McNiven, James D., and Dianna Cann. "Canadian Provincial Trade Offices in the United States." Pp. 167–183 in *States and Provinces in the International Economy*, edited by Douglas M. Brown and Earl H. Fry. Berkeley, CA: Institute of Governmental Studies & University of California Press, 1993.

McRoberts, Kenneth. "La question nationale québécoise." Pp. 123–137 in *La Révolution tranquille, 40 ans plus tard: un bilan*, edited by Yves Bélanger, Robert Comeau, and Céline Métivier. Montréal: VLB Editeur, 2000.

———. *Misconceiving Canada: The Struggle for National Unity.* Toronto: Oxford University Press, 1997.

Mearsheimer, John J. *The Tragedy of Great Power Politics.* New York: W. W. Norton & Company, 2001.

Meernik, James, Eric L. Krueger, and Steven C. Poe. "Testing Models of U.S. Foreign Policy: Foreign Aid during and after the Cold War." *Journal of Politics* 60, no. 1 (1998): 63–85.

Michaud, Nelson. "Quebec and the Americas: A Federated State's Answer to the Challenges of Continentalization." Paper presented at the 2003 biennial meeting of the Association for Canadian Studies in the United States, Portland, OR, 20–23 November 2003.

———. "Souveraineté et sécurité: Le dilemme de la politique étrangère dans l'après 11 septembre." *Études internationales* 33, no. 4 (December 2002): 647–665.

———. "Bureaucratic Politics and the Shaping of Policies: Can We Measure Pulling and Hauling Games?" *Canadian Journal of Political Science* 35, no. 2 (June 2002): 269–300.

———. "Federalism and Foreign Policy: Comparative Answers to Globalization." Pp. 389–415 in *The Handbook of Federal Countries 2002*, edited by Ann L. Griffiths. Kingston, ON: McGill-Queen's University Press, 2002.

———. "Genèse d'une politique syncopique: la défense du Canada et le livre blanc de 1987." Ph.D. dissertation, Université Laval, 1998.

———. *L'énigme du Sphinx.* Québec: Presses de l'Université Laval, 1998.

Michaud, Nelson, and Kim Richard Nossal. *Diplomatic Departures: The Conservative Era in Canadian Foreign Policy 1984–1993.* Vancouver: UBC Press, 2001.

Michelman, Hans J., and Panayotis Soldatos, eds. *Federalism and International Relations: The Role of Subnational Units.* Oxford: Clarendon Press, 1990.

Middlemiss, Danford W. "Canadian Defense Policy: An Uncertain Transition." Pp. 119–134 In *Canada Among Nations 1989: The Challenge of Change*, edited by Maureen Appel Molot and Fen Osler Hampson. Ottawa: Carleton University Press, 1990.

Middlemiss, Danford W., and Denis Stairs. "The Canadian Forces and the Doctrine of Interoperability: The Issues." *Policy Matters* 3, no. 7 (April 2002): 1–40.

Middlemiss, Danford W., and J. J. Sokolsky. *Canadian Defense: Decisions and Determinants*. Toronto: Harcourt Brace, 1989.

Milner, Mark. *Canada's Navy: The First Century*. Toronto: University of Toronto Press, 1999.

Mingus, Matthew. "Transnationalism and Subnational Paradiplomacy: Is This Perforated Sovereignty or Are Democracy and Civil Society Just Reaching across Borders?" Paper presented at the annual conference of the Public Administration Theory Network, Anchorage, AK, June 2003.

Minifie, James. *Peacemaker or Powdermonkey? Canada's Role in a Revolutionary World*. Toronto: McClelland & Stewart, 1960.

Minister's Advisory Board on Canadian Forces Gender, Employment, Integration and Equity. "Successes and Opportunities: 1999 Annual Report."

Minister's Advisory Board on Canadian Forces Gender Employment, Integration and Equity. "Summary of Recommendations: How to Improve the Grade, 2000 Annual Report". <http://www.forces.gc.ca/site/reports/CFGIEE/annex 5-e.htm> and <http://www.forces.gc.ca/site/reports/CFGIEE/4a-e.htm#obj>.

Mirus, Rolf, and Nataliya Rylska. "Should NAFTA Become a Customs Union?" Pp. 359–76 in *NAFTA in the New Millennium*, edited by Edward D. Chambers and Peter H. Smith. Edmonton: The University of Alberta Press, 2002.

Mitrany, David. *The Progress of International Government*. London: George Allen & Unwin, 1933.

Molot, Maureen Appel, and Norman Hillmer. "The Diplomacy of Decline." Pp. 1–33 in *Canada Among Nations 2002: A Fading Power*, edited by Norman Hillmer and Maureen Appel Molot. Don Mills, ON: Oxford University Press, 2002.

Moravcsik, Andrew. "Negotiating the Single European Act: National Interest and Conventional Statecraft in the European Community." *International Organization* 45, no . 1 (Winter 1991): 19–56.

Morin, Jean, and Richard H. Gimblett. *Operation Friction, 1990–1991: The Canadian Forces in the Persian Gulf*. Toronto: Dundurn Press, 1997.

Morris, Lynn Lyons, Carol Taylor-Fitz-Gibbon, and Marie E. Freeman. *How to Communicate Evaluation Findings*. Beverly Hills, CA: Sage Publications, 1987.

Morrison, Alex. "Canada and Peacekeeping: A Time for Reanalysis?" In *Canada's*

International Security Policy, edited by David B. Dewitt and David Leyton-Brown. Scarborough, ON: Prentice-Hall Canada, 1995.

Morrison, David R. *Aid and Ebb Tide: A History of CIDA and Canadian Development Assistance*. Waterloo, ON: Wilfrid Laurier University Press and The North-South Institution, 1998.

Morrison, William. R. *True North: The Yukon and the Northwest Territories*. New York: Oxford University Press, 1998.

Morton, Desmond. *Understanding Canadian Defence*. Toronto: Penguin/McGill Institute, 2003.

———. *A Military History of Canada: From Champlain to Kosovo*. Toronto: McClelland & Stewart, 1999.

Mulroney, Brian. "Address by the Right Honourable Brian Mulroney, 24 November 1989." Ottawa: PMO Press Office, 1989.

Munton, Don. "The Limits of American Hegemony and the Impact of Norms: Canada and the Invasion of Iraq." Paper presented at the annual conference of the International Studies Association, 16–20 March 2004, Montreal, Canada.

Nash, Knowlton. *Kennedy and Diefenbaker: Fear and Loathing across the Undefended Border*. Toronto: McClelland & Stewart, 1990.

Nation at Risk: The Decline of the Canadian Forces. Ottawa: Conference of Defence Associations, 2002.

National Defence: Manpower Study. Ottawa: Department of National Defence, 1965.

National Defence: Report on the Plans and Priorities—2000. Ottawa: Department of National Defence, 2000.

Neatby, H. Blair. *William Lyon Mackenzie King*. 3 volumes. Toronto and Buffalo: University of Toronto Press, 1963.

Nethery-Castro, Jody, and Marc Rousseau. "Québec, Francophonie, and Globalization." *Québec Studies* 32 (Fall 2001/Winter 2002): 15–35.

Nevitte, Neil. *The Decline of Deference: Canadian Value Change in Cross National Perspective*. Peterborough, ON: Broadview Press, 1996.

New Partnership for Africa's Development (NEPAD). "About NEPAD." 2002. <http://www.nepad.org/inbrief.html>.

Newman, Peter C. *Titans: How the New Canadian Establishment Seized Power*. Toronto: Viking, 1998.

Nicolaides, Kalypso. "International Preventive Action: Developing a Strategic Framework." Pp. 23–72 in *Vigilance and Vengeance: NGOs Preventing Ethnic Conflict in Divided Societies*, edited by Robert I. Rotberg. Washington, DC: Brookings Press, 1996.

Noël, Alain, and Jean-Philippe Thérien. "From Domestic to International Justice:

The Welfare State and Foreign Aid." *International Organization* 49, no. 3 (Summer 1995): 523–553.

Nord, Douglas C. "Northern Foreign Policies: Tensions between Canadian and American Visions—Past and Present." Pp. 291–309 in *Northern European and Baltic Sea Integration*, edited by Lars Hedegaard and Bjarne Lindström. Berlin: Springer-Verlag, 2003.

Nossal, Kim Richard. "Canada: Fading Power or Future Power?" *Behind the Headlines* 59, no. 3 (Spring 2002): 9–16.

———. "Canadian Foreign Policy After 9/11: Realignment, Reorientation, or Reinforcement?" In *Foreign Policy Realignment in the Age of Terror*, edited by Leonard Cohen, Brian Job, and Alexander Moens. Toronto: The Canadian Institute of Strategic Studies, 2002.

———. "Pinchpenny Diplomacy: The Decline of Good International Citizenship in Canadian Foreign Policy." *International Journal* 54, no. 1 (Winter 1998–99): 88–105.

———. *The Politics of Canadian Foreign Policy*. 3rd ed. Toronto: Prentice-Hall, 1997.

———. "The Democratization of Canadian Foreign Policy: The Elusive Ideal." Pp. 29–44 in *Canada Among Nations 1995: Democracy and Foreign Policy*, edited by Maxwell Cameron and Maureen Appel Molot. Ottawa: Carleton University Press, 1995.

———. "The Democratization of Canadian Foreign Policy?" *Canadian Foreign Policy* 1, no. 3 (Fall 1993): 95–105.

———. "Cabin'd, Cribb'd, Confin'd? Canada's Interest In Human Rights." In *Human Rights in Canadian Foreign Policy*, edited by Robert O. Matthews and Cranford Pratt. Kingston, ON: McGill-Queen's University Press, 1988.

Nye, Joseph S., Jr.. *Bound to Lead: The Changing Nature of American Power*. New York: Basic Books, 1991.

———. "Soft Power." *Foreign Policy*, no. 80 (Fall 1990): 153–171.

———. "Transnational Relations and Interstate Conflicts." Pp. 367–402 in *Canada and the United States: Transitional and Transgovernmental Relations*, edited by A. B. Fox et al. New York: Columbia University Press, 1976.

O'Brien, Robert, Anne Marie Goetz, Jan Aart Scholte, and Marc Williams, eds. *Contesting Global Governance: Multilateral Economic Institutions and Global Social Movements*. London/New York: Cambridge University Press, 2000.

O'Hanlon, Michael. *Technological Change and the Future of Warfare*. Washington, DC: Brookings Institution Press, 2000.

Oliver, Dean. "The Canadian Military after Somalia." In *Canada Among Nations 1998: Leadership and Dialogue*, edited by Fen Osler Hampson and Maureen Appel Molot. Don Mills, ON: Oxford University Press, 1998.

O'Neill, Michael. "Great Britain: From Dicey to Devolution." *Parliamentary Affairs* 53, no. 1 (January 2000): 69–95.

Op APPOLO, Canada's Military Contribution to the International Campaign against Terrorism. <www.navy.forces.gc.ca/mspa_operations/operations>.

O'Reilly, Marc J. "Following Ike? Explaining Canadian-US Co-operation during the 1956 Suez Crisis." *The Journal of Commonwealth & Comparative Politics* 35, no. 3 (November 1997): 75–107.

Organization for Economic Cooperation and Development. *Geographical Distribution of Financial Flows*. Paris: OECD, various years.

Organski, A.F.K. *The $36 Billion Bargain: Strategy and Politics in US Assistance to Israel*. New York: Columbia University Press, 1990.

Our Place in Canada, A Summary Report. St. John's: Royal Commission on Renewing and Strengthening Our Place in Canada, 2003.

Owens, Admiral William. *Lifting the Fog of War*. New York: Farrar, Straus & Giroux, 2000.

Paquin, Stéphane. "Paradiplomatie identitaire et diplomatie en Belgique fédérale: le cas de la Flandre." *Canadian Journal of Political Science* 36, no. 3 (July–August 2003): 621–642.

———. *Paradiplomatie identitaire en Catalogne*. Sainte-Foy, Québec: Presses de l'Université Laval, 2003.

Pastor, Robert A. "North America's Second Decade." *Foreign Affairs* 83, no. 1 (January/February 2004): 124–135.

Patton, Michael Quinn. *How to Use Qualitative Methods in Evaluation*. Beverly Hills, CA: Sage Publications, 1991.

Patry, Bernard, M.P. *Partners in North America: Advancing Canada's Relations with the United States and Mexico*. A Report of the Standing Committee on Foreign Affairs and International Trade. Ottawa: 2002.

Pauly, Louis W. *Who Elected the Bankers? Surveillance and Control in the World Economy*. Ithaca, NY: Cornell University Press, 1997.

Peacekeeping Operations, Operations Land and Tactical Air 3. B-GL-301-003/FP-001. Ottawa: National Defence Headquarters, 1994.

Pearson, Geoffrey A. H. *Seize the Day: Lester B. Pearson and Crisis Diplomacy*. Ottawa: Carleton University Press, 1993.

Pearson, Lester B., with John A. Munro and Alex I. Inglis, eds. *Mike: The Memoirs of the Right Honourable Lester B. Pearson*. Volume 3: 1957–1968. Toronto: University of Toronto Press, 1975.

———. *Mike: The Memoirs of the Right Honourable Lester B. Pearson*. Volume 2: 1948–1957. Toronto: University of Toronto Press, 1973.

Pearson, Lester B. *Mike: The Memoirs of the Right Honourable Lester B. Pearson*. Volume 1: 1897–1948. Toronto: University of Toronto Press, 1972.

———. *Words and Occasions*. Cambridge, MA: Harvard University Press, 1970.

———. "Force for U.N." *Foreign Affairs* 35, no. 3 (April 1957): 395–404.

———. "The Development of Canadian Foreign Policy." *Foreign Affairs* 30, no. 1 (October 1951): 17–30.

Pearson, Michael. "Humanizing the UN Security Council." Pp. 127–151 in *Canada Among Nations 2001: The Axworthy Legacy*, edited by Fen Osler Hampson, Norman Hillmer, and Maureen Appel Molot. Don Mills, ON: Oxford University Press, 2001.

Pettigrew, Pierre. "Dancing with the Elephant: Contending with an Assertive Super Power in Trade and Global Diplomacy." Address to the Empire Club, Toronto, 25 September 2003. <http://webapps.dfait-maeci.ca>.

Pickersgill, J.W. *My Years with Louis St Laurent: A Political Memoir*. Toronto and Buffalo: University of Toronto Press, 1975.

Pierson, Paul. "The Path to European Integration: A Historical Institutionalist Analysis." *Comparative Political Studies* 29, no. 2 (April 1996): 123–163.

Poe, Steven C. "Human Rights and the Allocation of US Military Assistance." *Journal of Peace Research* 28, no. 2 (1991): 205–216.

———. "Human Rights and Economic Aid Allocation under Ronald Reagan and Jimmy Carter." *American Journal of Political Science* 3, no. 1 (1992): 147–167.

Porritt, Edward. *Sixty Years of Protection in Canada, 1846–1907*. London: Macmillan, 1908.

Porter, Tony, and Duncan Wood. "Reform without Representation? The Transnational Dialogue on the Global Financial Architecture." In *Debating the Global Financial Architecture*, edited by Leslie Elliott Armijo. Albany, NY: State University of New York Press, 2002.

Potter, Evan H. "Canada and the World: Continuity and Change in Public Opinion on Aid, Trade, and International Security, 1993–2002." *Études Internationales* 33, no. 4 (December 2002): 697–722.

———. "Niche Diplomacy as Canadian Foreign Policy." *International Journal* 52, no. 1 (Winter 1996–1997): 25–38.

Pratt, Cranford. "DFAIT's Takeover Bid of CIDA." *Canadian Foreign Policy* 5, no. 2 (Winter 1998): 1–13.

Prime Minister's Office. *Notes for a 24 November 1989 Address by the Right Honourable Brian Mulroney*. Ottawa: PMO Press, November 27, 1989.

Privy Council Office. *The Role and Structure of the Privy Council*. 1999. <http://www.pco.gc.ca>.

Protocol for the Assessment of Nonviolent Direct Action (PANDA) [Computer File]. <http://www.wcfia.harvard.edu/ponsacs/panda.htm>.

Pue, W. Wesley. *Pepper in Our Eyes: The APEC Affair*. Vancouver: University of British Columbia Press, 2000.

Radwanski, George. *Trudeau*. Toronto: Macmillan, 1978.

Rausch, Ulrike. *The Potential of Transborder Cooperation: Still Worth a Try: An Assessment of the Conference of New England Governors and Eastern Canadian Premiers*. Halifax: Dalhousie University Centre for Foreign Policy Studies, 1997.

Ravenhill, John. "Federal-State Relations in Australian External Affairs: A New Co-operative Era?" Pp. 134–152 in *Paradiplomacy in Action: The Foreign Relations of Subnational Governments*, edited by Francisco Aldecoa and Michael Keating. London: Frank Cass, 1999.

Ray, James Lee. *Global Politics*. Boston: Houghton Mifflin, 1998.

Rayfuse, Rosemary. "Reference re Secession of Quebec from Canada: Breaking Up Is Hard to Do" *University of New South Wales Law Journal* 21, no. 3 (1998): 834–844.

Reilly, John E. *American Public Opinion and U.S. Foreign Policy*. Chicago: Chicago Council on Foreign Relations, 1999.

Reinharz, Jehuda. "ChaimWeizmann as Political Strategist: The Initial Years, 1918–1920." Pp. 271–294 in *Essays in Modern Jewish History*, edited by Frances Malino and Phyllis Cohen Albert. East Brunswick, NJ: Association of University Presses, 1982.

Reisman, Simon S. "The Issue of Free Trade." Pp. 35–51 in *US–Canada Economic Relations: Next Steps?* edited by Edward R. Fried and Philip H. Tresize. Washington, DC: The Brookings Institution, 1984.

Reitz, Jeffrey G., and Raymond Breton. *The Illusion of Difference: Realities of Ethnicity in Canada and the United States*. Toronto: C. D. Howe Institute, 1994.

Report of the Auditor General of Canada to the House of Commons. "Peacekeeping." FA1-1996/1-6E. Ottawa: May 1996.

Report of the 1996 National Forum on Canada's International Relations. Address by Lloyd Axworthy. Ottawa: Canadian Centre for Foreign Policy Development, 1997.

Report of the Special Joint Committee of the Senate and House of Commons on the Constitution of Canada, 4th Session, 28th Parliament 1972.

Report of the Standing Committee on Foreign Affairs and International Trade, *Partners in North America: Advancing Canada's Relations with the United States and Mexico*. Ottawa: December, 2002.

Reumiller, Lt. Col. Ernest. "Canadian Perspectives and Experiences with Peacekeeping: General Policy Considerations." In *Conflict Resolution and Peacemaking/Peacekeeping: The Irish and Canadian Experience*, edited by Padraig O'Gormaile and Ray Murphy. Galway, Ireland: Association for Canadian Studies in Ireland, 1997.

Rhodes, Martin. "The Future of the 'Social Dimension:' Labour Market Regulation in Post-1992 Europe." *Journal of Common Market Studies* 30, no. 1 (March 1992): 23–51.

Richter, Andrew. "A Question of Defense: How American Allies Are Responding to the U.S. Missile Defense Program." *Comparative Strategy* 23, no. 2 (April–June 2004): 125–141.

———. *The Revolution in Military Affairs and Its Impact on Canada: The Challenge and the Consequences.* Working Paper 28. Vancouver: University of British Columbia Institute of International Relations, 1999.

Riesman, Simon S. "The Issue of Free Trade." In *U.S.–Canada Economic Relations: Next Steps?* edited by Edward R. Fried and Philip H. Tresize. Washington, D.C.: The Brookings Institution, 1984.

Rioux, Jean-Sébastien, and Douglas A. Van Belle. "The Influence of Le Monde Coverage on French Foreign Aid Allocations." Paper presented to the Canadian Political Science Association Annual Meeting, Québec City, May 2001.

Rioux, Jean-François, and Robin Hay. "Canadian Foreign Policy: From Internationalism to Isolationism?" Norman Paterson School of International Affairs Discussion Paper no. 16. Ottawa: Carleton University, 1997.

Ripsman, Norrin M. "Big Eyes and Empty Pockets: The Two Phases of Conservative Defense Policy." In *Diplomatic Departures: The Conservative Era in Canadian Foreign Policy, 1984–93*, edited by Nelson Michaud and Kim Richard Nossal. Vancouver: UBC Press, 2001.

Risse, Thomas, Stephen C. Ropp, and Kathryn Sikkink, eds. *The Power of Human Rights: International Norms and Domestic Change.* New York/Cambridge: Cambridge University Press, 1999.

Ritchie, Gordon. *Wrestling with the Elephant: The Inside Story of the Canada-US Trade Wars.* Toronto: Macfarlane, Walter & Ross, 1997.

Robertson, Scot. "The Defence Review: Attacking the Strategy-Resources Mismatch." *Canadian Military Journal* 3, no. 3 (Autumn 2002): 21–27.

Robertson, Terence. *Crisis: The Inside Story of the Suez Conspiracy.* New York: Atheneum, 1965.

Robinson, Basil. *Diefenbaker's World: A Populist in World Affairs.* Toronto and Buffalo: University of Toronto Press, 1989.

Robson, William B. P., and David Laidler. *No Small Change: The Awkward Economics and Politics of North American Monetary Integration.* Toronto: C. D. Howe Institute, 2002.

Rochlin, James. *Discovering the Americas: The Evolution of Canadian Foreign Policy Towards Latin America.* Vancouver: UBC Press, 1994.

Rodal, Berel. *The Somalia Experience in Strategic Perspective: Implications for the*

Military in a Free and Democratic Society. Study prepared for the Commission of Inquiry into the Deployment of Canadian Forces to Somalia. Ottawa: Canadian Minister of Public Works and Government Services, 1997.

Rosenau, James N. *Along the Domestic-Foreign Frontier: Exploring Governance in a Turbulent World.* Cambridge: Cambridge University Press, 1997.

Rosenstock, R. "The Declaration of Principles of International Law Concerning Friendly Relations: A Survey." *American Journal of International Law* 65 (1971): 713–735.

Rosner, Gabriella. *The United Nations Emergency Force.* New York: Columbia University Press, 1963.

Roussel, Stéphane. "Fortress North America." In *Fortress North America? What Continental Security Means for Canada,* edited by David Rudd and Nicholas Furneaux. Toronto: The Canadian Institute of Strategic Studies, 2002.

Rowley, Charles K., and Robert D. Tollison. "Rent-Seeking and Trade Protection." Pp. 217–237 in *The Political Economy of Rent-Seeking,* edited by Charles K. Rowley, Robert D. Tollison, and Gordon Tullock. Boston: Kluwer Academic, 1988.

Royal Canadian Military Institute. *A Wake-Up Call for Canada: The Need for a New Military.* Toronto: Royal Canadian Military Institute, 2001.

Royal Commission on the Economic Union and Development Prospects for Canada. *Report.* Vols. 1 and 2. Ottawa: Minister of Supply and Services, 1985.

Rubin, Barnett R. *Blood on the Doorstep: The Politics of Preventive Action.* New York: Century Foundation Press, 2002.

Rudner, Martin. "Canada, the Gulf Crisis and Collective Security." In *Canada Among Nations 1990–91: After the Cold War,* edited by Fen Osler Hampson and Christopher J. Maule. Ottawa: Carleton University Press, 1991.

Rummel, Rudolph J. *War, Power, and Peace.* Beverly Hills, CA: Sage Publications, 1995.

Russett, Bruce. *Grasping the Democratic Peace: Principles for a Post–Cold War World.* Princeton, NJ: Princeton University Press, 1993.

Sakwa, Richard. *Gorbachev and His Reforms, 1985–1990.* London: Philip Allan, 1990.

Sands, Christopher. "How Canada Policy Is Made in the U.S." In *Canada Among Nations 2000: Vanishing Borders,* edited by Fen Osler Hampson and Maureen Appel Molot. Don Mills, ON: Oxford University Press, 2000.

Saunders, Alan. "Pondering the Arctic Council." *Northern Perspectives* 19 (Fall 1991): 2–5.

Savoie, Donald J. *Governing from the Center: The Concentration of Power in Canadian Politics.* Toronto and Buffalo: University of Toronto Press, 1999.

Sawer, Geoffrey. *Modern Federalism*. London: C. A. Watts and Co., 1969.
Scharfe, Sharon. *Complicity: Human Rights and Canadian Foreign Policy: The Case of East Timor*. Montreal and New York: Black Rose Books, 1996.
Schmitz, Gerald. "Democratizing Trade Agreements: Contesting the 'Corporate Millennium'?" Paper presented at the Annual Meeting of the Canadian Political Science Association, Québec City, 30 July 2000.
Scrivener, David. "Arctic Environmental Co-operation in Transition." *Polar Record* 35 (Fall 1999): 51–58.
———. "From Ottawa to Iqaluit: Towards Sustainable Arctic Cooperation?" *Environmental Politics* 7, no. 4 (Winter 1998): 136–141.
———. *Environmental Cooperation in the Arctic: From Strategy to Council*. Oslo: Norwegian Atlantic Committee, 1996.
Secretary of State for External Affairs. *Foreign Policy for Canadians*. Ottawa: Information Canada, 1970.
Securing an Open Society: Canada's National Security Policy. 2004. <www.pco-bcp.gc.ca>.
"Securing Our Future: Report of the Standing Committee on Finance." *House of Commons Committee Reports*. 2001. <www.parl.gc.ca>.
Senate Standing Committee on Foreign Affairs. *Canada–United States Relations: Canada's Trade Relations with the United States*. Ottawa: Minister of Supply and Services, 1978.
Sens, Allen G. *Somalia and the Changing Nature of Peacekeeping: The Implications for Canada*. Ottawa: Commission of Inquiry into the Deployment of Canadian Forces to Somalia, 1997.
Shamsie, Yasmine. *Engaging with Civil Society: Lessons from the OAS, FTAA and Summits of the Americas*. Ottawa: North-South Institute, 2000. <http://www.nsi-ins.ca>.
Sharp, Mitchell. *Which Reminds Me . . . A Memoir*. Toronto and Buffalo: University of Toronto Press, 1994.
———. "Canada-US Relations: Options for the Future." *International Perspectives* 3 (Autumn 1972).
———. *Foreign Policy for Canadians*. Ottawa: Queen's Printer for Canada, 1970.
Sikkink, Kathryn, and Jackie Smith. "Infrastructures for Change: Transnational Organizations, 1953–93." Pp. 24–44 in *Restructuring World Politics: Transnational Social Movements, Networks and Norms*, edited by Sanjeev Khagram, James Riker, and Kathryn Sikkink. Minneapolis: University of Minnesota Press, 2002.
Sinclair, Jim, ed. *Crossing the Line: Canada and Free Trade with Mexico*. Vancouver: New Star Books, 1992.

Singer, David J., and Melvin Small. *Annual Alliance Membership Data, 1815–1965* [Computer file]. ICPSR version. Ann Arbor: University of Michigan Mental Health Institute, Correlates of War Project [producer]. Ann Arbor: Interuniversity Consortium for Political and Social Research [distributor], 1991.

Siplon, Patricia. "Acting (UP) Globally: The Internet, AIDS and Activism." Paper presented at the annual meeting of the American Political Science Association, San Francisco, CA, September 2001.

Sisto, James E. P. "How Do Canadian and US States View the Importance of Their Cross-Border Counterparts?" *Canada-United States Law Journal* 27 (2001): 139–145.

Skelton, Oscar D. *The Day of Sir Wilfrid Laurier.* Toronto: Glasgow Brook, 1916.

Skilling, H. Gordon. "The Helsinki Process." In *Human Rights in Canadian Foreign Policy*, edited by Robert O. Matthews and Cranford Pratt. Kingston, ON: McGill-Queen's University Press, 1988.

Sloan, Elinor. "Canada and the Revolution in Military Affairs: Current Response and Future Opportunities." *Canadian Military Journal* (Autumn 2000).

Smith, Constance. "Dollarization and Its Alternatives: Currency Arrangements under NAFTA." Pp. 377–396 in *NAFTA in the New Millennium*, edited by Edward D. Chambers and Peter H. Smith. Edmonton: The University of Alberta Press, 2002.

Smith, Denis. *Rogue Tory. The Life and Legend of John G. Diefenbaker.* Toronto: Macfarlane, Walter & Ross, 1995.

———. *Diplomacy of Fear: Canada and the Cold War 1941–1948.* Toronto: University of Toronto Press, 1988.

Smith, Gordon, and John Hay. "Canada and the Crisis in Eastern Zaire," in *Herding Cats: Multiparty Mediation in a Complex World*, edited by Chester A. Crocker, Fen Osler Hampson, and Pamela R. Aall. Washington, DC: US Institute of Peace Press, 1999.

Smith, Graham. "Federation, Defederation and Refederation: From the Soviet Union to Russian Statehood." Pp. 157–173 in *Federalism: The Multiethnic Challenge*, edited by Graham Smith. London: Longman, 1995.

Smith, Peter J. "The Dream of Political Union: Loyalism, Toryism, and the Federal Ideal in Pre-Confederation Canada." Pp. 148–171 in *The Causes of Canadian Confederation*, edited by Ged Martin. Fredericton, NB: Acadiensis Press, 1990.

Smith, Peter J., and Elizabeth Smythe. "Globalization, Citizenship and Technology: The MAI Meets the Internet." *Canadian Foreign Policy* 7, no. 2 (Winter 1999): 83–105.

Sokolsky, Joel J. "The Bilateral Defence Relationship with the United States." In

Canada's International Security Policy, edited by David B. Dewitt and David Leyton-Brown. Scarborough, ON: Prentice-Hall Canada, 1995.

———. "Realism Canadian Style: The Chretien Legacy in Foreign and Defense Policy and the Lessons for Canada-U.S. Relations." Lecture given at the Woodrow Wilson International Center for Scholars, Washington, DC, 15 January 2004.

———. "Realism Canadian Style: National Security Policy and the Chrétien Legacy." *Policy Matters* 5, no. 2 (June 2004): 1–44.

———. "A Seat at the Table: Canada and Its Alliances." Pp. 145–162 in *Canada's Defence. Perspectives on Policy in the Twentieth Century*, edited by B. D. Hunt and R. G. Haycock. Toronto: Copp Clark Pitman Ltd., 1993.

———. "Parting of the Waves? The Strategy and Politics of the SSN Decision." In *The U.S.-Canada Security Relationship: The Politics, Strategy, and Technology of Defense*, edited by David G. Haglund and Joel J. Sokolsky. Boulder, CO: Westview Press, 1989.

Special Joint Committee of the Senate and House of Commons, *Independence and Internationalism: Report of the Special Joint Committee on Canada's International Relations*, Ottawa: Queen's Printer, 1985.

Spry, Graham, "Canada, the United Nations Emergency Force, and the Commonwealth." *International Affairs* 33, no. 3 (July 1957): 289–300.

Stairs, Denis. "Myths, Morals, and Reality in Canadian Foreign Policy." *International Journal* 58, no. 2 (Spring 2003): 239–256.

———. *The Conduct of Canadian Foreign Policy and the Interests of Newfoundland and Labrador*. St. John's: Royal Commission on Renewing and Strengthening Our Place in Canada, 2003.

———. "Trends in Canadian Foreign Policy: Past, Present, and Future." *Behind the Headlines* 59, no. 3 (Spring 2002): 1–7.

———. "Foreign Policy Consultations in a Globalizing World: The Case of Canada, the WTO, and the Shenanigans in Seattle." *Policy Matters* 1, no. 8 (December 2000): 1–44.

———. "Liberalism and the Triumph of Efficiency in Canada-U.S. Relations." *ISUMA* 1, no.1 (Spring 2000): 11–16.

———. "The Policy Process and Dialogues with Demos: Liberal Pluralism with a Transnational Twist." Pp. 23–54 in *Canada Among Nations 1998: Leadership and Dialogue*, edited by Fen Osler Hampson and Maureen Appel Molot. Don Mills, ON: Oxford University Press, 1998.

———. "Canada and the Korean War: The Boundaries of Diplomacy." In *Partners Nevertheless: Canadian-American Relations in the Twentieth Century*, edited by Norman Hillmer. Toronto: Copp Clark Pitman Ltd., 1989.

———. "Present in Moderation: Lester Pearson and the Craft of Diplomacy." *International Journal* 29, no. 1 (Winter 1973–1974): 143–53.

Standing Committee on National Defence and Veterans Affairs. *Facing Our Responsibilities: The State of Readiness of the Canadian Forces*. Ottawa: Report of the Standing Committee on National Defence and Veterans Affairs, 2002.

Standing Committee on National Security and Defence. *For an Extra $130 Bucks: Update on Canada's Military Financial Crisis*. Ottawa: Report of the Standing Committee on National Security and Defence, 2002.

Standing Senate Committee on Foreign Affairs. *Canada-United States Relations: Canada's Trade Relations with the United States*. Ottawa: Minister of Supply and Services, 1978.

Stecher, Brian M., and W. Alan Davis. *How to Focus an Evaluation*. Newbury Park, CA: Sage Publications, 1991.

Stevens, Paul. *The 1911 General Election: A Study in Canadian Politics*. Toronto: Coop Clark, 1970.

Stevenson, Brian. *Canada, Latin America and the New Internationalism*. Kingston, ON: McGill-Queen's University Press, 2000.

Stevenson, Garth. *Unfulfilled Union*. Toronto: Macmillan, 1982.

Stohl, Michael. *The Purdue Political Terror Scale*. Codebook, 1993.

Stone, Frank. *Canada, the GATT and the International Trade System*. 2d ed. Montreal: The Institute for Research on Public Policy, 1992.

Strange, Susan. *Mad Money: When Markets Outgrow Governments*. Ann Arbor: University of Michigan Press, 1998.

———. *States and Markets*. New York: Basil Blackwell Press, 1988.

———. *Casino Capitalism*. Oxford: Basil Blackwell Inc, 1986.

Studer-Noguez, Isabel. *Ford and the Global Strategies of Multinationals: The North American Auto Industry*. New York: Routledge, 2002.

Stursberg, Peter. *Lester Pearson and the American Dilemma*. New York: Doubleday and Co., 1980.

———. *Lester Pearson and the Dream of Unity*. Toronto: Doubleday, 1978.

———. *Diefenbaker: Leadership Lost: 1962–1967*. Toronto and Buffalo: University of Toronto Press, 1976.

———. *Diefenbaker—Leadership Gained: 1956–1962*. Toronto and Buffalo: University of Toronto Press, 1975.

Suzuki, Eisuke. "Self-Determination and World Public Order." *Virginia Journal of International Law* 16 (1976): 779–862.

Tanner, Leesa. "Gender Integration in the Canadian Forces: A Quantitative Overview." Paper presented to the conference "Women in Uniform: Exploding the Myths; Exploring the Facts," Women's Research and Education Institute, Washington DC, December 1998.

Tarr, G. Alan, and Ellis Katz, eds. *Federalism and Rights*. Lanham, MD: Rowman & Littlefield, 1996.

Tarrow, Sidney. "Transnational Politics: Contention and Institutions in International Politics." *Annual Review of Political Science* 4 (2001): 1–20.

Taucar, Christopher Edward. *Canadian Federalism and Quebec Sovereignty*. New York: Peter Lang, 2000.

Telford, Hamish. *Expanding the Partnership: The Proposed Council of the Federation and the Challenge of Glocalization*. Montreal: Institute for Research on Public Policy, 2003.

Tennberg, Monica. *The Arctic Council: A Study in Governability*. Rovaniemi, Finland: University of Lapland Press, 1998.

The Canadian Forces and Interoperability: Panacea or Perdition? Halifax: Center for Foreign Policy Studies, Dalhousie University, 2002.

"The GATT and Canadian Interests: Summary of the Proceedings of a Research Symposium." Pp. 1–20 in *Canada and the Multilateral Trading System*, edited by John Whalley. Toronto: University of Toronto Press, 1985.

The International Commission on Intervention and State Sovereignty. *Responsibility to Protect: Research, Bibliography, Background*. Ottawa: International Development Research Centre, 2001.

The International Institute for Strategic Studies. *The Military Balance 2002–2003*. London: Oxford University Press, 2002.

Thérien, Jean-Philippe. "Le Canada et le régime international de l'aide." *Études internationales* 20, no. 2 (June 1989): 311–340.

Thérien, Jean-Philippe, and Carolyn Lloyd. "Development Assistance on the Brink." *Third World Quarterly* 21, no. 1 (February 2000): 21–38.

Thérien, Jean-Philippe, Louis Bélanger, and Guy Gosselin. "La politique étrangère Québécoise." Pp. 255–278 in *Québec: État et société*, edited by Alain G. Gagnon. Montréal: Québec Amérique, 1994.

Thompson, John Herd. "Playing by the Washington Rules: The U.S.-Canada Relationship, 1994–2003." *American Review of Canadian Studies* 33, no.1 (Spring 2003): 5–26.

Thomson, Dale C. *Vive le Québec Libre*. Toronto: Deneau, 1988

———. *Louis St. Laurent: Canadian*. Toronto: Macmillan, 1968.

Thordarson, Bruce, *Lester Pearson: Diplomat and Politician*. Toronto: Oxford University Press, 1974.

———. *Trudeau and Foreign Policy: A Study in Decision-Making*. Toronto: Oxford University Press, 1972.

Thorup, Cathryn. "The Politics of Free Trade and the Dynamics of Cross-Border Coalitions in U.S.-Mexican Relations." *The Columbia Journal of World Business* 26, no. 11 (Summer 1991): 12–26.

Tullock, Gordon. "Welfare Costs of Tariffs, Monopolies and Theft." *Western Economic Journal* 5, no. 2 (June 1967): 224–32.

United Nations Development Program. *Millennium Development Goals.* 2000. <http://www.undp.org/mdg/Millennium%20Development%20Goals.pdf>.

United Nations General Assembly. *Report of the Secretary-General on the Prevention of Armed Conflict.* New York: United Nations, June 2001.

United States Government. National Security Decisions Directive Number 90. *US Arctic Policy.* 14 April 1983.

Uslaner, Eric M. "The Democratic Party and Free Trade: An Old Romance Restored." *NAFTA: Law and Business Review of the Americas* 6 (Summer 2000): 347–62.

Van Belle, Douglas A., Jean-Sébastien Rioux, and David M. Potter. *Media, Bureaucracies, and Foreign Aid: A Comparative Analysis of United States, the United Kingdom, Canada, France and Japan.* New York: Palgrave Macmillan Press, 2004.

———. "A Comparative Analysis of the News Media's Influence on British, French, Japanese and U.S. Development Aid Bureaucracies." Paper presented to the Annual Meeting of the American Political Science Association, San Francisco, CA, September 2001.

Van Rooy, Alison. "Civil Society and the Axworthy Touch." Pp. 253–269 in *Canada Among Nations 2001: The Axworthy Legacy,* edited by Fen Osler Hampson, Norman Hillmer, and Maureen Appel Molot. Don Mills, ON: Oxford University Press, 2001.

Vile, M. J. C. "Federal Theory and the 'New Federalism.'" In *The Politics of New Federalism,* edited by D. Jaensch. Adelaide: University of Victoria Press, 1977.

Viotti, Paul R., and Mark V. Kauppi. *International Relations Theory: Realism, Pluralism, Globalism, and Beyond.* 3rd ed. Needham Heights, MA: Allyn and Bacon, 1999.

"Vision 2010—The Integrated Navy." Chief of the Maritime Staff. <http://www.dnd.ca/navy/marcom/intro_e.htm>.

Waite, P. B., ed. *The Confederation Debates in the Provinces of Canada, 1867.* Toronto: McClelland & Stewart, 1963.

Walker, Graham F., ed. *Independence in an Age of Empire: Assessing Unilateralism and Multilateralism.* Halifax: Center for Foreign Policy Studies, Dalhousie University, 2004.

Walker, Henry James. "Henry Clayton and the Secession Movement in Alabama." *Southern Studies* 4, no. 4 (Winter 1993): 341–360.

Waltz, Kenneth. *Theory of International Politics.* Reading, MA: Addison-Wesley, 1979.

Wapner, Paul. *Environmental Activism and World Civic Politics.* Albany, NY: SUNY Press, 1996.

Waruszynski, Barbara. "Determining the Canadian Pulse on Defence Matters." *Defence Matters* 2, no. 5 (July 1997): 12–17.

Watkins, James D. "The Maritime Strategy." *US Naval Institute Proceedings* 4 (January 1986): 11–14.

Watts, Ronald L. *Comparing Federal Systems in the 1990s.* Kingston, ON: Institute of Intergovernmental Relations, 1996.

Waverman, Leonard. "Post-NAFTA: Can the United States, Canada and Mexico Deepen Their Economic Relationship?" Pp. 55–79 in *Beyond Mexico*, edited by Jean Daudelin and Edgar J. Dosman. Ottawa: Carleton University Press and Canadian Foundation for the Americas, 1995.

Welch, David A. "The New Multilateralism and Evolving Security Systems," in *Canada Among Nations 1992–93: A New World Order?* edited by Fen Osler Hampson and Christopher Maule. Ottawa: Carleton University Press, 1992.

Wheare, K. C. *Federal Government.* London: Oxford University Press, 1953.

Wilkinson, Derrick G. "International Trade Policy and the Role of Non-central Governments: The Recent Canadian Experience." Pp. 202–210 in *Foreign Relations and Federal States*, edited by Brian Hocking. London: Leicester University Press, 1993.

Williams, Glen. *Not for Export.* 3rd ed. Toronto: McClelland & Stewart, 1994.

Williams, Gwyn. *The Search for Beulah Land: The Welsh and the Atlantic Revolution.* New York: Holmes & Meier, 1980.

Williams, Robert J. "Federalism and Cultural Diplomacy in Canada and Australia." In *Foreign Relations and Federal States*, edited by Brian Hocking. London: Leicester University Press, 1993.

Wind, Marlene. *Sovereignty and European Integration: Toward a Post-Hobbesian Order.* New York: Palgrave, 2001.

Winham, Gilbert R. *Trading with Canada: The Canada-US Free Trade Agreement.* New York: Priority Press, 1988.

Winslow, Donna. *The Canadian Airborne Regiment in Somalia: A Socio-cultural Inquiry: A Study.* Ottawa: The Commission, 1997.

Winters, Barbara. "The Wrens of the Second World War: Their Place in the History of Canadian Servicewomen." Pp. 280–296 in *A Nation's Navy: In Quest of Canadian Naval Identity*, edited by Michael L. Hadley, Rob Huebert, and Fred W. Crickard. Montreal: McGill-Queen's University Press, 1996.

Wolfe, Robert. "See You in Washington? A Pluralist Perspective on North American Institutions." *Choices* 9, no. 4 (April 2003): 1–24.

Wood, Duncan R., and George A. MacLean. "A New Partnership for the Millennium." *Canadian Foreign Policy* 7, no. 2 (Fall 1999).

Wood, Duncan , "The G7, International Finance, and Developing Countries." In *Shaping a New International Financial System: Challenges of Governance in a Globalizing World*, edited by Karl Kaiser, John J. Kirton, and Joseph P. Daniels. Aldershot, UK: Ashgate, 2000.

Wood, Robert E. *From Marshall Plan to Debt Crisis: Foreign Aid and Development Choices in the World Economy*. Berkeley: University of California Press, 1986.

Woodrow Wilson Center for International Scholars, Canada Institute. "Realism Canadian Style: The Chrétien Legacy in Foreign and Defense Policy and the Lessons for Canada-U.S. Relations." <http://wwics.si.edu>.

Worth, L. Kinvin. "Notes for a Comparative Study of the Origins of Federalism in the United States and Canada." *Arizona Journal of International and Comparative Law* 15, no. 1 (Winter 1998): 33–56.

Young, Oran R. *Arctic Politics*: Conflict and Cooperation in the Circumpolar North. Hanover, NH: University Press of New England, 1992.

———. "The Age of the Arctic." *Foreign Policy*, no. 61 (Winter 1985–86): 160–179.

Young, Oran, and Gail Osherenko. *Polar Politics: Creating International Environmental Regimes*. Ithaca, NY: Cornell University Press, 1993.

Zaslow, Morris. *The Northern Expansion of Canada, 1914–1967*. Toronto: McClelland & Stewart, 1988.

Zimmerman, David. "The Social Background of the Wartime Navy: Some Statistical Data." In *A Nation's Navy: In Quest of Canadian Naval Identity*, edited by Michael L. Hadley, Rob Huebert, and Fred W. Crickard. Montreal: McGill-Queen's University Press, 1996.

Zirakzadeh, Cyrus Ernesto. *A Rebellious People: Basques, Protests, and Politics*. Reno: University of Nevada Press, 1991.

NEWSPAPERS, NEWSMAGAZINES, NEWSLETTERS, NEWS AGENCIES, ONLINE RESOURCES, & POLLING AGENCIES

Action Nationale.
Agence France-Presse.
Associated Press (AP) Online.
Bout de Papier.
Canadafreepress.com—Politically Incorrect.
Canada Leader-Post.
Canada News Wire.
Canada World View.
Canadian Business and Current Affairs.
CanWest News Service.

BIBLIOGRAPHY

CBC News.
CNEWS.
CTV.ca.
DFAIT News Release.
Dispatches (the Canadian Army's "Lessons Learned Newsletter").
Economist.
Edmonton Journal.
<europa.eu.int>.
Financial Post.
Gazette (Montreal).
Globe and Mail (Toronto).
Guardian (Charlottetown).
Halifax Chronicle Herald.
Halifax Herald.
Hamilton Spectator.
International Conciliation.
Ipsos-Reid.
Jane's Defence Weekly.
Kingston Whig-Standard.
Le Devoir (Montréal).
Los Angeles Times.
Maclean's.
Maple Leaf.
Monthly Trade Bulletin (Industry Canada).
Montreal Star.
National Post (Toronto).
New York Times.
<north.cbc.ca>.
Nova Scotia Department of Finance.
Nunatsiaq News.
Ottawa Citizen.
Peace and Environment News.
<pm.gc.ca>.
Portage Daily Graphic (Manitoba).
Reuters News.
Standard (St. Catharines, ON).
<strageis.ic.gc.ca>.
The Canadian Forum.
The Daily Camera (Boulder, CO).

Time.
Toronto Star.
Washington Post.
Windsor Star.
Winnepeg Free Press.
<www.acdi-cida.gc.ca>.
<www.angusreid.com>.
<www.bankofcanada.ca>.
<www.carc.org>.
<www.carleton.ca/cifp>.
<www.chrr.org>.
<www.dfait-maeci.gc.ca>.
<www.foreign-policy-dialogue.ca>.
<www.freedomhouse.org>.
<www.ftaaalca.org>.
<www.icrc.org>.
<www.ichrdd.ca>.
<www.ligi.ubc.ca>.
<www.mri.gouv.qc.ca>.
<www.navy.forces.gc.ca>.
<www.nepad.org>.
<www.onesky.ca>.
<www.parl.gc.ca>.
<www.pco.gc.ca>.
<www.peacebuild.ca>.
<www.ploughshsares.ca>.
<www.sasktrade.sk.ca>.
<www.snipercountry.com>.
<www.tbs-sct.gc.ca>.
<www.torontofreepress.com>.
<www.tradeagreements.gc.ca>.
<www.undp.org>.
<www.wcfia.harvard.edu/ponsacs/panda.htm>.

SURVEYS
CUSO, Aug. 2003.
International Development Research Centre, Aug. 2003.
Project Ploughshares, Aug. 2003.
UNICEF Canada, Aug. 2003.
Youth Millennium Project, Aug. 2003.

Index

Page references appearing in italics refer to tables and figures.

3-D policy, 14, 195, 204, 229
9/11, 4, 17, 19, 43, 66, 68, 124, 152, 226, 329, 338, 354, 420, 422–423, 505, 514; post-9/11, 1, 13, 18, 68, 352, 411, 505–506, 514, 522, 524; pre-9/11, 2, 348, 397, 401

Abbas, Mahmoud, 353
Accompanying Convention on Certain Conventional Weapons, 499
Afghanistan, 66, 79n77, 114, 178, 189, 199, 350, 380, 411, 416–417, 422; Canada, working in, 203, 206; Canadian Forces (CF), in, 168, 181–182, 414–415, 426, 483; Canadian International Development Agency (CIDA), in, 180; International Security Assistance Force (ISAF), in, 70, 80n101, 166, 170, 380; U.S. leading Operation Enduring Freedom, 170, 414
Afghan Campaign, Canadian Forces (CF), in, 168, 182, 414–415, 426, 483
Afghan National Army, 168, 415

Africa, 13, 15, 137, 139, 141–146, 199–200, 205, 211–212, 223, 225–227; CIDA, in, 216
African Union (AU), 226–227; Summit in Durban (2002), 227
Agence de Coopération Culturelle et Technique (ACCT), 135, 141, 143–144, 145–148, 157–158, 220. *See also* La Francophonie
AIDS crisis, NGOs addressing the, 494
Alaska Boundary Dispute (1903), 26, 28, 292
Alaska, state of, 106, 412
Alberta, 40, 106, *114*, 115, 117, 118; trading with China, 118; trading with Russia, 118; trading with South Africa, 118
Algeria, 153, 226
Alliances, of Canada, 58
Allied: Command European Land Force in Norway, 61; Germany, war against, 293; missions the Balkans, 168
Al-Qaeda, 5, 10, 66, 228, 329
Americas, 199; CIDA, in the, 216

577

Amnesty International, 133, 156, 247
Amsterdam, Treaty of, (1997), 379–380. *See also* European Union
Andean community, 369
Anglo-Japanese alliance, 31
Anglo-U.S. alliance, 340
Angola, 351
Annan, Kofi, 166, 196, 351, 424; 2001 *Report on the Prevention of Armed Conflict*, 192
Annexation Manifesto, 85
Anti-Americanism, 355
Anti-personnel land mine treaty. *See* Axworthy, Lloyd; International Campaign to Ban Landmines; Landmines Convention; Mines Action Canada; Ottawa Process; Ottawa treaty
Anti-submarine warfare (ASW), 54
Arab-Israeli War (1948–1949), 339, 346
Arafat, Yasir, 353
Arctic, 7, 8, 10, 15, 295–296, 309–310, 396; Arctic Council, 9, 15, 289–312; Arctic Monitoring and Assessment Program (AMAP), 307; Canadian Forces (CF), in, 412; Canadian policy towards, 15, 297, 302, 425; Canadian-U.S. negotiations, 15; Conservation of Arctic Flora and Fauna (CAFF), 307; Environmental Protection Strategy Conference (Finland), 298, 301; policy, 5; Protection of Arctic Marine Environment (PAME), 307; University of, 308, 310; U.S. policy, for, 296, 301–302. *See also* Circumpolar; Inuit Circumpolar Conference
Argentina, 281

Articles of Confederation, 439
Asia, 2, 15, 70, 97, 137, 199–200, 205, 211, 219, 223, 228, 274, 293, 318; Canadian Forces (CF), in, 216; Canadian International Development Agency (CIDA), in, 216; Commonwealth, countries in, 343; crisis, 279; Québec offices, in, 119; reform process, 279; South East, 199
Asia-Pacific Economic Cooperation Forum (APEC), 500–501
Asian Development Bank, 217
Association of Indigenous Peoples of Northern Russia, 302
Atlantic Alliance, 341, 402. *See also* North Atlantic Treaty Organization
Auditor General (AG): 1996 study, 173; 1998 report, 65; Audit, 67. *See also* Fraser, Sheila
Atlantic Alliance, 402
Australia, 106, 110, 166, 258, 281, 340, 348, 350, 381, 400–401, 514, 523; gender integration in the Navy, 474
Authoritarianism, 16
Auto Pact (1965), 38, 100n23
Austria, gender integration in the Navy, 474
Avro Arrow, 54
Axworthy, Lloyd, 21, 64, 179–181, 284; 2002 Keith Davey Lecture, 419; action towards anti-personal land mines, 42, 399, 419, 498–499; action towards child soldiers 510n33; action towards proliferation of small arms, 510n33; Axworthyism, 419; consulting with NGOs, 42, 496, 510n33; Foreign Affairs minister, as, 43, 168, 178, 308, 323, 397, 419, 496, 497, 498–499, 522; human security

INDEX 579

agenda, 42, 235, 332, 397, 457, 483, 498; Liberal Foreign Policy Handbook, writing of, 495; soft power capacity, 498–499, 507. See also Anti-personnel land mine treaty; Human Security; International Campaign to Ban Landmines; Landmines Convention; Mines Action Canada; Ottawa Process; Ottawa treaty
Aznar, Jose Maria, 351

Balfour Report, 33
Balkans, 380, 414; Canadian Forces (CF) Allied missions in the, 168
Bamako Declaration, 156
Bangladesh, 211, 221–223
Bank for International Settlements' Basel Committee on Banking Supervision (BCBS), 280
Bank of Canada, 34
Barre, Raymond, 146
Bavaria, 444
Beatty, Perrin, 60
Beaudoin, Louise, 151
Belgium: federal constitution (1995), adoption of, 106; gender integration in the Navy, 474
BENELUX countries, 386n29
Bennett, Richard B., 31; promoting Imperial trade, 31
Bergeron, Stephane, 330
Berlin Wall, dismantling of, 3, 296
Bernard, Daniel, 156; Bouchard-Bernard deal, 151
Bernard, Louis, 151; Secretary of the executive council, 151
Bertrand, Jean-Jacques, 139
bin Laden, Osama, 5
Binational Planning Group (BPG), 68

Black, E. P., 141
Blair, Tony, 351, 354, 394, 400; government of, 399
Bloc Québécois, 101n37, 175, 181, 330, 351
Blue Helmets, 13, 165, 166, 167, 168, 170. See also peacekeeping
Boer War. See South Africa
Bohemian index, 115–116
BOMARC, 54
Bongo, Omar, 143
Bonn, 57
Borden, Robert Laird, 29–30, 34, 44; government of, 35
Bosnia, 70, 194; Canadian Forces (CF), in, 172, 181, 348, 380, 414, 483; Srebrenica, massacre in, 189; Stabilization Force (SFOR), in, 70, 81n101, 114
Bouchard, Lucien, 149; Ambassador in Paris, 150–151, 155; Bouchard-Bernard deal, 151; Québec premier, 6, 133
Bourassa, Henri, 28, 46n10
Bourassa, Robert, 153
Bourguiba, Habib, 136
Boutros-Ghali, Boutros: Organisation internationale de La Francophonie, Secretary-General of, 133; United Nations Secretary-General, 158, 191
Boxboard Manufacturers' Association, 101n29
Brazil, 281, 327, 514, 523
Breton, Gilles, 302
Bretton Woods, 33–34; conference, 273, 522; economic system, 3; financial institutions, 277. See also General Agreement on Tariffs and Trade; International Monetary

Fund; World Bank; World Trade Organization
British-Columbia (BC), 85, 106, *114*, 115, 117, 121–122, 412; arrangements with South Africa, 121; trade missions, 122
British North America, 445
British North America Act of 1867 (BNA Act), 27, 85, 442–443
British Royal Air Force (RAF), 467
Bulgaria, 373
Burundi, 134
Bush, George H. W., 62; administration of, 41, 301–303; new world order, 21, 62, 513
Bush, George W., 5, 11, 17, 43, 226, 351, 352, 394, 400, 414, 422–423, 514; administration of, 227, 237, 348–349, 354, 396–397, 421
Business Council on National Issues (BCNI), 94, 102n41

Cabinet, 23–25, 27, 37, 42, 172–173; Secretariat for, 25
Cadieux, Leo, Defense Minister, 74n25
Cadieux, Marcel, 136, 138
Cairns Group, 381
Calhoun, John C., 439
Camdessus, Michel, 276
Cameroon, 153, *222*, 351
Camp David, 38
Campbell, Gordon, 122
Campbell, Kim, 48, 397
Canada in the World (1995), 28, 194, 222, 496, 498, 519
Canadian Alliance party, 12, 350–351
Canadian Battery Manufacturers' Association, 101n29
Canada Cast Iron Soil Pipe Association, 101n29

Canadian Centre for Foreign Policy Development (CCFDP), 42, 496–498, 505
Canadian Chamber of Commerce, 101n29
Canadian Charter of Human Rights and Freedoms (1982), 39, 235, 459, 473, 492, 495
Canadian Chemical Producers' Association, 100n29
Canadian Conflict Prevention Committee (CCPC), 196–197
Canadian Conflict Prevention Initiative (CCPI), 190, 196
Canadian Council of Chief Executives (CCCE), 102n41
Canadian Council of Furniture Manufacturers, 101n29
Canadian Federation of Independent Business (CFIB), 90, 102n40, 102n44
Canadian Grocery Bag Manufacturers' Association, 101n29
Canadian Forces (CF), 11, 51, 54, 57–58, 62, 67, 71, 170–171, 173, 175, 178, 181–182, 426, 521; 3rd battalion of the Princess Patricia's Light Infantry (3/PPCLI), 415; in Afghanistan, 168, 181, 415, 426, 483; Airborne Regiment (CAR), 78n69, 171, 177; Air-Sea Transportable (CAST) Brigade Group, 75n31; Allied missions in the Balkans, 168; American surveillance (Aurora), 58; Annual Report of The Chief of the Defense Staff, (1999–2000), 466; Argus surveillance aircraft, 58; in Arctic, 412; in Bosnia, 172, 181, 348, 380, 414, 483; C-5 fleet, 63; Canadian Women

in the South African Military Nursing Service, 467, 469; Canadian Women's Army Corps, 469; Centurions, 58; Chief of Maritime Staff (CMS), 460; contributions to NATO, 174, 186n46, 210, 414–415, 522; Cougar close fire-support vehicles, replacement of, 63; in Cyprus (1964), 174, 522; diminished capabilities, 66; EH-101 helicopters, cancellation of, 62, 418; Employment Equity Act (1986), 460; F-18 fighter, 58, 61, 63, 78n73; gender equity, 460–461; in Germany, 61; HCMS *Preserver*, 418; HCMS *Protecteur*, 418, 470; Labradors, cancellation of, 62; in Lebanon, 348; Leopard tanks, 58; Maritime Command (MARCOM), 426, 458, 461, 464, 467, 470, 471, 473, 479, 481–483; Mixed Gender Units (MGU), 471; Non-Commissioned Members (NCM), 475, *476*; in NORAD, 176, 425; nuclear capability, 37; nuclear-powered attack submarines (SSNs), 59, 76n42; peacekeepers, 177; Permanent Joint Board on Defence, 33; Reserve Officer Training Corps (ROTC), 466; Royal Canadian Air Force (Women's division), 468; Royal Canadian Air Force Medical Branch and Nursing Service, 468; Royal Canadian Army Medical Corps Nursing Service, 468; Royal Canadian Navy (RCN), 29, 457–458, 467, 469, 470–473, 519; Royal Canadian Navy Nursing Service, 468; Sea Kings, cancellation of, 62, 418; Sea Kings, replacement of, 63, 77n62; in Somalia, 171; in Suez, 522; Victorias, 418; *Vision 2010–The Integrated Navy*, 471–473, 481–482; Women's Royal Canadian Naval Service (Wren), 468–470; working with U.S. troops, 417. *See also* National Defense, Department of

Canadian foreign policy: Golden Age, 4, 10, 22, 26, 35–36, 44, 55, 524; Northern agenda, 295; northern dimension, 291; Northern diplomacy, 296; reevaluation of, 2; scholars of, 3, 213, 229, 241, 246

Canadian Hardwood Bureau, 101n29

Canadian Human Rights Act (1978), 459

Canadian Human Rights Tribunal, 459, 471

Canadian Imperial Bank of Commerce (CIBC), 273

Canadian International Development Agency (CIDA), 190, 195, 202, 239, 243; in Afghanistan, 180; in Africa, 216; in the Americas, 216; in Asia, 216; in Central and Eastern Europe, 216; foreign aid programs, 2, 14, 118, 200, 205, 210, 212, 216, 229, 236, 239; in Middle East, 216; NGOs, working with, 219; Official Development Assistance (ODA), 14, 209–230; Peacebuilding Fund, 180; Peacebuilding Initiative, 180; *Strengthening Aid Effectiveness* (2003), 216, *Sustainable Development Strategy 2001–2003: An Agenda for Change*, 218; White Paper, *Sharing Our Future: Canadian Assistance to International Development*, 217

Canadian Manufacturers Association (CMA), 88, 101n29
Canadian Manufacturers and Exporters (CME), 102n39
Canadian Paint Manufacturers' Association, 101n29
Canadian Particle Board Association, 101n29
Canadian Printing Ink Manufacturers' Association, 101n29
Canadian Toy Manufacturers' Association, 101n29
Canadian Truck Trailer Manufacturers' Association, 101n29
Canadian University Service Overseas (C.U.S.O), 204
Cardinal, Jean-Guy, 138
CARICOM, 369
Canergie Commission on Preventing Deadly Conflict, 192
Carter, Jimmy, 39, 240
Catalonia, 106, 108
Cellucci, Paul, 352, 391
Chamberlain, Neville, 402
Chanak crisis, 32
Charest, Jean, Quebec government of, 120
Charter Task Force (1986), 459
Cheney, Dick, as U.S. Vice-President, 118
Chevrier, Lionel, 139
Child soldiers, 198, 201, 510n33. *See also* Axworthy, Lloyd
Chile, 320, 351; in hemispheric bilateral accords (1997), 98n1; North American Free Trade Agreement (NAFTA), bilateral trade with, 96
China, 222–223, 227, 281, 349; Pierre Trudeau, relations with, 39; Québec office, in, 119; trading with Alberta, 118
Chirac, Jacques, 394
Chrétien, Jean, 2, 4, 5, 14, 17, 18, 45, 62, 133–134, 173, 181, 237, 348, 397, 418, 421; Cabinet, 21; Clinton-Chrétien Summit (1997), 306; government of, 41–42, 66, 78n69, 91, 170, 277, 284, 338, 350, 352, 354, 397, 399, 421, 507, 514, 522; Prime Minister, 42, 66, 80n89, 168, 182, 225–227, 275–277, 282, 305, 330, 349, 400–401, 420, 505, 514
Christian Democrats. *See* European People's Party
Christie, Loring, 34
Churchill, Sir Winston, 33
CIDA, in Central and Eastern Europe, 216
Circumpolar: Affairs, 308; North, 293, 295, 299, 302–303, 309–310. *See also* Arctic; Inuit Circumpolar Conference
Civil-Military Cooperation (CIMIC), 180
Civil rights, 18, 458
Civil society, 18; notions, 18; participation, in Canadian Foreign policy, 7, 9, 18, 195, 203, 220, 224, 325, 494, 496, 506, 518
Civilian control: objective, 463; subjective, 463–464
Clark, Joe, 21, 151; government of, 144, 243; Progressive Conservative Party, leader of, 350; Secretary of State for External Affairs, 298
Clarkson, Adrienne, Governor-General, 289–290, 312, 414
Cleveland, Grover, 29

INDEX 583

Clinton, Bill, 103n58, 305, 348, 514; administration of, 276, 281, 302–303; Clinton-Chrétien Summit (1997), 306; foreign policy, 303; supporting North American Free Trade Agreement (NAFTA), 103n58
Clinton-Chrétien Summit (1997), 306
Cold War, 2, 5, 37, 42, 54, 59, 61, 64, 175–176, 191, 236, 241–242, 246, 252, 254–255, 259–260, 290, 293–297, 299, 301, 317–323, 333, 342, 347, 390, 394, 412, 422, 447, 465, 482–483; diplomacy, 341; post–Cold War, 20, 493, 498, 513, 521; post–Cold War UN interventions, 13, 170; postwar era, as the, 2, 52, 53, 55; U.S. interest, in, 340
Colombo Plan (1950), Canadian participation in, 216
Colonialism, 33; countries emerging from, 36
Combat-Related Employment of Women (CREW), 459, 470
Committee on Government Representatives for the Participation of Civil Society (CGR), 503
Common Market, 368, 370
Commonwealth, 52, 134, 137, 138, 141–142, 153, 156, 200, 213–214, 220–222, 236–237, 279, 318–320, 340–341, 350, 424; Asian countries of, 343; Indian membership, 52
Comparative advantage, theory of, 88
Confederal Group of the European United Left—Nordic Green Left (GUE/NGL), 374
Confederate Constitution, 440
Confederate States of America, 439
Confederate Union, 440

Confederation, of Canada, 52, 83, 85, 413, 442
Conference Board of Canada, 329
Conference of Defence Associations, 67
Conference on disarmament (1921), 31
Conference on Security and Cooperation in Europe, 240
Conflict: prevention, 7, 8, 13, 189–195, 205–206; resolution, 13, 14, 16, 210. *See also* Peacebuilding; Peacekeeping; Peacemaking
Congo, Democratic Republic of (DRC), 148, 199–200, 227. *See* also Zaire
Conservative Party of Canada (PC), 11, 12, 30, 38, 40, 42, 83, 88, 92–93, 95–96, 101n37, 181, 393, 396, 495, 500, 521
Constitution, of Canada, 438–439, 443
Constitutional Act (1982), 93
Continentalism, 89
Coolidge, Clavin, 319
Co-optive power, 267
Corn Laws (1846), 84–86, 98n4
Costa Rica: in hemispheric bilateral accords (2002), 97n1; North American Free Trade Agreement (NAFTA), bilateral trade with, 96
Cote d'Ivoire, *222*
Council for Canadian Security in the 21st Century, 67
Council of Canadians, 500
Council of the Federation, 125
Council of State Governments (Eastern Region), 121
Cuba, 87, 92, 503; Missile Crisis (1962), 37; Pierre Trudeau, relations with, 39; Soviet missiles, in, 37
Currie, Arthur, 413

Cyprus, 170; Canadian Forces (CF), in (1964), 174, 522
Czechoslovakia, Soviet occupation of, 57

Dalai Lama, 122
Dandurand, Raoul, 30
Davos. *See* World Economic Forum
D-Day, 2, 33
Debray, Régis, 147, 149
de Gaulle, Charles, 136–137, 151, 158
Delors, Jacques, 375
Democrat Party, 103n58, 181, 395
Denmark, gender integration in the Navy, 474
d'Estaing, Valéry Giscard, 142, 144, 146
Developing countries, 3
Dialogue on Foreign Policy, 505
Diefenbaker, John George, 17, 36–38, 54, 89, 346, 392, 394, 419; government of, 54; Kennedy, tension with, 37
Dingly tariff, 29
Diori, Hamani, 139–140; Léger-Diori constitution, 140
Dixon Entrance, 412
Dodge, David, 369
Domestic independence, 2
Dominion, of Canada, 26, 32, 445
Dori, Hamari, 139, 140
Dulles, John Foster, 342, 343–344
Dupuy, Michel, Ambassador in Paris, 147

East Timor, 242
East-West conflict, 242, 254
Eden, Anthony, 339, 341, 342–346; Eggleton, Art, defense minister, 170
Egypt, 153, 174, 213, *221*, 222–223, 226, 341, 343, 347

Eisenhower, Dwight D., President, 37, 340, 342; administration of, 341, 344–45, 352
Elizabeth II, Queen, 19n8
Emergency Financing Mechanism (EFM), 278
Emergency and Preparedness and Response (EPPR), 307
Emergency Standstill Clause, 279
Environment, 15, 18, 211, 501, 504
Estonia, 447
Ethiopia, famine relief of 1984, 41
European heritage, of Canada, 2
Europe, 2, 15, 16, 33, 40, 42, 52, 54, 56, 58, 60–61, 70, 84, 97, 142, 274, 289, 293–294, 318, 354, 390, 393, 524; Canadian Forces (CF), in Central, 216; Canadian Forces (CF), in Eastern, 216; colonial powers, 339; Imperialism, 340, 413; Québec offices, in, 119. *See also* European Community; European Economic Community; European Union
European Centre for Conflict Prevention (ECCP), 196
European Community (EC), (1993), 368, 370, 375, 377, 382, 440–441; employment, anywhere in the, 376; fiscal barriers, reduction of, 376; financial services, opening of, 376; movement of capital, in the, 377; public procurement markets, opened in, 377; physical barriers, removal of, 376; Single European Act (SEA), The 1986, 370–372, 376, 377, 382, 386n21; single European market, 376, 386n30; technical barriers, elimination of, 376; Treaty of Rome (1957), 375. *See also* Rome

INDEX 585

European Democrats, 374
European Economic Community (ECC), (1957), 375
European People's Party (Christian Democrats), 373
European Regional Development Fund (ERDF), 388n40
European Roundtable of Industrialists (ERT), 375
European Union (EU), 9, 16, 106, 108–109, 281, 321, 365–366, 369, 371, 373, 377–378, 380–381, 386n27, 402, 432, 440, 518; BENELUX countries, 386n29; Canada, relations with, 9, 365, 379, 382, 383, 526; Central Bank (ECB), 374, 378; Commission, 371, 373, 374–375, 377, 383; Committee of the Regions (CoR), 386n27; Common Agricultural Policy (CAP), 380–381; Common and Foreign Security Policy (CFSP), 378–380; Community law, 374; constitution, 383, 440; Council of Ministers, 375, 378, 386n23; Council, of the, 372, 373, 375, 376, 386n23; Court of Justice (ECJ), 371, 374–375, 383, 386, 474; Economic and Monetary Union (EMU), 377–378; economic integration, 366; European law enforcement organization (EUROPOL), 380; fishing disputes with Newfoundland and Labrador, 124; Force in Bosnia and Herzegovina (EUFOR), 380; foreign minister, 383; foreign policy, 374; High Representative for Foreign Policy, 383; inner six, 386n29; Justice and Home Affairs (JHA), 378, 380; members, 371; Parliament, 373–374; political economy, 7; president, 383; sub-national regions, recognition of, 106; subsidiary, notion of, 108; Treaty of Amsterdam (1997), 379–380; Treaty of Maastricht (1993), (TEU), 9, 16, 374, 377, 379, 384n9, 386n21, 388n42; Treaty, on (TEU), 377

Fabius, Laurent, 149
Fading power, 338
Federal budget deficit, of Canada, 2, 513
Federalism, 138, 433–435, 442, 444–445
Finance, Department of, 15, 34, 217, 266, 284
Financial Stability Forum (FSF), 278, 280
Financial system, of Canada, 274
Finland, 289, 300, 308
Fisheries, 1, 32
Flanders, international role, 106, 108, 124–125, 444
Foreign Affairs and International Trade, Department of (DFAIT), 11, 168, 178, 225, 239, 266, 284, 308, 310, 317, 497–499, 502, 504–506, 522. *See also* Foreign Affairs of Canada
Foreign aid, 8, 14, 15; Canada towards, 2, 14, 118, 200, 210, 212, 229, 236, 239; Canadian International Development Agency (CIDA), programs for, 2, 14, 118, 200, 205, 210, 212, 216, 229, 236, 239
Foreign Affairs, of Canada (FAC), 11, 15, 42, 64, 105, 168–169, 172, 173–176, 179–181, 190, 195, 228, 321, 324–327, 333, 517, 520–521

Foreign economic policy, of Canada, 89, 380, 382
Foreign Investment Review Agency, 40
Fox, Vicente, 332; administration of, 331
Framework Agreement for Commercial and Economic Cooperation (1976), 382
France, 2, 3, 11, 12, 16, 32, 84, 135–156, 173, 214, 274, 277, 283, 340, 342, 344, 346–347, 349, 351, 372, 390, 400–401; colonialism, 339; culture, 13; Élysée Palace, of, 149; gender integration in the Navy, 474; trade missions with Québec, 106; trading with Mackenzie, Canadian government of, 27
Franco-African Summit of 1977, 142
Franco-African Summit of 1980, 144
Francophonie, La, 1, 5, 6, 8, 10, 12, 15, 41, 119, 121, 133–134, 135, 137, 138, 143, 147, 152, 154–159, 175, 213–214, 220–222, 516; Beirut, Summit (2002), 152, 155, 157; Charte de la Francophonie, 158; Grand Baie Summit (1993), 154; Hanoi Summit (1997), 158; Monton, Summit (1999), 153–155; Permanent Council of, 156; Senghor University, 157. *See also* Agence de Coopération Culturelle et Technique; Boutros-Ghali, Boutros; TV5
Fraser, Sheila, 66. *See also* Auditor General
Free Trade Agreement (FTA) (1988), 41, 348; Canada-U.S. free trade agreement (CUSFTA), 368–370, 377, 384n8, 388n42, 495, 500; Free Trade of the Americas (FTAA), 84, 92, 96–97, 326, 501–504; November 1999 Ministerial in Toronto, 503; November 2001 Ministerial in Quito, 503; Québec, support of the, 119
French Company of the West Indies, 84
Functionalism, 52, 53

G-7, 275, 278, 279, 280–283, 285; Canada, member of, 274; Summit in Birmingham (May 1998), 279; Summit in Cologne (June 1999), 284; Summit in Halifax (June 1995), 275–279; Summit in Williamsburg (1983), 149
G-8, 14, 15, 226, 266–267, 272, 274, 275, 279, 281–282, 284–285, 339, 517; Africa Action Plan, 225, 228; Summit in Genoa (July 2001), 225; Summit of Kananaskis (June 2002), 14, 212, 225. *See also* New Economic Partnership for Africa's Development
G-10, 278
G-20, 15, 43, 266, 278, 282, 339, 522
G-22, 278, 281, 285n1
Gabon, 137–138, 143; affair (1968), 138; Québec, relation with, 119, 137
General Agreement on Tariffs and Trade (GATT), 33, 89–91, 97, 99n20, 112, 366, 381; Article 24, Section 12 of the, 112; Kennedy Round (1963–1967), 90; Tokyo Round (1973–1979), 90–91, 94–95; Uruguay Round (1986–1994), 97, 367, 381, 388n42. *See also* World Trade Organization
Gérin-Lajoie, Paul; doctrine, 112; Québec's minister of Education, 136
Germany, Federal Republic of, 16, 32,

57, 106, 173, 273, 277, 349, 351, 372, 390, 400–401; Allied war, against, 293; Canadian Forces (CF), in, 61; Federal republic of, 57; gender integration in the Navy, 474; Landers, 109; Ontario, missions in, 117; trading with Saskatchewan, 123
Globalism, 212
Globalization, 12, 24, 105–108, 112, 114, 116, 118, 120, 124, 125, 154, 190, 277–278, 281, 285, 326, 370, 385n14, 493, 515
Gorbachev, Mikhail, 60, 295–297
Gotlieb, Allan, 394
Governor General, of Canada, 19n8, 24, 38. *See also* Clarkson, Adrienne
Graham, Bill: as Minister of Foreign Affairs, 505–506; as Minister of National Defense, 171
Gray Lecture. *See* Louis St. Laurent
Great Britain. *See* United Kingdom
Great Depression, 31, 273
Green, Howard, 37
Greenland, 293
Grey, Earl, 28
Gross Domestic Product, 14
Group of Greens/European Free Alliance (Verts/ALE), 374
Group of the Alliance of Liberals and Democrats for Europe (ALDE), 374
Guinea, 351
Gulf War (1990–1991), 62, 148, 237, 414–416, 421. *See also* Iraq

Haiti, 12, 14, 194, 211, 222
Hammarskjöld, Dag, 190, 344, 345–346
Hard power, 64
Harkness, Douglas, 38

Harper, Stephen, 11, 24, 168, 350, 423, 457, 522, 524; government of, 522
Head, Ivan, 141
Health care system, 2
Healy, Denis, British Defense minister, 74n28
Heeney, Arnold, 340, 343–344
Hees, Georges, 38
Hegemonic stability theory (HST), 269–270
Heinebecker, Paul, 350
Hellyer, Paul, 55
Helsinki Final. *See* Conference on Security and Cooperation in Europe
Helms-Burton Act (1994), 399
Hemispheric Social Alliance, 504
Henry Clay's American System, 86, 98n10
Highly Indebted Poorest Countries (HIPC), 283–284
Hillier, Rick, 178
Hitler, Adolf, 340, 341
Honduras, 222
Howe, Joseph, 443
Howard, John, 351
House of Commons, 10, 23–24, 44, 45n1, 172–173, 175; Standing Committee on National Defense, 67. *See also* Standing Committee on Foreign Affairs and International Trade
HSBC, 274
Hudson's Bay Company, 291
Human rights, 7, 8, 13, 14, 114, 134, 156, 191, 198, 204, 223, 235–260, 318, 323, 324–328, 501, 504, 520, 522; NGOs, promotion of, 244; Saddam Hussein violating, 354. *See also* Canadian Human Rights Act; Canadian Human Rights Tribunal; International Criminal Court

Human Security, 4, 14, 64, 71, 106, 178–180, 193, 206, 228, 265, 317–318, 494, 523; agenda, 320–328, 330, 332, 333; rhetoric, 333. *See also* Axworthy, Lloyd
Humanitarian crisis, 251, 254
Hungary, Soviet Union in, 340, 343–347
Hussein, Saddam, 5, 349, 352–353, 422; government of, 337–338, 411, 421; human rights, violation of, 354; possessing nuclear weapons, 401–402, 421

Iaccoca, Lee, 423
Iceland, 289, 293, 308
Idaho, state of, 106
IFA reform, 277–278, 281–283
Ignatieff, Michael, 4
Immigrants communities, of Canada, 245
Imperial conference (1926), 33
Independence/Democracy Group (IND/DEM), 374
India, 29, *221*, 281, 320, 341, 514, 523; Commonwealth, member of, 52
Indochina, 36
Indonesia, 199, 222, 281
ING DIRECT, 274
Inner six, 386n29. *See also* European Union
Interdependence, 392–393. *See also* Sovereignty
Intermediate Range Nuclear Forces, 1987 Treaty, 60
International Association of Insurance Supervisions (IAIS), 280
International Bank for Reconstruction an Development (IBRD), 273
International Campaign to Ban Landmines (ICBL), 499–500. *See also* Anti-personnel land mine treaty; Axworthy, Lloyd; Landmines Convention; Mines Action Canada; Ottawa Process; Ottawa treaty
International Commission on Intervention and State Sovereignty, 203; Report on *The Responsibility to Protect*, 192
International Court of Justice. *See* United Nations
International Criminal Court (ICC), 510n33, 517
International Development Research Center (IRDC), 204
International Financial Institutions (IFIs), 217
International law, 432, 436–438, 444, 446
International Monetary Fund (IMF), 33, 217, 273, 278–279, 280–282
International Organization of Securities Commissions (IOSCO), 280
International Policy Review (2004), 201
International role, of Canada, 1, 3, 27, 36, 42, 45, 53, 65, 174, 200, 202, 203–205, 338, 513–514, 523
International Security Assistance Force (ISAF), in Afghanistan, 70, 81n101, 380
International trade, 11, 15, 83, 106, 115, 116
Internationalism, 52, 169, 321, 501; liberalism, 237
Inuit Circumpolar Conference, 295, 300, 304
Iran, 242. *See also* Nuclear proliferation
Iraq: Iraqi police, Canada working with, 203; Québec, against war in,

350, 400–401; sanctions against, 211; U.S. presence in Iraq, 1, 114, 348–349, 351–352, 355, 383, 394, 397, 400, 518; war in (2003–), 69, 114, 338, 350, 352, 415–416. *See also* Gulf War; Hussein, Saddam
Israel, 175, 213, 349; gender integration in the Navy, 474; North American Free Trade Agreement (NAFTA), bilateral trade with, 96
Israeli-Palestinian conflict, 353. *See also* Six-Day War
Italy, 32, 372, 400; gender integration in the Navy, 474
Ivy League, 392

Japan, 215, 273, 283, 293, 321, 375
Jamieson, Don, 243
Johnson, Lyndon B., 38; Vietnam policy, 398
Johnson, Pierre-Marc, 151
Jordan, gender integration in the Navy, 474
Julien, Pauline, 139

Kampuchea, 242
Kassebaum, Senator Nancy Landon, 479
Kemal, Mustafa, 32
Kennedy, John F., 17, 37; Diefenbaker, tension with, 37; Kennedy-Diefenbaker relation, 393, 396; liberalism, 396; President, 392, 394, 396
Kennedy Round. *See* General Agreement on Tariffs and Trade
Kenya, 227
Kerry, John, 422–423
Kierans, Eric, Trudeau Cabinet minister, 74n24
Kimberley Process, 198

Kinshasa arrangement, 139
Klein, Ralph, 118, 351
King, William Lyon Mackenzie, 30–32, 33–35, 44, 88; Prime Minister, 89, 403, 413
Kissinger, Henry, 402
Korean War (1950–1953), 36, 52, 77n57, 469
Kosovo air war, 60, 399
Kyoto protocol, 119, 517; Québec, signing the, 119

Labour Party, 394
Lalonde, Marc, Prime Minister principal's secretary, 138–139
Landmines Convention, 499; NGOs supporting, the, 499–500. *See also* Anti-personnel land mine treaty; Axworthy, Lloyd; International Campaign to Ban Landmines; Mines Action Canada; Ottawa Process; Ottawa treaty
Landry, Bernard, 150–151
Landymore Report (1964), 470
Lapointe, Ernest, 32
Latin America, 9, 15, 13, 199–200, 242, 274, 276, 289, 317–335, 524; governments, 326, 328; policy, towards Canada, 319; Québec offices, in, 119; relations with Canada, 333; security, 7
Latvia, 447
Laurier, Sir Wilfrid, 28, 29, 84, 86–89, 93, 95; administration, 86; defending free trade, with United States, 29; League of Nations, 30, 34
Lebanon, Canadian Forces (CF) in, 348
Lee, Steven, 497
Léger, Jean-Marc, 140; Léger-Diori constitution, 140

Léger, Jules, Ambassador in Paris, 136
Lesage, Jean, 135
Lévesque, René, 143–144, 149–151, 441
Liberal Caucus Committee on External Affairs and National Defense, 495; Liberal Foreign Policy Handbook, 495. *See also* Axworthy, Lloyd
Liberal Party of Canada, 11, 41–42, 81n96, 83, 88, 91–92, 95–96, 101n37, 181, 229, 303, 341, 393, 400, 402, 495–496, 500; defense policy, 56; "Red Book" (1993 election platform), 495–496
Liberal Party of Québec, 120
Liberalization of investment, 97
Liberia, 199, 227
Lithuania, 447
Lodge, Henry Cabot, 345–346
London World Conference on Wheat, 31
Long Term Capital Management (LTCM), 279
Libya, 227

Maastricht, Treaty of (TEU), (1993), 9, 16, 374, 377, 379, 384n9, 386n21, 388n42. *See also* European Union
Macdonald, James, 32; 1971 Defense White paper, 42
Macdonald, John A., 24, 27; national policy, 84, 86, 87–88, 91, 93–94
MacEachen, Allan, as Secretary of State for External Affairs, 142
MacGuigan, Mark, 146; Secretary of State for External Affairs, 145
Machinery and Equipment Manufacturers' Association, 100n29
Mackenzie, Alexander, 27; trading with France, 27
Madrid Conference (1991), 349

Malawi, 227
Mali, *222*
Manitoba, 115, 117, 123
Manley, John, 4; Deputy Prime Minister, 352; Foreign Affairs Minister, 329–331
Marchi, Sergio, 502–503
Martin, Louis, deputy minister of intergovernmental affairs, 151
Martin, Paul, Jr., 11, 14, 64, 68, 112, 171, 181, 237, 352; Finance Minister, 43, 275, 277, 279, 282, 284; government, 427, 522; Prime Minister, 22, 43, 166, 168, 229, 354, 382, 394, 418, 422–423, 520, 522
Martin, Paul, Sr.: Secretary of State for External Affairs, 38, 43, 135–137; Senator, 139
Masse, Marcel: minister of defense, 61; minister of intergovernmental affairs, 139
Mbeki, Thabo, 225, 227
McCallum, John, Defense Minister, 171, 181, 349
Meech Lake Constitutional Accord, 45, 93, 101n37, 514
Meighen, Arthur, 30
Mercosur, 367, 369
Mexico, 281, 318, 320, 329–332, 351, 368–369; crisis, 277–278; gender integration in the Navy, 474; NGOs, supporting the Zapatistas rebellion, in, 494; in North American Free Trade Agreement (1994), 97n1; ties with Québec, 119
Middle East, 9, 15, 16, 43, 310, 337–338, 342, 345, 350, 353, 354; Canadian Forces (CF), in, 216; Canadian International Development Agency

(CIDA), in, 216; Canadian security policy towards, 7, 339, 342, 348; crisis, 518; United Kingdom, interest in the, 340, 341; United States policy, in, 338; war, 343. *See also* Arab-Israeli War; Israeli-Palestinian conflict; Six-Day War

Middle power, 3, 8, 13, 53, 71, 174, 179–180, 339, 347, 353–355, 420, 427, 525; Canada, as a, 53, 169, 174, 338–339, 355, 365, 414, 523

Military: capability, 7, 9, 53, 412, 418, 479; effectiveness, 7, 8; professionalism, 463, 465; security, 8. *See also* Canadian Forces; National Defense, Department of

Millenium Round, in Seattle (1999), 501

Milosevic, Slobodan, 65

MINERVA (1994), 460

Mines Action Canada, 499. *See also* Anti-personnel land mine treaty; Axworthy, Lloyd; International Campaign to Ban Landmines; Landmines Convention; Ottawa Process; Ottawa treaty

Mitterand, François, 146–149, 151, 153–154

Mobutu, Joseph, 139. *See also* Congo; Zaire

Montana, state of, 106; relations with Saskatchewan, 123

Moldova, 155

Morin, Claude, Québec deputy minister of intergovernmental affairs, 139, 145–146

Most-favored nation (MFN), 367. *See also* World Trade Organization

Mugabe Robert, 227. *See also* Zimbabwe

Mulroney, Brian, 2, 11, 41, 43–45, 58, 84, 91, 92–95, 149–153, 157, 397; CEO, as a former, 41; government of, 21, 60, 62, 243, 398; *Independence and Internationalism*, foreign policy report, 59; Prime Minister, 40, 65, 155, 297–298, 300, 412

Multilateral Agreement Investment (MAI), 500–501, 504

Multilateralism, 5, 13, 15, 16, 33, 89–90, 97, 134, 180, 210, 219, 275, 317, 337–339, 349, 354, 393, 398, 425, 505, 516–517, 520

Mundell-Fleming theorem, 387n35

Nasser, Gamal Abdel, 339, 340–341, 343, 346, 348; Suez Canal, nationalization of, 345

National Capital Branch of the Canadian Institute of International Affairs (CBCIIA), 297

National Defense, Department of (DND), 10, 51, 60, 63–65, 67–68, 70, 169, 176–178, 180, 195, 228, 416, 460; 1964 White Paper 53, 72n8; 1971 White Paper, 57; 1994 White Paper, 42, 62, 67, 77n63, 417, 427, 520; Advisory Board on Canadian Forces "Gender Integration, Employment and Equity: Successes and Opportunities: 1999 Annual Report," 460; Army, 415–417; budget, 55, 80n94, 171, 182; Council employment policies, 459; Criminal Code, 468; Defense Structure Review 57, 58; Liberal's defense policy, 56; Manpower Study (1965), 458; *Shaping the Future of Canadian Defence for 2020*, 65; Strategic

Defense Initiative (august 2004), 425. *See also* Canadian Forces
National Energy Program (NEP), 40, 100n27
National Forum for Youth, 506
National Forum on Canada's International Relations in Ottawa (1994), 496–497
Nationalism, 434; Post-Nationalism, 322
Near East, 341
Nehru, Jawaharlal, 340
Neoliberalism, 237–238
Netherlands, gender integration in the Navy, 474
New Brunswick, 117, 120, 121, 150, 153, 443; exports from, 85; foreign trade missions 120; Team Canada Atlantic, in, 120, 129n48
New Democratic Party (NDP), 81n96, 91, 181, 351, 500
New Economic Partnership for Africa's Development (NEPAD), 212, 225–226, 228, 233n44, 517; U.S. participation in, 226. *See also* G-8, Summit of Kananaskis
New England Governors–Eastern Canadian Premiers Association, 120–121, 123
Newfoundland and Labrador, 116–117; fishing disputes with EU, 124; Royal Commission on the future of the of, 124; trade missions, 124
New Zealand, 340, 381; gender integration in the Navy, 474
New world order, 21, 62, 513. *See also* Bush, George H. W.
Niche interoperability, 426
Nigeria, 226

Nixon, Richard, 39, 396; Nobel Peace Prize, 13, 16, 38, 55, 122, 347
Non-central governments, 107
Non-governmental organizations (NGOs), 41, 134, 180, 195, 197–198, 244, 307, 492, 497, 502–503, 516; addressing the AIDS crisis, 494; against neoliberal globalization, 494; building school, 211; in humanitarian activities, 499; impact on policies, 494; operating overseas, 200, 228–229; in peacekeeping activities, 499; promoting human rights, 244; in Sierra Leone, 202; supporting the Landmines Convention, 499–500; supporting the Zapatistas rebellion in Mexico, 494; using Internet technologies, 501; working with Axworthy, 42; working with CIDA, 219
Normand, Robert, 145
North, 290, 292–294, 304, 309, 312; agenda, 295; defense of, 1, 81n95 366; dimension, 291; diplomacy, 296; security, 1, 68–69, 81n95, 333
North American Aerospace Defense Command (NORAD), 1, 13, 36, 37, 54, 290, 294, 426; Canadian Forces (CF), in, 176, 425
North American Customs Union (NACU), 370
North American Free Trade Agreement, of 1994 (NAFTA), 41, 97n1, 108, 112, 118, 124, 276, 317, 319–321, 330, 333, 366–370, 382, 384n8, 388n42, 392, 396, 492, 500, 503; Article 105, 112; Bill Clinton, support from, 103n58; Chile, bilateral trade with, 96; federal-state clause,

111–112; Québec, support of the, 119; side agreements on environment, 386n25; side agreements on labor, 386n25
North American Monetary Union (NAMU), 371, 385n17
North American Security Perimeter (zone of confidence), 329, 330
North Atlantic Treaty Organization (NATO), 3, 16, 34, 36, 52, 57, 58, 135, 165, 166, 168, 174–175, 177, 181, 290, 293, 333, 340, 344, 347, 351, 424, 480; Article 2, 34; Canada serving into Composite Force, 61; Canadian Forces (CF), contributions to, 174, 186n46, 210, 414–415, 522; Canadian participation in, 55, 61, 169, 418; Charter, 34; International Security Assistance Force (ISAF) in Afghanistan, 70, 80n101, 166, 170, 380; peacekeeping missions, 70, 170, 172, 210; Pierre Trudeau, opposition to, 39; North Korea, 77n57, 87. See also Nuclear proliferation; Korean War
Northern Foreign Policy Conference, 304
Northern Forum, 302
Northwest Passage, legal status of, 60, 292, 296, 412
North Pole, 289
North-West Rebellion (1885), 467
Norway, 300, 347, 353, 514, 523; Allied Command European Land Force, in, 61; gender integration in the Navy, 474
Nova Scotia, 114, 117, 122, 443
Nuclear proliferation: in Iran, 227; in North Korea, 227

Obanjo, Olusegun, 225
Oceania, 15
Office of International Relations and Protocol (OIRP), 118
Official Development Assistance (ODA), 14, 209–230
Ogdensburg statement, 33
Olso Accord (1993), 353
Ontario, 114–115, 116–118; trading with Germany, 117
Operation Allied Force. See also Kosovo air war
Operation Desert Storm, 77n57. See also Gulf War
Oregon, state of, 106
Organization of African Unity (OAU), 143, 225–226; Lusaka Summit (July 2001), 225
Organization of American States (OAS), 16, 320, 322, 324, 332; Canadian participation in, 41, 317–319; General assembly, 324–325; Permanent Council of, 327; Summit of the Americas (Guatemala-1999), 325
Ottawa Process, 504. See also Anti-personnel land mine treaty; Axworthy, Lloyd; International Campaign to Ban Landmines; Landmines Convention; Mines Action Canada; Ottawa treaty
Ottawa treaty, 4, 42, 179, 499. See also Anti-personnel land mine treaty; Axworthy, Lloyd; International Campaign to Ban Landmines; Landmines Convention; Mines Action Canada; Ottawa Process
Ottoman Empire, 32
Ouellet, André, 303

Overseas development assistance, 7, 8, 283

Pacific Northwest Economic Region (PNWER), 106, 118
Pakistan, 351
Pan American Union (1908), 319. *See also* Organization of American States
Paris-Québec City Accord, 136
Paradiplomacy, 5, 10, 12, 105–106, 108, 110, 112, 114–115, 116–117, 120, 124; Québec, activity of, 119
Parliament, of Canada, 23, 27, 32, 41, 44, 94, 110–111, 239, 243, 330, 420, 502
Parliamentary Sub-Committee on Equality Rights, 459
Parti Québécois (PQ), 120, 143, 433; proto-diplomacy, of the, 120
Peacebuilding, 13, 180, 204
Peacekeepers: Canadian Forces (CF), of, 177; defenders of, 2. *See also* Blue helmets
Peacekeeping, 5, 7, 8, 13, 14, 53, 165, 169, 171–174, 176–182, 311, 323, 461; Canada, actions towards, 2, 56, 176, 182, 195, 210, 235, 317, 347, 457, 479; North Atlantic Treaty Organization (NATO), missions of, 70, 170, 172, 210; operations, 70, 168; United Nations (UN), missions of, 70, 174, 177, 180, 209
Peacemaking, 8, 13, 323
Pearson, Lester B., 13, 16, 21, 26, 35–36, 38, 43, 136–138, 168, 175, 189, 206, 209, 342–344, 346–347, 353–354; government of, 55; Minister of External Affairs, 173–174, 338, 341, 352; Pearsonalities, 39; Pearsonian internationalism, 39, 45, 65, 516; Prime Minister, 56, 134–135, 174, 348, 396; speech at Temple University, 38; Suez diplomacy, 347, 350
Pelletier, Gérard: Canada's ambassador in Paris, 145; Secretary of State, 138, 139, 140, 141
People's Summits, 504
Pettigrew, Pierre: Foreign Affairs Minister, 11; International Trade Minister, 369
Pluralism, 212
Poland, 155, 400
Political economy, 6, 8, 9, 16
Pompidou, Georges, 151
Pope, Joseph, 28, 34
Portugal, gender integration in the Navy, 474
Post-colonial institution, 12
Powell, Colin, as U.S. Secretary of State, 349, 402, 422
preferential trading arrangements (PTA), 367, 369–371, 378, 388n42; article XXIV, 367. *See also* World Trade Organization
Preventive diplomacy, 190
Price, George Lawrence, 413
Prime Minister's Office (PMO), 11, 22, 24–25, 37, 44
Prince Edward Island (PEI), 116–117; Trade Team, 123
Pritchard, Neil, 342
Private Council Office (PCO), 11, 22, 24–25, 37, 44
Pro-Canada Network (PCN), 500
Prodi, Romano, EU Commission President, 382
Progressive Conservatives. *See* Conservative Party of Canada

INDEX 595

Proportional representation system, 23
Protectionism, 12, 86–87, 89, 91, 93–96, 273; British, 85

Qualified majority voting (QMV), 372
Québec, 4, 12, 17, 92, 93, 116–117, 119, 133–159, 438, 440, 442–443, 446; 1998 Free Trade Agreement (FTA), support of the, 119; against war in Iraq, 350, 400–401; Convention on Protection of Children and Cooperation in Respect of Inter-country Adoption, supporting the, 120; delegation in Paris, 136; Francophone immigrants, selection of, 115; international role, 136, 142–143, 147, 432, 444, 447; Kyoto Protocol, signing the, 119; National Assembly, 110; nationalist sentiment, 29–30; North American Free Trade Agreement, support of the, 119; office in Asia, 119; office in China, 119; offices in Europe, 119; offices in Latin America, 119; offices in United States, 119; Optional Protocol to the Convention on the Rights of the Child on the Sale of Children, Child Prostitution and Child Pornography, supporting the, 119; paradiplomacy activity, 106, 119; *Reference case*, 17, 431–432, 438, 441–443, 447; relation with Gabon, 119, 137; ties with Mexico, 119; trade mission with France, 106. *See also* United Nations

Reagan, Nancy, 31
Reagan, Ronald, 39, 41, 60, 295–296, 398

Realism, 212–213, 236–237, 393, 461–462
Reciprocal Trade Agreements Act of 1934 (RTAA), 89, 99n20
Reform Party, 172
Republican Party, 348, 393–394, 402, 439
Responsible government, concept of, 23
Revolution in Military Affairs, 65
Rey Report, 278
Reykjavik summit (1986), 60
Robertson, General Lord, 80n94
Robertson, Norman A., 25, 45n3, 342–343
Robichaud, Louis, 139
Robinson, Basil, 37
Rocky Mountain Trade Corridor, the, 118
Romania, 155, 373
Rome, Treaty of, (1957), 375. *See also* European Community
Roosevelt, Franklin D., President, 33, 44, 89, 413
Roy, Bernard, 151, 152
Royal Bank, 273
Royal Canadian Mounted Police (RCMP), 292
Royal Commission on the Economic Union and Development Prospects for Canada, 91
Royal Commission on the Status of Women (1971), 459, 470
Rubber Association of Canada, 100n29
Rules of origin (ROO), 367. *See also* General Agreements on Tariffs and Trade; World Trade Organization
Russia, 227, 274, 279, 281, 289, 300, 349, 351, 400–401; Association of

Indigenous Peoples of Northern Russia, 302; Saskatchewan, missions in, 123; trading with Alberta, 118
Rwanda, 134; genocide in, 189, 498

Sami Council, 302
Saskatchewan, 117; in agriculture, 122; mission to Russia, 123; relations with Montana, 123; in Trade and Export Partnership, 122; trade missions, 122; trading with Germany, 123
satellite power, 3
Saudi Arabia, 281, 339
Scheffer, Jaap de Hoop, 80n94
Scotiabank, 273
Scotland, 436
Seattle, Millennial Round (1999), 501–502. *See also* World Trade Organization
Senate, of Canada, 10
Senegal, 12, 141, 148, *222*, 226
Senghor, Léopold, 136, 138, 141–143, 144, 145, 146; Senghor University, 157
Service Women in Non-Traditional Environments Role (SWINTER), 459, 470
Severe Acute Respiratory Syndrome epidemic (SARS), 124
Sévigny, Pierre, 37–38
Sharp, Mitchell: Secretary of State for External Affairs, 39, 40, 90, 170; Third Option, 42, 100n27
Siddon, Tom, 298
Sierra Leone, 199–200, 227; NGOs, in, 202
Simon, Mary, 304, 308
Singapore, gender integration in the Navy, 474

Single European Act, The 1986, 370–371–372, 376, 377, 382, 388n42. *See also* European Community
Single member simple plurality, 23
Six-Day War (1967), 349
Skelton, O. D., 34–35
Smart Border, 81n95
Smoot-Hawley Tariff Act (1930), 273
Socialist Group in the European Parliament (PSE), 374
Society of the Button Industry, 101n29
Society of the Plastic Industry of Canada, 101n29
Soft power, 64, 71, 178, 204, 311
Softwood lumber, 1, 124, 411
Solinas, Carlos, 331
Somalia: Canadian Forces (CF), in, 171; inquiry, 78n69
South Africa, 4, 14, 41, 226, 242, 281, 514, 523; apartheid in, 4; arrangements with British Columbia, 121; Boer war in, (1899–1902), 26, 28, 467; gender integration in the Navy, 474; international sanctions, to, 14; trading with Alberta, 118
South Korea, 281, 400
Sovereignty, 15, 17, 414, 423, 433–434, 438–439, 446, 452n45; Canada, protection of its, 42, 52, 56, 57, 330, 411–412, 425, 427, 445, 518; Québec sovereignty, 7, 9, 17, 92, 125, 137, 140, 144, 412, 431–432, 437, 441–442, 514
Soviet Union, 3, 54, 56, 57, 293–297, 346–347, 420, 447, 464–465; arms control negotiations, with United States, 57; Communist Party, 76n41; defensive defense, 60; fall of, 498; glasnost, 59, 76n41; in Hun-

gary, 340, 343–347; missiles, in Cuba, 37; Perestroika, 59, 76n41; reasonable suffiency, 60
Spain, 349, 351, 400; gender integration in the Navy, 474
Sri Lanka, 242
Stabilization Force, in Bosnia, 70, 380
Standing Committee on Foreign Affairs and International Trade (SCFAIT), 102n44, 308, 502
Standing Committee on National Defense, 67
Stirn, Oliver, 145
St. Laurent, Louis, 21; Gray Lecture, 35 as Secretary of State for External Affairs, 26, 35–36, 52, 72n3, 341–343, 346; Stogran, Pat, 417
Strange, William, 469
Subnational entities, 8, 12
Sudan, 199, 227
Suez crisis (1956), 13, 16, 36, 174, 209, 339–40, 343, 346, 348, 352–353; Canadian Forces (CF), in, 522; Canal zone, 342, 344. *See also* Nasser, Gamal Abdel; Pearson, Lester B.
Suharto, Hadji Mohamed, 501
Summit of the Americas, in Guatemala City 1999, 325
Summit of the Americas, in Quebec City (2001), 503
Supreme Court, of Canada, 17, 431, 433–434, 438, 442–444, 447
Sweden, 348, 514, 523; gender integration in the Navy, 474
Switzerland, 153

Taliban, 5, 66, 350, 411, 415
Tanners Association of Canada, 101n29
Team Canada, 122, 124–125
Temple University, 38

Terrorism, 2, 18, 66, 190, 329, 352, 390, 424, 465, 506
Thatcher, Margaret, 41
Thibault, Laurent, 102n44
Third Option: Mitchell Sharp, policy of, 42, 100n27; Pierre Trudeau, policy of, 39–40, 90, 100n27
Third World, 144, 340
Tobin tax, 277–278
Tokyo Round, 90–91, 94–95. *See also* General Agreement on Tariffs and Trade
Toronto Board of Trade, 85
Toronto Centre for Financial Supervision, 280
Toronto Dominion, 273
Trade and Investment Enhancement Agreement (TIEA) in 2004, 382–383
Trade: liberalization of, 83–87, 89, 93, 279; Québec, role in liberalization of, role in trade liberalization, 97; relations, with the United States, 89, 389, 395, 396
Trade Negotiations and Agreements website (TNA), 502–503
Tremblay, Alain, 168
Trudeau, Pierre, 4, 11, 39–40, 42, 45, 48n31, 56, 138, 139, 140, 142–144, 146–149, 320; against NATO, 39; anti-Americanism, 42, 56; government, 57, 58, 141, 240; National Energy Policy, 396; peace initiative, 40; Prime Minister, 53, 74n24, 90, 169, 523; pro-Communist, 56; relations with China, 39; relations with Cuba, 39; Third Option, 39–40, 90, 100n27; U.S. Foreign policy, 348
Truman, Harry S., President, 480; 1947 Doctrine, 36

Tunisia, 148
Turkey, 32, 211, 281, 339, 373
Turner, John, 95, 149
Tuskegee Airmen, 480. *See also* United States, Racial integration.
Tutu, Desmond, 122
TV5, 154

Uganda, 242
Unilateralism, 5, 425
Union for Europe of the Nations Group (UEN), 374
United Kingdom (UK), 2, 3, 10, 16, 29, 32–33, 135, 238, 341–343, 347–351, 372, 436, 445; British Hudson's Bay Company, 84; Conflict Prevention Pools, 195; Empire (British), 27, 29, 32, 110; gender integration in the Navy, 474; Great Britain, 2, 3, 27, 31–32, 57, 84, 90, 214, 258, 273, 280, 283, 318–319, 340–342, 344, 346, 400–401, 413, 424, 440; interest in the Middle East, 340, 341; Parliament, 33; protectionism, 85
United Nations (UN), 3, 5, 13, 14, 34, 36, 39, 55, 135, 156, 165–167, 170, 172, 181, 190, 192, 196, 337, 342–344, 346, 348, 350, 352, 354–355, 389, 421, 424, 521; *Agenda for Peace*, 191; Children's Fund (UNICEF), 204; Conference on Disarmament, 499; Conference on the Role of Civil Society in Conflict Prevention, 190; Convention on Protection of Children and Cooperation in Respect of Inter-country Adoption, 120; Convention on Racial Discrimination and Covenants on Economic and Social Rights and Civil and Political Rights, 240, 244; Development Report, 320; Economic, Social, and Cultural Organization (UNESCO), 155; emergency force (UNEF), 343–345, 347–348, 353; General Assembly, 175–176, 229, 343, 345–346, 348; impartiality, 166; International Court of Justice, 412; Millennium Goals, 228, 517; missions, 13, 166, 170, 176, 177–178, 348, 522; Optional Protocol to the Convention on the Rights of the Child on the Sale of Children, Child Prostitution and Child Pornography, Québec supporting the, 119–120; reform, 205, 510n33; Security Council (UNSC), 34, 165–166, 173, 178, 349, 350, 351, 353, 402, 421. *See* also Annan, Kofi; Boutros-Ghali, Boutros; Hammarskjöld, Dag
Union Party, 30, 46n15
United States, 3, 4, 6, 7, 9, 10, 11, 13, 15–16, 31–33, 40, 42, 46, 58, 61, 65–66, 68–70, 83, 85–86, 89–91, 97, 106, 114, 134–135, 156, 166, 169, 175, 179, 213, 227–228, 238, 253, 266, 270, 273–276, 280–281, 283, 289–290, 293–296, 300–301, 304–305, 307, 310–312, 318–320, 327–329, 333, 338, 343–344, 346, 350–351, 353–354, 365, 370, 375, 381, 390, 392, 396–397, 400–401, 411–413, 419–423, 434, 457, 463, 515, 517, 524; 54–40 or Fight, 292; American Revolution, 439; Arctic policy, 296, 301–302; arms control negotiations, with Soviet Union, 57; bilateralism, 22, 516; Canada, defense partnership with, 71; Canada, economic dependence on the,

40; Canada, relations with, 22, 38, 90, 174, 175, 319, 348, 352, 373, 379, 389–394, 398–399, 402–404, 421, 424, 505, 516–517, 522–523; Canadian exportations to, 368; checks and balance, 23; Coast Guard, 412; Civil War, 27, 85, 438–439; Congress, 391, 398, 466; Defense, Department of (DOD), 474, 481; Elgin-Marcy (Reciprocity) Treaty, 85; foreign economic policy, 271–272; foreign investments in Canada, 371; foreign policy, 17, 56, 422; gender integration in the Navy, 474–479; hegemony, 317; in Iraq, 1, 114, 348, 351–352, 355, 383, 394, 397, 400, 518; interventionism, 235; isolationism, 413; Jacksonian system, 24; led in Operation Enduring Freedom in Afhanistan, 170, 414; missile defense system, 81n96; national security, 17; Navy (U.S.N), 457–458, 467, 473–475, 479; NEPAD, participation in, 226; Pierre Trudeau, foreign policy towards, 348; policy in the Middle East, 338; protectionism, 272; Québec offices, in the, 119; racial integration, in the armed forces, 480; *realpolitik*, 343; reciprocity with, 89; security concerns, 332; states, 12, 106; State Department, 247; trading with, Canadian government of Laurier, 29; unilateralism, 168, 174–175, 181, 516, 518; War on Terror, 352
Uruguay Round. *See* General Agreement on Tariffs and Trade

V-J Day, 3
Védrine, Hubert, 514

Versailles Peace conference (1919), 30, 32
Victoria I, 28
Vietnam, 148, 153, 155; War, 38
Voit, Jacques, 145

Wade, Abdoulayé, 225
Wales, 436, 444
Wallonia, international role, 106, 108, 124–125
Washington, state of, 106
Weapons, of mass destruction (WMD), 18, 348
West European Union (WEU), 379
Western alliance, 53, 339–340
Western Europe, 215
Western Governors' Association meetings, 122
Western Interstate Energy Board, 118
Western Premiers' Conference, 122
Westminster: 1931 Statute of, 33; style of government, 25, 110, 436, 423n23
White House, 1, 21, 37, 345, 352; Millennium Challenge Account, 227
Wilkie, Agnes W., 468
Wilson, Michael, Minister of Finance, 59
World Bank, 211, 273, 277, 280–282
World Economic Forum, 225, 233n44
World Trade Organization (WTO), 84, 97, 99n20, 366, 501–504; Doha Round, 381; most-favored nations (MFN), of, 364. *See also* Preferential trading arrangements; Seattle
World War I, 2, 26, 29, 32, 52, 351, 412, 468; Conscription crisis of, 351
World War II, 2, 15, 16, 32–33, 52, 54, 134–135, 158, 209, 291, 293, 318, 337, 351, 401, 412, 480; post–World War II, 4, 26, 51, 53, 321, 338, 375;

post–World War II Canadian foreign policy, 4, 18n2, 35; pre–World War II, 318, 320
World Wars, 16
Wrong, Hume, 53

Yelstin, Boris, 300
Youth Millennium Project (YMP), 204

Yukon territory, 106
Yukon Field Force (1898), 467
Yugoslavia, 222, 498

Zaire,134, 138, 156, 186n51. *See* also Congo; Mobutu, Joseph
Zimbabwe, 211, 227. *See also* Mugabe, Robert

About the Editors and Contributors

Patrick James is Professor of International Relations at the University of Southern California (PhD, University of Maryland, College Park). James is the author of ten books and more than one hundred articles and book chapters. Among his honors and awards are the Louise Dyer Peace Fellowship from the Hoover Institution at Stanford University; the Milton R. Merrill Chair in Political Science at Utah State University; the Lady Davis Professorship of the Hebrew University of Jerusalem; the Thomas Enders Professorship in Canadian Studies at the University of Calgary; the Senior Scholar award from the Canadian Embassy, Washington, DC; the Eaton Lectureship at Queen's University in Belfast; and the Quincy Wright Scholar Award from the Midwest International Studies Association. He is a past president of the Midwest International Studies Association and the Iowa Conference of Political Scientists. James recently completed a five-year term as editor of *International Studies Quarterly*. He is vice president, 2005–2007, and president-elect, 2007–2009, of the Association for Canadian Studies in the United States.

Nelson Michaud (PhD, Laval) is Associate Professor of Political Science and International Relations, Chair of the Groupe d'études, de recherche et de formation internationales (GERFI), and Chair of the Laboratoire d'étude sur les politiques publiques et la mondialisation at the École nationale d'administration publique. He is Fellow of the Canadian Defence and Foreign Affairs Institute; Researcher-Member of the Institut Québécois des Hautes Études Internationales; Associate Researcher at the Centre d'études interaméricaines; and Research Fellow at the Centre for Foreign Policy Studies (Dalhousie University). He has taught at Dalhousie and Laval Universities and has been invited as a guest professor at the Canadian Royal Military College. His research has been published in leading refereed journals, as chapters in collective works, and as encyclopaedic articles. He has also authored some books and coedited with Kim Richard Nossal (Queen's) *Diplomatic Departures: The Conservative Era in Canadian Foreign Policy 1984–1993*. He was awarded the Excellence in Research Award from the Université du Québec network (2005) and the Excellence in Research Prize from his own institution (2004), and *Le Journal économique* recognized him among its top research scholars in 2003. Nelson Michaud has appeared as analyst/commentator on radio, television, and in dailies. Prior to his academic career, Dr. Michaud worked for nine years with the Canadian federal government mainly as policy analyst.

Originally from Montreal, **Marc J. O'Reilly** is Assistant Professor of Political Science at Heidelberg College, where he teaches courses on Canadian foreign policy and other international relations subjects. His work on Canadian foreign policy has appeared in *The Journal of Commonwealth & Comparative Politics*, *The American Review of Canadian Studies*, and *International Public Opinion and the Bosnia Crisis* (Lexington Books). He is also the author of *Bittersweet: The Creation of an American Empire in the Persian Gulf, 1941–2005* (Lexington Books).

Jeffrey M. Ayres is Associate Professor of Political Science at Saint Michael's College (Colchester, VT), where he teaches and specializes in international relations and international and comparative political economy including transnational political processes and global and regional governance. Additional research interests include social movements and Canadian/North American politics. He is the author of *Defying Conventional Wisdom: Political Movements and Popular Contention against North American Free Trade* (1998), as well as articles, book chapters, and reviews on the above topics.

Thomas G. Barnes is Professor of History and Law Emeritus and Co-Director of the Canadian Studies Program at the University of California, Berkeley. He is the author of a number of articles on Canadian history with an increasing emphasis on the Canadian military, at war and in peace. He is a former president of the Association for Canadian Studies in the United States.

Bethany Barratt is Assistant Professor of Political Science at Roosevelt University in Chicago. She is the author of a forthcoming book, *Human Rights and Foreign Aid*, and has authored articles on human rights, foreign aid, and counterterrorism, as well as U.S., British, Canadian, and Australian foreign policy. Her work has appeared in *Political Research Quarterly, The Journal of Homeland Security and Emergency Management*, and *Understanding Human Rights Violations: New Systematic Studies* (2004).

David Carment is Professor of International Affairs at the Norman Paterson School of International Affairs, Carleton University (Ottawa), and Fellow of the Canadian Defence and Foreign Affairs Institute. He serves as the principal investigator for the Country Indicators for Foreign Policy project. In 2002–2004, he served as Carleton's Director of the Centre for Security and Defence Studies. In 2000–2001, he was a fellow at Harvard University's Belfer Center. He is the recipient of several teaching and research awards, including a Petro-Canada Young Innovator Award. He is the author of several books, including *Peacekeeping Intelligence, Conflict Prevention: From Rhetoric to Reality, Using Force to Prevent Ethnic Violence: An Evaluation of Theory and Evidence*, and *Conflict Prevention: Path to Peace or Grand Illusion?* His current research focuses on developing failed-state risk assessment and early warning methodologies and evaluating models of third-party intervention.

Neal Carter is Associate Professor of Political Science at St. Bonaventure University (St. Bonaventure, NY). His main areas of research focus on Canadian politics, political psychology, identity, and conflict processes. He has been published in such journals as *Mobilization, Peace and Conflict Studies*, and *Political Psychology*. He has also contributed book chapters on ethnic conflict and political psychology.

Greg Donaghy is Head of the Historical Section at Foreign Affairs Canada. He is the editor of several volumes in the series Documents on Canadian External Relations, as well as the editor of three collections of essays on post-war Canada: *Uncertain Horizons: Canadians and Their World in 1945* (1995); *Canada and the Early Cold War, 1943–1957* (1999); and (with Stéphane Roussel) *Escott Reid: Diplomat and Scholar* (2004). His recent publications include *Tolerant Allies: Canada and the United States, 1963–1968*.

Charles F. Doran is Andrew W. Mellon Professor of International Relations at the School of Advanced International Studies (SAIS), Johns Hopkins University. He directs the Center of Canadian Studies at SAIS and is also a Senior Associate at the Center for Strategic and International Studies in Washington, D.C. Among his many publications on Canada are *Forgotten Partnership: Canada–U.S. Relations Today* (1984) and *Why Canadian Unity Matters and Why Americans Care* (2002). A past president of the Association for Canadian Studies in the United States, he is a recipient of the Donner Medal for distinguished scholarship in Canadian Studies and the Governor General's Award, the highest award for scholarship in the field.

Athanasios Hristoulas is Professor of International Relations and Director of the National Security Program at The Instituto Tecnológico Autonomo de Mexico (ITAM). He also regularly teaches at the Mexican Naval and Army Staff colleges. His research interests include civil-military relations, Mexican defense and national security policy, as well as Canada–Mexico–U.S. relations. He has published articles in *The Journal of Politics*, *Etudes Internationales*, *Comercio Exterior*, and *Foreign Affairs en Espanol*. Recent publications include the edited volumes *Las Relaciones civico-militaren el nuevo orden internacional* (2002) and *La Politica y Gobierno de Canada* (2005) and a chapter in *The Rebordering of North America* (2003).

Axel Hülsemeyer is Assistant Professor of Political Science at Concordia University in Montreal. His work has been published in several journals, among them *Review of International Political Economy* and *The World Economy*. He is the editor of *Globalization in the Twenty-First Century: Convergence or Divergence?* (2003), author of *Globalization and Institutional Adjustment: Federalism as an Obstacle?* (2004), and coauthor with Julian Schofield of *Introduction to International Relations: A Reader* (2004).

Carolyn C. James is a Visiting Professor at Columbia College in Columbia, MO. She has received multiple awards for excellence in teaching and is a Fellow with the Centre for Military and Strategic Studies at the University of Calgary. She has written articles and book chapters on international security, foreign policy, and civil-military relations that have appeared in *Terrorism and Political Violence*, *Journal of Security Studies*, *Journal of Military and Strategic Studies*, *Naval War College Review*, and the *Canadian Journal of Political Science*. She currently serves on the governing council of the International Studies Association (ISA) Foreign Policy Section and is President of ISA's Midwest Section.

Michael Lusztig is Associate Professor of Political Science at Southern Methodist University (Dallas, TX). His research focuses on the politics of trade and Canadian constitutional politics. He is the author of a number of scholarly articles and two books, *The Limits of Protectionism: Building Coalitions for Free Trade* (2004) and *Risking Free Trade: The Politics of Free Trade in Britain, Canada, Mexico and the United States* (1996). His current research focuses on the roots of liberal republicanism in Canada.

Koren Marriott is a law student and L.L.B. candidate at the University of Ottawa. She is a graduate of Carleton University's Norman Paterson School of International Affairs. After graduating from Carleton, she worked in the nongovernmental sector on issues relating to conflict prevention, foreign policy, and children and women in armed conflict. Her current studies focus on areas in international law, national security, human rights, and constitutional law.

Kimberly Marten (formerly Kimberly Marten Zisk) is Professor of Political Science at Barnard College, Columbia University. She is the author of three books on international security issues. The most recent is *Enforcing the Peace: Learning from the Imperial Past* (2004), which received the *ForeWord* Magazine Gold Award for the best book in political science published by an independent press. Her two major current research projects focus on Central Asian security issues and the warlord problem in Afghanistan, Somalia, and elsewhere.

James T. McHugh is Professor of Political Science and Chair of the Legal Studies Program at Roosevelt University. He has done extensive writing and research on international and comparative law, including in relation to Canada and Quebec. He is the author of *Comparative Constitutional Traditions* (2002), *The Essential Concept of Law* (2002), and (with James S. Pacy) *Diplomats without a Country: Baltic Diplomacy, International Law, and the Cold War* (2001). He contributed a chapter to *Canada Observed: Perspectives from Abroad and from Within* (2000) and has published articles in *International and Comparative Law Quarterly, Québec Studies, Social Science Journal, American Review of Canadian Studies*, and *Review of Politics*.

Douglas C. Nord is Professor of Political Science at Wright State University (Dayton, OH). He is a specialist in the politics of the Circumpolar North. He has written widely on Canadian and American foreign policies affecting the region, including a recent book chapter discussing tensions between Canadian and American foreign policies in the Arctic. He has also worked on the development of collaboration among scholars in the North, including serving as one of the founding organizers of the Circumpolar Universities Association. He is coeditor of *Higher Education across the Circumpolar North: A Circle of Learning* (2002).

Jason Rich is a doctoral candidate at the University of Connecticut. His current research interests include comparative foreign policy and diplomacy, the dynamics of international coercion and compellence, and asymmetrical warfare.

Andrew Richter is Assistant Professor of Political Science at the University of Windsor. His research interests include Canadian foreign and defense policy, weapons proliferation, and how technology affects the use of force. His most recent book is *Avoiding Armageddon: Canadian Military Strategy and Nuclear Weapons* (2002). He has published articles in numerous journals, including *Comparative Strategy, International Journal, Naval War College Review*, and *The American Review of Canadian Studies*.

Jean-Sébastien Rioux holds the Canada Research Chair in International Security at the Institut québécois des hautes études internationales (HEI) at Laval University, where he is also Assistant Professor of Political Science. His research interests focus on foreign policy analysis, conflict processes, and third-party intervention in conflict. His research has been published in *International Studies Quarterly, Canadian Journal of Political Science,* and *International Politics.* He is coauthor (with Douglas Van Belle and David Potter) of *Media, Bureaucracies and Foreign Aid: A Comparative Analysis* (2004). He has traveled extensively to study stabilization missions in Bosnia (SFOR) and in Afghanistan (ISAF). He has also been participating in peacekeeping training missions with the Lester B. Pearson Peacekeeping Center in Canada and at the International Peacekeeping School in Mali, West Africa. His next book will examine peacekeeping in Central Africa.

Richard Vengroff is Professor of Political Science at the University of Connecticut. He has published articles on Québec and Canadian Politics in the *Canadian Journal of Political Science, Canadian Public Administration, International Journal of Canadian Studies, American Review of Canadian Studies, Québec Studies,* and *Issue.* He has also contributed several book chapters. He is currently completing a study of Québec municipal consolidation and is the codirector of a project with the Roper Center (Storrs, CT) to create a Canadian I-Poll data set. He has served as vice president of the American Council on Québec Studies, was the campus project director for a FIPSE-funded North American Mobility Grant, and has been a participant in a USIS-funded NAFTA faculty exchange research program.

Duncan Wood is Professor of International Relations at Instituto Tecnológico Autonomo de Mexico (ITAM). At ITAM, he directs the Undergraduate Program in International Relations, the Canadian Studies Program, and Think Mexico. He is the author of *Governing Global Banking: The Basel Committee and the Politics of Financial Globalization* (2005) and coauthor with George MacLean of *Introduction to Politics: Power, Participation and the Distribution of Wealth* (2000). He is coeditor (with Athanasios Hristoulas and Claude Denis) of *Canadá: Política y Gobierno en el siglo 21* (2004). His research interests include oil reforms in Mexico and Canada-Mexico relations, as well as remittances and economic development.